CONTEMPORARY COMMUNITY HEALTH SERIES

CLIFFORD W. BEERS

CLIFFORD W. BEERS

Advocate for the Insane

NORMAN DAIN

UNIVERSITY OF PITTSBURGH PRESS

Published by the University of Pittsburgh Press, Pittsburgh, Pa., 15260
Copyright © 1980, American Foundation for Mental Hygiene
All rights reserved
Feffer and Simons, Inc., London
Manufactured in the United States of America

Library of Congress Cataloging in Publication Data

Dain, Norman.
  Clifford W. Beers, advocate for the insane.

  (Contemporary community health series)
  Includes bibliographical references and index.
  1. Mental health services—United States—History.
2. Mental health services—History. 3. Beers,
Clifford Whittingham, 1876–1943. 4. Mental illness—
United States—Biography. I. Title. II. Series.
RA790.6.D36   362.2′092′4 [B]   79-24290
ISBN 0-8229-3419-1

The statements of fact and expressions of opinion in this book
are the sole responsibility of the author.

Grants from the American Foundation for Mental Hygiene and the Maurice Falk Medical Fund made possible the writing and production of this volume.

For Phyllis, Bruce, Ted

Contents

Contents

Illustrations

xiii

Foreword

The American Foundation for Mental Hygiene is pleased to introduce this significant biography of Clifford Whittingham Beers, the sponsorship and guidance of which has been a major activity of the Foundation.

We consider ourselves fortunate to have obtained the scholarly interest and skill of Professor Norman Dain to undertake this important task of portraying the life and times of the founder of the mental hygiene movement. We believe Professor Dain's work enables greater appreciation of Mr. Beers' formidable personality and contributions and is a uniquely worthwhile addition to historical literature.

A special word of commendation is due to the officers and trustees of the Foundation for their sustained interest in this project. We are also indebted to Stanley P. Davies, the distinguished mental health pioneer, for his valuable advice, and to the Maurice Falk Medical Fund for financial assistance.

William T. Beaty II, Secretary
American Foundation for Mental Hygiene

Preface

An anomaly in a field of endeavor where traditionally achievement has come from practitioners — doctors, scientists, and other professionals — Clifford Beers is probably the nation's first example of a successful consumer advocate. He was active in an era before that term was used, a layman who fought a lifelong battle against mental illness in himself and in his family, and provided the impetus for the development of a national mental health movement.

With publication of his book, *A Mind That Found Itself,* Beers set the foundation of a nationwide movement to promote mental health. Founder of the National Committee for Mental Hygiene (now known as the National Mental Health Association) and the American Foundation for Mental Hygiene, Inc., Clifford Beers aroused the national conscience to act on behalf of the mentally ill.

Despite his achievements, Clifford Beers died profoundly disappointed, convinced that his life's work had been in vain. If he had lived but a few more years, he would have seen, for example, the passage of the National Mental Health Act, the establishment of the National Institute of Mental Health, and the growth of new national initiatives to fulfill two of his lifelong goals: prevention of the onset of mental illness and increased attention to the humane treatment of mental patients. Perhaps then he could have derived some satisfaction from knowing that his movement would indeed survive.

It is pleasing to me personally to see this book published, which so thoroughly documents the early roots of the mental health movement, particularly those parts which emphasize the importance of the efforts of private citizens and the impact of volunteerism. In this field of public health, progress has always been closely dependent on the collaboration of many professions and groups in our society, and on the attitudes and will of many citizens. Today, this partnership between the public and private sectors is even more pronounced. Recent moves toward closer cooperation between the NIMH and voluntary associations such as the Mental Health Association and the American Foundation for Mental Hygiene, Inc., are perhaps the finest tribute we can pay to Clifford Beers.

Bertram S. Brown, M.D.
Former Director
National Institute of Mental Health

Acknowledgments

Through the years that it took to research and write this book, numerous persons and institutions kindly assisted me. The Board of Trustees of the American Foundation for Mental Hygiene, Inc., which sponsored the work, gave me much encouragement, facilitated my work in many ways, and provided financial aid. William T. Beaty II, secretary of the Foundation, was especially helpful, as were Gordon E. Brown, president, Philip B. Hallen, and Eric T. Carlson, M.D. Mr. Hallen, as president of the Maurice Falk Medical Fund, arranged for research grants from the Fund and has been always generous with moral as well as financial support. Robert A. Koch, counsel for the American Foundation for Mental Hygiene, gave useful advice at the beginning of the project, when Arthur Rosenthal, currently the director of the Harvard University Press, was also helpful. Several trustees of the Foundation were good enough to read the manuscript of the book: Gordon Brown, Eric T. Carlson, Philip Hallen, Helen P. Langner, M.D., James H. Wall, M.D., and William Beaty II. The Foundation also asked Stanley P. Davis, Ph.D., formerly general director of the Community Service Society of New York City, to read the manuscript, which he kindly did. Nina Ridenour, Ph.D., formerly secretary of the Ittleson Foundation, not only granted me an interview, but gave the manuscript a critical reading.

The members of the biweekly seminar of the Section on the History of Psychiatry and the Behavioral Sciences of the Department of Psychiatry at Payne Whitney Psychiatric Clinic, New York Hospital—Cornell University Medical Center, New York City, with which I have been associated for years, listened patiently to and commented helpfully on my presentations of my ideas about this book. Oskar Diethelm, M.D., for many years chairman of the Department of Psychiatry, also read the first completed draft of the manuscript, as did Jacques Quen, M.D., whose detailed comments helped me to clarify the text. Very special appreciation goes to Dr. Eric T. Carlson, the founder and guiding spirit of the Section on the History of Psychiatry and the Behavioral Sciences. He not only read the manuscript with his customary care, but has also always been generous with his knowledge, his time, his support, and his great good will and concern.

I am indebted to all those who shared with me their memories of Clifford Beers: Bianca Artoni Avela; Ralph S. Banay, M.D.; Earl D. Bond, M.D.; Col. Edmund Bullis; Clarence B. Farrar, M.D. (who also showed me Beers papers in his private collection); Helen Frost; Jack Griffin, M.D.; Marion Kenworthy, M.D.; Emily Martin; Grace E. O'Neill; Irving S. Reeve (who also kindly allowed me to see the Beers home in Englewood, New Jersey); Nina Ridenour, Ph.D.; George F. Stevenson, M.D.; William B. Terhune, M.D.; Christine Robb Thomson; M. Towey; and Margaret H. Wagenhals. Drs. Oskar Diethelm and Phyllis Greenacre discussed with me their memories of Adolf Meyer.

This book depended heavily on permission granted me to consult various manuscript collections and institutional records. Mehadin K. Arafeh, M.D., superintendent of Connecticut Valley Hospital, allowed me to see the case records of Clifford Beers and his aunt, Henrietta Cooke Robinson. Francis Braceland, M.D., senior consultant and formerly chief of the Institute of Living, Hartford, Connecticut, gave me access to Clifford Beers' case record there. R. W. Brunell, Jr., executive director of the Connecticut Association for Mental Health, had the minutes of the Connecticut Society for Mental Hygiene copied for me. Professor Gerald N. Grob of Rutgers University saved me a good deal of time and trouble by allowing me to peruse his microfiche file of the William A. White correspondence in the National Archives. Jack Griffin, M.D., general director of the Canadian Mental Health Association, made it possible for me to examine its archives and other material. Alan R. Gurwitt, M.D., director of the Clifford W. Beers Guidance Clinic, New Haven, Connecticut, gave me access to material relating to Beers' work in Connecticut, and the Reverend Alvin D. Johnson of the First Baptist Church, New Haven, sent me some Beers material. Janet Koudelka, curator at the Welch Medical Library, Johns Hopkins University Medical School, made the Welch Papers available to me. Emily Martin allowed me to see her Beers collection before it was deposited in the Archives of Psychiatry of New York Hospital–Cornell University Medical Center. Joan B. Surrey of the Howard Colman Library, Rockford College, Rockford, Illinois, sent me copies of the Beers-Lathrop correspondence in the Lathrop Papers. Eunice E. Winters granted me permission to see material from the Adolf Meyer Papers in the Welch Medical Library. I wish also to acknowledge the access I was given to the following sources: the Beers and Emily Martin Collections in the Archives of Psychiatry, New York Hospital–Cornell University Medical Center; Clifford Beers' case record at Butler Hospital, Providence, Rhode Island; the Menninger Foundation Archives, Topeka, Kansas; the Rockefeller Foundation Archives, Hillcrest, Pocantico Hills, North Tarrytown, New York; the Carl E. Beers and Henrietta Cooke Robinson case records in the State Records Center, Rocky Hill, Connecticut; and manuscripts and other material in the Yale University Library.

At the University of Pittsburgh Press, Frederick A. Hetzel, the director, Louise Craft, editor, and Beth Luey, editor, were unusually understanding, helpful, and wise collaborators with whom it has been a pleasure to work.

I want to express my deepest appreciation to my wife, Professor Phyllis Dain of Columbia University. As in all my published work she has contributed to this book to such an extent that she comes close to being a co-author. As critic she forced me to clarify many misty ideas, as editor she gave the book whatever grace it possesses, and her technical knowledge of sources and citations brought a badly needed consistency and clarity: Much of whatever is valuable in this book I owe to her efforts.

Introduction

In 1908 Clifford W. Beers' *A Mind That Found Itself* appeared, published by the venerable firm of Longmans, Green and endorsed by William James and other notable Americans. The book brought Beers immediate fame and became a classic of that genre of books written by former mental patients to expose conditions in mental hospitals and to depict their own struggles with mental illness. *A Mind That Found Itself* is the best work of that kind yet published and probably the best known. It was in its time extraordinary and has remained so, not only on account of its literary quality, intelligence, and vivid descriptions, but because of the role it played in launching Clifford Beers into a lifetime career as founder, organizer, and chief fund raiser and propagandist of the modern mental health movement both in the United States and on the international scene. Even after seventy years the book is still timely, speaking to many of the issues raised by reformers and radicals in the 1960s and 1970s.

Beers felt psychologically compelled to write and publish *A Mind That Found Itself* and thereafter to retell his story again and again for the rest of his life. He did this also in the service of a grand design that would bring happiness and peace to mankind by creating and maintaining an organized effort to change the status of the mentally ill, to alter public attitudes toward them, to improve their conditions in mental institutions, and finally to understand and prevent mental illness. His life is the story of a man's struggle to create out of his personal experiences and psychological needs a public career that would give meaning to his sufferings and transcend them to benefit other sufferers. He thus gained a place in history, distinguished associates and friends, and many honors. His success was all the more remarkable because he was able to turn his shameful status as a former mental patient into an instrument for reform, and himself into an object of admiration.

Yet whether Beers and the mental health movement — the two are almost inseparable — succeeded in fulfilling their objectives is open to question, and Beers himself questioned this toward the end of his life. Today, nearly two generations after Beers' death in 1943, and in the midst of yet another movement for change in the mental health field, the issue is acutely relevant. Contemporary radical thinking about mental illness and ways to deal with it, as well as historical writing on the subject, questions the value and achievements of all mental health movements and their leaders, past and present, and challenges central assumptions about mental illness and its treatment. In the modern era mental illness, involving as it has the state in its management, has always been a politico-economic as well as medical, religious, and social matter. Heightened consciousness today of this reality has politicized the field as perhaps never before.

Until the late nineteenth century, critics of institutionalized mental health care in the United States (which dates back to the middle of the eighteenth century) objected mainly to shortcomings in achieving generally accepted goals: cure, humane care, and safekeeping of mental patients, usually in hospitals, and at minimal cost to society, which would thus be protected against possible harm from deranged people. The so-called medical model of mental illness — the view that it is a bodily disease like other disease, in this case a disorder of the brain, and amenable to treatment by physicians — became by the nineteenth century commonplace among trained physicians and educated lay people. Its acceptance was considered a sign of enlightenment and a prerequisite for a new optimism about the cure of mental illness; it underlay the establishment of new mental hospitals designed to practice moral treatment, a humanistic therapeutic system developed by Philippe Pinel and others in Europe and by Quaker reformers in England and the United States. In the 1840s and 1850s, under the impetus of Dorothea Dix and her friends, public hospitals for the insane were built in many states, a few to offer indigent and lower-class people this new treatment that had up to then been available mainly to upper-class patients in private or corporate hospitals.

After the Civil War there was a change, and for the worse. The failure of hospital care to sustain the high rates of "cure" promised by moral treatment set a tone of pessimism that dovetailed with new theories of social Darwinism and their corollary, reverse evolution, or degeneration of those who supposedly were genetically unfit. The giant state institutions lapsed into custodialism and came to house many old people, alcoholics, and social deviants as well as the mentally ill. Some of the few humanitarian reformers and psychiatrists who were active in the post–Civil War years doubted whether mental hospitals could by their nature help psychotic people and whether physicians in such hospitals knew better than lay people what they were doing. An even smaller number of people perceived inherent defects in institutionalization under the best of conditions and proposed alternative ways of caring for some of the insane in the community. Still, until the mid-twentieth century, almost no one seemed to doubt the validity of mental illness as a medical reality and to question the need for mental hospitals. Critics generally sought to improve hospital conditions and develop the science and art of psychiatry, not to eliminate hospitals and psychiatry. This was true of Clifford Beers. For all his sharp criticisms of the mental health power structure, he became, through both temperament and force of circumstance, committed to working almost wholly within established institutions and with establishment figures.

The classic modern historical approach to the problem of mental illness also accepted hospitalization and psychiatry as essentially progressive and benevolent. This outlook was best expounded in Albert Deutsch's standard history *The Mentally Ill in America,* published in 1937 with Clifford Beers' help and under the auspices of his American Foundation for Mental Hygiene. Adopting a basically progressive view, Deutsch saw the primary goal of reformers from the earliest founding of hospitals as always a therapeutic one, an attempt to give the mentally ill proper medical treatment leading to cure, though it was only with the advent of the National Committee for Mental Hygiene founded by Beers in 1909 that both the knowledge and the organization necessary to the task were finally present. Deutsch was not unaware of the harsh, ineffective, and custodial treatment that most of the mentally ill suffered throughout American history, but he had no doubt that progress was continual, and he regarded the shock therapy and psychoanalysis introduced in his own time, together with a growing concern for prevention through public education, as evidence of such progress.

During the past generation or so, from the 1950s but especially in the 1960s and 1970s, the progressive and medically oriented approach has been challenged by historians, social scientists, psychiatrists, social activists, and former mental patients and their supporters. Early in this period, psychiatrist-historians J. Sanbourne Bockoven and Eric T. Carlson and historians Gerald N. Grob and myself, rediscovering a lost period of reform in the first half of the nineteenth century and tracing its rise and decline in specific institutions, questioned the evolutionary, progressive historical model and posited instead a cyclical one of reform and retrogression. My own work has been particularly concerned with the class nature of mental health movements as well as their political contexts and with the inherent difficulties of programs designed to help people unable to function normally in capitalist society. All these writers, plus other, younger historians who now became interested in the field, nevertheless accepted the reality of mental illness as a clinical entity, albeit one highly sensitive to and perhaps even greatly determined by societal forces. Their work coincided with a new concern for the fate of the mentally ill, when the discovery of new psychopharmacological agents transformed hospital psychiatry and, through their effectiveness in controlling symptoms, facilitated new modes of living for mental patients, both in and out of hospitals. This was also a time of activism in behalf of the rights of dependent and institutionalized people to freedom and adequate treatment.

These trends were accompanied by ideological challenges to conventional concepts of mental illness and to hospitalization. Best known have been the writings of Dr. Thomas Szasz, who denied that mental illness existed as a medical phenomenon and accused mental hospitals and indeed mental health movements of creating the illusion that they were dealing with a clinical disorder; in reality they were sanctioning society's tendency to label misfits or deviants insane and to justify their involuntary incarceration in hospitals. Sociologist Erving Goffman, studying "asylums" as enclosed or total systems, saw no benefit to mental patients from hospital life, which infantilized them and was itself responsible for much of the behavior that psychiatrists considered symptomatic of insanity. The British existentialist psychoanalyst R. D. Laing, a counterculture hero of the 1960s, went a step further in arguing that schizophrenia, the most prevalent form of mental disorder today, was the logical, even healthy, response of people to a sick society, and that the descent into schizophrenia could produce a healthier personality. Laing acknowledged the contribution of Pinel and other eighteenth-century reformers in moving insanity from the theological to the clinical sphere as a great step forward for humanity. But he and his followers believed that subsequently the psychiatric profession, mental hospitals, and mental health movements, in being committed essentially to preserving the status quo, worked against the real needs of those people society labels schizophrenic. Among historians, David Rothman has concluded that the major purpose of pre–Civil War hospital-building in the United States was not to cure patients but to control social deviance in a changing society: the goal of therapy was never a serious motive for reformers. Similarly, the influential French philosopher Michel Foucault has depicted hospitalization of the mentally ill as a process that developed to serve the needs of a divided society rather than those of the patients.

Partially influenced by these new critics, but also impelled by the social activism of the 1960s, a number of new antipsychiatry organizations both in the United States and in Western Europe have emerged. Composed mainly of mental patients, former patients, and radical practitioners in the mental health professions, this growing movement tends to combine Szasz's and Laing's positions with a "Marxist" analysis of society, together with a blend of psychoanalysis, existentialism, structuralism, and anarchism. Basically, mental problems are seen as a product of the irrational, contradictory, and exploitative nature of capitalism and its hierarchical power relations; psychiatry is seen as a major force in the pacification of the lower classes and their potentially revolutionary allies. These activists, influenced also by the thinking of European writers like Jacques Lacan, Félix Guattari, Gilles Deleuze, and Michel Foucault, see the goal of the mental health professions as normalization, the removal of individuality that is nonconformist and therefore threatening to the capitalist social system. What the mental health movement has described as progress is depicted by the new activists and theorists as merely improved methods of social control. They do not usually deny that people may need psychological help, but they usually insist that such therapy should be voluntary self-help or help from a nonmedical source. Ultimately the solution is seen as the destruction of capitalism and its replacement by a new, humane, communitarian society. (That socialist societies have so far nowhere resulted in the elimination of mental disorders as a serious health problem does not seem to bother some of these new ideologues; others realize that socialism is also power-oriented and therefore no solution.)

This ideological ferment calls into question the attitude of a biographer of Clifford Beers, one of the foremost activists in the mental health field and to date the most famous former mental patient turned crusader. How I see Clifford Beers is spelled out in the following pages and summarized in the epilogue; essentially the book must speak for itself. But in the light of the current controversies over mental illness and its history, I do feel obliged to discuss my own assumptions in writing about Beers. I believe that there is a phenomenon that Western societies, and all other societies with the relevant records — past or present, capitalist, socialist, or what have you — have traditionally called "insanity" or its equivalent; that is, that there have always been a certain number of people unable to function adequately by the standards of their day on account of mental or emotional problems. I also believe that we are still at a primitive state in our knowledge of the mechanisms of mental illness; we are in what biologist Lewis Thomas called the "nontechnological" stage of medicine, in which heavy expenditures of funds and effort are required to treat disorders whose underlying mechanisms (which may be biochemical or social or of some other origin) are as yet unknown.

As for mental health movements, they have always had, in my view, divergent and conflicting goals. Therapy and humane care have never been the only objectives of reformers; there was also the wish to rid society of a disturbing class of people, including some who were not insane by contemporary medical standards. I do believe, however, that many reformers were genuinely concerned for mental patients' welfare. That the institutions they established were only partially successful — and indeed sometimes mistreated patients and may have made some of them worse instead of better — is probably as much a reflection of the nature of mental disorder as of our social system. In the absence of a cheap technological therapy for most forms of mental disorder, provision for long-term care of patients, with all the problems entailed, became necessary. Before hospitals undertook this function, there was no golden age of community care; the mentally ill would more often than not be left to fend for themselves (or to rot in jails or almshouses) in a world that was not necessarily kind and humane for being "precapitalist." No reforms, radical or otherwise, have succeeded in resolving that oldest of problems, how to bring mentally disordered people into a relationship with the rest of the population that is compatible with the interests and needs of both. The attempt to do so is a significant feature of the history of reform movements.

Both critics and supporters of such movements often tend to paint them in one color. Radicals (who have much justice on their side) seem to argue that since capitalism is exploitative, all its institutions serve *only* exploitative ends. From this perspective, mental hospitals, schools, libraries, and other institutions, including the family, are exclusively or essentially instruments of exploitation or social control. On the other hand, those who see the system of care of mental patients positively, despite its faults, often ignore or underplay the extent to which social control, class interests, bureaucracy, politics, and in general nonmedical and antipatient interests have molded the way mental patients are treated. Supporters stress progress in drug therapy, for example, without recognizing that these scientific advances are often used, today as in the past, to immobilize the hospital population for the convenience of staffs and to save money by reducing the need for active treatment, which is expensive. Radicals tend to ignore the role of personality and of the individual in the history of mental health movements and to focus exclusively on social forces. Traditionalists tend to minimize the significance of class and of conflict and to center their attention on institutional accomplishments and psychiatric theories and give short shrift to how patients have fared. The more ideological or political or self-justifying the outlook, the more likely the tendency to interpret the past as if it were simply an older version of the present, and in the service of the present, regardless of evidence.

Serious study of how reform movements actually grow and evolve, of the actual role of leaders, of the interplay of medico-scientific and social forces as they impinge on leadership, has been in short supply. This biography of Clifford Beers is conceived as a contribution to such a literature. I hope that it will reveal the process whereby the modern mental health movement was formed and depict the relationship between the movement and its founder, within the social contexts that helped to shape them both, and all in terms of the available evidence. I reject the all too common tendency to subordinate the significance of evidence to theoretical or ideological considerations (no matter how attractive the latter may be). No position is tenable if it runs contrary to the evidence. That the sources at any given time may not be adequate to support strongly a particular thesis is no justification for ignoring or contradicting them in order to validate a thesis. I accept Thomas Henry Huxley's concept of the "great tragedy of Science — the slaying of a beautiful hypothesis by an ugly fact." I have not forsworn generalizations, but I have attempted to keep them within recognizable relation to the evidence and to avoid putting forward the obvious as a great discovery. I must also admit that despite a decade of research and thought, I do not have more than an imperfect understanding of Beers. I know of no theory of personality that seems adequate for that task. Nor do theories about the role of socioeconomic forces in personality development appear to me as more than suggestive. I have tried to see Clifford Beers with the critical eye of the present but as a man of his time, not of ours, as a man who tried to do good and to do his best.

CLIFFORD W. BEERS

‡ 1 ‡

Early Years:
Crisis and Collapse

As Clifford Whittingham Beers, descending slowly from the high excitement of mania, celebrated his twenty-seventh birthday in the Connecticut State Hospital for the Insane, he had no doubt that society would soon reward him with fame and fortune.[1] Family history, however, afforded no outstanding forebears to justify his hopes for a famous future. His paternal ancestors were obscure Englishmen who came to the British Colonies in North America from Gravesend, Kent, about 1635. All that is known of Clifford Beers' paternal grandparents is their identity: Anthony Beers, a native of Newtown, Connecticut, who married Betsy Ruggles, from Brookfield, Connecticut. As Clifford viewed the matter, neither his father, Robert A. Beers, nor his father's two long-lived sisters broke with the Beers tradition of mediocrity. Robert Beers was born in Buffalo, New York, on December 13, 1825, but spent most of his life in New Haven, Connecticut, engaged in a wholesale provision business with his sister's husband, Samuel E. Merwin, a former lieutenant governor of Connecticut. This business provided a modest living for the numerous members of the Beers family, of which Clifford was the fourth of five surviving sons. The partnership terminated in the early 1900s, when the business was sold.[2]

In his mother's family Clifford also found little distinction. His mother, Ida Cooke Beers, met and married Robert Beers, twenty years her senior, in Marietta, Georgia, in 1863. She had been born in Savannah on July 17, 1843, the oldest daughter of the eight surviving children of Nathaniel Minto Cooke, a native New Yorker, and Harriet Mullryne Schroeder, a Savannah woman of partly German extraction.[3]

Nathaniel Cooke became a homeopathic physician, a profession he had to abandon while still young because of eye disease. In his later years he lived on a small farm in Georgia paid for by a son-in-law. One of his daughters described him as vacillating and high-strung, with a volatile temper and changeable moods, often in despair nearly to the point of suicide because of his blindness. His wife Harriet's ancestry boasted a marriage into British nobility and several prominent professional men in the American colonies.[4]

3

Harriet Cooke was said by one of her daughters to have borne up better under her troubles than her blinded husband, although probably not so much through fortitude as through immaturity. A poor housekeeper, she reared her children somewhat haphazardly, instilling in them the idea that they were "southern ladies and gentlemen and should scorn work," just as she did.

And so did most of them, at the expense of Clifford Beers' parents. Perhaps because she was the eldest daughter of an ineffectual mother, Clifford's mother Ida, unlike her siblings, worried about everyone else's troubles as well as her own. Once settled in New Haven after the Civil War, she felt bound to bring into her home and support her four maiden sisters and bachelor brother. The remaining sister married and remained in Georgia. For many years Ida Beers ran her large household (including five sons) with limited help from her sisters. The brother and two sisters married late in life, so that during Clifford's childhood and youth his uncle and aunts lived in the house; the two maiden aunts remained until his mother's death in 1914.[5]

Ida's sisters did lighten her burden by each adopting a child as her special responsibility, relieving Ida of taking full charge of all but the eldest boy, George. Understandably, then, the personalities of the sisters, as surrogate mothers, were important in the lives of the Beers boys.

All but one of the Cooke relatives were eccentric and unstable. The exception, Aunt Annie, nicknamed "Old Ironsides," inculcated in Clifford the importance of associating with the "best" sort of people. Aunt Clifford, for whom Clifford Beers was named, was a pretty, fastidious, white-haired woman who studiously avoided unpleasantness and was generally regarded as "peculiar, erratic, and non-dependable." Aunt Henrietta Cooke Robinson, the youngest of the twelve Cooke children, was always considered "delicate." She barely learned to read and write, was allowed to do much as she pleased, and suffered from sick headaches. To the amazement and disapproval of her relatives, she married in 1909, at the age of fifty, a "respectable, kind-hearted laborer" whom she met on the street. They moved frequently because Henrietta could not get along with people, who called her "crazy." Continuing threats of suicide may have led her husband to commit her to a private sanitarium in 1918 and the next year to the Connecticut Hospital for the Insane, where she died. Uncle Nathaniel Cooke always "had wild schemes for making money"; in the meantime he was satisfied to live off Robert Beers. He suffered from "nervousness," his sister Henrietta said, and never revealed a sense of responsibility "or more than a vague sense of right and wrong." In about 1909 he married a widow with a little money who supported him thereafter.[6]

Finally there was Mary L. Cooke, Aunt Mame, Clifford Beers' caretaker. She had, Henrietta recalled, a "high" temper and was "flighty, erratic and nervous"; she liked to refer proudly to her southern upbringing which, she believed, gave one "an over abundance of culture."[7] Aunt Mame "delegated herself as a sort of mother [to me] at the time I was born," Clifford wrote. She "practically raised me."[8] In her eyes Clifford "was a king who [could] do no wrong." When he was ill she would sleep with an ear cocked for his slightest movement and would immediately come if there was any unusual noise. He called her "a sort of substitute parent" and characterized himself as her "pet nephew."[9]

What of Clifford's mother, Ida Beers? An old friend of the family described her as sympathetic to pain and suffering and "very active-minded, keenly interested in the political news of the day and a great reader of good literature."[10] But her sister Henrietta said that her nature was gloomy, and Clifford Beers' case record noted that his mother was of a "rather nervous temperament."[11] Several letters he wrote to her indicated that she was delicate and timid and did not leave home much.[12] Clifford remembered her as liking a good sermon, freely expressing her opinions, and showing a taste for literature, and he credited her with having great sympathy for unfortunate people and being strongly opposed to injustice.[13] But of her qualities as a mother he said little, although his letters to her were affectionate and solicitous. When he was recovering from his breakdown he wrote her that she had "been a good mother to us all. I fear the Beers Boys have neglected to tell you how good a mother you have been."[14]

Robert Beers seems to have been an affectionate father, albeit somewhat formal and elderly. (He was fifty-three when Clifford was born.) From all accounts and as his photographs portray him, he was a genial, courtly, kindly, bearded gentleman who wore a top hat almost from morning to night and saw good in everyone.[15] Clifford never heard him say an "unclean word, a profane word, or an unkind word to or about anyone."[16] Although he saw his own good traits in his father — vigor, independence and an "unusual and never-failing amount of optimism and persistence of purpose" — Clifford did hint at a certain lack of strength and of emotional involvement with his family in Robert Beers, an unwillingness to "clean up trouble" and a reluctance to confront unpleasantness.[17] He never became entangled in family quarrels, which was quite a feat, considering that a wife, five sons, four difficult sisters-in-law, and a shiftless brother-in-law were living under his roof and on his income.

Although Clifford Beers claimed that his undistinguished ancestry did not irk him,[18] he continued to search for more prominent antecedents. He finally satisfied himself in this respect and in 1935 gave the fruits of his efforts to a journalist. He had decided that he was a "great-great-great grandson of Joseph Ruggles, son of Rev. Benjamin Ruggles and Mary Woodbridge Ruggles" and could therefore boast descent from "Colonial Governor William Leet of Connecticut and Thomas Dudley, third Governor of Massachusetts Bay Colony."[19]

The prime motive of Beers' researches into family history was pride, but he was also interested in evidence of mental instability, although usually obtuse in perceiving it. Neither he nor the man who helped him search his genealogy in the 1930s reported discovering any mental abnormality in the various families,[20] nor did Beers ever describe his maternal aunts as being anything more than high-strung. He did concede that something had gone wrong when the Beers and Cooke strains merged, an incontrovertible conclusion. None of the five surviving children of Robert and Ida Cooke Beers (a sixth died in infancy), that apparently unexceptional, hard-working, middle-class couple, escaped serious neurological or emotional disorders. One died young of a probable brain tumor that precipitated epilepticlike seizures, and the other four, including Clifford, died in mental hospitals, two of them by suicide. Ironically, it was through Clifford's psychiatric experiences that the Beers name finally achieved a measure of fame.

‡

In the manic stage of his illness Clifford Beers had grandiose ideas about his future and therefore of the significance of the facts of his life and genealogy. When his excitement abated, he became embarrassed at the thought of writing a largely personal autobiography, especially as his aim was to expose and reform mental hospitals. He therefore decided to "eliminate as much of the personal equation as possible."[21] Consequently his published autobiography contains little about his personal life before his mental breakdown, and information from other sources is scant. There is enough, however, to assess the quality of his childhood and youth.

He was born on March 30, 1876, and grew up in a small frame house in New Haven, Connecticut. His early years were marked by the serious illnesses common to children of the time—"colora [sic] Infantium," diphtheria, rheumatism, colic, chickenpox, earache, toothache, and measles. By the time he was five or six years old his health improved. He spent many summers at his grandfather's farm in Marietta, Georgia, and there developed a fond feeling for Georgians.[22]

Beers remembered himself as being so active that he could not sit still long enough to read books, particularly those required at school, which he thoroughly disliked. He did love to read newspapers, especially reports of murders, scandals, and other sensational events, and would fight with his younger brother Samuel for the first chance at the lively *New York World*.[23]

He enjoyed the usual activities of boys living in a small city with open country nearby. He liked to roam the woods, often with a friend. They tried to tame little patches of wild flowers in their own yards; jack-in-the-pulpit, violets, columbine, bloodroot, and forget-me-nots "were our stock in trade." Always enterprising, he and another boy started to raise bullfrogs for sale, contriving an elaborate tank from which the frogs promptly escaped. Then there was gardening and yard work to do for pay, and in winter shoveling snow and tending furnaces, which in retrospect Clifford considered good discipline but disliked at the time and sometimes found too strenuous.[24]

The odd jobs he did to earn pocket money reflected more than an ethic that children should learn the virtues of work. The Beers family did not suffer a lack of necessities, but neither did it have the resources for more than a modest standard of living. Nevertheless they were not poor. Photographs show all five boys and parents dressed in well-cut clothes of good fabric, even a velvet suit for one boy and a Scotch plaid outfit for Clifford. There is a well-fed, comfortable look about the group of good-looking sons and their parents, although all were invariably solemn and Clifford always sad-eyed. At a time when most children had only a grammar school education, four of the five Beers boys completed high school; at least two, William and Clifford, went to college (the latter with the help of his uncle Samuel Merwin),[25] and all worked at white-collar jobs. It was also a Victorian family: when Mrs. Beers was about to give birth to her youngest child, Clifford and Will were "bundled off" to spare their "modesty," which Clifford thought "a waste of good money" as he knew what was going on anyway.[26]

There were pretensions to gentility in the insistence that Clifford, who showed no musical talent, learn to play the piano. The end came when his mother took him to hear the great Josef Hofmann: "Shortly afterwards I stopped taking piano lessons!"[27]

One lesson Clifford Beers did not learn at home, his wife commented many years later, was self-control.[28] Probably somewhat neglected by his overburdened mother, indulged by an easygoing removed father and fond, erratic aunts, and struggling for attention with four active brothers (two of them as loquacious as he), he grew up self-indulgent, willful, and insecure. At the Skinner Grammar School one teacher, he remembered, wanted to expel him for "continued misbehavior." This conduct included a tendency to talk too much, and to be "pert and sassy."[29]

Beers believed that his "chronic restlessness" (which in a later day might have been designated hyperactivity) accounted for his teachers' insistence that he take an entrance examination for high school instead of being admitted automatically. To this "injustice" he responded in characteristic fashion, by scoring second in the citywide examination. After thus proving himself he again relaxed, so that his academic performance at Hillhouse High School, which he entered in September 1891, was not better than at grammar school.[30]

At high school Beers concentrated on accomplishing extracurricular goals, which interested him much more than his studies and which displayed his flair for management and organization. He accepted election to one fraternity but refused to become a charter member of another because he felt he

Ida and Robert Beers with their five sons. Clifford is at the extreme right.

"was good enough for the best," Gamma Delta Psi, to which he was the first man elected from the class of 1894. Shortly thereafter he became assistant business manager of Gamma Delta Psi's biweekly school newspaper, *The Crescent,* and then succeeded to the managership. In that position he enlarged the paper, made a profit, acquired a taste for business, and also had the satisfaction of seeing some of his jokes in print. The Banjo Club interested him because he wanted to run it. In a few weeks he learned to play the banjo well enough to join and then did become the manager; under his leadership the club obtained commissions to play in local churches, sometimes for money. In his senior year his classmates elected him chairman of the Promenade Committee, a position second to that of class president. Beers boasted that he organized the best and largest promenade that "any class ever gave." He made so much money from selling advertising space that the "box-holders" received a return on their contributions.[31]

The *Courier* of New Haven, in an editorial about his election, described Clifford Beers as "a young man of exceptional executive ability . . . a born diplomat. He has arranged matters for the promenade in a manner which has pleased the board of education, the class and all concerned. In him the committee has a first class chairman." Also in the leadership of the class were two young men, Herbert Fisher and Paul McQuaid, who were to remain Clifford Beers' lifelong friends and supporters.[32]

The only sport Beers engaged in was tennis, to which he gave his all. The summer he was sixteen he played four thousand games, frequently for ice cream sodas. Since he often won, it was lucky for him that his opponents did not always pay their debts. Beers won the singles championship, spurred by the taunts of girls in the audience who, he imagined, felt he had ignored them, when in truth he was just shy with girls.[33] Whether the girls fired his fighting spirit is not important except for the fact that he told the story, which illustrates his lifelong view of himself as the subject of other peoples' hostility or contempt, which led him to rise to the challenge to prove his worthiness. It is tempting to conclude that as a child he felt rejected by his mother, and, thinking himself somehow to blame, believed that he did not deserve love and attention, which he badly wanted and endlessly sought.

‡

Side by side with Clifford Beers' depiction of apparently "normal" activities of a middle-class child growing up at the end of the nineteenth century, he described his inner anxiety. Much of the information about this aspect of his childhood and youth derives from his introspective writing during his manic phases in 1902 and 1905. At that time, by comparison with his buoyant feelings, his previous state seemed to him to have always been somewhat depressed. In consequence, he tended to stress excessively the pathological or prepsychotic aspects of his past. He was not wholly unaware of this bias and admitted that at least during the first three years of high school he had considered himself normal and that only in retrospect did his health appear fragile. He characterized himself from age six to ten as "extremely nervous and very diffident." "When I was seven or eight years old I had the same peculiar feelings I had during the last two years. I simply seemed to leave the earth entirely and lose myself in space." He had many of the "nervous tricks common to nervous children," such as nail-biting, which he finally overcame when he was twelve upon the offer of a reward of money, an inducement he could seldom resist. The neat appearance of his unbitten nails then convinced him finally to stop the habit.[34]

He saw himself as having been a "hyper-sensitive" child worried about the ordinary occurrences of life, tortured by a morbid self-consciousness, and so shy that "after putting off kilts and donning short trousers — for which most boys are only too eager — I hid behind doors and pieces of furniture." At eleven, he wished himself dead when, because he was deemed too young, he was "denied the privilege of participating in a parade in which many of my friends were to march and uphold the flag and honor of the country. This wish to die was not a momentary flash of disappointment; it remained the subject of my morbid contemplation during part of an afternoon spent alone in my room."[35] He seldom would speak to strangers, a problem that endured into his teens. When he was thirteen or fourteen he became depressed and remained so until about sixteen; he also suffered from severe headaches about three times a week during his fifteenth year. His depression coincided with his first "love affair," an unrequited affection for the "one and only girl I ever thought I loved," he wrote when he was twenty-six.[36] He admitted masturbating to a mild extent when a boy and to having nocturnal emissions, which disturbed him enough to try patent medicines such as Fowler's (without success) and to consult his family physician and godfather, Dr. B. H. Cheney. His addiction to sensational newspaper stories was morbid, he thought, and accounted for his dwelling "on the accounts of criminal cases and the like" during his first mental breakdown.[37]

Although Beers avoided discussing the possible origins of his boyhood problems, he did note one source or embarrassment, a skin color "more like that of a Cuban or a Portuguese" than an American, which his mother blamed on some Portuguese boys who had annoyed her when she was pregnant with him. Playmates teased him about his swarthy complexion, and his brother Sam, sharp-tongued like himself, made Clifford cry by saying that his face was "dirty and it never will be clean." When he went to heaven, he asked an aunt, would he be white "like other boys?" He imagined himself a dark and ugly duckling in a family of fair and handsome sons, although his hair and eyes were not dark and photographs show him to be as good-looking, if not more so, than his brothers.[38]

Despite all his adolescent problems, real or imagined, Clifford seems to have been an outgoing, aggressive boy, popular among his peers, who accepted his leadership and friendship and respected his ability to get what he wanted. He had many friends, some of whom remained devoted to him throughout his often troubled life.

As the time for graduation from high school drew near he had to decide what he would do afterward. Although indifferent to a college education he evidently felt no great pressure to seek a job, so for lack of anything better he would go to Yale. He chose the Sheffield Scientific School, which had a business course, rather than the more prestigious Yale College, because of his interest in a business career and perhaps also because its curriculum was only three rather than four years. The difference in status probably did not bother him, as he never cared about academic achievement. He always proudly considered himself a Yale man and remained interested all his life in alumni affairs.

‡

As Beers prepared late in June 1894 to take the entrance examination for the Sheffield School a calamity befell his family. After returning from a fraternity banquet at four o'clock in the morning, Clifford had just fallen into a sound sleep when his mother rushed into his room on the top floor. Sam, Clifford's next oldest and most lovable brother, was in a convulsion and seemingly near death.

Sam lived but continued to suffer for the following six years from what Dr. Cheney called convulsions of epileptic form. Physicians at that time hesitated to tell patients that they had epilepsy; it was considered closely allied to mental illness, and both disorders were thought to be hereditary and incurable in the majority of cases. One supposedly inherited not the actual illness but a predisposition in the form of a weak nervous system. The Beers family shared this view, which made Sam's condition even more shocking because they had no knowledge of epilepsy or "insanity" in the family.[39]

The onset of such afflictions, moreover, was thought by both physicians and lay people to derive significantly from an immoral way of life. Just as serious-mindedness, work, moderation, and control of the emotions safeguarded one against mental illness, so self-indulgence, idleness, excessive indulgence in alcohol, and sexual activity exposed one to its dangers. Clifford could find no evidence of such dissipation in Sam's life, so why did this happen? The only possibly bad habit he had was to keep very late hours and then get up early to go to work.[40] Sam himself thought his illness originated from a fall years before when he struck the back of his head.

Sam's rational state prohibited placing him in a mental institution and the family could not afford a nurse, so Clifford, who was free that summer and the oldest son still at home, took care of him. Almost a year later, in May 1896, Sam was sent on a sailing trip around the world from which he returned unimproved. He stayed home for a while, lived on various farms in Connecticut, then in a doctor's home, and finally died in early July 1900 in a Hartford hospital. An autopsy disclosed a large tumor at the base of the brain, which in the end caused total blindness by pressing on the optic nerve.

From the moment Clifford understood the nature of Sam's condition he lost his peace of mind. Sam took his illness with equanimity, but Clifford could not, especially as he had to care for him, though the family rallied around and tried to do their best. He wanted desperately to escape his responsibility before his own strength gave out; he "was crushed by the load—mainly mental" that he was carrying. He "inwardly rebelled" at his "fate."[41]

It may be that Clifford was suffering from guilt over secret wishes that his brother might die and thereby free him of the burden of caring for him, and that to justify these "unworthy" feelings he argued that Sam's illness undermined his "own health and wreck[ed] [his] nervous system."[42] Another source of worry was the fear that he himself was fated to be struck by "nervous" disease, not only because of Sam's experience but also because his older brothers, George and William, had gone through emotional crises in their youth. Clifford called the years twenty-four to twenty-seven the "Beers Boys Climacteric."[43]

He felt sure that the suffering he endured through a period covering nearly six years, coinciding with the illness and death of Sam, "was more acute than that endured [by] Sam during his six year siege with epilepsy." He believed that he had tortured himself into what he later described as an "acute stage of neurasthenia," which today would be called psychoneurosis.[44]

During this time, except for a few months' absence, Beers was a student at Yale, where even during the first semester he managed to pass his exams.[45] He claimed that he did average work but had "trouble remembering things, particularly studies such as geometry." Sitting in class was very difficult, especially if he might be called upon to recite. He felt terrified lest his "psychic convulsion" be converted into a physical one—that is, that he would have an epileptic seizure in public. His nerves seemed to be snapping "like so many minute bands of rubber stretched" beyond the breaking point.[46] When forced to recite he would sweat, he recalled, odoriferously, profusely, and in colors, "from coffee color to blue-pink etc." Indeed he claimed that to the day of writing in 1905 he continued "to perspire similarly—but less odoriferously and of more cheerful colors—when in an excited condition."[47] When called upon to speak he usually said he was unprepared, and it seems that his instructors excused him when he explained that his brother was ill. Yet when he could no longer be so exempted he performed well enough, though often he felt "stage struck from tip to toe and limp as a dish rag" afterwards.[48]

During his last year at Yale Beers sought help from Dr. Cheney several times, especially before examinations, when he asked for a "nerve sedative." Cheney attributed Clifford's mental state "entirely" to his having cared for Sam for so long, and reported that he passed his exams "creditably and seemed to recover his spirits." He recalled, too, that he had never noticed any symptoms of melancholia in Clifford before or during his college career.[49]

Beers recalled that he had avoided the theater for the same reason as he did speaking in class. All pleasure was impossible if there was a chance he would suffer an attack of epilepsy in a public place. Since Beers considered his brother's "epilepsy" a reflection upon himself, if he became ill in public his own insecure self-image would suffer a severe if not intolerable blow. Even going out into society proved too painful. He slept fairly well but complained of not feeling refreshed upon waking but rather exhausted; his "nerves ached." Sometimes he would take "two or three drinks for the effect."[50]

Later Beers felt convinced that he had been "insane during [the] last two years" of his college career.[51] Yet, according to his own later reports, at the same time as he was undergoing excruciating torment, he functioned well, especially in activities that interested him, and his classmates never suspected his distress, which was probably exaggerated in retrospect.

As in high school, Beers managed at college to achieve all his goals, most of them extracurricular. Like his friends, he contented himself with just getting by academically—a "gentleman's C" was enough. He would read only the books he absolutely had to, still preferring newspapers; he professed to dislike imaginative literature, including Shakespeare (a course he had to repeat), and to be attracted only by "facts." His considerable energies were expended in social and business activities. Promptly elected to the secret society of his choice, Berzelius, the one his brother William had joined, he never missed a meeting in three years, even when his anxiety kept him from going to classes. In November 1895, at the peak of his inner panic, he became editor of the biweekly *Yale Record* and edited its twenty-fifth volume; the following March he was appointed business manager.[52] He was able to go downtown to solicit advertisements for the paper and could "hustle an add [sic] when I couldn't go near a recitation." He had no difficulty in studying.[53] He earned enough money (between four and five hundred dollars) to pay part of his tuition, passed all his examinations, and in June 1897 received his diploma within the prescribed three years.[54]

During his junior year (1895–1896), supposedly his worst time psychologically, Clifford Beers was also listed as chairman of the class of 1897 historians and as a member of the triennial committee; he was asked to write about his freshman year for his class book. In the class bulletin for that year he was cited for his "brilliant recitations" in English. He was also writing jokes for the *Yale Record,* a few of which were published in *Life Magazine.* In a class census he got twenty out of ninety-nine votes as the wittiest, placing him third in that category, and at least seven men chose him as the biggest bluffer, three, the "most to be admired," and four, the "most original."[55]

His claim that he shunned social life is contradicted by his own statement that when he "occasionally 'got on a skate with the boys at college,' 'three or four beers would do the job.'"[56] And his nicknames, "High Ball," "Cliff," and "Whit," do not fit the somber tones with which he depicted his college years. One of his many friends noted years later that he was "quite the life of the party" with the "knack of flavoring sound sense with piquancy that makes the delightful companion." He enjoyed verbal jousting, especially if he found someone as "sassy" as he, "if indeed that ever happened."[57] His eyes shining intensely in his swarthy, good-looking face, which at one time sported a thick mustache, Clifford Beers was an attractive man. Although of average height (5′ 9½″) and physique, he struck an impressive figure because of the vigor and charm of his personality. No one doubted that he would distinguish himself in whatever he did. Neither his close friends nor his acquaintances ever "had any suggestion of the mental torture that reached a climax when he returned to New Haven in 1900 for his triennial celebration at Yale. He cloaked his fears so well that we learned with something like chagrin that our companion had been hitched to a spectre for years."[58]

‡

Upon graduation Beers felt well enough to look for a job away from home, in New York City. To tide him over until the move he took a job for twelve dollars a week at the New Haven Tax Commission Office. Fourteen months later he finally landed a job in New York with Hoggson Brothers, interior decorators at Forty-fourth Street and Fifth Avenue. He was ecstatic. It was not very exciting work, consisting mainly of making himself useful, including running errands, and paid little, only six dollars a week, but it was considered a coup for a neophyte.[59] "You have every right in the world to be enthusiastic over it," wrote his brother Will. "Your natural business instincts will carry you through, as they always have in the past."[60]

In September 1898 he began work at Hoggson's. The hours were longer than at the tax office, but he did not mind, for now he had "something to work for."[61] He surprised himself by feeling somewhat nostalgic for his parents' home, and he went back to New Haven on many weekends to see friends and relatives and kept up with affairs at Yale.[62]

"Something to work for" soon proved insufficient. It was not that after eighteen months he was earning only eleven dollars a week, but rather that he found the details of the work unbearable and craved an opportunity to exercise his own initiative. "Dabbling with silks, and satins, wallpaper—figuring etc. got on my nerves—and to tell the truth I must have got on the nerves of my employers—for I was very far from being an efficient office-boy-bookkeeper-errand runner, or rather errand crawler."[63] As usual, he imagined that his employers were critical of him; in fact, they had raised his salary by five dollars a week in a year and a half and had extraordinary faith in him. Even Beers admitted later that, despite his crankiness, some of his fellow employees did him many favors.[64]

But he was not one to accept a subservient position for long. He left Hoggson's for a new job at about thirteen dollars a week with Bankers Life Insurance Company, a small firm on downtown Nassau Street, whose president was an intimate family friend with whom he was living on Eighty-third Street. His spirits lifted only temporarily, even after he received a $600 commission for insuring a college friend for $25,000. The clerical work, mainly bookkeeping, did not suit him, and he "played the play-game to the limit rather than the work-game," seeing various friends living in New York City and occasionally entertaining his aunts on visits from New Haven.[65] In 1902, after his breakdown, he told his brother George, "I went crazy on Simon pure deviltry . . . My morals were so loose that they would have made an excellent rattle for his Satanic Majesty."[66] Whether this meant relations with women is not clear. He was certainly interested in women all his life and was attractive and charming enough to appeal to them; later evidence that he had venereal disease indicates that he satisfied his sexual appetites somewhere.[67]

As in his college days, he fluctuated between high spirits and feelings of depression, continuing "to have . . . more or less nervous days, weeks, and months." When he felt low he would, as before, resort to alcohol.[68] Some indication of his difficulties must have been transmitted to his fellow employees for he requested one of them "to let up on the standing joke, which had to do with [his] medicine-taking-mania and to discourage others, when the subject came up." During this time January 1900, he imagined he had "Bright's Disease, Neurasthenia, Cerebro Spinal Meningitis, Articular and Intercostal Rheumatism, Gout, Nervous Dyspepsia, Cirrhosis of [the] Liver, Psychical Epilepsy, Mania, . . . Enlarged Spleen, Torpid Liver, Nephritis, Bronchitis, Appendicitis, Heart [burn] (chronic) and hundreds of other ailments." The only concrete sign of any disorder found by the company physician was that Beers' eyes were bloodshot.[69]

Finally his anxiety became acute. In March 1900 he suffered a severe "grippe" that kept him home for several weeks and to which he attributed his ensuing depression: "Despair seemed to clutch at my heart." From that time, he wrote in an unpublished autobiography, "I was never free from . . . acute depression. . . . I grew more and more nervous—slept less and less—brooded more and more—indulged in a few things I might better have left alone—hoping thereby to bolster up my drooping vitality." His distress intensified from March to June, surpassing anything he had previously experienced. He became suspicious of "everyone and everything" and imagined that certain fellow employees were trying to do him in. On June 15 he had a most horrifying experience: although able to answer questions he could not speak. His hand was too unsteady to copy records and his vision too blurred to read words and figures clearly. His nervous system "seemed tied up in a knot," and he felt as though he "would fly apart." As usual, no one apparently detected his mental state.[70]

Beers decided to take his two weeks' vacation immediately. He made hurried arrangements to go to New Haven, and, conscious of an impending calamity, burned many of his personal papers. Among these were his "literary efforts which had failed of publication in the college paper," but which he had "jealously cherished for several years," including a book of several hundred squibs. Also destroyed were certain letters, "one of them really compromising," and "some things which were meant for me and me alone."[71]

Arriving in New Haven, he went to the family home at 30 Trumbull Street, where none of his relatives seemed to take his complaints very seriously: he had been a neurasthenic for five years and they assumed that his ups and downs would in time disappear. It may be, too, that they were preoccupied with Sam, who was then close to death. Clifford's old fear of epilepsy returned. He had in the past told friends that he would "rather die than live an epileptic," but never really threatened suicide because he always felt he would escape Sam's fate. But on June 18 or 19 he concluded that he would indeed succumb and "began to think of suicide in case [he] did . . . have an attack."[72]

He worked out alternative plans. A nearby sandy beach seemed an ideal spot to drown oneself, or perhaps the North Haven meadows. He had to reject a watery death, though, because he lacked the "courage" to go out of doors, much less to go any distance away. Then he had a delusion that the long-feared epileptic seizure had occurred. Time was running out. He must act quickly before someone discovered him during a seizure and made suicide impossible. The following day he took to bed and scarcely talked, ate, or slept; he could not read. The family fetched two physicians to examine him; they found nothing seriously wrong.

The next day Clifford decided that the only sure way to self-destruction was a leap from his window. He asked to see the doctor, to whom he said only that his "bowels were paralyzed etc. etc."; he was given some appropriate medicine. In retrospect he considered himself "absolutely insane" at this time, but neither his relatives nor his physicians were aware of it.[73] Apparently only an extravagant exhibition of violence or incoherence, or both, could convince anyone that Clifford suffered from some sort of mental disorder—an old, popular misconception. Even Dr. Cheney's lifelong observation of Clifford Beers did not enable him more than any lay person to recognize his true mental state.

Beers did dissemble. He remained quiet when Aunt Mame and his mother spent some time with him. Finally at midday, when left alone, he went to the window and opened the blind, but instead of jumping climbed out, hung from the sill, and let go. This ambivalent method of suicide almost surely saved his life. He landed squarely on both heels, "miraculously" not on the concrete walk or a nearby iron grate, but on a two-foot square piece of earth; as he fell he struck the building with his arms, which may also have broken his fall. One heel bone was crushed and most of the small bones in each arch were broken; he injured his back and was cut slightly on the fore-head.[74]

The family was eating dinner in the dining room when Clifford fell past the window. Carl rushed out and brought him into the house. He had evi-dently lost consciousness; when he came to he explained that he thought he was going to have an attack of epilepsy and wished that "it was all over." He then exclaimed, "Oh, I don't see why I did it." He thought his back was bro-ken but was able to raise himself. Doctors were sent for and Clifford remem-bered hearing them talk. They finally decided to send him to Grace Hospital, and in the afternoon his father and Aunt Mame came to visit. Clifford, be-lieving he had disgraced his family, felt too ashamed to see them.

From the moment he struck earth in his suicide attempt, Beers claimed to have lost all terror of an epileptic attack. Instead he suffered fears of police persecution, first for attempted suicide, then for numerous crimes that he could not recall. The iron bars on his window at Grace Hospital he associ-ated not with his suicide attempt but with incarceration by the police. Most of his delusions were auditory: he imagined hearing voices of friends, rela-tives, and policemen discussing his heinous acts against humanity. He also found that everything had a saline taste. He felt guilt-ridden over unspeci-fied youthful indiscretions and considered them all subject to police investi-gation; then he conceived himself the perpetrator of all the crimes he had ever read about in newspapers. When medical students discussed obstetrical cases in his presence he thought he must be mixed up in a malpractice suit. Upon first entering the hospital he could not speak, so that confession of all these crimes was not possible; later when he could speak he would not, for fear of implicating his family.

During the three or four weeks he lay in Grace Hospital, his feet in casts, Clifford was visited almost daily by his father and by his brother George, who would drop in on his way home from work. There is only one reference to his mother in Clifford's detailed accounts of that time. When one night the doctors feared he might die, George brought their mother to see him:

He came and told me that mother was downstairs and asked if I wished to see her. I believe I told him no. For me to see any of the relatives I had brought such suffering and disgrace upon — was torture — so it was not strange that I did not care to see any of them. Later in the week when the crisis was passed — for they could not tell whether the shock

to my spine would cause meningitis or not — or cause death itself — I
began to grow stronger. I began to eat and when relatives came I paid
some attention to them, though I don't believe I talked any.

He does not mention whether he saw his mother again but talks affection-
ately of his father's visits and those of his childhood friend John Veitch.[75]

By the time Beers left Grace Hospital he suspected that everyone there
was a police spy trying to force him to confess his many crimes. He therefore
refused to speak, except for a few words. Still Dr. Cheney did not recognize
that he was psychologically disturbed, and he was discharged.[76] At home he
protested when George, who had taken responsibility for him and had
promised not to employ anyone who had attended him at the hospital, did so
anyway because of a scarcity of nurses. It did not matter that Clifford had
scarcely seen this woman; he remembered her and it reinforced his suspi-
cions of the hospital staff and encouraged him to question the authenticity
of his family members. His condition deteriorated to the point where he
thought his real relatives were under arrest and languishing in jail. Again he
refused to speak. By then there could be no doubt that he was disturbed, and
in August 1900 the family decided to sent him to a mental hospital.[77]

‡ 2 ‡

Stamford Hall

The realization that Clifford was disturbed enough to be hospitalized must have been calamitous for the family, as it has been for most families, but especially so for the Beerses. Sam, after suffering for six years, was dying. Now Clifford, the promising young businessman and lively companion, sat mute and unreachable. And who knew whether he might not again attempt suicide? There probably seemed no alternative but to institutionalize him.

By this time, the beginning of the twentieth century, hospitalization of those thought to be mentally ill was widely accepted in the Western world. Although a stigma remained attached to mental illness, few urban families would find it practical to secrete their afflicted relatives as Mrs. Rochester was at Thornfield Hall. The "modern" idea that mental disorder was always a natural disease to be treated medically and in special institutions had taken hold, if still feebly by 1847 when Charlotte Brontë published *Jane Eyre,* certainly strongly by the 1900s.

Mental patients in the eighteenth century were admitted to the first British North American hospitals with the hope of restoring them to sanity as well as protecting them and society from harm. Conditions in these hospitals left much to be desired, but the patients probably fared better there than outside.[1] Some lucky ones were treated kindly and received medical care from respectable physicians like the eminent Dr. Benjamin Rush. Later, in the early nineteenth century, partly under the influence of developments in England and on the Continent, new kinds of mental hospitals were built. They practiced "moral treatment," a total therapeutic environment based upon the belief that the mentally ill responded best to kindness, moral suasion, and a regimen as nearly normal as possible. Most forms of harsh physical punishment were, in theory, to be eliminated and physical restraints kept to a minimum. The prime object, again in theory, was cure, the mood hopeful.

The early successes of this movement were undermined in the 1850s and thereafter. An influx of impoverished immigrants, among a host of other factors, helped to overcrowd and then lower the standard of treatment in the state hospitals that at Dorothea Dix's prodding had begun to proliferate and

19

eventually came to hold the vast majority of patients. After the Civil War a renewed emphasis on somatic therapy among physicians, together with a revival of belief in the incurability of insanity, helped to erode the psychological or "moral" aspects of moral treatment, even in the best and least crowded hospitals. In state institutions, which catered largely to the poor, the major goal became custody at the lowest possible cost. Reported recovery rates declined sharply, and the optimistic attitudes of the prewar decades gave way to widespread pessimism.

In cases of manic-depressive psychoses (of which Clifford Beers' illness was thought to be an example) nothing much was done for patients but to provide an ordered existence, care for their physical needs, control their outbursts, and see whether time would be a healer. Patients were lucky, though, if that was all the treatment they got. Hospital superintendents did not sanction abuse of patients, but the prevailing mood did not discourage it, and they did approve of physical restraints (strait jackets, for example) to curb "violent" behavior.

Not a great deal more was then understood about mental illness than a century before. There was no accepted theory of mental disorders and little research in the field; one major breakthrough, proof that paresis or general paralysis was a final stage of syphilis, was still to come; Kraepelin's more accurate description and classification of mental disorders was just appearing in the United States; Freud's writings had yet to electrify or horrify American psychologists and psychiatrists. There were a few psychiatrists interested in reforming mental hospitals, but they had so far effected little change in the majority of institutions, and a mental hygiene movement started in the 1880s was short-lived.

For middle-class families in the Beerses' situation there were several choices of mental institutions. They could commit Clifford to a public mental hospital, which would be free if he was deemed indigent but which would require him to be legally declared incompetent to handle his affairs and thereby stigmatized. Another possibility was a private hospital, which could charge steep fees, but which did not require official branding of a patient as insane. In addition, the treatment might be better, and it would be possible to buy a great variety of services for the patient and so possibly increase his chances for recovery and make him more comfortable. There were two types of private mental hospitals, those operated for profit (the proprietary) and the nonprofit (the corporate). Proprietary hospitals abounded in England, but in the United States they were still few and their reputation was undistinguished, their main advantage being the secrecy they offered. The corporate hospitals, however, were considered among the best mental institutions in the United States. They had led the transformation of care of the insane in the early nineteenth century and had maintained their preeminent position, although not their high recovery rates. Their fees were not necessarily lower than those of the proprietary hospitals, but the range of rates put them within the reach of many middle-class patients. However, secrecy was not so easily preserved as in the proprietary institutions, which would often mask their real function by calling themselves sanitariums or rest homes and by categorizing psychotic patients euphemistically as "nervous," "exhausted," or "neurasthenic."

Clifford Beers eventually experienced treatment in all three types of hospital, but the one first chosen by his family was proprietary, even though they could not afford the expense and had to accept the help of his generous uncle Samuel Merwin.[2] That they did so indicated hope for a speedy recovery and a desire to keep the matter quiet. If complete secrecy proved impossible, one could always say the patient was not insane but had merely had a nervous breakdown, which the family may have wanted to believe anyway.

‡

On August 11, 1900, almost two months after his suicide attempt, Beers entered Stamford Hall, in Stamford, Connecticut, owned by Dr. Amos Givens and advertised as treating nervous and mental diseases and opium and alcohol addiction. He spent eight months there, of which the primary record is his own, in unpublished memoirs and letters and in *A Mind That Found Itself,* published eight years after the fact, supplemented by other contemporary evidence. Although the available sources are not definitive, they provide a fairly full account of Beers' experiences, which as a rule he faithfully described.

During his entire stay at Stamford Hall, Beers claims to have remained virtually mute and to have retained his delusions of persecution.[3] Because of his foot injuries he was confined to his room during the first months; only after the casts were removed did he move about somewhat, but even then fear of police prosecution led him to hide the extent of his physical recovery. Despite all his psychological distortions and physical incapacities he remained mentally alert, especially in reference to the treatment he received.

Dr. Givens, the proprietor of Stamford Hall and an object of Beers' criticism, summarized his condition at the sanitarium in a letter to the superintendent of the Connecticut State Hospital. When Beers arrived he was "profoundly depressed, muttering to himself, sleeping about three hours in the night; bowels were constipated; was very anaemic, ankles needed careful attention; sighed a good deal; answered questions when urged to do so. When his clothing was taken to him, he said it looked like his but was not his; when his relatives came to see him, he said they looked like his relatives, but were not. . . . He stated he had had a seminal emission twice a week, and had had for some time." Upon discharge his general condition had improved somewhat. He had gained a few pounds, slept better, took his food more readily, ate at the table, and walked about the grounds. Givens thought that "sexual exhaustion" (a euphemism for masturbation) was a complication in Beers' case.[4]

Considering the extent of Beers' withdrawal and the clues he supplied about his psychological state, Givens' report was superficial and indicated the inattention to patients' mental conditions that tended to prevail, not only at "sanitariums" like Stamford Hall, but at most mental hospitals. And Dr. Givens did not mention any trouble he had had with Beers.

As for Beers' account, although he was critical of Givens, he did acknowledge that he improved under his care to the extent that his delusions of persecution eventually abated, but not before he first went through a painful period of highly intensified illusions, delusions, and hallucinations. Before his eyes moved horrible pictures that were flashed on screens by detectives: first a series of bloody crimes, then a chamber of horrors (reminiscent of something he had actually seen some years past) where a gorilla holding the gory body of a woman underwent a metamorphosis "strictly in accordance with Darwin's theory": the creature became manlike and repeatedly plunged a dagger into the woman's breast. His senses of smell and touch were affected; familiar foods tasted peculiar because detectives had poisoned them; his clothes did not feel real and must have been planted by detectives. His relatives were dead and those visiting him were detectives in disguise. Even the kindest attendant was his enemy. All wanted to force a confession from him. At times he would refuse to swallow medicine, even a sugar pill, because he imagined it "saturated with the blood of loved ones," the mere touching of which was to shed their blood. He was afraid he would reveal his guilt. But cautious as he was, he was not immune to normal influences and could not resist ice cream, which he would eat fast, before it melted.[5] He contemplated suicide as a way out, but how could he evade the constant police surveillance?

Because they feared another suicide attempt, Beers' relatives paid for attendants to watch him day and night. The quality of these men (about a dozen during the first weeks) greatly distressed Clifford, as did their rough handling of him. Some were "positively disgusting in appearance and habits. They were almost tramps—in dress, speech and action. They cursed like pirates [using] the most obscene language . . . chewed [tobacco] incessantly and spit in proportion." He believed that the police deliberately placed them there to torture him.[6]

These protestations cannot be brushed aside as exaggerations. Difficulties in finding competent attendants for the mentally ill long antedated Clifford Beers' experiences, and continued low pay, long hours, lack of training, and poor working conditions ensured the perpetuation of the problem. The medical staffs, too, except for some superintendents, tended to be inexperienced and untrained. The level of medical education in the United States was generally low, and specialized training in psychiatry was almost nonexistent, so that most mental hospital staff physicians were young men just out of medical school who learned on the job, while dealing with the patients.

Beers accused the assistant physician at Stamford Hall, a Dr. Hodgson, of mistreating him. His feet still in bandages, Beers sat on his bed and refused to answer the doctor's questions (afraid to talk lest he reveal his crimes or his ability to stand trial for them). The doctor "cuffed" him and, still not evoking a response, "took hold of my arm and jerked me from the bed—throwing me heavily on [the] floor." In the published autobiography Beers describes the incident: "Suddenly . . . as a petulant child locked in a room for disobedience might treat a pillow, he seized my arm and jerked me from the bed."[7]

This affair was witnessed by an attendant, Frank B. Wordin, who had taken charge of Beers a few weeks after his admission and became his protector, albeit Clifford did not then so recognize him. In an unpublished autobiography, Wordin recalled that Hodgson wanted to put Beers on his feet after the casts were removed so that he would not be crippled and became angry when Wordin suggested a more gradual and less painful approach. The physician then pulled Beers up so violently that he fell forward into Wordin's arms.[8]

Beers, like most emotionally troubled people, tended to see everything in terms of the effects of his own behavior; that is, he was what psychiatrists call *self-referent* (a characteristic that did not entirely disappear when he recovered). To him, in the incident concerning his feet, the physician acted immaturely: frustrated and insulted by what he took to be Beers' disobedience and disrespect, he punished him; he looked upon Beers not as mentally ill but as a normal person and expected normal responses from him. At the same time, Beers declared that if the physicians had explained his condition to him in a rational way—that is, if they had granted him a measure of rationality—things would have gone much better. Wordin, the attendant, also saw the staff as insensitive and sometimes needlessly cruel, but, interested in justifying and inflating himself, he described Dr. Hodgson's behavior as a reaction to his own insubordination. (We do not have the doctor's interpretation.)

Wordin's relationship with Beers illustrates the key role that an attendant could play in relation to a disorder whose symptoms were behavioral and which could be influenced by everything and everyone in the environment. It also indicates the kind of personal involvement that an attendant could develop with a patient in his care. Because of the nature of mental illness, a sensitive, intuitive attendant might be more successful in helping a patient than a busy doctor. More likely, of course, the opposite would happen, and Beers' account of other hospitals focuses upon the adverse effect of attendants on patients' conditions.

Wordin was that rarity, a devoted and capable attendant, but there was a price to be paid for his dedication. His history as a nurse for private patients shows that he would become extremely possessive and controlling. He would stand for no interference, and if a patient improved he would take sole credit. When he became Beers' attendant he disobeyed doctors' orders and acted as his protector against the rest of the staff. So assiduous were his attentions that it was assumed he had either known Beers previously or was related to him. Inevitably he would come into conflict with the staff, about whom he believed Clifford's accusations of cruelty and self-interest, although he acknowledged that sometimes it was their methods rather than their aims that had been wrong.[9] And when in 1906 Beers sent him the Stamford Hall section of *A Mind That Found Itself* for comment on its accuracy Wordin replied that it was too moderate.[10]

When financial considerations forced Beers' transfer to another building where he would have a private room but share only one attendant with fifteen or twenty other patients, Wordin objected. It was "rather mean" of Givens to send Beers to a ward where he would have to associate with a lower class of patients, especially since Wordin "had done so much to bring him around . . . and now [Givens] was trying to undo all that had been done."[11] But Beers liked his new quarters. No longer under constant supervision, he had more time to himself and could relax without fear of revealing his improvement and thus could stave off his imminent prosecution. He evidently had also begun to talk and to read.[12]

Beers depicts Givens as willing to do almost anything to make money, but Wordin indicated in his memoirs that this was not so. For example, Givens refused to give morphine to an addicted patient even when he threatened to leave the hospital.[13] Still, he probably was as inept and insensitive as Beers charged, although not so much from cruelty as from ignorance and an unwillingness to take the time to mitigate patients' fears and frustrations. Kraepelin's classic description of such cases as Beers' was probably not known to Givens. On the subject of feeding, for example, which caused Givens such concern, Kraepelin wrote, "Feeding often causes great difficulty because the patients resist vigorously on account of lack of appetite or in consequence of delusions . . . they suspect poison. *Kindly persuasion,* patient waiting for the right moment" in most cases lead to the goal.[14]

Beers' treatment, however, was not at that time exceptional in a proprietary hospital; it was probably much the same as that given most depressed patients with similar symptoms — decent physical care but indifferent, unskilled attention to emotional needs. His family was not satisfied. Partly on Wordin's advice they removed him from Stamford Hall in March 1901 and placed him in Wordin's care at his family's home in Wallingford, Connecticut.

‡ 3 ‡

The Hartford Retreat

Beers arrived at Wallingford on March 13 and stayed a little over three months. Everyone was kind to him and Wordin gave his usual attentive care, but Beers remained depressed and withdrawn and suffered from fear of his "enemies." Wordin allowed him considerable freedom, even letting him wander about the community unattended — a serious mistake, Beers recalled, because his delusions were coupled with a hostility so fierce that "had I had a Gatlin gun I would [have] shot everyone in sight — and then myself."[1]

The Beers family, discouraged, debated sending Clifford back to a mental hospital, possibly even one for the incurably insane, which would be less expensive. Under the best of circumstances, mental disorder tends to be a long-term, difficult condition that taxes a family's patience, optimism, bank accounts, and finally even sympathies. In an era of widespread pessimism among physicians about curing insanity, it would probably have been unusual for an afflicted family to remain hopeful, especially since most physicians thought that any recovery would most likely be exhibited within the first year after onset. Up to this time Beers had been depressed and was erroneously considered a victim of dementia praecox (schizophrenia), which had a very pessimistic prognosis.[2]

Before any decision could be made, Clifford arrived in New Haven for a visit home during which he was totally uncommunicative. The previously reluctant family members were compelled to agree that Clifford must be hospitalized again. George's views and actions were especially important, as he was now named Clifford's legal guardian or conservator. George had been in the produce business with his uncle and aging father, but by 1903 he had become treasurer of the Sheffield Scientific School at Yale. He had his father's cheerful temperament plus intelligence, common sense, reliability, and strength of character. Not only Clifford but all the Beers and Cooke household turned to George when in trouble: he was the real head of the family.[3] Many letters from Clifford show his attachment to George and his wife and how much he counted on George's support and concern and looked forward to his letters and visits. One of the surest ways to send him into de-

25

spair was to deprive him of contact with George, a weapon that hospital physicians were quick to use.

George decided to place Clifford, not in an institution for incurables, but in the Hartford Retreat (renamed the Institute of Living in 1943), Connecticut's oldest corporate mental hospital and, under its first superintendent, Dr. Eli Todd, a pioneer in offering the new moral treatment. Although the Retreat retained a commitment to humane care, by the time Clifford Beers arrived in 1901 moral treatment as a therapeutic system and its attendant optimism had disappeared, and the Retreat had lost its position as the most successful mental hospital in the United States. No other institution supplanted it, for there appeared to be few outstanding therapeutic successes anywhere. The Retreat's superintendent, Dr. Henry P. Stearns, who served from 1874 to 1905, had at first advocated nonrestraint and other improvements, but by 1901 he was old and ill, and conditions had deteriorated. The care offered at the Retreat was no different from or better than that at similar corporate hospitals, and its limited resources inhibited innovation.[4]

‡

On June 11, 1902, ten days after he visited his family, Beers left Wordin's care with a cold farewell (he considered Wordin his enemy) and entered the Hartford Retreat, committed by the Probate Court. He recognized the city of Hartford and shortly after arriving realized that he was in a hospital again. He was not unhappy to be there, though. Here we can see the danger of the sweeping condemnation of all institutionalization so common today. For Beers at this stage of his depression, the hospital was preferable to living in the community. The physical setting was soothing: his quarters were comfortable and "though the view was a restricted one, a vast expanse of lawn, surrounded by groups of trees—patches of primeval forest—gave the place an atmosphere which was not without its remedial value." It was pleasant and peaceful, especially for the untroublesome and undemanding patient who observed the hospital routine and did as he was told. After breakfast at 7:30 A.M., patients able to go out were taken for a walk on the hospital grounds in good weather, while others could stroll on the lawn or sit under the trees. After a noon lunch, active patients again spent several hours out of doors doing whatever they wished, with an attendant always watching. At about 3:30 all patients returned to their rooms for the rest of the day; those who wanted to attend the almost daily religious services might do so. There were some lawn games and indoor games like checkers and cards and occasionally a dance in the evening; a piano was available; the women could sew or knit. The small library contained old books, mainly nonfiction, as imaginative literature was still considered injurious to disturbed minds. It was a dull existence, without active individualized programs to engage patients' interests and energies.[5]

Beers felt content, or as content as one could be who thought he must soon face death after a trial for various crimes. Whenever he heard the bell ring in the administration office — several hundred times a day — he thought his time was up. He still regarded certain persons as detectives and continued to misinterpret what was said to him: for example, the phrase "We'll straighten you out yet" meant to him a hangman's rope. Nevertheless, delusions of touch, smell, sound, and sight no longer plagued him, though he later said that he occasionally still heard voices while he was at the Retreat. Being among other disturbed people was comforting; he had found his stay in the community at the Wordins difficult not only because the complexity of normal life was too much for him but because being surrounded by sane people had made him too painfully aware of his own condition, his "mental inferiority." At the Retreat he felt better, for "many of my associates were, to my mind, vastly inferior to myself." He also was pleased that attendants and physicians treated him kindly.[6] He needed to feel secure and respected, and as long as he remained passive the hospital could fulfill this need. The hospital was small (only 154 patients in 1904),[7] so patients could get individual attention and there was some feeling of intimacy.

Still, Beers was afraid to reveal his improved condition. At first abjuring his recently acquired habit of reading, he soon read books, magazines, and even his mail secretly. Although the still weakened condition of his ankles limited his physical activity and he walked flatfooted for months, he was stronger than he let on. Afraid of arrest and trial, he feigned weakness.[8] The detailed case reports corroborate Beers' own account of steady progress.[9]

Finally, a year after his admission, in the summer of 1902, he began "to talk a little, on the sly, to a few patients," who could not testify against him because they were "crazy." This was the first clear break in his conviction that all the people he met were detectives and therefore untrustworthy. He made a friend, another patient who had also been in the insurance business, to whom he confided his disbelief in the identity of his visitors. This man, he said, "did perhaps more than anyone to get me well. It was he, with his insatiable curiosity, who made me talk."[10] At the same time, he continued to look for opportunities to commit suicide before his improving health became so obvious that the police could put him on trial. If his "reason" had not come back when it did, he insisted, he would definitely have killed himself, a doubtful contention considering how successfully he had always managed to avoid doing so. Hoping to filch a spikelike tool from the hospital's lawn mower with the intent of using it on himself when he came to trial, he did not pick it up when he saw it lying on the path: the police had left it there to trap him and were watching his every move. Other plans proved equally infeasible.[11]

His delusions were on the wane. He had already begun to abandon the notion that the police falsified all the information he was receiving. The hospital record for July 1, 1902, notes that he appeared to be a little "brighter" and to show some interest in what was happening around him. By July 20 he was answering questions, and on August 15 he "reads his paper, converses pleasantly . . . and appears much brighter."[12]

Beers decided to test his family's verity. His friend, who could go to town, suggested that he search the New Haven telephone directory for the Beerses' addresses; Clifford did not answer, as he would have previously, that the phone book was a false document printed to fool him. Then, urged by his friend, he wrote to George telling him to bring the letter (mailed outside by the friend to avoid police interception) on his next visit as evidence of his identity. The letter of course created great excitement at home. George phoned the physician in charge of Clifford's case and wrote to Clifford, who made the doctor assure him that George's call was genuine. As soon as George appeared on August 30 with the letter, Clifford was convinced, without reading it, that he was indeed his brother. That moment, "all was changed"—his delusions vanished. At this "culminating moment of . . . gradual re-adjustment" he instantaneously moved from a "condition of absolute insanity" to comparative sanity. Then, sitting under a tree all afternoon, he poured out to George in detail what he had been suffering.[13]

In fact, Clifford was prepared before seeing George to accept his existence and had been steadily shedding his delusions. On the day of the meeting his physician wrote that Clifford said he now believed that "his people are not dead and recognizes that he has been deluded. A visit from his brother was what finally convinced him of this fact."[14] From then on Clifford considered himself not really ill, but merely elated, and if not wholly sane, not really insane. Like many lay people, he equated so-called rationality with so-called sanity, when actually he was moving not from "absolute insanity" to relative sanity but from one to another stage of his disorder.[15]

‡

From depression Beers passed into mania. It was at this time that doctors diagnosed him as a manic-depressive. He reveled in the simple activities of life—eating, walking, reading, playing the piano, singing, writing, and, above all, talking. Silent for years, now he wouldn't stop. "I fear that the doctors . . . will almost regret that I am on earth again, as I give them . . . an earful every time they get within range." He slept only a few hours a night, seemed tireless, and gained great joy from everything he did, although he could not concentrate on any one thing for very long. New vast projects filled his mind, and everything took on new significance as an act of God. He counted the duration of his illness in days, hours, minutes, and then seconds—68,947,200 from June 23, 1900, to August 30, 1902. He developed delusions of grandeur and became "extremely abusive toward those who [did] not entirely agree with him"—so much so that in September the freedom of the grounds that had first been given him was withdrawn. That some people doubted his sanity at this time amazed him. He never felt so mentally alert. For the first time in his life he now knew what mental health was, he told Superintendent Stearns, for until the day he recognized George, he had never been quite sane: as far back as his early childhood he had had feelings of dissociation from reality.[16]

He started on "the greatest literary debauch on 'Bughouse' records." His friends and relatives, from whom he had felt alienated for so long, were now sent lengthy and frequent letters telling about his marvelous recovery. They became so long and he wrote them so fast (thirty and then forty words a minute, he claimed) that the hospital ran out of paper and gave him wrapping paper which he cut into foot-wide strips. Some of his missives, pasted together, extended over fifty feet — an extraordinary accomplishment, he thought, for one who previously never could sit down and write an article of any length and would write a "fair letter" only with great difficulty and much recopying. To Clifford's annoyance his letters were permitted to go only to George, who would not forward them.[17] But he kept on writing.

His growing elation soon got Beers into trouble. At first, he recalled, he had "behaved pretty well," his excitement expressing itself in letter-writing and playing the piano. "Then I began to get more dictatorial as my expansive ideas got a better grip. I wanted many things and wanted them *on the spot* and any delay on [the] part of those who came in contact with me . . . called forth a long line of highly spiced talk. . . . This . . . abusive language at first did not seem to bother either Dr. A . . . the assistant physician, or the attendants — but in three or 4 weeks time it began to get on the[ir] nerves — and the more I irritated them the more they irritated me."[18] The case record described one incident that Beers never reported. Although the story illustrates the typical behavior of a manic person, he probably felt ashamed of it. Allowed to go to town for a haircut, he at first would not pay the barber, then "finally yielded," and then "attempted to steal [the money] . . . [and] entertained all present with an exaggerated account of his experiences at the Retreat and the cruel treatment which patients receive."[19]

By September 13, two weeks after he had recognized his brother, Beers was placed in the "4th hall" — the violent ward. The hospital record notes that the transfer pleased him very much, as he wanted "to see the whole of the institution in order to write a book on insanity, thereby making millions of dollars." He said later that he had been deliberately provocative in order to see for himself how violent patients were treated. What actually precipitated the move was Clifford's frustration and anger at having been completely cut off from George, an apparent effort by "Dr. A" (the physician who had authority over Clifford's case) to reduce his level of excitement.[20]

It was not George's fault but Dr. A's, Clifford believed. "For six months I was at war with assistant physicians . . . [but] there is only one . . . who I really dislike. I do not hate him either. I simply despise him. . . . He tortured me cruelly and for personal spite." Clifford had begun by liking and respecting Dr. A. Even after they had argued he could write to Aunt Mame that the physician was "a keen proposition and with few exceptions I would rather have his opinion . . . than anyone I know of." But Dr. A would not spend time with him. During his depressed period Clifford rebuffed Dr. A's attempts to make conversation, and when he came out of his depression and wanted to talk, Dr. A scarcely listened. "It is part of the duty of the Assistant Physician to listen to what a patient had to say even though what he says is the quintessence of crazyness," Clifford complained to Dr. Stearns. He wanted desperately "to talk to sane people" of his own class. The attendants were good and well-meaning, but he could not converse with them.[21]

Beers later recalled that he had been starved for the company of an educated man like Dr. A whose "studied and ill-disguised avoidance of me only served to whet my desire to detain him whenever possible."[22] All his life Beers craved the respect of men in important positions; it gave him confidence in his own worth. Dr. A's rebuff, at a time of great vulnerability, was shattering.

Their first serious conflict came when Dr. A would not let Clifford call George. Clifford consigned him to hell. Dr. A got "'huffy' just as if a sane man had said the same thing," and said, "Mr. Beers, unless you can stop using such language I'll have you put on the 4th ward." Clifford threatened to put the doctor in the "gutter" where he belonged. To the fourth ward Clifford went, and Dr. A told George not to call, write, or visit. Clifford was very upset — his desire to investigate the violent ward notwithstanding. It was not nearly as homelike there as the ward he had been in. The walls were bare of pictures, wooden benches and hard chairs stood in place of comfortable seats, the hardwood floors had no rugs, stern rather than friendly attendants watched over the patients, and there was the ever present threat of restraint by strait jacket and isolation in a padded cell. Clifford was in and out of this ward for the next eight weeks.

Worst of all was to be incommunicado. "Come up at once," Clifford wrote George. "Dr. A . . . has put me in the padded cell for telling him to his face what a blankety blank fool he is. Have done so several times during the past two days, but not until he had treated me as a mangy yellow cur that *he* himself is. I shall continue to tell him what I think of him just as long as he continues to treat me as he is at present." Clifford also asked other people to telephone him and wrote to the judge who committed him to the Retreat to find out whether Dr. A was depriving him of his legal rights by forbidding him to phone George.[23]

That George acceded to Dr. A's request to keep away from Clifford is understandable. Not only was he following doctor's orders, but he knew from experience how excited Clifford was and that the level was accelerating. For example, on September 17, Clifford was writing to George when a "tune flashed through my brain which I have not remembered at all in over two years. I went at once to the piano—played the tune and accompaniment without error first off and returned to writing inside of three minutes. Don't tell me I'm crazy. I may be close to it but I have skipped over the border into the land of geniuses."[24]

The next day he sent an eighty-five-page letter, one of several written that day, to Superintendent Stearns, complaining about Dr. A and describing his plans for the future. He would make Yale the world's greatest university, and he intended to write a "book on neurasthenia, psychical epilepsy, insanity and the care of the insane," which he knew would become a "classic."[25]

He also presented a scheme to reform present hospital conditions (the germ of the movement that he actually did later launch). With money from tycoons like Andrew Carnegie, John D. Rockefeller, J. P. Morgan, and the Vanderbilts he expected to finance, as had Morgan in steel, a "Billion Dollar Charity" designed to treat every known disease and called the "Beers Trust Association." He of course would be president but without salary; he would earn a living by writing. History would celebrate him as the "greatest man, with one exception, who ever lived."[26]

These and other plans were revealed to Dr. Stearns on September 18, but Beers still did not get to see him, or the steward, whom he also wanted to see, or obtain "satisfaction" from Dr. A. He then rammed a heavy wooden chair through a glass window in the dining room so that the steward, who was in charge of the building, had to come. Beers demanded to go back to his old ward and have Dr. Stearns take over his case. In return he "agreed to do the right thing." His request was granted. On September 23 he was returned to the third hall, assigned an attendant to accompany him outside the hospital, and given writing material and other things he wanted.[27]

He resumed writing long letters (eight to fifteen or more pages on large paper) to his friends, outlining his plans to be a famous author and to make his wide-ranging reform movement his "life work." At the first opportunity he was "going to write a book" on the subject of insanity. Success would certainly be his, for God had at least twice saved his life and no doubt for a purpose.[28] He remained highly excited and uncontrolled, he admitted later. His delusions of grandeur giving him a "pretty good opinion" of himself, he "undertook to run everything," and he even struck an attendant who tried to take an unwilling new patient out for a walk. Dr. Stearns, who broke up the fight, was grieved to "see a Yale man acting like a rowdy."[29]

Stearns understood manic-depressives well and knew how to manage Beers.[30] Recognizing his excited condition as disturbing to all concerned, but evidently not wanting to banish him to the violent ward, Stearns sent him to the relatively isolated and sparsely occupied annex, where he devoted himself for a few days to reading, writing, and a new enthusiasm, drawing. Now

he would be a great artist as well as a famous writer, and he demanded artists' materials as well as writing paper.[31]

Then trouble began again. On October 12, the hospital record reads,
"[Beers] has had several personal encounters with his attendant. Destroys his
own property, books, pictures, etc., as well as that of the Retreat. When not
granted any demand he may make, he threatens to break windows, etc." He
boasted to George that he could "without exertion keep the entire staff of
this Insane Asylum on the run—and they admit it." A few days later, the
hospital record notes, "sought to strike attendant with a platter and threatened to 'brain the first doctor who dares to poke his nose into the Annex.'"
The reason he became so angry, Clifford explained, was that the attendants
were going to confiscate his collection of corncobs. A souvenir collector
from childhood, and now seeing himself as an "embryonic Raphael" who
should preserve mementos of his development, Clifford fought for his corncobs. Dr. A, acting in place of the ailing Dr. Stearns, put him back in the
fourth hall and refused him books and all drawing and writing materials. He
was "ignored" until he smashed the glass globe around the light in his cell,
for which conduct an attendant allegedly choked him so hard that he could
not get up or talk for twenty-four hours. Then followed what he called his
"false suicide attempt," which the hospital authorities thought genuine and
foiled only by discovering him in time. Considering his excited condition
and past history of unsuccessful tries at suicide, Beers is probably to be believed when he says that the hanging he rigged up with the bedclothes (which
the hospital record says nearly strangled him) was intended as a sham. Since
manic patients are, however, often unable to weigh risks, the "show" may
have become "real." When Dr. A arrived, "probably hoping to find me
dead," Beers proceeded to tell him "what I thought of him."[32]

That evening Dr. A returned with several attendants to place Beers in a
strait jacket, which he acknowledged "was all right enough," but the doctor
pulled and tightened the jacket excessively, which Clifford always believed
he did out of vindictiveness. When asked to loosen the arms Dr. A tightened
them and left, not to return until eleven the next day. Unable to take a full
breath or move his arms, Beers "suffered the tortures of a hundred damned
one" [sic]. How long Beers was kept immobile is not clear, probably for
twenty-one nights and part of the corresponding days. He also said that his
attendants punched and choked him and otherwise physically abused him
when he was obstreperous or would not immediately obey them and that the
padded cell was cold, poorly ventilated, and without a toilet.[33]

Another incident that embittered Beers involved forced feeding. The hospital record notes that on October 25 he refused medicine but yielded when
he saw preparations for administering it by nasal tube; the next day he was
given the medicine by oesophageal tube. Beers related that he would not take
his night medicine because Dr. A had denied him various requests and that

he had given in when threatened by the nasal tube. But Dr. A insisted that he must pay for his obstinacy. For five minutes the doctor tried to tube-feed the medicine, the only result being that Beers suffered a bloody nose; Dr. A then switched to a wooden feeding device. All this time Beers was immobile in a strait jacket. The mild dose of medicine that finally got into his stomach failed to put him to sleep.[34]

Beers considered these procedures not only cruel, vengeful, and unethical but traumatizing:

> When I was placed in straight jacket my mind was clear though in excited state. When I reached [Connecticut State Hospital after leaving the Retreat] my mind was greatly confused and whereas I could on Oct. 8, play 200 tunes on piano I could scarcely recall 20 a month later — numb fingers for over 2 months as result of 1st night in St. JK. [Dr.] A . . . put the screws on. My brain felt on night of Oct. 18 like it did on 22 & 23 of June 1900 [the time of his first suicide attempt]. . . . Was promised food by [Dr.] A . . . but got none.[35]

Superintendent Stearns, a "fine man" who "did everything for me," was, Beers insisted, unaware of the abuse he suffered; otherwise he would never have countenanced it. He tolerated no "slugging" at the hospital except in self-defense and would fire attendants who disobeyed. Stearns later corroborated his judgment and said that never in all his experience had he had a patient in whom he took "such an interest and had such a desire to help . . . back to health." Beers had caused him "more worry than any patient he ever had." By that time, though, Stearns' health was failing rapidly and he seems to have lost contact with what went on in his institution.[36]

‡

Although we do not have the Retreat physicians' (especially Dr. A's) opinions of Beers' case — the hospital case records briefly describe his behavior — it seems that they were following the prescribed approach to manic-depression, from which they assumed Beers to be suffering. Except for the apparent lack of the hereditary factor, he seemed to fit the typical case as then seen. During the depressed stage, Stewart Paton wrote in his authoritative *Psychiatry* (published in 1905 and based substantially on Kraepelin's *Textbook on Psychiatry*), there were no effective drugs. The patient could only be encouraged to be active and measures taken to prevent his committing suicide. In the manic stage it was important to reduce excitement to a minimum. A "suitable narcotic or sedative" would help, as would iron, strychnine, and arsenic tonics. Prolonged or continuous baths might cut short an attack of mania, and the patient should be kept in bed. In any case there was no really effective therapy; the disease would eventually run its course and the patient would improve. Another influential theory, promulgated by neurologists George Beard and S. Weir Mitchell, was that insanity was a pathological intensification of fatigue which could be treated by bed rest.[37] It was also believed that manic patients could die of exhaustion if left unrestrained.

Kraepelin's influential text, adapted by Dr. A. Ross Diefendorf, lecturer in psychiatry at Yale, and published in 1902 (the year Clifford Beers, still manic, was to meet Diefendorf at the Connecticut Hospital for the Insane, where he was assistant physician and pathologist), also emphasized creating a calm environment for the manic-depressive patient: "all forms of external irritation" should be eliminated, including "visits of relatives, long conversations, letters, etc." Since "unrestrained activity tends to increase the excitement," the patient must be kept quiet through "confinement in bed," warm baths, and various drugs, as necessary. During the depressed phase, the transition from depression to mania, and then the convalescent phase, care must be taken to prevent suicide attempts. But great "tact and patience [can render even an apparently] dangerous patient quite tractable." The nurse must "avoid all use of discipline, and above all be frank and truthful."[38]

This "rest cure" approach that attempted to reduce stimuli, to calm rather than to humor a manic patient and find outlets for his boundless energy, although not followed at the Retreat to the point of requiring absolute bed rest, seems to have been central to Beers' troubles with Dr. A. What Beers considered "mean" or "cruel" might have been the application of the latest teaching on the medical management of highly excited patients. His critique really applied more to the misconceptions psychiatrists had of such patients' feelings and needs rather than to deliberate mistreatment, though certainly some physicians were insensitive, unsympathetic, and just plain unskilled and even cruel in handling "troublesome" patients.

And Beers, of course, may have exaggerated the events and no doubt viewed his relationship with Dr. A, who evidently deeply hurt his pride, in somewhat distorted form. At the time of the conflict he was very excited and later, writing in retrospect, he was again slightly excited. He also admitted, probably in 1903, that the letters complaining about his treatment had been "all written with blood and vitriol" and should be discounted.[39] But he never forgave Dr. A, and he never made up stories; almost every conflict he describes—if not always his interpretation of it—can be verified from other sources.

Beers considered the treatment he received punitive and therefore unprofessional. In his view, the staff (except Dr. Stearns and the steward) reacted to his "misbehavior" as if he were a "normal" person, to the point of taking his obscenities and insults personally and then repaying him cruelly, thus exacerbating his condition and wounding his self-esteem. If he had been humored and handled intelligently, he claimed, he would have caused little trouble. The worst thing was to be deprived of communication with George and then of paper and pencil. He realized that the restrictions on communicating with friends were probably justified, since he was in such an excited *"though sane* state of mind." Even so, if allowed to write in moderation he would have been spared much suffering.[40] "It is needless to say I was in a great state of mental excitement for 4 months after 'coming to' but had I been handled properly by competent attendants and assistant physicians I would never have lifted a finger."[41]

Finally Beers raised the real issue, as pertinent today as it was when he wrote. He desperately needed sympathetic human contact, a therapeutic environment. So why assign to him unsympathetic physicians and attendants? Why not the type who would be flexible and friendly, the sort who "never resorted to force if argument failed," who would ignore insignificant transgressions and avoid arguments? Why try to make his "unruly personality" adjust to uncongenial people? After all, he was the sick one, why not adjust to his needs? Such a flexible policy "would have cost attention and perhaps inconvenience. But would not the reward have been worth the pains? And if hospitals exist for the purpose of restoring patients to health, was I not of right entitled to all such benefits?"[42]

But the experience was all just as well. "Without it some very important events which will some day happen, could not have happened — as they will be the direct result of my torture etc.," he told George.[43]

By that time he was out of the Retreat. For when George finally heard about Clifford's troubles he immediately transferred him to the Connecticut Hospital for the Insane. Financial considerations also played a part. Without Uncle Samuel Merwin's help the family could not afford to keep Clifford in a private hospital.[44] As long as there was hope of a fairly quick, foreseeable recovery, Uncle Merwin was ready to pay, but as this hope died the financial burden seemed to be unwarranted.

‡ 4 ‡

Connecticut Hospital
for the Insane

On November 8, 1902, fourteen months after entering the Hartford Retreat, and nearly two and a half years after jumping out of his bedroom window, Beers was admitted as an "indigent" to a state hospital, a course that his family had wanted to avoid.[1] But this time there was no choice; they had exhausted the other possibilities. And at Connecticut Hospital for the Insane, at Middletown, although he was to experience and witness abuses even worse than those at the Retreat, Beers finally "recovered."

The case records at the Connecticut Hospital (later the Connecticut State Hospital and now the Connecticut Valley Hospital) are not copious, but they are more extensive than those at the Retreat and from Stamford Hall. There is an ongoing record weekly, semiweekly, monthly—whenever, it seems, there was something considered worth reporting—as well as a summary of his case a few weeks before Beers was discharged.

The hospital physicians diagnosed him as having "Manic Depressive insanity" in "maniacal form" for about three months. His "psychosis of sudden or sub-acute onset" followed a "depression attack of some 18 months." This "psychosis" was "characterized by marked psychomotor unrest, numerous expansive ideas, a pronounced feeling of well being, destructive habits, perfect orientation, excellent memory for both remote and recent events, incoherent train of thought with a tendency toward circumstantiality, irritability, egotism, mischievousness, inability to apply himself to any one thing for but a short time, and no insight till subsidence of excitement, etc." He was not catatonic. His physical symptoms were: "exaggerated patella reflexes, tremor of tongue and hands"; the etiology: "worry over care of brother the initial factor"; treatment: "baths to allay excitement, tonic for general condition. Nourishing diet, quiet rest in bed during acute symptoms; later light and systematic out of door exercise will probably hasten convalescence." The prognosis was "good for present attack, will no doubt suffer from another at some future day."[2]

Beers relates in *A Mind That Found Itself* that upon admission he was "as

36

tractable . . . mild-mannered, and, seemingly, right minded" as any patient in the hospital, so much so that he was assigned to the best ward.[3] He wrote George that the attendants were thoughtful, anticipating his wants; the head attendant, an educated, tactful man, noticed that the heels of his shoes needed repair and had them fixed in time for his "debut at the Ball," a square dance for the patients. Clifford thanked George for sending him money to buy several attendants briar pipes; they would be appreciated, as in state institutions attendants seldom received tips. He enjoyed the days, which he spent writing, drawing, reading, walking, and playing the piano, and found the food surprisingly good. The attending physician, Dr. Albert Thomas of Baltimore, was "a regular thoroughbred, who is sufficiently southern, to enter a large room and say [once], 'Good evening, Gentleman,'—to 10 or 15 men and each and every man feels as though he had had a personal interview. That is the kind of man to have for a doctor, and not one of the type, who tried to 'do me.'"[4]

With all the talk of well-being, the letter is poignant. Clifford entreats George to visit, not only because he wants to see him and wants him to bring the *Yale Record* and drawing materials, but also so that they could settle things. "This waiting—for something definite *must stop—I can't stand it.*" He was a pauper, living on the state in borrowed clothes "and seemingly abandoned by everyone." If he could only establish connections in the business world he would earn enough "to make you wish you had hustled a little more as my conservator." And why had George on his last visit left early so that he could call on his ill ex-bookkeeper? Was a bookkeeper more important than a brother? George must fulfill his most important request, to be allowed to come home for Thanksgiving, even if he had to be "handcuffed & muzzled" or put in a "H.R. Corset or in a cattle car" on the way. If George refused he would have himself "'habeas corpused,' go to N. H.—and eat in jail."[5]

The hospital record depicts Beers as not nearly so calm and quiet as he claimed. He was, it said, restless and talkative, telling whoever would listen about his scheme for building and laying out new towns, insane hospitals, and immense corporations.[6] But Beers later insisted that he had self-control: in response to an attendant's challenge to keep quiet for fifteen minutes he did so for twenty-four hours.[7] That exploit took place on November 20, before Thanksgiving, when, the hospital report noted, he had been "extremely active, somewhat meddlesome," and had scattered unfinished drawings and bits of writing all over his room. Considering how incessantly he had been talking, his silence was a feat indeed, if all that provoked it was a dare and the wish to show that he could control his behavior. In his autobiography he spoke of how hard it was for him to keep quiet for so long, but he never mentioned what the hospital record noted, that Beers handed a physician a piece of paper on which he had written, "I am suffering from an attack of psychic epilepsy."[8] Could he have had a recurrence of the old fear that had inhibited his speech several years before?

The next day, the hospital record continued, he resumed his chatter but would not discuss his muteness. The following morning, November 22, he barricaded himself in his room, shouting, "I am a bad man, a raving maniac! When in this condition at the Hartford Retreat it required the combined efforts of four men to hold me. I will smash the skull of the first man that puts his head into this room. I have provisions for a number of days and will open the door for no one except the Governor of the State." When staff members finally got into the room he struck the physician but otherwise offered no resistance when he was caught and transferred to the violent ward. On the contrary, he was "jovial and highly pleased" and boasted that he had concocted the episode to break the monotony of the ward and "to get a taste of the worst as well as the best the state offered."[9]

Beers' version in *A Mind That Found Itself* connects this escapade with George's refusal to take him home for Thanksgiving. Angry, he vowed to carry out his threat to escape and decided it would be easier to get out of the violent ward on the ground floor than from his present quarters, which he found "entirely too polite." He "craved excitement—action," and had an "intense desire" to investigate the violent ward. So the day after he had been speechless he collected all kinds of junk and reading material and messed up his room with it. The next morning he ate a double breakfast, stuffed his pockets with bread, and then barricaded himself in his room. In his excitement he forgot, overlooked, or lacked the patience to do something about his roommate, a defenseless, depressed young fellow who therefore remained shut up with him. When asked to open the door Beers refused, good-naturedly but emphatically. He had been treated well so far, but he knew there were wards where helpless patients were brutalized and he would not open up until the governor of the state, the judge who had committed him, and his brother George came to the door. "When they arrive we'll see whether or not patients are to be robbed of their rights and abused." His action, Beers wrote, was "rightly construed as symptomatic of elation; and the doctor acted wisely in refusing to be reassured." Then Beers became vituperative, upon which Dr. Thomas, possibly fearing for the life of Beers' roommate, tried with the attendants to force the transom open. Beers gave "blow for blow" and it remained in place. When Thomas and the attendants finally pushed aside the barricade, they rushed in and threw him on the bed. The physician choked him "in a scientific manner," so skillfully that no serious bruises were left. Beers claimed to have enjoyed the whole thing—the drama was great and it was all a "huge joke, with a good purpose behind it."[10]

He then stayed in the violent ward for over three months. The hospital record describes him as "elated and happy" there, noisy, singing, whistling, talking, fighting, very destructive to bedding and clothing, and highly irritable, swearing vehemently at his caretakers.[11]

Beers' worst experiences in the ward took place while he was in "seclusion," a euphemism for isolation, without clothes or shoes, in cold, bare, poorly ventilated cells. Some of these cells were entirely without furniture, with only "felt ruggets" to lie on, and located in a corridor called the "Bull Pen" where, in Clifford's words, "maniacs" were incarcerated and allowed to rant and rave to their "heart's content." It was unbelievably noisy, "a pocket edition of the New York Stock Exchange during a panic." During this month in seclusion, he claimed, he went without a bath (which was better than having one, since the attendants would bathe several patients in the same water), had to breathe foul air, did not get enough food (he claimed to have lost twenty pounds in less than two weeks), and "nearly froze to death —wasn't warm once." Even when moved to a room with a bed he was still left in his underwear, which was one reason he tore up the little rugs. Partly to keep himself warm and partly just for the satisfaction of destroying hospital property, he would weave the felt strips into a sort of suit for himself each night; every morning the attendants had to cut him out of it. He also used the strips to invent an antigravity device.[12]

Beers had enormous energy and nothing much to do. The doctor would not give him pencil and paper, and the attendants were too lazy to take the patients out for their prescribed daily walk. Eventually he did manage to find a pencil stub and something on which to write his many notes of complaint—all ignored. Then began noisy demonstrations in which he was joined by a young neighbor. Together they sang and talked all night; when the assistant physician appeared they scolded him for neglecting them. Their "indiscretions" landed them in the Bull Pen, where their performances were even more flamboyant until they were separated from each other.[13]

Beers' respect for Dr. Thomas deteriorated, though he never felt so intensely hostile to this physician as he did to the Retreat's Dr. A. Dr. Thomas continually implored Beers to act like a gentleman. But without clothes, sufficient food, warmth, and "sane companionship," he would not. Only better treatment should have and would have evoked better behavior, Beers felt.[14] A number of years later Dr. Thomas recalled the brilliant but very sick Clifford Beers. In a state of hypermania he would never sleep, no matter what drugs he was given. He was very contentious, explosive when opposed, and resentful of any limitations, but was always a gentleman, always aware of the need to be a man with a cause.[15]

In Beers' long letters and statements about asylum conditions, and later in his book, he criticized Dr. Thomas and the other physicians at the Connecticut Hospital, not for cruelty or brutality, but for ignorance, incompetence, and toleration of a "lax system of supervision" of attendants, the real culprits. He realized that because they were poorly supervised and completely untrained, these uninformed, uneducated men, even the few with good intentions, were easily tempted by the helplessness and unruliness of the patients into gross laziness, neglect, and brutality. Unable to compete for jobs in the outside world, they were trapped together with the patients in a vicious circle of violence. The patients in ward four were "violent, noisy, and troublesome" — that was the nature of their illness — and they were abused just because they were so and were too weak physically and mentally to care for themselves. The attendants, most of them the "brute-force type," found it easy to take advantage of them and to neglect them.[16]

Beers found it particularly annoying that they would not give him enough to drink. One night he asked for some water. The attendants refused, with curses; he replied in kind. Overcoming the barriers he erected, they forced their way into his room, then one of them "punched, knee-ed, choked and *kicked* me for fully 4 or 5 minutes. . . . The attendants claimed next day that I had called them sons-a-B's — maybe I did — though I don't believe I did at all. What of it? This is no young ladies' boarding school. We are supposed to be crazy and irresponsible. Should a man be nearly killed because he swears at an attendant? Both of these attendants swear like pirates too." The next day he showed his bruises to the doctor, who did not disbelieve him but had to take the attendants' word against his.[17]

As his excitement diminished Beers learned to avoid such incidents, but most of his wardmates could not, and he sometimes got into trouble for defending them. Some were older men suffering from final stages of paresis or dementia; others were incapable of controlling their behavior or taking orders. They were abused unmercifully and continually. Beers claimed to have seen fifteen men, "many of them mental and physical wrecks, assaulted just as brutally as I was and usually without cause." (Later, in *A Mind That Found Itself,* he gives the number as at least twenty out of forty.) Patients were kicked, choked, hit, and then abandoned, to the point where deaths sometimes occurred, "a polite way of saying that murder had been committed here." He could not say whether women were treated similarly, but he had reason to think so.[18]

Beers finally came out of seclusion a few days before Christmas. The "most galling deprivation was at last removed. That is, my clothes were restored." He was given a better room, writing and drawing materials, and more freedom. He could now write to George, and he believed that some of his less "blood-curdling" letters were forwarded, so that George found out about his sufferings. The next six weeks in the violent ward were rather pleasant, although there was no reading matter and few diversions. Back in the nonviolent ward, he now went outdoors and could read, write, and draw. His room became a center for "the most irrepressible and loquacious characters in the ward," whose sometimes "obstreperous," angry, threatening behavior he "controlled by tact," testing his theory that violent patients could be easily handled if attendants did not perceive them as "challenges."[19]

The hospital record notes that he showed improvement but remained restless, talkative, defiant, boastful, and meddlesome.[20] He was upset because George had not written to him for ten weeks, even if he did understand that George felt he could not "very well handle" him in his excited state. George should not listen to "misguided physicians" but come up and see for himself how things were.[21] He kept himself busy writing letters, drawing, working out his grandiose plans for New Haven, and inventing a flying machine and a hammock that would automatically "overcome every motion of the ship" and enable an engaged man to make "as much love as his sense of propriety would permit" in some secluded spot. He felt that his creative powers were at their zenith, to the point where he began to write bad poetry, some of it on a handkerchief decorated with his drawings.[22] A note to the editor of *Life* told of his newfound artistic talent and gave as an example a small, mediocre sketch of a detail from *The Anatomy Lesson* copied from *McClure's Magazine*.[23] His sense of humor had returned, but since manic patients characteristically enjoy jokes and word plays it is often difficult to know whether his sometimes extravagant declarations were made in jest or were manifestations of his mania, or a combination of both.

Beers was aware that he was excited, but he reveled in this symptom, which he hoped to retain, as he had "literary ambitions and the automatic association of ideas makes the work easier." He knew he did not keep to his "Goal idea"; neither did Shakespeare, "but there were no alienists in existence in those days, which accounts for the fact that his fertile imagination was never put behind the bars of a jail or asylum." The doctors "exhibited" him occasionally at clinics: "My specialty is my ability to indulge in Delusions of Grandeur." Some of his ideas should rightly be considered "fairy tales," but others were "quite sensible and feasible." If he were free and had never been crazy he could make a "pot of money out of some of them."[24]

He improved enough by early March to be transferred to a quiet ward.[25] In late February or early March he sent George a list of relatives and friends to whom he wanted to write. From his comments and George's answers (mostly yes) it seems that in the past his recipients had found Clifford's letters disturbing and that he had tried to circumvent George's subsequent restrictions by asking them to be couriers for him. Now he promised that if he were permitted to write to Aunt Em it would be a letter "without a 'kick' in it," and that he would first send it to George for his perusal; he also would not enclose letters to be sent to others.[26] He began to stop dating his letters from the violent ward "Prison Ward," even when he was still there, and wrote an affectionate note to his mother, who had been ill.[27] His Uncle Nathaniel Cooke was very much affected by the "feverishly bright" letter he received from Clifford: "How dreadful it is that medical science cannot straighten out a brain as brilliant as [Clifford's] would be. It all makes me feel dreadfully sad."[28]

George approved visits from friends and said Clifford could take shorthand lessons from a fellow inmate. This was important to him, as he wrote so much — twenty to thirty letters a day, including a long reprise to his mother of a sermon he had just heard at chapel. Dr. Thomas recalled that Beers wrote all the time and, if not given long rolls of paper, would steal toilet paper and write on the full roll, much to the irritation of the other patients who had to share the bathroom. The problem was finally solved by giving Beers wrapping paper.[29]

Some of Beers' longest letters reflected his increasing preoccupation with exposing asylum conditions and promoting ideas for reform. A sketch he made during that winter shows himself, elegantly bearded and formally dressed, orating to an absorbed group of important-looking men. The left margin contains the caption: "Whittingham C. Beers delivering an address before the Connecticut Legislature in the Capitol Building Hartford Connecticut — February [?] 1903. His bill for the correction of abuses now existing in Insane asylums was passed without a dissenting vote, within 10 minutes of the conclusion of B. de Bug's speech." The right margin reads: "The Bill of Rights for those declared legally, to be insane, gives the inmates of public and private Insane asylums all the rights of an American citizen, except absolute Freedom. No attendant or physician will be allowed to assault a patient, and a patient can write letters to any lawyer or his conservator as often as he desires."[30]

‡

In lieu of speaking directly to the legislature, Beers wrote to the hospital physicians and important men of affairs, including a lengthy exposition of his experiences and plans to President Theodore Roosevelt. (Letters to such persons as a rule were not mailed out.) His legislative reforms, "like the Red Cross," would "be world-wide in scope," Beers told Roosevelt. He would also establish a new town, Beresford (named for himself), peopled entirely by "perverts (mental, physical and moral)," which would become the largest city in Connecticut and have access to the sea by diverting the Connecticut River. He would start a printing press there, write books, edit magazines, build a textile factory using his own inventions, enlarge New Haven, replace the state capitol, etc., etc., etc.[31]

As time went on, Beers' ideas became less expansive. He intended to write a book which would "cause a stir in literary, religious and even political circles." In order to be able to use technical language he would take a course at Yale Medical School, which would make him the "most expert alienist in this country," able to diagnose any and all mental illness.[32]

He continued to be very much concerned with his correspondence, which became wide — he estimated that during this time he received some three hundred letters and wrote many more than that — and which had always been a sore point in his struggle for his rights. Since his book would be based in part upon the letters he wrote, he made it a policy to request their return to him from all recipients; his letters would serve in lieu of a diary.[33] He also made carbon copies of his letters and other writings and may have planned to dictate his memoirs into a phonograph.[34] George's continued control of his mail was exasperating.[35]

Finally George relented. Clifford thanked him "for letting me write to 'any of the boys.' Those four words cover a multitude of sinners."[36] In reply to his rather effusive letters he received warm but careful ones from his friends, explaining why they could not easily visit him, although one did make plans to come. His friends found Clifford's manic period "delightful," one recalled years later, not only because it gave hope of his recovery but because of "the literary fulminations, bundles of yellow wrapping paper some twenty or thirty pages thick, mailed from Hartford or Middletown. They were vivid descriptions of life in the institutions, kindly, humorous comments on his 'classmates' and some very salty characterizations of doctors and men in charge. We also got some pretty reproductions of the Gibson girl, the arch-type of the period, when he became interested in drawing while a patient." His recovery became a source of concern and then "wonder and admiration, as he, defying grim circumstance and iron convention, plodded upward from a padded cell."[37]

Beers was allowed to go to town, properly escorted, and on one of these excursions managed to send a thirty-two-page communication to the governor of Connecticut by leaving it among some periodicals in a stationery store. This missive, written elegantly in ink on parchment, was enclosed in a thick wrapper, addressed and stamped, and bore strict instructions to the finder to mail it.[38]

In the letter Beers introduced himself and declared that he was "in the Crazy Business" and therefore understood aspects of it about which the governor knew nothing but, as chief executive of the state, ought to know. To ensure a hearing, he mentioned prominent people he knew, most notably his Uncle Samuel Merwin, who had been lieutenant governor of Connecticut and had run for governor. He then briefly gave his own history and vividly described his experiences at the Hartford Retreat and the Connecticut Hospital. All asylums were alike, "though some are of course worse than others." In his story of the Hartford Retreat, Beers absolved Dr. Stearns of guilt and blamed Dr. A for his sufferings there. He also gave details of his treatment and the brutality, even murder, inflicted upon other patients in the violent ward at the Connecticut Hospital.

One way the governor could bring about reform in the Connecticut Hospital was to hold a "private-'star-chamber'-investigation," conducted in a spirit of friendliness. Beers would act as "State-Attorney and question doctors and patients." He must have the governor's assistance to be able to gather information from patients all over the hospital; he could get more out of a patient in five minutes than the governor could in an hour. He was an "expert extractor of hard-luck stories." Physicians could get little from patients, who trusted only one another. If such a quiet investigation were held, reforms could be instituted without publicity; Beers could then continue his reform efforts at other hospitals and point to the Connecticut Hospital as a model institution. He wanted no one discharged "as a result of any damaging testimony. My scheme is to lay bare the abuses — suggest and put in force new rules etc., and make doctors, attendants et al., obey those regulations or submit to discharge. . . . There is only one doctor — who I wish to put out of business, and that is A . . . , who for personal spite tortured me. In doing it, he violated the ethics of his profession — and he is unfit to have under his care human beings who in many cases would not fight for their rights as I did." He apologized if his letter was at all "fresh," but as he had "an Insane License" he did not hesitate to say what he thought. "What's the use when one is caged like a criminal?"[39]

Beers did not wait for an answer — which he expected but did not receive immediately, much to his annoyance[40] — but carried on his reform campaign by means of communications to Dr. Noble, the superintendent of the Connecticut Hospital, and Dr. Thomas.[41] He also sought legal advice from his friend Paul McQuaid, a lawyer. Did an inmate of a mental hospital have the right to communicate with his conservator, no matter what his condition? Did he have freedom to send mail without interception or tampering by the hospital staff? Was there a state law providing for punishment of attendants who abused insane patients? Was it legal for the conservator of a mental patient to control his mail, to have all letters addressed to others first forwarded to him and then to hold them up or destroy them? Had not such a patient the right to mail letters direct to his probate judge? Also, how could he obtain a writ of habeas corpus? He did not want to cast aspersions on George, who had treated him well, but who, on the advice of "damnably dull doctors," had made "'divers different' errors of judgement."[42]

Dr. Thomas tended to consider Beers' letters and manifestos as devices to gain extra privileges, a charge Beers denied but, according to Thomas' record, later admitted. He was, Thomas wrote, still "mischievous," "boastful," "expansive," sometimes "incoherent," elated, "irritable," and very active.[43]

Beers called Dr. Diefendorf "Dr. Indifferent Duffer," a typical manic play on words, and told him that if he needed corpses for dissection all he did "was press a button and the attendants did the rest." The doctor laughed but admitted there was "too much brutality here."[44] Beers recalled years later that he had addressed a request to "Dilly-dallying daffy Dafendorfer, The damnably indifferent Duffer" and then got what he wanted from him.[45] Most of his wit was directed at Dr. Thomas. After a row over the veto of Beers' plans to have his best friend Johnson Veitch visit him, Beers wrote to

Thomas one account of the argument in the form of a dispatch to the *New York Sun,* with the headline: "A Fractious Fanatic confined in the Connecticut Hospital for the Insane at Muddletown, Ct. mentally assaults a superior mannered inferior assistant Physician." The story began: "Dr. A. C. Thomas, of Louisiana, who is holding down a job, which should be held down by a native of Connecticut, narrowly escaped annihilation at the vocal cords of one C. W. Beers, a maniac who for over four months has been a thorn in his crown of horns." Dr. Thomas, a man of attractive personality and "executive ability," would make a good superintendent of an asylum outside Connecticut. He would not, as he undoubtedly hoped, succeed Dr. Noble to the superintendency, as it was unwise to appoint an assistant physician to such a post. That had happened to Dr. Noble, who was as a result hampered in changing the system of giving assistant physicians, some of them "young lightweight youths, fresh from college," entire charge of wards.[46]

That evening Beers castigated Dr. Thomas for being a "stickler" for unimportant details of conduct and then for being unconcerned about the real welfare of his patients. The placing of "'Hotel de Lunney' on back of an envelope, prior to mailing same, sends shivers up and down your spinal-column of propriety. Yet at the same time, you permit helpless mental wrecks to be brutally assaulted on wards under your sole care, and never lift so much as a finger to put a stop to the practice, and probably never would, if you *knew* that news and proof of such inhuman treatment, would never be made public."[47]

A couple of days later Beers received a troubled letter from Paul McQuaid, who asked if he really meant to leave the hospital and urged him to rely on the judgment of George and the hospital authorities. He should not let his troubles with Dr. Thomas preoccupy him, though no doubt the doctor was a "ninkempoof." He carefully informed Clifford that inmates of asylums were wards of the state and therefore the objects of its care and protection, and that attendants and physicians were servants of the state and held to the "strictest responsibility." If they went beyond using force to "repel or restrain a violent patient" they would be guilty of the crime of assault. Clifford was correct in thinking that the opening of his mail by hospital physicians was in violation of a federal statute; only his conservator had that right. And habeas corpus was a procedure used only in the extreme case where a recovered patient is denied discharge.[48]

Oh, no, Beers answered, he did not despise Dr. Thomas. He was "a young man of ability . . . clever—foxy, tricky, fair and unfair, truthful at times—a choice liar when he cares to be; in fact he is the style of man I like. He keeps me guessing—consequently I enjoy 'bucking up against' him." He had beautiful manners and "generally did the right thing at the right time except when I exert myself to irritate him when he invariably does the wrong thing." After he completed his "post-graduate course" under Beers' tutelage, Thomas would be "a pretty good sort of fellow." And he, Clifford, was "exceedingly happy" and had no desire to leave the hospital. No one could completely recover so soon after such a serious illness, and besides he had certain things to accomplish first. He had to inform himself thoroughly on the proper treatment of the insane, so that he could "do the thing up in such a thorough manner that the abuses will be done away with at one stroke of the President's [Roosevelt's] pen (a sample of le delusion de grandeur)." He then again asked legal questions about patients' correspondence.[49]

By this time he had decided that Dr. Thomas' refusal to permit John Veitch's visit was "a blessing traveling incognito," as now Veitch was to come on his birthday, March 30. George decided against visiting then; instead he sent a sober birthday message: "Hoping your birthday will find you well and that when your next birthday arrives, you will have regained a normal mental condition."[50] Thomas kept his promise to parole Beers in care of Veitch, who took him out to dinner and then for a walk. Beers told Dr. Thomas, "I've had a fine time. I wish I was twins so I could have twice as many birthdays. This is what I need, a little liberty, not enough to intoxicate me, but enough to permit me to get around a bit and see things."[51]

Veitch wrote George afterwards that he had had Clifford on his mind almost constantly ever since. He appeared "so *almost* sane that it would seem all one had to do was to sit down and reason quietly with him and restore his reason completely." Although the doctors did not hold out much hope, he could not "help hoping in spite of them." Clifford was "in excellent spirits and was the best of company," and had not shown the "slightest sign of excitement or nervousness." He discussed public affairs, mutual friends, and his experiences intelligently but was prone to digress and talk of his own plans and activities. Veitch thought that a weekly visit from someone would tend to interest Clifford gradually in the outside world and draw him away from his own inner world.[52]

Clifford agreed. He had already begun a campaign for more freedom. In witty but respectful words, he requested from Dr. Thomas (and, more soberly, from Dr. Noble) the freedom of the grounds and a transfer to a ward where he would have more to do and more congenial company and would not have to go to bed so early. He was not sleeping well. This he asked for as a birthday gift: it was customary in some countries to grant liberty to certain criminals on their birthdays.[53] In a letter to George, Clifford begged to be allowed to go to New York City for a few days with an attendant. He was not feeling well. Occasionally he had disagreeable dreams and sometimes felt the way he had during his depressed period. He now understood that everything in the outside world was the same as before his illness, that his perceptions had been distorted, but he needed more contact with reality. He had mainly to mingle with all kinds of mentally ill people in an atmosphere that was enough to depress "a less optimistic nature" than his. "I have not as yet tasted of Liberty, though I have tasted of Death, as few have." If only he could "get a glimpse of the world, which for over two years had in my imagination practically ceased to exist." He wanted to see and to mix with sane men and women on an equal footing. New Haven would not be good—he would be stared at as a curiosity; New York offered crowds and anonymity. He would spend most of his time at the Metropolitan Museum, see the sights, and visit with some friends. Nothing else would free him "entirely from the damnable dreams." He realized that they were a form of "hallucinations which consciousness quickly dispels," but he feared that he might go to sleep and dream a dream from which he might not awake for months.

The prospect of a relapse did not worry him if he could be assured that Dr. Diefendorf would discuss his condition with him scientifically. "Just prove to me that my delusions etc. are those of an insane man and I'll feel easy. Had I been talked to properly during my siege I would have recovered months earlier. I had among other things Delusions of Reference. Everything done and said in my presence I thought referred to me in some way. Had I known that what I thought was due to the condition of my brain, I would have got over the 'detective idea' months earlier" and recognized George much sooner. In any case he wanted badly to go to New York; he would find a way to earn the money himself. (He evidently had some project afoot for doing artistic work for *Life* and perhaps other magazines.)[54]

The trip was vetoed, though John Veitch told George that he couldn't help thinking that "Clifford knows what is good for himself."[55] Clifford continued to agitate for better conditions. Dr. Thomas' policy of treating all patients alike was wrong: it was "absurd" to expect a man brought up in refinement to be satisfied with conditions suitable for "uneducated hodcarriers."[56]

Clifford confided to his father plans for his future that were more realistic than before. He wanted his sketches shown to two professors for their opinion of his talent. It would be good if he could earn a living by his art rather than in business, which was too confining, though he intended to write some insurance on a commission basis. He would rather stay in an insane asylum than do clerical work, which he had always loathed. He would not do anything that "'gets on my nerves.'" Then his fantasies took over: he would go to Paris to be an artist if he could get his freedom; he would pay all his expenses and repay the "several thousand already borrowed."[57]

Finally there came news of the governor's reaction to his letter. (Evidently the governor had acknowledged it but Beers never received his note.) John W. Coe, a business associate of Beers' Uncle Samuel Merwin and a close friend of the governor's, had read Beers' letter and was coming with George to see him. The governor had been impressed enough by his statements to visit Dr. Stearns at the Retreat.[58] Beers, delighted, asked Coe for at least an hour's time, though "3 or 4 would be none too long for me—though you might object to [the] risk [of] being talked to death." One advantage of his visit would be to impress upon the medical staff that Beers could "force them into doing away with the inhuman abuses . . . here."[59]

He could not resist writing Dr. Thomas a long I-told-you-so letter and warning him that he would "not mince words and the list of abuses to which patients under your care are subjected will not be any feather in your cap. Men are still being abused." Beers then gave details and repeated his warning: "Mr. Coe will get my stock of information and don't you forget it and . . . he is Gov. Chamberlain's intimate friend. . . . I am not attacking you personally. I simply am trying to change the method of treatment in this institution and I think I shall succeed."[60]

On the day of Coe's visit, Beers wrote out a twelve-page memorandum outlining his demands for unlimited parole of Middletown and vicinity, describing all his experiences, and detailing his observations of brutality in the violent ward of the Connecticut State Hospital. He suggested that the doctors could stop the brutality by blacklisting attendants the way insurance companies listed rejected risks; that the food could be varied without extra expense; that a private reception room be provided; that the best attendants could be obtained by paying higher wages than other states; and that Dr. Noble should teach the attendants that it was possible to handle patients like Clifford Beers easily and without force.[61]

The visit with Coe and George went off well for Clifford. To him, conversation with sane men who could point out the distortions in his thinking was just what he needed. He felt freed of "a lot of peculiar notions" and decided to accept Coe's advice to "quit acting as a Regulator for this institution" and start to reform himself. His reform efforts had "had a moral effect which will produce good results," but he realized that he had done as much as he could to correct abuses "while I am classed as a mental incompetent."[62]

Five years later, in *A Mind That Found Itself,* Beers expressed disappointment about his effect on the governor. At the Retreat, Dr. Stearns, hurt by Beers' criticisms, told the governor what a troublesome patient Clifford Beers had been, and the governor never met Dr. A. Perhaps because Beers' letter had stressed conditions at the Retreat, the govenor did not intervene at the Connecticut State Hospital. "My failure to force the Governor to investigate conditions at the State Hospital convinced me that I could not hope to prosecute my reforms until I . . . regained my liberty and re-established myself in my old world."[63] (In fact it does appear that an "informal investigation" took place at the State Hospital after Clifford's discharge: Dr. Noble wrote Beers in late December 1904 that John Coe and then Governor Chamberlain visited the hospital that month and both had spoken "very pleasantly regarding you.")[64]

At the time (the spring of 1903), however, Beers felt gratified that he had accomplished some good at the State Hospital. He acknowledged that it would be in his own best interest to moderate his reforming zeal, but he intended to keep on the doctors' trail "in a quiet sort of way" until he was discharged. "Then if they backslide they will hear from me through the Governor, whose son and private secretary was a classmate of mine at Yale."[65] As Coe and George suggested, Clifford gave notice to Drs. Noble and Thomas of his intention to stop agitating for reform, especially as efforts were being made to correct abuses. The Connecticut State Hospital was the best he had been in and was superior to most state asylums in the United States. "Cut out the physical abuse of patients by brutal attendants and there will be left but little room for criticism." He even admitted that the violent ward was being administered better. But since he was no longer concentrating on reform, he needed "other ways of getting rid of excess energy. A parole will be just the thing and for a starter why . . . not . . . a parole of the grounds." He would live up to any conditions and, if not, would take his "medicine without a kick."[66]

Most gratifying was the news that several attendants were discharged for brutality within a week after Coe's visit. Dr. Thomas fired them on the spot "on the strength of a statement made by the patient assaulted. Formerly all such protests were ignored . . . and . . . let me state plainly that I am responsible for the change. The patients recognize that fact and so do the doctors though they of course do not admit it."[67] Beers sent a note (probably surreptitiously) to one of the discharged attendants, expressing his joy and telling him to "get out in the world and hustle for a living and find out how worthless you are." At the same time he wrote to the head attendant of the violent ward, warning him in a "friendly" spirit to be careful, as now any attendant who struck a patient except in self-defense would be fired. "Insane men appreciate kind treatment and if you will make them your friends you will find them obedient. . . . I consider you one of the best attendants here, except that you are (occasionally) too strong for your job."[68]

At this time George received a letter from a man, possibly a patient at the hospital, advising him to allow Clifford to do what he wanted to do. "Whatever criticism may . . . attach to C[lifford]'s methods the fact remains that he may do some good & we hope that he has done. I have no advice for him because of the fact that he *acts—he acts—* in this alone lies his strength & progress. If he acts into a mistake he will also act out of it. We should look to him in a measure as he has his own methods & is very interesting as a study." The writer then gives his opinion that only "reasonableness" would "help the insane problem"—nonrestraint and the cottage system.[69]

To Dr. Thomas a triumphant Clifford Beers wrote an uncharacteristically friendly letter expressing his pleasure at the discharges and noting the "excellent" effect they had had. Most of the attendants were unambitious men afraid to compete in the outside world, so that threat of discharge was an effective way to modify their behavior. Since Beers had badgered Dr. Thomas for months with his protests, it was now only fair that he show appreciation for the doctor's action. He had clashed with him "for the fun of it as there is some satisfaction in fighting a man, who is perhaps sharper than I am."[70]

The honeymoon with Dr. Thomas did not last, though Beers' communications to him became somewhat milder. The major points at issue during that spring of 1903 were Beers' wish for parole of the grounds, transfer to another ward, and the old demand that his correspondence be unsupervised. He could be trusted. If he sometimes lied it was because the doctor had not been candid with him and had not treated him as a trustworthy man. If he sent forbidden letters to attendants along one of his "many underground railroads" it was in retaliation for the doctor's tampering with his correspondence with outside persons. For the same reason he had smuggled magazines, sketches, and notes—well written and unobjectionable, Dr. Thomas acknowledged—to women patients whom he met at dances. In sum, he behaved the way he did because he was balked in his perfectly reasonable and understandable requests.[71]

Beers desperately wanted the parole, which he believed would do more for his "complete recovery than any one thing." Thomas finally granted him four hours a day outdoors, but this was unsatisfactory, for he had to go to the arbor with a "pack of lunatics and under guard." He could not bear being forced into such close quarters "with a lot of jabbering and cursing men."[72]

Patients in worse condition were transferred to the better wards—why not he? He needed more activity—to play the piano and speak to more congenial and less disturbed people.[73] He became so annoyed by the nocturnal noisemaking of a fellow patient, who was always quiet at the approach of a night watchman, that he wrote Dr. Thomas a note of complaint. If someone in authority "will disabuse him of the idea that he is exempt from a taste of the 'Bull Pen' I'm sure it will be quieter on Ward 2S at night."[74] The advocate of tactful handling of excited patients urges the physician whom he had berated for insensitivity to subdue another patient by threats—so he, Clifford Beers, would get a night's sleep!

He continued to write to various friends and relations, his letters becoming shorter and less extravagant. One was to his former caretaker Frank Wordin, thanking him for his kindness at the Retreat and explaining the delusions he had been laboring under then. He told a woman friend in New Haven that he had made up his mind to be open and honest about his having been insane, and he wrote George a warm birthday letter, warning him not to work so hard, as all the Beers boys were high-strung and subject to breakdowns of one sort or another. And since he expected to be discharged soon, would George give some thought to what he might do out in the world. He was still considering writing insurance and studying art. What was George's opinion?[75]

Although it seems to be true that Beers had stopped his crusade for asylum reform, he evidently had not entirely given up the fight. He not only intended to keep a quiet watch over conditions but, when declared legally sane, planned "to put on the finishing touches" to his reform work.[76] He was delighted to hear from Coe again, who said that he would like to call on him with the governor sometime during the summer.[77] To his friend Vic Tyler he confided that he still had plans to reform mental hospitals in the United States and vindicate his own sufferings. "Without intentionally throwing boquets [sic] at myself, I do not hesitate to say that not one patient in 500 would have dared do as much kicking as I have; and as I seem to be one of the few with sand enough in my spinal column, brains enough in my cranium and *friends* enough on the outside to accomplish something I feel it my duty to do what I can to make life in insane asylums throughout this country a little less like Hell itself." Perhaps the best way to do this was to create a "system of espionage," with "spotters" whose presence would intimidate attendants — all of them cowards — into treating patients better.[78]

Beers became more involved in family affairs, wanting to hear all about his brother Will's wedding in Erie, Pennsylvania.[79] He wrote his parents an affectionate letter on their fortieth wedding anniversary and in lieu of money sent his drawings as a gift. He assured them that he did not attribute his illness to the "sins of the father's etc.'" but to uncontrollable circumstances. Nevertheless he did not intend to marry, much less have children. If by any chance he did marry he would have to find some woman "interested in Psychiatry who wishes to study eccentricity at close range and at more or less expense to herself." Aware as he recovered of the financial drain his illness had been on his family, he wished his parents long life and well-deserved prosperity, from "one who has done more than his share to postpone a state of chronic prosperity which seems to be at hand."[80] His mother wrote to him every Sunday, and various friends and family members visited him, offering what he regarded as essential to his full recovery: a sober and realistic sounding board for his projects.[81]

Gradually he won the privileges he had sought. In July Dr. Thomas finally gave him parole of the grounds and of the town, and he could walk as much as five miles a day. He gained twenty pounds, ate well, and his deportment was considered "excellent." He was even allowed trips home alone.[82]

He pressed his project to go to New York to study art and sell enough insurance to pay his board. The hospital physicians approved, but George wanted to explore the situation more fully.[83] Finally, at the end of July, George wrote that he had seen Clifford's friends in New York. They "will be glad to see you again," and George thought that he would "be able to arrange matters as you wish to."[84] Despite his characteristic exaggerations about being a great artist — which diminished as time went on — Clifford's goals were modest. He hoped to make at least part of his living as an illustrator, which, he was told, required only temperament and ability coupled with hard work. He needed to study the human figure, as he had so far concentrated on heads, of which the hair came out best; he had developed a secret method for drawing hair; perhaps he might "make a specialty of it."[85]

The time for discharge finally came (September 10), and Clifford wrote to George that he was not afraid of a relapse but wanted to guard as best he could against such a contingency. "On the principle of 'preparing for war in time of peace,'" he wrote out eight instructions for George to follow in case he did have trouble in the future: First, if recommitment proved necessary he should be placed in the Connecticut State Hospital at Middletown. Second, relatives and friends were not to refuse to write to him even on the advice of a doctor. Only when Clifford requested them to stop writing should they do so. Third, he must have the right to write to George as often as he wished, with George to supply stamped envelopes and instruct the physicians not to hold up any letters to him, which was illegal (here he quoted Connecticut law). Fourth, no matter how long or "'ratty,'" all letters must be forwarded to George, who could then censor them. Fifth, George or someone he selected should come to the hospital once a week "to examine my person and see that I am not being abused as I was last winter. Don't depend on telephone messages from those in charge of me." George should visit fairly frequently until Clifford approached normality, "as I always will, even if I have another whirl." Sixth, even when on the "'war path!'" Clifford wanted to see some of his friends, who would get their money's worth, for he was sure to be at least interesting. Seventh, while elated, he should have a special attendant, whatever the cost, as it would speed his recovery. Humoring him would be therapeutic, in contrast to being locked up without exercise, food, or air. Eighth, Clifford must have all the drawing materials he wanted. Had he had them at the Retreat he would have caused little trouble. "Damn the theory held by some doctors that a brain the condition mine was should be given nothing to occupy it except abuse etc. I have theories of my own on the subject and I am sure I'll get well quicker if I am allowed to amuse myself with something in which I am interested." And finally, he wanted to tell George how much he appreciated the way he handled his case. "I can say no more now than simply 'Thank you!', but you can bet I never said it before when it meant as much."[86] Clifford Beers, as Veitch suggested, knew better the kind of treatment he needed than some of the doctors who practiced psychiatry.

‡ 5 ‡

Back in Circulation

Beers went home on September 10, 1903, with the good wishes of the staff, including Dr. Thomas, who in the case record described his recovery as only "fairly satisfactory" and predicted a recurrence of the illness.[1] Beers had his own forebodings, but he put on an optimistic face. His friends greeted him as "one risen from the dead" and avoided talking about his illness until Beers, anxious to put them at their ease, directed the conversation to the subject — a tactic that enabled him, he believed, to resume warm and easy relationships. One childhood friendship that he renewed, according to later recollections, was with Clara Jepson, who took an uncommonly sincere interest in his plans.[2]

By late October or early November, when no one could accuse him of running away, Beers went to New York. With borrowed money he rented a room with board on West Seventeenth Street between Fifth and Sixth Avenues, at the northern edge of Greenwich Village, and apparently played with the idea of taking art courses. He had no "regular occupation." The anonymity of the city was a joy: treated like "everyone else," he could regain his self-confidence. After only a week, the "commercially supercharged" atmosphere revived his "business instincts" and he again dreamed of conquering the houses of Mammon. At the same time his artistic impulse languished and with it all desire to study art. Three months later he had a job with the firm that had first employed him five years before, Hoggson Brothers.[3]

In an early draft (1905) of his book, Beers claims that during those three months he kept a sharp "lookout for some man with courage enough to employ" him. In the published version he lands a job by "merest chance," through a social call to Hoggson Brothers, with whom he had kept in communication during his illness. Actually, during his visit he learned that Hoggson Brothers had begun a program to build bank buildings completely furnished and ready for occupancy. Beers offered to tell them of any bank about to be remodeled or built; if he could get a contract for Hoggson, a commission might be arranged. When Beers did hear about such a situation in Erie, Pennsylvania, in January 1904, he called upon W. J. Hoggson, who

53

offered to pay the expenses of a trip to Erie and give him a commission if he closed the deal. Beers left for Erie on January 20 and stayed a month so that he could see other bank presidents who expressed an interest in building new quarters.[4]

The experience of speaking to respectable men of affairs, who listened attentively and sometimes even signed contracts for their new buildings, was gratifying to a man who just a few months before was being exhibited to Yale medical students as a manic patient with delusions of grandeur. This was the right kind of work for him, without set working hours or petty office routines, and with freedom to use the considerable persuasive power, charm, and business acumen he had displayed in high school and college. "Exhilarated," he planned to earn enough to repay all the debts he had accumulated since 1900 and hoped to be able to send his parents on a long-planned trip to the South next year.[5]

George was skeptical. Clifford's expectation of earning $5,000 a year would require negotiating a vast amount of business. And since Clifford had only $13.45 left of the money lent to him, he would do well to refrain from telling "others the amount of business you think you shall do." In any case he should remain on commission rather than on a salary.[6]

According to Clifford Beers, Hoggson had been doubtful that someone without architectural experience could succeed at the work, but when Beers returned from Erie with contracts he changed his mind and offered him a regular job at $750 a year, with all expenses paid. Beers accepted with the understanding that if he did well he could work on commission. He began work on February 26, 1904, and for twenty months traveled from forty to fifty thousand miles, to over two hundred cities and towns in every state east of the Mississippi except Florida and the Carolinas. The approximately fifteen hundred interviews he was able to get yielded him a small but creditable number of confirmed contracts.[7]

In later years, W. J. Hoggson recalled the events that led to Beers' re-employment, and his version is somewhat different. One day Hoggson was astonished by a visit from Beers,[8] "who came to ask if we would take him back." It was a dilemma: to rehire Beers might hurt the firm's position, but if refused he would not easily find another job. Hoggson decided that "a man was worth more than a business." Beers' old job would be too confining, so they must create one that would place him outdoors. He would "travel first-class, stop at the best hotels, and visit [banks in] all cities and states east of the Rockies" to build up a file on their building needs and plans, information that later served as the basis for over three hundred banks built by Hoggson Brothers.[9]

The difference between Beers' and Hoggson's public versions is interesting. Hoggson focused on his own altruism. Beers wanted to demonstrate his self-assurance and to encourage other former mental patients in their search for employment. The job came to him, he said, because he impressed Hoggson so well: all ex-patients should be as aggressive as he was, for success depended upon convincing the employer of one's vigor and capability. The other necessary element was the kind of "common-sense view of insanity" that Hoggson displayed.[10]

What probably really happened was that Hoggson Brothers was contemplating going into the bank-building business, and when Beers came along they decided to give him a chance, the Erie trip being a trial run. Beers realized at the time that they had done him "a great kindness" and he felt deeply in their debt.[11]

Although life on the road seemed to suit him, it had disadvantages. There was a good deal of time in strange cities with nothing to do. To fill up the lonely hours he wrote letters and read books, which stimulated a growing "literary impulse." He read "Macauley's Essays on Bacon, Hastings, and Pitt; Camille; De Quincey's Confessions of an Opium Eater; Eliot's Essays; Middlemarch and Les Miserables." The *Confessions* were disappointing: he had experienced much more interesting and varied "phantasmagoric visions and physical conditions" than De Quincey. The deepest impression was made by Hugo's novel of "suffering Humanity." He dreamed of it by night, and by day the strain of reading made his head ache and set his "brain . . . afire." He grew increasingly excited and became filled with an irresistible and "mildly mad desire to write." He, too, could write a book that would "arouse sympathy for and interest in that class of unfortunates" in whose behalf he felt it his "peculiar right and duty to speak," although just when he would begin to do so he did not know. There were other signs of mounting excitement: incessant talking, loss of weight, and great physical as well as mental activity without fatigue.[12]

Then came the spur needed to start his reform work. Some time after Thanksgiving, W. J. Hoggson wrote that he was satisfied with Beers' work: he was "the right man in the right place" — a precious sign of approval. Upon leaving the hospital, Beers had decided to initiate his reforms only after first reestablishing himself in the business and social world; now he had that assurance. He was suddenly transformed into a dedicated reformer uninterested in the pursuit of money, the "comparatively deadening routine of commercial affairs."[13] His position and his prospects, Clifford wrote George, surpassed those of other men his age. "I naturally feel that I have made 'good' and have a perfect right to act as though I had never been a mental incompetent." Anticipating criticism, he said that he could not be expected to conduct himself as George did: George was "safe, sure, conservative; I am fairly safe, usually sure, but willing to take lots of chances." He could take care of himself, and he intended to ask for advice as he went along. Because George's primary concern was to safeguard the job with Hoggson Brothers, he could not judge Clifford's ideas objectively, but in any case Clifford did not intend to launch his scheme immediately.[14]

Clifford did seek advice. He visited the physicians at the Retreat and at

Middletown; they listened to him politely and respectfully, but unknown to him they considered him in an excited and potentially dangerous condition if left untreated. Then he borrowed one hundred dollars from his friend Victor Tyler for a trip to Washington, D.C., to win the support of President Roosevelt and Secretary of State John M. Hay for his plan. President Arthur T. Hadley of Yale (to whom Clifford probably had entrée through George's position as treasurer of the Sheffield School) dissuaded him from going. Agreeing that Clifford's scheme, if properly managed, would do much good but that it was too wide-ranging, he advised that it be put on paper before prominent men were asked for help.[15]

So instead of going to Washington, Beers went the next day, New Year's Day, 1905, to the Yale Club in New York City, where in three days he wrote fifteen thousand words detailing his experiences and his plans for reform, which he hoped to present in a book that would have the same effect on mental illness as *Uncle Tom's Cabin* had on slavery: "Why cannot a book be written which will free the helpless slaves of all creeds and colors confined today in asylums and sanitariums throughout the world?" He would rather write such a book than do anything else.

He also diverted himself by writing to friends, who discovered serious signs of elation in the letters.[16] One such letter led George Beers, Vic Tyler, and John Veitch to confer in New Haven about Clifford. Knowing that he intended to tell Hoggson Brothers about his plans, George phoned New York twice that day to dissuade him.[17] It was too late. Clifford could not cancel the scheduled dinner at the Yale Club where he was to give the Hoggsons the opportunity to dismiss him if they judged his plans incompatible with their firm's interests. Under George's desperate pleading to save his job, Clifford agreed to avoid the subject if he could and to return to New Haven the next day. But at the dinner he could not evade his employers' direct questioning and had to unfold his ideas. They were favorably impressed but warned him against acting hastily; his philanthropic activity would be a full-time job and one that might endanger his health and perhaps even lead to a serious relapse. Despite their misgivings, the Hoggsons assured Clifford that he could conduct a reform movement and remain in their employ as long as he fulfilled his business obligations, but they thought it would be best for him to wait until he was forty.[18] Clifford saw that this advice was sensible, but he was not about to take it.

He did go home on January 4 to see George, who told him he was somewhat elated and should drop his schemes at least temporarily. Then, upon George's insistence that he be hospitalized, Clifford chose a "voluntary commitment" to the Hartford Retreat but insisted upon being granted certain privileges: all the reading and writing material he wanted and the right to procure books and supplies at will in return for his accepting the condition that he be accompanied by an attendant on visits to the city.[19] He convinced himself that he could do no better than remain at the Retreat for several weeks, devoting himself to writing. His old enemy, Dr. A, had resigned some months before, so he feared no mistreatment, and his awareness of his elated condition probably helped him to accept the prospect of hospitalization with equanimity, and perhaps with relief.

‡

Clifford Beers entered the Retreat in 1905 under much different conditions than the first time. In place of the depressed, largely mute, fearful, suspicious man of three and a half years before stood a confident, somewhat exuberant businessman who won concessions from hospital officials before agreeing to sign in as a "voluntary" patient.

His composure was not shared by his family, and he felt obliged to write reassuringly to his parents and Aunt Mame. No one but the immediate family needed to know about his condition. Letters sent to him should be addressed to the family home in New Haven and forwarded to the Retreat. Clifford wrote on stationery from a Hartford hotel and asked Aunt Mame to have his personal papers put in safe storage by George, who had done just the right thing in hospitalizing him, difficult as the decision must have been.[20]

At the Retreat Beers wrote and read, walked and talked, and frequently attended the theater in Hartford. On one occasion he did some business: while his attendant stood unobtrusively outside the door he talked with the cashier of the Phoenix National Bank about a building contract that Hoggson Brothers later signed for $150,000.[21] The Hoggsons were supportive. N. F. Hoggson assured George that "everything would be all right," and W. J. Hoggson visted Clifford and told him not to worry: his case was no different from that of any other employee who became ill, and his job was waiting for him. This news was a great relief. Despite his complaining, Clifford enjoyed the free-lance character of the work, and it would not be easy to get another job. W. J. Hoggson also confessed to Clifford that he, too, suffered from mental troubles and that of the two of them he probably felt more uneasy most of the time, as he worried day and night about his business.[22]

‡

While at the Retreat, Clifford Beers wrote his most ambitious work yet, "My Autobiography," 176 manuscript pages which, with later deletions and additions, formed the basis for the first chapters of *A Mind That Found Itself*.[23] He also drafted a 14-page version of his plan to establish a national mental hygiene organization and jotted down all sorts of impressions and thoughts. Funding his movement would present no great difficulty, he judged, as his research revealed that Americans gave in 1904 over $95 million for educational and philanthropic purposes and from 1893 to 1905, $695,410,000. This was a philanthropic age: John D. Rockefeller had recently endowed an institution for scientific research relating to the cause and treatment of scarlet fever. "The death of a favorite grandson led him to do this. Is it unreasonable to suppose that some rich man or men would become interested in my scheme because of the death or recovery of some relative afflicted with mental disease? I think not."[24]

Still, he had some trepidation about presenting his life story to the public. He considered anonymous publication and sought justification for his plans in the lives of famous men like Disraeli and Theodore Roosevelt. Although his future was uncertain, he must "turn what looked like certain failure into an assured success." In fact, "what real success I have had thus far has been founded on my supposed afflictions. I hope to succeed as a result of my trials and if I can carry out my plans I will base my success on temporary failure." He hoped that his health would hold up long enough for him to accumulate sufficient money to ensure his income for the rest of his life. He had been a financial drain on his family for too long.[25]

Cesare Lombroso's *The Man of Genius* fascinated Beers, for if he himself was not a genius he believed that he had "the peculiar mental organization which Lombroso uses to prove that all geniuses are abnormal." From Stearns' *Insanity, Its Causes and Prevention,* he learned that insanity was on the increase as a result of the growing mental activity produced by the forces of civilization and that in time this trend must put insanity on society's agenda for immediate attention and resolution.[26] Clearly, then, his own interest in the subject only anticipated what must inevitably become central to government officials as well as physicians and lay people. His chosen work would not forever remain neglected, nor would he long have to wait for society's recognition.[27]

Family loyalty and a protective attitude toward women probably prevented Beers from writing candidly in his autobiographies about the mental health of his mother and aunts, a reticence sharply contrasting with his willingness to discuss his brothers' problems. And he never revealed in his extant correspondence or diaries the fact that one of his aunts died in a mental hospital. But during this second stay at the Retreat one quotation from Stearns that Beers copied and marked for special notice indicates that he was not insensible to his family's psychological make-up:

It is not necessary that the tendency toward unstable mental action should be fully developed in the parent in order that it may so happen in the child. Parents who have for years been very odd or singular in their habits of life, manner of speech and mental actions [beginning here Beers marks the quotation]; those who are subject to periods of depression, and are accustomed to look on the dark side of daily experiences; mothers, who more often have been all their lives "nervous" or irritable and easily excited [here Beers' emphasis ends] impress more or less profoundly those characters & conditions on their offspring.[28]

Beers tried to mitigate his relapse by stressing the success that would flow from it and by explaining its occurrence. The emotional impact of reading *Les Miserables,* he felt sure, was a key factor. Hugo's "forceful and epigrammatic style" stimulated him to literary endeavor, the subject matter affected him profoundly because of his own terrible experiences, and Hugo's ability through his writing to effect reforms was an accomplishment that Beers hoped to emulate.[29]

After two weeks at the Retreat, Beers gave his father a different explanation for his relapse. The "excited condition" of his brain was due "to some change in the brain tissue or condition of the blood, which comes on of its own accord and in spite of anything one can do. . . . In a nutshell: when I'm normal, I am normal—and when not, I am just a little abnormal—due to some peculiar physical condition, rather than to anything I do in the way of living, so long as I live temperately."[30]

Despite his awareness that feeling a strong literary impulse usually indicated the onset of excitement, Beers searched within himself for a long-term interest in and talent for literature in order to find a healthy origin for what he recognized as his "literary symptoms." He could point to his joke-writing in high school and college, as well as his extensive letter-writing—from five hundred to eight hundred personal letters written during the past year. These interests were, like the whole course of his life, preordained: "Destiny controls." He considered himself a fatalist; although he tried to shape his career, he realized that "only in unimportant details can action of my own in any way alter the decreed order of events." As a youth he had believed in God but not in a "Future Life, in Immortality." His doubts relating to immortality faded after he became mentally ill and felt the "gentle hands of God sustain" him in his trials. With this conversion came a desire "to do good in this world" so that he would enjoy immortality in the next.[31]

These were speculations written during the early days at the Retreat. By the end of the second week he was calming down, gaining weight, sleeping more, eating well, and writing and talking less.[32] His descriptions of his activity and condition are corroborated by the brief hospital case record. He improved to the point of being given unlimited parole on January 26 and then a discharge on the 30th, less than a month after his commitment. One item that Beers did not note anywhere is his confession to hospital physicians that he "recently had Gonorrhea and still has it," an indication that he did not spend all his time on the road reading in hotel rooms.[33] His frankness about his illness never extended to sexual experiences and feelings.

Beers attributed the return of his "slightly disturbed state of mind . . . to normal within a surprisingly short time" to the physicians' permissiveness. Because all his reasonable requests were granted and others refused politely, he caused no one any trouble. This experience, he thought, validated his views on the proper treatment of the insane, as well as his opinion that most maniacs were the "product of unfair, cruel and unscientific methods of treatment."[34] He was here reiterating a point that he made often (and one which was "discovered" and became current among mental health critics in the late twentieth century): the conditions of institutionalization can themselves not only exacerbate but produce symptoms of mental disorder.

Beers' relapse and stay at the Retreat confirmed his resolution to press for reform. The weeks he spent in the hospital, by enabling him to elaborate his ideas, established more firmly than ever the belief that his goal was attainable. Perhaps also the recurrence of his excitement made him want ever so much more to obliterate the disgrace of mental illness by changing the public's attitude and achieving fame. He felt that he had made a concrete start in his life's work by writing his autobiography, which in revised form he intended to show to prospective donors to his movement. When he returned to work for Hoggson Brothers, he was therefore in no mood to abandon or postpone the rewriting and publication of his autobiography or the founding of some sort of national organization to implement his reform proposals.

‡ 6 ‡

Writing the Autobiography

The doctors designated Clifford Beers improved, not recovered. He thought he was fine, especially since after only a few days out of the hospital he helped to compose and edit a booklet, *Some Bank Work,* published for Hoggson Brothers. But he did postpone work on his autobiography, intending instead to compose many letters and talk as much as he could about his life in order to clarify his ideas. His friends would just have to suffer through it—what else were friends for, if not to help one another?[1]

His chance to write letters came during a five-month business trip, when it became evident to his correspondents that he was still excited. George warned Clifford to "*cut out all your schemes* for the present and *confine yourself to the business of Hoggson Bros.* If you don't it may cause you trouble. When do you expect to even up your expense account?" He did not lack faith in Clifford's plans, but they must be feasible and Clifford had to prove that he could control himself for an extended period.[2]

Despite his friends' advice to stick to business, Beers was determined to write his autobiography and soon. He also was afraid of another relapse, so that he was alert to danger signals and during the months on the road was preoccupied with self-examination and self-justification. Besides his own experience he could draw upon the information in the books he had been reading on mental disease, which were discouraging in their implications for his mental health. The standard works of the day held out little hope for a permanent cure for manic-depressives, whose disorder was supposed to be cyclical and who would never be entirely symptom-free.[3] In March, when he found himself writing very fluently and with a "tendency to digress," Beers wondered whether he was on the verge of a period of elation. He thought not, though he warned himself to put on his "hot-air brakes." Not that high elation was unpleasant: albeit "without doubt an abnormal condition of mind," it was a very "7th Heaven of Supreme contentment." By July he noted real signs of excitement: buzzing in his ears, compulsion to write, trouble sleeping.[4] A portion of a letter to Thomas R. Lounsbury, his English

61

professor at Yale whom Beers had asked for literary advice, indicates his state. Enclosing a turgid ode to Niagara Falls that he had written, he said:

> Finding myself in a blank-verse mood I went to Niagara, early in March 1905, with the intention of writing a poem, describing Niagara, in my own feeble way.
>
> One of my delusions de-grandeur predictions was this: "Some day I will write a poem that will make Dante's Divine Comedy look like a French Farce."
>
> Let it go at that until I do, and in the meantime believe me more modest that [sic] that remark would indicate.[5]

Beers probably did aspire to outdo Dante some day. He was controlled enough to realize that he had to modulate the egotism characteristic of his excitement by a few modest statements, but one suspects that he secretly hoped one day to look back upon his braggadocio as prophetic.[6] Sometimes swinging widely in the same letter between sobriety and euphoria, he would say openly what other people secretly felt or wished were true. The conviction of his genius so pervasive in his manic writings never completely disappeared. Throughout his life he would periodically come up with extravagant boasts, yet he usually retained enough insight to make them in a half-humorous way.

Increasingly frustrated by opposition from friends and relatives, and despite his knowledge of symptoms, Beers insisted upon his normality. It was just that he had changed. "I appreciate the fact that the C. W. B. of 1905 is not the C. W. B. of those years prior to it. Yet, because I am unlike, in many ways, what I once was, no one has a right to complain, as I am surely in a healthier and happier state of mind than ever before. My letters being at times egotistical missals [sic], are not for that reason unnatural. . . . The high flown language, the isolated lofty ideas are not written with studied effect." To friends who advised him to take his time he showed impatience. "Would they with a million dollars worth of satisfaction, and at least $50,000 in cash [from royalties] within reach be more patient than I am? I think not." His brothers wanted him to concentrate on his business career. William's attitude particularly irked him: "I gave my bro. Bill a chance to learn all about my schemes and . . . he preferred not to hear what I had to say; later on he will want to get on my band wagon but when he does he will have to buy a ticket." Aunt Em should preserve his letters: "I should hate to have my early efforts fall into unfriendly hands." Afraid he might be hospitalized against his will, he wrote in his notebook, "See F. L. and make him legal representative — one who will protect my legal rights should my desire to push my schemes annoy relatives or friends and cause them to restrain me."[7]

Apprehension that Clifford would lose his job and suffer a serious relapse was not the only reason for the family's attitude. They did not want him to make his history of mental illness public. But he had to, Clifford told his father. A policy of frank admission would gain him respect; besides, too many people already knew about his past. He himself felt "as unconscious of [his] past as is a man whose life has been uniformly uneventful," though he understood very well the "sense of disgrace now so generally associated with insanity, . . . a psychological relic of the Dark Ages." To overcome this prejudice, people must stop speaking about insanity as if it were the "unpardonable sin" and make it as much a subject of discussion as physical illness.[8]

That Clifford Beers was entirely free of a sense of disgrace is questionable. Many years later he believed he had discovered in a passage from Horace Walpole the psychological origin of his impulse to write: "Whosoever hath anything fixed in his person that doth induce contempt hath contempt also a perpetual spur in himself to rescue and deliver himself from scorn." By producing a sort of *Uncle Tom's Cabin* about the mentally ill and establishing an organization to reform asylums, he could give meaning to his suffering, vindicate himself, compensate his family for their sacrifices, and remove the shame he and his relatives had felt because of his illness.[9]

He was in no mood to heed the warnings of his friends and relatives or the counsels of psychiatric authorities against "excitement, physical or mental" to prevent recurrence of manic-depressive symptoms. His mission to reform the condition of the insane was God-given: "One's career is shaped for him" by God and can be "carried to a successful conclusion provided [one] tries to do the right thing all the time." Ignoring the pronounced eccentricity on his mother's side of the family (characteristics that Paton believed would turn up in a manic-depressive's family "even when a history of definite symptoms of alienation" was absent), Beers found in the absence of insanity in his family tree proof that he was a tool of God rather than a toy of the devil.[10]

Another, more mundane consideration prompted him to persist in his planning for reforms: the tedium of life as a traveling salesman. "Without my literary ambition which keeps me interested in reading and writing," he confessed to his mother, "life on the road would be an uninteresting one." "Stranded in an ugly, dirty, railroad town, an exceptionally poor hotel, mean weather, I have had a very enjoyable time, simply writing." Or he would read literary classics for two to three hours a day. When he first started traveling it was immensely satisfying to talk to bank officials and negotiate business deals; now an order for a sixty-thousand-dollar building scarcely gave him a thrill. Reading Mill's essay *On Liberty* was much more interesting and pleasurable.[11]

At the end of July he asked for a raise in salary. His outstanding debts amounted to $4,100, of which $1,000 was incurred while he was at college and another $1,200 since he came out of the Connecticut State Hospital; the remainder was lent during his hospital stays. He had had to continue borrowing because his salary of $7.80 a week did not cover "legitimate expenses," even though he was making an effort to live within his expense account by "spending night after night" in his hotel room. He also deserved more money. Had he not just secured three contracts in Kentucky and West Virginia? And was not his work crucial in gaining contracts elsewhere? All he wanted was to make a comfortable, secure living.[12]

His letter brought a salary increase and, to his surprise, retroactively. This recognition of his worth could not, however, rekindle his commitment to business. Instead, the ease with which he wrote to Hoggson convinced him of his literary skill and of his ability to start writing his book. He had also by then received from Professor Lounsbury a heartening reply to his somewhat excited letter. Lounsbury encouraged his literary and organizing efforts, provided he exercised proper judgment, and he offered to criticize his manuscript. As for writing, the key thing was to have something to say, "granted of course you can write some."[13]

Still Beers could not get much further than composing a dedication "To Humanity." It did not seem to matter that he had already written two versions — the fifteen-thousand-word highly autobiographical plan dashed off at the Yale Club in early January and "My Autobiography," composed at the Retreat a few weeks later. Indeed, in his later discussion of the creation of *A Mind That Found Itself* he ignored these not inconsiderable early writing efforts. At most he had intended to show the Yale Club version to a few prominent men whose support he sought, and the Hartford Retreat autobiography he considered too "indelicate or worse" to be published, though since it was a record of what one insane man thought, he planned to publish its important facts in his autobiography.[14]

He therefore dated the start of the first draft of the book that was to become *A Mind That Found Itself* as August 1905. It was spurred by what Beers presented, characteristically, as a key event. Finding himself in the Berkshire Hills on business and hearing that Joseph Choate, the lawyer, diplomat, socialite, and philanthropist, had a summer home nearby, Beers decided to try to see him. Undaunted by his lack of an introduction, he wrote his own, a piquant composition asking for a few minutes to present a subject of interest to Choate. Choate granted an appointment the next morning, when he advised Beers to put his ideas in writing and promised to read the manuscript and help in any way he could. Busy men, he said, would not give the hours needed to hear Beers out, but they might read about his project at leisure.[15]

Beers was galvanized into action. Choate's matter-of-fact attitude toward the insane encouraged him to expose his past illness: "a person's dread of insanity and antipathy towards the insane or those who have been insane and have at least temporarily recovered varied in indirect proportion" to his intellectual superiority. Superior men like Choate and Theodore Roosevelt felt less fear or hostility to the insane because geniuses and the insane "only differ in degree." Two days later Beers took off for the Boston Public Library to see if it had any book of the kind he wished to write; if not, he would "work all the harder." At the end of August he finally overcame his writing block. On a lonely Saturday in Worcester, he decided to try dictating to a stenographer and found himself easily telling his life story. The idea of using a stenographer must have been on his mind for several weeks at least, if not more: an earlier entry in his notebook reports that he had inquired about stenographers' rates and calculated the cost. He evidently did not employ a stenographer until after he saw Choate, though.[16] As always, Beers needed encouragement and approval from important people. Without that stimulus it was difficult for him to act, no matter how much he talked, though he had the courage – or audacity – to approach such men and the cleverness to attract their interest.

‡

From August 26 through October, in Worcester and then in New York, Beers dictated from memory some eighty thousand words in ninety hours. Each morning he would talk for three hours, then put the stenographer's notes in a safe deposit vault. The total product was, he realized, a repetitive and discursive story that had to be pruned; before showing it to philanthropists he would have to redictate it, which he did.[17] During the first few weeks he stayed away from New Haven, so that his "well-meaning but perhaps over-zealous relatives" would not see his excitement. No matter how precarious his health and how exhausting the experience of reliving "the trials and the torture of [his] unhappiest years," he was determined to finish the manuscript.[18]

When George did hear about the manuscript, he made no objections but advised Clifford not to tell the other relatives. Clifford tried, but with fame and fortune finally awaiting him and certain issues to be settled it was hard to remain closemouthed.[19] What, for example, should he do about his name, Clifford, which he did not care for? (In the hospital he would often sign letters Whittingham C. Beers.) He wrote to the Reverend Richard Whittingham of Aiken, Maryland, who had given him his middle name during baptism, asking permission to use the name Whittingham Beers in the book. "Clifford" was too boyish, too romantic, "a bit effeminate," and indeed he had been named for an aunt. Cliff and Whit, which some of his closest friends called him, struck him as undignified. The Reverend Whittingham thought that Clifford was a perfectly respectable name, so Clifford Whittingham Beers it remained.[20]

The many people who came to know of the manuscript were all sworn to secrecy. Some were contacted to gain information for the book, and others to offer professional opinions.[21] Beers also sent both Dr. Diefendorf and Dr. Thomas of the Connecticut Hospital what he had written. Diefendorf encouraged him and became a confidant; to Thomas the story was "intensely interesting," but he wondered whether others not so personally involved would tolerate the "tediousness of detail with a tendency to repetition." He would reserve judgment, though, until he read the entire work.[22]

During the first three weeks of dictating, Beers had continued his business activities in the vicinity of Worcester. Then he asked for and received two weeks' leave without salary to enable him to work on the manuscript undisturbed in New York; he planned thereafter to try to do his bank business from New York. He had that "peculiar and almost indefinable feeling of subconscious confidence" that seldom preceded an "unsuccessful attempt to do a thing."[23] The leave enabled Beers to complete the biographical part of the story. Greatly relieved, he could now go home to New Haven. He was again granted time off to edit his first draft, a "literary spree," he told a friend, that "was in a way, a period of elation without many of its characteristic symptoms." Intellectually and emotionally spent, he was then glad to resume traveling for the Hoggsons, this time going south: he would "cool" his brain by "daily contact with the more prosaic minds of men of business."[24]

What Beers finally completed was only the first part of his prospective book, consisting of an introduction and the story of his life. The second part, never fully written, was to contain a description of methods, old and current, of treating insanity; a scheme to establish a "psychiatrical" hospital in every state, as well as sanitariums for scientific treatment at minimum cost; and finally a description of an organization similar to the Red Cross, to carry out these and other reforms and to conduct research, educate the public, and write model statutes. This "society" must be kept free of political, religious, sectarian, or any other divisive belief or activity and should be connected with a university, preferably Yale. "As it will be for the good of humanity every human being regardless of race, creed or color should be allowed to contribute towards its success if he so desires." Beers did not expect to hold a salaried position in his society. All he hoped for was an advisory relationship while he continued to work for Hoggson Brothers and to write part-time. As for his mental state, he felt sane enough for "everyday purposes," and though he expected to experience periods of elation and depression he had learned from doctors that between these extremes he would be normal. As long as he remained in good physical health he believed that the "worst that can happen to me is a temporarily active mental condition."[25]

He began to send copies of the revised draft to relatives, friends, psychiatrists, and other influential men and women. Claiming expert knowledge neither as a psychiatrist nor as a writer, only as a former inmate of mental hospitals, he rejected advice that contradicted the hard-earned lessons of his hospital years or that seriously criticized his plan to found a reform organization, but was open to any other comments from qualified people. To ask for advice from those who knew psychiatry, administered hospitals, or understood good writing posed no threat to his self-image; on the contrary, it gave him reassurance.

George, of course, received a copy, which he read carefully. He hoped Clifford would be able to carry out his plans, which would be mainly "only a question of money and time," the object being "certainly most worthy." Clifford could count on him for help in any way possible.[26] From friends, including a former professor at Yale, Clifford also received praise and encouragement, as well as some criticism.[27]

The superintendent of the Danvers Insane Hospital at Hathorne, Massachusetts, Dr. Charles W. Page, an advocate of moral treatment whose articles on nonrestraint Clifford had read, responded encouragingly. Page read the manuscript to his medical staff, all of whom were intrigued by the account of Beers' "abnormal mental conditions" and hospital experiences; he intended to read certain portions to the attendants, so that they might as a result "stop and consider more frequently, just how their actions and treatment of patients would appear to themselves as well as to others, if described in newspapers and books." When the manuscript was printed he would insist that his staff read it as part of their training. Beers' descriptions of his "depressive and manic symptoms" were more comprehensive than any report they had ever read, and, though his particular case was not common, his analysis of his symptoms was valuable in showing the workings of his mind under stress. Further, his "claims, suggestions and discussions" gave the patient's point of view, "a picture which is too seldom borne in upon the minds of hospital officials and employees, but which, if sufficiently comprehended by them would . . . modify somewhat their attitudes and actions toward certain patients."[28]

The book might be more effective, Page suggested, if Beers confined his statements to his own observations and experiences and eliminated the names of the hospitals he was describing. (The latter point was also made by Beers' friend Paul McQuaid, and Beers finally did delete the names, along with "unnecessary epithets and caustic allusions.")[29] Although Beers' nonvindictive attitude toward these hospitals was commendable, Page said, did he not vitiate his arguments by first severely criticizing and then recommending them as being "as good as the best"? Then there seemed to be an inconsistency in his bitter condemnation of one physician (Dr. A), who "at the most, showed lack of sympathy and judgment in applying the strait jacket and in forcing the stomach tube to give medicine," and at the same time his admiration for another (Dr. Thomas), who "took you by the throat, threw you on the bed and choked you into submission."[30]

Beers never fully came to grips with these criticisms, probably because his view was such a mixture of rational, logical thinking and emotional carry-overs of whose nature he was not fully aware. His portrayal of the two assistant physicians reflected the perceptions of their behavior that he had had at different stages of his disorder. None of the versions of his autobiography — published or unpublished — fully conveys what the contemporary documents forcefully do: that Clifford Beers, so needful of others' esteem, felt that Dr. Thomas respected him and Dr. A did not.

Page also had a point in noting Beers' contradictory evaluation of the hospitals. Beers was proposing a thorough reform that would be based on the needs of all patients — individualized treatment, attendants who would receive skilled training, nonrestraint techniques to control violent patients, and, most of all, a humane attitude that included permitting uncensored letter-writing, freedom of the grounds, and some sort of activity to occupy patients' time and energy. At the same time, because of his own experiences, he was so obsessed with the mistreatment and brutality meted out in the hospitals to highly excited, violent patients that to the extent that nonviolent patients were *not* physically abused he could praise the very same institutions as places where the majority of patients were treated well. He maintained this position even when he himself showed that nonviolent patients would often be mistreated if they caused trouble, created extra work, or did not respond as expected.

Some of Beers' receptiveness to criticism reflected his uncertainty as a writer and perhaps the realization that his somewhat excited state during the book's composition had interfered with his ability to organize the material and to exercise sound literary judgment. Unconcerned with brevity and precision, he tended to repeat himself and sometimes wrote in circles. Or, his sense of injustice and his reform aims uppermost in his mind, he would break into an irrelevant sermon about the terrible conditions of the mentally ill or introduce a long digression about nonrestraint or the need for a reform organization. The result was a story badly needing order, economy, and stylistic grace — that is, needing an editor. In March 1906, after he had been writing for six months, Beers found one, his old friend Herbert Wescott Fisher, who worked in a law office.[31]

When Beers asked Bert Fisher to correct errors in the first chapter, his detailed editorial criticisms were so helpful that Beers wondered whether he would do the same work for the entire manuscript, for pay. Fisher would take no money; he would do the editing at his leisure and doubted he could work on the whole manuscript. Beers sent him twenty dollars anyway as a token of good intentions.[32] Fisher became deeply involved in the work, recommending changes in style and organization sentence by sentence. Although many others read the manuscript and Beers later acquired other editors, no one but Fisher did such detailed and extensive editing.

In letters written a few years later Beers speaks glowingly of Clara

Jepson's help and inspiration, a "supposedly Platonic collaboration" that grew into love and then marriage. Much later, in the 1930s, he paid tribute to his wife's influence in deleting superfluous passages from *A Mind That Found Itself*.[33] She did help him with his later writings, including important letters; just how much she contributed to *A Mind That Found Itself* is not clear. In the acknowledgments section of the first edition she is not mentioned even obliquely, but during the year of its publication (1908) Beers privately thanked her for encouraging him from the time he first left the hospital in 1903. The extant documents of 1906, when he and Fisher were working on the manuscript, include few letters to or from Clara Jepson and no reference to her. She may well have been in the background giving moral support, though, and Beers did send her a copy of at least part of the edited manuscript. By then he had begun to be interested in marriage, which he had previously ruled out, but he dared not marry until he proved himself permanently healthy and had met the right woman, one of exceptional courage who would consider him a "fair risk." At the end of the year he was sending Clara a birthday present.[34]

On the whole, Beers accepted Fisher's excellent editorial advice, though he chafed under the yoke of "correct composition" and yearned to have his work be "artistic, if not technically perfect" and to be judged by its sincerity rather than its simplicity.[35] Fisher's judgment was as a rule sound, but not always. Because he considered that information about Beers' early years would be of no particular value to psychologists or psychiatrists, much less to the reading public, he encouraged Beers' tendency to give sparse attention to his life before the traumatic event of his youth—his brother Sam's illness. This advice was unfortunate, since there is so little documentary evidence of Clifford Beers' first twenty-four years, and of course psychologists and psychiatrists even at that time would have been interested.[36]

When Fisher favored reticence about the return visit to the Hartford Retreat in 1905, however, Beers demurred. That would be a "fatal error," he said. "The moment I consciously suppress any facts of importance . . . my story will cease to ring true." He also intended to mention the elation he experienced while writing the book: "What care I if people do consider me subject to periods of mental excitement, if that activity results in the production of MS to be edited when I am in a comparatively stupid state of mind?"[37] But he vetoed Fisher's suggestion to include, for comic relief, some of the letters written during his manic state. They might detract from the book's "dignity and convincingness." Later he thought that his "Elation Letters" might make up a special chapter and even had them mimeographed, but they were never published. Beers, the jokester, had nothing against humor even at his own expense, but he never ridiculed himself. Nor did he want people made too aware that he had ever behaved "disreputably." His story must be taken seriously and he must be portrayed as in command of most situations.

Not only, then, must he show himself as having the best of the many arguments he had had in the hospital, but he must not appear undignified. Otherwise the reader might question the accuracy of his memory and the validity of his interpretations. A sober treatment was necessary to achieve his aim of correcting popular misconceptions of insanity and breaking down stereotypes of the insane. For the same reasons the book must not be illustrated. He did not object in principle but wanted no one but himself interpreting his visions. After the book's publication he sent to a prominent psychiatrist "ornamental illustrations" that he had apparently created, perhaps for inclusion in a second edition, but was advised against making them public.[38]

By June 1906 Beers felt that his ability to write had improved enough under Fisher's tutelage for him to rewrite the rest of his story in good style, though Fisher continued to edit everything he wrote. Beers did not need to dictate any more but could put his thoughts directly on paper, a knack that he attributed to his habit of writing letters in his mind.[39] By August he hoped to complete a second draft and then "head for Oyster Bay under proper auspices of course." He felt confident of a warm reception there from President Roosevelt, who had just the other day sent "representatives to Chicago to investigate the charges made by the author of 'The Jungle'" (which Beers believed were untrue). Surely, then, the president would look into Beers' charges which of course were true. On the advice of friends, Beers desisted from approaching Roosevelt; nor did he send an open letter to him composed a few months later in which he sketched a comprehensive plan of governmental action that foretold by some fifty years the federal program in mental health and illness developed in the 1960s under the National Institutes of Health. Roosevelt, Beers suggested, should create a committee of psychiatrists, pathologists, psychologists, and others to investigate the cause, cure, and treatment of the insane, to work out model legislation for the insane, and to establish an international clearing house for information relating to mental illness. These functions would be performed under federal auspices, the best means of gathering and disseminating information. Also needed was a supplementary private organization whose work would "be a more personal affair and one in closer touch with the individual citizen" and which should be in existence before the publication of his book in order to take advantage of the sweeping interest in reform that it would stimulate.[40]

As work on the manuscript approached completion, Beers, always keen to provide for any contingency, wanted to ensure that his plans would be executed in case anything should happen to him. George Beers had suffered a "general but not serious, nervous break-down," which could have caused Clifford anxiety on two counts—the possible loss of a stable, dependable influence in his life, and the reminder of his own perhaps hereditary susceptibility to breakdown. If he should succumb again to mental illness, his book must not be published until he recovered, he told Fisher, as the success of his reforms depended upon his own ability to follow up the interest that the book would generate. In case of his premature death, he asked Judge R. W. Taylor, a family friend, to implement as many of his projects as possible. Over a period of eighteen months he wrote a half-dozen wills instructing relatives about the disposition of his manuscript, and he tried to decide upon a literary executor.[41] Would Bert Fisher be willing to serve? If so, he must see that the book was published and that, among other things, it should be copyrighted in every country where it would be likely to be read, "surely Great Britain, Germany, Austria, perhaps Russia, Japan, etc., also Norway, Sweden and Denmark . . . years hence after my plans have been executed, I may get . . . a 'Nobel Prize' of $40,000." Fisher agreed to be literary executor but felt obliged to tell Beers, "I expect your book to be a valuable contribution but of course not a masterpiece, and . . . I expect to see your personal efforts for reform fruitful, but not revolutionary. This is enough to reward any man for living."[42]

As favorable comments on the revised draft began to come in, Beers' attention turned almost wholly to working on the book. The editor of *Life* thought that the preface and first three chapters (edited by Fisher) were very much better than when he had first read them. Annie Trumbull Slosson, a writer, agreed: "It is strong, terse and not at all diffuse or rambling." Beers should take the hint, Fisher urged, and tighten up the rest of the manuscript.[43] At this point Beers acquired a second editor, Ada Comstock, professor of English at the University of Minnesota (and later to become president of Radcliffe College), in order to get a woman's point of view, one that would help him to delete anything offensive to women. But Comstock turned out to be less forthright in her criticism than Fisher, who forced Beers to expunge his most vigorous figures of expression on the "altar of conservatism."[44]

‡

In early July 1906, Beers received encouragement of which even he had scarcely dreamed and which was to prove a landmark in his life. Wanting an estimate of his book's "psychological worth" from the leading American psychologist, he introduced himself to William James one day while he was in Boston.[45] James, famous by then as a philosopher as well as a psychologist, not only was interested scientifically in psychological phenomena, but also had a personal concern with mental disorders, although it is not apparent that Beers knew this. Alice James, his sister, suffered attacks of hysteria in her youth and remained an invalid until her death in 1892, and two younger brothers were neurotic, one of them an alcoholic. James' own adult life was, in his latest biographer's words, "a struggle to overcome crippling neurosis" and ward off insanity. In his youth he suffered a period of "unbearable melancholy fear" that he later described in *The Varieties of Reli-*

gious Experience. "So great was the panic that William dreaded even to be left alone in the daytime", his biographer wrote, "and he wondered how other people could live unconscious of 'that pit of insecurity beneath the surface of life.'" As a professor at Harvard he took his students to observe patients in asylums and at one point was treating in his home "four 'melancholics,' as his wife called them."[46]

Intensely alive emotionally as well as intellectually, always interested in psychic experiences, sympathetic to human suffering, James was attracted to the obscure former mental patient, lively and witty like himself, who boldly approached him, and he agreed to read his manuscript. Beers sent the completed first part to James on June 9.[47] By July 1 James had finished it and wrote to Beers in his characteristically enthusiastic way:

> Having at last "got round" to your MS, I have read it with great interest and admiration for both its style and temper. I hope you will finish it and publish it. It is the best written out "case" that I have seen; and you no doubt have put your finger on the weak spots of our treatment of the insane, and suggested the right line of remedy. I have long thought that if I were a millionaire, with money to leave for public purposes, I should endow "Insanity" exclusively.
>
> You were doubtless a pretty intolerable character when the maniacal condition came on and you were bossing the universe. Not only ordinary "tact" but a genius for diplomacy must have been needed for avoiding rows with you; but you were wrongly treated, and the spiteful assistant M.D. at the Retreat deserves to have his name published. Your report is full of instructiveness for doctors and attendants alike — it ought to be published by some one of the Journals devoted to insanity *first*. I should think they'd be glad to take it in spite of its length.
>
> The most striking thing in it to my mind is the sudden "conversion" of you from a delusional subject to a maniacal one — when the whole delusional system disintegrated the moment one pin was drawn out by your proving your brother to be genuine. I never heard of so rapid a change in a mental system.
>
> "Psychology" knows nothing of the thing you write about. It is only an affair of acquaintance with concrete types. If anyone talks "psychology" in this matter, he's an ass.
>
> You speak of re-writing. Don't you do it. You can hardly improve it, except a possible omission of some of your side jokes which are not needed.
>
> I shall keep the MS a week longer. I wish to impart it to a friend.[48]

Beers was ecstatic. That such an eminent man should support him, an "honorless prophet" among relatives and friends who considered his book merely an advertisement for himself, was immensely gratifying. Although his family still cautioned him against disappointments, they were now convinced that "prematurely expressed ambitions and plans of mine are not to be regarded as symptoms of a disturbed mind."[49]

If Beers was overjoyed by James' "encouraging opinion," he was not overawed. True, he replied to James, he had been a "pretty intolerable character" in the hospital, which was partly why he did not mention the name of the malignant Dr. A, who in any case had given up psychiatry and who, representing a type found in almost every hospital, should not be singled out by name; nor should the other men guilty of abuses. All were victims of a vicious system. For the same reasons, he had decided not to name the hospitals, which had, after all, provided him with such good material for a book. After it was published Dr. A would no doubt eventually be found out and "sweat blood." But Beers, rather than having a "feeling of revenge to satisfy," felt only contempt.[50]

To Dr. Page he wrote that if any hospital in which he had been a patient failed to adopt nonrestraint policies before his book reached the printers they would "find themselves under the disturbing rays of an aroused public opinion." At that time Diefendorf told Beers that some people at the Connecticut State Hospital hoped the book would not be published, but Diefendorf told him, "Let it go, the sooner, the better."[51]

Beers understood psychiatrists' fear of revelations of hospital conditions, but he meant to shock his readers into action. His main object was not to expose hospitals but to improve conditions, not to convince doctors and attendants but to educate the "general public, and relatives and friends of the insane," who would then force physicians to eliminate abuses. For this reason he rejected James' advice that he first publish the book in psychiatric journals. He also turned down James' suggestion not to rewrite; since he intended to base his career on the book, he wanted to gain a reputation as a "writer of good English."[52]

On the road again for the Hoggsons, he worked hard to improve the style of the first part and to bring the narrative up to date. Still in the outline stage was the second part, his reform plan and miscellaneous materials, which he looked forward to writing, as he "dearly [loved] to preach" and enjoyed "lam-basting humanity, or a deficient specimen of that interesting aggregation of flesh and blood." The arguments with his two editors about his moralistic digressions continued. "Down with the critics!" Beers told Bert Fisher. "Naturalness is a law of nature; technique a necessary, yet sometimes superfluous consideration." But he acquiesced in the plea to eliminate duplication and finally asked Fisher to rearrange the completed manuscript (including the prospective second part.)[53]

By late summer Beers' literary energy had wound down, not to return until October, but he felt uneasy about taking time off again from work, although he hoped his future success would enable him to compensate his employers for any advantage he might have taken of their good nature. He persuaded the Hoggsons to hire a southerner to work in the South (where Clifford had already scouted business prospects) and to give him a leave of absence to prepare the manuscript for publication. The Hoggsons not only gave him the time but paid his salary through November and December, until he refused to accept any more money, and he remained officially in their employ.[54]

The revisions and the writing of the second part took longer than expected, but by February 15 the whole thing was done (Beers took care to have it copyrighted soon afterward), subject to revision by various critics, expecially the indispensable Fisher. The next step was to arrange for publication. At Judge Taylor's suggestion Beers turned to William James, to whom Russell H. Chittenden, head of the Yale Sheffield Scientific School, had at Beers' request vouched for his character and the validity of his story. Would James write the preface? Beers asked in a two-hour interview. James was unbelievably helpful. He suggested that his July 1 letter to Beers serve as the preface, gave permission to use his endorsement at will, and offered to write a letter of introduction to his own publisher, Longmans, Green.[55]

This was the beginning of a warm relationship that lasted until James' death in 1910. James was aging, he was busy, he suffered from heart disease. Yet he gave Clifford Beers his time, his advice, his friendship, and eventually his money. He even read Beers' poetry, which he thought not nearly so good as his prose.[56] Beers kept him informed about negotiations with publishers, sent him additional chapters and the entire revised manuscript to read, and even asked him to write a letter to convince Hoggson Brothers to grant him another leave of absence. The Hoggsons were impressed enough by James' graceful letter to give Beers unlimited leave and the freedom, when he came back, to work whenever it suited him, an arrangement that promised a "happy combination of literature, commerce and philanthropy [that] will enable me," Beers told James, "to support myself in healthful comfort and enjoy life to the full."[57] He was never to return to Hoggson Brothers.

He felt "pure happiness closely akin to elation itself," a sensation that he experienced rarely during "these prosaic days of normality." If, he told James, he had the "choice between the use of your name in the furtherance of my project, and the use of millions of dollars of one or a dozen of our men of vast wealth, I should have chosen the good name rather than the great riches. . . . Having won that which money cannot buy, my project— of itself—will win the other." He was forthright enough to tell James that he, Beers, had known just what to do: "the way to get what one wants is to go after it frankly." One must "ask the right person, in the right way at the right time." And he would not take James' advice to publish under a pseudonym: he felt most comfortable with those who knew his history, and besides, too many people did. More important, "I must fight in the open."[58]

Beers wrote to Longmans, Green, asking for their terms of publication, without telling them anything about the book or sending them the manuscript, though he may have enclosed James' letter. Understandably, Longmans, Green, although receptive, would not do any business until they knew the nature of the book. Why Beers was so uncharacteristically cryptic is not clear. Perhaps he thought that James' word would be enough, or he might have felt apprehensive enough to want to set the scene for a rejection. Longmans, Green was a conservative firm that might not advertise the book sufficiently, so that, he told Aunt Mame, he half hoped their terms would be unacceptable and he would have to find a more aggressive publisher.[59]

Longmans, Green, favorably impressed by the manuscript that Beers finally sent them, did hesitate to publish it because it was designed to be the basis of a reform movement that might affect the house's reputation. "How a firm can cheapen itself by playing a part in a worthwhile reform I cannot for the life of me see," Beers told James, and he tried to convince Longmans, Green that it would do them honor to publish the book. He formulated detailed plans for reaching all sorts of people through proper reviewing media and advertising campaigns (which could be financed by wealthy men); he expected to sell ten thousand copies the first year.[60] To buttress his case he obtained letters from prominent people. From Professor Lounsbury came a statement that the manuscript exceeded in interest "any novel which I have read in a long, long time." Professor Wilbur Cross of Yale attested that he had read the story "with the same absorbing interest as, say, The Opium Eater." (Years later Cross, who had become governor of Connecticut, recalled Beers' "amazing book" that he saw in its "first inchoate form" and remembered that Beers "kept damning" him for criticisms that he "finally accepted for the most part.") President Hadley of Yale told Beers he could refer any publisher to him for a recommendation.[61]

On James' advice and with George Beers' approval, Clifford negotiated for a publication contract on a percentage basis. Clifford would pay production costs; Longmans, Green would issue and distribute the book for a percentage of the gross earnings; and Clifford would own the plates and also receive a percentage of the gross earnings, the rates graduated in relation to sales.[62] Early in April 1907, less than two weeks after receiving the manuscript and reassured that Beers did not intend to launch a sensational advertising campaign, Longmans, Green agreed to publish on his terms. "With the magic names of 'James' and the confidence-inspiring imprint of the oldest publishing house in the world stamped on my book," Beers exulted to Paul McQuaid, he really would be famous. But to Clara Jepson he confided that the thrill was disappointingly mild, perhaps because he had believed all along that Longmans, Green would accept his terms. Yet, "if I have failed in my search for the *sensation* of success, I find great satisfaction in announcing my success to certain skeptical ones. *We* are, indeed, vindicated."[63]

76 ‡ Clifford W. Beers

Dampening Beers' pleasure was the recent death of his uncle, Samuel Merwin. He was the one man above all who, Beers felt, should have lived to see him a famous author and reformer. Uncle Sam had financed his college education, had made it possible for him to go to Stamford Hall rather than a state hospital when he was first taken ill, and had subsequently been interested in his work. Even in death he was a benefactor, having left Clifford a small legacy. Clifford decided to dedicate his book to him instead of to humanity, as originally planned. The text was sent to family members for their approval: "Dedicated to the memory of my uncle, Samuel Edwin Merwin, whose timely generosity I believe saved my life, and whose untimely death has forever robbed me of the opportunity to prove my gratitude." (In response to criticism that his words implied a disbelief in an afterlife, he revised the dedication to read "robbed me of a satisfying opportunity.")[64]

Clifford Beers was always most appreciative of the help he received. Although unabashedly egocentric and never hesitating to ask favors—money, time, effort, letters, sympathy—he always fully and publicly acknowledged assistance and was ready with voluble expressions of thanks and with information to benefactors about his progress. To Bert Fisher, who shared most intimately the writing, rewriting, and finally the triumph of James' approval and the publication contract, and without whom the manuscript would have been "an everlasting offense in the eyes of discriminating readers," Beers promised remuneration as well as help in his career. The unselfish, sacrificing way in which Fisher helped him was "one of the gratifying experiences of my life." "When I think of the work you have done for me, I tremble (almost) at the thought of the terrible mess I should have made of things had I blissfully gone ahead alone."[65]

Beers prized his personal attachments, which seemed to be warm, loving, and caring. He had the gift of binding people to him, including even hospital attendants and physicians to whom he had been a good deal of trouble. His behavior was not always lovable, but he himself must have been, and this, together with his intelligence, wit, and inventiveness, brought him unstinting devotion from a lot of people. His family and friends really cared about him, supported him financially, worried about his health, and enjoyed his successes: "Nothing could be better nor more encouraging," wrote his cousin. "We share your happiness in your work although we may at times have been rather skeptical of its results."[66]

‡

Beers still did not feel ready to send his book out into the world. Besides the money to finance publication, he wanted further expert opinion on the manuscript from psychiatrists and pledges of support from wealthy people for his reform movement. The publication of the book had to be coupled with the founding of a reform organization; otherwise the impact of both events would be lost. The book would educate and stir the public; but before it appeared, the manuscript had to convince philanthropists to finance an organization so that the aroused public would have a vehicle for action. To interest wealthy people would be difficult. There had been much encouragement to publish the book, but not so much for the reform plans. If important men like William James and G. Alder Blumer, superintendent of Butler Hospital in Providence, Rhode Island, who knew well the problems of the mentally ill, hesitated to endorse a reform movement, how could lay people be expected to give their money? It was necessary, Beers concluded, to gain additional support from psychiatrists so that his story would be invulnerable to attacks from the medical profession. He must demonstrate his willingness to accept and profit by criticism, and he must be ready to delete exaggerations, unfair generalizations, and possibly erroneous statements.[67]

A sample of the kind of criticism Beers could expect came from Dr. William McDonald, Jr., of Butler Hospital, whose basic objection was that Beers, in not sufficiently considering the viewpoint of the hospital staffs, had unfairly described their behavior. Without doubting Beers' veracity he questioned his judgments.[68] Beers' insistence, for example, that to be protected from abuses patients must have the right to see visitors without notifying hospital officials was too simplistic. There were all kinds of unwelcome visitors: people eager to satisfy their morbid curiosity; unscrupulous lawyers and relations who might take advantage of the patients' condition to persuade them to sign away property or money; "yellow" journalists eager for "thrilling" stories. And what about the patients' right to privacy?

There was also, McDonald continued, no guarantee that if the physicians had worked actively to overcome Beers' delusions he would have recovered much earlier, something Beers was not ready to acknowledge until many years later. (In 1937 he wrote, "The manic-depressive psychosis from which I suffered is a highly recoverable form of mental trouble, and psychiatrists, aside from treating a patient with consideration, cannot do very much to bring about a cure until recovery has actually set in.")[69] And, along with other knowledgeable readers, such as Dr. Noble, superintendent of the Middletown Hospital,[70] McDonald wondered about the instant return to reason at the Hartford Retreat. Clifford must have been already emerging from his depression or he could not have made a friend or devised a plan to test George's authenticity. He must realize that he had not regained his reason but was only shifting from depression to elation, and that he could not accuse physicians of neglect because they would not listen to his manic chatter. Nor were *all* attendants incompetent, insensitive "hirelings," nor *all* hospitals using padded cells and violent wards. Hospital administrators had, moreover, a blacklist of brutal attendants. Finally, Beers furnished plenty of evidence to show that in his period of high excitement he made trouble for himself. In other words, McDonald was saying that Beers had not been objective enough in recalling his experiences.

Far from being distressed by such criticism, Beers expressed delight. The points raised were "the very ones a hostile critic would have singled out for the purpose of discrediting the book," and he would try to incorporate them.[71]

His revisions did not fully satisfy McDonald. There was still the "insinuation . . . to the effect that the physicians have done little or nothing toward improvement of conditions. . . . If you knew . . . the attitude of the public mind toward insanity you would not wish to see the experiment tried of 'Packing all the drugs and all the doctors in the land over the seas and of installing in their places a body of amateurs with no equipment but consideration and sympathy.'"[72] McDonald was referring to Beers' contention (not unique to him) that "a knowledge of men is of more importance than a knowledge of medicine" in caring for the insane and that if physicians "would substitute tact for drugs . . . statistics would show a startling increase in the number of recoveries." He had imbibed from writers on psychiatry the view that science would find a cure for mental disorder, yet his own experience had shown that the greatest weakness in mental hospitals was a lack of sympathy for the patient. Until the time, therefore, that science would furnish the ultimate answers, humanitarian reforms would prove most effective. He nevertheless modified his statement to read, "It is the quality of heart rather than the quantity of mind that cures or makes happy the insane."[73]

He would not, however, change his declaration that scandalous conditions could be found in any institution, although he did agree to modify a caustic paragraph attacking the "tongue-binding ethics of the medical profession" that prohibited physicians from criticizing colleagues and correcting abuses, and he did admit that physicians had made progress in treating mental illness and reducing public apathy. He also responded to McDonald's challenge to his call for hospitals for incurables. How could anyone be sure who was incurable? McDonald asked. And what of the psychological damage done to people so deemed? Beers deleted the passage but never recognized that his support of the establishment of psychopathic hospitals to treat supposedly treatable psychotics was open to the same criticism because, in effect, patients would be initially divided into the recoverable and the unrecoverable.[74]

On several basic issues Beers refused to concede to McDonald. He insisted, first, that while he was manic he had interpreted events accurately; second, that while writing the book he had remembered equally accurately what had taken place in the hospitals; and third, that the hospital staffs, not he, bore responsibility for his suffering. Without these assumptions the book would lose much of its significance as a reform document. At the same time, he was careful to give the heads of the Hartford Retreat and the Connecticut State Hospital the opportunity to comment on his manuscript. Evidently he did not care about Givens' opinion; both Stamford Hall and Givens were too obscure. Stearns of the Retreat was dead, so Beers sent the manuscript to his successor, Dr. Whitefield N. Thompson, who found the story fair. At the Connecticut State Hospital, Superintendent Noble commented briefly on an early draft and agreed to read it in revised form. But although Noble and Thomas read the revised version, neither sent opinions or suggestions for changes, and when Beers went to see them at the hospital they were away. He concluded that, "having let them read my story for the purpose of accepting suggestions I now feel that I have a right to print what I please."[75]

But he did not have the opinion of the principal psychiatrist in the country, as he had that of the leading psychologist. (He may have known by then that James' word would not count much with most of the psychiatric-neurological establishment; the schism between psychology and psychiatry runs deep.)[76] Who was the leading psychiatrist? A natural person to ask was the medical reformer and writer Stewart Paton, whose views were sympathetic to Beers' own and who had influenced his thinking through his widely read text, *Psychiatry,* which advocated prevention as the primary aim of the mental health professions. Paton had given Beers permission to reproduce in his autobiography a chapter, "The Modern Hospital for the Insane," and now he suggested the right man for Beers to see. This was his friend Dr. Adolf Meyer, a Swiss-born, European-trained neurologist-psychiatrist who had come to the United States in 1892. If he could win Meyer over, Beers believed, "all the other psychiatrists would follow."[77]

Still only forty-one, Meyer was on his way to becoming the dominant figure in American hospital psychiatry. Already he had successfully introduced from Europe ideas and methods that were to transform the field. In his work at Kankakee State Hospital, Illinois, then at Worcester State Hospital, Massachusetts, and currently as director of the Pathological Institute at Ward's Island in New York City (later Manhattan State Hospital), he had instituted systematic record-keeping, programs of scientific research closely linked to clinical work, an awareness of Kraepelin's classification and delineation of mental illnesses, and, above all, an optimistic therapeutic approach that considered the patient's total life history and environment — in other words, the beginnings of modern hospital psychiatry. He was also in a position to carry his ideas beyond his own hospitals through his appointment as professor of psychopathology at the Cornell University Medical College.

Brilliant, rigorous, imperious, completely devoted to his work, and genuinely sympathetic to mental patients, Meyer had the intellectual sophistication and force of personality to effect reforms in hospitals and changes in the thinking of his colleagues. He had early made contact with a small group of outstanding men who between 1890 and 1909 "developed the most sophisticated and scientific psycho-therapy in the English-speaking world." This was the "Boston school," which Meyer came to know when he was clinical director at Worcester State Hospital (1896 to 1902) and had taught at Clark University, then a leading center of academic psychology. The Boston school included William James, Harvard neurologist Dr. James Jackson Putnam, philosopher Josiah Royce, psychologist Hugo Munsterberg, psychiatrist Morton Prince, and the superintendent of McLean Asylum, Edward Cowles. Meyer was especially close to James and Putnam. Just as James consulted Meyer about psychiatry, Meyer was greatly influenced by James' psychological thought.[78]

Meyer would be just the person to grasp the potentialities of Clifford Beers' work and to help him launch both the autobiography and a reform movement. At the least he would look at the manuscript, especially upon the recommendation of William James and Stewart Paton. Beers sent it to him at the end of September 1907, and a week later the two men met for the first time. Beers' impressions, expessed to Clara Jepson, were shrewd:

> Last evening, if evening extends from 6:30 to 11:30 P.M., I discussed my book and project with Dr. Adolf Meyer, — one of the finest men I have ever met. In appearance Dr. Meyer is much like Professor Chittenden of Yale. In methods, Dr. Meyer is much unlike Dr. Beers of New York, New Haven, and Hartford — and elsewhere. I am, as you probably know, not the most conservative person in the world. Dr. Meyer, to my mind, is a conservative of conservatives, in methods, though not at heart, for there he is a real reformer. Being a scientist, he is careful and exact, and slow to jump at conclusions. He weighs every word, not consciously but through habit.[79]

There were at least four meetings between the two strong-minded men (with Mrs. Meyer present as a referee) during which they spent some twenty hours talking about the manuscript; they also discussed it by mail.[80] Thus began a close collaboration, and a critical one for Beers. Meyer edited the manuscript and then wrote long journal reviews of the published book, and he became Beers' chief sponsor, advisor, and coworker in founding the reform movement.

Meyer's criticisms were probably the most influential and painstaking of all Beers had received (except Fisher's, which were more stylistic than substantive). Beers regarded Meyer as the one critic who could keep him from "slopping over" and hurting "the cause." He "tore parts of [the] story to pieces," and Beers was generally willing to put them back together again as recommended, although he was concerned that the book's quality as his unique story not be edited out of existence. Many of Meyer's objections resembled McDonald's. Beers' harsh judgment of hospital physicians, for example, gave offense. Beers, anxious to please and trying to understand Meyer's viewpoint, "read carefully" an address Meyer had given to hospital superintendents; he then rewrote a "destructive" paragraph into a "*constructive*" one. He would try to give credit to physicians for their good work, and he thanked Meyer for his "invaluable advice which will take the wind out of the sails of unfriendly critics." To Clara he wrote that he would go over the manuscript again "for what seems the thousandth time — and look for the rhetorical short-circuits likely to cause heart-burnings among the elect who are about to be dragged into the lime-light."[81]

The "flavor" of the manuscript displeased Meyer. It reflected too much Beers' "hypercritical" and unbalanced judgment during his manic period. Beers, not realizing that he had been an excited patient looking for trouble, gave too much credence to the perceptions he had at the time, and he confused the ability to speak coherently with being mentally sound: "it is action and capability of adaptation that count in mental disorders more than ability to talk." This was the "one point on which the success of the book will turn more than any other." Meyer tried to soften his criticism in a postscript: "I want to assure you that I greatly appreciate your willingness to meet me half way. I can easily see that even now you may feel differently from me about some of the events. But we can talk the points over whenever you wish to see me about them."[82]

After going over the manuscript with a "fine-tooth comb" and convincing Beers to make innumerable changes, Meyer approved publication. Not that he considered the book foolproof, but he had done the best he could. A few years later Meyer said that he had not mentioned certain features that he hoped Beers would spontaneously correct in the second edition and that on other points Beers could not be convinced. These were, for example, "such things as the description of the bull pen which should be brought up to date and the false impression Beers conveyed that 'the mind that found itself' reached a recovery where he says it did; I tried to balance the chapter by some wisdom at the end of it."[83]

Publicly, in a review of the published book written for the prestigious *North American Review* in 1908, Meyer gave the impression that on all but a few points he agreed with Beers' interpretations, including the Bull Pen episode, whose existence he explained as shaped by problems in dealing with troublesome patients.[84]

Thirty-five years later, however, Meyer told the editor of the *American Journal of Psychiatry* that "a good share of the writing was done in a state in which adequate insight could hardly be expected. There never was a complete understanding, although he was ready to see that the period from which he took the title of the book was the transition from depression into excitement. . . . He never on his own account asked the treating physicians to tell their side of the story, so that the book will not be a fair document." Perhaps Meyer was unaware that Beers did give superintendents and attending physicians opportunity to comment on his narrative; as for the title, originally he intended to call the book *Reason Triumphant,* but no one liked it, so he chose *A Mind That Found Itself* from a long list of possibilities.[85]

As Meyer realized at the time, Beers had attempted to comply with his criticisms, even when he could not either fully comprehend or fully agree with them. He tried to temper his condemnations, eliminate hostile remarks, and modulate his absolute judgments, but he continued to believe what he had first written. The result was an ambivalent book. For example, despite his insertion of statements indicating high elation during his troubles at the Retreat and the state hospital, Beers still gave the impression that he had acted in an essentially rational manner and that his demands on the staff were sensible. Even if he had sometimes unbearably provoked them, as a patient he had a right to decent treatment no matter what he did. On the other key question, his so-called sudden return to reason, he was not consistent. He presented evidence, as McDonald noted, that he had been gradually emerging from his depressed, delusionary state, and he called his epoch-making meeting with George "the culminating moment of my gradual readjustment"; in the next breath he spoke of an "apparently instantaneous return to reason." He realized the difficulty of determining the line between sanity and insanity, but in his case "the elapsed time between a condition of absolute insanity and comparative sanity was scarcely appreciable." The "very instant" he saw George "all was changed," his delusions vanished, his "mind had found itself." That momentous day was his "second birthday."[86]

Did he mean that he regained his reason but not his sanity? That was unlikely, for except when Meyer prompted him, Beers equated the ability to reason with sanity. This was the old idea that reason existed separately from emotion and the "insanity" was a disorder only of the cognitive process. If his perceptions became accurate, his imagination less morbid, his thought less confused, he considered himself sane, despite his accelerating excitement after he saw George. Later, revising the book for the third edition, he considered including a note "explaining [the] degree of sanity" that he had achieved and qualifying his statement about "regaining my reason," but he did not do so.[87]

The encounter with George remained the highlight of *A Mind That Found Itself.* It appealed to Clifford Beers' sense of the spectacular as well as his tendency to dramatize himself. It also served a more crucial purpose. Since he dated his newfound writing talent and his determination to describe his experiences and reform mental hospitals from the time he recognized George, it was important to give credibility to his exposés by making clear that they emanated from a "sane" mind. If he was to be successful in his campaign, he must convince the public that his mind had been intact both during his mania and when he was writing the book. His description of the crucial meeting was vivid and passionate: "Untruth became Truth. My old world was again mine. . . . That the Gordian knot of mental torture should be cut and swept away by the mere glance of a willing eye is like a miracle; but not a few insane persons recover their reason — or, more scientifically expressed, reach the culmination of their hitherto invisible process of readjustment — in what might be termed a flash of divine enlightenment, though very few have documentary evidence to prove their instantaneous return to life." No man could be born again, but he believed he "came as near it as ever a man did. To leave behind what was in reality a Hell, and, in less than one second, have this good green earth revealed in more glory than most men ever see it in, was a compensating privilege which makes me feel that my suffering was distinctly worth while . . . for have I not before me a field of philanthropy in which to work — a field which, even in this altruistic age, is practically untouched?"[88]

Whatever Meyer may have thought about the final manuscript, Beers was happy with the result of their collaboration: "I feel that my story is "practically bomb-proof, as far as criticism goes," he wrote.[89] He also felt encouraged by possibilities that had arisen of reaching the two great philanthropists, Andrew Carnegie and John D. Rockefeller, with hope centering on the latter. The era of massive private philanthropy through the foundations that the new American tycoons established had only just begun, and their philanthropic specialties, organized in a businesslike way, were just developing. No individual or foundation had yet shown an interest in mental illness, though medical projects were becoming popular.

Andrew Carnegie was not a likely prospect. He had given funds mainly for libraries and education, enterprises that would supposedly help individuals rise in the world as he had. The Carnegie Institution was founded to promote scientific research, and in his famous essay on wealth Carnegie had listed hospitals as worthy objects for philanthropy. But later he declared that hospitals, like prisons, were a public rather than a private responsibility, and he refused requests for money for medical purposes with the comment, "That is Mr. Rockefeller's specialty. . . . Go see him."[90] Rockefeller, through the influence of his close business associate and advisor, the Reverend Frederick T. Gates, had indeed claimed medicine, among other things, as an object of the philanthropy he was practicing on an unprecedented scale. In 1901 the Rockefeller Institute for Medical Research (Gates' idea) had been established, and a year later the General Education Board, with Gates as president. In June 1907 Beers met Anson Phelps Stokes, Jr., secretary of Yale University, member of a well-known banking and philanthropic family, who suggested that Rockefeller would be more likely than Carnegie to support Beers' reform organization, and he offered to place the manuscript before Gates. The clever Baptist minister, businessman, and innovator in philanthropy had a special and informed interest in medical research and education, and he had asked Stokes to bring to his attention prospects for large philanthropy.[91]

Beers wrote James, "Success is at hand." Stokes had great influence with Gates, who had a son at Yale and planned to send three others there—a sign that he would give a Yale man a fair hearing. James should expect to receive inquiries, and perhaps he might "bring pressure on the situation" through his friend and former student, the psychologist Charles Strong, Rockefeller's son-in-law. The likelihood that Gates would want opinions from experts led Beers also to turn to Paton for help. Would Paton be ready to leave Princeton for New York at a moment's notice to advise Gates should he be asked to do so? And would Paton kindly send Beers' manuscript to Dr. Weir Mitchell, the famous neurologist and novelist, whom Beers had failed to reach on his own?[92]

Paton gave Beers "pretty good proof of his interest in the cause" by promising that he would, if need be, return from Naples, where he was planning to travel shortly. The man to enlist at this point was not Mitchell, Paton advised, but the highly influential William Welch, chairman of the board of the Rockefeller Institute for Medical Research and professor of pathology at Johns Hopkins Medical School, then the leading medical school in the United States. At the end of September, at about the same time that Beers first sent his manuscript to Meyer, he met Paton at the Yale Club in New York to receive cards of introduction to Welch. For the next few weeks, in between consulting with Meyer about the manuscript and making revisions, Beers saw medical notables in Baltimore. He met the assistant superintendent of the University Hospital (son of James' friend Professor Charles Eliot Norton of Harvard) and had lunch with Paton's brother-in-law, Dr. Lewellys F. Barker, physician-in-chief at Johns Hopkins Hospital and a specialist on the nervous system who was interested in psychotherapy and with whom Beers left his manuscript. He spoke several times with Welch, who said, Beers reported to Meyer, "If my opinion were asked I should say that the most urgent need in medical education in this country today is the need of Psychiatric Clinics at our several medical schools."[93]

Paton also volunteered to put Beers into contact with a certain wealthy man, but Beers wanted to negotiate with only one philanthropist at a time. When Stokes offered to introduce him to Robert de Forest, legal advisor to Mrs. Russell Sage, who had just inherited her husband's immense fortune, Clifford again declined. If Rockefeller refused to finance his project he would approach first Carnegie and then Mrs. Sage; these three could best furnish the large sums he required, some ten to twenty million dollars. Only if turned down by them would he approach smaller fry. Nevertheless, he would like to have de Forest's opinion of his reform plan so that he could better answer any questions that Gates might ask; no philanthropist had as yet commented on his manuscript. And he still wanted to reach President Roosevelt.[94]

Not until October did Gates finally reply, in a letter to Stokes which, although negative regarding any forthcoming money, was not discouraging. Gates read the manuscript with interest, but he could not then even investigate Beers' project. For one thing, the new Rockefeller Institute was intended to act as Rockefeller's agency in everything connected with medical education, and it was still in its infancy. Gates, along with his wife and sister, who also read the manuscript, was enthralled with the part telling Beers' personal story; thereafter their interest waned. The book should therefore, he advised, conclude with the end of the narrative, which would be the part that would influence people; the opinions of experts and the other informational material should go into an appendix. In a subsequent letter written directly to Beers he declared his faith that the book would "become a classic in its line, and if properly launched, it will have a great and immediate popular success and produce a profound impression throughout the country." If there was a need for a society of any kind, or special hospitals for treating mental illness, they had all best come after publication of the book.[95]

Beers decided to follow Gates' advice, which would not cause printing hardships, as the last part was not yet at the printer. He was aware that Gates' criticism had been made by others, "but not until an authority laid down the law could I see clearly the advantage to be gained by omitting some of the concluding chapters of my story." What gave Gates' literary advice such weight he did not explain. No doubt it was its connection with a lot of money, a source of authority Beers respected greatly — even to the point of considering Gates worthy of a dedication for the "timely and convincing criticism" that saved the book from having a "fatal ending." Beers also decided to stop searching for financial backers and to concentrate on getting his book published; fund-raising on a large scale would be futile until the book appeared in print. However, encouraged by Meyer and other psychiatrists, he began to solicit "moral support" by enlisting temporary trustees for his national society. On Meyer's advice he requested William James to revise one of his letters that was to appear in the introduction to *A Mind That Found Itself* so that it would be "critic-capturing, suspicion disarming" and endorse the movement. "With my book and 'remedy' vouched for by you and Dr. Adolph [*sic*] Meyer," Beers wrote James, "it will be only a brave, or very ignorant critic who will dare attack it [the book] unfairly."[96]

James revised the letter, dated November 10, 1907, to read as follows:

Dear Mr. Beers:
    You are welcome to use the letter I wrote to you (on July 1, 1906) after reading the first part of your MS. in any way your judgment prompts, whether as preface, advertisement, or anything else. Reading

the rest of it only heightens its importance in my eyes. In style, in temper, in good taste, it is irreproachable. As for contents, it is fit to remain in literature as a classic account "from within" of an insane person's psychology.

The book ought to go far toward helping along that terribly needed reform, the amelioration of the lot of the insane of our country, for the Auxiliary Society which you propose is feasible (as numerous examples in other fields show), and ought to work important effects on the whole situation.

You have handled a difficult theme with great skill, and produced a narrative of absorbing interest to scientist as well as layman. It reads like fiction, but it is not fiction; and this I state emphatically, knowing how prone the uninitiated are to doubt the truthfulness of descriptions of abnormal mental processes.

With best wishes for the success of the book and the plan, both of which, I hope, will prove epoch-making. I remain,

Sincerely yours,
Wm. James

Beers was pleased and appreciative: the letter was a "clincher." James thanked Beers but thought "the millions of a Rockefeller will help your cause far more than the 'reputation' of a James."[97]

The book was in press during the fall of 1907 while Beers was soliciting contributions or loans to finance publication. Would Meyer help by writing an opinion, to be used confidentially, "regarding the value of my story, the good it will do and the feasibility of the method offered"? Meyer immediately complied.[98] But the time was not propitious for raising money because of the "threatened 'financial panic.'" Five men whom Beers approached, including Anson Phelps Stokes, refused his appeal for a thousand dollars. The president of the newly formed Russell Sage Foundation, John H. Glenn, would consider helping only if the book were issued as a Sage Foundation publication, which Beers would not permit.[99] Finally, as before, help came from an intimate: his brother George supplied endorsed notes on which Clifford borrowed the money to print a first edition of three thousand copies at a cost of $2,100, and earlier his friend Vic Tyler had lent him money toward publication costs.

The work on which he had been concentrating so much hope and labor would finally reach the public, and under the most impeccable auspices. An obscure young man who only five years before lay immobilized in a strait jacket would be, by virtue of that experience, on his way to the fame that had existed only in fantasies envisioned while he shouted and shivered in a padded cell.

‡ 7 ‡

Publication of
A Mind That Found Itself

Various delays postponed publication of *A Mind That Found Itself* until March 1908, when it came out in New York and London. The dust jacket included a revised version of Lounsbury's letter of the year before, and the introduction consisted of William James' letters of July 1, 1906, and November 10, 1907, prefaced by the following paragraph:

> A story so strange as to challenge belief must needs be presented in a way especially calculated to inspire confidence. Thanks to Professor William James of Harvard University, I am able to cut off incredulity at its source by quoting his opinion. That which has already enlisted the support of one of the most eminent psychologists in America is entitled at least to a respectful hearing from laymen.

After the table of contents came a page with the following statement: "This book is written by one whose rare experiences impel him to plead for those afflicted thousands least able to speak for themselves."[1]

The text was 363 pages, divided into four parts, plus appendices. The first part, nearly two-thirds of the book, was the narrative of Beers' mental illness. The second part consisted of a critique and analysis of the treatment of patients. The next part continued the autobiography through Beers' writing and editing of the book, including eloquent appreciations of all the help he received, mention of the scientists who made the work "authoritative," the statement that the "managements of the two hospitals so fully discussed have exhibited rare magnanimity (even going so far as to write letters which helped me in my work)," and acknowledgment of "the active encouragement of casual but trusted acquaintances, the inspiring indifference of unconvinced intimates, and the kindly scepticism of indulgent relatives, who, perforce, could do naught but obey an immutable law of blood-related mind." Then the burden was shifted to the reader: "If the reader does not now feel that he would like to do something to help those unfortunates for whom I speak, then either I have failed to present my story convincingly, or the reader's love of fair play and his moral nature are of a false kind." Part 4 discussed proposals for reform followed by appendices containing reprints of papers and speeches documenting the text. The final lines of the text read: "For twenty centuries the cry of the insane has been and today is: 'Torment me not! Torment me not!'"[2]

Beers' considerable efforts to make the book authentic and authoritative, together with the intelligence, vigor, and intensity of his presentation, had created a document that was to have a remarkable impact. It did for the mental hygiene movement, Anson Phelps Stokes said years later (when he was canon of Washington Cathedral), "what Thomas Paine's 'Common Sense' did for the cause of American Independence, or what Harriet Beecher Stowe's 'Uncle Tom's Cabin' did for the freeing of the slaves. It proved an irresistible combination of facts and arguments based on personal suffering which made a profound appeal to the intelligent and philanthropic public."[3]

There had previously been sensational exposés of the treatment of the mentally ill—by reformers, former inmates, and inmates—but few, if any, like Clifford Beers'.[4] The most famous revelations up to then in the United States had been made by Dorothea Dix, a compassionate observer whose tireless investigating, writing, and lobbying resulted in the construction of approximately thirty public mental hospitals in the United States and Europe where there had been only a handful before. Beers became in some ways her parallel, half a century later, but to spark his movement he drew on his own experiences to produce a powerful and convincing account written from the inside, by a victim of the system.

Former patients had before then described their ordeals in pamphlets and books that tended to be poorly written vindications of their sanity and condemnations of those who had confined them. The best-known such case in the United States was that of Mrs. E. P. W. Packard, who wrote about the State Insane Asylum at Jacksonville, Illinois, where she spent three years as an involuntary patient. She claimed that her husband committed her merely because she refused to accept his religious beliefs and that she was only one among many sane people held in the asylum against their will. As a result of her campaign, the superintendent of the Jacksonville asylum was dismissed and the Illinois legislature enacted in 1867 a statute to protect prospective mental patients by requiring a jury trial to decide on commitment. The law was a dubious reform in that the decision as to an individual's sanity was vested in a lay jury and the public proceedings often caused great embarrassment to the person being judged, so that psychiatrists had since been trying to change it.[5]

The many other exposés in the nineteenth century by journalists as well as former patients were similar to Mrs. Packard's in describing treatment in asylums as cruel and inhumane, but most went beyond credulity, so that they were not effective propaganda, at least among the educated public that could have effected changes. Another class of exposé literature, by its nature scarce and ephemeral, derived from patients still in hospitals. Then there was the group of writings, of which Daniel Paul Schreber's *Memoirs of My Nervous Illness* is perhaps the best known,[6] in which the author was interested in either expounding his particular form of delusion or simply expressing himself.

An account of asylum life similar to Clifford Beers' and by a man with similar purposes was written seventy years before *A Mind That Found Itself* by J. T. Perceval, a British army officer and son of a prime minister. He had become mentally ill in 1830 and spent some three years in two expensive private mental hospitals which he described in narratives published in 1838 and 1840.[7] Perceval's catalogue of abuses included practices no longer used in 1900—cold baths, bloodletting, and confinement on straw in an "out house," but his purpose was similar to Beers': to "stir up an intelligent and active sympathy, in behalf of the most wretched, and the most oppressed, the only helpless of mankind, by proving how much needless tyranny they are treated [with]—and this in mockery—by men who pretend indeed their cure, but who are in reality their tormentors and destroyers."[8] He also had discussed various therapeutic systems with the hospital physicians and others and, again like Clifford Beers, went beyond writing to establish in 1845 the Alleged Lunatics' Friends Society. In 1851 he published *Poems by a Prisoner in Bethlehem* and in 1859 gave evidence to a Select Committee for Lunacy established by Parliament. Until his death in 1876, the year Clifford Beers was born, he also wrote occasional letters to the *Times* on the lunacy laws.[9]

Beers, who liked to portray himself as the only former mental patient with the talent and courage to expose asylum conditions effectively and start a reform movement, seems to have been unaware of Perceval's work, as were most people. All the same, Beers was right about himself. If he was not the only man of his kind, he was the most famous and most effective, in his own time and beyond. *A Mind That Found Itself* combined the desires to expose, reform, and inform without denying his own illness. He had no doubt that he had been disturbed and had to be hospitalized; highly intelligent and alert throughout his illness, he was able, even while at the hospital, to view events in some measure from the vantage point of the physicians and attendants he encountered, although he did not absolve them of responsibility. He was not wholly innocent of self-justification, but he was mainly concerned with disclosing the misunderstanding and damage created by inappropriate, insensitive, ignorant modes of treatment that neglected the real feelings and needs of the patient. In so doing, he wrote a classic account of the course of his illness that offered unusual insights into the mental processes and sensibilities of a delusional, depressed, and then manic person. Partly because he was aware of the sensitivity of hospital superintendents to irresponsible, sensational criticism and wanted his book to be taken seriously, he had gone to unusual lengths to make it bear the impress throughout of consultation with leading specialists in mental illness and of familiarity with the psychiatric literature and psychiatric trends. The result was a unique, largely successful attempt to interweave the nature and progress of his disorder with the kind of care available to him, together with well-considered suggestions for reform. It was the best and most influential account then published of a mental patient's experiences — not only more dramatic, more immediate, and more powerfully written than any other, but temperate enough to convince readers with the most sophisticated knowledge of the subject; it had the backing of important people and a highly reputable publisher; and it was issued at a time of renewed interest in humanitarian reform and, in psychiatry, of new ideas and fresh optimism.

‡

Although Beers wanted public attention drawn to the book, he did not want to alienate the psychiatric profession, already made sensitive by the exposés of mental hospitals published in the popular press. Yet he had to take the risk of sensationalism if he were to publicize the book and move masses of people. One way to deal with this problem was to ensure that notices by responsible reviewers would appear in reputable newspapers and journals, as well as medical publications. He sent two hundred prepublication copies out for review and prepared the ground for reviews in the old and respected *New York Sun, Nation,* and *North American Review* by communicating with their editors and leaving page proofs with prospective reviewers.[10]

The campaign was on the whole successful. The major American and some British newspapers and periodicals published articles, reviews, or editorials and in some cases all three. There were at least eighty-five reviews and editorials, plus twelve medical reviews (including one from *Lancet* and another from the *Rivista di psycologia applicata*).[11]

The general periodicals emphasized three aspects of the book: Clifford Beers' humanitarian call for reform, especially the idea of a national reform society; his terrible experiences and unfair treatment (albeit he was troublesome and had possibly exaggerated or misinterpreted events); and the book's truthful and convincing quality. Reviewers characterized it in forceful terms: "remarkable"; "vivid"; "elegant"; "strikingly well written"; "of poignant interest"; "exceedingly interesting"; "more fascinating than any novel"; "extraordinary . . . in point of subject matter and form." It was "a convincing subjective study"; "a text for . . . reorganization of the 'system' of management of the insane"; "a classic . . . obvious even to the unitiated"; "one can hardly release the book while reading Part 1." Newspaper reviews and editorials were similar. The book was "powerful," "one of the most remarkable books published in recent years," a "human document," "of intense interest and of deep significance," "a masterpiece on insanity," "sure to make a sensation among . . . humanitarians." The general consensus was that reforms were necessary and must be implemented.

Predictably, some of the press coverage was lurid. For example, the *Boston Herald* headlined a two-column review as follows:

BRUTALITIES TO INSANE TOLD BY YALE MAN WHO WAS A VICTIM

Clifford W. Beers, Crazed for Few Years, Relates His Experiences in Three Asylums in Connecticut in Book Which He Hopes Will Start National Reform Movement

BEATEN WHEN HE ASKED FOR A GLASS OF WATER

Kicked and Left in Corner on One Occasion—Is Now Recovered and Has Secured Aid of Prof. James of Harvard, Joseph H. Choate and Other Scientific Men[12]

Beers spent three hectic days before the book's publication date trying to keep the New Haven newspapers from waxing sentimental or worse, sensational. He wanted to protect both the "cause" and himself. For had not a prepublication article in the *New Haven Evening Reporter* used a question mark after the title: "A Mind That Found Itself?" Years later he called this a typographical error and confessed how much it had upset him, especially as he knew that there were some people who thought that he should return to a mental hospital for more treatment.[13]

The *New Haven Union* was stirring up sentiment for investigating mental institutions in Connecticut, a campaign that Beers tried to modulate by suggesting to the governor that if the "people" wanted conditions probed, Dr. Meyer and Dr. William L. Russell, medical inspector of the New York State Commission in Lunacy, were the men to do the job. He also reassured Dr. Noble that if the hospitals were investigated they could use the reports to gain more financial aid from the state legislature. At Beers' urging the editors of the *New Haven Journal Courier* and *Register* opposed the "ill-advised clamor" of the *Union,* but they would allow him no more interference.[14] William James advised that Beers' efforts to control the nature of reviews was futile and wearing: Beers' "cerebral health" was "too precious to add that sort of burden to it."[15]

But even James was disturbed by a long article on the book that was featured in the Sunday *New York Times*, with a banner headline: "The Story of Two Years in Asylums for Insane. Yale Graduate Who Had Gone Mad Suddenly Regained His Reason, but Was Unable to Convince Keepers of His Sanity." This piece, purporting to be a review of *A Mind That Found Itself,* focused almost entirely on Beers' descriptions of hospital abuses, complete with the most sensational quotations from the book. It ended with remarks that Beers made in an interview, where he discussed the projected National Committee for Mental Hygiene and mentioned the prominent roles of William James and Adolf Meyer, along with others who had agreed to be honorary members. Beers was careful to point out that the public, instead of dwelling on abuses, should see to it that mental hospitals received sufficient financial support and should, through state societies for mental hygiene, try to raise the standard of treatment.[16]

The *Times*'s writer's obvious sensationalism aside, his treatment of the book indicated that some of the modifications Beers had inserted to satisfy his psychiatric critics confused the issues instead of clarifying them. His own perceptions, forcefully presented, made the most lasting impression on the unsophisticated reader. For example, the article notes that although Beers was "perfectly sane, he could not convince the keepers that he was." A few lines later: "One day, suddenly and unaccountably his clouded brain cleared, the delusions which vexed his disordered mind vanished, and from sheer insanity and profound depression his mind swung back to comparative sanity and clear perception." He was also described as getting into trouble only because he had decided to uncover abuses and determine their extent, which resulted in the book's being written.[17] Two days after this "review" appeared, the *Times* published a letter from a former asylum inmate praising both Clifford Beers and the *Times* for devoting so much space to his book.[18]

But William James was so angry about the sensationalism and the "wilful misstatements" that he sent off a "piercing" letter of protest to the *Times* editor.[19] Meyer was apparently concerned about the use of his name in connection with what he considered unfortunate publicity for mental hospitals, and Beers was worried about Meyer's concern as well as about the general effect of the *Times* "blast." As to the latter, however, he assured Meyer that after the "reporters have had their inning, the Editors will clear the atmosphere," and that Russell thought the article would help the cause. Beers forswore talking with reporters "except for the purpose of doing what I can to keep them within bounds," and he promised to try to keep Meyer's name out of print. He also proposed to neutralize the *Times*'s article by sending a personal letter to each mental hospital chief in the United States, telling them that the proposed National Committee would be a cooperative venture involving hospital superintendents. He would also call attention to positive reviews of his book in respectable journals and enclose a copy of a sympathetic *New Haven Courier* interview with himself.[20] Meyer vetoed the plan.

James' letter to the *Times* was not published, but, as Beers had predicted, there did appear a corrective editorial comment several days later. The editors affirmed their high estimate of *A Mind That Found Itself* but said that Beers had taken "only a narrow view" of insanity and its treatment; he had condemned conditions on which "superintendents have been working for years." He "admitted the fact that the asylum superintendents and only in less measure their subordinates, down to the worst of the attendants, were themselves like the patients, victims of an evil system of public economy, [but] he did not make plain just where the responsibility lies." The *Times* thought that the authorities were doing the best they could with limited resources and had themselves pointed out the need for higher standards, which "unfortunately" required more money.[21]

From the conservative *New York Sun,* whose managing editor had promised to place *A Mind That Found Itself* "in the hands of the right person," came a critical editorial declaring that the book failed to throw "any new light on what happens in institutions that are mismanaged." Meyer replied to this one, informing the editors that "such a first-hand account and direct illustration of the nature of the difficulties and discussion of concrete reforms is a document such as has not been produced before."[22]

On the whole, Beers had little cause for complaint about the general trend of newspaper coverage, although negative comments in two leading New York papers would be disturbing. The notices (many of them several columns long) in a wide range of U.S. and British newspapers were overwhelmingly favorable, sympathetic, intelligent, and free of the melodrama and pandering to thrill seekers that might have been expected in the heyday of "yellow journalism." Reporters and reviewers were much impressed by James' and Lounsbury's endorsements; by Beers' background as a Yale graduate and businessman of "superior attainments" and of "high intellectual attainments";[23] by his being the nephew of a former lieutenant governor of Connecticut; by the inclusion of documents by experts; and most of all by the sincerity and literary quality of his prose and the sobriety of his reform proposals. Most of the articles hoped that the book would contribute toward more humane and enlightened care of the mentally ill.

Reviews in the general periodicals were more sophisticated and critical than those in newspapers but were on the whole favorable. A recent (1971) evaluation of the reception of *A Mind That Found Itself* in leading general magazines contends that it was greeted "with condescension and incredulity." A reading of these reviews, in such magazines as the *Nation, Dial, Independent, Outlook,* and others, indicates, on the contrary, that although the reviewers did lean to pessimism about preventing and curing insanity and were not optimistic about effecting improvements in the treatment of the insane, they found the book believable in its narrative and commendable in its intent to enlighten the public and reform hospital conditions. It was a "remarkable and grimly engrossing book," a "veritable human document."[24]

The old, respected *North American Review,* still a leading vehicle for intellectuals, gave the book to Adolf Meyer to review, apparently at Beers' suggestion.[25] In his careful, balanced way Meyer discussed the significance of the book and revealed the striking impression Beers had made upon him. Allowing that mental hospitals were probably much better than the public and even the medical profession would admit, he exclaimed, "But alas! there are many defects in them, and the experience of Mr. Beers was more strenuous than that of the average patient, yet, as I have said, it may prove to have been for the good of many." His book would "if anything can, . . . rouse a sentiment among all, that there is much to be done for the amelioration of existing conditions by those who are willing to lend their intelligence, good sense and civic instincts to a great cause." It was unique among "abuse" and antihospital literature in presenting so fairly "the undoubted hardships" to which the author was subjected: "He does not make them stand out as the one outrage or trouble in the world; he looks fairly at the situation; he takes advice as to his interpretations and recommendations. If he expresses himself more drastically than an outsider or a physician would, we can easily excuse him, for he himself had to endure the things which he tells."

Meyer concluded that "unimaginative officials, uninformed of what is going on in the world, and penurious legislative censors of expenses and a misinformed public govern too many hospitals, and will continue to do so unless help is offered." Beers rightly realized the need for an organization of citizens to bring to the public "the warnings and suggestions which can only be obtained from a study of the actual wrecks. These are the balancing factors without which his plea would easily share the fate of the numerous outcries of the past."

Beers had aptly indicated the kind of information needed and was willing, even anxious, to give the work of informing and reforming over to an organization that would represent "the entire movement of mental hygiene, and give the special needs a balance and proportion which they have never attained in the past." Meyer approvingly quoted James' praise of the book as a classic but said that its most "valuable effect " was in "drawing the reader to a striking and fascinating personality, direct and sensible, and promising to become an excellent champion for a great cause."[26]

Notices in medical and psychiatric journals (to which Meyer also contributed with a review in *Psychological Bulletin*) were favorable but not uncritical. The book was considered valuable for its portrayal of how a sick mind worked, particularly in a depressed state,[27] and Beers' reform proposals also met with approval. One commentator, however, stressed that hospitals were better in 1908 than in 1900, some questioned the accuracy of Beers' version of events, and several worried that lay people would misinterpret the depictions of hospitals. These negative remarks apparently only mildly expressed the feelings of the many hospital superintendents who were, in the recollection of Dr. Earl Bond, a young psychiatrist in 1908, "bitterly antagonized" by the book.[28]

Beers had prepared himself for skeptical comments. He had been in communication with the superintendents at the Hartford Retreat and Connecticut State Hospital, and now he had Frank Wordin sign a sworn statement attesting to the truth of the incidents described at Stamford Hall. A year before he had obtained affidavits from a lawyer swearing to the truth of charges of brutality at the Lexington, Kentucky, asylum.[29] He also asked Meyer to vouch for his story. Meyer contacted Dr. Noble, who must have confirmed Beers' account of events at his hospital, for Meyer, in a "To Whom It May Concern" letter, stated his conviction of the book's accuracy.[30] In the *Psychological Bulletin* review, Meyer said that "searching inquiries have failed to bring forth any demonstrations of misrepresentations." There might be errors of interpretation, but they were "trifles in comparison with the vivid description of events." Anticipating, too, the inevitable questions that would arise about Beers' current condition, Meyer declared that he was "fully restored."[31]

Another important professional review appeared in the organ of the American Medico-Psychological Association (later the American Psychiatric Association), the *American Journal of Insanity,* predecessor of the *American Journal of Psychiatry.* It was written by Dr. Clarence B. Farrar, assistant physician and director of the laboratory, Sheppard and Enoch Pratt Hospital; associate in psychiatry, Johns Hopkins Medical School; visiting physician, Bay View Asylum (and in years to come, the long-term editor of the *Journal*). Farrar adopted a clinical approach to the book, which, he said, could not "be taken without a liberal grain of salt," as it gave the erroneous impression that Clifford Beers' case was extraordinary, that the transition from depression to mania was rare, and that Beers had presented a "fair statement of conditions from the view-point of a sane man, inasmuch as the author recovered."[32]

Farrar raised a more serious question, one that he thought the evidence strongly suggested and which in his view influenced any evaluation of the book: Was Beers fully recovered? Maniacal patients commonly failed to gain adequate insight into their illness long after the passing of the acute phase and after their discharge from the hospital. Further, projects and ideas conceived during "morbid excitement" might form the basis for activity after "virtual recovery." Sometimes "a permanent change seems to have taken place . . . new or previously latent powers" appear, together "with a broadened view of the world, with an abiding desire, withal honest and wholesome, to effect philanthropic reforms, and a constitutional hypomanic state which betrays itself at every turn, which is always busy, always in the way, always bristling with magnificent schemes, but always fantastic, visionary and ineffectual."[33]

This characterization seemed to Farrar to apply to Beers. His book was an outgrowth of pathologic excitement; he had devised reform plans not in his depressed but in his elated stage. That he did not understand his disorder was shown by his insistence on his sudden return to mental health when he recognized George. Considering his claims about his "rare experiences, his marvellous escape from death and a miraculous return to health after an apparently fatal illness," Farrar concluded that Beers' mental health was suspect. Even some of his reforms were dubious: demands that preachers circulate among the insane, that relatives should in all cases visit patients, and that patients' letters be forwarded without exception were too simplistic.[34] Farrar believed it likely that Beers' illness had reoriented his personality and created a reformer who was still not in a full state of mental health.

Beers himself went further in his self-analysis, insisting that his passage into mania was the turning point in his life, giving him a much improved memory, the ability to draw, an interest in literature, and a new concern for his fellow beings. He was not restored to his former self but had discovered a new self more healthy, more creative, more satisfying than the old.[35] Although he knew he had been elated while writing the first draft and was ever alert to his mental condition, Beers did not consider that his book showed signs of excitement.[36] (It had certainly gone through enough editors' hands.) What he knew, and what Farrar did not at that time seem to see, was that Clifford Beers did not in a crucial way fit Farrar's model of an unrecovered manic patient: he was not all talk and no accomplishment. Excited or not, visionary or not, he *had* written the book, he *had* obtained the endorsement and help of prominent people, he *had* had it published by an esteemed publishing house, he *had* enlisted the support of well-known psychiatrists for his reform plans.

Farrar, withal, considered the book "very valuable and timely" as a "human document, an autopathography" and as an exposure of admittedly terrible conditions. His criticisms and reservations, Farrar said, should not "detract from the interest and value of the work," which although perhaps not suitable for every lay person, could be perused "with profit" by every physician and nurse involved with mental disorder for the insight that Beers gave into patients' psychology and for his "abundant suggestions" for proper, individualized treatment.[37]

In an equivocal review in the *Journal of Abnormal Psychology,* Ernest Jones, the British psychiatrist and disciple of Freud, agreed with much of Farrar's analysis. Jones did not doubt the overall truth of Beers' story and accepted its general tendency; indeed, he recommended it as essential reading for everyone concerned with mental hospitals. Yet it seemed to him to be strewn with evidence of "impaired insight into the morbid manifestations from which the writer had recovered" and so could not, without corroboration from other sources, be taken as an accurate depiction of contemporary hospital care.[38]

Morton Prince, editor of the *Journal of Abnormal Psychology,* told Beers that he wished it had been "practicable" to have given a "deeper analysis" of his mental condition. Would Beers write a paper for the *Journal* to this effect? Psychiatrists very badly needed detailed accounts by patients of their mental life. And it would be a good idea for Beers to deliver a paper on nonrestraint to a group of psychiatrists. Such a discussion would do more toward carrying Beers' suggestions into effect "than all the public agitation imaginable." Anticipating late-twentieth-century criticisms of mental hospitals, Prince suggested that the real difficulty was not so much the low quality of attendants, as Beers claimed, "as the principle of 'institutionalizing' the attendants and the younger physicians." Prince soon wrote again to Beers in his capacity as trustee of an estate, asking whether the firm Beers was connected with would consider a contract to reconstruct a building in Boston.[39] Beers' old hope that his book would bring business to Hoggson Brothers was not so wild after all.

Although much pleased by Prince's letter, Beers had to refuse his request to give talks and write articles. He was too overwhelmed by the correspondence growing out of the book's appearance. Much as he agreed that it would be worthwhile to present more material on his psyche, he would have to postpone indefinitely writing about it. As for delivering a speech, he did not have "'nerve'" for anything—certainly not for public speaking. Perhaps after the reform movement had taken more definite shape he could speak with some authority about reforms. "Then will be the time for me to begin to speak and I have a feeling that when I *have* to speak I shall be able to do so—as I wrote when I *had* to write."[40]

‡

The book elicited letters from all sorts of people, many of them having read a copy that Beers sent along with a request to become an honorary trustee of his proposed national society. His correspondence embraced prominent physicians, university presidents, professors, social workers, reformers, hospital superintendents, businessmen, and politicians as well as mental patients and former mental patients, to whom he replied with tact and understanding. A typical letter of the last type, from a woman of an apparently prominent Pennsylvania family, confirmed through her own experiences what Beers had written, and expressed the "pride and pleasure" felt by the many inarticulate sufferers whose feelings he had conveyed "so powerfully." She sent along memoirs of her treatment; others gave Beers brief summaries. A man fearful for his mental health wrote a long letter describing his situation and stating his intention to read *A Mind That Found Itself.* Beers advised his correspondent against reading it and recommended another book less apt to be disturbing. To an anxious mother he gave assurance of his confidence in the Hartford Retreat and the Connecticut Hospital for the Insane: "You may place your daughter in either institution."[41]

A former superintendent of mental hospitals attested "to the great value of non-restraint, kindness, sympathetic interest in and personal attention to, as well as absolute honesty in the care of and dealings with the insane."[42] Another superintendent, convinced of the importance of "intelligent cooperation" and "good will" among workers in a mental hospital, was persuaded to buy fifty copies of *A Mind That Found Itself* to be placed on the wards for attendants to read.[43] A San Francisco lawyer was so impressed by the book's "immense value" that he was sending copies to the governor of California, certain members of the Insanity Commission, and physicians in mental hospitals; a businessman from Canton offered to do the same in Ohio.[44]

Praise and an offer to help Beers' "good cause" came from Dr. William Russell of the New York State Commission in Lunacy, with whom Beers probably became acquainted through Meyer. William Welch, who read the book "with great interest," did not see how it could "fail to be of great service." Since the greatest need was, first, for improved care of early and curable mental cases and for borderline cases that could be prevented from passing into an insane state, and second, for better instruction of students and physicians in psychiatry, Welch hoped that Beers would give priority to the establishment of psychiatric hospitals and wards in connection with general hospitals, university clinics, and medical schools.[45]

The celebrated Weir Mitchell read nearly every line with the "utmost interest." The book confirmed his own views that individualized treatment was "impossible for the hordes of persons collected in asylums and sanitariums" and that there were only two reasons for committing anyone to an asylum: "Poverty and Peril." The executive secretary of the National Association for the Study and Prevention of Tuberculosis, Dr. Livingston Farrand, found the book "one of the most striking and convincing documents" he had ever seen and promised his "hearty cooperation" in building a reform movement. Jacob Riis assured Beers the same, as did the psychologist Robert Yerkes. Beers sent a copy of the book to President Roosevelt, along with a request that he serve as an honorary trustee; he was told that the president was too busy to concern himself with the matter. Many years later Roosevelt's daughter, Ethel Roosevelt Derby, who became a member of the National Committee for Mental Hygiene, said that her father had read the book and found himself "enormously interested" in it.[46]

The warm reception of *A Mind That Found Itself* was not reflected in its sales, which failed to fulfill Beers' expectations. He attributed the slow sales to the public's misconception that the book was a treatise on insanity and therefore not especially readable, a situation that would change, he told William James. Although the book did not become a best seller, it became a steady one. Within six years there were five printings, with 4,500 copies sold and 500 given away. The reading public was aware of the book, medical and psychiatric professionals certainly knew of it, and Beers received a good deal of attention in the press. His success would be measured, James told him, not in sales but in the establishment of a permanent reform organization within five years of publication.[47]

Beers agreed. He had given up thinking that all that was needed was the indignation and passion aroused by his book, that the public would rise up spontaneously and demand reform. Action would come only with organization and the sustained labor of dedicated workers like himself. Otherwise the autobiography (and himself with it) could fade from public consciousness, achieving status as a minor classic but accomplishing little else. He came to see the book as creating a constituency and a potential leadership for the reform movement, so that its appearance had to be coordinated with the emergence of a national society. This timing was as important for him personally as it was for the "cause." He obviously had no intention of going back to work for Hoggson or any other business; in some way he would have to earn his living from the reform work to which he now meant to devote his life.

✝ 8 ✝

A Reform Movement Launched

While *A Mind That Found Itself* was in press Beers had gone ahead with great energy to start his national society, the aim being to announce its formation simultaneously with the book's publication. The money for its activities would come later. Because his ideas were still amorphous and had to be worked out as he went along, and because he tried to follow the advice of others, especially Adolf Meyer, the picture kept changing.[1]

The "To Whom It May Concern" statement that Meyer had supplied to help Beers raise a loan was also to be used in starting the reform movement, as was his letter to Beers written a month later accepting an honorary trusteeship in the proposed organization. The statement expressed Meyer's concept of the reform movement and Beers' role in it. In meeting Clifford Beers, he wrote, he had had "an unusual experience in finding . . . a man without a chip on his shoulder, but with a sound and worthy conviction that something must be done to meet one of the most difficult but also lamentably neglected fields of sociological improvement." At the same time that Beers drew upon his own experience, impressions, and thinking, he had such an open mind and willingness to accept advice and consider other viewpoints "that it looks as if we had at last what we need: a man for a cause" — a cause whose difficulties would be "insurmountable" to anyone without "the personal experience and instinctive foundation for what equals a religious vow of devotion of his life to a task before which others become opportunistic if not indifferent." Clifford Beers deserved help "in the work which will be one of the greatest achievements of this country and this century — less sensational than the breaking of chains but more far-reaching and also more exacting in labor." A "Society for Mental Hygiene" was needed to put an end to conditions almost unfit for publication. What officialism would never do alone must be helped along by an organized body of people who are seriously devoted to the cause.[2]

Meyer gave the organization the name "Society for Mental Hygiene," and although the term *mental hygiene* had been used before, Beers came to believe that he and his associates gave it meaning. They certainly gave it cur-

100

rency, but as late as 1936 he did not wish to be asked "just what it did really mean."[3] In 1933 Meyer discussed why he had suggested the term: he wanted to take the new organization beyond the idea of mere reform of psychiatric hospitals and legislative investigations toward "an intimate study and public education in favour of those factors which make for mental health in a positive, creative, and not merely a passive or mending way." Medical leaders in 1907 did not have such a view and had to be educated to it; the new Rockefeller Institute, full of promise for achievements in medicine, had made no major provisions for psychiatry or even neurology.[4]

Meyer and Beers acknowledged the difficulties inherent in the work and were at this early stage in general agreement on its broad aims, but where and how to begin remained a problem. There were few models. No viable citizens' organization existed for mental health, and those in other health fields were just finding their way. Social services were developing at the turn of the century from local, private charities into public undertakings on the municipal and state level, spurred and supplemented by new kinds of local citizens' groups—the urban settlement houses, local health centers, the City Club and Citizens Union in New York, groups working for tenement reform, the New York State Charities Aid Association (which had a Committee on Insanity)—with a political orientation and a sense of the need to help people by changing their social conditions. (The emphasis by activists on helping the objects of charity to improve their lives through community organization came later; this was still the noblesse oblige period.) Clifford Beers' notion of a mental health movement—and certainly Meyer's—did not then or later encompass political activity beyond working for needed legislation and eliminating political influence in state hospitals; and, their growing interest in prevention notwithstanding, they never seriously considered the role of the existing social structure or social ethos in mental illness. Whatever they did, they would work within the current socioeconomic system, which they did not question, and with the governing elite of that system, with whom they felt most comfortable.[5]

Organizing on the national level to cope with health problems was at an early stage. The American Red Cross (founded in 1881 and chartered by the federal government in 1900) tended to be crisis-oriented and was not devoted to one specialty. There was the Association for the Study and Prevention of Tuberculosis, founded in 1904, to which Clifford Beers frequently referred. But the tuberculosis movement had had its troubles with schisms, which he wanted to avoid. His society would do in the field of mental and nervous diseases "what is now being done by those interested in prevention and cure of tuberculosis," but the work would be broader in scope, as it would "necessitate the education of the public for all time."[6]

Beers knew of the citizens' organizations but did not make a serious study of them, though he later consulted with their officials. One thing he was sure of—he would work within no existing group: "I am open to no argument that does not contain at least the germ of an entirely new organization," he told Bert Fisher, who had advised him that "other things—education board and Carnegie Scientific research centers—are coming into use, [so that] a big central benevolent monopoly is possible."[7]

There had been a precedent in the United States for the kind of organization that Beers and Meyer were proposing. In 1880 a group of charity workers and neurologists founded the National Association for the Protection of the Insane, with the aims of eliminating political control of asylums, raising standards of medical treatment, providing for borderline cases and the non-institutionalized insane, encouraging clinical and pathological research, expanding and upgrading psychiatric education, and educating the public about the causes and treatment of insanity.

This movement lasted only a few years. A struggle between lay people and neurologists over its goals, the death in 1883 of its most influential leaders, Drs. George Beard and Harvey B. Wilbur, and the withdrawal of another resulted in the demise of the organization before it had a chance to develop practical programs. The lay members were concerned with the welfare of the insane—unfair commitment procedures, inordinate power of superintendents, harsh treatment of patients, mechanical restraints—which led them to question the primacy of medical experts and even to deny the value of mental hospitals. The neurologists' concern for the patients centered more heavily on "scientific" than on humanitarian motives. Their medical specialty, which began by focusing on injuries to the nervous system, had come to encompass insanity. Anxious to bring a "scientific" approach to bear upon mental ailments, and competing with the alienists who ran mental hospitals, the neurologists criticized the management of those hospitals, particularly state hospitals, which had lapsed after the Civil War into custodialism and, in neurologists' eyes, incompetence. But this did not mean allowing lay people to dictate paths of reform, so that neurologists "inevitably disapproved of efforts to discredit experts or medical control of asylums" and questioned "the wisdom of extended collaboration with laymen." The neurologists quickly shifted from condemnation to support of asylums, and not only on account of the medical profession's tendency to close ranks in the face of criticism from lay people. By the mid-1890s, neurologists and psychiatrists were moving toward a *modus vivendi,* a sign of which was the invitation to Weir Mitchell to deliver a critical evaluation of psychiatry before the American Psychiatric Association in 1893. The neurologists were increasingly coming into positions of power in mental hospitals and acknowledging that conditions there had improved, and it was becoming more common for physicians interested in mental disorders to study neurology.[8]

It is possible that Beers knew as early as 1905 of the existence of the National Association for the Protection of the Insane, although he later said he discovered it in a review of his book,[9] but whether Meyer was aware of it and its problems is not clear; by the time he arrived in the United States the movement had died out. Meyer's statements about Beers' work indicate that he had some of the same fears as the neurologists in the National Association and wanted to guard against "uninformed" participation, a concern that he expected Beers, with his willingness to take expert advice, to share. In return Meyer was willing to give Beers, who had the time and motivation, a measure of responsibility in the movement.

Beers agreed for the moment, although he had always had a more militant view of the public's role than Meyer, who opposed a frontal attack on hospital physicians and wanted knowledgeable lay people under professional direction to help create the legal and financial conditions that would enable reform-minded hospital physicians to improve care. A mental health organization was needed to educate the public and to exert public pressure for change directly on the hospital physicians, to be in Meyer's words "the body of the informed and active citizens and representative of the . . . communities," which had always been Beers' position. As William Russell put in in a letter to Beers, "You are quite right in thinking that an aroused public sentiment is necessary to effect any great improvements in the care of the insane; without this, even earnest and enlightened workers cannot obtain either sufficient funds, or eliminate selfishness and inefficiency in applying them."[10]

Beers also accepted the prevalent psychiatric focus on prevention, an emphasis that had grown as confidence in therapeutic techniques waned. Believing that insanity was a disorder of the brain and nervous system and that acquired characteristics could be inherited, psychiatrists thought that bad habits or unhealthy ways of life could adversely affect the offenders' brains and those of their offspring. This "pessimistic" outlook was in tune with social Darwinist theories popular among the middle and upper classes after the Civil War and then with ideas stylish at the turn of the century that doomed the depressed and criminal classes to progressive degeneration and final obliteration. To psychiatrists and neurologists unwilling to become mired in hopelessness, the process was reversible. A healthy life-style could save people from insanity, hence the importance of educating the public as a means of preventing mental illness. Neither Clifford Beers nor his psychiatric colleagues carried the argument further to consider the socioeconomic conditions that might inhibit people from taking their advice on the right way to live.

As Beers had conceived before meeting Meyer, the new organization would also be concerned with encouraging the establishment of "psychopathic" hospitals or units connected with university hospitals and medical schools, a program that would enable teachers, students, scientists, and practitioners to work together to accomplish three interrelated goals: provide the best care for patients, give modern training to students and specialists, and conduct research into mental illness. The society might also distribute funds to the states for psychopathic hospitals if the states would furnish sites and endowments (a clear imitation of Andrew Carnegie's mode of donating public library buildings); money might also be forthcoming for cooperative sanitariums to compete with and eventually eliminate the proprietary sanitariums. The society would also be concerned with promoting psychiatric research and education, perhaps in concert with the federal government, which could sponsor research under the auspices of the National Academy of Sciences.[11]

The conception of the work of a national society for mental hygiene at the time it was first organized was wide-ranging, although no one, Clifford Beers included, expected that everything would or could be done at once; nor had he or anyone else worked out a specific, practical program of action. That would have to evolve as they moved ahead with organizational work. Beers' approach was pragmatic, subject to change and suggestion. Still, his first idea, originally developed at the Hartford Retreat, remained the same: the organization by him of a national movement to help the insane, correct abuses, and sponsor scientific research, with the moral and financial help of important people. He had always been enterprising, a good organizer and a successful salesman. At college he had had ambitions to conquer the business world; through his experiences with mental illness and mental hospitals his talents and aspirations turned away from making money to working for a cause that touched him deeply. Instead of being a tycoon of business he would be a pioneer in philanthropy. Not Dorothea Dix but the powerful men of his time—Andrew Carnegie, John D. Rockefeller, Theodore Roosevelt—were his ideals. He was and remained all his life a mixture of the conventional and unconventional. He took pride in being a Yale man, loved to dine at the Yale Club, dressed well, respected money, craved contact with important men and women, and exulted in their approval. Yet he utilized these inclinations in the service of a movement that would aid people traditionally considered tainted if not damned and that required, indeed derived from, his willingness (or compulsion?) to expose himself as one of them, to become not only, in his friend Bert Fisher's words, a "professional philanthropist,"[12] but a professional former mental patient.

During the fall and winter of 1907–1908, while his book was in press, Beers, in consultation with Meyer, Stokes, and others, began to work out the form the national society would take. In time it would appeal to the public for membership and its work would be complemented by state societies that would cooperate with hospital officials, but it would be brought into existence by the establishment of a board of honorary trustees. These thirty to fifty prominent men and women would stand as sponsors of the cause "in their respective communities," and would probably evolve into a sort of advisory group. The movement must be placed "in the hands of the right men, otherwise reformers of vary [sic] degrees of incapacity will pop up in every state and hinder rather than help reform," or rival organizations might develop. The society would eventually be incorporated, adopt by-laws, and appoint officers. Its actual work would be done by the "active trustees," a small group (about five) chosen by the honorary trustees that would have "absolute power, subject only to restrictions imposed by the honorary trustees." This scheme was suggested to Beers by the so-called Des Moines plan of municipal government, in which five elected commissioners ran the city's affairs, a recent innovation of the municipal reform movement.[13]

What of his own position? Although encouraged by his collaborators to think about working for the society as a salaried executive secretary or assistant secretary, he was willing for the moment to leave the question in abeyance, thinking it best that at first he serve both as an honorary trustee and as an unsalaried "active trustee," but with the eventual prospect of a salary. He was afraid that a desk job requiring "doing certain things at certain times" would get on his "artistic" nerves. Perhaps he could be a field secretary without salary, working free-lance around the country "à la Hoggson" in such a way as not to endanger his health—that is, doing work "not of too exciting a nature and therefore likely to burn energy faster than I can generate it." For the time being he was satisfied to give Meyer and other professionals the control (on paper at least). And Meyer was convinced that Clifford Beers was "the man for the cause" who could organize the movement and then play a role in it under the guidance of psychiatric experts like himself.[14]

As replies to invitations to serve on the honorary board arrived, it became obvious that its members had to be guaranteed that their only duty was to lend their names to a good cause. Beers bowed to reality and reduced the trustees' obligations to just that. William James, who was privy to much of Beers' thinking, was the first person to agree to serve, which proved, predictably, to be an invaluable drawing card. His acceptance letter was intended to be used: he hoped that "most of the gentlemen whom you have thought of as possible trustees will feel as I do, that it is not only a duty, but a privilege to promote so humane a cause."[15] With the help of Meyer's testimonial, James persuaded his friend, the Boston banker and philanthropist Colonel Henry Lee Higginson, to become a trustee. Another friend, the Plummer Professor of Christian Morals at Harvard, Francis G. Peabody, "well known in philanthropic circles," with "a reputation for prudence and judgment," told James yes: he found in *A Mind That Found Itself* "a rare note of rational and hopeful plan."[16]

In December 1907 Beers appealed for membership on the honorary board to a broad group of men and women to whom he sent page proofs of his book with covering letters, varying somewhat depending upon the recipient (and without details as to plans for the society they were asked to sponsor). In approaching people, Beers made use of all the friends and acquaintances he could: his brother George, Bert Fisher, Ada Comstock, and Judge Taylor as well as Anson Phelps Stokes, Adolf Meyer, William Welch, and William James — anyone who could smooth the way.

The list of prospective trustees was drawn up in consultation with James and approved by Meyer and Stokes. Included were many academics: the presidents of Cornell, Clark, Stanford, and Brown Universities (the last "representing Baptist and Rockefeller interests") and of the Universities of Virginia, Michigan, and Minnesota; the former presidents of Cornell University, Andrew White, and of Columbia University, Seth Low; Russell Chittenden, the head of the Sheffield School at Yale and member of the Committee of Fifty set up in 1893 to investigate alcoholism; and psychologists J. Mark Baldwin of Johns Hopkins and Joseph Jastrow of the University of Wisconsin. There were physicians Frederick Peterson of Columbia University (former president of the New York State Commission in Lunacy), Weir Mitchell, and William Welch, and influential religious personages like the Reverend Lyman Abbott, Congregationalist editor of the *Outlook*; the Reverend Henry Van Dyke of Princeton University, author and preacher, "representing Presbyterians"; Professor George E. Vincent of the University of Chicago ("son of Bishop Vincent — Methodist"); Cardinal Gibbons of Baltimore and Archbishop Ireland of St. Paul ("representing Roman Catholics"); and, presumably to represent Jews, the founder of the Ethical Culture Society, Felix Adler, Secretary of Commerce and Labor Oscar Straus, and the financier and philanthropist Jacob Schiff. Other philanthropists and businessmen, plus potential links to them, were Joseph Choate, Robert de Forest ("representing Sage interests"), President Henry Pritchett of the "Carnegie Foundation" ("representing Carnegie interests"), Cornelius Vanderbilt, George Foster Peabody, Colonel J. J. Astor, Helen Gould, and Mrs. Emmons Blaine, daughter of the late Cyrus Hall McCormick and philanthropist Nettie Fowler McCormick. The conservationist Gifford Pinchot was included as a "reformer" and a "way to the President's ear," as was, no doubt, Roosevelt's daughter, Mrs. Nicholas Longworth. "Representing Government" was the secretary of state, Elihu Root, and representing the judiciary, Supreme Court Justice David Brewer and Judge Taylor; Whitlaw Reid, the former editor of the *New York Tribune* and now ambassador to Great Britain, was included "to aid reform in England. There's as much to be done there as here." Then there were the reformers and social workers: social gospel advocate Josiah Strong; Edgar Murphy ("prominent in 'child labor' legislation crusade"); Jane Addams of Hull House; Bert Fisher's brother Irving, professor of political economy at Yale, "Chairman, Committee of 100 on Public Health"; and Louisa Lee Schuyler, the founder of the New York State Charities Aid Association and reformer of New York state laws relating to the mentally ill. Prominent journalists were Colonel Henry Watterson, St. Clair McKelvey, and the president of the Associated Press, Melville H. Stone.[17] Other names were added later, for example, President Arthur

Hadley of Yale, reformer Jacob Riis, the president of the General Federation of Women's Clubs, and several judges.

Proposed by Beers as active trustees were, besides himself, two psychiatrists, Adolf Meyer and August Hoch, pathologist and assistant physician at Bloomingdale Hospital in White Plains, who, Beers noted, "ranks with Dr. Meyer in the field of Psychiatry." Another would be Julia Lathrop of Chicago, the first woman on the Illinois Board of State Commissioners of Public Charities, a colleague of Jane Addams and friend of Adolf Meyer from his Kankakee Hospital days, and one "who has done more than any other woman in the country to help improve the conditions among the insane." The fourth would be George McAneny, a well-known New York reformer and organizer and president of the City Club, who was recommended by Stokes as an "ideal secretary for the society."[18]

The response to the appeal for honorary trustees was on the whole positive. The few declinations tended to be gracious and complimentary; and a number of tentative acceptances became definite upon assurance that the position would entail no obligations beyond the use of the trustee's name. Even refusals, like Lyman Abbott's, were useful. As editor of *Outlook,* Abbott, although sympathetic to Beers' cause, could not serve on the board of an organization; he felt moreover that he could do more for the cause through his journal than as a trustee. Beers concurred. All he wanted was an official statement that he could show to others. Abbott complied, giving his reasons for declining, endorsing Beers' work, and wishing him success.[19] Another rejection that Beers considered understandable was that of Weir Mitchell, by then almost eighty years old,[20] but other refusals were not always accepted. Beers would try again, either with another letter giving more names and additional information or by having friends intercede for him.

From Julia Lathrop, who may not have known of the scheme to appoint her an active trustee, and to whom Meyer had also written, came an acceptance of honorary trusteeships for both herself and Jane Addams. Lathrop considered *A Mind That Found Itself* "touching and appealing," written in "admirable literary form." For some time she had felt that a national society should be formed for the study and treatment of insanity, from a social as well as a medical standpoint, and she was willing to follow Beers' lead. There were "many indications of a strong revival of interest in the care of the insane and I cannot but believe that we shall within a few years see the insane treated generally as sick persons." Another prospective active trustee, August Hoch, agreed to become an honorary trustee. The time was ripe for Beers' undertaking, he thought, and he had no doubt that the book and the society "will do a great deal of good."[21]

By the end of January 1908, twenty-two out of twenty-eight people approached had accepted.[22] Welch, who himself tried unsuccessfully to enlist several influential friends, told Beers, "You ought to be proud of what you have accomplished. Don't believe that those near the work can fully appreciate it." James wrote, "Hurrah for everything, except the recalcitrant millionaires," a reference no doubt to the difficulty of recruiting moneyed men or their representatives to the cause.[23]

A few days after the publication of his book, Beers made a public announcement of the formation of a National Committee for Mental Hygiene and of plans to set up a Connecticut society as well.[24] McAneny had convinced Beers and Meyer that the national society would have a good deal more independence if it were not a dues-paying membership organization but a fairly exclusive body of men and women who could work unhampered by commitments to a membership, on the model of the "efficient 'National Child-Labor Committee.'" Hence the name National Committee for Mental Hygiene.[25] There were already thirty-two "honorary members": William James, Anson Phelps Stokes, Jr., Russell Chittenden, Adolf Meyer, Henry Lee Higginson, Dr. J. Montgomery Mosher of Albany Hospital, Francis G. Peabody, Henry Van Dyke, J. Mark Baldwin, Lewellys F. Barker, Irving Fisher, Judge Robert W. Taylor, Sherman D. Thacher, an educator, of Nordhoff, California, (formerly at Yale), the well-known Chicago physician Dr. Henry B. Favill, Julia C. Lathrop, Jane Addams, Katherine Felton, a social worker in San Francisco, August Hoch, President David Starr Jordan of Stanford University, Stewart Paton, William Welch, President Cyrus Northrop of the University of Minnesota, President Benjamin Ide Wheeler of the University of California, Melville E. Stone, Horace Fletcher (writer and lecturer on nutrition and friend of Chittenden and George Beers), President Jacob G. Schurman of Cornell University, Boston sociologist and social worker Robert A. Woods, President W. H. P. Faunce of Brown University, legal scholar George Wharton Pepper, President James B. Angell of the University of Michigan, Gifford Pinchot, and Frederick Peterson. These were, as Welch described them, "responsible and influential" men and women. They were not, however, the cross-section of the American establishment that Beers had had in mind. The committee was weighted with academics, reform-minded physicians and psychiatrists, and liberal social worker–reformers. There was nothing surprising in this and nothing wrong with it and Beers did not complain, but the group did not exude the aura of wealth and power that he sought. He still hoped to add President Roosevelt, Elihu Root, Oscar Straus, William H. Taft, Cornelius Vanderbilt, Cardinal Gibbons, and others.[26]

Nor had he given up hope of help from Frederick Gates and, through him, John D. Rockefeller. In response to the gift of a bound copy of *A Mind That Found Itself,* together with a request for an interview, Gates allowed Beers to come to his office. He would try to see him; if not, his associate Starr J. Murphy, who had read the book and was interested in the subject, would, but Gates would try at least to "grasp your hand for a moment."

Murphy saw Beers and, while not absolutely ruling out any aid from Rockefeller, was not encouraging. It was unlikely that Rockefeller would give money to the cause of the mentally ill: he preferred to support projects that others would not, and mental illness, he felt, was the responsibility of the public. Beside, Beers' plans were vague and unshaped.[27]

Actually by that time, after much discussion and persuasion, his plans had become more practical. A year earlier Dr. Page had recommended that he first start a state society in Connecticut, where "you understand the conditions, and where the hospital officials evidently stand ready to support your views." And one of William James' friends, Dr. Henry P. Walcott, chairman of the Massachusetts Board of Health and trustee of McLean Hospital, would not join the National Committee because he thought that only state societies could do any "practical good."[28] Beers did envision a network of state societies doing local work, but he wanted to create a national society first. Once it seemed to be under way and his book's appearance was guaranteed, he could listen to other suggestions, mainly from Meyer and McAneny, whose opinions he greatly respected, the first as a psychiatric authority and the second as an experienced organizer of charities and reform groups. While helping him to work out the form and function of the national society and to recruit honorary trustees, they concluded that the actual work of reform would best be launched on a state level with the founding of a state society of mental hygiene in Connecticut. This organization could work out a model plan for other states to copy—a prerequisite, Meyer came to believe, for the inauguration of an effective national campaign. This change would not mean abandoning the national organization Beers had worked so hard to form, but rather leaving it temporarily quiescent in favor of the work in Connecticut. Unlike the National Committee, the state societies would be membership organizations and would appeal to the public for support without competing with the National Committee.[29]

Beers reluctantly agreed to the new plans and gathered names of those willing to be honorary members of the Connecticut Society. The actual working leadership would be provided by a small group of active trustees and officers; later a general appeal for money would be made to fund work to safeguard the mental health of the public, including protection of the interests of asylum inmates.[30] Beers managed to convince himself of the rightness of his new course, which reflected not only his own views but those of Meyer, Welch, and Paton that reform should be effected through work with existing hospitals and medical schools and under the aegis of medical experts.[31] "It begins to look as though your friend, Dr. Walcott, was right when he advocated that the crusade should be begun in a single state," Beers wrote James. Now that the National Committee was organized Beers was content to expend his energy in one state for a while, "for I realized that the National Committee must have an example to point to if it is to carry the campaign into all states. The situation in Connecticut could not be better. The hospital authorities are willing to co-operate, the press is under control, and the public, while it wants something done, seems willing to leave the doing of it to the projected Society for Mental Hygiene."[32] Upon receipt of this news, Walcott withdrew his objection to serving as an honorary trustee of the National Committee.[33]

‡

Clifford Beers seemed on the way to success. His book was published with much favorable comment, and through it he had managed to interest dozens of important, famous, intelligent men and women in joining his cause, even if only nominally. Lyman Abbott, Anson Phelps Stokes, George McAneny, and Julia Lathrop went further in promising to help him in any way they could. Men of the stature of William James, Adolf Meyer, Stewart Paton, and William Welch advised him, encouraged him, vouched for him, befriended him, and — in the case of Meyer and James — worked closely with him, worried about his health, and risked their reputations for him.

Why was he able to elicit such enthusiasm, support, even affection and devotion? He had a compelling personality — charming, clever, witty, energetic, frank, articulate, audacious, persuasive, ostensibly unselfconscious. He knew how to appeal to people, how to use them, from whom to take advice and when, and all without giving offense. Most of all, he was determined, and aggressively so. Although amenable to criticism and willing to listen to suggestions, once he was convinced of the rightness of a course he pushed ahead like a well-mannered bulldozer. He was adept at having one success breed another: each notable added to his list persuaded the next one to sign up, and he shrewdly interwove his book with the founding of the National Committee. And his book was very well done. James' imprimatur helped, but ultimately the story had to stand on its own merits. He had created a persuasive combination — a well-written, powerful, emotional book accompanied by an appealing entreaty to join other important people in a good cause, the improvement of the horrible conditions the book described.

Beers' timing was also apt in a broad social sense, as some of his collaborators realized. In the two decades before the United States entered the First World War, social, economic, and scientific conditions seemed to coalesce into a favorable environment for the kind of work he was proposing. Just as Dorothea Dix in her pre–Civil War crusade had ridden the crest of a wave of all sorts of social reform and of economic development that together produced the will and the means to provide decent care for the insane, so did Clifford Beers half a century later. His life experience, personality, and style of work were different from Dix's, as were the kinds of changes he sought (in a sense he had been a victim of the decay of her accomplishments), and he would go beyond her in his many-sided concern for progress in mental health. Yet his basic aim was the same, and his personal tragedy had occurred and his plans had matured during a similar period of widespread criticism of social, economic, and political institutions and of campaigns, radical and nonradical, to transform them—the Progressive Era. A number of significantly placed psychiatrists can be considered participants in this movement. They knew that conditions in mental hospitals were bad and were already trying to improve them when Beers came along, and their scientific thinking was undergoing a metamorphosis that could give a theoretical underpinning to their reform efforts. They shared the optimism, moral fervor, commitment to an enlightened elite leadership, and, to a lesser extent, the environmentalism that characterized Progressivism as a whole.[34]

A predominant technique used by Progressives to bring social and economic problems to public attention was the publication of moralistic, albeit factual, exposés in the style of the evangelistic preachers of an earlier day in the belief that the public, once informed, would act to eliminate the ills. Implied was faith in the ultimate goodness of people, who could be counted upon to change conditions for the better and be changed by them. The complaints about American society reflected a pervasive optimism that human problems could be solved if only people were aroused and guided by elite leaders. Science and technology had already brought the wireless, telegraph, electric light, locomotives, the telephone, the automobile; why not similar miracles in the social sphere if people tried hard enough?

At the same time, advances in medicine and surgery that seemed to promise the conquest of disease had spread to the United States from Europe and with them a determination among knowledgeable physicians to raise American medicine from its low state. This would be done by promoting medical research and improving medical education, work in which William Welch was a prime mover. Under William James' influence, psychology had become a scientific discipline, and psychiatry was emerging from its postwar doldrums, with a resultant optimism among young psychiatrists anxious to make their mark in the world.

There was also a lot of money for social and scientific projects. The source would be not the government, as in western Europe, but private wealth. The industrial and financial development that contributed to the intensification of many social ills—urban slums; poverty; unsafe, unsanitary, inhumane working conditions; exploitative wages; child labor; poor public health; municipal corruption; concentration of economic power and consequent monopoly control of prices and resources—had created the immense private riches from which their owners would fund programs of social amelioration. Medicine in particular presented a fruitful field for philanthropy. Compared with other areas, it was politically neutral but still humanitarian, and it offered great possibilities for research. And rich people as well as the masses caught diseases or went mad. Elitist-minded progressive physicians, though more socially oriented than most of their colleagues in the traditionally conservative medical profession, did not think deeply about the relationship between the social system and health problems. Accepting the existing social structure (unlike many lay reformers), they did not hesitate to seek money from the rich and powerful to finance organizations to cope with serious diseases.

The large-scale, nationally organized, lay-medical voluntary societies so much a part of the American social landscape in the twentieth century were coming into being. Despite the fiasco of the National Association for the Protection of the Insane and the problems of the antituberculosis movement, it seemed clear to progressive physicians and lay public health activists that ways had to be found for physicians and lay people to work together. A hallmark of the period was the development of social medicine: recognition of the social component of disease and of the need to educate the public about health and disease, to mobilize support to pass health laws, and to obtain funds for health care and the prevention of disease. A bilateral organization like the one Clifford Beers conceived in 1907–1908 was among the first of several established within the next few years. After the National Committee for Mental Hygiene came the American Association for the Study and Prevention of Infant Mortality in 1909, the Society for the Control of Cancer in 1913, and the American Social Hygiene Association in 1914, to name a few.[35]

Closely allied to all these efforts was the new profession of social work, whose practitioners were a major force in the Progressive movement and who increasingly saw a causal connection between socioeconomic forces and criminality, alcoholism, mental disorders, and other forms of social deviance, as well as many widespread "physical" diseases.[36] Not only were social workers active in the various health organizations, but they initiated health and nursing services in settlement houses and community health centers and began to work as supporting staff in hospitals. The Massachusetts General Hospital in Boston first employed a social worker in 1906; in psychiatry the concern of Louisa Lee Schuyler with "eleemosynary charity for after-care" (in Adolf Meyer's words) was increasingly replaced by active social work for patients and their families. From 1904 Meyer's wife, Mary, gave pioneering service as a volunteer psychiatric social worker in New York, and Meyer dated the first employment of a professional psychiatric social worker anywhere as 1905.[37] These workers investigated the home conditions of mental patients in order to improve diagnosis and help speed recoveries; it was also thought that if other family members in incipient stages of mental illness could be reached, further damage might be prevented. Meyer, whose awareness of the social aspects of psychiatry had been heightened during his Illinois days by Julia Lathrop, focused particularly on aftercare. Before meeting Clifford Beers he had helped to organize an aftercare program for the New York State Charities Aid Association in which social workers would look into conditions that had led to patients' breakdowns and help them when released to readjust to their home environments. Meyer and others also sponsored public lectures on insanity aimed at general practitioners and interested lay people that discussed the organization of some sort of "movement toward prophylaxis and the development of sound interests"; schools, hospitals, courts, and other institutions would be involved "in the advancement of mental hygiene." "The whole trend of modern psychiatry," wrote Meyer in 1907, "is in the direction of the extension of work beyond the hospital walls and therefore needs a system of popular education."[38]

In the late 1920s Meyer discussed the scientific factors that had led to the mental hygiene movement. First was the "pivotal committal to a personal standpoint," that is, a concern with individual personality that evolved at Worcester State Hospital, where he had in 1903 formulated his concept of adolescence and "of the constitutional types of make-up and personality types, leading to the concept of habit disorganization as one of the topics of concern in psychiatry." Second, there was the work of psychologist Boris Sidis, who with William James' help had developed a research institute in Boston along principles similar to those guiding Morton Prince "but dealing more with minor psychoses than with multiple personalities and the study of the co-conscious, Prince's special interests." Finally, there was the allied work of psychiatrist William Alanson White, superintendent of St. Elizabeths Hospital in Washington, D.C., and neurologist Smith Ely Jellifee of New York, who were to become advocates of psychoanalysis. These three developments signified a new focus on the "living patient — clinical, psychopathological, and dynamic" — that "became the central characteristic of the American movement destined to reach its culmination in mental hygiene."[39] In 1935 Meyer summarized the process: "In place of the passive descriptive psychiatry of the older tradition, limited to 'insanity' and 'asylums,' and the mainly prognostic-dogmatic, diagnostic-nosological newer psychiatry of Kraepelin, concerned with classification rather than therapy, a biological, dynamic psychiatry which included the whole of human nature had arisen to pledge itself to research and teaching, based on an interest in daily work with patients."[40]

Meyer did not stress explicitly enough the growing interest in the psychogenesis of mental illness. This interest arose partly from disillusionment with prevailing theories of etiology and their accompanying sterile therapies (described as "simply a pile of rubbish" by Charles Hill in his presidential address before the American Medico-Psychological Association in 1907),[41] and partly out of the new ideas emanating from Freud and his contemporaries, Bleuler, Jung, and others, and from the psychological research in the United States done by men such as William James and G. Stanley Hall. Psychiatrists and neurologists like Charles Page, Charles Dana, August Hoch, the young William White, and Adolf Meyer himself became deeply concerned with the nonsomatic aspects of mental disorder. In 1908 Meyer published a paper on "The Role of Mental Factors in Psychiatry" in which he insisted that in hereditarily predisposed people learned habit patterns rather than brain lesions could cause insanity.[42] James had encouraged him "to explore nervous and mental disorder from a directly psychological outlook, without recourse to underlying somatic hypotheses such as nutrition of the nervous system or the malfunctioning of the cerebral cortex."[43]

This trend was discernible in the 1880s. George Beard, writing in *American Nervousness, Its Causes and Consequences,* blamed the poverty, worry, hopelessness, and envy created by contemporary American society for the prevalence of neurasthenia; Weir Mitchell's famous rest cure employed a whole pattern of psychological techniques.[44] In psychology, G. Stanley Hall, first at Johns Hopkins and then at Clark University, was deeply interested in psychopathology and in relating psychiatry to the psychological study of mental abnormality. His biographer summarizes his contribution: "he shared at a very early stage in the modern reform of American psychiatry toward more enlightened asylum care, toward scientific study and treatment, and toward the understanding of psychological pathology in mental illness." Hall greatly influenced in this direction Edward Cowles, the medical superintendent of McLean Hospital, one of the oldest progressive private nonprofit mental institutions in the United States, who came to study with him in 1887–1888. Upon returning to McLean, Cowles established one of the first research laboratories in an American mental hospital.[45]

Historically, a tacit (if not an explicit) rejection of somatic theories and therapies in favor of an environmental, psychological approach seemed to go hand in hand with reform efforts, a trend that is discernible in the relationship of environmentalism to reform in general. The problem in psychiatry was that physicians and psychologists wanted badly to be "scientific," which seemed to mean somatic; but with some exceptions—paresis, for example—somatic ideas and techniques did not cure mental patients and tended to downgrade humane care. Any effective movement to give such care had to believe in a theoretical system that justified a focus on psychological factors in etiology and therapy. By the turn of the century, despite advances in somatic medicine that promised progress in psychiatry as well as in other fields, it was becoming scientifically respectable to be interested in the workings of the mind apart from its material basis. That was also where much of the intellectually stimulating work was being done.

Although reform-minded psychiatrists did not surrender wholly to the environmentalism of Progessivism, they did temper their belief in the primary role of heredity in mental illness with a renewed interest in the role of the environment in shaping human nature and behavior. They sought to picture psychopathology as partly the product of the environment and not so exclusively that of hereditary predispositions and moral laxity. And if environmental and psychological factors could cause mental illness, they could also perhaps cure it and, even better, prevent it — all reasons to try to create a hopeful, therapeutic mood in mental hospitals and in the community that would support materially and morally the hospitals' new efforts.

By the time Clifford Beers appeared on the scene, reform-minded psychiatrists were ready to act, and sophisticated lay people stood willing to help. In Beers, Meyer and his friends had found the man who could translate their ideas into action, work for which they had neither the time nor the temperament and for which he had both.

‡ 9 ‡

The Connecticut Society and
Founding the National Committee

Beers spent the early spring of 1908 soliciting charter members for the Connecticut Society for Mental Hygiene, which was founded by thirteen people on the afternoon of May 6 at the Stokes home in New Haven, a historic house that later became the Yale Faculty Club. Among the members of the temporary executive committee was Dr. Diefendorf, who expressed confidence in Beers and in his plans—thus certifying his mental health—and moved that he be appointed acting secretary, which the meeting approved. (Later he was named executive secretary at twenty dollars a week, finally achieving a salaried position again.) Beers, who had staged the whole thing, found it amusing; years later he cited Diefendorf's statement as evidence of the suspicious atmosphere in which he began his work.[1]

The New Haven papers carried the news. The *Journal Courier* article included the text, written by Beers, of a prospectus for the society's work, and the *Evening Register* published an editorial by Everitt G. Hill, the editor (whose name appeared a month later on a list of prospective members of the society), headlined "A Great Work Begun"; he marveled at the rapidity with which the mental health movement was started, scarcely two months after *A Mind That Found Itself* came out. The first meeting of the Connecticut Society for Mental Hygiene was "an historic occasion . . . the beginning of a movement that in less time than one would dare to think will spread over America.[2]

Beers' prospectus gave, in Meyer's words, an "excellent sketch of the directions in which a State Society for Mental Hygiene can enter upon concrete work."[3] It proclaimed that the society's aim was to "become a permanent agency for education and reform in the field of nervous and mental diseases, an agency for education always, for reform as long as radical changes may be needed." The press was to be aroused, as were the pulpit and "innumerable other channels," and the public sentiment thus stimulated would eventually result in more generous appropriations by the legislature and thereby in higher standards of treatment at the state hospitals, including the adoption of the principle of nonrestraint. Hospital officials would take an active

116

part in the work; instead of legislative investigations, reports of commissions of experts would be used as a means of reform. "A most important function of the Society will be the waging of an educative war against the prevailing ignorance regarding conditions and modes of living which tend to produce mental disorders." To protect patients' legal rights, a committee of experts would write a model set of statutes; to help discharged patients cope with "the struggle for existence," aftercare committees would be appointed. Each town should have a local committee to give "First-Aid" to the insane (something like the crisis clinics started in the 1960s and 1970s) and to send men and women to hospitals to take an interest in friendless "but responsive" patients. The society should be given the official right to hear complaints about hospitals, and the legislature should pass a statute, framed by the society, that would reward good attendants. Finally, the society would try to have created in Connecticut model mental hospitals, courses in psychiatry at the medical schools, a psychopathic hospital, and model sanitariums — all to be financed by wealthy people.[4]

At the next meeting of the society, June 6, one hundred and five members were enrolled (including President Arthur Hadley of Yale and several prominent faculty members), and a constitution and by-laws were adopted. The objects of the society were listed as "(a) to protect the mental health of the public at large; (b) to improve conditions among those actually insane and confined; (c) to encourage and aid the study of nervous and mental disorders in all their forms and relations, and to disseminate knowledge concerning their causes, treatment and prevention." Although officially a board of directors formed the ruling body and would elect officers and appoint an executive committee, matters were to be left to the executive committee and the executive secretary, Clifford Beers.[5]

He was pleased. The progress made since his book's appearance surprised even him, he confessed to William James in the first letter sent from the society's office to the "first person to stamp my book as a work of value." (Beers always liked to note "firsts" and to mark anniversaries.) The constitution and by-laws, he thought, would serve as a workable model for any state, and "it should now prove easy to introduce the Connecticut plan into other States under the auspices of the National Committee for Mental Hygiene," which he hoped to launch soon. He was seriously considering making the national organization, like the Connecticut Society, a dues-paying membership association with the honorary trustees as directors. With such an assured income the organization could be self-supporting, which would make it easier to attract contributions for special programs. At first both national and state work would have to be supported "by a few with money to give"; then there would be a general appeal for funds. The fact that he had already raised a thousand dollars for the Connecticut Society in cash and guarantees from only six persons was a sign that the national movement would easily get what it needed.[6]

Clearly Beers' concept of his job in Connecticut was to found an organization there, start it going, and then move on to his real interest, the national movement. He wrote to Clara Jepson, his "friend and helper, and the most consistent supporter" of his belief that he could carry out the plans outlined in his book: "On this day, June 30, 1908, the organization of the first Society for Mental Hygiene ever founded was completed. I venture to predict that on June 30, 1910 few, if any States in the Union will be without an organization such as recently founded in Connecticut."[7]

‡

Founding the movement in Connecticut had been fairly easy; national organization would be harder and would require a great deal more money than the Connecticut Society's few thousand dollars. Complicating matters was Beers' impatience to start national work coming up against Meyer's cautious reluctance, a problem that caused a three-year struggle between the two men. Beers had other advisors, but he relied heavily upon Meyer, whose opinions carried weight everywhere and who was a formidable and magnetic personality.

After the Connecticut Society was founded, Meyer began to doubt whether a national organization could raise funds until a "definite plan of work" was devised. He urged therefore that its formal establishment wait until Beers formulated such a plan and Meyer could himself explore certain questions whose answers would help to develop a national program of prevention, cure, and reform.[8] But before his investigations could be completed, Meyer was thrust further into power and prominence and given an opportunity to put his clinical and educational ideas into practice. In the middle of June 1908 Henry Phipps, Andrew Carnegie's business associate, pledged to the Johns Hopkins Hospital money to build a psychiatric clinic (the famous Phipps Clinic) and to fund a professorship and chief of psychiatry and necessary assistants. Meyer was to be the professor and chief.

This chance to create one of the first modern psychopathic hospitals in the United States, associated with its leading medical school and committed to research and teaching as well as the best treatment available, was the fulfillment of one of Beers' dreams, and one for which he could claim some credit. Some newspapers played up the connection between Phipps' gift and Beers' book: The *Philadelphia North American*'s headline ran "Will Insanity's Germ Be Found? The Phipps Gift for the Study of Lunacy Inspired by One Who Lost His Mind"; the caption under Beers' picture read: "C. W. Beers, Author of the Book That Touched the Millionaire." Similar articles appeared in other newspapers.[9]

Welch wrote Beers about it. "You may look upon the benefaction as one of the fruits of your efforts," he said, and went on to relate that Phipps had become interested in mental disorders as a result of a passing remark by Welch, who sent him, along with a long letter, a copy of *A Mind That Found Itself* with numerous passages marked. Phipps' son, John S. Phipps, also procured a copy. "When I told Mr. Phipps later how much pleased you would be with his gift, especially as I could say that your book had influenced him, he himself expressed his pleasure at this." Welch wanted Beers to know this because the newspaper accounts did not give the story sufficient attention. Phipps would "appreciate" a letter from Beers, if he had not already sent one. Lewellys Barker, the physician-in-chief at Johns Hopkins Hospital, also wrote to Beers, saying that Phipps "told us he was taking your book with him to read carefully while abroad," and Stokes related that Phipps' son said that *A Mind That Found Itself* had without doubt influenced his father. Soon after the announcement of the gift, the younger Phipps indicated a wish to meet Clifford Beers and hear about his plans, and then Henry Phipps himself, responding to an invitation from Beers, accepted membership in the National Committee and later expressed interest in meeting Beers.[10]

In reply to Welch's letter Beers could not resist a reminder that the previous fall he had prophesied that Johns Hopkins would receive a psychiatric clinic within the year. Both Welch and Barker had "smiled the smile of hope and, what seemed to me, psychiatric suspicion. . . . I deliberately placed myself in a position to be temporarily misunderstood, feeling confident that I should have the last laugh. This is a habit of mine which affords me much amusement and in which I, as a 'certified dreamer,' feel privileged to indulge."[11]

Meyer, though, minimized Beers' contribution, saying only that *A Mind That Found Itself* had a "relation to the maturing of the plans of Mr. Phipps."[12] At the opening of the Phipps Clinic in 1913, Meyer gave major credit, as he did on various occasions years later, to his friend Stewart Paton, who while at Johns Hopkins had educated Welch and William Osler about the importance of psychiatry and had interested them in the German clinics. These three, plus the president of the university's board of trustees, were the most responsible for Phipps' gift, Meyer said. He mentioned neither Beers nor his book.[13]

By the time the Phipps Clinic opened, Meyer and Beers had come to an open break, which might account for Meyer's neglect even to mention the role of *A Mind That Found Itself,* an acknowledgment that would not have detracted from any kudos to Paton and the others. In 1908 they were still friendly, although some strain was beginning to show. Years later Beers came to believe that Meyer had not wanted him to feel the book had influenced Phipps for fear that he would ask Phipps for money. This may well have been so. Meyer wished to postpone the founding and funding of a national organization, and he had put off implementing Beers' compromise offer to form a temporary organization with himself as acting secretary.[14] Meyer wanted time to influence Beers, who was in his view a manic-depressive personality whose condition hindered successful work. He had to be reeducated, trained to control his manic propensities — especially an inclination to overemphasize organization and promotional activities at the expense of substantive programs, which took time to develop. Beers, knowing well his tendency toward what he called "hot air," doubted whether it was realistic to expect that anyone but a man of his temperament could single-mindedly devote himself to reform. And one may indeed wonder whether the reform spirit by definition is not antithetical to the cautious, safe, conservative personality into which Meyer wanted to transform Beers, in his own image.

Meyer was also in an awkward position as both Beers' chief advisor and the prospective chief of the Phipps Clinic: he probably was afraid to appear to be taking advantage of Phipps, who might not appreciate Beers' enthusiastic begging. Beers realized this but would not be deterred. His success in founding the Connecticut Society and the announcement of the Phipps gift convinced him that this was the time to ask for help. He was also deeply in debt and desperately needed the income that a general secretaryship in a national organization could provide. Having more confidence in James "as a beggar" than in Meyer, whom he had asked to approach Phipps, Beers wondered whether James would just mention to Phipps that his work so far had been financed "with considerable difficulty."[15]

He sent along to James a copy of a letter he had written to Meyer explaining his situation. He was unable to pay his fair share of the upkeep of his parents' home, where he was living, and he owed his brother George $3,600 for the publication of the book. George had not been in good health in recent years, a consequence, Clifford believed, of the "strain incident to my illness and all the difficulties which grew out of it." Although Clifford would not permit himself to worry about the past, the future did disturb him, and he was fearful of the results if George could not take a long rest and be relieved of the obligation of supporting Clifford. "And one reason why I perhaps impress you as seeming at times to be in a great hurry to achieve some of my purposes and reap part of the pecuniary reward which seems almost within reach is that I should like to be in a position" to rid George of this burden. Clifford explained to William James that George "suffered from some so-called 'vaso-motor disturbance,'" although "he is not at all nervous and among his friends is really famous for his poise."[16]

That Meyer refused to ask Phipps for money was understandable; what bothered Beers was Meyer's attitude. Meyer advised Beers to cut his activity to suit his financial resources. "Do as nature does: Nature shapes her aims according to her means." The future would take care of his debts. Meanwhile, take the "vacation you want and *can* take." Meyer may actually have been worried more about Clifford's health than about his finances. Earlier he had warned him: "Do not forget to take . . . two days off each week for good wholesome rest. I want you to *look* as strong as you feel energetic. . . . I say this because Dr. Mabon [superintendent of the hospital at Ward's Island] remarked that you did not look well and that kind of impression are [*sic*] quickly spread by those who have an interest in seeing something pathological in a man's plans."[17]

But how, Beers wondered, could he take a vacation "except by adding to my debts?" Several years later he noted that not to "spend money that you have not got" was "pretty advice, from one who encouraged me to undertake my work, and to continue it, when he knew I could get no money except from the N.C. . . . for which I had been told repeatedly I was to work."[18] These feelings he expressed not to Meyer but to James. To have followed Meyer's counsel, he wrote, "would have resulted in irreparable damage to my health and might have prevented my ever completing the book or assuring life to the project by giving it momentum." In any case he intended to "give Phipps a chance to assist him." If Phipps only knew that Beers' activity had been financed by his family he might at least clear up the $2,900 owed to George. The book was selling well enough to have already reduced the debt by $700, but not fast enough to clear it all soon. "The main question is — what shall be done in the meantime?"[19]

James wrote from London: "You seem to be doing splendidly, . . . I enclose to you an order . . . for $1,000.00 to which extent I am only too willing to bleed for the cause. So you need not think of paying me till you become a millionaire." He added that he was writing to Phipps urging him to become a trustee of the National Committee.[20]

This generosity was a touching surprise. When Beers had earlier received a postcard from James saying that he could not afford to help financially, he assumed that all James could do was intercede with others in his behalf; he had not the slightest suspicion that James would himself contribute. James was "as fine a friend and generous a supporter as any man engaged in a distressing work may hope to find."[21]

By October 1908, nothing had happened regarding a job with the National Committee, but there was promising news for the movement. The hope that other states would follow Connecticut's lead seemed about to be fulfilled in Illinois, where Julia Lathrop and Jane Addams were active, together with Dr. Henry Favill, a Chicago physician and friend of Meyer's who had accepted an honorary trusteeship on the national committee.[22] The prospect of a mental hygiene society in Illinois led Beers to reopen an issue that was to loom large in his relations with Meyer — the role to be played by hospital physicians in national and state mental hygiene societies. In a long letter to Meyer (and a similar one to Lathrop with a copy to Favill), Beers stated his position. He had wanted to include hospital psychiatrists in the leadership of the National Committee, just as the national antituberculosis movement had recruited heads of sanitariums caring for tubercular patients. The committee needed the expert knowledge of psychiatrists as well as the appeal that their participation would have for a public as respectful of physicians as Americans were. But on the state level psychiatrists should not be identified with the mental health society; rather they should work from the outside, and the society should cooperate with them as an independent body "representing the taxpayers and the public."[23] Meyer believed that medical staffs of state hospitals should not only take an active part in the state societies but serve as officers. (There had been enough evidence, especially in Illinois where political interference with hospital administrators had a long and ignominious history, for Meyer to distrust lay activities.) Beers had acquiesced in accepting hospital physicians into the Connecticut Society, and to show his sincerity had asked Dr. Noble to join. Noble declined, feeling he could do more by remaining independent, although his mind might be changed as the society's policies solidified, a position, Beers discovered, typical of hospital physicians. They wanted to be assured that the work of a mental hygiene society would not conflict with their interests. Beers therefore wished to exclude them from the society, at least at first.

There was another problem. For example, the state hospital at Middletown needed half a million dollars to eliminate overcrowding and to build a psychopathic pavilion and a nursing home; other state hospitals needed similar improvements. But would state legislatures appropriate the money if the society campaigning for funds had hospital physicians as members and officers? Therefore Beers advised that the projected Illinois society temporarily forgo having physicians in its leadership. Everyone he spoke to but Meyer concurred, so Beers felt "no longer in doubt" on that point. His mind was still open about the composition of the National Committee, an issue he hoped to discuss in November with as many honorary trustees as could be gathered for a meeting. At the end of the letter Beers admitted that he was not really "wedded to any especial policy either for the State Societies or the National Association" and was "willing to give up ideas held at present" if he could have a chance to discuss them with Meyer.[24] The letter was less a declaration of independence than a demand for an interview with Meyer, who sometimes refused to speak to Beers when he disapproved of his actions.

Meyer did agree to talk the matter over but had to say that Beers' "attitude called their relationship into question." After all, "since I am a physician of the state system I might also become an obstacle to your aims and those of your society." A well-developed movement of hospital physicians and public men would give the former the "moral strength to go to any legislative body without looking like a man who 'comes with a letter of recommendation written by himself.'" To follow majority opinion was, of course, Beers' right, but it happened that in this instance the majority held a position fraught with problems for the future.[25]

Meyer communicated his private thoughts to Julia Lathrop before he saw Beers. He was "on the point of breaking with Mr. Beers on this issue." If the movement was limited to lay people and excluded officers of state hospitals from membership, "I withdraw from the Committee, although Mr. Beers naively thinks that my difference of opinion would not interfere with my remaining a director, though somewhat inactive. I have not the slightest intention of figuring as an advertisement of a policy which I consider the most detrimental and the chronic sore of the problem of insanity in this country. The things have got to be done with and through the physicians of the hospitals, even if they get done slowly that way." Meyer then discussed the impression that Beers had made recently on a Dr. Barrett, who was probably the well-known psychopathic hospital director, Albert Moore Barrett, from Michigan:

It is perfectly obvious that his advisors favor a lay-movement because they do not wholly trust him and do not want to become implicated in a questionable move. The trouble with Mr. Beers has been that he is infinitely more concerned with securing funds than with doing other work. He is in the undesirable position of a philanthropist who wants to make a living out of his philanthropy. If he is assigned his place as a determined worker he is all right, but if, as Dr. Barrett said, he tried to impress on others that he is the "whole push" of the movement, that he appoints the officers of the association, etc., he is evidently making a mistake and justifies the lack of confidence and the disguised advice to make the thing a laymen's movement and a lobby for the legislature to secure appropriations and what not. I may be somewhat naive on that score, but I do not believe that appropriations can be maintained for any length of time on mere emotionalism. The sooner we spread among intelligent co-workers a correct knowledge of useful facts and an interest in helping us, the feeling of seriousness of the issue will come very naturally in our legislative bodies. There will be enough people who will ask before the election of a man whether or not he takes a sound stand or merely subordinates the problem to the political game.

The chief difference of opinion between himself and Beers, Meyer said, was "that he is bearing in mind organization and chiefly organization, whereas I rather dread premature organization before a sufficient number of people know the best ways of cooperating with hospitals. . . . If we should organize a society now composed of persons not capable of an interest in that sort of a programme we would retard the perfectly feasible and eminently necessary step forward for quite a number of years to come. . . . Personally I am more than ever decided to cut loose from any movement which does not make cooperation with the hospitals and the ultimate raising of the hospitals to leadership of the movement the principal aim." It was also unfortunate that Beers had been more or less promised the secretaryship of the National Committee: "only a man who had the absolute confidence of the hospitals on ground of well recognized knowledge of the ins and outs of the problem, should take that position so as to protect Mr. Beers against over-taxing and to give him the field in which he really can do most."[26]

The interview the two men had must not have been pleasant for Beers, especially as it came on the heels of a complaint from Phipps that the information Beers had sent him was too voluminous. Beers normally bombarded anyone he considered important to the cause with long letters and documents of all sorts, and during the fall of 1908 he realized that he had perhaps written more letters than ever. One of his victims was Phipps. Meyer, warning Beers about overwhelming prospective donors with "big ideas" in lengthy communications, said he believed more firmly than ever that the financing of the movement must be placed on a "more sober and judicious" basis.[27]

Beers probably would have been crushed by Meyer's attitude if he did not by then have something else of great importance in his life. For the past year affection had been growing between himself and Clara Jepson, in spite of their having "sagely resolved never to fall in love with each other."[28]

In September 1908 he finally declared his love. Clara kept him waiting for a "complete answer" for several months but gave enough encouragement to make him feel that life was "one unbroken and happy dream" and to enable him to modulate his obsession with the movement, thus making it easier for him to do his "duty" toward it.[29] It was not until a year or so later that he was really sure of her and that they definitely planned to marry. Because of his insecure financial status their relationship was kept secret from his professional colleagues and most of their friends and acquaintances. There was not only the problem of whether Clifford was healthy enough to be a husband or should father children. He had no money — only debts; no full-time job — or none that he wanted; and no position — save that of notorious former mental patient with some important friends. Clara, a conventional middle-class woman of thirty-four (a year and a half older than Clifford) had no income and did not work for a living. Although well educated (she had graduated from Smith College in 1898) and well traveled, she was not trained for any profession, and the strict Victorian outlook of her family precluded her undertaking an independent life.

She lived at home with her parents, Benjamin and Mary Louise (Wiswell) Jepson. Her English-born father, a musician, had since 1863 been in charge of all music instruction in the New Haven public schools; Clifford Beers claimed to have received his first star at grammar school from him. One of her two elder brothers, Arthur Jepson, with whom she was very close, was university organist, director of chapel music, and professor of music at Yale, so there was an indirect Yale connection between Clifford and the family through mutual friends and acquaintances.[30] The Jepsons were apparently cordial to Clifford, but they certainly could not have considered him a brilliant match for their much doted upon daughter. Clifford himself could not think of marrying Clara or even of announcing their engagement until he had a stable source of income and a good position, which was one more reason for him to push hard to activate the National Committee.

Meanwhile, he had his love and the prospect of eventually consummating it in marriage to sustain him. He also had in Clara a confidante totally on his side and one who was highly intelligent and had good judgment, however much her father had babied her. Clifford, passionate and gregarious, had always been interested in women and probably had had casual affairs, but up to then he had not allowed himself to think seriously about a woman. His attitude toward women, at least the "respectable" kind, was idealized.[31] Clara's love, he felt, would spur him to be less selfish and become, like her, always generous and thoughtful, and as "complete a man as Fate intended." The achievement of "a man's higher self depends largely upon the woman to whom he looks up." "Those men who don't find a good woman to adore and cherish and love never can know the degree of development of which they are capable." How immensely lucky he felt to have found such a woman, who gave him unconditional support in what he was trying to do. She had a mind "as fine as spun gold," a heart "true through and through."[32]

So, after meeting with Meyer in the fall of 1908 and hearing his criticisms, Beers could bounce back with a revised plan for the movement that represented a capitulation to Meyer. The national and state organizations would be under physicians' control. Perhaps Welch, the most influential member of the American medical profession, would be president of the national association. (Welch declined the honor and suggested someone from the Midwest "such as Frank Billings or Favill.")[33] The general secretary should be, as Meyer said, a person knowledgeable about mental hospitals, Meyer's friend Russell, for example. Meyer himself should properly be chairman of the executive committee; Beers' only reservation was that the chairman must believe an "aggressive campaign looking toward the education of the public and the organizing of State societies throughout the country and the securing of a large membership for the National Association" was just as important as gaining support from hospital physicians. (Actually Beers was in no position to set any conditions; at that point he would have been only too glad to have Meyer serve.) The unique function of a national association would be to facilitate physicians' efforts to tell the public what needed to be done.

Beers thanked Meyer for saving him "from making a disastrous move (for I believe the adoption of the policy I had in mind a week ago would have proven disastrous, or at least seriously hindered progress)." As for his being general secretary, he had at the outset believed he would do better to limit himself to "writing and talking in the interests of the cause." Only later, upon others' urging, (who, if anyone, did urge him Beers did not say) did he aspire to the job. All along, however, he had secretly worried that the "burden of responsibility" might bring on a "recurrence of either depression or elation," especially as every physician he knew warned him against overwork. So he welcomed Meyer's suggestion that he serve as a field secretary under a general secretary with full responsibility.[34] After some amending, Beers' statement received Meyer's approval, but not without a caution against premature action: "I . . . hope we shall not be 'launched' and financed, before we have formulated that mere bagatelle, the work."[35]

Nevertheless Beers resumed his search for more honorary trustees for the national association. He sent his book to author James Bryce, then British ambassador to the United States, who replied that he had heard well of it. Then a friend arranged introductions to the governor of Connecticut, George L. Lilley, and to Gifford Pinchot, and Welch urged Cardinal Gibbons to lend his name to the national movement. In a warm letter of acceptance to Beers, the socially aware, liberal cardinal said that he could scarcely remember "ever having read anything which stirred me so deeply, or left upon my memory stronger or more vivid impressions" than *A Mind That Found Itself*. Beers was delighted and triumphant; this was one of the most gratifying letters his book had elicited.[36]

‡

During this time Beers was also working for the Connecticut Society. When not out trying to raise money, he answered letters seeking information about the society's work, and spoke and wrote to people asking advice for themselves and friends. Another new activity was public speaking; the University Club of Cleveland, for example, invited him to talk on mental hygiene.[37] By the November 1908 meeting of the Connecticut Society, Beers had obtained just enough money and pledges to finance its activities.[38] At this meeting Diefendorf proposed a plan dear to Meyer's heart. This was the formation of an aftercare committee to help discharged patients readjust to the outside world by finding them jobs, giving them money and advice, and generally looking after them. Such a program, which the society approved, would make it possible for many more patients to leave the hospital and would also prevent relapses.[39] In January Clifford described his first aftercare "case". It involved a woman who appeared at Beers' home at midnight after leaving Boston to escape recommitment to Worcester State Hospital. Beers, while in Boston on other business, intended to see several people to whom the woman referred him and to interest two Bostonians who did aftercare work there; he also persuaded the woman to agree to an examination by two psychiatrists and to accept their recommendation. "The more familiar I become with after-care work," he told Meyer, "the more convinced am I that it is the very foundation of the mental hygiene movement and too valuable a privilege for a State Society to give into other hands."[40]

Meyer of course was pleased. There was "nothing more fascinating, nothing more instructive and more sound as a foundation for our mental hygiene work, and in the end, nothing more keenly appreciated and warmly supported financially" than aftercare work. He hoped that every discharged patient would come for help, for each needed it. The best plan would be to train hospital people to do the casework.[41]

As Meyer well knew, this work was not what most interested Beers or what he considered most important, even in Connecticut. He was more concerned with convincing the public of the "necessity for granting liberal appropriations to the State Hospitals."[42] Out of this came an "Outline of a Plan for the Improvement of Conditions among the Insane in Connecticut," written by Beers, which was to be sent to several thousand citizens along with an appeal to join the society. The plan pointed out the inadequacy of the state's support of its two public hospitals (at Middletown and Norwich), condemned the serious overcrowding there, and called upon the legislature to increase its appropriations to these hospitals, to build a new one west of the Connecticut River, and to erect a psychopathic pavilion and a nurses' home at the Middletown institution.[43] The society—that is, Clifford Beers— also pushed for legislation establishing a commission to study the problem of insanity, a course that Meyer strenuously opposed as possibly leading to an "old-time investigation" and because it was a "step from the top before the proper foundation was laid." Russell, however, thought that the commission should be given even more investigatory power than the bill provided and that eventually Connecticut should create a Commission in Lunacy with a "first-class man" at its head.[44] The bill failed to pass, partly because Meyer persuaded Beers that it would alienate the hospital physicians.

‡

A tug of war had been going on between the two men about organizing on a national scale, Meyer urging caution, patience, and delay, and Beers seemingly acquiescent but pushing for action and for a search for money. Meyer hammered away at the need for a specific plan. For example, he said, President Schurman of Cornell University told Russell that a nonrestraint campaign would not arouse great public interest because hospital abuses had already declined. Men like Schurman were looking for "*issues* and these cannot be issues of organization but must be issues of demonstrable activity for the benefit of practical improvement in the care of the insane and in mental hygiene." Beers' interest in distributing literature to the public would not yield this "practical improvement."[45]

Beers refused to accept Meyer's fundamental point. Going along with the idea that the national organization should start out in safe hands, Beers affirmed the recommendation that it be at first a national committee with a membership of prominent people and closed to the public. All the more reason, then, for beginning the work without waiting to prepare detailed plans: as in the child labor movement, a few interested individuals would organize, plan, and execute the work. An outline of policy should be sent to the board members for discussion, and if it was approved a national committee should be formally organized, officers elected, and an executive committee appointed that could begin to work, if only on a small scale at first. The experience in Connecticut had shown that the moment a definite organization was formed people would begin to "take increased interest," plans would follow, and money would come.[46]

Beers also rejected Meyer's strictures against educational measures to prevent insanity. Considering Noble's favorable response to this aspect of the proposed program, he suggested that McAneny, Glenn of the Russell Sage Foundation, Livingston Farrand of the National Tuberculosis Association, and possibly some hospital superintendents should be consulted. As for more specific issues, there were enough in the printed scope of the work of the Connecticut Society and in the outline of policy for the National Committee "to warrant the prompt founding of the National Committee." Few, if any, national organizations, he pointed out with justice, had ever started work with plans as specific as these. In order to stir Meyer to action, Beers mentioned that he had sent the outline to James and Stokes and that he was calling for the formal founding of the National Committee. Meyer then said he was willing to call an organizing meeting of the National Committee in due time once he and Beers could put together a concise version of the outline.[47]

In a further attempt to move Meyer, Beers reported that Robert Woods, the Boston sociologist, William James, and Dr. Noble considered the plans for a national committee in excellent shape, sufficient to found the organization. James was more interested in this movement, his wife said, "than in any other work with which he is identified." He even volunteered to write an appeal for money to John D. Rockefeller, something he would not do for anyone else. Similarly, Stokes told Beers that he had refused at least a hundred requests that he introduce people to Gates, "but you are the only person I have ever been willing to send to Mr. Gates." Surely, then, the national committee would not fail to get a lot of money.[48]

Beers discussed with James the advisability of inviting Charles Strong, James' friend and former student and Rockefeller's son-in-law, to join the National Committee. It was a good idea to have as members "unofficial representatives of philanthropists of the ten-million-dollar-class, namely, Mr. Rockefeller, Mr. Carnegie and Mrs. Sage," not so much to secure an endowment "as for the purpose of one day persuading Mr. Carnegie and Mrs. Sage to build clinics and model sanitariums, etc." Dr. John Shaw Billings, director of the New York Public Library, board chairman of the Carnegie Institution, and a prominent physician and planner of Johns Hopkins Hospital, might serve "as a Carnegie ear-trumpet"; Carnegie looked to him for advice, and he had cordially acknowledged a gift of *A Mind That Found Itself.* As for Mrs. Sage, her advisor, Robert de Forest, might change his mind and join now that plans were more definite. Would James write to these three men? It would smooth the way for Beers, who also intended to solicit John S. Kennedy, president of the board of trustees of Presbyterian Hospital in New York, to which he had just given a million dollars. If Kennedy consented to serve as a member, "it will not be long before the Presbyterian Hospital has funds in hand for building and maintaining wards wherein nervous and mental cases may be treated" and "blaze the way for all general hospitals."[49]

James spoke to Strong and wrote to Billings but was not acquainted with de Forest. On second thought he worried about Strong suspecting "the Rockefeller cat in the meal," so that Beers should give him a chance to talk with Strong and "feel his pulse." (By the way, James wrote, he had had a letter from Dr. Giolio Cesare Ferrari, head of the provincial asylum of Bologna and editor of the leading Italian psychological review, praising *A Mind That Found Itself.* It ought to be translated, Ferrari said, and all asylum physicians ought to read it. It had influenced his own work already.)[50] Strong agreed to join the committee, but Beers, on James' advice, decided to keep it quiet. "I think he is a little sensitive as to that whole relation and we mustn't let him walk into a trap, or resign after publicly joining us," James wrote. Strong himself, after learning that his father-in-law was going to be approached for money, withdrew his acceptance in a cordial letter to Beers.[51]

James had already written a draft of his Rockefeller letter, which Beers took to Baltimore with Meyer's blessing, to show to Welch, who thought it "splendid." One reason for optimism, Welch thought, was that the Rockefeller people (Gates and Murphy), who were interested in psychiatry, felt chagrined that Phipps had been the one to give the first psychiatric clinic; they might want to make their big splash by financing the National Committee. Although nothing was sure and negotiations were only beginning, Beers felt confident that in two or three months there would be a Rockefeller gift, especially after he read Rockefeller's statement in *World's Work* that it was best to give money to organizations that "know all the facts, and can best decide just where the help can be applied to the best advantage."[52]

Meanwhile Beers and Meyer were preparing for the meeting to found officially the National Committee that Meyer finally agreed to call for February 19, 1909, at the Hotel Manhattan. Attending were Adolf Meyer, Julia

Lathrop, Lewellys Barker, Frederick Peterson, August Hoch, Anson Phelps Stokes, Jr., Russell Chittenden, Jacob G. Schurman, Marcus Marks (a merchant), Horace Fletcher, a representative of Dr. Favill, and Clifford Beers. Afterwards Meyer gave an informal dinner at which Beers' father was also present.[53]

The group established the National Committee for Mental Hygiene, and adopted rules and regulations (based on those of the Committee of One Hundred, a public health reform organization). Officers were elected and an executive committee appointed. Favill was president, with Welch (who had sent Beers his "assurances of my interest in you and the movement which you have espoused") and Dr. Charles B. Bancroft (head of the New Hampshire State Hospital) as vice-presidents.[54] The executive committee consisted of Meyer as chairman, Bancroft, Chittenden, James, and Lathrop — a mix of psychiatrists and prestigious lay people. Beers and Meyer's "Outline of Policy" was accepted without changes. It listed six goals for the National Committee: to protect the mental health of the public; to raise standards of care for the mentally ill and those threatened with mental illness; to promote the study and dissemination of information about the causes, treatment, and prevention of insanity; to gather data on treatment; to enlist aid from the federal government; and to help establish state societies for mental hygiene. These goals would be attained through aftercare programs, the elimination of prisons as receptacles for the insane pending their final disposition in hospitals, the development of techniques of popular education, the creation of a subdepartment of public health in the federal government, and the establishment of a national organization of distinguished people who could offer advice to federal and state legislatures. Finally, the "Outline" stated, in what were obviously Meyer's words, the formation of local societies presupposed "the existence of a productive and efficient agency, consisting of and funding those who will be practical exponents of the necessary work rather than mere propagandists" — in other words, the National Committee. The founding members, convinced that a large sum of money was crucial to the committee's work, then decided to submit an appeal to Rockefeller for funds (perhaps a million dollars) because of his interest in medical research.[55]

Late that night Beers wrote to Clara. February 19 "will ever be one of *our great* days. The events of today will shape and hasten the complete realization of our highest destiny." If only Clara had been there. At one end of the dinner table sat Clifford's father, at the other, William James. "Upon analyzing my emotions I discovered that my feeling toward Mr. James has developed into positive affection. And I'm proud of it — and proud of you for making my heart over with the sensitive tone it has become."[56]

He refrained from expressing disappointment at not being appointed provisional or acting secretary, a job he wanted regardless of his protestations. He turned to one man on whom he could always count — William James.

Would he move to appoint Beers secretary, without salary, since no one had been designated to attend to correspondence and other business which would inevitably come up? In order to work for the movement to his full capacity, he should be identified officially with the National Committee. Otherwise he was "in an anomalous position — and a rather delicate one," for he could not make any move without seeming to usurp rights that he had surrendered when he turned his "'divine rights'" over to the National Committee. As acting secretary he "could keep the 'pot-a-boiling,' a privilege I crave as Dr. Meyer is prone to delay unless prodded — gently. He has so many interests that he sometimes lets mental hygiene drift for days or even weeks at a time. With me 'on the job' officially, this is not likely to happen." Besides, Meyer's judgment was not to be trusted in matters of "business policy, organization, propaganda and finance. I have found him in error too often during the past year and a half . . . with reference to these subjects." For example, Meyer had originally opposed making a wide public appeal for membership dues, a policy that had worked in Connecticut. He had also been against the formation of state societies everywhere but now accepted what he previously considered a "hobby of mine." And only after his "mind had come through the fog it so often has to penetrate before arriving at its final conclusion" had Meyer come round to advocating an endowment for the National Committee.[57] (Actually, Meyer had assumed, incorrectly it turned out, that his and other prominent physicians' endorsement of the mental hygiene movement would persuade millionaires to give an endowment so that a public appeal would be unnecessary. As for the state societies, Meyer remained wary of new organizing efforts.)

The ever agreeable James raised the question with Meyer, who appointed Beers secretary pro tem "on account of the financial advantages that should come your way as the natural and well deserved reward for your labors." Receiving the secretaryship made the founding a complete success for Beers. "Everything was done that I wished done and nothing done that I did not wish," he told his friend John Veitch. "At last I have a real job. The next thing to do is to help secure funds for . . . a real salary."[58]

In a letter thanking Meyer, Beers decided to forgo a salary until the National Committee appealed to Rockefeller. He then described his work in Connecticut, which was going "satisfactorily." The emphasis was on educating the public as to "After-Care and Before-Care"; money would come as a consequence of effective "concrete work." Then Clifford twisted the lion's tail. Experience had already shown that good publicity brought results. For example, the newspapers gave the society such good coverage that nearly 10 percent of the New Haven residents receiving the first appeal (190 persons out of 2,000) joined, with all but 20 percent of these paying their dues; in Waterbury, 40 new members came from a mailing of 400 letters. In Hartford, however, where the local press had ignored the society, 2,000 appeals brought only 50 memberships. Since newspapers would willingly publish articles on mental hygiene, perhaps the National Committee could prepare some on the society's work.[59]

Predictably, instead of praise Meyer sent a reprimand: "No sooner do I mention the arrangement for the secretaryship . . . than I see you sitting on the fence flapping your wings. The part which I have most at heart [aftercare] seems to be quite secondary. It is not the number of people you get into the thralls of membership dues that is going to count, but getting some work under way apart from legislative propaganda."[60] Beers was not intimidated. His organizing and legislative activities, he replied, could be done without interfering with aftercare work. He must, moreover, prove to Rockefeller that there was a "wide-spread interest in mental hygiene" and that a state society, once founded, could be self-supporting. As for flapping his wings, he could also sometimes fly.[61]

‡

A controversy that developed at this time over the name of the National Committee indicates the relations among Beers, Meyer, and James, as well as their concern for Rockefeller sensibilities. The dispute seems to have been sparked by James' report to Beers that Strong had questioned the use of the term *mental hygiene* as "flabby and evasive" and also "misleading," for it did not suggest the real subject, insanity. Why not say "National Committee on Insanity," a name that might better appeal to Strong's father-in-law, John D. Rockefeller? James agreed.[62]

In this case Beers took Meyer's part. The term *mental hygiene,* although not "all-satisfying," was the best yet found to express the broad purposes of the National Committee to protect sanity as well as fight insanity. It was infinitely better than "insanity," which had such negative connotations. The committee "would render humanity a great service, if through its activity the words 'insane' and 'insanity' were formally rendered obsolete." To Meyer, Beers wrote that he preferred the term *mental hygiene* but was not categorically opposed to the use of the word *insanity* for the National Committee; it must not, however, be used for the state societies, which would have much more direct contact with the public.[63] (Even the use of "mental hygiene" carried a stigma: in order to avoid embarrassing recipients of its educational materials, the Connecticut Society for Mental Hygiene omitted its name from the envelopes.)[64] James, unconvinced, told Meyer that "mental hygiene" did not *"bite,"* that many people would think it had something to do with "mind-cure" or "new thought." "Insanity" was the "straighter term, as a better fighting appellation, and one better understood."[65] But the term *insanity* gave Meyer a "cold shiver." *Mental hygiene* was constructive, "chosen because we have to outgrow both the term insanity and the connotation of the narrower psychotherapy, such as deserves that name, and the unfortunately often admixed psychoquackery." In approaching people it would be an advantage "to take a constructive attitude rather than essentially a fighting term."[66]

Would not "insanity" "be a better name for fighting, and so to speak for advertising purposes?" James replied. "I fear the loss of *popular prestige* at the outset if we use the somewhat insipid term of mental hygiene. *Scourges* fix attention more than *ideals*."[67] Meyer responded sharply: "The term 'insanity' has been a misfortune to psychiatry and will continue to be so." It covered only a small part of the work to be done, and if "mental hygiene" was insipid it was time to show people "that what is good in it implies no hocus pocus and offers plain and simple and strong and reliable help to success in living." If "insanity" were to be used he would withdraw from the National Committee:

> It is not after all a question whether we should create or clip enthusiasm among *workers*. Moreover the very thing I abhor in this movement is the advertising. . . . It is just the fact that people believe that the catch word "insanity" needs no interpretation, that makes it so objectionable. We are not in for a popular campaign at once, but for work on definite matters which will shape their own campaigns. It is not ideas versus scourges, but concrete achievements versus the know-it-all conception; not launching a boom, but giving a chance to some natural and strong developments.

Rockefeller and his advisors would be reached by evidence of "concrete instances of work" rather than words. "By the way, would it not be well to let the donor say whether he wants to immortalize himself with a Rockefeller Foundation for Insanity? . . . If, *in the end,* a change of name, should be the salvation of the cause, I shall say God speed."[68]

Beers urged James to accept "mental hygiene." "If this be treason, please make as little of it as possible." The merits of "mental hygiene" would "grow on you. At first I didn't like it much, but I do now."[69] James gave in, but apparently discontent with "mental hygiene" persisted, for the following month Meyer confided to Beers that he rather liked the term *mental health* suggested by Strong and would keep it as an alternative to "mental hygiene," which was still his first choice.[70] "Mental hygiene" it remained.

Beers felt content. He celebrated his thirty-third birthday — an "important, happy, healthy and prosperous" day — by finishing work on the National Committee's appeal for money. Before another year passed, he confided to Aunt Mame, he would be out of debt and receiving an income of "at least $5,000 a year." He thanked her for "the brush-broom, and the doilie for Mrs. Meyer," and the candy and the love she had sent.[71] Aunt Mame had made the gift in appreciation for all that the Meyers had done for Clifford, her "king who can do no wrong."[72]

‡ 10 ‡

"The Ox and the 'Wild Ass' "

Although he did have much to be happy about, Beers was as usual overoptimistic. For the next three years the National Committee remained quiescent while he and a few active members tried to find financial support.

Their first big effort was the appeal to Rockefeller. Beers, Meyer, Russell, James, and other members of the executive committee worked on this during the spring of 1909, with Clifford the most heavily involved. This activity, together with his work for the Connecticut Society, fully occupied him. In mid-March Beers had suggested, with Meyer's approval, that Meyer and Russell each submit to him notes for a Rockefeller appeal, to be blended into a document that the executive committee, plus Russell, could comment upon. The work of amalgamation, plus the addition of statistics on mental illness, was what Beers had finished on his birthday.[1] The divergences between Meyer and the others then broke out — and then again and again for the next two years. Reflecting differences in approach and temperament as well as in principle, the conflict dominated Beers' work during that time, he always pressing for action, to get the National Committee moving, and Meyer always pulling back, preferring caution and assurance of success.

James reworked the appeal to make it "sharper and more smiting" and added a preamble of "highly generalized character," which Meyer disliked because of its uncomplimentary attitude toward hospital psychiatrists in particular and its pessimistic attitude in general. What to do? It was necessary to satisfy Meyer, but, "Experience teaches me that the only way to insure [progress]," Beers wrote Russell, "is for us not to turn everything over to Dr. Meyer who, because of his many duties, is forced to let matters drag."[2]

Meyer's notes for the appeal indicate that ambivalence was also responsible for his procrastination. He advanced cogent arguments for an independent organization like the National Committee to work for the improvement of psychiatric care and to educate the public to correct "deviations of moral experience" by proper habit training. Through contributions from "the powerful and enlightened individuals who have organized the property of our country," the committee would overcome the financial and political obsta-

134

cles that had stymied such work in the past. At the same time he warned: "Example: not preaching! Money to report *examples* [of work] and to show them. Let's ask it [money] as we get ready. Or do we have to get ready in order to do justice to the money obtained before we are ready to even venture on a plan?"[3] He had no confidence that the National Committee could effectively make use of a large endowment, yet here he was composing an appeal for just such an endowment. Unlike Beers, Meyer did not like to take chances, especially with other people's money. Nevertheless, with Mrs. Meyer there as usual "to pour oil on the troubled waters,"[4] Meyer had Beers to dinner, which resulted in a new draft of the appeal that Meyer could accept; it was basically a restatement of the goals and means in the "Outline of Policy" adopted by the National Committee. Meyer approved inclusion of the original James version with the documents submitted to Rockefeller, and he suggested that Beers' name be mentioned as a field worker: "It will make the appeal stronger."[5]

At last, by the end of May, the appeal was completed. James' accompanying letter to Rockefeller, dated June 1, 1909, stated that institutions in the United States were "deplorably inferior" to those in Europe, gorged with inmates, managed by second-rate physicians, run on a "sodden" regimen, and hard to get into and out of. Public opinion remained uneducated: "what should be regarded as a common functional disease is handled as a social stigma." Routine and safety rather than prevention and cure were the first considerations. In order to achieve the latter objectives, a tremendous campaign must be launched by a national committee. James ended with a reference to *A Mind That Found Itself,* which had convinced him and others of the need to act.[6] He also wrote another note to Rockefeller to accompany a copy of the book: "I think that if you once begin it, you will not wish to stop reading, and that your sympathy will 'warm' to the philanthropic purposes of the author. He is a rarely disinterested man." Stokes was to present the appeal in person to his friend Gates, through whom requests to Rockefeller were usually funneled. All seemed in good order: even Meyer conceded that "the whole thing will I believe make a good showing."[7]

Gates promised to consider the appeal seriously. He was especially interested in knowing from Meyer whether there was a physical cause of insanity, and inquired how many copies of Beers' book had been published and sold.[8] Gates' interest in the book coincided with a favorable notice of it by Dr. Ferrari, whom Meyer called one of the best men in Italy, and who, James informed Beers, had found a good translator and was looking for a publisher. Shortly thereafter Beers learned that Dr. Katzen Ellenbogen had already translated half his book into German. He gave Ferrari permission to publish his book in Italian, provided that the translation was faithful and that it include the revisions he was making for a second edition. And what did Ferrari think about organizing a mental health movement in Italy? If Ferrari were willing to take an active part in such work, Beers would forward information regarding the plans of the National Committee.[9]

The revisions projected for a new edition of *A Mind That Found Itself* included a new paragraph, suggested by Meyer and revised by Fisher, designed to show that in childhood Clifford Beers suffered from a distorted personality that predisposed him to a mental breakdown when the pressures of life increased. Beers also intended to say that his disorder might have been prevented if only he had been warned in advance and that relapses in manic-depressive illness could be eliminated by avoiding certain types of strain. Would Meyer give him a brief statement for the book, and as part of the fight for prevention, to that effect? Meyer refused. Psychiatry did not know enough to assert definitely that Beers' illness had been avoidable. "Most certainly with your whole make-up relapses are preventable," he said, and he felt "considerable certainty that even your actual attack might have been preventable," but there were too many ifs involved to be really sure. On Meyer's and Fisher's advice the new paragraph was not inserted in the second edition.[10]

The response on the issue of relapse may have been in part an effort by Meyer to reassure Clifford Beers. Not only had George Beers had "nervous" problems, but a younger brother, Carl E. Beers, was taken seriously ill in the fall of 1908. After residence on a farm and then in a physician's establishment, Carl was sent to a private sanitarium in New Haven and in 1910 to the Hartford Retreat. At Bloomingdale Hospital (the psychiatric division of New York Hospital in White Plains), to which he was transferred a year and a half later, his condition was diagnosed as dementia catatonia.[11]

The following summer, while waiting for Gates' reply to the Rockefeller appeal, Clifford Beers took a long vacation, his first "real rest" in a long time, something that Meyer had been urging upon him. He spent six weeks on the Connecticut shore, most of the time as guest at the Jepsons' summer home. By then he was Clara's acknowledged suitor within the family, which that summer gave him a "taste of real home-life." Upon returning to New Haven, he decided to destroy his memorabilia, "the accumulation of a lifetime." He had "been in the habit of hoarding . . . old letters . . . from childhood days," and now he disposed of the contents of two trunks, after which he felt "greatly relieved."[12] He apparently feared that these letters contained uncomplimentary material which would reflect unfavorably on him when a biographer came to write about his life.

In August, Stewart Paton invited Beers to his summer home in Maine, a visit that gave the two men a chance to discuss at length the cause and Beers' role in it. Paton's opinion regarding his future, Beers wrote Mrs. Jepson, "convinces me that before many months I shall have 'arrived' indeed. And then I shall be able to prove, if proof be needed, that the confidence placed in me by Mr. Jepson and yourself was deserved. . . . Clara is a jewel beyond price, and a man to prove himself worthy of her must measure up to the highest standards."[13] Paton suggested that Beers write a "constructive work" as a sequel to *A Mind That Found Itself,* something that Clara had also mentioned. Accordingly Clifford set to work when he got home: "in honor of the day" a year before when he had told Clara he loved her, he began writing on September 3, and in less than two weeks finished a detailed outline to send to Paton and Meyer.[14] (This project was never pursued further.)

‡

The prompt decision expected from Gates did not come, and Beers' financial situation continued to deteriorate, forcing him to reopen the issue of a salary from the National Committee. Meyer refused to see him, but Beers "was not to be put off. . . . especially in view of earlier promises regarding salary." He turned to Stokes, who agreed to place a letter from Beers before Meyer.[15]

Could he ask for a salary as secretary pro tem without endangering negotiations with the Rockefeller people? Beers wrote. He considered himself as devoting full time to the National Committee, since his work for the Connecticut Society was designed to discover a model plan which the National Committee could use in its work. "I have, in fact, reached a point where I can no longer ask residents of Connecticut to give pecuniary support to the Connecticut Society." Only when he received a salary from the National Committee would he resume fund-raising in Connecticut. In fact, he had accepted no money from the Connecticut Society since last June 26. He had been living on borrowed money for four years, a situation for which he could not hold anyone responsible, but there it was nonetheless.[16]

At this time (early October), his friend Vic Tyler came to his rescue with a check and a canceled note for one hundred dollars. "I'll be damned if I want your note. . . . I am sick of so much business between friends," Tyler wrote. "You are doing a great work and I would like to help that, to say nothing of you. Your family are making sacrifices to help you and some of your friends can do a little occasionally. If it will ease your soul to pay me some day all right but I do not need your note to insure that." Beers was to let him know when he needed another three hundred dollars.[17]

Beers meanwhile had spoken with Meyer about plans for future work as justification for receiving a salary. In an obvious attempt to appease Meyer, he focused on aftercare, but he developed such an elaborate and impractical scheme that Meyer exploded: "The idea to go to every place [in Connecticut] to persuade some people [to form aftercare committees] is directly contrary to everything I ever urged. Start on some actual case and draw on help as needs arise and as information accumulates, but do not load a scheme on the hospitals which . . . even a modicum of sense on their part would condemn." Beers asked Stokes to pass on his pleas for support to Gates, and asked James to send a supporting letter. This time James must not give his own money: Beers was not that desperate. To Meyer, Beers wrote of his inability to contribute to the support of his parents, who might as a consequence have to give up their home of forty-six years.[18]

The answer that finally came from Gates, via Stokes, was discouraging. Gates had "some pretty serious questions as to the plan outlined" and doubted that the General Education Board would help the National Committee. Money could be obtained, Stokes believed, for "doing definite things, such as after-care for instance."[19]

So willy-nilly Beers was pushed into aftercare work, whose value, he admitted to Meyer, it had taken him over a year to appreciate fully. On Meyer's urging, in order to win hospital superintendents' support for aftercare activities, he had immersed himself in aftercare literature, from which he extracted excerpts for a pamphlet to be published by the National Committee for distribution to psychiatrists. Meyer found an early version "rather attractive," and at a meeting at the Century Club after hearing the disheartening news from Gates, Meyer, as chairman of the National Committee executive committee, agreed to publish it and to try to raise money at once for a salary for Beers.[20]

At this time Paton revealed himself as Meyer's active ally in suspending national activity. Beers, he said, should rather choose a few individuals and educate them about mental hygiene; this is what Paton had done at Johns Hopkins. "Meyer and myself, will help you all we can in New Haven. The cause is hopeless unless you can get the sympathy and backing of the men in the hospitals. Begin with them." The American sin of big talk should be avoided until there was something to boast about. Six instances of well-cared for aftercare cases would prove more valuable than any amount of propaganda. When all was going well in Connecticut, then Beers should try to stir up interest elsewhere. Just a few days later, after he had seen Paton, Meyer retracted his agreement to print the pamphlet on aftercare.[21]

Beers could not back down. Hospital superintendents and members of the Connecticut State Board of Charities were expecting the pamphlet, and physicians who would attend the meeting he was organizing to hear Meyer speak on aftercare would get more out of the talk if they had a chance to read the pamphlet first. Further, hospital men like Russell, Thompson, and Noble thought it was valuable, and its publication might help to convince hospital physicians to join and support the Connecticut Society. Since Meyer did not want to pay for it (although he finally did), Beers solicited money from Vic Tyler to print proof sheets of part of the pamphlet for distribution prior to the meeting.[22] This incident is an example of how Meyer encouraged and then discouraged Beers and, indeed, many people with whom he was associated in a position of power.

The maneuvering necessary to arrange the meeting at which Meyer was to speak indicated the difficulties in dealing with the hospital men. The way to win them over to the Connecticut Society for Mental Hygiene was to try to eliminate threats to their position. To remove the suspicion that Diefendorf was using the society as a power base for himself, he resigned from the society.[23] Then Drs. Givens and McFarland, "the *present* powers in the Connecticut Society of Alienists," would not allow the meeting to be held under the latter group's auspices. Beers therefore invited hospital superintendents, trustees, and members of the State Board of Charities, among others, to an open meeting, with no obligation to endorse his society or any particular program. Wanting also to avoid any impression that the National Committee wanted to take over in Connecticut, he suggested that Paton — considered by the state hospital physicians as a wealthy man dabbling in psychiatry, with little understanding of their problems — not be present.[24]

Contrary to Meyer's forecast, and as Beers predicted, the meeting was a success. Meyer's talk, "The Social Service Movement for Hospitals for the Insane and the Connecticut Society for Mental Hygiene," was well received by a responsive audience. Paton sent Beers congratulations and an invitation to visit him in Princeton at his expense. Beers, now convinced that the hospital men were beginning to trust him and would soon come into leadership of the Connecticut Society, thought he would hasten the process by assuring them that the society would no longer "try to effect legislation or suggest policies for the State Hospitals."[25]

By this time, Meyer had become somewhat more sympathetic to Beers' demands for a salary, but when Beers took an unannounced trip to Boston to study aftercare practices, Meyer exploded. Beers' "deception" and "financial extravagance" in going to Boston a day after bemoaning his indebtedness convinced Meyer that he could not "afford the expenditure of energy along the lines of restraining [Clifford Beers]. . . . I always feel that I deal with a man who ought not to be exposed to too serious a strain." If only he could stay with the Connecticut work, then the National Committee would be in a better position to secure for him "lasting rewards rather than a huge pile of soap-bubbles."[26]

To keep Beers active in Connecticut, something had to be done to relieve his financial difficulties. Meyer therefore asked him to estimate a minimum salary for himself, which must come through the Connecticut Society and be for work done in Connecticut, not for the National Committee. Beers must first go through an apprenticeship in "concrete work" in Connecticut before venturing elsewhere and engaging in propaganda. "I would rather pay the interest out of my own pocket than get the National Committee into a wrong move" in order to get Beers out of debt.[27]

Meyer's letter arrived while Beers was in Baltimore to speak with Cardinal Gibbons about the role of the Roman Catholic church in the mental hygiene movement; he also intended to go to Washington to discuss his plans with National Committee members Gifford Pinchot and Surgeon General Walter Wyman.[28] The trip also gave him a chance to see Welch, who encouraged his quest for a salary of four thousand dollars a year (a substantial amount in those days) and offered to speak to Phipps. But when Welch saw Meyer's letter he reconsidered: "My interest in you is a sympathetic one. My opinion of the plan of work, however, depends largely on what Dr. Meyer has to say." Just at that time Phipps volunteered a contribution to the expenses of the next National Committee meeting, which did not seem to make any difference in Meyer's attitude.[29]

Instead Meyer threatened to resign from the National Committee if his policies were not accepted. Beers should talk to Paton, which he did, challenging Paton to specify any actions of his over the past six years that had "*hurt* the cause or alienated the support of any person whose support is worth having." Meyer meanwhile advised Paton to point to errors such as Beers' promotion of a bill setting up an investigatory commission in Connecticut and his accumulation of debts on the assumption of future income. "I should like to act in harmony with you when I see him," Meyer wrote. Paton as a result also threatened to resign from the National Committee if it paid Beers' salary; he would try himself to raise money to pay him through the Connecticut Society, and even to take over his debts, if only he stayed in Connecticut and kept the National Committee inactive. When it came to actually soliciting funds for the salary, however, Paton had to ask Beers where to turn.[30]

The pressure from Paton and Meyer forced Beers to agree to confine his work to Connecticut. He tried to prove his sincerity to Meyer by describing his social work cases and asking for advice. By social work he meant assistance of all sorts. For example, to a husband worried that his wife was mistreated in the state hospital, Beers lent twenty dollars so that he could see for himself; he then obtained work for the man, whose trip to the hospital assuaged his fears. "I discover," Beers wrote Meyer, "and I hope you, too, see evidences of it, that my *point of view* is getting to be that of the hospital physician and psychiatrist."[31] Meyer remained unconvinced.

Beers had by then (early 1910) achieved an important "success" in this respect. A majority of the additional directors of the Connecticut Society were trustees of mental hospitals and members of the State Board of Charities, and the four leading hospital superintendents in Connecticut, Drs. Noble, Pollock, Thompson, and Buel, agreed to accept membership on the executive committee. Then Beers' entire slate of officers for the society was elected (including Dr. George Blumer of Yale Medical School as president). Jubilant, Clifford told Clara: "Part of your vindication—and mine has come." It proved that "other as yet unattained ambitions and hopes will be achieved." He longed for the day when he could declare his love and the fact that only Clara's help enabled him to succeed.[32]

Only a few weeks later he heard that the Connecticut hospital men were having second thoughts about joining the society, which might in the future come into conflict with state hospital policies. Beers had so completely adopted Meyer's position that he suggested that the society's constitution and bylaws be changed to limit its activities to social service work and public education. This done, the superintendents came in. He had not betrayed the society, Beers reassured a mistrustful correspondent. The physicians now in leadership would be its strongest supporters.[33]

Beers thought he had achieved the goal his advisors kept saying was prerequisite to national activity. A year's additional work would "make it possible for the National Committee to inaugurate a *national* movement," he told Paul McQuaid and his wife, to whom he owed money. "Then I shall, as it were, come into my own with respect to salary, prestige and opportunity to use all of my energy." He predicted he would "soon be on Easy Street," and thanked the McQuaids for helping to finance the Connecticut Society for the past few months.[34] Meanwhile he could not resist giving Clara, his "Queen," for her thirty-fifth birthday "a little band and bond of gold set with a very little solitaire," an expression of his "birthday-love in a way at least suggestive of the life-long token and pledge yet to come."[35]

‡

Although he was doing what Meyer and Paton advised, Beers still received nothing but promises from them in the matter of salary. Meyer continued to insist that any salary be for work in Connecticut and not as secretary of the National Committee. For the time being, Beers confided to James, he would "humor Meyer and Paton" and go along with Meyer's "conservative" estimate of his worth at $1,800 a year. James should not lift a finger to help him. That Meyer and Paton "are doing something in my interests. . . is cause enough for letting them alone." He would try to be patient. He had to be. "It is quite obvious," Meyer wrote Paton, "that there is no special hurry" as far as Beers' debts were concerned. The only prompt action required was to raise money for a salary. But all Beers heard from Meyer was, "Your cause is not forgotten!"[36]

With the completion in February of the Connecticut Society's prospectus, Beers considered it "converted into a model State Society . . . an achievement [that] would bring . . . the promised pecuniary assistance" from Paton and Meyer.[37] Meyer was stirred to communicate with Stokes regarding action from Gates on the National Committee's appeal. One might say that, having done nothing, Meyer was hoping for a miracle to relieve him of the responsibility for finding money to pay Clifford a salary. Beers, in Stokes' office when the letter came, drafted a reply from Stokes saying that Gates was not likely to help an inactive organization with unsettled policies and plans and that therefore a meeting had to be called to activate the National Committee.[38] At the same time Meyer wrote to Blumer of the dangers of giving Clifford a high salary: "To tell the truth I should not like to put him into a position in which he could flap 'eagle's wings' too freely. It would not be safe for him."[39]

Apparently Meyer was not above using the argument that to become active on a national scale would be detrimental to Beers' mental health but that work in Connecticut presented no such threat. Meyer probably believed what he wrote, but one cannot help noticing that this fear of his was not compatible with his original estimation of Beers. Meyer had recognized that the reform work he encouraged Beers to enter would require him to dedicate his life to the cause. Indeed it was Beers' great energy and devotion as well as his willingness to take advice that initially convinced Meyer that he was the man for the cause. Now that Beers seemed resistant to his guidance and Meyer could devise no convincing plan of national work, he saw the very qualities that fitted Beers for the role of reformer as a threat to his mental health.

Blumer took Meyer's letter to Chittenden, who sent him to Beers, who drafted replies for them to send to Meyer. Beers described these moves to James: "I have at last got my arguments before Dr. Meyer without so much as appearing on the horizon. It seems too good to be true." He also sent copies of the Stokes, Chittenden, and Blumer letters to guide James in responding to any communication from Meyer, who must of course never learn of these transactions. James could also encourage Chittenden and Blumer to hold firm. Meyer's and Paton's "reactionary tendencies" stemmed from "their having overemphasized the relative importance of the psychiatrical phases of the work. Though they are of course, vitally important, certain other phases are deserving of attention first, viz., organization of the National Committee and the financing of the work." Meyer and Paton, as scientists, found it impossible to act even though they wanted to, whereas Chittenden and Stokes, men of affairs, had no difficulty in doing so.[40]

The Blumer and Chittenden replies to Meyer resembled that sent by Stokes: recommendations to call a meeting of the National Committee and to have it pay Beers' salary, on the grounds that the work in Connecticut provided a model state society to which the National Committee might point as evidence of the feasibility of its goals. Chittenden added that Beers had "a certain degree of personal magnetism that makes presentation of a matter attractive to many people," and Blumer noted that Beers' "great enthusiasm would lead one to think that he did not always perhaps use proper deliberation. I had this impression . . . but I now know that he never takes any important step without consulting the members of the National Committee who live here."[41]

Beers confided his real plans to James. What was needed was to have the National Committee win support from Gates to found state societies, with the Connecticut Society, now almost self-supporting, as an example for other states to follow. There must be strict secrecy about this, for he was "*supposed* to be content to work in Connecticut exclusively, for a while yet."[42] Even if Meyer never saw this letter, he knew Beers well enough to suspect he would never be satisfied to work in Connecticut and was continually hatching grand schemes for the National Committee.

Meyer's replies to Blumer, Chittenden, and Stokes praised Beers' Connecticut work and his willingness to learn, a judgment that Meyer seemed loath to express directly to Beers. Meyer also confided misgivings about holding him back. "I feel at times that I should not stand in the way of Mr. Beers and his desires—to work up something of an organization of . . . national scope." Beers would raise the money more readily than anyone else, but would it produce results? Unless he earned his "spurs in the Conn. Society . . . I should feel much more comfortable to either get the organization described in the appeal or to retire to a well defined local problem" such as the Phipps Clinic, where work could be done by example.[43]

It appears that Meyer did not, in principle, object to work on a national scale even before local work showed the way, provided the work was well funded. But again, as when he composed the Rockefeller appeal, Meyer revealed his ambivalence. He feared Beers would produce little of value in a national organization, and he did not want him to have the influence that would naturally come to him as the principal fund raiser—which would be the case if a large grant of money were not initially forthcoming. Meyer's "solution" was to insist upon local work and upon training Beers as a psychiatric social worker, thereby reducing the possible role of lay people in the movement. This tendency to reorient the mental hygiene movement to being under physicians' control is also revealed in the nature of the work that Meyer proposed for both the National Committee and the Connecticut Society, as well as his criticisms of the activities for lay people. Meyer called for the organization of clinics as the prime activity for the National Committee, however difficult it would be to obtain funds for them, while the Connecticut Society would assist hospitals in aftercare and other social work. He virtually denied the value of public education by lay people, and he played down the significance of organization and fund-raising, areas in which lay efforts could be especially useful. The initiative and control would lie with the hospitals. Meyer was not completely unaware of the tendency of his thought, although he never clearly defined its direction. That he had always felt a need to proceed cautiously was as far as he ever went toward admitting that he was changing his mind about the value of a mental health movement in which lay and medical members shared control. His criticisms of Beers were really a rejection of any leadership role for lay people in the mental health movement, and his complaints about Beers' grandiosity and financial irresponsibility were in part a disguise for this change in his thinking.[44]

Meyer realized that the kind of movement he was actually proposing would be difficult to fund, and he also knew that he had "not the rudiments of a talent" for fund-raising. In his naiveté, he told James, he had assumed that no action should be taken until the Rockefeller people responded to the appeal, so that he pleaded guilty to undesirable delays, and he did not "bear the feeling of guilt well." Clifford Beers had done good work. "He had much to learn and still does; but he will do it. I shall always help him all I can. The best way to please a man is to please him to his complete satisfaction, of course." He felt sure that the program in Connecticut, "a very commendable beginning of the real work," would do that.[45] It is difficult to understand how Meyer could possibly believe that aftercare work in Connecticut would ever give Beers the satisfaction he sought. Probably Meyer sought to justify his position in a way that would be more acceptable to Beers' supporters.

As for himself, Meyer would resign from the National Committee if it was activated; he would thereafter make his contribution to the cause through the Phipps Clinic. He warned Chittenden about starting a national organization with a man at the center who was in debt; it would lead to "mortgaging a philanthropic movement."[46]

Beers correctly understood that the real issue was the nature of the National Committee. Meyer and Paton were shaping its policy to suit their own ends, which revolved around the Phipps Clinic and an erroneous concept of the National Committee's program as "exclusively psychiatric," Beers told James, when it was really "essentially missionary and educational." Just as Meyer wanted Beers to learn scientific caution, Beers had hoped that Meyer would become through experience more of an activist. Meyer's renewed request for information about Beers' finances was insulting, and despite having done nothing to raise money he "now had the 'nerve' (there's no other name for it) to ask me to continue to leave my personal affairs in his and Dr. Paton's hands." Beers would do his own begging and thereby "escape obligations which might later prove embarrassing. Besides, how could Meyer and Paton raise money for me personally, when they are so opposed to my coming into rights, a position and a salary I have already earned?" They simply wished to buy his inactivity. Some people did not even want Meyer to head the National Committee. According to Stokes, Gates had been given a bad impression of Meyer through the writings submitted with the appeal, and Stokes as well as Chittenden and Blumer now believed that the National Committee would stand a better chance with the Rockefeller Foundation if Meyer stepped down.[47]

James found it "part of the irony of human destiny that I, a mere metaphysician and sponsor of cranks, should be having a vote in this momentous practical matter." Previously James had argued that Meyer was indispensable to the National Committee, so that his resignation would look bad. Now he felt it unfortunate that Meyer wish to resign, but if he could not work in a more aggressive movement "it is perhaps better that he should."[48] James could see both sides: "it is a case of the ox and the 'wild ass' not working well in double harness." Meyer, the scientist, sought to create a movement bit by bit, and Beers, the graduate of lunatic asylums, favored the big movement; Meyer hoped that Beers' experience in Connecticut and his own in Baltimore would suggest how to add content to the movement, whereas Beers would let the content arise from action. Either position was tenable, but Beers' would save years of time even it if was more risky. Meyer was a "splendid creature on the purely psychiatric side; and it may well be that the people from whom we hope for the big endowment . . . will see things much as he does. He evidently is sure they will. 'Tis the way all 'critical' judges feel when asked to back creative minds: they shake their heads." James thought that Beers was the movement's "chief asset and content." "You are a creative mind and a successful propagandist — witness the Conn. Ass'n.! — and things grow under your touch in unforeseeable ways. The great task will be to find someone to work along side of you, and in cordial partnership, *immediately*." James later told Beers that what he had already accomplished warranted giving him freedom to try to do more, and that valor and discretion had always characterized his actions.[49]

Except for George Beers and a few close friends like Vic Tyler and Professor Chittenden, no other person gave Clifford Beers such consistent support as William James. James considered himself impractical, and he felt happy to help an activist like Beers. As Ralph Barton Perry pointed out, James "accepted Carlyle's gospel of work in his answer to the great question, 'What Makes Life Worth Living?' With Carlyle he admired heroic action," without which life lost its significance.[50]

Beers was concerned about James' health. Upon receiving a letter from James which seemed to be a last farewell, Beers wrote what he had "long intended to do":

Not until today when I read your letter and its message: Well, good success! and good bye! Your friend — did I sense the depth of my affection for you. No matter how many friends come as rewards in my work, none can ever take your place. The circumstances which gave rise to our friendship cannot recur. . . . you had faith in me, and weren't afraid to say so.

Many a time when facing a difficult situation . . . have I said, "Well, if so and so won't do it, Mr. James will" — and you always did.

May you live as many years as *I* want to live, and may the fear of my heart which inspired the writing of this letter prove unfounded![51]

James reassured Beers that he was "*much* more comfortable" than since a year past. "You are most responsive and recognizant of human beings . . .

and it 'sets me up' immensely to be treated by a practical man on practical grounds as you treat me. . . . you are not only a moral idealist and philanthropic enthusiast, (and good fellow)! but a *tip-top man of business* . . . and to have actually done anything . . . you can regard as having helped . . . is an unwonted ground . . . for self-gratulation. I think that your tenacity of purpose, foresight, tact, temper, discretion and patience, are beyond all praise, and I esteem it an honor to have been in any degree associated with you."[52]

James sent Beers a copy of a letter from Henry Walcott remarking that Dr. Copp, the executive officer of the Massachusetts State Board of Insanity, was "much impressed with Beers's mental soundness" after speaking with him several times. "What an encouragement such a case is," Walcott said. James had also gone to President Eliot of Harvard, a member of the General Education Board, to ask about a grant of ten to twenty thousand dollars for the National Committee to get started. Gates, Eliot said, had never brought the National Committee's appeal before the General Education Board, which would in any case almost certainly turn it down. Meyer's resignation at this point would not look good.[53]

Despite telling James that Meyer's withdrawal would be best, when Meyer wrote in a seemingly conciliatory way to Chittenden, Beers was relieved. His hurt feelings at Meyer's derogatory remarks about him did not prevent him from recognizing that if Meyer could only compromise enough to allow some progress in the National Committee he must be retained as chairman of the executive committee.

Meyer, however, tried to resolve the impasse in a way that would hardly please Clifford Beers. He suggested that Beers work as an inspector of the male wards in the New Jersey State Hospital at Trenton, where a series of accidents needed investigation. "It would be a remarkable experience."[54] This job as a glorified attendant was offered by the superintendent of the hospital upon Paton's request to make a place for Beers for a year or two while the affairs of the National Committee were taking shape. Beers held Paton, not Meyer, responsible for this maneuver. What he did not know was that Meyer wrote to Stokes that Beers was "in no way prepared for a leading position in the movement, notwithstanding his admirable devotion, and I think it would be a wrong to him and to the cause not to realize that."[55]

Aside from objecting to Beers' financial extravagance and penchant for organization and propaganda, Meyer also argued that unless he was restrained from exercising a free hand or taking a leadership position he might suffer a relapse of his mental disorder. Throughout their relationship, Meyer monitored Beers' mental health, advising him to take frequent vacations, not to work too intensely, to leave certain organizational decisions to others, and above all to be conservative financially so as not to place undue strain upon himself. This concern for Clifford Beers' mental health was characteristic of psychiatrists and lay people who worked with him through-out his public life. The issue of his mental health always lay near the surface, so that when he became involved in controversy it was frequently used as a weapon against him.

The National Committee meeting was scheduled, notwithstanding Meyer's objection, for April, and with him still as chairman of the executive commit-tee. He tried to muster support for his viewpoint. Urging Bancroft to attend the National Committee meeting to counter James and the New Haven con-tingent, Meyer estimated that Beers could develop "if properly directed and held down . . . but he will always be a man requiring control." He had hoped that Beers would bring the right people, like Bancroft, into the Na-tional Committee, but that did not happen; some thought its goal was to re-form asylums; a few, to help Clifford Beers.[56] Ironically, at this time a letter from Mary C. Acker, a hospital trustee and aftercare worker whom Meyer greatly admired, commended Beers for the "fine basis upon which your in-defatigable interest and energy has placed the Conn. Soc. for Mental Hy-giene! As a pioneer you are to be *congratulated,* and I hope other States will model their work after yours."[57]

The New Haven men were perfectly willing to have Meyer plan the scien-tific aspects of the work, but they no longer had faith in his ability to oversee the kind of organization they envisaged. Most of them could not understand his reluctance to act; there seemed to be plenty to do once funds were se-cured. Blumer assumed that Meyer, "after helping to organize the move-ment, wanted to back out unless he could have complete control." He was carrying out a policy of "'Masterly inactivity.'"[58]

‡

At the April meeting of the National Committee, Meyer acquiesced in the decision to set up a finance committee to raise funds for the appointment of a medical director and then a secretary.[59] But privately he objected. In a con-fidential letter to Russell Chittenden, Meyer accused Beers' New Haven friends of stirring him up with assurances of the correctness of *"his* 'Na-tional' policy. . . . 'National' is a dangerous word for a man of Beers' consti-tution and manic depressive temperament. I truly blame myself for not having demanded its elimination from his program before entered upon. . . . We may say what we will, there is a Mental Hygiene Problem and a Beers problem being welded together in a disastrous manner." Encouragement from Stokes, Blumer, and especially Chittenden led Beers to believe he could solve his personal financial problems through the National Committee. All this could not be discussed at the meeting in his presence, which was unfor-tunate, since policy must not be determined by "unexplained untempered inspirations of a manic-depressive temperament." Beers "ought not to be encouraged to think that what he has done in Conn. is an *achievement* for the National Committee today." At best a "meager beginning" had been made. Experienced people like Bancroft, Glenn, and Folks (the influential secretary of the State Charities Aid Association of New York), badly informed by Beers, were predicting failure for the cause. Beers must be taken in hand. He was "too good a man to be made expansive, if expansive, he may indeed promise to give money for things in which no mortal can make good." To use him in fund-raising entailed a "two fold risk, that of inflaming him with reduction of his real capacity and that of misleading the giving public."[60]

When Beers eventually learned of Meyer's virtual repudiation of the action of the National Committee, he wrote that if he died prematurely Chittenden must "assume this sacred trust and fight it out along the lines so effectively laid down by him at the meeting of the Committee held on April 9, 1910."[61] Beers stayed very much alive, and Chittenden, appointed chairman of the financial committee, stood firm. As a result, Meyer resigned as chairman of the executive committee. What was needed, Meyer said, were "foci of strong local work," to which he would contribute more at the Phipps Clinic "than by helping to create a very uncertain central bureau insufficiently attached to any of the agencies on which we must depend for the actual work."[62]

Hurt and angry, Beers expressed his feelings, as usual, to James. From James, at Bad Nauheim for a cure, he received a characteristic message: "It is evident that propagandism and 'Science' take two quite different orders of mind. I fully believe in propagandism and 'fighting it rough,' so long as you're around. I shall be here till July 1st getting patched up. I need it sorely."[63] This was probably the last communication Beers received from James, who came home to die. There is nothing in Beers' papers to indicate his feelings about James' death, but they must have been deeply sad, as James had been such a faithful and lovable friend ever since Beers had presented himself, young, unknown and probably excited, to the famous psychologist-philosopher four years earlier. Mrs. James and her son, William, an artist a few years younger than Beers, maintained a friendship with him for years thereafter.

With Clara Jepson, of whose existence as Clifford Beers' fiancée Meyer and the others were apparently ignorant, Beers was his usual optimistic self. From St. Louis, where he was attending the National Conference on Charities and Corrections as an invited speaker, Clifford wrote her that he felt satisfied. His two years of work in Connecticut had been "surely productive of results. And now that hampering millstones have been shaken off — I assume Dr. Paton will follow Dr. Meyer into the deep sea of oblivion (so far as the National movement is concerned) I should soon swim to shore. The thought occurs to me that I have the unusual capacity for overcoming obstacles and opposition." He felt that he had saved the cause. Previous failures to finance the National Committee were blessings in disguise. "Think what a calamity—for me personally—it might have been had Mr. Gates endowed the National Committee last summer and placed the control in Dr. Meyer's hands!"[64]

Nevertheless Beers feared that Meyer's resignation from the National Committee altogether would not only provoke a crisis, but would make it difficult to recruit the right medical director even if funds were raised for the next few years' work. Beers therefore urged Meyer to remain a member of the National Committee, whose planned work did not differ from Meyer's concepts. "Or, is it that *I* am the rock on which, if you resign, you force the . . . Committee to split?"[65]

Meyer for his part mistakenly thought that the psychiatrists supported him and the lay people opposed him. "We physicians will have to be the responsible persons in the movement," he told Bancroft.[66] But Russell, for example, seriously considered taking the job as medical director and urged Meyer to remain a member of the National Committee. Russell, of whom Beers was fond, also tried with Meyer's approval to substitute for him as Beers' advisor. "I shall do my best to take your place in serving as a mentor for him, but I cannot expect to have your success," Russell told Meyer. "Alas," Meyer replied to Russell's plea to stay in the National Committee, "I know of no remedy but of a change of mind among his [Beers'] friends and advisors."[67]

Meyer confessed that he tried to write to Beers, but all his drafts were too harsh; Beers in turn felt that Meyer was both thoughtless and cowardly in not communicating with him for months. In the letter that Meyer finally sent, which was critical enough, he explained his own failings as due to "unwillingness to cross your path any more than was absolutely necessary," and that he felt he was being punished for his "excessive confidence in the goodwill and capacity of cooperation of others."[68]

Beers matched criticism for criticism with Meyer, and it is apparent that a very sore point involved his indebtedness. He considered his debts the moral responsibility of the National Committee. He could "never forgive Dr. Meyer who is conversant with the situation, and George's state of health, for breaking his solemn promise to lift or shift the debts which George and yourself are still carrying," he told George's wife. "The criticism and humiliation to which I have been subjected as a result of my failure to 'arrive' more promptly, is nothing compared to the feeling which comes over me when I think of the burdens you and George must carry, especially as George is feeling unwell." Clifford had gone so far as to call upon the National Committee, through Chittenden, to pay his creditors in case of his death in a state of insolvency. In return he offered the National Committee his $1,000 life insurance policy and all royalties from the sale of his book until the amount defrayed for his debts was reimbursed.[69]

He laid the blame for the quarrels on Meyer's change of heart concerning the secretaryship of the National Committee. Further, he himself had always been cooperative, willing to serve an apprenticeship in Connecticut and indeed to continue to do so while the National Committee plans took shape, "provided a subsidy is granted to the Connecticut Society by the N.C." Meyer misunderstood his motives. Not "advancement to more conspicuous and remunerative posts," but "pressure of worry and uncertainty" about the "nervous" illness of George and Carl Beers, "which has been my portion for so long (and which our family has had to share) are the two causes of my restlessness." This was the first open admission by Clifford Beers that he was restless and that his brothers' troubles seriously disturbed him.[70]

Beers reassured Meyer that he had no intention of abandoning his commitment to a "medical-lay plan rather than one in which the lay element was to be predominant."[71] The extent to which Beers had absorbed Meyer's opinions is seen in replies at this time to correspondents who wished to start societies in other states. "At present," Beers advised one, "*workers* rather than organizers are needed. Though I may seem to have begun work by 'organizing,' you should remember that I studied the problem and wrote and published a book before I gave any time to the mere work of organizing a Society."[72] Finally Meyer, Russell, and Beers met to discuss their differences, but with no resolution of the issues. As a result, Beers vowed never to "lift a finger to keep [Meyer] in the work as an active member of the National Committee." He assumed some responsibility for the break, but the brunt had to be borne by Meyer, by then regarded by almost everyone as an isolated personality who was primarily at fault.[73]

After further unsuccessful negotiations, Meyer resigned both as chairman of the executive committee and as a member of the National Committee. He did not, however, seek to lead a procession out of the National Committee. Indeed, he hoped that Favill would stand by the cause and help it succeed; it needed his "level judgment and keen practical sense."[74]

But Favill did resign as president of the National Committee, although not from the organization altogether. He was probably influenced as much by his own impression of Beers as by Meyer's views. Their first meeting in St. Louis at the social work conference was a disturbing experience that convinced him that Beers was "going straight toward a breakdown. He is worried, tense, aggressive, expansive and opinionated." He argued logically but was out of touch with reality and was developing feelings of persecution which in "his specific difficulty are very threatening." Beers may not have been feeling well at that time. Writing to Clara, he assured her that he felt rested and would keep within his "limit of energy and recuperation." He intended to be "very careful" with Favill, but he was determined to make "it quite plain that delay is not tolerated." When he later found out about Favill's impression of him, he was quite distressed.[75]

Whatever his condition that spring, it passed, and it seems not to have been an issue with anyone on the National Committee but Meyer and Favill. By the time Meyer resigned in December he was considered to be an autocrat unable to cooperate with others. Only Paton and Favill took his part, and they remained members of the National Committee, as did Hoch, who with Russell tried to keep Meyer on. Beers had become sufficiently disgusted with the whole situation to give up such efforts, and Meyer's resignation became final on December 28, 1910.[76]

‡

Clifford Beers had taken a long time to get to this point. At least since his onset of mania in the Hartford Retreat he had had problems with strong, older men in positions of authority on whose approval his physical and psychological well-being depended. If, like Stearns and James, the men were kindly, understanding, and supportive, he could get on with them and even develop affectionate friendships that did not preclude criticism but did assume mutual respect. In his relations with Meyer, whose personality was not warm but who exhibited a sincere interest in him, he did try very hard to please. Not only did Beers need Meyer, but he respected his opinions and judgments, especially as they were working in a new field in which no one felt too sure of his ground. Given their personalities and proclivities, however, together with the very real problems involved in establishing a mental hygiene movement, there was a good chance at the outset that their relationship would founder.

Meyer consistently doubted Beers' mental stability and thought he needed to be kept in line. This professional judgment fed into Meyer's inclination to control every aspect of anything with which he was associated in a position of leadership. Former students of his who worked at the Phipps Clinic have reminisced about Meyer's austere, forbidding manner, accentuated by a pointed black beard and piercing eyes, and about the authoritarianism and ambivalence that kept his staff insecure and fearful of him. As he had done with Beers, he alternately encouraged and discouraged them.[77] He could not easily tolerate opposition, nor could he compromise on issues he considered important. Although not opposed to innovation, he was, as Beers observed the first time they met, careful, deliberate, and reluctant to move until he felt safe and sure. Unable to appreciate the value of Beers as a promoter, all he saw were the negative aspects of such work. He wanted a man with a passionate devotion to the cause but then tried to limit this powerhouse of activity to conservative, safe channels, to build a movement slowly, deliberately, brick by brick, upon a proper foundation.

Meyer knew that Beers had not the temperament for such a mode of work, but he thought he could change him. A believer in "habit training" as a basic means to correct imbalances in human character or mental states,[78] Meyer hoped to replace the satisfactions Beers derived from grandiose organizational and propaganda schemes with those to be gained from working with former patients and their families. But, like someone who married a clearly incompatible spouse in order to change her, Meyer was fated to be disappointed, and not only because he lost faith in Beers and found his expansive personality and incessant activity intolerable. Equally important were Meyer's doubts about any useful purpose to which Beers' talents could be put. Meyer urged that the National Committee be allowed to evolve out of the experience of local work because he had no clear vision of a national organizations's role, or of the place of untrained lay people in it.

Meyer's stress on localism and on the mental hospital as the coordinating center of mental hygiene activity in the surrounding community applied to his own work at the Phipps Clinic, which was to serve a region of Baltimore, and had its counterparts in two other types of institutions providing local social and health services. The first was the neighborhood settlement house, of which he had learned much from Jane Addams and Julia Lathrop, and the second, the health centers that had sprung up subsequent to the settlement houses and which in New York City were well under way during the years of his collaboration with Beers.[79] Meyer may also have yearned for the neat institutional structure of his native Switzerland, where mental hospitals were small and very much more integrated into the community than similar institutions in the United States.[80]

Clifford Beers shared Meyer's hopes for better care for mental patients but did not see himself as a quiet social worker. His models were neither the scientifically minded psychiatrists nor the compassionate social workers, but the captains of industry from whom he hoped to extract money. Just as these bold entrepreneurs had revolutionized and conquered the world of material production, he would revolutionize and conquer the mental health field, first in the United States and then throughout the world. Steeped as he was in the mundane details of recruiting members to the Connecticut Society, he never lost the vision that had come to him in the Hartford Retreat, and he never really assumed mere organization was the answer, especially as he had always hated humdrum office work. Once he set up an organization and got it running smoothly, the routine tasks could be left to others. He would be, first, the founder, the man who originated and brought to fruition a new idea, then the advisor, idea man, and trouble shooter. During the first phase he would be willing to do all or almost all the work, even the details. But not later. He wanted to turn his attention to the more important programmatic matters that only he would have the imagination and drive to initiate. Less rigid than Meyer and not usually as insistent on his own way, Beers was nevertheless almost as controlling in his determination and drive. Neither man was easy to know, but where Meyer was intimidating, Beers was approachable, if often exasperating.

Meyer gave his side of the controversy many years later in a private conversation:

> I was very busy with Beers, as long as I was able to stand it, and then . . . I broke loose. . . . I wanted him to train himself somewhat . . . instead of just being a collector of money, to learn something of what he wanted to get the money for. He hobnobbed with Chittenden and Blumer. We decided he ought to have his way. I told him I felt obliged to withdraw in case the thing could not be carried out, so that I felt the work should be on a foundation of knowledge and not merely of dreaming.[81]

Beers also later reminisced, but in drafts of speeches and therefore more circumspectly. The National Committee, he recalled, almost foundered in 1910 on the "rocks of an empty treasury" and the "pessimistic outlook" of those members who were disheartened and doubted its usefulness. There were, he wrote in a passage later deleted, several "sincere persons" who "could think only in terms of independent laboratories, scientific research and psychiatric training, without seeing the tremendous value of a centralizing and coordinating agency that could bring harmony and efficiency into the field and act as a powerful lever for public education in mental hygiene."[82] Beers was nonetheless aware of his own shortcomings. Speaking at Meyer's seventieth birthday dinner in 1937, he announced Meyer's appointment as honorary president of the National Committee and praised his "vision and courage" in endorsing *A Mind That Found Itself,* helping to launch the mental hygiene movement, and staying with it as long as he did. It was not easy, he acknowledged, for one whose methods of work were so "conservative and thoroughgoing" to collaborate with an aggressive, daring young man in a hurry to bring his plans to a head. As William James said, and Beers quoted him, it was a case of the "ox and the 'wild ass'" not being able to work together in double harness.[83] Less witty and more clinical commentators might say it was a classic clash between manic-depressive and obsessive-compulsive personalities.

✣ 11 ✣

Phipps "To the Rescue"

Clifford Beers no longer had to worry about what Meyer thought, but he determined that, by following a course similar to the one Meyer advocated, he would demonstrate that his resignation was unwarranted. So, although the Connecticut Society did hire a social worker (with the title of field secretary) to take over much of the aftercare work, Beers continued actively as executive secretary and also accepted an appointment to the Committee on Defectives of the Connecticut State Board of Charities.[1]

He received and replied to a steady stream of letters from former patients and their friends and other interested parties. Some told of terrible conditions and sought help in changing them; others asked advice and assistance in the care of friends and relatives. A few wanted Beers' opinion about establishing state mental hygiene societies, toward which Beers took a Meyerian wait-and-see position. In reply to an appeal from a physician who had read *A Mind That Found Itself* and wanted to enter the mental hygiene field, Beers suggested that he and his wife work as nurses or attendants in a state hospital, preferably in Connecticut, the advance guard of the movement. In time such people as they would be in great demand by the National Committee to serve as secretaries of field work for state societies of mental hygiene, but they must first make good as "nurses among the insane."[2] In dealing with calls for help from those with psychiatric problems, Beers worked with psychiatrists (including Meyer). He would suggest that such people either consult a particular psychiatrist or follow the advice that he would obtain for them from a psychiatrist.[3]

Beers' relationship with Meyer continued to obsess him. He especially felt the need to justify himself to Russell, who greatly respected Meyer and who was considering taking on the medical directorship of the National Committee, as well as to counteract any damage that Meyer's defection might do to the cause. Outsiders might consider it odd that the leading psychiatrist in the United States had bowed out of the National Committee, and there was no telling what Meyer might say. Beers therefore compiled a confidential, detailed record of his relations with Meyer, entitled "Troubles with Meyer,"

154

that ran to over eight hundred typed pages, a copy of which he sent to Russell. The handwritten version, entitled "Troubles with Dr. Meyer" was, he told Clara, his "supplementary Autobiography."[4] Except for a few important letters Beers had not seen and some portions of letters that revealed his role in Stokes', Blumer's, and Chittenden's responses to Meyer's letters, it contained copies of almost all the relevant correspondence and documents and added up to a persuasive case for Beers' position. Certainly Meyer, whose own records were in disarray, could not compete with Beers on this level, even if he had wanted to, which he evidently did not. Since Meyer never made any open moves against either Beers or the National Committee, Beers never showed his compilation to more than a very few people. The fact that he spent so much time on it, however, indicates how deeply the struggle with Meyer had affected him.

Beers was also busy organizing the third annual meeting of the National Committee, held in New York on January 28, 1911, which gave him a vote of confidence. Favill's resignation as president was accepted, as was Meyer's from the organization, the latter with regrets and thanks for all he had done and the wish that he "may continue to give us his cooperation and advice and at some early date join our forces officially again." This action Beers considered "extremely fortunate," as it opened the way for Meyer to reenter the committee in the future and give it counsel in the meantime. The group reaffirmed the objectives of the National Committee as adopted at the founding meeting and reelected Bancroft as vice-president with the presidency remaining vacant; Blumer was elected chairman of the executive committee, which included Hoch and Russell; and Chittenden retained the chairmanship of the finance committee, which included Favill.

Then, "to overcome the unfounded fear held at one time by a few members of the National Committee that its work might be launched on a national basis under lay leadership," it was voted unanimously to employ a medical director, "under whose leadership it is hoped that Mr. Beers's work may be continued." Beers was elected secretary at a salary of $3,000 a year beginning February 1, 1911, to serve until an active medical director was appointed. Then, with Beers absent from the room, the finance committee was directed to "secure if possible the sum of $5,000 in contributions given for the specific purpose to be presented to Mr. Beers in appreciation of his important and devoted services during the past four years in laying the essential foundations for the work of the Committee."[5]

Probably in preparation for this action, Stokes had asked Beers to explain his financial status. Altogether, Beers replied, he owed $8,000: $2,800 to George, $1,000 to Vic Tyler, $1,600 to two New Haven banks on notes endorsed by Tyler, and one "floating indebtedness" of $600. (What had happened in regard to James' $1,000 is not clear; it may be that upon his death the "debt" was cleared.) Beers estimated that if unpaid back salary and expenditures of his own were included, he had lost at least $22,400 to the cause.[6] On the basis of these figures, a gift of $5,000 would pay off most of his actual debts, and he felt satisfied, contrary to Russell's fear that he might not be. Beers so assured Hoch, who had succeeded to Meyer's place as director of the Psychiatric Institute on Ward's Island and also, it seems, to Meyer's role, along with Russell, as Beers' advisor and collaborator. Receiving a flat $5,000 was greatly preferable to having been voted $8,000 in back salary, which would have generated criticism, Beers said. Besides, the National Committee's obligation to him was entirely a moral one, which it had clearly recognized. The next step was for the executive committee to formulate a definite plan of work. He would be happy now to "follow 'leads' not make them" and would "find pleasure in awaiting orders and following them explicitly when given."[7]

Since Favill's successor as president had not been decided upon at the meeting, Beers again appealed to Welch, whose acceptance would help the committee raise money to hire Russell as medical director. The exceedingly busy Welch turned the job down, accepting instead one of the two vice-presidencies. Lewellys Barker, physician-in-chief at Johns Hopkins Hospital, Paton's brother-in-law, and an early supporter of Beers and convert to psychotherapy, then took the presidency.[8]

Beers felt gratified that Jane Addams had come to the meeting and thanked her for contributing to "re-establishing harmony in our organization." She, not being privy to what had been going on, found the meeting "somewhat bewildering," so that Beers had to fill her in. Meyer had, he said, "by conjuring up fears for the Committee's future, made a mountain out of a mole-hill," as shown by the fact that his intimate friends Hoch and Russell took responsibility as members of the executive committee for formulating a program that was in substance "the one originally suggested and advocated by Dr. Meyer."[9] Both Hoch and Russell, Beers told Julia Lathrop, felt that Meyer's resignation "was not warranted by the *facts* (though possibly by his temperament)" and that everything within reason had been done to keep him in. Stokes, also attempting to counter any impression that Meyer's withdrawal either reflected or portended the failure of the National Committee, described Meyer as "utterly lacking in executive ability" and as one under whose guidance the affairs of the National Committee had "languished."[10]

A sign to Beers that harmony had been restored and that he had been vindicated was Favill's presence at a joint meeting of the executive and finance committees, as well as Favill's work on the National Committee's "Forecast" and "Plan of Work."[11] These plans, as developed by Hoch and Russell, included a survey of mental institutions similar to Abraham Flexner's recent influential study of medical schools, with the aim of preparing a report on the care and treatment of the insane that would discuss public education, facilities for patients awaiting commitment, and methods of commitment, admission, and aftercare. The data gathered would make the National Committee's office a national clearinghouse for information on insanity.[12]

Although he was involved in program planning, Beers' primary activity was searching for funds. Several prominent men, including Welch, gave him letters of introduction to philanthropists and endorsed the National Committee's proposed activities.[13] Phipps gave the first contribution, $1,000, not to the National Committee but to the $5,000 fund for Beers. Stokes advised Beers to send a *"brief"* note of thanks and to remember that Phipps spoke of having been deluged with printed matter and statements from Beers in the past.[14] Because the onset of summer would make it difficult to raise money, Phipps was then asked to lend the National Committee $4,000. Meanwhile Professor Morris Loeb, president of the New York Foundation and a member of the National Committee, was persuaded to grant $3,000 for Beers' 1911 salary. A few days later Phipps lent the National Committee $1,000 to give Beers; if it could not raise the balance, he told Chittenden, "let me hear from you." Beers gave the money to his father. That Phipps felt kindly toward Beers is also indicated by his offer of a copy of Vallery-Radot's *Life of Pasteur,* which he had had privately printed in a small edition.[15]

Money for the National Committee was more difficult to find. Beers still hoped, through Gates, to interest Rockefeller, who had never officially turned down the original appeal. But Gates refused to give him an interview: the regular procedure of submitting a written request for Rockefeller funds had to be followed.[16]

Beers had no time to be disappointed. The next day he heard from Welch news that gave him, he recalled later, "the greatest thrill of my life."[17] Welch thought he could convince Phipps to give $50,000 to the National Committee. Welch needed a statement of its purposes, its plan of organization, and the results that could reasonably be expected from its work, "especially along the lines of amelioration of the condition of the insane," in which Phipps was interested. Rockefeller was not in the mood to give to any new philanthropy, so that an interview with him, which Welch could probably get for Beers, would not do much good. (Rockefeller's attitude at this time may have been influenced by public criticism of him and by the federal government's antitrust action against his Standard Oil Company of New Jersey.) In composing an appeal to Phipps, Welch advised Beers to consult Stokes and Chittenden; with their advice, plus Blumer's, Beers, Hoch, and Russell wrote a letter containing the information Welch suggested. Welch also received specific assurance from Russell that the National Committee was the best organization to receive Phipps' donation.[18]

Beers was concerned about what Meyer might say. He could not conceive that Meyer would oppose the Phipps gift and the National Committee's plan, since, he told Welch, "I know the purpose in view is one he originally approved of," but if so, Beers wanted to know it. Evidently there was nothing to worry about; Meyer had decided to keep out of the National Committee's business altogether. Welch urged Beers not to be impatient and assured him that the money would be forthcoming, probably in ten to twenty days.[19]

With the Phipps fund in view, preliminary work was begun on the survey of the conditions of the mentally ill. John Koren, editor for the American Statistical Association and a Bureau of the Census expert in charge of, among other things, statistics on the insane, volunteered to compile a summary of the laws governing commitment and care of the insane in the various states. Beers accepted this offer, with the promise that the National Committee would publish the results, which it did in 1912.[20]

Soon thereafter Phipps gave $50,000 to the National Committee for surveys and offered an endowment for the same amount, provided an additional $200,000 was raised within the next two to three years.[21] A few days later Phipps invited Beers for an automobile trip with him[22] and, a week later, to lunch at the Metropolitan Club, where he said he did not want his gift made public, because it would prevent others from contributing. He expressed his conviction that Beers was embarked on a "noble career" for which he should be relieved of all worry and burdens. "Make other people work for you, whenever you can. That's the secret of success." On the way from the club to Phipps' home, where Beers met Mrs. Phipps, Phipps warned him to be careful—"Your life means too much to the cause"—and insisted, over Beers' demur, on discussing his debts. "Why not. . . . That's why I invited you to call upon me." Then, Beers later told Clara, "Mr. Phipps, as a result of what I suggested he might call a 'spontaneous pecuniary combustion,' insisted upon giving me a check for $5,000 to use as I please —a check given 'to the man,' 'not to the organization.'"[23]

Beers could now pay his debts, with special thanks to George and Louise Beers and Vic Tyler, all of whom had supported him for years, but he kept the source of his windfall secret even from George. As he explained to Mrs. William James, in whom he was wont to confide, "I have reason for desiring to have it appear I am still in debt, because $3,000 is still due me from the National Committee under its vote of Jan. 1st." Feeling that the National Committee had a moral obligation toward him and assured that Phipps' check was a personal one, Beers feared that the committee would not pay him the remaining $3,000 if his newfound solvency became known. Upon Beers' request, Welch approached Gates for the $3,000 and got $1,000; Phipps then converted his original loan of $1,000 to an outright gift. Altogether, by the spring of 1912 Beers had received enough money to pay all his debtors. The outstanding $2,000 out of the $5,000 pledged to him by the National Committee would therefore, when paid, constitute an asset. Not until the end of June, six months after the fact, did he divulge to the National Committee that Phipps had privately given him $5,000.[24]

‡

Now that he had a salary from the National Committee, Beers could forgo one at the Connecticut Society, for which he remained executive secretary without pay. To finance its work he got eight guarantors to make up any deficits incurred from October 1, 1911, to October 1, 1913; seven of the eight also gave three hundred dollars each for the current year's work. This money, plus the thousand dollars that dues brought in, seemed to secure the organization for a while at least.[25] Relations between the Connecticut Society and the hospitals developed in the direction Meyer had advocated, so much so that Beers protested that the social worker was giving all her time to the Yale-affiliated New Haven Hospital. There had been no objection to her organizing a social service department there, but when the hospital asked for her services for several more months Beers refused.[26] At the same time, at the request of George Blumer, then president of the Connecticut Society, he compiled an outline of the activities of a social service worker. The list emphasized that administrative duties and other obligations be reduced to a minimum in favor of attention to actual casework.[27] So successful was the society's social worker that Beers concluded that such a person could "do more to help the average prospective patient than . . . the general practitioner lacking specialized experience. Timely advice given by social workers will save many people from mental collapse.[28]

Unfortunately the Connecticut Society's solvency did not last beyond 1913, when lack of funds forced the social worker to resign, and Blumer would not hire a successor until existing debts were cleared and funds for at least the next three years were assured. Possibly the headquarters could be moved to the New Haven Dispensary, which offered the additional advantage of close contact with the visiting nurses and patients who needed advice. Apparently Beers must have raised the money, for several months later (December 1913) a new field secretary, Miss V. M. MacDonald, was in the office.[29]

By then he had been easing out of work for the Connecticut Society. When the National Committee began in 1912 to claim his full time, he commuted to New York City daily from New Haven, so that he could not see people who sought his advice through the Connecticut Society. When he finally moved to New York in 1914 he surrendered his position in Connecticut to a Mrs. Dragget, who in his view made a success of the society.[30] Several years later he anticipated with pleasure going to mental hygiene meetings at which representatives of his "little Connecticut baby" were to speak in public "without 'papa's' bossing the affair."[31] His interest in the Connecticut Society had little of the intensity inspired by the National Committee. As long as the Connecticut Society did its work reasonably well he could keep hands off; if not, it must expect to hear from him.

Beers also found himself launched in an activity that he had previously avoided, public speaking. Although an effective talker on a one-to-one basis or at a small meeting, he had felt that his forte in communicating with a large public was writing. He made his first public appearance, at the National Conference on Charities and Corrections in St. Louis in 1910, only on Julia Lathrop's urging. In 1912 she again asked him to speak, this time before the newly organized Illinois Society for Mental Hygiene. Years later he confessed that this early speech-making was "the most painful experience of my normal life (I might as well use the phrase). I was in terror of my first speeches," especially when they had been prepared in advance. One way to conquer his fear was to talk extemporaneously, so that he claimed later that he could never write a speech.[32] From all accounts his oratory was successful. If he was not quite so eloquent and witty on the podium as on paper, his dynamism and charm lent his remarks a persuasive force that was hard to resist.

In Chicago in 1912 he did read from a written text that gave a modest, realistic evaluation of his role as founder of the National Committee. Although he did not know it at the time, he said, he now felt obliged to admit that his idea was not new, that he had subsequently learned that a similar society had existed from 1881 to 1883, the National Association for the Protection of the Insane. He claimed not originality of concept but the ability to crystallize an existing interest and to focus it in such a way as to "produce tangible and lasting results." Organizing a society on paper was easy; the hard part was to formulate a plan of activities. As he saw it, his job was that of "politely pestering the professionals until they had committed their thoughts to paper and reread them, and the thoughts of others, often enough to accept all as their own."—no mean achievement when working with the "ultra-cautious class of physicians known as psychiatrists."[33]

‡

By February 1912 the National Committee was based in New York, and Beers wrote his "first long-hand letter" on its new stationery to Clara Jepson. "Four years and three months from the first acceptance of membership—Mr. James's—to this happy day, with the organization completed, an office all but opened in New York, 'under medical direction,' and $50,000 in the treasury, more promised, and almost no personal debts standing between us and our heart's desire!"[34] Finally they could marry. Clifford wrote of their four years' courtship as a beautiful experience that enabled them to know each other better than most couples did before marriage: "I think, dear, we have managed a difficult matter with great skill. To love and be loved, to have laid the foundation for a career, for two careers, to have won a complete vindication, all at so early an age as ours is no small achievement. The future is assured and safe and will bring us increased happiness." Theirs had been "a real romance—one which a great writer might easily weave into a story of unsurpassing interest."[35]

All the same, the waiting had not been easy. Such a long engagement would have been an ordeal for almost any couple at that time (even at their ages they had to think about taking a chaperone along on a trip). In this case there was the added burden of keeping the relationship secret from Clifford's professional colleagues at the same time as his drive for a salary and settlement of his debts came in great part from his wish to marry. Then there was the anxiety created by his brother Carl's illness, by George's "nervousness," and by the reluctance of Clara's father to give her up. And Clara had to listen to Clifford's troubles and face besides "criticism and gossipers" on account of her relationship with a man with nothing to give her but hopes.[36]

As Clifford realized, it took a good deal of courage and faith for Clara to attach herself to him. Her family and friends, as well as she herself, were conventional and her father possessive. Apart from a European tour during 1902-1903 with a female companion and then her brother Harry and his wife —during which she picked up a knowledge of French and an acquaintance with Italian that would stand Clifford in good stead in their later travels and overseas correspondence—she stayed mainly at home in New Haven, sheltered and doted upon by adoring parents. She was also, in the mode of many young women of her generation and class, "delicate," suffering from "stomach" and "nerves." Clifford was always talking about protecting her, from what dangers it is not clear, since throughout her long life she exhibited a hardiness that belied her so-called frailty. Even during their courtship Clifford found her health delicate but her stamina extraordinary.[37] A photograph taken during Clara's European tour shows a small, slim, dark-haired, self-confident, stylishly dressed, handsome young woman.[38] Clifford thought she had every quality he could ever want—beauty, intelligence, sensitivity, stability, judgment, courage, charm—all of which he extolled in many effusive letters.

Clara Jepson did not accept her position at home without a struggle, albeit mostly an inward one. From the time she was in college she had wanted independence, but not until she developed a relationship with Clifford Beers did she achieve a measure of it, and then only under her father's eye. She was caught between two worlds. "You can't realize," she wrote, "how a girl brought up as I was must necessarily submit entirely to those in authority. Nor how hard it was for her to follow the dictates of her own mind. College taught me such a different point of view and gave me the courage of my convictions but even now that I am a woman grown, I have to fight many times to be allowed to manage my own personal affairs. I suppose it is the English idea of absolute obedience which doesn't accord with the American idea of independence."[39]

Clara's relationship with Beers grew slowly, with hesitation to commit herself and concern for what her father would say. Described in later years as "reserved, self-effacing and gifted,"[40] Clara apparently found it difficult to put her feelings on paper, however strongly urged by her faithful correspondent, Clifford, or "K," as he often signed himself. This reluctance to express herself to a man may account for the absence of a substantial body of letters from Clara in reply to Clifford's outpourings, often written just after he had seen her.[41] But she wanted him to be more affectionate, and under Clara's prodding his letters became quite ardent, especially as the years went by and they were still not married. He sent her flowers (usually violets), valentines, a hair from her head that he had found and tied into a love knot.[42]

Clifford Beers attributed all his success, real and hoped for, to Clara. She edited at least some of the documents he was working on before their marriage and in one case reworked some of Meyer's suggestions for the Rockefeller appeal; Clifford frequently asked her opinion. Many years later she said that she seldom interfered with his work and then only in matters of health, not policy. However, during the struggle to get the Connecticut Society and the National Committee going, Clifford continually spoke of the value of her advice. Her interest and help were "all the moral support I need to keep me at my task. With you behind me — or beside me, I feel that I could defy the whole world — if there were need of doing so."[43] Clara, much as his secretaries did later, acted as the sounding board Clifford needed.

Something of the formal Victorian quality of their relationship, as well as Clifford's feelings of insecurity in relation to Clara, is indicated in an affectionate letter from him during the summer of 1911: "I don't think you know how many satisfactory statements you made this morning . . . how many uncertainties you did away with. To be told that you would have sent for me during your illness had your condition been so serious as to warrant doing so is a comforting, if tragic thought." Should either of them die before "we reach a definite understanding — an engagement — the survivor shall be considered as having been engaged to marry the other." Clara, touched, felt herself "fortunate . . . to have such a lover, one especially who can express what he feels." She had to scheme to meet him privately so they could kiss; her father might not allow her to walk down a wood path alone to meet him, it was too dangerous (by then she was thirty-six years old).[44]

By this time Clara's mother, who had been sympathetic to Clifford, had died and he had to contend with the domineering Benjamin Jepson, whose "one great consolation" was having his "little Clara to lean upon."[45] After the National Committee was established in New York and Clifford's salary assured and his debts paid, it was a "unique proposal" made by Jepson that, according to Clifford, "proved to be the element needed to precipitate action," that is, finally to plan the wedding. What may have been involved was that the couple make their home with him, which they did until his death in 1914, which left Clara with a "reasonable income."[46]

Clara and Clifford W. Beers.

They were married in New Haven on June 26, 1912, and left for Boston and then Maine for their honeymoon. On the wedding day Beers announced his marriage to Phipps and several other friends on the National Committee and, three days later, to Mrs. James. In all these letters he explained why he had not revealed his engagement and noted that although he had sought no advice about marrying, he felt gratified that his psychiatrist friends believed it was "the very best thing for me to do." He had won "not only a wife, but a companion and helpmate whose qualities of heart and mind are recognized by all who know her."[47]

One crucial issue on which Clifford and Clara Beers agreed was not to have children, a consideration that may have eased the long wait to be married and may also have helped to pacify her father. Clifford felt strongly that, because of the mental illness in his family, all the Beers brothers must remain childless, to the point where he reproached his brother William for fathering a child.[48] This conviction contradicted his belief that mental illness could be prevented, a cornerstone of his movement; but he realized that prevention was not a sure thing and believed that it did not in any case preclude hereditary predispositions. Not one Beers brother had escaped "nervous" troubles. As of 1912 Sam had died of a neurological ailment and two others, Clifford and Carl, had had serious breakdowns from which Carl showed little sign of recovering. Why take chances with future generations? Therefore, Clara and Clifford never had children, never wanted them, and seemed to live happily together for many years. Throughout his marriage Clifford remained as tender and grateful to Clara as when he courted her those four long years.[49]

✣ 12 ✣

The National Committee in Action:
The Salmon Years, First Phase

William James had said that *A Mind That Found Itself* could be considered a success if Clifford Beers managed to found a permanent national mental health organization within five years of its publication. Beers had done it in four. He could look forward to a new life as a married man and as a paid official of a national organization backed by money and prestige. The job now was to accomplish its goals, and for this a medical director must be found. The position was not especially attractive. The National Committee had only enough money to pay someone for a few years, the program had to be organized almost from scratch, and, although the officers and members were professionally and socially preeminent, the work was in a field still having to establish its respectability among many physicians and the lay public. Of course, these very conditions offered a challenge for someone who was either in an uncertain position himself or wanted to strike out on new and uncertain trails, or both.

Russell, who declined the job because of the National Committee's still shaky future and his own better prospects as a hospital superintendent, suggested another candidate.[1] This was Dr. Thomas W. Salmon, originally considered as a statistical consultant.[2] He was approved by the National Committee and Clifford Beers and began work in March 1912.

Beers' new collaborator was his contemporary, with a personality quite different from Meyer's but in its own way as complex. Moody, sickly, sensitive, yet cheerful, optimistic, and athletic, Salmon had a deep concern for mental patients and a capacity for unending work in their behalf. This commitment, together with wit, informality, and impatience with red tape, routine methods, and smug superiors, was bound to appeal to Clifford Beers. In his crusading zeal and rebelliousness against hypocrisy and conventional wisdom, Salmon outmatched Beers. Yet in some basic ways he was quite different: his nature was retiring, his persuasive technique gentle, his demeanor modest and self-effacing. And he was something of an eccentric, which Beers really was not. Salmon had no money sense, he was absent-minded, hated punctuality, was careless about his dress, and procrastinated end-

165

lessly. At the same time, he had a great fund of common sense as well as both vision and the ability to do systematic scientific and statistical work.

Salmon's career had been undistinguished. He had had, like Clifford Beers, a tortuous road to travel: illness and death in his family, financial troubles, his own physical illnesses, a large family to support on a meager income, inability to cope with the practical demands of medical practice, and the frustration of dealing with bureaucratic officials resistant to change. The job with the National Committee gave Salmon the chance finally to come into his own.[3]

He had entered psychiatry by accident and without any special training. A financial failure as a young general practitioner, he joined the New York State Health Department as a bacteriologist. His investigation of a diphtheria epidemic at Willard State Hospital in 1901 so impressed his superiors that they appointed him bacteriologist for all the New York State mental hospitals. At Willard State he met Russell, who brought him into staff psychiatric conferences and discussions. In 1904, after becoming an officer in the U.S. Public Health Service, he was assigned to give psychiatric examinations to the thousands of immigrants, most of them from eastern and southern Europe, pouring into the port of New York. Shocked by the conditions he found, Salmon tried to improve the facilities for mentally ill immigrants, but his superiors disapproved and punished him by transfer to the Marine Hospital in Boston. In 1911 he took a leave of absence to work as chief medical examiner of the Board of Alienists of the New York State Commission in Lunacy; he was to study foreign-born patients in the state hospitals. He made the first graphic statistical charts the state hospitals ever had and devised a uniform system of reporting admissions and discharges that the National Committee for Mental Health and the American Psychiatric Association later adopted nationwide. He got into trouble again by trying to help mentally ill immigrants, who, upon discovery of their disorder, would be returned to their native country in the worst ships' quarters and, because the authorities and relatives back home were not informed of their arrival, were abandoned at the debarkation point. Eventually these conditions were ameliorated through the agitation of Salmon and others.

Salmon's motives were not only humanitarian. Drawing unwarranted conclusions from statistics, he maintained that there was a greater frequency of mental disorder, especially the incurable varieties, among the "new" immigrants from southern and eastern Europe than the "old" (a position commonly held half a century earlier by many leading hospital superintendents in relation to an earlier "new" mass of immigrants, the Irish Catholics).[4] Salmon, a leading physician said at his death, was "a bulwark against the rising flood of guests who were already, to his discerning eye, unfit to share in the social privileges of our country." His biographer, the eminent psychiatrist

Earl D. Bond, commented similarly on Salmon's efforts to effect better control over the entrance of immigrants.[5]

Salmon's "distinctly alarmist and, at times, racist" stance on immigration[6] would not disqualify him from working for the National Committee. Clifford Beers considered him a "humanitarian at heart and every minute of the day."[7] Most National Committee members, mainly highly placed white Anglo-Saxon Protestants with a scattering of upper-class Irish Catholics and upper-class Jews of German origin and only a few people like Addams, Lathrop, and Riis with liberal social views, probably shared Salmon's attitude, if not his intense conviction. This was the heyday of a new nativism in reaction to the "new" immigrants from cultures considered alien to the Anglo-Saxon model. If all the southern and eastern European peasants and Russian and Polish Jews could not be kept out—and there were efforts to do so—the "worst" of them could be: under amendments to the 1907 Immigration Restriction Act, immigrants afflicted with the so-called social disease of anarchism or with physical and mental diseases, along with criminals and paupers, could be refused admission into the United States.

The first formal step taken by the National Committee's executive committee after Salmon's arrival in March 1912 was to pass a resolution, at his request, urging Congress to enact legislation requiring that mental examination of entering immigrants be conducted by physicians trained to diagnose mental illness. This step could be seen as advantageous to the immigrants themselves, allowing them the benefit of professional judgment of their mental condition; another purpose was to have the law work more effectively in screening out undesirables. The National Committee's position was at the time moderate, as was that taken later in relation to eugenics: it eschewed the extremist call for sterilization of "inferior" persons—the insane, the criminal, the vicious, and the mentally defective—but did favor intervention to limit reproduction by the mentally defective. At the same time, clearly influenced by and in some ways actually a part of the liberal social work movement during the Progressive Era, the National Committee did endorse reforms that would reduce stress upon the poor: "sanitary factory conditions, wholesome foods, tenement inspection, child labor laws, juvenile courts, and special provisions to enable pregnant and nursing women to remain at home."[8] These social-political questions were not, however, a major preoccupation of the National Committee and certainly not of Clifford Beers, who went along with the official positions taken on them during the Salmon years and who was for a time busy mainly with the organizational and fund-raising aspects of the work.

Because there were no funds for his salary for more than two years, Salmon was not given the title of medical director; instead he was called director of special studies. At the same time, he remained officially with the

Public Health Service, which extended his leave of absence until the end of 1913.[9] He remained as director of special studies through 1914, and then as medical director from 1915 until he went on leave to the army in 1917, returning in 1919 and serving until 1922.

‡

Clifford Beers founded the National Committee, put it on its feet, and kept it there; Thomas Salmon got it moving. In Beers' words, Salmon placed the organization and the entire movement "on a sound and scientific basis,"[10] and it was largely regard for Salmon that finally interested the Rockefeller Foundation in the National Committee's work. During his first five years from 1912 to 1917, the National Committee was mainly concerned with collecting statistics and other information about the incidence of mental disorders and mental deficiency, determining the status of legislation relating to mental disorder and the mentally ill, and, by means of surveys and other studies, investigating the condition of the insane in various institutions. Some work was also done to inform the public about these conditions and to enlist support for programs to improve them, mainly through the surveys and studies.[11]

Like Meyer, Salmon doubted the wisdom of the National Committee's beginning its work with a popular campaign to prevent mental illness. The subject, he said later, "could hardly be discussed because of the prejudice and misinformation that were so general. What needed to be done was to educate the public toward a better attitude which the growth of humanitarian ideals was fostering in other fields. To this end surveys were undertaken to determine the actual conditions of the mentally ill."[12] This work, which carried out the plans formulated by Russell, Hoch, and Beers in 1911, seemed to be a judicious course for the National Committee. Actually it took a certain amount of courage, as psychiatrists both within and outside the organization worried that an investigation of the status of the insane might take on a muckraking character.[13] Even the very respectable Flexner report on medical education, which the National Committee leaders regarded as a model, had made quite a few medical school administrators unhappy. Salmon and the National Committee, convinced that their first obligation was to help the insane poor by investigating and reporting their condition, went ahead notwithstanding, the first survey being a report on the "Wisconsin System" in which inmates lived in "cottages" instead of very large buildings. As a result of this and of Salmon's survey of all Wisconsin mental institutions and of state legislation affecting the mentally ill, the Wisconsin Board of Control adopted several of his recommendations and the University of Wisconsin appointed a professor of psychiatry to direct the scientific work of all state hospitals for the insane in Wisconsin and to initiate mental hygiene extension activities in the university.

Other surveys followed, including a census of public mental institutions in the United States, which turned up 21 percent more institutions than were known by the Bureau of the Census. The most significant consequence of these surveys was to convince many states to eliminate dual systems of state and local care of the mentally ill in favor of total state control. In some cases the surveys led to reforms: new institutions were built and methods of treatment improved. A survey of South Carolina, for example, revealed such horrible conditions that the General Assembly voted six hundred thousand dollars in 1915 to reconstruct state hospitals and drafted more humane legislation relating to the mentally ill. The Texas survey prompted legislation to establish modern scientific psychopathic hospitals and to provide for the removal of the mentally ill from almshouses and jails to hospitals. (Nevertheless, by 1930 five states still used jails and almshouses for the insane.)

In 1915, in response to requests from state officials, the surveys were expanded to include the "feebleminded," and the Rockefeller Foundation began its support for such work, which included surveys of the incidence of mental deficiency in Nassau County (New York), Connecticut, Georgia, Louisiana, Pennsylvania, Indiana, Colorado, California, and the cities of Scranton and New York, and the pioneering clinical study by Dr. Bernard Glueck of the psychopathology of crime at Sing Sing Prison.

Some of the National Committee's activities were carried out in collaboration with other groups, partly because it did not have the resources to work independently. For example, the Children's Bureau of the U.S. Department of Labor, newly established under Julia Lathrop, agreed to print and distribute many of the committee's pamphlets. *Survey Magazine* submitted to the committee for revision or editing all manuscripts bearing on mental hygiene; the *Journal of the American Medical Association* referred to it for reply all inquiries received on the subject; and *Modern Hospital* requested the committee to conduct a "Department of Mental Hygiene" in its pages.

As its founders had hoped, the committee influenced medical schools to provide some psychiatric education for their students. In 1915 Harvard Medical School gave a course in mental hygiene for public health officers, and the medical school of New York University did the same in its general curriculum. There also appeared at this time three important medical textbooks that included chapters on mental hygiene.

However, as the work of the National Committee evolved, it soon became apparent that these limited educational changes were not enough. Under Salmon's influence and despite his interest in the institutional surveys, there was a shift in the National Committee from concentration on hospital care to interest in the psychological aspects of the environment in schools and penal institutions. The committee came gradually to focus on outpatient services in special clinics and on programs of prevention, diagnosis, and treatment in various community social agencies. This was the first time reform efforts were carried beyond the walls of hospitals and systematic attempts were made to apply theories of mental health and disease to people in a variety of social institutions. As a result there was a shortage of psychiatrists qualified to do such work, since most had been trained to deal with the severe mental disorders requiring hospitalization. In order to increase the number of specialists working with nonhospitalized and less serious cases, the National Committee proposed and eventually received funds to create training fellowships.

Clifford Beers' goal of having the National Committee serve as a clearinghouse for information was realized in various ways. A summary of laws of various states was compiled and published, the nucleus of a library was established, and then the National Committee began issuing a widely used annotated bibliography of mental hygiene. To answer requests for help from former patients and their relatives, the staff compiled lists of various institutions, commitment laws, facilities for treatment, and names of psychiatrists throughout the country.

To bring its information to the attention of the public, lay and professional, the National Committee started an educational campaign. Articles were placed in leading magazines, and Salmon and others lectured all over the country. Over ninety thousand copies of four articles on mental hygiene were printed and distributed to physicians, nurses, and relatives of mental patients. In 1917 the National Committee's own periodical, *Mental Hygiene,* was created to disseminate information and news to both physicians and lay people; it immediately became the standard journal in the field. An exhibit was created that utilized Salmon's interest in statistics and graphs as well as his persuasive writing and artistic talents to tell the story of mental illness. It was shown in many cities and at numerous meetings. The International Congress on Hygiene and Democracy set up a special "Subcommittee on Mental Hygiene"; this action, together with recognition from the American Medical Association and the American Medico-Psychological Association (later the American Psychiatric Association), gave scientific standing to the National Committee. Along with Salmon, the committee was also credited with helping to launch a movement to form a department or division of mental hygiene in the U.S. Public Health Service.[14]

These varied activities made the National Committee the chief agency for creating psychiatric awareness in the United States and for promoting the new field of social psychiatry and the notion of mental health. It had yet to develop, in William Alanson White's words, a "comprehensive program, an adequate statement of principles scientifically founded and practically workable," mainly because no one had yet defined such principles. Propelled by faith and working pragmatically, the movement was able fairly quickly to place mental hygiene as a medical and social goal on a firm footing, a considerable accomplishment.[15]

‡

All this took money, and Phipps' gift was only a start. Funds had to be found to ensure Salmon's salary and to underwrite long-range activities. This was mainly Beers' job, along with arranging meetings, keeping minutes, attending to various routine matters, and organizing local societies for mental hygiene. The officers of the National Committee, as well as Salmon, helped Beers by writing letters and appeals, seeing certain prospects (like the Rockefeller Foundation people), and furnishing leads and introductions. They all assumed that it would take approximately a decade to prove the value of the National Committee to the community, which would then finance the work through public subscriptions. In order to achieve such results, financial stability from private sources must first be achieved, and this became Beers' responsibility. He also spoke occasionally about his work before various groups, such as a mental hygiene conference in 1913 at Raleigh, North Carolina, or the Fifth Annual Conference of Charities and Corrections,[16] and attended meetings of the American Medico-Psychological Association. He traveled considerably, usually without Clara. Notices of his activities continued to appear in newspapers and magazines, including his picture in *Every Week* among a group of "Men Who Started Wrong." What he thought about being in the company of pugilist John L. Sullivan, novelist R. W. Chambers, editor George Lorimer, revivalist Billy Sunday, and a former train robber turned politician is not known.[17]

He kept up his friendships and his connection with Yale and his former classmates, and, though little is known about his personal life at that time, he apparently maintained his family ties, especially with George and Louise Beers. The Beers family continued to be afflicted by mental illness. Not only was there little improvement in Carl, by then at Bloomingdale Hospital in New York, but now William was displaying signs of a breakdown. According to friends this was too much for their mother, Ida Beers, who "lost initiative and gave up to her worries" about her four troubled sons. She died in 1914 at the age of seventy-one. Ninety-year-old Robert Beers followed his wife to the grave two years later.[18]

An incident involving Carl Beers indicates how Clifford had changed under the tutelage of his psychiatric colleagues and the exigencies of the movement they had started together. On January 16, 1913, the *New Haven Evening Register* reported that Clifford Beers intended to "sue 'both civilly and criminally' the management of the Bloomingdale Hospital because of abuse visited upon [Carl Beers] by attendants." This story was both untrue and embarrassing, because Clifford Beers' good friend Dr. Russell was now medical director of that hospital. Beers immediately informed him that the report was a fabrication from beginning to end, and he also sent a denial to the *Register*'s editor, with the demand that it be printed in its entirety. Ironically, the same day the newspaper story appeared, Beers had given an interview to its source, a former attendant at Bloomingdale, and convinced him to drop his campaign of exposure on the grounds that it would be an ineffective means of reform.[19]

Not only did Beers fear to threaten his good relations with Russell and other hospital men, but he did not want such a prestigious institution as Bloomingdale put in a bad light through airing of charges that he felt were exaggerated if not false. It would harm the movement, in which hospital men like Russell were so prominent. By depending upon the medical establishment, Beers had joined it. Instead of investigating directly or initiating a quiet inquiry into conditions at Bloomingdale, which after all was no more esteemed than the Hartford Retreat where he himself had suffered, he hushed up the matter. Through his alliance with the hospital physicians and other "important" people whose help he had needed and whose friendship he enjoyed, he had put himself in the position of soft-pedaling if not actually abandoning at least some aspects of the cause for the good of the cause.

And the cause (or at least the National Committee) seemed to need money more than anything, certainly more than bad publicity for one of its leaders. The problem was twofold. Beers felt that they key objective was to obtain an endowment to provide a stable income for operating expenses. Foundation officials, however, did not want to ensure the life of an organization independent of the quality of its work and therefore preferred to support special projects or furnish seed money for programs that would eventually be self-supporting or taken over by local, state, or federal agencies. In 1915 the new Rockefeller Foundation, object of endless hopes and efforts of Beers and his friends, began to give the National Committee grants for special surveys and other projects but would not supply funds for an endowment or for general operating expenses (a policy that gave the foundation a measure of control over the committee's work). But the more a foundation gave earmarked funds, the more dollars must be raised for administrative and routine activities, so that Beers would be distracted from the search for an endowment to the pursuit of gifts to meet the current operating budget, which by 1915, when the Phipps money ran out, had grown to forty thousand dollars a year.

For more or less routine contributions he would send a form letter to prospective donors, along with a copy of his book and other literature; the recipients would be asked to give anywhere from a hundred to a thousand dollars.[20] Certain people were also seen in person. Beers would approach anyone he knew or had access to. His former employer J. Hoggson, for example, gave a hundred dollars after a forty-five-minute interview[21] and was later made a member of the National Committee's finance committee. Much attention was given to reaching the wealthiest men and women, especially the women (who tended to be more interested in social-work-oriented philanthropies), which meant keeping track of family fortunes and of any possible special interest heirs and heiresses might have in medicine, social work, psychiatry, or mental illness.

Although Beers would seek out any wealthy person, he thought his chances greatly improved if, as was common in most extended families, some member had a mental problem. With his psychiatric connections, such knowledge almost inevitably came to him. It was not that his medical friends deliberately gave him hints, although that cannot be ruled out. Rather, as the National Committee became the central agency for psychiatric reform in the United States, few prominent members of the profession failed to come to its offices or attend its annual meetings or other functions, and however carefully they protected their patients' identities, the fact that a member of a rich family was under psychiatric treatment became known. If Beers found out, he might use the information, but discreetly. He spoke freely about his own mental illness, but he respected the reluctance of most people to reveal its existence in their families.

He tried not to approach prospective big donors cold. Before asking for an interview he would send them his book. Then because he knew that these people, prey to all sorts of solicitations, were difficult to reach, he would try first to enlist as an intermediary someone well known to them, often a member of the National Committee. In some cases it took months and even years to make the necessary contacts. It also took a lot out of Beers, whose intense talks with donors drained even his abundant energy. And though he enjoyed hunting for big game, as he put it, and loved being in his quarry's company, it was not without a subtle feeling of disdain that he did so. He copied in his notebook for 1915 a quotation from Charles Lamb: "The aristocracy of the future will not be that of wealth and social position but that of usefulness. The rich man and the highborn man will make way for the man who does something for his country and his fellow man."[22]

Sometimes prospective donors checked up on Beers. For example, in the spring of 1914 the private secretary to Julius Rosenwald, president of Sears, Roebuck & Company and a philanthropist, asked William A. White his confidential opinion of Beers, who was to have an interview with Rosenwald. White, who had met Beers just the previous summer, was "very greatly impressed, not only with the earnestness of the man and with his ability, but with his substantial sanity. His ideas are clear, well formulated, eminently practical and sane, and in my opinion you need not have the slightest hesitation in . . . accepting at face value what he tells you." It was through his energy alone that the Connecticut Society for Mental Hygiene was formed and that subsequently the National Committee, which was doing excellent work under Salmon, "was put aright." Beers was giving himself "without stint" to the cause, and White thought that "hospital superintendents and charitable organizations throughout this country ought to welcome him and help him in every way."[23] This recommendation apparently did not move Rosenwald to give the National Committee money, but White in time became Beers' good friend.

Another millionaire whom Beers stalked was the new automobile tycoon, Henry Ford. Although not as committed to philanthropy as Carnegie or Rockefeller, Ford had shown interest in medical causes in his gift to the Detroit General Hospital (later the Henry Ford Hospital). The way to him was through his wife, who asked Beers to communicate first with the family pastor and intimate friend, Dr. Samuel S. Marquis, dean of St. Paul's Cathedral in Detroit and a man much interested in social questions. Encouraged by Marquis, Beers composed a twenty-one page exposition of the situation of the National Committee that may have been written while he was somewhat excited.[24]

There was a real urgency. The time, December 1913, was critical for the National Committee, as he explained to Marquis. It had only enough funds to carry on for another year. Worse yet, it might lose Salmon, whose leave of absence from the Public Health Service was due to expire. Since there was a moral obligation to use the remaining money for work in the field, not for operating expenses, where would Salmon's salary come from? The committee had counted on Rockefeller money, but the only offer finally received from the Rockefeller Foundation was to put Salmon on its own payroll and lend him to the National Committee on a temporary basis, contingent on an annual evaluation of the arrangement, a proposition that both Salmon and the National Committee rejected. The organization badly needed a guaranteed income for at least ten years. Phipps' offer of an endowment if matching funds were raised had lapsed through failure to secure such funds; Phipps was too old and sick to be approached again, and his sons were not good prospects, their father having "exhausted all the philanthropic impulses of the family."[25]

Marquis was impressed enough to obtain for Beers an interview with Mrs. Ford in the family home in Detroit. Beers described the experience in a thirteen-page letter to Clara. He spent longer than planned, about two hours, with Mrs. Ford, who had read *A Mind That Found Itself;* she found it "'intensely interesting' and expressed her desire to help." Young Edsel Ford joined his mother in listening to Beers, who by then was going on at "full tilt" about his struggles as a pioneer in mental hygiene. As he had hoped, Mrs. Ford saw an analogy between Beers' experiences and her husband's difficulties in raising capital for the Ford Motor Company, and she also confided that as the wife of a man with a "big and absorbing idea . . .

she scarcely knew she had a husband." His wife felt the same, confessed Beers, trying to create a "bond of sympathy" between Mrs. Ford and Clara Beers. Then, acting upon Marquis' suggestion, he appealed to the Fords' sense of rivalry with the Rockefellers—a technique he would often use when dealing with the very rich. The Rockefeller Foundation, he said, was trying by "unfair dealings" to lure Salmon away from the National Committee. Like a starfish, the foundation wanted to smother the oyster, the National Committee, and "even now unless funds were secured elsewhere, might suck the oyster into its greedy maw." He became so carried away that he forgot the time, and there was Henry Ford at the door. The two men had a brief, cordial conversation and Beers finally left. He was thrilled: "To have been introduced to him by his wife in their home—and to have made the acquaintance of the son and heir—is getting pretty close to the throne under the best of auspices." And the monarch had even wanted to help him on with his coat![26] But that throne bestowed no largesse upon Clifford Beers. Despite further solicitations several years later,[27] Henry Ford never gave anything to the National Committee.

Possibly influenced by Otto Bannard and Russell Chittenden's (treasurer of the National Committee and chairman of its finance committee, respectively) interpretation of the Rockefeller Foundation's proposal to save Salmon for the National Committee, and no doubt moved to hyperbole by the chance to net Ford money, Beers had overstated to Marquis the foundation's attitude. From June 1913, in response to a simple request for information about the National Committee, the foundation's officials had been barraged with statements, pleas, and endorsements in behalf of the committee from Salmon, Beers, Welch, Chittenden, Stokes, Bannard, and Homer Folks. The campaign had its effect: negotiations progressed as far as the discussion stage, including an interview between Salmon and John D. Rockefeller, Jr., president of the foundation, and others; Beers wanted to see Rockefeller, too, but got only as far as Jerome D. Greene, the foundation's powerful secretary.

In October the foundation's board considered the National Committee's request for forty thousand dollars annually for ten years. Although favorably impressed with the committee's work and plans and with the quality of Salmon and Beers as executives, and convinced of the importance of mental hygiene, the board, still trying to determine the new foundation's direction, was unprepared to make definite long-term commitments. Further, the board members believed that heredity, mental hygiene, alcoholism, and venereal disease were related and had to be approached as one broad problem whose solution called for coordination of several lines of research "under adequate scientific supervision," a difficult job requiring cautious planning. But they did want to help the National Committee relieve the Salmon crisis, which was immediate; hence the offer, with no guarantees or binding agreements, to put Salmon on the foundation's staff and lend him to the National Committee for at least a year, with the prospect of cooperation between the committee and the foundation in the future and without precluding some sort of direct aid to the committee later. This proposal was, contrary to Beers' assertion, agreeable to Salmon but not to the National Committee, especially Bannard and Chittenden, who regarded it as selling Salmon to the Rockefeller Foundation—an unfortunate and mistaken view, according to Greene. The only way out, as Chittenden and Bannard saw it, was for the National Committee independently to raise the money to pay Salmon, which no doubt accounted for Beers' hasty end-of-the-year appeal to the Fords.[28]

Salmon remained at the National Committee, on leave from the Public Health Service and still as director of special studies. Where his salary came from is not clear, nor what guarantees, if any, were given him, though he had wanted them. For 1914, at least, it seems that he was not paid from Rockefeller Foundation funds; perhaps part of the Phipps money went toward his salary. It is also possible that the Rockefeller Foundation people gave him some assurances privately about the future. In any case, in 1915 the Phipps fund would be exhausted and Salmon would again have to decide what to do. The National Committee had thus to deal with what Beers later termed its "third crisis."[29]

The committee conducted a campaign for funds, including an approach to the Rockefeller Foundation for money for surveys and Salmon's salary. Beers send a hundred copies of his book to wealthy people known to have supported charitable causes. Five responded. Among them were Mrs. Elizabeth Milbank Anderson, a liberal contributor to many social welfare and public health agencies and founder of the Milbank Memorial Association, and Mrs. William K. Vanderbilt, the socialite wife of the wealthy sportsman and art collector, each of whom pledged five hundred dollars a year for five years and asked Beers for more information about the National Committee's work. Mrs. Vanderbilt also gave him a letter of introduction to her cousin, Mrs. E. H. Harriman (widow of the railroad builder), who, more interested at that time in the mentally deficient than the insane, gave Beers only a handclasp and a cup of tea, which he did not care for.[30]

Then Mrs. Anderson promised to give ten thousand dollars annually for four years if Mrs. Vanderbilt would do the same. It would be better, Beers replied, if Mrs. Anderson gave the money free and clear. He asked her to write to Chittenden, stressing the need to devise a plan to raise an endowment of at least five hundred thousand dollars before the end of 1919 and pointing out that the budget for the next four or five years could be increased by accrued interest on gifts received for endowment during this period. Beers added a confidential postscript indicating that the National Committee had reached an accommodation with the Rockefeller Foundation, resulting in the latter's paying Salmon's salary as medical director for 1915 and 1916.[31]

The National Committee thus accepted the conditions it had rejected a year before; that is, Salmon would be a member of the foundation's permanent staff, assigned for at least two years to the National Committee. Influential men like Welch, Stokes and Simon Flexner (a member of the foundation's executive committee) played a role in the foundation's decision to hire Salmon,[32] as did Adolf Meyer, who evidently kept in touch with what was going on at the National Committee. In a strong letter urging support for Salmon, he said that Salmon's reports were "level-headed and judicious"; if the United States were to catch up with Europe in psychiatry the facts must be discovered upon which scientists would base their work, hence the importance of Salmon's proposed surveys. Some members of the National Committee, Meyer wrote, considered Beers "the principal asset, whereas others probably would rather assign his propagandist nature to a secondary position." It seemed to him that the "constructive programme, which I believe I was largely responsible for while I was chairman of the Executive Committee, should be capable of development quite apart from a propagandists [sic] spirit." In a second letter he maintained that the surveys would improve conditions in hospitals.[33] Meyer was the only one who brought Beers' name into the picture at this time; everyone else seems to have been concerned with Salmon and the National Committee's executive committee, about which there was some question. Beers probably never discovered what Meyer had said; if so he would have responded immediately to Meyer's self-serving attack upon him, especially as he had been trying as hard as he could to save Salmon and his surveys.

The urgent appeals for relief of victims of the European war made the Rockefeller Foundation decide to confine its help to the National Committee to the arrangement to keep Salmon.[34] What would happen after Salmon's two years with the National Committee ran out remained to be seen, Beers told Mrs. Anderson. Unless the National Committee managed by then to place itself on a firm financial footing, the foundation would entice Salmon away, he thought. If the committee could secure a guaranteed annual budget of at least twenty thousand dollars through 1919, then Salmon would stay, paid either by the committee or by the foundation. "Now is the time to forever win for our National Committee the complete independence it so well deserves" (and which Mrs. Anderson, by implication, could supply).[35]

Preventing Salmon from going to the Rockefeller Foundation and preserving the National Committee's autonomy seem to have preoccupied Beers during these years. In fairness to the foundation, its officers do not seem to have sought to deprive the National Committee of Salmon. The arrangement was a way to give him financial security and the National Committee stable leadership, since the foundation was a permanent, firmly financed organization and the committee was always in financial peril.[36] Foundation officials also wanted to see how things would go at the National Committee, or they might want to use Salmon eventually for their own activities. That the National Committee was doing useful work for which Salmon seemed essential soon became apparent to Greene. "The good already done by the National Committee is incalculable," he said in 1915 at its annual meeting, "and the Rockefeller Foundation has done nothing in its first two years of life of such indisputable value to the community as is done by assuring to the Committee the continuation of Dr. Salmon's services." At the end of 1916 the foundation extended Salmon's services to the National Committee indefinitely.[37]

Still, Greene and his colleagues were careful men who wanted their money to be used well, so they would try to make sure the National Committee went in the proper direction and was in competent hands. The National Committee did not become wholly dependent upon Rockefeller Foundation money, but the contributions from that quarter became substantial enough for foundation officials to gain, subtly and gently, a measure of power over its affairs. Initially, Greene, counseled by Flexner, Welch, and Paton, considered proposing the reorganization of the National Committee's executive committee, perhaps with a foundation representative as a member, and from time to time he made various suggestions to Salmon as to projects and modes of work, with emphasis on the need for systematic planning and the maintenance of the "highest scientific standards." Evidently deciding that the foundation would not yet itself enter mental health work, its officials channeled requests for mental hygiene studies and programs to the National Committee, which increasingly came to act as its arm in that field.[38]

Beers therefore had some reason to feel apprehensive over the foundation's role in the National Committee. If so, his sentiments were far from clear-cut. By the end of 1914, when Salmon's future was in doubt and the National Committee was waiting to hear from the foundation (several months before the note to Mrs. Anderson about the need to be independent), Beers was as anxious as anyone else to get Rockefeller money and ready to pay a price for it. On his own initiative he wrote Welch a "personal message" intended to be passed on to Greene; to make sure, as usual, he gave a copy to Stokes for the same purpose. Both men acquiesced and also sent Greene their own appeals in behalf of Salmon and the National Committee. Beers made two points in his letter: first, something had to be done to keep Salmon, who, if he returned to the Public Health Service would "be lost to private agencies for all time"; and second, Beers' own fund-raising work was being hampered by the foundation's slowness to act, as it was difficult to approach the wealthy people to whom he had access until he knew what the foundation would do. What in his view should it do? It should make three commitments to the National Committee: fifty thousand dollars for the surveys; a guarantee of Salmon's salary for at least five years; and ten thousand dollars a year for routine operations and to hire an assistant medical officer to help Salmon. From other sources, namely Mrs. Anderson, ten thousand dollars a year for five years could be obtained. In a postscript, Beers mentioned plans to incorporate the National Committee and suggested that the Rockefeller Foundation, should it "help finance the work of the National Committee," could "of course, secure such representation" on the committee as it might desire and could also recommend changes in the bylaws before the incorporation took effect.[39]

How much this letter influenced Greene is not known, and the decision six weeks later to guarantee Salmon's employment was short of Beers' requests, but Welch's and Stokes' notes must have carried some weight. This support, modest as it was, from the greatest philanthropic foundation established up to then was an immensely important achievement for the National Committee, the culmination of years of work and hope and a tangible sign of confidence in its future. Beers could not have been really unhappy about it, especially as it may have helped him finally to convince both Mrs. Anderson and Mrs. Vanderbilt to pledge funds for operating expenses, ten thousand dollars each annually for operating expenses of the National Committee for four years, which would tide it over until 1919.[40]

In the middle of February 1915, a week after Beers had told Mrs. Anderson about the Rockefeller role, the Anderson and Vanderbilt gifts, plus the arrangement with the Rockefeller Foundation as to Salmon, were announced at the National Committee's annual meeting, attended by Greene. A few days later Beers sent, along with a copy of Greene's remarks at the meeting, a gracious, grateful note to him. Later that year the foundation gave its first grants for special projects, $22,800 for "surveys of the care and treatment of the insane" in sixteen states, for which Beers again wrote Greene a warm note of thanks. "The nation-wide survey of the care and treatment of the insane will, more than any other one thing, achieve the purpose I had in mind when I published my book," he said.[41]

The next year Beers brought off a big coup. Not only did he get five thousand dollars each from Mrs. Willard Straight (daughter of the financier and sportsman William C. Whitney and a cofounder with her financier husband of the progressive *New Republic*) and from Mrs. Mary Rumsey (Mrs. Harriman's daughter and a leader in social welfare in New York City who had introduced him to Mrs. Straight), but he managed, after a good deal of negotiation, to extract from Mrs. Anderson a pledge of one hundred thousand dollars toward an endowment. (In this case, too, she was concerned about what Mrs. Vanderbilt, then in Europe doing war work, would do, but Beers persuaded her that he would not let Mrs. Vanderbilt get away and was only waiting for the right moment to approach her.) Mrs. Anderson's offer was conditional on the National Committee's raising an additional nine hundred thousand dollars to create a million-dollar endowment; she would give fifty thousand when four hundred and fifty thousand dollars was pledged from other sources, and then ten thousand on each one hundred thousand dollars obtained, until the full million dollars was reached. She expressed herself as "well satisfied with all that has been accomplished since Mr. Beers first stirred my interest in the work and I feel that we all owe him a debt of gratitude for the important part he has taken in focussing public attention on a subject of such vital concern to the community."[42]

Everyone at the National Committee was of course pleased. Otto Bannard, the treasurer, agreed that Beers was "a wonderful asset," and Beers received several notes of congratulation.[43] He sent copies of all these letters to George Beers for the family to see; he hoped to be rewarded with a raise in salary the following year.[44] Especially gratifying was Mrs. Anderson's warm acknowledgment of his own work. It gave him prestige on the National Committee and would make it easier to raise more money. "So far as I know," he told her, "your method of helping pioneer workers to secure gifts from others is unique. By expressing appreciation of the one whose task it is to solicit funds you at once increase in a donor the impulse to give. If a book is ever written on the psychology of getting and giving, you should be its author, so generous is your attitude in regard to both."[45]

At the same time Beers, Salmon, and others were trying to get the Rockefeller Foundation to meet the salary of an associate medical director to take some of the burden from Salmon. Greene advised the National Committee to use its own money to pay for such a position; it was not a good idea for the foundation, by paying the salaries of two National Committee executives, to appear to have such an influential role in its administration. The committee evidently did find the necessary money to employ an assistant for Salmon—Dr. Frankwood W. Williams, the successful executive director of the Massachusetts Society of Mental Health, who came as associate medical director on January 1, 1917.[46]

Besides fund-raising, Beers helped to establish mental health societies in various states, some of them growing out of the sentiment aroused by National Committee surveys.[47] The First Convention of Societies for Mental Hygiene was held at Johns Hopkins University in Baltimore under the auspices of the National Committee on May 25, 1914, just preceding the seventieth annual meeting of the American Medico-Psychological Association there. Fourteen societies, some independent and some subordinate to charity or health organizations, were listed on the program. The first was the Connecticut Society, then the National Committee, and then by date of founding those in Illinois, New York State, New Jersey, Massachusetts, Maryland, Pennsylvania, Texas, Canada, South Africa, Dallas, North Carolina, Dayton, and several others in process of organization. Paton was the presiding officer and Beers acted as secretary. He, Salmon, Barker, Welch, and representatives of the various local societies were among the speakers. The tone of the meeting was optimistic and action-oriented. In his speech, Beers expressed his gratification at the extensive organizational activity in so many places, including Australia and Mexico. He also heard himself acclaimed and applauded as the founder of the entire movement.[48]

He was no doubt much pleased, as he was when Dr. Aaron Rosanoff, "one of the ablest psychiatrists in [New York] State's service," told Beers that what he had done "will cause posterity to remember you." That kind of compliment would not, Clifford told Clara, interest his brother George, "as he is quite willing that posterity should look after itself, or themselves, but to one of my make-up, doing something for posterity is satisfying. If there is any 'beyond,' it would seem that those who do something for posterity will have greater rewards than those who do not."[49] Beers always felt the need to vindicate himself to those who doubted or criticized him, in either the present or the past. For although he and the National Committee accomplished much, it was not without strain.

‡

However removed Beers was supposed to be from policy-making, his fund-raising could not easily be divorced from program decisions. The situation was compounded by his habit of working behind his colleagues' backs. For example, there was his letter to Mrs. Anderson with the mention of the Rockefeller Foundation menace, along with other correspondence along the same lines, at the same time as he was soliciting Rockefeller Foundation support. Then he told no one but Salmon about the Vanderbilt gift, which he announced as a surprise at an executive committee meeting. What bothered the executive committee was not only the secrecy but the condition Mrs. Vanderbilt attached to her gift — that part of it be used to start a magazine, a project Beers had advocated since at least 1909.[50]

George Blumer, then chairman of the executive committee, finally sent Beers a frank letter criticizing his "somewhat Jesuitical" methods. In the future, Blumer suggested, all matters before the executive committee should be discussed openly, without prior prompting of members by Beers. There was no objection to having his opinions presented if he did so in writing and equally to every member. Beers had always shown one "very great weakness as an officer of an organization," the assumption that having originated the movement he must be the "master mind in its control." He "attempted to make the organization a one-man organization," and when thwarted on an issue tried to circumvent the executive committee, a tactic calculated to alienate the institutional psychiatrists, who were admittedly bureaucratic but whose resignation would present the executive committee with serious problems. Then Blumer revealed that the executive committee's refusal to give Beers authority to organize state mental hygiene societies while on a transcontinental trip stemmed from lack of confidence in his judgment. He had given the impression that Mrs. Vanderbilt had insisted on the journal when in fact he had. Finally, Beers "nagged" Salmon to do things that Salmon considered of no importance. Of course, Beers, a "most persuasive talker," would have a "thousand specious explanations of all these things," but facts were facts and could not be talked away; they must be faced for the good of the cause, Blumer concluded.[51]

As Blumer predicted, his admonitions, which could just as well have been written by Meyer five years before, were futile. Penciled on the back of Blumer's letter was a note in Beers' hand: "Successfully refuted in all important particulars, when I talked with Dr. Blumer on March 6th/15. Dr. Blumer went off 'half-cocked.'" Beers defended his actions (although he realized he might have made a "psychological error" or two in dealing with the psychiatrists on the executive committee), and said, with some justice, that the executive committee was too slow to act; that it only wanted to do surveys; that Salmon was a procrastinator, to the extent of unconscionably postponing a reply to an important letter from the secretary of the Rockefeller Foundation. In other words, Beers had to act as he did in order to get anything done.[52]

A few months later Beers was on the offensive, criticizing the executive committee and explaining his view of Salmon in a long letter to Chittenden. The hospital men—Russell, Mabon, and Hoch—who tended to dominate that committee, stymied action and treated both Salmon and himself as "lowly members of their hospital staffs—as subordinates who are to do as they are told." Believing that Salmon acquiesced in their conservatism, Beers did not try to oppose them for feat of "reviving the old charge that 'Mr. Beers wishes to run things.'" Now he understood that Salmon, "were he not so generous and so interested in the welfare of the National Committee, would resign." The latest affront had been the executive committee's decision finally to publish the journal on the condition that Dr. McFie Campbell, Meyer's assistant at the Phipps Clinic, be the editor. Salmon should be the editor, Beers insisted: not only was he eminently qualified but it would enhance both his and the National Committee's prestige if its medical director had the job. Salmon said he was too busy, but Beers knew better. Like the girl who objects to being kissed when asked but happily accepts her fate if kissed without being asked, Salmon would gladly accept if just handed the job with no questions.[53]

Beers had been at work. Salmon wanted to start the journal and was rebuffed by Hoch, Mabon, and Russell, who thought the time was not ripe and objected to being manipulated by Beers, who was behind the project. So then Beers played on both Salmon's and Hoch's feelings, suggesting to Salmon that his prestige and usefulness were under attack, and then to Hoch that Salmon was unhappy, which led to the decision to publish the journal but frustrated Beers' wish that Salmon be editor. It was to change this latter situation and weaken the opposition so that he could have freedom of action that Beers wrote to Chittenden. "I personally feel under obligation to Mrs. Vanderbilt," who wished the journal to be edited by the active officers of the National Committee, he said. "I am sure that you must feel that Mrs. Vanderbilt's expressed desire shall not be over-ruled except for good reason." Then he revealed his deeper motive: "What sort of controlling committee shall we create to keep our Executive Committee as at present constituted from committing such a serious error of judgment as is shown in its handling of the matter at issue?" There was a remedy: fill the three vacancies on the executive committee with lay people. In this way Russell, the chief obstacle to progress, could be outvoted or might resign; Russell, conscious of his conservatism, had already considered resigning.[54] (That Russell was instinctively opposed to new ideas was well known, so that he may well have made life difficult for Beers and Salmon.)[55] In case all did not go as planned, Chittenden should write a letter to Beers supporting Salmon as editor of *Mental Hygiene*. But all would go well, Beers predicted, for Mabon was willing to reopen the issue and recommend Salmon as editor. And if placing new members on the executive committee did not get for Salmon what he wanted, then a joint meeting of the executive and finance committees, plus a few selected people, would have to thrash the problems out.[56]

On the whole, Beers got his way. Hoch, Mabon, and Russell did compromise. Against their better judgment they voted to publish *Mental Hygiene;* Mabon agreed to propose Salmon as editor; and all three approved adding three lay people to the executive committee. They had to be pushed, though, which Beers found exasperating. What he did not seem to realize was that he, too, had to be "managed," that if people finally surrendered it might not have been because they were convinced he was right but because they were worn down by the struggle. It all meant much more to him than to most of the others, who had other jobs and other concerns.[57]

With regard to the value of *Mental Hygiene* to the National Committee and the mental hygiene movement, Beers judged correctly. As with much that he initiated, it is necessary to distinguish between his methods and the value of what he proposed to do. Frequently he had a better sense of what was possible and worthwhile than the psychiatrists who directed the fortunes of the National Committee. His complaint that the executive committee depreciated the value of a journal in favor of almost exclusive attention to surveys apparently described the situation accurately. Under such conditions, since he initially did not have the votes, the only way to establish a journal was through machinations.

During the prewar period, Beers and Salmon were in alliance on most issues and got along fairly well, although Beers felt that Salmon was not aggressive enough in exposing abuses in mental hospitals, and in some ways Beers irritated even the low-keyed Salmon. This went beyond annoyance at Beers' "nagging" (for Salmon was indeed a procrastinator) to a distaste for his style of work, especially when it might affect the fate of the National Committee. On the whole, Salmon liked and respected Beers. He could even be amused rather than angry when Beers outwitted him or did erratic things. The respect and regard were mutual enough for Beers to take advice from Salmon, who considered it his responsibility to curb Beers' impetuosity, dampen his sometimes extravagant proposals, and keep him away from people he annoyed.[58] So when in 1916 Beers communicated with the Rockefeller Foundation regarding an endowment, general expenses, and support for an associate medical director for the National Committee, it was not to Salmon's liking. Beers later ascribed this attitude to Salmon's resentment of anyone but himself going near the Rockefeller people, who were his "private preserve." Realizing how sensitive Salmon was on the subject, Beers did not cross him but felt it was too bad, since Salmon was "too timid and delicate" about advancing the National Committee's interests, bound up as they were with his own; further, Salmon was not interested in money and so was not an aggressive fund raiser. All this may have been true, but Beers seemed unaware, first, that Salmon did ask for an assistant, and, second, that he objected to Beers' energetic insistence and worried about his effect upon the Rockefeller Foundation's officials. The dispute did not reach the breaking point at this time.[59] Beers, knowing how important Salmon was to the National Committee, kept away from the foundation for the time being.[60]

The prospects for the National Committee were auspicious. Mrs. Anderson's proposal had made the possibility of gaining an endowment real, and the Rockefeller Foundation had demonstrated serious interest in its work. Although financial security was still not ensured, the committee's continued existence was no longer in doubt. The results of a prepublication solicitation for the journal *Mental Hygiene* were encouraging: 350 subscriptions came in.[61] Frankwood Williams, the new associate medical director, although not Beers' first choice, had an orientation congenial to his, combining an interest in popular education with psychiatric practice and research. Williams expressed his concept in *Mental Hygiene,* which came out in January 1917 under his, not Salmon's editorship, Salmon having taken instead a place on the editorial board. Willliams wanted to make the journal nontechnical, aimed at "leaders of the community" but readable by ordinary lay people.[62] The composition of the editorial board was impressive but strongly representative of the hospital men and of Meyer's circle. In addition to Salmon there were Blumer, Campbell of Johns Hopkins, Paton, Hoch, and Walter E. Fernald, M.D., superintendent of the Massachusetts School for the Feebleminded, whose presence reflected the National Committee's interest in a new field.

The first issue of *Mental Hygiene* set forth the goals of the movement as then conceived not only by the editors and the National Committee but by several contributors who were influential advisors to Clifford Beers. The most obvious characteristic of the articles was the extension of the scope of mental hygiene beyond the traditional medical model. The foreword (possibly written by Williams) explained that a general realization was emerging that "mental factors underlie not only inability to make a living and the gross disorders of conduct but all the social activities of man." New information in the field "no longer benefits only the mentally sick," but was used in the children's court, prisons, schools, factories, "wherever intelligent attempts are being made to direct human activities."[63] The president of the National Committee, Lewellys Barker, thought that the survey work was well enough advanced to warrant entering new fields like eugenics, "to provide for the birth of children endowed with good brains, denying, as far as possible the privilege of parenthood to the manifestly unfit [and also] to supply all human beings . . . with the environment best suited to the welfare of their mentality." Medical men and then the public must be educated to the fact that "anomalies of feeling and abnormalities of behavior are as much subject to natural laws as are disorders and defects of the intellectual processes."[64]

Beers contributed an article describing his own changed outlook as a consequence of his work in the National Committee. Originally he had thought only in terms of the treatment and prevention of insanity, but in trying to carry out this goal the National Committee "soon found itself called upon to help also the mentally deficient, the epileptic, the inebriate—in fact all of the mentally abnormal groups." The primary aims of the movement now included the conservation of mental health, prevention of mental disorders and mental defects, and improvement in the care and treatment of those suffering from these conditions. He did not mention eugenics or take any position on a key issue, the relative roles of heredity and environment in human development.[65]

These attitudes, which reflected the various scientific and social ideas current at that time as well as changes in psychiatry, were not fully accepted by the hospital psychiatrists, so that there was still a difference of opinion in the National Committee. For example, Russell's article in *Mental Hygiene*, "What the State Hospital Can Do in Mental Hygiene," placed the hospital in the center of the mental hygiene movement in general and the National Committee in particular.[66] Other key people, including Salmon, were moving away from mental hospital work, which Salmon, though deeply concerned with improving the conditions of hospital inmates, nevertheless considered "less important perhaps than any other when the broader conception of mental hygiene is borne in mind." He would expand the field to include schools, prisons, and indeed the whole society: in time the movement could reasonably hope to help reorient the minds of men and women to make "adjustments which will permit the spirit of humanity and charity to rule instead of envy and malice, vengeance to give way to justice, war to peace, despair to hope." Salmon's concept of community mental health thus diverged from that of Meyer and his circle in that it was not an extension of hospital psychiatry but a reversal of the order of priority and a branching out to general social reform. The elimination of social problems would create favorable conditions for mental functioning, and healthy mental functioning would help to eliminate social problems.[67]

This trend in the National Committee, led by Salmon and influencing other organizations, could not help but please Beers, whose early dreams had been of an all-encompassing movement that would try to prevent mental illness. Still, although this goal might in the long run solve the problems of mental hospitals by eliminating the need for them, it did not necessarily help in the short run — that is, improve the conditions of those unlucky enough to be committed to state and other institutions. Meyer's "narrower" view might have offered more toward changing the mental hospitals than Salmon's.

‡

The outbreak of war with Germany in the spring of 1917 interrupted the programs of the National Committee and marked the end of its first period of activity under Salmon. At the suggestion of Paton and others to Surgeon General William C. Gorgas, the army initiated a program to screen emotionally unfit draftees and to treat soldiers who became mentally ill.[68] Most of the medical leaders of the National Committee entered government service, and the committee itself became engaged in war-related activities, including recruiting psychiatrists and neurologists for the armed forces, starting schools of military psychiatry, organizing records, printing medical examinations, and planning for the postwar psychiatric care of veterans. Salmon enlisted in the army, where he made an outstanding reputation by establishing military neuropsychiatry on a modern basis, planning and providing the leadership for psychiatric screening, and setting up treatment centers in France for soldiers who suffered from functional nervous disorder, or "shell shock" (a term he deplored). Presumably as a result of his work, the army and navy had a relatively low rate of shell shock victims (one-third less than that among soldiers serving on the Mexican border in 1916), and the U.S. expeditionary forces had only one-tenth of the suicide rate of the regular army in 1915.[69] Few, if any, psychiatrists who participated in these programs questioned the rightness of the war, for all they might have felt saddened by its horrors. They may have recognized that trench warfare and military life might be detrimental to mental health, but they took them for granted and regarded the situation as a job that had to be done in order to promote the Allied war effort and to minimize the suffering. They (and later commentators) regarded it as an accomplishment that their ministrations enabled emotionally stricken soldiers to go back to the trenches.

While Salmon was away, Beers had to work with several acting medical directors in succession at the National Committee. Williams was soon summoned to Washington; then came, briefly, Pearce Bailey, who looked to Beers for "advice in many situations—some of them," according to Beers, "of a medical nature." When the congenial Dr. Frank Norberry succeeded Bailey, Beers had an even freer hand; indeed, he said, he took the initiative in "doing things I felt I had a right to do in the absence of Dr. Salmon and Dr. Williams."[70] But there was not much to do; the war preoccupied the National Committee, as it did those in the mental health field generally. "Psychiatrists, neurologists, psychologists and nurses in all parts of the country have laid aside for the time being their civil duties and have taken their places in the military forces of the government: a big task confronts them," an editorial in *Mental Hygiene* declared. "In no previous war have mental and nervous diseases risen to such proportions."[71]

In addition to its services to the armed forces, the National Committee erected with Rockefeller Foundation funds a psychiatric wing at the marine hospital on Staten Island. That the navy approved the construction was a testament to the accomplishment of the National Committee in creating awareness of the need for psychiatric facilities in general hospitals and of the legitimacy of psychiatric treatment for servicemen. The Rockefeller Foundation also gave $25,000 for "special work in mental hygiene in connection with the American Army and Navy during the year 1918," and suggested that during the war and in Salmon's absence the National Committee should limit itself to work that promised significant results or that was necessary to complete important investigations in progress.[72] That the foundation could transmit such advice to the National Committee, with the obvious expectation that it would be followed, indicates how powerful it had become in the committee's affairs. Besides its role as employer of Salmon, it was the major source of funds for special projects, its contributions reaching $289,000, or 38 percent of the total gifts received by the National Committee up to mid-1920.[73]

Beers himself seemed to be somewhat indifferent to the war. This was probably not so much because of any pacifist feelings, his political views being as a rule conventional in the extreme, as because the war reduced the National Committee's ongoing programs, curtailed fund-raising, and made it impossible to organize any new state societies for mental hygiene. He was aware of events outside his purview, but he tended to see them as they impinged on himself and the National Committee. In February 1917 he expressed apprehension to George Beers that the auspicious future of *Mental Hygiene* might be threatened by the outbreak of war: the subscriptions that were expected to be generated by circularizing ten thousand more people would probably be lost if the United States entered the fighting. After war was declared, he confided, "When I organized the National Committee I did not realize it would be an engine of war,"[74] though he acknowledged the recognition that the National Committee, and himself indirectly, had won in its utilization by the war machine. Salmon, in France as chief of psychiatric work for the U.S. expeditionary forces, surmised that the extension of the work of the National Committee to the battlefields of Europe "must be a source of pleasure and pride to Mr. Beers,"[75] but Beers did not feel particularly happy.

The illnesses of his brothers Carl and William did not help Clifford's spirits. Carl's condition, diagnosed as manic-depressive by experts whom Clifford consulted, seemed to be hopeless; he did not even have lucid intervals. As for William, by 1917 he was at Bloomingdale Hospital, where Clifford visited him and was impressed with his progress, but a year later he still had not recovered. William was the only Beers brother to have offspring; Clifford, with his strong family feeling and no children of his own, followed the development of William's son with special interest.[76]

Clifford and Clara Beers seemed to be getting on well. During the hiatus at the National Committee, Clifford was not traveling so much, and on May 2, 1917, they left their Eleventh Street apartment in New York, where they had lived for three years near the National Committee headquarters on Union Square, for their "first real home," a modest frame house and garden in Englewood, New Jersey. At that time Englewood, on the palisades along the Hudson River, opposite Washington Heights in Manhattan, was a fashionable and affluent suburb where wealthy businessmen had year-round homes or summer houses, a fertile field for Clifford Beers in his search for benefactors of the movement. He enjoyed life there: "Everyone should live in an apartment in New York for a while to appreciate the privilege of living in a smaller city."[77]

Three years later he and Clara bought another house, on Sherwood Place, which was to be their permanent home in Englewood. Clifford found new and useful friends, among them Orlando B. Willcox, who helped him in his work in many ways, and Edwin R. Embree, Greene's successor in 1917 as secretary of the Rockefeller Foundation. He took up gardening and golf and sometimes even went to church. George must not take seriously reports that he held a pew in the Presbyterian church, he wrote: it was only that he avoided the Episcopal church, where the minister was a "sleep-producer." "My church is the Mental Hygiene Church, and I 'sit in' on Sunday, *occasionally,* where the preacher has a real message."[78] Pleasant as life in Englewood was, though, the Beerses eventually spent only about six months of each year there. Commuting to downtown New York during the cold months, when Clifford was busiest, was a chore, so they customarily spent the winter at the Hotel Holley on Washington Square West, not far from the National Committee office; during the summer, a slow time for fund-raising, since the rich were all on vacation, they usually went to Belgrade Lakes, Maine.

Although he could be irritatingly ebullient and exasperating at times, Beers still had his capacity for making friends, and through his work he acquired many warm, enduring friendships. H.O. Payne, who had been secretary to Dr. Walter B. James, president of the National Committee from 1919 to 1922 and then to Clifford Beers for three years, recalled that those who knew him well loved him for his charm and wit; others considered him a nuisance: "His persistency, and his refusal to take 'no,' literally, annoyed them."[79] He was intimate with only a few people—his brother George and boyhood friends like John Veitch, Vic Tyler, and Paul McQuaid—and he and Clara did not lead a very active social life. Clara had women friends with whom she would visit while Clifford was away, and sometimes, knowing that his absences were difficult for her, he would try to include her in his informal interviews. Her allegedly delicate health always concerned him; Clara "stood the moving well," he reported to George after they were installed in the Englewood house. Of course she had servants to help her, although getting them was a problem—one of the irksome consequences of the war for the middle classes: "It would be a fine thing if the Government would conscript competent servants and make them available for housekeepers," Clifford declared. Volunteer work for servicemen was too strenuous for Clara: "You are a good girlee," he assured her, "to refuse to be drawn into the cafeteria work. I wish you could do it but as you can't, you mustn't."[80]

Beers himself does not seem to have done much war-related work. With activity at the National Committee at a lull, he turned his attention to other things, among them a revision of his book, on which he worked on and off for years. Early in 1909, when *A Mind That Found Itself* had been out for nearly a year, he and Meyer had discussed plans for a new edition and ways to increase sales. Meyer thought the price of the first edition had been too high, but the problem lay elsewhere, Beers believed: the reviews, emphasizing that it was a treatise on insanity and an account of abuses, discouraged sales. The public must be assured that the book was readable and "anything but distressing."[81] Nothing came of Beers' schemes to have the National Committee take over the publication and distribution of the book; Longmans Green issued a new edition in 1910 which was reprinted in 1912; a year later a third edition, revised, was published. The additions consisted of a new "Postscript" that included objectives and plans for state and national mental hygiene organizations and other documents and was intended to serve as a sort of manual for prospective workers in the movement. It would be revised and inserted in each new edition in order to show the progress that had been made.

In 1916, contemplating a fourth edition, Beers proposed to publish excerpts from letters he had received (with permission from the writers) while he was organizing the National Committee. Not only would they furnish a graphic account of his early work, but the picture they would give of his success would counter the unflattering depiction of himself in the autobiography. Surely "no intelligent reader will find fault with me for wishing to leave a different and more normal impression of myself." Whoever read this appended section would know also that he had been correct in his initial estimate of the possibility of a mental health movement. More important, he hoped that revealing publicly what he had told philanthropists privately would make it easier to secure contributions for the National Committee. "After learning that I financed the preliminary work of the National Committee under great difficulties, those I have thus far appealed to seemed more willing to 'chip in.'" Worried about the probable bad taste of publishing material so complimentary to himself, Beers asked various people for their opinion. He also intended to include a list of the members of the National Committee, in expectation of which he asked Greene of the Rockefeller Foundation to sound out Mrs. Willard Straight about joining. The fourth edition came out in 1917 containing the additional material, which was also issued separately as a pamphlet. Half the printing costs were underwritten by the National Committee's treasurer, Otto Bannard, the chairman of the board of the New York Trust Company, whose offer to defray the entire amount Beers refused, reluctant to have others pay for his creation.[82]

During the war Beers also felt free to aid the cause in Canada, upon the request of Dr. Clarence Hincks, who, inspired by Beers' accomplishments in the United States, wanted to found a Canadian mental hygiene organization. On February 26, 1918, Beers spoke in a Toronto home to some two hundred people who had braved a thunderstorm to come. To Clara he confided how much he enjoyed the experience and how many compliments he received, some from leading citizens, about his relaxed style and frank discussion. A remark about his courage in speaking so openly "brought a round of applause that was somewhat disconcerting," and upon being thanked for his appearance he received a long ovation, which was "embarrassing," but "nice to remember." The next day the *Toronto Globe* reported that twenty thousand dollars had been contributed and that the "Canadian National Committee for Mental Hygiene" was launched. A member of the audience was quoted as saying, "I never saw people so enjoy being asked for money," which the reporter ascribed "to the fact that Mr. Beers manifestly and avowedly enjoyed himself."[83]

Beers may have been somewhat excited at this time, as he and Clara went to Atlantic City, often a sign in later years that he was elated and needed to go off somewhere to calm down.[84] He may also have felt elated because he had helped to arrange a good agreement with the Rockefeller Foundation. With Salmon away, and after Williams made a poor impression in his first negotiation for funds, Embree turned to Beers, with the knowledge of the National Committee's executive committee. Embree, unlike Greene, liked to be in touch with a variety of people. Beers therefore participated in the discussions about the allowances for 1918. Salmon cabled his satisfaction.[85]

Then Beers drew up for the National Committee a program that was adopted by the finance and executive committees. Proposed at a time when the National Committee was committed primarily to war work and its executives were on leave, the plan was both overambitious and unrealistic. At private gatherings in various cities, Beers would discuss the origin, scope, and growth of the National Committee's work and then appeal for contributions or pledges of money toward the goal of obtaining one hundred thousand dollars a year for ten years for general expenses and two million dollars as an endowment to assure a stable income. When these funds were raised, several associate medical directors would take charge of work involving nervous and mental diseases and mental deficiency; field secretaries would stimulate and supervise state societies and local committees for mental hygiene in various sections of the country.[86] Beers also asked for a raise in salary and for the still unpaid portion (two thousand dollars) of the sum voted him by the National Committee on January 28, 1911. He intended to use the two thousand dollars to defray fund-raising expenditures that were irregular and thus not a legitimate responsibility of the National Committee. The irregularity consisted in Beers' tendency to treat himself very well, to stay in the best hotels and in general act as if he were a lobbyist or fund raiser for some wealthy corporation or foundation. His request was refused, regretfully, with the suggestion that he find someone to donate money toward his extra expenses. Bannard and Coley also felt "extremely anxious" that he not "be too used up in this work . . . it is a great nervous strain and we do not want you to get too tired out so early in the year." They were obviously concerned about Beers' mental state. He reassured them. He would get the rest he needed: "it is the planning rather than the doing of work that seems to tire me," and now that he had worked out a plan, no one need worry about him.[87] The plan, so obviously impracticable, was never carried out.

The question of Beers' salary was settled a year later, when a joint meeting of the executive and finance committees voted to raise it from five to seven thousand dollars a year, beginning January 1, 1919, and thus to cancel the National Committee's moral obligation to pay him the two thousand dollars. This compromise came about, he believed, partly because he had abandoned his customary way of operating through one or another individual member of the finance committee; this time, before the joint meeting met, he had informed a number of members about the issues, so that no "atmosphere" would be created. He felt confident, he told George, that even without his intervention some substantial increase would have been given him, but "*I took no chances.* . . . I made up my mind to get my deserved reward for ten years or more of work. And now I have it." Now he could save enough money to ensure his own future, since he could not increase his thousand-dollar life insurance policy, the "family record" making him too high a risk for insurance companies.[88]

During the spring of 1918 he again agreed to help Hincks raise money in Canada and formally to organize a Canadian mental hygiene society. "Nothing that I am doing at present is so important as the Canadian work, and nothing is so interesting." He would speak in Quebec, Montreal, and Ottawa.[89] The Quebec meeting was a "complete success," Hincks told Dr. C. K. Clarke, medical director of the Toronto General Hospital; thirty of the city's most prominent citizens attended and twenty thousand dollars was raised. "The splendid result of the Quebec meeting is due as you no doubt have already suspected to the splendid appeal made by Mr. Beers. You will very well remember the diplomatic way in which he introduced the subject of finance in Toronto. His technique appears to improve with every meeting. During his remarks he won the complete sympathy of Sir Lomer Godwin, Premier of Quebec, and on account of this Sir Lomer made some very flattering remarks, and promised strong moral support," which influenced others to donate money. Salmon cabled from Europe his congratulations to Beers "on that splendid piece of work," the organization of the Canadian National Committee.[90]

By this time Beers had become confident of his speaking ability. At first he had preferred not having relatives in the audience, but at a meeting at the New York home of Mrs. Harriman—by this time won over to the National Committee, which had become involved with her interest, mental deficiency—he invited George, who might prove useful to him as a carrier of messages. The Harriman gathering finally gave him what he had "worked and waited for over ten years"—the opportunity to plead his cause "in person before such a distinguished and philanthropic group," the first meeting "of its kind held in this country."[91]

Edwin Embree attended the meeting and sent Beers a tactful but frank critique of his performance. The fifty-five-minute speech was "most interesting—in fact thrilling" and the audience remained intensely interested all the way through, Embree said. The speech was, however, excessively permeated by Beers' personal experiences, at the expense of a lucid, logical presentation of the mental hygiene problem and the "quite remarkable results" of the National Committee, about which few not already knowledgeable would have received any "clear conception."[92]

However much it may have enthralled the audience, the meeting failed to produce the expected gifts, and Beers felt that if the members of the National Committee would take as much responsibility as Hincks' colleagues did in Canada, "we should soon have the needed funds." "I cannot do the trick alone." He understood that the war was the main hindrance, so he would be "glad when peace times return and my own end of the work grows more active," he told George. A few days after the armistice was proclaimed he confided to Hincks, "Our work is beginning to boom, for which I am truly thankful. Competing with the Great War was beginning to be irksome. Now my ego will have a chance to expand again and I shall be able to plead our cause with pre-war vim."[93]

‡ 13 ‡

"Canning Salmon and
Bottling Beers"

Despite the failure to obtain an endowment to match Mrs. Anderson's pledge, the National Committee was in an excellent position at the war's end. The discovery that a considerable proportion of drafted men were rejected for armed service because of mental disabilities and then the sensational reports about "shell shock" – the horrors of trench warfare disabled almost as many men as did battle wounds – created a new public awareness of the seriousness of mental problems that proved critical to winning sympathy and money for the work of the National Committee. Precedents for the federal government's involvement in mental hygiene had been set before the war by immigration laws and in narcotics control and then during the war by military psychiatry, and Salmon later campaigned for federal mental hospitals for war veterans. Direct financial support for the national mental hygiene movement was, however, seen as coming primarily from private sources. The two major sources were individual wealthy donors, who might be tapped for large single gifts or smaller annual contributions for a specified time, and the foundations, which were potential donors for both big one-time gifts and substantial regular support. As a result of the revelations of the prevalence of mental disorders and of the effectiveness of the National Committee and its executives in coping with them in the armed forces, foundation leaders took a greater interest in financing the National Committee. Most influential were Salmon's accomplishments, for which he was awarded the Distinguished Service Medal. Not only did his work in instituting psychiatric screening of draftees and organizing psychiatric treatment for soldiers in the field offer clear examples of the practical nature of mental hygiene work, but they pointed up two of the National Committee's (and Clifford Beers') primary tenets, that prevention was more important than treatment and that psychological factors were crucial in all aspects of mental disorder.

The war's end led to stocktaking by the National Committee and its venture into new fields while it continued or resumed past programs. "Mental hygiene" was redefined to include the application of psychiatric knowledge to social problems in which psychological factors seemed to be fundamen-

193

tally important. In cooperation with other organizations, the National Committee increasingly dealt with mental disorders in the community. Prevention gained more attention, as did problems of delinquency and criminality, with special emphasis on children. Since many psychiatrists, partly influenced by Freud, believed that emotional disorders originated in childhood, the emphasis in both prevention and treatment began to shift to the young. Interest in the institutions with which children were involved—the family, schools, courts, and welfare agencies—led the National Committee to establish in 1921 demonstration child guidance clinics that acted as diagnostic, referral, and consultation centers for poor people in several cities. These clinics were financed by the Commonwealth Fund (a foundation established by the Harkness family, heirs to the fortune of a Rockefeller partner in the Standard Oil Company). After five years the child guidance work was continued by other organizations; it also stimulated research in the genesis of mental illness and led eventually to the extension of preventive and treatment services to the entire family, to the concept of an integrated program of services and research.[1]

Another National Committee project of the early twenties was to induce state institutions for the insane and for the mentally deficient to use its standard classification of mental disease and its uniform methods of collecting statistics. The U.S. Census Bureau asked the National Committee's help in preparing schedules and in gathering data for the institutional census of 1923, and finally the bureau took over the National Committee's entire system of collecting and tabulating statistics. The U.S. Public Health Service and the National Crime Commission also availed themselves of the committee's statistical service.

Surveys of the conditions of the institutionalized insane were continued by the National Committee, and research was conducted into alcohol and syphilis as causes of mental disorders. As the National Committee recognized early in its work, and as was pointed up during the war, the extension of psychiatric concepts and services required more trained psychiatrists, and finally in 1924 the Rockefeller Foundation and the Commonwealth Fund financed a training fellowship program.

These and many other activities gave the National Committee high prestige within the medical community as well as among the foundations. In effect it came to hold a virtual monopoly in its field of work. This success reflected glory on Clifford Beers but also gave him greater burdens, as it meant larger administrative budgets and therefore an endless race for funds, along with closer concern over what they were for and how they were administered. Although he was supposed to keep out of policy matters, Beers could not: temperamentally it was difficult for him, and, besides, funds and the way they were to be used were closely linked. At the same time, the organization had become complex and professionalized, so that he was perforce more on the periphery of some of its activities than during the founding years.

With Salmon still away he ventured at the end of 1918, with the approval of Bailey and Williams, to ask the Rockefeller Foundation to give the National Committee twenty thousand dollars for a postwar "reconstruction" program to remedy wartime backsliding in the care of the insane and help war veterans who had mental problems, and in so doing utilize the skills of the many physicians trained in psychiatry in the armed forces. The foundation rejected this plan, which was included in the grant request of the National Committee for 1919, in negotiations for which Beers actively participated and which in his opinion turned out to the committee's advantage.[2]

Salmon was meanwhile watching fretfully from France. In August, with the end of the war in sight, he had wondered about the Rockefeller Foundation's attitude toward his salary for the next year; "I am very anxious that Beers should not interfere," he wrote his wife. Later that year, when he heard that Beers was involved in the grant request, he was incensed: "I see where Beers kills the goose that laid the golden eggs as far as the National Committee was concerned." Russell, chairman of the executive committee, was to blame. "In spite of my solemn warnings Russell is permitting Beers to deal directly" with the foundation; this, on top of what Salmon considered inadequate support for his work by the National Committee, was too much, and he wanted "no more to do with them."[3]

Actually, Beers had not at all killed the goose: the Rockefeller Foundation, whose strong interest in medicine and public health had begun to crystallize at that time,[4] continued to subsidize the National Committee. Before the war the main contact with the foundation had been through Greene, who had wanted to avoid having to handle Beers.[5] In 1918, Salmon, three thousand miles away and preoccupied with battlefield problems, may not have realized that new leadership had come into the foundation. Greene's successor, Edwin R. Embree, had become a personal friend of Beers's, and there was also a new president of the foundation, Dr. George E. Vincent, a former adult educator, sociologist, and president of the University of Minnesota, an innovative administrator with whom Beers seems to have had an amiable relationship. Further, Salmon tended to be hypercritical of people; Beers, although he respected Salmon, saw him as an egotist who did not like his prerogatives usurped.

Beers was afraid that Salmon was considering whether he would resume the medical directorship of the National Committee. He had tasted success and a measure of power, and he saw possibilities for great work in mental hygiene after the war, other than through the National Committee, especially as he was being offered other jobs. Not only did he dislike the administrative duties at the National Committee, but he was annoyed that Beers had become more active during his absence, and he felt that important decisions were being made behind his back. He also attributed much of his frustration in dealing with neuroses and psychoses in the field to a lack of urgency about war needs in the National Committee and the Rockefeller Foundation. In his opinion, the committee was allotting him only a pittance and was not sending him enough good people, and the foundation's grants could not be used for his overseas activity. Salmon always felt insecure because of his former poverty and obscurity. He also felt very unmilitary on account of his informality and his compassion for the soldiers under his care whose emotional troubles tended, in his view, to meet indifference, if not contempt, from the army. He at times saw himself as an embattled knight-errant, a role not unfamiliar to him and apparently, despite his protests, not uncongenial either. Besides, he was an emotional man, prone to temper flare-ups.[6]

He was certainly irritated with Beers, who not only was consorting with the Rockefeller Foundation officials but in his grant appeal had "prattled" about the National Committee's great war work when in truth it had bungled the recruitment and training of personnel for army psychiatric work.[7] Even in a glowing tribute to him adopted by the annual meeting of the National Committee in 1918, Salmon saw Beers' hand and disliked the flattery. Although appreciative of the warm spirit it expressed, Salmon thought the words "awful bunk," and "altogether superfluous," evidence that "Beers' expansiveness gets contagious at times." He wished he "could make Beers understand that it is one of the things that make me feel like giving up the N.C. job," he told his wife.[8] Upon his return to the United States in 1919 he decided to resume his relationship with the Rockefeller Foundation where, in addition to directing the National Committee, he would be planning the foundation's own work in mental hygiene, a program under consideration by its officials, who gave him a substantial salary raise.[9]

Meanwhile, Beers had to find more money, the Rockefeller Foundation's contribution being only a part of the National Committee budget, which had for 1920 reached over $170,000, the biggest in its history. It was a difficult sum to raise, so much so that he asked Hincks to help him convince the members of the finance committee to give him more active assistance. In return he would take Hincks to see Salmon about getting Rockefeller Foundation money for the Canadian National Committee. The prospects were poor, though, since some members of the foundation were a "bit hostile to mental hygiene work" even in the United States.[10]

Salmon returned to the National Committee in the fall, but with the understanding that he would resign as medical director as soon as a successor could be found and that he would develop a prospectus of work in mental hygiene for the Rockefeller Foundation. To enable the National Committee to guarantee both a salary for a new medical director and a viable organization to work with, the Rockefeller Foundation for the first time voted funds for general purposes for the next five years.[11] Salmon was scouting for his replacement,[12] and so was Beers. He was determined that Williams, with whom he was having a dispute, would not get the job: "Dr. W—— is going to find that he must first win his spurs before he can safely stick them into me!"[13]

Actually Beers preferred Salmon to stay, mainly because of his connection with the Rockefeller Foundation, which wanted to delineate a division of mental health work between itself and the National Committee, something that would determine not only Salmon's relation to the two organizations but the kind and amount of support the foundation would continue to give the committee. Here Salmon's procrastination, his "unreal attitude toward time,"[14] might prove costly to the National Committee, for he neglected to write the requested memorandum on the subject. When one and then another reminder came from George Vincent, president of the foundation, Beers frantically called the National Committee president, Dr. James, who told him to find Salmon that night. Beers did and offered to "help in any way possible" to prepare the memorandum. Salmon got to work immediately and produced it for Vincent practically overnight.[15]

Salmon proposed the creation within the foundation of a division of mental hygiene that would in 1920 survey the opportunities for independent work in various areas: childhood mental diseases, including establishment of clinics; the social application of psychiatry (that is, social deviance); manpower needs in psychiatry and mental hygiene, including the opening of new psychopathic hospitals and the training of psychiatrists, social workers, and psychiatric nurses; and the founding of university psychiatric hospitals as centers for training, research, and care. The division might also provide consultation services for the mental health implications of other Rockefeller Foundation work. Two days after this statement came one from Dr. James on the National Committee's and Rockefeller Foundation's respective work in the field. The committee would be the public education, information, and organizing arm, and the foundation, the research and planning arm.[16]

Two days later Beers sent Embree a supplement to James' statement, a proposal for a community demonstration in mental hygiene, "a carefully planned attempt to apply intensively knowledge of mental diseases and their prevention to the practical management of certain phases of sickness, poor relief, child caring, delinquency and crime in a district having well-organized health and social activities." Beers had carefully worked out the whole program, which could well have been written fifty years later, when community mental health came into vogue. It included a budget of thirty-five thousand dollars to be expended in a district in upper New York State, in cooperation with local organizations, government agencies, and mental health clinics, to launch the following enterprises: studies of specific groups (mental hospital patients, inmates of almshouses and institutions for the mentally defective, people accused or convicted of crimes, juvenile delinquents, retarded and psychopathic children in public schools, children placed out or receiving public aid, and children in orphanages); psychopathic wards in general hospitals; first aid, aftercare, and social services for patients at the state hospital; family care of the insane; community supervision of the mentally defective; encouragement of better treatment of syphilis, "inebriety," and drug addiction; and popular education in mental hygiene.[17]

Beers was trying to see whether a well-supported program that combined insights of contemporary psychiatry and the broadened approach of the mental health movement could have a significant impact on a community. His proposal not only reflected the extension of mental hygiene to encompass socially deviant behavior traditionally considered sinful rather than sick and a concern for prevention; it also reaffirmed his (and Meyer's) original commitment to help the mentally ill and their families in a practical way. He may also have been influenced by the community health centers, related to the social welfare movement, that had sprung up in various cities while he was writing his book and organizing the national and local mental hygiene organizations. A good deal of this social work was done in New York, some of it financed and run by the same people whom Beers approached for support or by their friends. In terms of leadership and backing, the world of philanthropy, though wide-ranging in programs, was not large in numbers and was interconnected through families and friendships, so that someone like Clifford Beers could easily become conversant with what was going on. In any case, his was a far-seeing proposal.

The Rockefeller Foundation was not convinced by the various proposals for its relationship to the field of mental hygiene. Holding in abeyance a decision on the question, it gave sixty-four thousand dollars to the National Committee for ongoing programs, including surveys of the care and treatment of the insame and mentally deficient; action on Beers' demonstration project was postponed.[18] This deferment was no repudiation of Beers; indeed, it may be that the grant of sixty-four thousand dollars, a good sum and supplemented by the ten thousand dollars pledged for 1920 for operating expenses, was negotiated in part through his efforts. The foundation also appropriated Salmon's salary for 1920, with the understanding that he would continue on at the National Committee. Soon thereafter the foundation decided against setting up a division of mental hygiene and in favor of continued aid to the National Committee for special studies and surveys and the development of departments of psychiatry in important university medical centers. Foundation officials may have cooled toward Salmon, who now seemed mainly interested in the mental hospitals for war veterans being set up by the Public Health Service, which work Beers applauded.[19] Subsequent correspondence indicates that perhaps Vincent thought Salmon was spreading himself too thin and that Salmon was considering terminating his relationship with the foundation, a prospect that alarmed Beers. It wasn't that he loved Salmon so much, although he liked him, but his first concern was always for the good of the National Committee and for himself in connection with it. Beers was not ruthless, but he was calculating.

In an uncharacteristically pleading and apologetic letter, he asked Salmon to postpone his resignation until a new medical director was found; till then he should join Beers in publicly announcing his intention to stay with the National Committee for five years if necessary; by the end of that time, if not sooner, the National Committee should have adequate staff and funds, including an endowment, along with a successor to Salmon or to both himself and Salmon. Beers seems to have felt that the crisis of leadership in the National Committee involved himself as well as Salmon, that their fates were linked. If Salmon resigned prematurely, the whole burden of the National Committee would fall on him: "Together we can save the ship for all time. Alone, I don't know whether I can save it or not." Then Beers tried to placate what he believed to be Salmon's resentment of his relations with the Rockefeller Foundation, which had only existed through necessity and with the approval of the National Committee's executive committee. "I regret exceedingly that my efforts were misunderstood by you. I have not discussed any topic relating to our work with Mr. Embree since December 4th." Salmon reluctantly remained, as the Rockefeller Foundation did not want him to leave the National Committee, and discussion of the matter continued into 1921.[20]

Beers may have been concerned about the Salmon situation, but he was feeling buoyed up by his own work. In April 1920 he finally met the widow and children of Cyrus Hall McCormick (inventor of the reaper), one of whom had the year before given the National Committee a thousand dollars, and who were all very cordial to him. He intended to camp on their trail until they came through with ten thousand dollars a year for five years for general expenses and one hundred thousand dollars for endowment. He had reached them, he told George, at a "psychological moment": from various remarks dropped by H. F. McCormick (a son-in-law of John D. Rockefeller), he surmised that the "Harvester Company" would soon declare a stock dividend, which would mean "some new 'pin money' coming to the clan." Then Mrs. Harriman pledged twenty-five thousand dollars over five years. James and Fernald (the latter the chairman of the National Committee's committee on mental deficiency, a field in which Mrs. Harriman was interested) did the interviewing, "but I pulled the strings. I'm glad some others are learning how to raise money." If the McCormicks did give ten thousand dollars, all the National Committee needed to complete the year was eight thousand. "This is most encouraging—the best year we have had." By July, Clifford told George that the McCormicks were "about to come across—at least we believe so."[21]

In a memo written at the end of the month Beers reported that his 1919–1920 campaign had so far yielded pledges of $231,000. The McCormicks were sure to pledge $10,000 a year for the five years, plus $100,000 toward the endowment, and Beers was to interview the Mather family, leading capitalists in Cleveland; George Eastman, the photographic and film inventor; various rubber magnates in Akron (including Harvey Firestone); and other wealthy people. The National Committee had from its inception obtained in gifts and pledges $763,000 for all purposes, including $463,000 for general expenses and Mrs. Anderson's conditional pledge of $100,000 toward an endowment; out of the approximately $300,000 for special purposes the Rockefeller Foundation gave $289,000. (This meant that approximately two-thirds of the total funds for the National Committee were obtained more or less directly through Beers' efforts.) Since it is likely that the large special-purpose gifts would continue as long as an adequate general expense budget was secured, it was Beers' aim to do the latter. He wanted to get ten gifts of $100,000 each by 1924 for a million-dollar endowment and then proceed to get a second million. The future was "bright and *sure*."[22]

By this time he and Clara were settled in their new house in Englewood, to which they invited their families for a housewarming at Thanksgiving time. Clifford still leaned on George for advice — was the insurance he took on the house enough? — and kept him regularly informed of his doings. At the end of the year he was pleased to report a pledge of ninety-three thousand dollars from the Rockefeller Foundation and additional money from Mrs. Anderson and from Otto Bannard, and all his letters spoke contentedly of how busy he was. Evidently George spared him responsibility for their brother Carl, who was by then in the Connecticut State Hospital at Middletown, where Clifford would occasionally visit him. He was always concerned about Carl, but George seemed to be in charge of his interests. William was also still hospitalized, but his wife presumably took care of his affairs.[23]

The Salmon situation finally came to a head during the spring of 1921, when Vincent told Salmon tactfully but clearly that his "anomalous" relationship with the Rockefeller Foundation should be ended, as Salmon was no longer happy at the National Committee and the foundation had decided not to enter the mental hygiene field directly, so that there was no place for him in its organization.[24] Embree then declined Salmon's request that the National Committee be allowed to turn Rockefeller Foundation funds allocated for state-by state surveys of mental disease and mental dificiency into a general mental hygiene survey fund. He intimated, moreover, that the foundation would not continue indefinitely its support for the state surveys; it was time for the public to be solicited to finance such work. Beers, writing to Welch about the situation, supported Salmon on this point: to give up the state surveys, which cessation of Rockefeller Foundation funding would mean, would be to abandon the National Committee's most effective work and thus the mentally ill and the mentally deficient themselves. He realized that the Vincent-Embree regime at the foundation was not as wholeheartedly sympathetic to mental hygiene as its predecessor, and he worked behind the scenes, through Welch, to present the National Committee's case and to prevent loss of the foundation's support.[25]

Salmon resigned from the Rockefeller Foundation on May 4, 1921, to take a professorship of psychiatry at Columbia University (at a much lower salary) and to remain on at the National Committee until the end of the year, with the hope that the foundation would continue to support its work.[26]

The foundation's action had come as a shock to Salmon, who attributed it to complaints from the surgeon general about his aggressive campaign to get the federal government to care properly for mentally ill war veterans and to his protests against the new Harding administration's "callous indifference" to their condition. According to Beers, there were rumors in Washington that Vincent had tried to curb Salmon's militancy and that the Rockefeller Foundation's threat to cut appropriations to the National Committee was related to that situation. That the foundation's officials had expressed to Salmon disapproval of the use of its funds for activist programs is obvious from a letter in 1920 from Embree. In reply to a request to apply some of the survey money to the drafting of new state laws, Embree stated that the foundation was interested in gathering facts and making them available and in "demonstrations of feasible methods of controlling disease," not in programs undertaking "directly to influence public action or directly to effect legislation." Later he said that in originally funding the state surveys the foundation "had in mind not only and not so much the effect which would be produced in the states concerned, as a demonstration of the value of such studies."[27]

The Rockefeller Foundation was not unique among foundations in avoiding social activism and politics and concentrating on the much safer, less controversial fields of medical research and medical education. At the same time there is some indication, in a confidential letter from Beers to Welch, that there was some regret at the Rockefeller Foundation over the "late unpleasantness" regarding Salmon, which John D. Rockefeller, Jr., was said to have called a "series of misunderstandings."[28]

In any case the National Committee did not mean to give up Salmon without a struggle. Beers felt strongly that Salmon's "unusual vision and stimulating influence must, beyond any question, be retained. . . . His loss at this stage of our work would be irreparable." Salmon would stay on until January 1, 1922, and Beers hoped that enough money could be raised to keep him indefinitely.[29]

Salmon's eventual departure notwithstanding, the National Committee's prospects looked good. Its most faithful individual benefactor, Elizabeth Milbank Anderson, died on February 22, 1921, and left the committee an unrestricted bequest of one hundred thousand dollars, for which Beers took credit. He then persuaded the executive and finance committees to keep the money intact as part of the endowment, if at all possible. The major single beneficiary of Mrs. Anderson's will, the Milbank Memorial Fund (previously the Milbank Memorial Association), which was concerned with health and social problems, was under the control of her cousin, close advisor, and executor, Albert G. Milbank, to whom Beers now turned, without success, for money to ensure Salmon's continued service to the National Committee.[30] Beers also envisioned receiving substantial general support for the committee from the Milbank Fund.

The Rockefeller Foundation, perhaps as a result of Beers' and others' intercession, did not cut off the National Committee's survey funds, and it retained enough confidence in the committee's future to award a grant to enable four public health organizations, of which the National Committee was one, to achieve closer cooperation by occupying centralized offices on one floor of a new building in New York. The other organizations were the American Social Hygiene Association, National Tuberculosis Association, and National Organization for Public Health Nursing. All four, plus several other voluntary health agencies, had recently formed, with the blesssing of the Rockefeller Foundation, a National Health Council, a kind of secretariat that would run a statistical bureau and prepare educational materials. By the end of April 1921, the National Committee had moved from Union Square to the new headquarters on 370 Seventh Avenue, in the garment district.[31]

‡

As part of an effort to raise money, the National Committee decided to underwrite a new edition of one thousand copies of *A Mind That Found Itself*. Its size would be reduced by eliminating "all preaching" and also by using thinner paper, with the longer edition still available through the original publisher. Beers threw himself into the project, as he thought the cuts would improve the book's style. He wanted to retain the elementary propaganda and the appendix describing the mental hygiene movement, the latter to demonstrate that he had recovered and then successfully founded the movement. He also obtained an additional introduction by President Charles Eliot Norton of Harvard University and inserted letters praising the book, which would not only help the cause but would "rub out of readers' minds the weird picture of me which parts of my story of depression and elation must . . . give." To fulfill his literary ambitions for the new edition Beers again had Bert Fisher's help, this time for pay; he also asked Wilbur T. Cross, one of his English professors at Yale and now dean of its graduate school, to edit it. Cross agreed, but in going over the book he found little to do: "The trouble is that the book is deucedly well written."[32]

This new edition, the fifth, of *A Mind That Found Itself* was to be used in a crash campaign to raise an endowment of a million or more dollars, a large-scale effort for which the executive and finance committees thought they needed professional fund raisers. In June 1921 they discussed the matter with Charles Sumner Ward, a pioneering fund raiser whose technique, "the short-term intensive fund-raising drive," is still referred to as "The Ward Plan." Deeply religious and socially concerned, Ward had done most of his work for the YMCA, which he left in 1919 to establish his own commercial fund-raising firm, Ward, Hill, Pierce and Wells. His most celebrated assignment had been the promotion of Sir Wilfred Thomason Grenfell, an English medical missionary working among Labrador fishermen and Eskimos. In one year, by exploiting, among other things, Grenfell's books about his life, Ward had raised nine hundred thousand dollars to benefit the Labrador natives. Ward's skill in obtaining money and his interest in good causes seemed to be an apt combination for the National Committee, which received a grant from the Milbank Memorial Fund to hire him.[33]

He proposed to base the National Committee campaign on the Grenfell model, with Clifford Beers, whose book he thought was thrilling, as the hero. Salmon and several of the other psychiatrists wanted Ward to sell not Beers but mental hygiene and, specifically, prevention; improvement of the conditions of the insane was "the smallest not the largest part of our program," which should concentrate on educating the public. "We must fight wrong ideas with correct ones."[34]

Ward's approach won out for the moment. One of his employees, Cyrus P. Keen, would be in charge of the campaign, in consultation with Beers and the executive committee. The scope would be nationwide, headed by a committee of prominent people who would recruit a large sponsoring committee to organize locally. A major activity would be a series of "drawing room meetings," with Beers as the main attraction. The first city to be tackled was Boston where, in addition to small meetings, luncheons, and dinners, there was to be a large public meeting in Symphony Hall.

Preparations were hardly begun when Salmon announced his resignation as medical director several months before he was supposed to leave, news that disturbed Beers: "No money," he told Salmon, "will be likely to come to the [National Committee] unless you continue . . . at least nominally . . . as Medical Director. If money could be guaranteed equal to what we will lose when you leave that would be different. And if we could replace you by Dr. Campbell whose intellect, character, personality, prestige and experience in our field would keep us going you could resign. . . . Any other successor that we now know of would be but a 'shirt-front' and lead to failure." The problem was keeping Beers "awake nights." He wanted to prevent Frankwood Williams, then sharing the associate medical directorship with Dr. V. V. Anderson, from becoming medical director.[35] Under Beers' urging, Salmon again agreed to stay until the end of the year at the latest. Just a few weeks after this decision, the Commonwealth Fund gave a large grant for studies and field demonstrations "dealing with conduct disorders of children" that tended to produce delinquency, but on condition that Salmon remain as medical director until he got the work started.[36]

Beers, tired after working on his book, took a winter holiday in Florida, his and Clara's first, preparatory to the big campaign to be launched in Boston in January. Although he could not forget the problems of the National Committee, he and Clara enjoyed the Florida sun and cruised Biscayne Bay on a millionaire's yacht. He was happy to receive a telegram from Salmon announcing his decision to remain with the National Committee for an additional six months on a part-time basis, in some capacity other than medical director, as Beers had suggested before he left for Florida. His title would be "Medical Advisor"; for the time being there would be no medical director, the executive officers being Williams as director of the division on education, two other division chiefs, an executive assistant, a statistician, and Beers as secretary. Beers then wrote to Keen to try to exclude Williams from the fund-raising meetings. He considered Williams ineffective and not as impressive as Salmon, whom he really did not care to have either. Salmon encouraged Beers in opposing Williams' participation but also told him to stay out of Keen's hair: "Take care of yourself and do not bother with any detail but save yourself like the prima donna for the great performance."[37]

When Clifford and Clara returned from Florida, Clifford went alone to Boston, where for three weeks he was almost every day occupied with meetings, luncheons, dinners, teas, phone calls, and interviews, until he could take the pace no longer. There were also daily conferences with Keen. At first the two men got along well.[38] Keen thought Beers most accommodating: "Mr Beers has struck his stride in the personal solicitation. . . . The fine thing about Mr. Beers is that he is willing to throw away his preconceived notions as to how to do some things and adopt our suggestions on them." But Beers was amenable as long as he was allowed to dwell in his speeches on his own experiences and on his book. When the local committee, embarrassed by such an emotional appeal, wanted him to present a practical discussion of the National Committee's work, Beers refused; he also would not include a direct plea for money in his speech. Experience had taught him that people had first to be "cultivated," to be persuaded to read his book and "think it over"; they could be solicited later individually for contributions. Keen favored a more direct, less time-consuming approach.[39]

The disagreement erupted into continual bickering, with Beers complaining to the executive committee in New York that Keen's technique was unworkable. Beers had been told by wealthy people not to beg for money during the first interview; further, he needed more time than the fifteen minutes allotted him at meetings and then he needed time to follow up his talk with personal interviews.[40] To Clara he confided, "All the businessmen side with me against Keen's drive methods. They all say the big men can't be hurried." Still, he felt confident and relaxed. "There is a great deal of insomnia in Boston at present. A great many tell me that they sat up till 2 and 3 A.M. to finish my story." His summer's work editing the book, then, "was not in vain."[41]

The conflict between Beers and Keen went unresolved and reached, for Beers, the proportions of a crisis serious enough to elicit a spate of statements from him to the executive committee, and eventually to embitter and draw him away somewhat from the National Committee. He felt that his own approach to fund-raising had yielded valuable contacts in Boston, but Keen saw this as making his own efforts superfluous and accused Beers of sabotaging his work. Evidently already annoyed by what they considered Beers' earlier indiscretions in soliciting funds, the executive committee tried to bring him into line. It was recommended that the original campaign plan be followed, with Keen empowered to decide all differences and make all decisions.[42]

Beers retorted that the fault was not divided leadership, lack of teamwork, or his maneuvering behind Keen's back, but the abandonment of the original plan: instead of selling Clifford Beers as Ward had sold Grenfell, an "abortive attempt was made to 'sell' mental hygiene on its own merits as a health proposition." Beers had, moreover, understood that he was free to act independently in dealing with potentially heavy donors. Considering that he had ten years of experience in the field and was more expert than any officer of the National Committee in fund-raising, he felt particularly aggrieved and would have nothing more to do with the campaign until he could present his views at a meeting to settle the issues; he protested that meetings on the subject had been held without him. Finally, he threatened to resign: "Unless some plan is soon evolved whereby the Secretary of the National Committee can be treated with respect . . . and justice . . . he will soon begin to sever his connection" as a salaried official, a decision calmly arrived at and concurred in by his wife.[43]

In a draft of a paper titled "A Crisis, the Cause of It and a Remedy for It," Beers said that he had originally intended to remain as secretary of the National Committee until physically unable, and then to become honorary secretary, doing all he could to develop its plans and make it financially secure. Since his collaboration with Meyer in 1907 he had had to "fight" his way "through a cordon of psychiatrists" whose "drastic," "hasty," "unfair" criticism had dogged his every step. Improved organization and planning of the work had not ended the "psychiatric beating," so he believed it now "useless . . . to make further sacrifices of energy and perhaps of health and . . . happiness." He categorically denied Salmon's charge that he wanted to control the Boston campaign and would not submit to discipline. "If, as Dr. Salmon says, I am 'too individualistic' to handle individual donors under someone else's direction and methods, then let's admit it and plan my work accordingly." He would rather work under the finance committee, with its lay members, since his welcome with the executive committee, province of the psychiatrists, was no longer warm.[44]

The campaign was a failure, and it was Keen's fault, Beers insisted. It had cost sixteen thousand dollars to raise thirty-two thousand. Keen used "philanthropic blackmail" — reliance upon friendship among donors rather than interest as a spur to giving; it was the wealthy themselves who objected to his methods. Further, "in Boston, of all cities," Keen had chosen to chair the local committee, instead of a prominent banker "of the Higginson type," a dry-goods merchant; as a result, the campaign was waged not in State Street with gifts of a thousand dollars each but in the dry-goods and groceries district with gifts of two hundred and fifty dollars each.[45]

Beers finally got a hearing before the executive committee, which, while not canceling the contract with Ward (Salmon's fault, Beers claimed: he insisted in "excited moments" that Beers not "run things"), made several important concessions. After Keen prepared the way, Beers would manage his own personal interviews and luncheons, and he would no longer have to collect money from anyone, no matter how small the amount. "It is a wonder," he told Chittenden, "he didn't post me on a street corner with a tambourine in my hand." And he would in his appeals interpret the movement in terms of his hospital experiences. "This is what brings in money."[46] Beers understood that he did best when he could speak informally and at length to a small sympathetic group, preferably composed of people who had read his book. Further, requiring him, as Keen did, to appear hurriedly before a random assortment of people offended his dignity. It was one thing to tell his life story to a Mrs. Anderson, a Mrs. Harriman, a Mrs. Ford, and a Mrs. McCormick, another to talk as a former mental patient before a mass of lesser lights whose luminosity was not sufficient for him to bask in.

The executive committee also, at Beers' request, appointed a subcommittee to work out a statement of his duties, privileges, and rights. It consisted of three men sympathetic to him and only one a psychiatrist: Stephen P. Duggan, a political scientist and director of the Institute of International Education; his old friend Dr. Russell; and his confidante, Chittenden. To Chittenden he wrote: "As everyone says they can't get along without me (for financial reasons, anyway, if not because they love me) I assume my conditions will be agreed to."[47]

The Boston campaign became an academic question for Beers because of an acute case of laryngitis that he suffered in the spring of 1922. Then the executive and finance committees decided to terminate the contract with Ward's firm as of May 31, the stated reason being lack of funds to continue the campaign, although a confidential note indicated that the financial return "had been less than was hoped for." Beers felt that the whole affair, which had started auspiciously, had been botched by not using him effectively and by too didactic an approach to potential donors: "if you talk mental hygiene and childhood and mental mechanisms and Freud and all this stuff and get off into scientific talk you never get anywhere." He admitted that his own methods did not result in much public enlightenment, but they did elicit contributions, and enough money must be obtained to liquidate the National Committee's deficit and to finance a large-scale propaganda campaign to educate the public and get small gifts. "I don't want to spend much more of my life in this sharp-shooting stuff."[48]

Differences in personal style apart, the disagreement was real and involved two interrelated factors: the nature of the appeal for funds and the audience to whom it would be addressed. Would the appeal be educational and intellectual or emotional and personal? Would it be a mass public subscription campaign or one aimed at a small but very wealthy elite? Beers realized the need to do all of this, but not all at the same time; he gave first place to what he thought would raise the most money fastest — personal approaches to rich people with philanthropic impulses that would be stirred by emotional appeals. Keen had tried to follow a middle course, with disappointing results, and no one had yet come up with the kind of effective mass campaign tool for the mental hygiene movement that Christmas seals had proved to be for the tuberculosis organization; it was questionable whether mental hygiene could ever achieve that level of popular support. In any case, as Clifford Beers pointed out, an organization that lived from hand to mouth had to get enough funds to stabilize itself financially before investing in a mass effort.

During the Boston campaign, however, it was clear that a struggle of egos for power was at least as important as differences of opinion about the best way to get money. The acrimony was bad enough to cause Dr. Fernald to write Beers a cold reprimand. Keen, Fernald said, had not received everyone's cooperation because of the conflict within the National Committee's leadership that was essentially one of personalities and personal jealousies. The "painful scenes which mark too many of our meetings" were so intolerable that Fernald would not remain on the executive committee unless the squabbling stopped and each officer's status and scope of operation were clearly spelled out.[49]

The chagrin that this letter must have caused Beers was tempered by the news that Yale would confer upon him an honorary Master of Arts degree in June 1922, the twenty-fifth anniversary of his graduation from the Sheffield School. To Beers, such a confirmed Yale man, it was "the most inspiring message I have ever received."[50] His family and friends (including Dr. Russell) came to the ceremonies to hear Professor William Lyon Phelps present Clifford Beers and President James R. Angell confer the degree: "For your indomitable courage and devotion in turning to the enduring benefit of mankind experiences which have driven most sufferers to silence and seclusion."

The award was announced in the newspapers, and colleagues and friends sent congratulations. Duggan in his note alluded to the "pretty rough year" through which Beers had passed, but assured him that "to have had so fine an honor conferred upon you at the end of it ought to more than balance the irritation."[51] It did not, though, as a letter from Beers to his cousin indicates:

> As to the size of my head. It never has had a chance to swell because one or another of my psychiatric co-workers has periodically visited criticism upon me for one thing or another, frequently for the very things that brought commendation to me from lay associates. Though it is the psychiatrists that have made my work possible, it is the laymen who have given me courage to "carry on" all these years.[52]

To add to Beers' vexation, Frankwood Williams was appointed medical director. Williams was intelligent, thoughtful, well-meaning, and dedicated to the cause of mental hygiene, but he was neither brilliant nor innovative; nor did he have the wide reputation as a psychiatrist or researcher that Beers believed was needed in a medical director. At the beginning, in 1912, when its status was precarious and its potential undeveloped, the National Committee had had to hire an obscure and insecure man, but one with great possibilities. Salmon, with the money that Beers and others furnished and the confidence that the National Committee displayed in him, fulfilled his promise. He had the drive, imagination, and energy to realize many of Beers' ambitions for the organization and to project it into national and international prominence. Ten years later, with flourishing activities, a professional staff, and a position of leadership and influence, the National Committee had to settle for second-best in a director, which Beers feared would damage its chances to get the funds that would make such a job appealing to a first-class man, a frustrating prospect after all the years of work.

‡

Annoyed by Williams' appointment, disgusted by the mismanagement of the Boston campaign, and feeling aggrieved, despite the concessions of the executive committee, Beers turned his attention to a field that offered him new interest and satisfaction — international mental hygiene work. Years before, he had dreamed of ranging worldwide with his reforms. By 1918, the time had come to start. The National Committee's success and the fame of *A Mind That Found Itself,* together with Salmon's achievement abroad, had begun to spread the ideas of mental hygiene in England, France, and Canada. The Europeans led in theoretical, scientific work in psychology and psychiatry, but in the practical, social fields of public education and the prevention and treatment of mental disorders they were, with a few exceptions, at the same point and in some places behind where the United States had been before the founding of the National Committee. In the wave of reform that had begun a century before, the Americans had modeled their new institutions and their propaganda after the Europeans, especially the British. Afterwards Dorothea Dix visited Europe and was influential in having several mental hospitals built. In the twentieth century, the prototype for reform was the American National Committee, and the acknowledged leader of the movement was Clifford Beers, the quintessential American. As early as 1914 the organization of mental hygiene societies was reported in Canada, South Africa, Australia, and Mexico, but Beers (along with Salmon and others) considered his direct contribution to the founding of the Canadian National Committee in the spring of 1918 to be "without doubt, the beginning of an international movement in mental hygiene."[53]

Little could be done overseas until the war ended, so it was not until 1919 that Beers initiated plans for an International Committee for Mental Hygiene, for which he drew up a constitution and bylaws and began soliciting funds. William Welch agreed to serve as honorary president and approved Beers' intention to ask Sir William Osler to take the same post representing Great Britain. The actual presidency would be assumed for one year by Lewellys Barker, who would resign as president of the National Committee to do so. It was, Clifford told George, the "biggest thing I have yet formulated."[54]

At a dinner on February 4, 1919, given by Walter James, the new president of the National Committee, an "International Committee for Mental Hygiene" was created. Present at this meeting were key members of the American and Canadian National Committees and several other influential men, among them George McAneny, Stewart Paton, Wickliffe Rose (then head of the International Health Board), Anson Phelps Stokes, Adolf Meyer, William Welch, and George Vincent and Edwin Embree of the Rockefeller Foundation. The meeting was reported in the newspapers. "So many prominent names were connected with the proposal that the story was accepted as an important piece of technical news," the *New York World* said in a long article. "Probably few readers realized that this dinner marked one of the most dramatic achievements in world history and launched a movement in which every community on earth is vitally concerned."[55]

One of the objects of the new International Committee was to help found in other countries national mental hygiene organizations, whose work it would coordinate. Good advice on the matter was expected from Salmon, then on his way home from France. With his international prominence, Salmon was important; Mrs. Anderson had been persuaded to give five thousand dollars to the International Committee for initial expenses, conditional upon his approval, which he gave; he also accepted membership on the committee. He told Beers to go slowly in England: intervention by outsiders would be resented and English leaders should be encouraged to organize a national committee themselves. During his upcoming trip there to speak about neuropsychiatric war work, Salmon, a persuasive speaker, would try to put his audience in a mood to start such an organization.[56]

This cautious approach, common among the psychiatrists Beers had to deal with, did not suit C. K. Clarke, medical director, and Clarence Hincks, associate medical director, of the Canadian National Committee, who were more experienced in dealing with the British. Salmon was "pussy-footing," Clarke wrote, and did not understand the English; no address at the Royal Society would bring about action. "If you expect to accomplish anything by rousing the enthusiasm of the psychiatrists of Great Britain, you are making a mistake. We will never be successful if we depend on them, because it is the younger group who will bring us success." The "old 'stotin-bottle' class" was impervious to anything but a thousand years of persuasion. As in Canada, success lay only through people of wealth and influence. If the Canadians had waited for the medical profession they would still be waiting. Hincks' British friends confirmed his belief that the movement "would be relished if it were presented from American and Canadian sources." But at this time Beers was trying to keep Salmon at the National Committee and thus retain Rockefeller Foundation backing, so he felt constrained to go along with him.[57]

That it was Beers, not Salmon, who was the key to international activity is indicated by the lapse in the movement from 1919 to 1922, the years when Beers was deeply involved in raising funds for the National Committee, though in 1921 he did receive encouragement from several French psychiatrists.[58] The struggles around the Boston campaign led him to turn to international organizing just at the time a specific task presented itself in Canada. Hincks had managed to get the wife of the Canadian governor-general to lend her name to a drive that would get under way in October 1922 as "The Lady Byng de Vimy Fund for Mental Hygiene." She had read *A Mind That Found Itself* and very much wanted to meet Beers and to have his help in the campaign. Further encouragement also came from the establishment on May 4, 1922, of the National Council for Mental Hygiene of Great Britain, which cited the National Committee as the archetype.[59]

Also that year there appeared in England a book, *The Experiences of an Asylum Patient,* by Rachel Grant-Smith, who leveled against British asylums most of the same charges Beers had made against U.S. hospitals in 1908. In the introduction to Grant-Smith's book, Montague Lomax, author of *The Experiences of an Asylum Doctor,* called *A Mind That Found Itself* "one of the most striking illustrations possible of the reliability of a recovered lunatic's evidence. Not a shadow of a doubt has ever been cast upon the truthfulness" of his account.[60] The situation in France, Beers learned, was confused but hopeful, and the equivalent of national committees existed also in Belgium and South Africa.[61]

So that he could complete the organization of the International Committee, as well as work in Canada, the National Committee gave Beers a leave of absence from his routine duties as secretary for the fall of 1922. He planned to go to Europe for several months, and to prepare the way asked Dr. Ralph Noble of Australia, who was going abroad, to attend the forthcoming European Congress of Mental Hygiene in Paris. Noble was to tell the participants about the National Committee's work and to present Beers' plan to hold an international meeting in the United States in 1923 or 1924, the first international congress of mental hygiene. Noble was also to indicate how helpful Beers could be in organizing such a meeting and raising funds for it (a sum estimated to be more than twenty-five thousand dollars).[62]

Noble undertook the mission. The secretary of the European Congress, Dr. J. Genil-Perrin, and the president, Dr. Edouard Toulouse, agreed to have an international meeting in New York in 1924, he reported. They recognized that the movement had begun in the United States as a result of the efforts of Clifford Beers, whose name was mentioned frequently. The congress at Paris also heard of Beers' work from Dr. Helen Boyle, the prime mover of the National Council in England (and a descendant of the great chemist), who read a paper in which the American National Committee was held up as a model. There would be no difficulty in having the headquarters of an international movement in New York "and the organization of the same in your hands," Noble assured Beers.[63]

After receiving Noble's letter, Beers expressed his uncertainties about the future and so revealed how deeply he had been affected by the conflicts at the National Committee. Instead of a leave of absence he would have preferred an assignment to international work, an arrangement that would make it easier for him to raise money occasionally for the National Committee. There were many attractive features of work in foreign countries, although it would be a "sacrifice to home-life," especially for Clara. "However, now is the time for the international plunge. If there is not a whole-time career in that field I wish to find it out within the next two or three years, while still not too old to carve out some sort of career in the field of business or finance."[64] To become economically independent he hoped to have his salary paid by some wealthy individual, instead of the National Committee, he wrote one of its benefactors. Perhaps he would make a new life for himself by entering finance, where his "business and salesmanship impulses may find profitable outlet." In any case, "the events of the past few months indicate clearly that it will be best for all concerned, and especially for myself, if I am given, as it were, a 'quasi-sabbatical year' for the period ending September 30, 1923." His "Rooseveltian personality," as some had described it, needed freedom for a while. The change was painful but probably unavoidable, though he did not give up hope of returning to the National Committee: "I feel that the increased prestige which should come to me through the planned international developments can later be converted by me into funds for the endowment of the National Committee and for other purposes as well." To Noble he had admitted that expressing himself in international work was a way of dealing with his personal problems.[65]

A good deal of Beers' leave of absence, which extended to the end of 1922, involved helping Hincks in Canada. Hincks' methods were congenial to him. Not only did Hincks subscribe to the technique of going after rich and important people individually as well as through carefully planned meetings, but he would circulate at least three hundred copies of *A Mind That Found Itself* in Toronto a week before Beers arrived there. In less than a month one hundred thousand dollars was pledged, and all on a private, personal basis. The medical director of the Canadian National Committee, C. K. Clarke, wrote to Beers: "my impression about you is that if you were left to work out your own salvation you would achieve about the highest position possible in the world below, or even the world above, or in the world betwixt and between." If only Mrs. Beers had come to Canada; he would have liked to tell her how much Beers' friends there thought of him.[66]

His confidence restored, Beers again began to think of his status on the National Committee. He wondered whether "this showing will make our Executive Committee realize" the correctness of his methods. The finance committee, he suggested, should take over fund-raising and "put an end to the damage that has been done by the psychiatrists who imagine they are financiers." At the last annual meeting he heard he was missed, and he assumed that his prestige was restored. All he wanted was a "chance to act as freely as I have in Canada." He hoped, he told George, to work in the international field as well as for the National Committee, because without him the National Committee might go under. He realized that he was now being handled carefully, which pleased him well enough, but what he really wanted was action, a chance to work to full effect. "It will be easy enough to finance the National Committee if I can get from some of its members such help as Dr. Hincks gets from some of his officials."[67]

Without deprecating the success in Canada, it must be said that working there was not the same as working in the United States. First, at home Beers did not have a Hincks to help him. Hincks had the social connections to set up interviews with wealthy people and to recruit titled dignitaries whose endorsement was so important among Canadians. And the fact that Beers came to Canada as a famous visitor from the United States made it posssible for him to be featured as a star attraction whose presence constituted no threat to the Canadian activists in the movement. It also meant that he could act with a freedom that he had not had at home. Fernald speculated that if Beers could be "entirely dissociated from the 'cogs and wheels' of the . . . office," he "could accomplish the same thing in the U.S."[68]

Contrary to Beers' expectations, his welcome home at the National Committee was far from warm, and he soon became embroiled in a bitter struggle. As he saw it, executive committee members Salmon, Copp, and Kirby (a "cat's paw"), and also Williams, were trying to "bury" him. They had voted to extend the appointment of his replacement, a temporary financial secretary, for three months starting in December, when everyone knew that his leave ended January 1 and knew how successful he had been in Canada. This financial secretary was to organize fund-raising meetings and rehabilitate state mental hygiene societies. So Beers would be superseded not only as a fund raiser but also as a promoter of state societies. What was more, one of the conditions under which Williams accepted the position of medical director was that he rather than the finance committee (which was considered to be in Beers' power) would be in charge of the financial secretary. Beers discovered this information in a letter from Williams to the executive committee, a copy of which was left on his desk, probably by a staff member sympathetic to him.

Beers now felt fully justified in his opposition to Williams as medical director. Only a man with "sublime conceit" would take control over raising money without any experience at it. If at a prospective joint meeting of the executive and finance committees Beers' conditions for raising money were not met, he would sit out all fund-raising efforts and take the matter to the annual meeting. The situation must be corrected even if it caused "resignations in a dozen directions including Dr. Salmon and Dr. Williams." "There are plenty of good psychiatrists willing to come into the Executive Committee. And Salmon's continued connection is no longer vital as . . . he can do nothing more for us" with the Rockefeller Foundation; as for the Commonwealth Fund, Dr. Anderson was the National Committee's contact there, and they had already pledged fifteen thousand dollars for five years. Further, the executive committee, by using the Anderson bequest for general expenses rather than as an endowment, would wreck the National Committee. Salmon, Copp, Kirby, and Williams wanted to make him a "mere collector of gifts without anything to say regarding policies, plans, and personnel," and they must be stopped.[69] Beers would do everything to protect and restore his rights as secretary of the National Committee short of resigning. Nor would he keep out of the office or away from the active work of the organization until its affairs were put on an efficient and economical basis under an executive committee representative in character and composed of members anxious to serve. His strong stand, he said, was provoked by the frank admission "by some of the psychiatrists in the Executive Committee that there has been on foot for several months a definite plan to separate me from active work, including, I assume, no direct contact with plans, policies, and personnel." He quoted Russell as saying that if Beers intended "to enter into the work of the National Committee in an active way (except in the begging of money) the Executive Committee might as well resign." Beers would accept the "challenge"—let them resign and he would reorganize the National Committee. Correspondence among executive committee members and Williams confirms Beers' accusations about plans afoot to curb him and even to eliminate him entirely.[70]

Russell wrote Beers a tactful, reassuring letter telling him to calm down, explaining that it had been decided to change the finance committee in order to carry out Beers' plans for raising money. Russell expressed concern that Beers took the disagreements within the leadership so seriously and hoped he would understand that differences of opinion among a group of men associated with the movement for years did not mean they were indifferent to his interests. Nobody wanted to eliminate or disregard him; everyone was his "warm friend." It would be best for him to stand away from the "whirr of the machinery" of the National Committee and participate when needed in discussions of large questions of policy. There was plenty for him to do in helping to organize new groups, working on educational campaigns, doing international work, and, above all, planning fund-raising.[71]

Beers would not be soothed. He went to work gathering allies and wrote directly to Salmon, angrily spelling out his grievances, his feeling that Salmon had been trying to drive him out of the inner work of the National Committee. The result was turmoil and demoralization among the staff and harm to the organization's work. He could "establish a cordial basis for active cooperation at once," if Salmon would do what all retiring chief executives did, remove himself from the scene unless invited in for special advice. Finally, he had to tell Salmon how unfriendly his activities had been to him and how hurtful to Clara. "The feelings and happiness and health of my wife are, naturally, of more importance to me than the feelings of yourself, or Dr. Copp or anyone else." Salmon refused to resign from the executive committee and told Beers, "You can do more than I . . . to resolve the problem . . . if . . . you will cease asking for the resignations of those who differ with you on questions of policy." Everyone was as concerned as Beers "that the great work that is to be done shall not be interfered with."[72]

Actually, by this time Copp had decided that a reconstituted executive committee might be the best solution to a difficult problem. "I have the firm conviction," he told Russell, "that the elimination of Mr. Beers is the only salvation of the National Committee," but Copp could not "conceive any just basis on which" to accomplish this. "As founder of the National Committee he has certain rights which it would be ungracious and unjustifiable to ignore." Copp therefore could not join any move to force Beers out "against his will." A reorganized executive committee might be able to work better with him, so perhaps the members ought to resign; in any case, Copp was submitting his own resignation.[73]

Russell again tried to pacify Beers. "I feel that you are wasting your energies and exhausting yourself nervously. Do you not think that you may

ll if you are not careful?" Beers took umbrage. Why did Russell in-
dictated letter questions about his mental health? Last spring similar
from certain sources had started rumors in New York, Connecticut,
Chicago, and Canada. "Imagine fighting . . . ever since 1903 to rees-
reputation for mental stability and then, after many years of hard
ssful work finding that some of the mental experts who know me
iving or have given color to these hurtful rumors." The facts were
oked well, slept well, never weighed more, and was not overtired.
t that this question is raised whenever I become somewhat aggres-
ell theoretically superior officers of the National Committee some
e truths, sadly needed by a number of them who seem lacking in in-
conditions in its inner work that need immediate correction?"[74]
eers wrote what he considered to be a mollifying letter to Salmon.
f Salmon's resigning from the executive committee, why not ap-
rs to it, possibly ex officio. "Then the two men who have done
he National Committee could act on equal terms when decisions
policy, plans and personnel are made." Beers closed by expressing
nent of Salmon's casting aspersions on his mental health.[75]
oint meeting of the executive and finance committees, Beers man-
ive many of the issues brought into the open and to have himself
der the supervision of the finance committee, which would give
hand in his fund-raising so that he could "express" his "personal-
position of temporary financial secretary was abolished and the
d for the eventual appointment of an associate secretary to stand
rs when he became, as he expected, immersed in international
also promised to stay out of other staff members' affairs.[76]
atisfaction at this outcome was short-lived, and the congenial at-
he perceived was more the reflection of his own pleasure with the
han of reality. Several men were distressed about the way the
d gone and more so about Beers' condition. Salmon felt that al-
ers' moves to take over the "internal affairs of the organization"
hed, the fact that the finance committee was stacked with Beers'
uld allow him full leeway in running financial campaigns, and
e authority of the executive committee. The results would be in
f the Gods." Beers did not seem well. "He has gained weight, his
tremulous, he was excited and distractible and someone ought to
after him," especially as his wife was away.[77]
scovered the extent of feeling against him and the concern for his
n opening and reading a letter to Williams from Fernald, to whom
ptly drafted a reply. (Whether it was ever sent is not clear.) He
rnald for neglecting to make sure that his letter would not be
others, as it was not unusual for people in the office to read in-
ail not marked personal or confidential. Then Beers went on to

justify his recent behavior as necessary in the face of the conservatism and authoritarianism of the hospital superintendents on the executive and finance committees. He deeply resented that he, Clifford Beers, the outstanding figure in the mental hygiene movement, was being excluded from decision-making on the crucial issue of financing the National Committee. And he would not tolerate anyone who either thoughtlessly or otherwise threw suspicion on his mental health. Anyone who could not be "loyal enough to the organization" and to Clifford Beers to protect his "reputation for sanity . . . should resign" from the National Committee. If Beers himself revealed the troubles within the organization to outsiders, it was to protect himself against such attacks as Fernald's. As for the latter's claim that Beers lived on a sort of volcano, that seemed so only from the institutional psychiatrists' smug and conservative stance. He intended to give up active routine work for the National Committee as soon as he could develop the international side enough to yield him an adequate salary and a permanent position. Then he would concern himself only with the larger policies of the National Committee.[78]

Unless Russell, Salmon, Kirby, Fernald, and others were all deceiving themselves (or were not perceptive psychiatrists), Beers was in an excited state; even Hincks, his ally, was worried about his putting "too much strain" on his nervous system and stretching his "limit of endurance."[79] Other evidence includes the very long communications he was writing and his unusually strident accusations against his so-called opponents. His demands for a voice in the National Committee went beyond anything he had previously seemed to want. He sought equality with the medical director, and, because of the National Committee's financial straits, thought that he could command acquiescence. Finally, there was a certain grandiose tone to his writing.

As in past "crises," Beers found it hard to admit that he might be at fault, that he might have been difficult to deal with, or that he had to be handled, though he acknowledged that he always had trouble with the psychiatrists on the National Committee, from Meyer on. In his opinion, they were to blame: they never fully appreciated him, they were hypersensitive, conservative, jealous of their professional prerogatives, loath to give up power, unwise in their decisions, and always suspicious of his mental state. Unless the situation got too serious, though, as it had during the Boston campaign and its aftermath, Beers enjoyed "being under fire and having to fight opposition." As he once told Hincks, "I guess I ought to get a job blasting rock in tunnels and subways. Don't picture me as having a hard time in my work. I have to have some friction to make my wheels go round."[80]

Whether Beers was bound to clash with Salmon, as he seems to have been with Meyer, is another question. Salmon and he were not antithetical, but their temperaments were different and Salmon was an authority figure whom Beers felt he needed and yet had to challenge. Still, it seems that Beers looked upon Salmon as something of an equal: they were the same age and had together built the National Committee. Many of Beers' actions toward Salmon seem to have come more from opportunism than from emotional involvement. As long as Salmon was useful to the movement Beers tried to keep him. When his usefulness declined and conflicts arose, Beers was ready to let him go with few heart tugs and with a sense of doing righteous battle. Several years later he summed up that troubled year, 1922: "It's safer to can your Salmon than bottle your Beers!"[81]

Salmon had reasons apart from difficulties with Beers for feeling discontented with the outcome of his work at the National Committee. In losing the Rockefeller Foundation job and going to Columbia University, he had taken a cut in salary that forced him to establish a private psychiatric practice, and the problems at the National Committee obligated him to stay on longer than he wished. He was also unhappy about the unwillingness of the leaders of the medical profession, with a few exceptions, to play a significant role in its affairs. Physicians, he complained, "regarded mental diseases as a non-medical subject and mental hygiene as something which might be of interest to philosophers, social workers and 'uplifters' but outside the field of practical preventive medicine." Some improvement in this regard was occurring, but not a great deal.[82] At the same time Salmon felt defensive about what he had accomplished at the National Committee, which research-minded men like Paton criticized as being too oriented to the practical and not "scientific" enough and therefore out of touch with current research in related fields. On that account Paton had refused to serve on a campaign committee, which much disturbed Salmon, who apparently did not know that Paton had enough regard for him to support his Columbia University appointment.[83] Paton's view of the direction the National Committee should take was not new; it went back to its origins and to the disputes he and Meyer had had with Beers. But in his evaluation in 1922 of the National Committee Paton was perhaps not aware that its officials had for years expected that the Rockefeller Foundation would eventually take basic research in psychiatry as its domain.[84] Salmon may have felt that the more scholarly psychiatrists were put off by Clifford Beers' propagandistic inclinations, and therein may lie another source of his irritation with Beers. But if so, it would not have been justified, for it was Salmon, not Beers, who had determined the direction of the National Committee and bore responsibility for its programs. Indeed, Meyer's proposals in the 1920s for organizing community social work resembled the demonstration project that Beers rather than Salmon had wanted the Rockefeller Foundation to fund.

Whatever the reasons, by 1923 conditions at the National Committee had become difficult for everyone, so that the executive committee hoped Beers could channel his energies elsewhere. Beers for his part seemed to be tired of "sharp-shooting" after money; although there were new sources of funds to be tapped, the struggle of the National Committee to survive was difficult, the excitement of starting something new had gone, and he had always meant eventually to give up routine work and move on to some more creative and challenging activity. The doldrums had set in for him during the war and led him to Canada and then to larger conceptions of international work that intrigued him and that by 1923 suited his mood: "It is certainly a great opportunity and an interesting one. I am essentially a pioneer and cannot be completely happy or effective unless breaking new ground."[85] For the next decade, and in many ways to the end of his active life, international mental hygiene furnished him with an object of grand new scope for his energies and ambitions. The National Committee remained his precious first-born child in whose behalf he would always labor, but his interests broadened beyond it.

✡ 14 ✡

Branching Out

In the midst of the conflict at the National Committee, Beers had gone ahead with his international organizing. On December 11, 1922, there was a meeting of the organizing committee of the International Committee for Mental Hygiene attended by representatives from Canada, Belgium, and Brazil, as well as the United States (including Russell, Salmon, Clarke, and Hincks). The speeches must have soothed Beers' hurt ego. He was lauded as a modern counterpart of Philippe Pinel, the great psychiatric reformer of the French Revolution. Dr. Auguste Ley, professor of psychiatry at the University of Brussels and founder of the Belgian National League for Mental Hygiene, declared that if Beers could "come to Europe as General Secretary of the Organizing Committee to speak to various people it would be very important for the preparation of the Congress and also increase interest in the International Committee's plan." Duggan, chairing the meeting, commented that when Beers first outlined his international scheme in 1919, some people thought the time "was not yet ripe" to launch an international movement. "Events of the past four years have vindicated Mr. Beers's judgment in this important matter. Without any artificial stimulating there is now widespread interest in these international plans." It is not clear what was meant by "artificial," for, as Beers pointed out in his talk, mental hygiene activity abroad had grown from seeds planted by himself and others in the United States and Canada. The Canadian National Committee grew out of a talk between Hincks and Beers in 1918, the one in South Africa from correspondence with the National Committee, and the one in Australia from communications of Hincks, Williams, and later Beers with Professor E. Morris Miller of Hobart, Tasmania, and Dr. Ralph Noble of Sidney. A French physician wrote to Beers after reading his remarks before the New York Neurological Society as printed in the *Journal of Mental and Nervous Disease;* consequently the French League for Mental Hygiene was launched. In Belgium, Ley founded a league after talking with Beers, and the organization of the British National Council for Mental Hygiene grew out of Helen Boyle's visit to the United States and Canada.[1]

219

The encomiums were fine, but, as usual, moving ahead with plans for an international meeting required money, and as usual, Beers undertook to find it. In a few weeks he obtained funds to furnish an office for the organizing committee. He could then begin to "save the mental health of the world without having to do the work standing up or sitting on the floor."[2]

His next move was a trip to Brussels, Paris, and London to promote an international congress. Before leaving, he tried to clear his desk of the numerous letters that had piled up unanswered during the year (a measure of how preoccupied he had been with struggles within the National Committee). Luckily, Mrs. Payne, Dr. James' former secretary, hearing that Beers needed help, went to see him. The moment he spied her, he said, she recalled:

> "I'm going to Europe in the spring and you must get the names of all the outstanding professional and lay people over there . . . for I must formulate plans for the 1st International Congress. And you see my desk?" It was the old roll top type with which he never would part because he could chuck everything into it, shut it and no one could see the mess. "Well, all these papers must be sorted, indexed and filed because I can't ever find anything; and then you'll have to figure out ways and means of getting a lot more $1 and $5 a year members because I go after the big fish; and you must meet Miss Robbins who is cutting down my book by half — a lot of people don't read it because it's too heavy to hold; Miss Robbins has an M.A. so I call her my Meat Ax! and you can help her with that too, and you can have your desk over there and the new files there, and — "

When Mrs. Payne asked what there would be to do when these jobs were finished Beers laughed and said, "Honestly no one works with me very long, they can't stand too much of me, but I hope you and I will be in the same circus for a long time to come. I'll try not to crack the whip too often. Why don't you start right now." So the next morning she began three years' work in Beers' "cuckoo clock factory."[3]

Life at the National Committee had calmed down, according to Williams. Beers had kept his word to quit interfering in other people's work. The two men's personal relationship was "most cordial and friendly," and the effect on the work "most gratifying." Fernald wrote Beers a cordial note telling him of all the good things recently said about him at Yale — "You may not know it, but you are one of the sons of Yale that she is very proud of" — and expressing satisfaction with the "evidence of cordial cooperation in the staff" of the National Committee. "We have been like an aeroplane in a gale of wind, but it does seem now that we are straightening out, and we have another long period of prosperous work ahead of us."[4]

On May 2, 1923, after a week's vacation in New Hampshire, Clara and

Clifford sailed to Europe. Their tour took on the character of a triumphal procession of meetings with important public personages as well as medical men interested in the mental hygiene movement. Dr. Ley took them to see Gheel, the famous Belgian community where for several hundred years mentally ill people had lived in the homes and worked on the farms of the villagers. Then Beers had an audience with Cardinal Mercier at Malines and, the next day, with King Albert at the Royal Palace in Brussels.[5] In Paris Beers addressed a meeting of the French League for Mental Hygiene at the Sorbonne and met many Frenchmen, his doings were reported in the Paris edition of the *Chicago Tribune* and elsewhere, and he was introduced to members of the American financial elite, men like Morgan partner Thomas Lamont, also a philanthropist, and the U.S. ambassador to France, Myron T. Herrick. There was also an interview with Clemenceau, the wartime premier, who had once been a physician at the famous French mental hospital, the Bicêtre.[6] Clara was able to help Clifford immensely through her fluency in French. The trip was strenuous for her, especially as he wanted to see everything as well as meet people and serve the cause.[7]

Beers handled himself everywhere with aplomb. The Canadian National Committee's medical director, C. K. Clarke, who was on the Continent at that time, described Beers' success to Russell in a letter that Beers saw but had no hand in writing:

As you are aware, Beers is a trump card wherever he goes. Much as I admired his genius before, I am more than ever impressed with his success in Belgium and France. It requires a cool head to stand hobnobing with Kings and Cardinals without aero-planing to some extent, yet Beers seems to thrive on it without turning a hair.

The meeting in Paris at the Sorbonne Amphitheater was one of the most wonderful things I ever attended. Some three thousand people jammed in there and hundreds turned away from the doors. It was an event; undoubtedly Beers was the attraction and he received a marvelous reception. If he had gone into the air completely one could not have blamed him, but his coolness and good taste were remarkable. He spoke briefly in English, was modest and unassuming and made a palpable hit. I confess to being a little worried over the situation, for although I have always had faith in his ability to rise to a situation, it was interesting to see how he would take the tremendous ovation offered him. I was proud of him and felt more than ever that if anyone can put International Mental Hygiene across he can do it.[8]

The prospect for an international congress in the United States in 1925 looked good. Beers conferred about it with representatives of ten countries and discussed the organization of national societies in Italy, Spain, Czechoslovakia, Hungary, Denmark, and Sweden. He also was persuaded to lend his name to a foundation to be set up to finance a psychiatric ward in the American Hospital in Paris.[9]

Beers met someone who wanted to translate *A Mind That Found Itself* into French and was advised to give him permission.[10] In Paris he also became acquainted with Dr. Ferrari, the Italian reviewer and translator of his book, who delighted him by pointing out his resemblance to Benito Mussolini. Beers repeated Ferrari's words everywhere: Clifford Beers was the "Mussolini of mental hygiene." Even before this, Mrs. Payne recalled, Beers liked to think he was like Mussolini "both in look and dictatorial manner, but the resemblance applied only to the shape of the face, the high forehead and bald head, for his eyes were sympathetic as well as piercing and under bushy brows, and his smile was warm and contagious." Mussolini had just come into power, promising order and national glory for Italy. Ferrari wanted him as honorary president of the Italian organizing committee for the international congress and promised to have Beers presented to him (and probably also to the king of Italy) when he came to Rome. Many non-Italians admired Mussolini, and Beers, with his conventional political views, his acquaintances among upper-class Americans, and his near veneration of successful, powerful men, was likely to do so, too, although he was aware of Mussolini's totalitarianism. When he finally did visit Rome in 1927, four years after meeting Ferrari, he had nothing to do with the dictator, but as late as 1932 he was not averse to going to an international meeting in Rome the following year and being received by Mussolini (events that did not come to pass).[11]

From Paris, Beers went to London. Shepherded by Helen Boyle, he was interviewed by journalists and met the right people (which he hoped would gain him greater access to wealthy would-be donors back home), and was engaged to speak before the British Medico-Psychological Association and other distinguished groups. Although he wanted no general mass meetings, Beers did speak to an audience of possibly more than two hundred thousand people over the radio, which he found not as bad as he expected: "Talking to a metal disk isn't exactly inspiring, but once one gets going it is easy enough." He regretted not meeting English royalty; the British National Council of Mental Hygiene was still too new to receive royal recognition, but he felt sure that during his next trip he would gain an audience with the king and queen.[12]

A highlight of the London visit was Beers' attendance as an honored guest at the "First Ordinary General Meeting" of the National Council for Mental Hygiene, held on June 27. He was elected an honorary member after a laudatory nominating speech in which the National Committee was cited as having a "record of achievements to be proud of" and as being "the most powerful agency for the amelioration of the mentally afflicted that America has seen since the time of Dorothea Dix." The vehicle for the great movement was *A Mind That Found Itself,* "more than a classic in psychiatric literature . . . at once an inspiration, a message, an impelling force, a call which could not be resisted," whose power was already felt on three continents. "Honor be to him who in his own country has stirred men's minds to realise at last that the mental health of the people is the most important factor in human efficiency and in human happiness, and is the only true basis for the greatness of a nation."[13]

Upon arriving back in the States in July, Clara and Clifford Beers went to Maine, where Clifford mulled over the significance of his trip for his work at home. He thought that his triumphs abroad would win him greater credibility among his colleagues: once again he had proven his ability to gauge correctly the possibilities of creating a movement, this time on an international scale. In a letter to Duggan, chairman of the organizing committee for the International Committee (of which Beers was general secretary), he said that his success in Europe had depended upon his having had freedom of action and his being a foreigner and a layman, outside the struggle between competing factions. European psychiatrists were not interested in the thinking of their American colleagues about mental hygiene. "The only way to show them the best ways of doing it was to bring some of them to an International Congress in this country," which he, Clifford Beers, would organize. As founder of the movement and author of the book that sparked it, he could do more than any psychiatrist to form an international organization. "It isn't that I want to boss things just to satisfy my ego. I must more or less boss them—in the beginning, if I am to succeed in the none too easy task of getting the world movement going. Once it is going I shall wish to get away from the details, for I realize I should give my time to the things I can do because of my peculiar . . . niche in the work." The future looked bright for international work; Beers felt that a new career awaited him. The next thing was to find one hundred thousand dollars, not the originally estimated twenty-five thousand.[14]

Duggan agreed with Beers' assessment of the situation but worried about how the fund-raising could be done without deflecting money and interest from the hard-pressed National Committee, a concern shared by other executive committee members.[15] Russell, the pacifier, had no time to serve on the organizing committee for the International Committee but urged that Beers bury his resentment and invite Salmon to join. Russell also felt that no one person should "determine singly" how or by whom the congress should be organized or managed.[16]

Although Beers acquiesced in the request to include Salmon on his new committee, he could not accept "disaffection" from the international idea and a challenge to his right to act independently in international work. A hundred people had responded to his request for supporting opinions to use in appeals for funds for the congress, but none had come from Salmon,

Kirby, James, or Copp.[17] Beers deeply resented the implication that in focusing on international work he was neglecting his obligation to the National Committee. If his critics "lacked the constructive vision to see or believe in" his scheme to finance the National Committee through a successful international meeting they should "maintain a helpful silence." "Results are produced by people who have faith in success, not by those who scoff or criticize!"[18]

‡

In a private letter to Russell, Beers indicated that Salmon and company opposed him as a way of undercutting Williams' regime at the National Committee, and if they suspected Beers' expressed new confidence in Williams of being insincere they were wrong. Beers then tried to enlist Fernald in a scheme to eliminate Russell, Salmon, and Kirby from the executive committee; they could easily be replaced by "equally valuable — if not more valuable, psychiatrists. . . . You, as the leader in your special field, are indispensable."[19]

How Fernald felt about this maneuver is not clear, but he did continue on the executive committee and Salmon and Kirby withdrew their names from nomination before the December annual meeting of the board of directors.[20] Presiding was the National Committee's new and distinguished president, William Welch, an appointment that pleased Beers but gave more grounds for annoyance with Salmon. According to Welch, writing confidentially to Beers, Salmon had misled him into thinking the job was an honorary one and that there would be an active president to do the work; Welch was much too busy to undertake any new obligations. When he found there was only one president, he felt he had to accept to save embarrassment but that Beers must look for a new one for next year. Arrangements were subsequently made to accommodate Welch; in 1925 he took the position of honorary president and Dr. Charles P. Emerson, a well-known physician, became president. Evidently the struggles within the National Committee were kept quiet enough that Welch knew nothing about them; he still turned to Beers as the influential figure in the organization, and as president he "very charmingly and quite unwittingly sat on the top of a volcano and did not know but that he was on a bed of roses," Beers observed.[21]

The new executive committee seemed to Beers an auspicious one, although the chairman, replacing Russell, was also an institutional psychiatrist, Dr. Arthur H. Ruggles, superintendent of the venerable Butler Hospital in Rhode Island. "There is much poetic justice in the present situation," Beers wrote. "Those who were most active in trying to eliminate me from the active work of the National Committee and isolate me in international work or transfer me to that field prematurely, are now themselves eliminated, and

Dr. Williams and I are masters of the situation and intend to remain in control. We have the support necessary and, at last, an Executive Committee which will work with us harmoniously. The outlook for a Happy New Year was never better" — no doubt also because the executive and finance committees voted him a salary increase if the forthcoming fund-raising effort for the National Committee was successful.[22]

After all the acclaim abroad, Beers had to go back to money-grubbing for the National Committee. But this time it might not be too distasteful. It was decided that, in order to stabilize the general expense budget of the National Committee, he would conduct a campaign in Palm Beach at the end of January. It was a good time to raise money among the vacationers in Florida; the income tax had been cut and corporations were paying extra dividends.[23]

Before leaving for Palm Beach, Beers worked on the new issue of *A Mind That Found Itself* that Doubleday, Page Company, to whom he had transferred publication rights, was putting out, with plans for a big sales campaign. (Russell Doubleday found it "the most revealing, the most interesting, the most extraordinary book" he had read in years.)[24] If the Florida venture succeeded, he would be free to develop his international plans; he "was never happier" in his work. From all the controversy and bitterness, he had emerged with his role in the National Committee intact, his friends placed on the executive and finance committees, his relationship with Williams repaired, and his European tour confirming him as the luminary of the mental health movement. It was impressive. "I am quite sure now that I did not exaggerate your capacity to dodge the arrows of outrageous fortune," George Blumer told him.[25]

The Florida campaign started out well, but after a month Beers decided that the milieu was too languorous; it would take too long to get substantial results. He was looking forward to going back home to work with the National Committee's new treasurer and chairman of the finance committee, Frederic W. Allen, a Yale man and New York partner of Lee Higginson and Co., who had been impressed years before by *A Mind That Found Itself* and now promised to help Beers find money; he had important friends like Payne Whitney and George F. Baker, Jr.[26]

The failure in Palm Beach and the resultant crisis in the National Committee's financial affairs forced Beers to abandon temporarily his international plans.[27] On his own he kept the idea of an international congress in 1925 alive, appealing again to Embree to underwrite it. Embree, though personally sympathetic, had to refuse again; the Rockefeller Foundation had a policy of not financing international meetings.[28] Beers took the rejection as a blow: it would discourage donations from elsewhere and make it impossible to finance an international congress for a long time to come. "For, as is well-known, decisions of the Rockefeller Foundation, which is a sort of 'supreme court' in philanthropy, influence through force of example the decisions and policies of many other organizations of its kind." He hoped that "what the Foundation did not do for reasons of policy, Mr. John D. Rockefeller, Jr., himself may feel inclined to do in the interests not only of the Congress and our National Committee but the movement as a whole.[29] Nothing came of this suggestion or of the approaches to the Commonwealth Fund, so that the international congress had to be put off.

The National Committee's situation was a recurringly grave one that forced Beers each year to scrounge for thousands of dollars to meet current operating expenses. He would not have minded asking for money for special projects, but this constant "emergency begging" was "distasteful and a great strain." If only the National Committee could get at least a hundred thousand dollars a year for several years from "some public-spirited person of vision and wealth." That was the only way, as the "general public does not, and may never, understand and appreciate its work well enough to give it the financial support it deserves."[30]

Despite his weariness of the "emergency begging" and eagerness to move on to international work, Beers dutifully concentrated on finding money to meet the budget.[31] Mrs. Payne described how he worked:

Time, routines, schedules meant nothing to . . . Beers—he worked when in the mood, which was during the winter in his highly elated period. Each morning he had a new plan for raising money . . . and he would go down-town armed with his letters of introduction and wait in outer offices, all day if necessary, with chocolate bars in his pocket for lunch. He used to say, "It's when the potential contributor leaves his office for lunch that I catch him, maybe." After a couple of days of "sitting" he'd decide to take a rest and go to the sketching classes at the Arts Student's League or to a matinee.

When, during quiet days, Mrs. Payne tried to catch up with the backlog of work, Beers would burst into the office, command her to stop everything and listen to his latest scheme. He would try out all his ideas on her first. "Hundreds of letters, drafts of which had to be rewritten dozens of times before he was satisfied, would go out to what he called his first hand-picked list of potential $1,000 donors, and after signing them he never failed to add a postscript, for his contention was that every letter must carry the personal touch."

The winters were always hectic, it was then we disagreed, argued and fought. Time after time I would threaten to quit and he would invite me to do so; we worked at such high tension for so long at a time that I would wilt under the strain when it would suddenly occur to him that

I was exhausted and he'd order me to go home and not come back until I was rested. Sometimes he would bring me a matinee ticket to something musical "just to get away from me for a while," he would say. Or he would call me up to say, "I have a nice present for you, I'll be away for a couple of days and won't you miss me, I don't think." I could never be cross with Clifford for very long.

He only rarely let a rebuff get him down. One experience did disturb him, but it had a happy ending.

For days he had been trailing a very wealthy man, to whom he had a letter of introduction from one of our good friends who thought a substantial gift might be forthcoming. Clifford was depending on this potential contribution so much because for a month none of us had been paid. . . . The prospective donor had successfully evaded Clifford [and when finally cornered had turned him down cold]. "They say, if someone hands you a lemon, you can always make lemonade, but I'm just too tired to try." He talked on and on and I listened with sadness in my heart; one by one the lights in the outer office went out, everyone had gone; we sat in the darkness of his office looking across the Hudson and at the ferries taking their passengers home, but he didn't want to go home, tired as he was. The shrill ringing of the telephone shattered the quiet of the office. It was my husband wondering why I was not at home, for it was long after 7 o'clock. Together we walked down deserted 7th Avenue; it was cold and the sky was brilliant with stars, so I told Clifford to make a wish on the stars and we both did. I left him at 10th St. and he continued to Washington Square to the Hotel Holly.
    Next morning he did not come to the office so I telephoned the hotel and Mrs. Beers said he'd gone out but she didn't know where. About noon he blew in like a cyclone—"Lemonade," he shouted, "gallons of it," and he handed me a check for $25,000. "Know what," he continued, "early this morning I had a hunch, I'd make another try, so I went straight down to Mr. X's office and when I walked in his secretary said she was on the point of calling me up, because Mr. X wanted to talk to me; he told me that after my really eloquent talk yesterday about something of which he had never even heard, he decided the least he could do was to take a look at my book, and that once he dipped into it he couldn't put it down and spent most of the night reading it; said he felt it a privilege to help our cause, and that next year his contribution would be larger—now, how do you like that" . . . waving the check aloft for all to see, [he] spread the glad tidings that today the "ghost would walk."[32]

Beers accomplished a rapprochement with Salmon, whose renewed involvement in the National Committee seemed essential to solving its financial problems. He was anxious, Beers wrote Salmon, to resume their old, warm friendship, the loss of which had greatly pained him and cast a cloud over his work. Salmon invited Beers, Duggan, and Williams to dinner, where the discussion, focusing on the National Committee's fiscal situation, was friendly; "all old scores had been wiped off the slate" and the "complete harmony" would "without question, continue," Beers reported to Russell. Concluding that Salmon had influence with the Milbank Fund, Beers wanted Russell to convince him to press the fund for a five-year rather than a three-year grant for the National Committee's general budget. To Chittenden, Beers was more frank. Russell and Salmon had "adjusted to the new situation"—that is, to Beers' and Williams' control over the National Committee—so that a united front could be presented in the fight for funds. . . . harmony now prevails."[33] Beers had a tendency, after emerging victorious from one of his protracted, bitter struggles, to want to soothe the feelings of the "vanquished" and to feel he had erased rancor, when often the most aggrieved and hostile sentiments had been his own, so that the newfound amity reflected more the subsiding of his own feelings than the recovery of his "opponents."

Beers also looked to his book as a source of help. *A Mind That Found Itself* was being reprinted; from March 1908 to June 1924 there had been five editions and eleven printings. Although not every reprinting was a new edition, each contained changes and additions. Altogether twelve thousand copies had been distributed, half sold and the other half given away, usually to prospective donors, and fifty thousand people were estimated to have read it. From the letters he kept receiving from people who had just come across it, Beers concluded that it could still be marketed as a current publication. In a new effort to set up some sort of permanent source of money for the National Committee, divorced from immediate needs, he proposed to place the copyright in a trust or fund, the profits from sales to be set aside in perpetuity for mental hygiene work; the fund could also be the repository, on an international basis, for gifts for mental hygiene from individuals and foundations. The executive committee thought enough of the idea to allow Beers to appeal for funds for such a foundation, provided it did not detract from current financial needs.[34]

Beers was of course not alone in his fears for the National Committee's financial future, which gave him no peace and deflected him from what really intrigued him. For the first time, Embree, through conversations with Hincks, passed on advice to Beers about the course the National Committee should take. Embree was then still secretary of the Rockefeller Foundation, which had continued to allot annual grants to the National Committee but on a decreasing scale in expectation that with 1929 the contributions would stop entirely; this technique was calculated to stir the National Committee to develop "a broad basis for general support." Privately Embree told Hincks that he would be happy to cooperate with Beers and Williams in "shaping any policy that is good for the cause," but he hesitated to do so uninvited. Embree was expecting to become chief of a new Rockefeller Foundation division interested in human biology, which would place him "in a strategic position to foster mental hygiene development throughout the world." He believed that Beers, as founder of the mental hygiene movement, should have a distinguished position and be allowed free scope for his talents. Raising one hundred thousand dollars a year was too heavy a burden for one man. One way out was to shift part of the National Committee's work to a mental hygiene department of a university, with partial support from the Rockefeller Foundation. This plan would reduce the National Committee's general expense account to a reasonable thirty thousand dollars a year, which could be obtained from income on a million-dollar fund called the "Clifford W. Beers' Fund for Mental Hygiene." The National Committee's existence would be ensured, and the income could support a continuous educational campaign.[35] In other words, the research, training, and demonstration projects would be turned over to a medical school, with the National Committee focusing on public education.

Such a scheme was Beers' "only salvation," Hincks said. "While you are killing yourself in seeking large amounts for running expenses, you will be missing an opportunity to perpetuate the work." Hincks, by then medical director of the Canadian National Committee, had adopted Embree's suggestion for himself. Sponsored by the Rockefeller Foundation, Hincks would study mental health activities in Europe and the United States and then teach and do research at McGill University in Montreal for three months each year and give his other time to the Canadian National Committee in Toronto.[36]

Upon Embree's suggestion, Williams agreed to start a preventive mental hygiene program for students at Yale. As it worked out, Ruggles, the superintendent of Butler Hospital at Providence and chairman of the National Committee's executive committee, was asked instead of Williams to spend a year or two at Yale, to which Rockefeller's General Education Board and an anonymous alumnus each gave fifteen thousand dollars annually for five years to develop a department of psychiatry; there would be work with students and a small ward for mental patients created at New Haven Hospital. Beers, involved in the negotiations for Yale to obtain Ruggles' services, saw this as the beginning of the fulfillment of an old dream.[37]

Hincks also told Beers that the Rockefeller Foundation officials felt that the National Committee often asked for excessive amounts for projects, that its overhead was too high, and that some of the staff should be dismissed. Beers did not take this well. "Firing members of the staff in order to have less money to raise, when the work needs more and more money, would be an injustice to the cause. If the people now in charge of our National Committee cannot finance the Committee on a scale in keeping with the needs and demands, then they ought to get out and let some other group run the show." He would hate to live in a city where Embree was fire commissioner. "If money were scarce he would soon be supplying the Fire Department with garden hose and substituting Boy Scouts for trained firemen! Our National Committee is engaged in life saving quite as much as Fire Departments are, and necessary expenses must be met." The reason the Rockefeller Foundation thought the National Committee budgets were "grandiose" was that the foundation's officials had "a habit of beginning things in a small way and developing them slowly and very safely . . . but not always liberally enough for the best interests of the cause they happen to be helping. If the R.F. had been a real 'angel' to our National Committee all these years the mental hygiene movement would have developed twice as rapidly and twice as effectively as it has done." All kinds of projects were ready to be launched with enough money; it was not as though the National Committee had no idea of what to do.[38]

Beers just could not believe that wealthy people, once they were properly informed, would not provide the resources to deal with a health problem of such enormity. He talked from time to time about eventually building broad popular support that would yield a fairly predictable income, but he did not devote his efforts to it. He had no confidence, and with good cause, that it would be successful in a problematic field like mental health that was difficult to explain in popular literature, and he evidently did not care for that kind of work, preferring to operate through personal appeals to people with money who *should,* who *would* help if only he could get to them. Buttressing his unquenchable optimism and belief in the importance of his cause was his need to make his own suffering years ago meaningful by fulfilling God's design for him to do great work for mankind.

‡

However much he might want to, therefore, Beers could not relax his search for money — both to make up deficits in the annual budget[39] and to finance an endowment of three million dollars instead of the originally sought one million dollars, which he had never been able to acquire. By October 1925 he had managed to get forty-seven thousand dollars from seven of the eight persons he had interviewed, including five thousand from V. Everit Macy, who also agreed to join the executive committee. "This shows money can be gotten if I can get interviews," Clifford told George.[40]

Among the American moguls he had met in Paris was Cyrus H. K. Curtis, the Philadelphia publisher, who promised him an interview back in the United States. In April 1926, Beers, in Philadelphia, tried to reach Curtis but was told by a friend that the old man was interested in organs, not social problems (which was not exactly true), but his daughter, Mary Louise Curtis Bok, wife of Edward William Bok, the editor and peace advocate, was concerned with social welfare and was very generous as well. The morning of this conversation, Beers glimpsed his friend, William Lyon Phelps, at his hotel rushing for an elevator. Assuming, rightly, that Phelps was headed for the Academy of Music, Beers buttonholed him there and asked him if he knew Mary Bok. Phelps did and promised to help Beers reach her. Finding it impossible to draft a letter for Phelps to use in approaching Mrs. Bok because he could not "visualize her," Beers appealed to Phelps to write it, with the suggestion that she be asked to read *A Mind That Found Itself* and grant Beers an interview. Phelps did so, and rather involved maneuvering for the opportunity to speak with Mary Bok ensued.[41]

During this time Beers attended the American Health Congress in Atlantic City, where a merger of all the national health organizations into one superagency was being considered. Viewing this idea as a threat to the autonomy of the National Committee and to the special appeal it could exert, he quickly rallied its members against it. With the support of the American Cancer Society he was able to keep the resolution off the floor and thus "kill off for a long time to come" a plan he regarded as impracticable as well as dangerous.[42] So Clifford Beers played a role in the organizational fragmentation that has characterized voluntary health work in the United States.

Phelps finally arranged for Beers to see Mrs. Bok at the Curtis Institute of Music, which she had founded two years before in Philadelphia, but the presence of several of her friends cramped his style. She agreed, however, to see him in Maine during the summer and also gave him permission to communicate with her eldest son, W. Curtis Bok, a lawyer said to be influential with his mother and interested in prison reform. Beers, used to speaking with cool businessmen and to receiving rebuffs, noticed nothing unusual about his interview with Curtis Bok. But after reading *A Mind That Found Itself,* which greatly affected him, Bok felt he had been rude to Beers, an incident that led to a second interview and then another.[43] Bok discouraged any expectation of receiving a million dollars from his mother, then heavily involved in the Curtis Institute, but he promised to help Beers, who provided him with full information on the precarious financial plight of both the National Committee and himself and sent him a copy of Dorothea Dix's biography and also his own summer address in Maine. Bok, impressed, convinced his mother to see Beers in mid-August.[44]

At that time she told him that because she gave over half her income to the Curtis Institute she could not make a big gift to his foundation; Beers was then about to request money directly for the National Committee, when she interrupted with a plan of her own.[45] "You are," Beers quoted Mrs. Bok as saying, "the torch-bearer. You keep the flame alive. You have worries and anxieties over your financial future. You should be free to work out your destiny not only in relation to the National Committee, but to the Foundation and the international plans. I feel I can help most by freeing you, personally, from uncertainty regarding the future. If you will let me, I should like to guarantee your salary for a period of ten years." It would be ten thousand dollars annually. This payment was not contingent on Beers' being an officer of the National Committee or any other organization and would be made directly to him; if he should be alive at the end of the decade (when both she and Beers would be sixty), Mrs. Bok would take care of the situation then. The day after this offer, which Beers of course accepted, both he and Clara visited Mrs. Bok to thank her; the final agreements were received on August 30, 1926. These days were "the happiest Clara and I have ever known," Clifford wrote George. "We can now see daylight, having won at last a place in the sun." George could send the family's thanks to Mrs. Bok, but Clifford wanted to see his letter beforehand. Concerned that "some of the old 'gang' will probably feel that I shaped the gift in my own interests," he wanted George to express to Mrs. Bok appreciation for the fact that she had originated the idea.[46]

Beers had long dreamed of some such arrangement and at different times since 1917 had formulated schemes to give him and Clara financial security.[47] Surprising and gratifying, then, as was Mrs. Bok's gift, it was not in a sense completely unexpected. Not only had Beers been hoping for a long time to find a personal benefactor, but the very success of the mental health movement created the possibility that one would eventually turn up. Although sincere in claiming that in his fund-raising he always sought support only for the National Committee, in describing the mental hygiene movement to prospective donors he usually stressed his own difficulties and presented himself as the personal embodiment of the movement. And since his style was so personal he set the stage for receiving assistance for himself. Throughout his life in the movement he managed to win the financial and moral support of people just at the moment of greatest need — the Hoggson brothers when, first out of the hospital, he was looking for a job; William James, when his book was ready to be published; Henry Phipps, when he was penniless and wanted to marry — and now Mary Bok, when at the age of fifty he was still without a stable income. His faith in the coming of his personal savior and in the importance of his cause was vindicated again. Of course, owing partly to the work of the National Committee, mental hygiene had become popular among people like Mary Bok who were involved in social welfare, so much so that a professor at the New York School of Social Work wrote in 1926, "No social agency would dare make an appeal to one of the larger financial foundations today without including somewhere in the budget an item for individualistic mental hygiene, even if orthodox family case work was the intended function. Psychiatric social work . . . is the current fashion."[48] Still, Mrs. Bok gave the money to Clifford Beers personally, so forcefully had he struck her and her son and so crucial did they consider his role in the movement.

With his newfound financial independence from the National Committee, Beers intended "to focus upon the plans for a foundation, the International Congress, the International Committee and, perhaps, an International Institute." He had no intention of abandoning the National Committee, which he would aid in every way, but his dread of spending any more years as a mere solicitor of funds was gone (only temporarily, it proved). He would also be in a position to "talk frankly to the board of Directors," to force them "into action in helping to raise money." George Beers, delighted that Clifford would finally be freed from worry, as usual tempered his joy with a warning—this time that Clifford's new independence should not preclude the "necessity of working harmoniously with a considerable group of medical men and others." Clifford, conceding George's good sense, assured him that he would not be too aggressive with the National Committee. But he was now, for the first time, in a position to "point out to them that it must now become a self-supporting agency, with the *help of all,* and that I can't finance it without help. If the present membership won't play the game, then we must get new blood as soon as we can." But before acting he would get Chittenden's advice.[49]

Mrs. Bok had insisted that there be no public announcement of her gift, and Beers kept the news quiet, for he wanted to control to whom the news would go and when by preparing his own account, which he called "The Perfect Gift." This study on the art of extracting substantial contributions from people of wealth was also intended to absolve Beers from any imputation of self-serving by showing that the gift was Mary Bok's idea, not his.[50] The key technique in raising money, he pointed out, was to get potential donors interested enough to request interviews for themselves—that is, to give them a sense of obligation to explore the subject further; then success would be most likely.

As he usually did, or tried to do, with benefactors, Beers drew the Boks into his orbit. The semiannual receipt of his salary was always an occasion for writing to Mary Bok, as was her birthday; he kept her informed of happenings at the National Committee, turned to her for help in his fund-raising, and confided his troubles to her. Her son became involved in forming the foundation he was planning. And although Mrs. Bok could graciously turn him down when she chose, the friendship proved a distinct advantage to him through the years.

‡

The rejoicing at the National Committee over the Bok and Bok-related gifts was short-lived. A new crisis arose, one in which for once Beers was not the storm center but in which he became involved. Dr. Charles L. Dana, a prominent New York neurologist, resigned from the National Committee and its board of directors because of Medical Director Frankwood Williams' espousal of psychoanalysis. Williams had sponsored Otto Rank on his recent American tour and also took on private cases, a questionable practice for a medical director; worse, he practiced upon his patients Rankian methods, which Dana equated with Freudianism. Dana declared that Dr. Bernard Sachs, a world-famous neurologist and a vice-president of the National Committee, agreed with him.[51]

Beers, wanting to avoid a fight at the forthcoming board meeting, persuaded Dana to desist until Arthur Ruggles, chairman of the executive committee, could be consulted; Beers also felt that Williams' activities in behalf of psychoanalysis needed clarification. Williams was willing to have the "lid put on him a bit" so long as he remained medical director, and he acquiesced in Beers' proposal to hold a conference on the matter outside the board meeting. In Beers' opinion, the National Committee could not at that time dispense with Williams' services: he should be reappointed for a year, during which, if the matter of his activities and commitments could not be resolved, there would be time to find a replacement. Since Dana and Sachs were as fervently against psychoanalysis as Williams was for it, there must be a middle course. Dana, though, should be allowed to resign, as he would not be pleased with anything short of a categorical condemnation of the new theory, "and that can't safely be done, where so many psychiatrists more modernly trained than Dr. Dana, say that some forms of psycho-analysis are useful in treating some cases."[52]

Beers kept up with developments in psychiatry and was open to new ideas, so that he hesitated to support a denunciation of any form of dynamic psychiatry, especially as several men whom he greatly respected had embraced psychoanalysis, and many American psychiatrists had been analyzed by Jung during his American visit. The Swiss advocates of Freud had gained wide support in the United States, partly because Adolf Meyer at first endorsed certain Freudian principles, and in 1917 Isador Coriat claimed that psychoanalytic therapy was helpful in paranoia and manic-depressive disorder. The distinguished neurologist and editor of the *Journal of Nervous and Mental Disease,* Smith Ely Jelliffe, along with his close collaborator, William A. White, abstracted psychoanalytic literature from European journals as early as 1905 and 1906, and in 1913 founded the first psychoanalytic periodical in English, the *Psychoanalytical Review.*[53] Both men, especially White, were close collaborators and friends of Beers.

Further, the American Freudians tended to be optimistic toward their patients, an attitude that conformed with the National Committee's position. Freud himself, by comparison with most neurologists and psychiatrists, was a champion of environmental as opposed to hereditary explanations, as was his faithful disciple in the United States, Abraham Brill (translator of both Freud and Jung). Although Freud later emphasized constitutional factors, American psychiatrists in general remained even more optimistic than Freud's European followers. All, however, hoped that the benefits of psychoanalysis could be extended to the masses. In the United States, White, for example, made plans to experiment with psychoanalytic techniques in public mental hospitals. In 1913 he and Jelliffe edited what became perhaps the most popular textbook in American psychiatry, *The Modern Treatment of Nervous and Mental Diseases*. Influenced by psychoanalysis, they took a more hopeful view than previous writers had of the treatment of such disorders, including dementia praecox, which they saw as amenable to treatment and even prevention if environmental conditions were properly modified.[54]

Such thinking created a more favorable climate in psychiatry for a mental hygiene movement that stressed prevention. At the same time, conservative-minded psychiatrists and somatically oriented neurologists and neuropsychiatrists, like Dana and Sachs, found psychoanalysis absurd and antiscientific and fought hard against it. So although Beers would not reject psychoanalysis, he hesitated to alienate the anti-Freudians on the National Committee. He managed for a time to temper the storm over Williams' psychoanalytic interests, but the issue would not die. It went on to involve others like Dr. Charles Emerson, the president of the National Committee, himself neither a psychiatrist nor a neurologist, who took Dana and Sachs' part: far from being expendable, they were "the very backbone of our organization and each one is worth many from other fields of medicine or other professions."[55] Dr. Austen Riggs (for whom the famous psychiatric clinic is named) joined Dana and Sachs in making "charges" against Williams, who, deceived by the gentleness of the executive committee's objections to his attitudes, did not, in Beers' view, show sufficient concern over the matter.[56] Perhaps White, whom Beers invited to the next executive committee meeting, could reach Williams, who was as indiscreet as White was discreet. Especially offensive was Williams' advocacy of lay analysis, which even for Beers went too far. The National Committee, he told Ruggles, "should not be put in the position of officially approving such a questionable procedure" as having lay people practice psychiatry. White agreed with Beers that the most important thing at this time was to protect the National Committee. Williams "should make a concession to the opposition and temper his remarks"; it was possible to express oneself honestly but in a way that "did not offend other people." By then Beers, although not anxious to have Williams resign, decided that if most of the physicians close to the movement repudiated Williams, he would go along with his resignation. In any case, the National Committee would have to define its policy regarding psychoanalysis, which Williams had "prematurely . . . made an issue," thus jeopardizing its work. "Perhaps my original opinion of Dr. Williams as a leader was right after all," Clifford confided to George Beers.[57]

Williams may have made the necessary concessions. At any rate, he did not resign at that time, and the National Committee adopted no position on psychoanalysis. Several years later Beers commented that the committee was criticized for not taking a stand on such controversial issues as birth control, sterilization, and psychoanalysis. His defense was that the National Committee should be nonpartisan, a sanctuary for all sorts of opinions, and that a different policy would be fatal to the movement.[58]

‡

By the beginning of 1927, the struggle over Williams and psychoanalysis notwithstanding, Beers had managed to put the National Committee within five thousand dollars of its three-hundred-thousand-dollar budget, and during the next two months, he hoped to eliminate even that deficit; he had also received a pledge of one hundred thousand dollars toward the next year's budget. Prospects looked good enough for him to turn again to international work and to developing the foundation that he hoped would ensure the survival of the mental health movement in the United States. He planned to call it the American Foundation for Mental Hygiene. Evidence of confidence in the idea came in the form of a pledge of one hundred thousand dollars from Henry Walters, the wealthy railroad executive and art collector, toward the foundation's endowment, conditional upon its securing gifts and pledges of a million dollars by February 1, 1930.[59] Beers had also received encouragement from President Angell of Yale for his idea to establish an International Institute for Mental Hygiene at Yale.[60] From abroad came letters indicating interest in international mental hygiene, including a call for Beers to go to Europe during the spring of 1927, an invitation he could not take seriously until the current needs of the National Committee were met. By May this unexpectedly happened, when the McCormicks, whom he had been after for years, finally donated a large sum to the National Committee, which would make it solvent for two years. Beers believed that the end of its financial instability was at hand.[61]

In May Clifford and Clara Beers booked passage for France, where Clifford would attend the Centenaire de Pinel, a three-day celebration in Paris where his presence would be appropriate, he thought, as many people called him the American Pinel. His primary purpose in going was to participate in the June 2 meeting of the organizing committee of the International Committee for Mental Hygiene. The passage was pleasant, made more so by the opportunity afforded the Beerses to become better acquainted with fellow passengers Alexander James, William James' youngest son, and his wife.[62]

Twenty-five delegates from fourteen countries attended the International

Committee meeting, which was chaired by Beers, the general secretary and the American delegate. He also did most of the talking—in English, as he never learned French well enough—and other people's remarks were translated for him. As during this first trip abroad, Beers mediated between contending groups: for example, the German delegates, who through an "inadvertent" oversight by the French had not been invited to the meeting, were grateful to him for arranging their attendance. It was decided that the First International Congress would be held in April 1929 in Washington, D.C. Beers felt sure he could raise the money to transport a large European delegation to the United States; if not, the meeting would convene in Paris. He also was granted the job of permanent secretary general of the International Committee, a decision that reflected the delegates' regard for him and the practical necessity of having the secretariat located in the United States, with Beers the obvious choice to direct it. To him it meant, too, that he could implement his plan to create a "world-center and clearinghouse on mental hygiene in the United States"; he also told the International Committee of his hopes to create a fund to finance mental hygiene organizations all over the world.[63]

Besides meeting, feasting, and touring, Beers hoped to do some business. Mary Bok and her father were in Rome, where he planned to go to familiarize himself with the work and organization of the International Institute of Agriculture preparatory to organizing the secretariat of the International Committee for Mental Hygiene. Mrs. Bok had just given seven million dollars to the Curtis Institute of Music; perhaps he would meet her in Rome and get some money for his foundation. An unsolicited gift of a thousand dollars from a woman who had followed his work since his first visit to Paris helped Beers to meet his expenses, which had risen unexpectedly high, and he and Clara went to Rome, fortified by a personal letter from the U.S. ambassador at Paris to his counterpart at Rome. Though yielding no Bok money, the Italian trip was useful in impressing upon Beers the importance of making his international organization independent of any government. He and Clara then went to Geneva to inspect the offices and arrangements at the League of Nations, then back to Paris for a rest, and on to London for Beers to give a speech before embarking for home on June 29.[64] Upon his departure from Europe, Beers received a letter from his Italian translator, G. C. Ferrari, thanking him for his international work:

The great work of mental hygiene in America is universally recognized, thanks to the numerous and excellent publications in your particular paper. But you, with your personal charm (which happily has endowed you with the "perfect gift"), have greatly helped to reunite in a unique alliance first the desires and then a few scattered workers, and even the pioneer of the idea, in this old and disillusioned Europe.

The cordiality with which the assemblage has wished you to remain the Secretary General of the movement and the active head of the future Congress, has been the best proof of the identification which one makes in Europe between the mental hygiene movement and Mr. Clifford Beers.[65]

The European trip had been stimulating but not relaxing, and the Beerses went from New York to Maine for their usual summer vacation. While there they heard that Salmon had drowned in a boating accident. Beers wrote to his widow, expressing his regret not only at Salmon's death but that he and Salmon, because of their "markedly different temperaments," had never quite reached the friendship he had hoped for. Always feeling in debt to Salmon, Beers tried to help his wife have her brother admitted into an old-age home, and when in 1938 she objected to her husband's biographer, he actively supported her.[66]

After Salmon's death Beers lapsed into inactivity through almost the entire fall and winter. Whether he had gone into a low period of a recurring high-low cycle, possibly exacerbated by the news of Salmon's drowning, or whether his own and the National Committee's temporary financial solvency created something of a void in a life intensely devoted for so many years to achieving that state, is hard to say. He felt that he lacked a strong impulse to work and hoped that something interesting would come along to prod him into "efficient" activity.[67]

The international congress had again to be postponed, which was just as well, since there was not enough money yet for it and Beers seemed to be having trouble reviving his enthusiasm for the work. The secretary of the American Psychiatric Association, Earl Bond, asked for the delay to 1930 in order to avoid a conflict in 1929 with the first joint session of the American Psychiatric Association and the American Association for the Study of the Feebleminded. In 1930 these two organizations would be willing to meet simultaneously with the international congress on mental hygiene and so consider it as part of their annual meeting.[68]

It was also hard to find money for the American Foundation for Mental Hygiene, which was to be incorporated in order to give it legal status, to meet the conditions of several substantial bequests and pledges already made, and to receive and administer the expenditure of fifty thousand dollars that Beers hoped soon to have for the congress.[69] The foundation was incorporated on May 24, 1928, under the laws of Delaware. Its chief function would be to serve as a repository for contributions made to further mental hygiene work, done primarily but not exclusively under the aegis of the National Committee. In drawing up the legal documents for incorporation, Beers had the counsel of W. Curtis Bok, who was also named a trustee and who wrote, at Beers' request, a "Lincolnesque Preamble" to the certificate of incorporation.[70] The preamble declared that:

Science takes exception to the law that only those whom Nature deems the fittest shall survive. Nature has . . . the remedies for the torture of a broken mind or body, and science is upon the march in search of those remedies. . . . The knowledge so gained forms a sacred trust of civilization for the maintenance of the strong, for the refitting of the weak and sick to their health and opportunity, and for their deliverance to a useful life in the community and that pursuit of happiness which is the proper promise of creation.[71]

This statement clearly renounced the Darwinian pessimism of the late nineteenth century in favor of a twentieth-century concept of optimistic perfectibility that had also characterized the eighteenth- and early nineteenth-century periods of reform in this and other fields. Added is the strong belief in the power of science to solve the mysteries of mental disorder and point the way to mental health and thus to human happiness. Such a conviction motivated the founding of the National Committee, and the ultimate ideal remained the discovery by scientists, not necessarily in the National Committee, of medical solutions. Beers' book sensitized people to the seriousness of the problem of mental disorder; faith in science and a quickening of interest in social reform, together with the propensity of American millionaires to do something useful with their excess money during the boom days of the 1920s, made the cause of mental hygiene attractive to people searching for a nonradical way to ameliorate social conditions and for a nonthreatening explanation of human misery.

The growth of the mental hygiene movement, concomitant with and indeed stimulating the development of psychiatry and psychoanalysis, also offered the possibility of finding answers to the age-old human plagues of war and aggression so horribly evidenced again in the First World War. Perhaps the solution would be found in studying the human psyche scientifically. The twenties were a time of profound disillusion and bitterness, especially in Europe, over the failure of the war and the postwar peace settlements to bring lasting peace and a better life. Mental hygiene might hold the key to an understanding of behavior and its manipulation in the cause of peace through knowledge, education, and treatment. This hope helps to explain the appeal of mental hygiene at this time and particularly the enthusiasm that Beers was able to generate for international work. As was pointed out in 1928 by Professor C. E. A. Winslow of Yale, the president of the Connecticut Society for Mental Hygiene:

After all, this problem is clearly not only a dominant problem in the field of public health but it is going to be *the* dominant problem in the field of public health and human relationships. The conservation of the body is a matter of some importance but, after all, the conservation of the brain power and the emotional power of the human race is a far higher goal, and that is the goal which has been set by this movement.[72]

Tangible encouragement of the international movement came in the receipt by the foundation of the expected fifty thousand dollars from the estate of Mrs. John I. Kane for the international congress and a very faint hope that it could get some of the estate of thirty million dollars left by the philanthropist Payne Whitney. Beers was also pleased by the attention that the nineteenth annual meeting of the National Committee, held November 8, received. It had broadened from a small meeting of members to one attended by over four hundred physicians, psychologists, educators, social workers, and lay people from all over the United States. The *New York Times, Tribune,* and *World* prominently reported the proceedings, which included the announcement of the formation of the American Foundation for Mental Hygiene and plans for the international work.[73]

Despite all the good news and publicity, the National Committee was again in financial trouble, so Beers had to concentrate on getting more money into the foundation. His optimism regarding the continuance of the McCormick contribution, which had constituted half the National Committee's operating budget for the past two years, was not borne out, and although he was able to obtain another substantial bequest, actual receipt of the money would have to wait until the donor died. The strain of this work, Beers believed, accounted for the eye trouble he began suffering. He asked the advice of the ophthalmologist-in-chief at Johns Hopkins Hospital; perhaps he had "shown too much vision" during the past two decades, he quipped.[74]

Possibly more publicity would be the answer for the National Committee; it had helped other organizations. Would Mary Bok write to Adolph Ochs, publisher of the *New York Times?* Beers had met him when they both received honorary degrees from Yale in 1922, and Ochs had read *A Mind That Found Itself* and had otherwise shown interest in his work, but the acquaintance was not strong enough for Beers to approach him on his own. Mrs. Bok complied, with the result that Ochs expressed willingness to publish material helpful to the cause.[75] Much as he wanted publicity, though, Beers was wary of what he considered vulgar popularization of mental hygiene. The mass media did not appeal to him, except where he could more or less control what they reported. A couple of years later, when a feature writer for the *New York World Telegram* approached him for help in starting a daily feature on mental hygiene for the women's page, he put her off: it would take time to work out, "if, indeed, it can be formulated at all. Daily doses of authoritative mental hygiene advice are difficult to concoct. Unless done well, they would do harm, rather than good."[76]

Articles in newspapers might be useful, but they would not directly bring in the five million dollars needed to meet the quarter of a million dollars in annual expenses of the National Committee.[77] To the obvious and persistently asked question of why the National Committee did not scale down its expenses in order to avoid the perpetual crises caused by budget increases and to relieve him of constant fund-raising, Beers replied that the current budget was already a minimum one that a "rapidly growing concern" could not reduce without destroying its usefulness "and so impairing its prestige as to make rehabilitation later not only difficult but, perhaps, impossible." He managed by the middle of 1929 to raise all but fifty thousand dollars of general expenses.[78]

Most of Beers' time had to be devoted to looking for money, but he could not ignore the International Congress scheduled to open on May 6, 1930, the twenty-second anniversary of the mental health movement. Despite delegation of details to an administrative secretary and his not being concerned with the program (which was Frankwood Williams' responsibility), Beers had to be involved in the planning. In April he held the first full meeting of the committee on organization for the congress, exclusive of foreign members; fifty-six people attended, including Adolf Meyer and other chiefs of hospitals, officers of various professional organizations related to mental hygiene and psychiatry, directors of social work agencies, chairmen of departments at medical schools, heads of private schools, and foundation officials, including the director of the Commonwealth Fund[79] — a roster of leading figures in social work, psychiatry, and education that must have been a source of satisfaction to Beers. He had already received a good deal of recognition in the United States, but the Europeans seemed up to then to appreciate his work more. Now the international esteem, culminating in the congress, seemed to increase his prestige at home. William Welch, as usual, marveled at Beers: "How you accomplish it all, I do not understand, but I know no one else would accomplish all that you have done." It was a long time, Beers replied, since he had "had such an inspiring opinion from anyone," and it strengthened him for the hard jobs lying ahead. If Beers was pleased enough by Welch's "bouquet" to pass it on to George to show to Aunt Mame, he must have been overjoyed to hear that President Herbert Hoover had agreed to serve as honorary president of the congress, and if possible to address the opening session. He had no inhibition about sending Hoover a copy of *A Mind That Found Itself* to read in preparation for the congress.[80]

Still, the National Committee's ongoing crisis was a continuing irritant, interfering with Beers' vacation plans and a trip to Europe to speak at the first mental health conference in London. "It's a damned shame, I think, that I have to go around with a tin cup begging for a work that the very rich ought to step up and finance," he told George. Clifford always kept in touch with George, who remained his closest confidant, and through him with the rest of the family, but during these years he did not seem to see his family much. Through a family agreement he took responsibility for supporting Aunt Mame; George Beers and their cousin, Caroline (Carl) Dudley, looked after the still hospitalized Carl Beers.[81]

Beers also kept Mrs. Bok posted on his affairs, with the result that she came through with twenty thousand dollars to take care of the National Committee's expenses for the rest of 1929.[82] This gift enabled Beers to go ahead with plans for his next project, the twentieth-anniversary dinner of the National Committee, which offered a chance to renew contacts with interested people and potential supporters. He managed to get five hundred people to attend what was essentially a tribute to himself and one that he justified by pointing to several gifts that came in immediately thereafter and by the publicity and interest it stimulated. The *New York Times,* true to Ochs' promise, printed a feature article three days after the dinner under the head: "Twenty Years of Work for Mental Hygiene. The Movement Founded by Clifford W. Beers, Who Was Once a Patient in a Connecticut Institution, Has Grown to Activity in Many Foreign Countries." William Welch was toastmaster; William A. White, president of the international congress, President Angell of Yale, and Clifford Beers spoke; and telegrams were read from Henry Phipps and Alfred E. Smith, former governor of New York State, who proclaimed his long-term interest in mental hygiene.[83] Welch talked about Beers' great role in the movement: unlike other great movements in the health field, whose origins were obscure and complex, the mental hygiene movement

> is just one man and one book. Other books have been written by those who have gone through mental disturbances, but no book in any way in my judgment, is comparable to his. It is of interest to psychologists, to psychiatrists, of interest to humanitarians – to all who are interested in great social movement. . . . Dangerous as judgments of one's contemporaries may be as to the historical niche which one may occupy, . . . Clifford Beers's name is imperishable in connection with the launching of this great movement.

Angell also paid tribute to Beers:

> I think it is entirely impossible to over-estimate the courage and devotion which he has shown in building up this extraordinary movement, with absolutely no limit to the personal sacrifice which he has been willing to make, bringing as it has, literally to thousands upon thousands of people, a fresh courage to face life, a fresh hold on human happiness, and a fresh belief in the essential value of human living. This, I think, is a great achievement.[84]

By then, in spite of the deepening economic depression, things were beginning to look up for the National Committee and certainly for the international congress, support for which was substantial. Beers was able to get Thomas Lamont to serve as treasurer of the congress, a nominal appointment but one that would give cachet.[85] Even Adolf Meyer had agreed to be a vice-president.

Once the congress was under way, and under distinguished auspices, financial backing became easier to get. Besides the original fifty thousand dollars for expenses, there came from the Commonwealth and Rosenwald Funds ten thousand dollars each for the traveling expenses of foreign delegates expected to deliver papers; later five thousand dollars each was received from the Milbank Memorial Fund and the Metropolitan Life Insurance Company, and through Welch, eight thousand dollars from the balance remaining in the treasury of the defunct International Congress on Hygiene and Demography; the registrations at the congress itself were expected to yield a good deal (actually one hundred thousand dollars). At the end of 1929, Beers had improved the situation of the National Committee as well: he and Ruggles convinced Henry Walters to convert his conditional gift to the foundation into an unconditional contribution of one hundred thousand dollars, which, Beers told Walters, gave him "one of the greatest thrills I have ever experienced in my work." The money would give stability to the foundation and help to attract other gifts; it would also enable the foundation to come to the aid of the National Committee in financial crises and would free Clifford Beers from worries and allow him to achieve new successes through the international congress.[86]

‡ 15 ‡

The First International Congress
on Mental Hygiene

The First International Congress on Mental Hygiene was perhaps the acme of Clifford Beers' career. Certainly that is the way he regarded it. Running six days, from May 5 through 10, 1930, it was a hectic affair filled with scientific sessions, field trips, luncheons, dinners, and receptions—all packed with thousands of delegates, among them leading practitioners, researchers, and theoreticians in mental hygiene, psychiatry, social work, and allied fields from all over the world. Beers was in the middle of it all, rushing around in an old-fashioned straw hat whose bobbing in the lobbies, reception rooms, and meeting halls marked his presence everywhere.[1]

From forty-one countries (including the United States and its possessions) came 3,042 officially registered participants; the crush was so great that many more probably attended than were registered. There was representation from the major nations of Western Europe and also from Eastern Europe, the Soviet Union, India, Japan, Siam, Venezuela, the Union of South Africa, Cuba, Costa Rica, the Dominican Republic, and Uruguay. Besides Herbert Hoover as honorary president, William A. White as president, and Thomas W. Lamont as treasurer of the congress, the vice-presidents included the chief of the U.S. Children's Bureau, the secretary of the interior, the surgeon general of the U.S. Public Health Service, the presidents of Yale University, the American Psychiatric Association, American Neurological Association, American Association of Psychiatric Social Workers, American Association for the Study of the Feebleminded, and the American Psychological Association, the leading American psychiatrist, Adolf Meyer, and the leading physician and medical educator, William Welch of Johns Hopkins. There were also honorary vice-presidents from twenty-seven countries. Participating organizations included national mental hygiene societies from twenty countries, twenty American state mental hygiene societies, fifty-two U.S. professional and voluntary organizations and government agencies in allied and related fields, and the League of Red Cross Societies, the International Council of Nurses, and the Health Organization of the League of Nations.[2] Prominent psychiatrists, social workers, and other specialists (including Meyer, Russell, Glueck, Brill, Ferrari, Franz Alexander, Karl Menninger, Helene Deutsch, and Otto Rank) delivered papers and participated in the discussions, and Secretary of the Interior Ray Lyman Wilbur, himself a physician and former professor and dean of the medical school at Stanford, addressed an "International Dinner" that opened the Congress. The unanticipated arrival of so many delegates from so many countries led to the addition to the program of three "world view" meetings so that the congress might get an "adequate world view of mental hygiene work and its development," since the planned program was organized by topic rather than by countries. Also, to meet popular demand, a special postcongress session was held on May 10 to enable the Russians to give a more extensive picture of mental hygiene in the Soviet Union.[3]

Several months before the congress opened it had become apparent that more than the fifteen hundred delegates originally expected would come, and Beers could not manage all the details by himself. Upon the recommendation of the Red Cross and after checking with the State Department, he engaged H. Edmund Bullis, a retired U.S. Army colonel, to help organize practical arrangements, especially the supervision of living arrangements and social functions for the foreign delegates. As Bullis remembered it, the official program, for which Williams was responsible, was the only competently organized part of the congress. Everything else was a mess—room reservations, registration procedures, field trips, receptions, the opening banquet. (On the morning of the banquet only eight reservations had been received and only sixteen by evening; the cooks kept killing more chickens as more people took tickets. By the time of the dinner a crowd of sixteen hundred had turned up.) Except for William A. White, who had a way of smoothing things over, Bullis found the committee of psychiatrists that he worked with hopeless in dealing with ordinary problems; they could not agree on anything and had no experience organizing a large meeting. He had to do the job himself, with the loan of experienced people from banks and elsewhere to manage the registration, collect money, and take care of the innumerable details of running such a large meeting involving so many foreigners.[4] Evidently Beers did not concern himself with the minutiae or even the overall management of the congress; one participant remembered that he left various jobs unfinished.[5] He was understandably on edge, and, as secretary general of the congress, was busy mingling with the dignitaries, renewing friendships he had made in Europe, and making others.

The first day so many delegates crowded the registration desks that two policemen had to be brought in to keep order. Eventually lines formed and several thousand people were moving slowly along, when Beers came up to the head of the line with two distinguished European delegates. Told he would have to wait his turn, Beers insisted: he was Clifford W. Beers, founder of the movement, secretary-general of the congress. Bullis' assistant neither knew nor cared. Finally Bullis, tough and efficient, came out and he, too, refused to let Beers and his guests register; it might cause a fuss. Beers' face blackened with anger and he stamped away. For days he refused to talk to Bullis, who learned later that no employee ever dared to cross Clifford Beers. By the end of the week Beers had relented and admitted that Bullis' systematic management had ensured the success of the congress, which was the "top experience" of his life. Would Bullis come to work for him? No, Bullis replied, "You're the most impossible bird I ever worked with." Beers, he recalled, "didn't get mad; things would roll off his shoulder." Bullis also found the idea of working with psychiatrists distasteful, and he thought the National Committee staff was incompetent.[6]

Beers was probably quite excited; he didn't sleep much, and he looked tired. Rumors must have circulated about his condition, and when people began coming up to him to suggest that he needed a vacation he decided to make a public announcement on the subject, which he did several times. He had several opportunities, as he spoke at the opening dinner, the inaugural session, and the closing luncheon, and greeted guests at a reception held at St. Elizabeths Hospital by White. At the reception he admitted that he might be difficult to live with under the present hectic conditions, but "I am never happier than when I am busy." The next day he assured the luncheon audience that he was not overworked, only "extremely active," as others had done the real work of the congress; after it was over, like a fireman between fires, he would take it easy. "When we went out to Dr. White's reception in a taxi, as we got into the yard there the taximan said, 'The receiving ward?' (Laughter) That is an absolute fact. I said, 'No, please, the reception ward this afternoon.'"[7] His wit and buoyancy were so engaging that he could get away with all kinds of egocentric remarks and leave an audience laughing and charmed. Hincks a few years later described him as a speaker:

> Beers adopts a natural conversational style with no attempt at oratory—
> he is fluent, unstudied, intimate and with extemporaneous flashes of
> wit and insight that immediately disarm and, at the same time, intrigue
> an audience. As is the case with his writing there is directness and sim-
> plicity. And, while he is frequently facetious in referring to himself and
> to his psychiatric colleagues, there is always a note of seriousness for
> the work in which he is engaged—for his baby—for the mental hygiene
> movement. He invites you to laugh at him if you will, but not at his
> health movement, that has high aspirations for the improvement of
> our civilization.[8]

He was determined to get his due as the moving force in mental hygiene. He enjoyed all the references to him in various speeches, formal and infor-mal, and relished any chance to speak in front of an audience or serve on reception lines. In the picture of the founders of the congress he stood up front in the central group, with Welch and Meyer nearby. When a panoramic photograph of the delegates was arranged on the White House lawn during a reception there, Beers saved himself a place in the middle, next to President Hoover. Just as Hoover came over a woman stepped in beside him. Beers told her bluntly that he was the founder of the movement and was going to stand next to the president; she would have to stand somewhere else. Hoover looked a little surprised, the woman moved, and the picture was taken with Clifford Beers in his place of honor.[9]

The high point of the congress was the inaugural session on Tuesday evening, May 6, 1930, at Constitution Hall, where some three thousand people gave him a standing ovation. In boxes around the auditorium were diplomatic representatives from many of the countries participating in the congress, and on the stage sat the foreign delegates and congress officials. Welch presided over the meeting, where the delegates, all in formal dress, were greeted by White, Ruggles (chairman of the committee on organization), and Beers.[10] In his presidential address White discussed Beers' creative response to his sufferings and called him "the genius of whose mind among a million saw opportunity where no one else had seen it for a century," one who not only devoted everything he had to the mental hygiene movement, but was "willing to strip his soul and tell his experiences to the world in that wonderful book of his." He had brought the impossible to pass.[11]

Beers made a witty, graceful speech in which he acknowledged the contributions of his wife, his friends, and his associates (Adolf Meyer among them) to the growth of the movement and to his own career. He also talked about the difficulties of financing the movement and predicted that in time it would be liberally supported: mental health was an interesting and widespread problem, it was being increasingly realized that the solution to social problems had to encompass mental factors, popular awareness of mental hygiene was growing, and the American Foundation for Mental Hygiene was proving successful. The success of the movement was due not only to his and the National Committee's efforts, but to the work of many people in all countries. He looked forward to the second congress, "to be held in Paris, the city in which Pinel, during the French Revolution, when mass madness was so evident, demonstrated at that historic hospital, the Bicêtre, that the so-called insane were not possessed of demons, but were, in fact, sick people deserving of humane care and the best of treatment."[12]

The congress received a good deal of notice in the press, which was fully represented at the proceedings by the Washington papers, the Associated Press and other services, reporters and feature writers from various press syndicates, magazines, and out-of-town papers like The *New York Times,* whose correspondent wrote especially clear and accurate reports of the sometimes abstruse discussions of mental health problems.[13] Beers figured prominently in many of the news reports and feature articles. *Time,* for example, devoted several columns to the meeting and ran a picture of him. Columnist James Hay, Jr., in the *Washington Post,* wrote a paean in mixed metaphors: "He is a star, satrap and superman among all those amazing persons who have transformed difficulties into stepping stones, risen Phoenix-like from the ashes of their own destruction, and, taking running starts from the bogs of obscurity climbed without aid . . . to the glittering top of the Tower of Fame."[14]

All this would have been exhilarating for anyone, and certainly for Clifford Beers, who saw an old dream fulfilled and who, after seemingly endless struggles for recognition and money, was receiving homage from so many distinguished men and women. Beyond that, he was immensely pleased that what had first been regarded almost thirty years before as a delusion, a manifestation of his insanity, should have come to pass. His presumably wild ideas were actually sane. Bold as he was in referring to his past and even to his present condition, instrumental as he was in trying to change popular misconceptions of mental disorder and to remove the stigma from its sufferers, he still could not freely transcend the shame of insanity.

‡

No one could deny that the convening of the congress under such impeccable auspices was a triumph for Beers and for the National Committee. In private, though, there were some doubts about the value of the accomplishment. The Rockefeller Foundation had declined again to contribute toward the congress, this time because it did not meet its criteria for support of meetings: "When the Congress seems of out-standing importance [and] when it seems thoroughly justified as a mechanism of the wise promotion of the field which it represents."[15] That long-time and ardent supporter of Beers and the National Committee, William Welch (whose connection with the congress almost convinced the Rockefeller Foundation to support it),[16] publicly praised the conference.[17] Afterwards, he wrote his private thoughts to Simon Flexner in a letter that Flexner described as a "rare burst of discouragement." The congress, Welch said, "was rather terrible as an example of rousing the public before the foundation of sound knowledge and doctrine had been laid. With good psychiatric and neurological institutes something might be done in mental hygiene, but it would have to be at first so elementary as to lack altogether the spectacular appeal now made for this subject." Flexner noted that Welch, although he considered the mental hygiene movement "one of the great movements of all time," wanted to "create a sound, scientific basis for the care of the mentally sick."[18] Welch's assessment expressed the feeling among several leading physicians (mostly but not only nonpsychiatrists) that the National Committee had oversold mental hygiene to the public, that there was not yet enough information to back up various prevailing ideas about how to treat and prevent mental disorders, and even that the specialty of psychiatry was based on not very firm ground. And Edwin Embree, by then with the Julius Rosenwald Fund, was said to have commented after the congress, "Well, my attitude towards mental hygiene is entirely different than my attitude ten years ago. It really has the greatest charter in the world for human betterment. It, however, has been oversold and people are expecting too much."[19]

The congress did bring together a great, enthusiastic crowd of all sorts of people, but the men and women who presented papers and gave commentaries were mostly all well-known, learned European professors. The major papers (forty-eight in all) were not read in their entirety but distributed to the delegates in three languages—English, French, and German—and summarized by their authors at the formal sessions, which included comments on the papers and discussion from the floor. Besides the meetings, displays, and press and information services, there was a consultation service for those wanting advice on any aspect of mental hygiene work. The program was developed with the aim of producing "significant contributions from leading thinkers and workers in all countries to the philosophy and practice of mental hygiene."[20] A number of the papers reflected some of the most advanced and pioneering thinking and programming in the field, especially those from a psychoanalytic point of view, which has always been criticized for its lack of scientific validation. So here could be ground for disapproval from men like Welch, one of the founders of scientific medicine in the United States and leader of a profession traditionally conservative and suspicious of purely psychological explanations of illness. Indeed, at the congress considerable objection was taken to Freudian ideas.

But what really offended Welch and like-minded people were the seemingly boundless optimism and enthusiasm for mental hygiene, the turning away from concentration on mental disorder and the mentally ill toward investigation of "normal" behavior, and the emphasis on prevention through proper child guidance and public education. One of the stated purposes of the congress expressed this view:

Through news and comment resulting from the Congress, to arouse greater world interest in mental hygiene, and secure greater acceptance of the idea that mental disease can, in large measure, be prevented, and that greatly increased governmental and philanthropic expenditures for mental health will find justification in lives saved for productive activity and will be good public policy.[21]

This trend—emergent at the turn of the century, noticeable in the 1920s, and quite evident by 1930—reflected the shift from biological and hereditary explanations to a focus on socially produced environmental causes of mental disorder. Hence prevention could be an objective to be realized through a campaign of public education. And although few people in the mental hygiene movement itself extended the concept to call for a radical transformation of the social environment, interest in the issue can be seen by the extra session held at the congress on mental hygiene in the Soviet Union. This more socially oriented approach moved mental hygiene beyond psychiatry and attracted people interested in social reform, in the amelioration of human suffering, and in effecting basic changes in behavior and thus helping to create a better social order and greater possibilities for human happiness. These themes were expressed again and again at the congress.[22]

Sir Maurice Craig, chairman of the National Council for Mental Hygiene of Great Britain, asserted that it was "becoming increasingly evident that the mental-hygiene movement is one of the greatest medical movements of modern times," one that "will increasingly continue to save many persons from the severer forms of mental disturbance." Its value extended into all "human matters and activities." The movement's concentration on prevention conformed to contemporary medical developments: "The whole trend of modern medicine is toward prevention of disease." Further, "this wonderful International Congress will mark a new epoch in medicine, an epoch that I verily believe will prove to be second to none in its value for the alleviation of suffering in the human race." From James Angell, president of Yale University and a psychologist, came the suggestion that the movement was in the "most strategic position to exercise leadership, for it has the entree into all sorts of social organization engaged with the problems of men and women." His hopes went beyond the "diminishment of social maladjustment" or "mere betterment of public health" to a "more basic objective," the "enrichment of the quality of life." And Barry Smith, general director of the Commonwealth Fund, said, "More and more I think we are coming to believe that perhaps the greatest value of the child guidance clinic or the mental hygiene clinic in general lies in its educational work, in its being a center for the education of the community." The emphasis on prevention reflected, Dr. Haven Emerson, professor of public health administration at the College of Physicians and Surgeons of Columbia University, pointed out, the "relative failure of . . . curative medicine," which could not restore more than 25 to 30 percent of patients admitted to mental hospitals. Like Beers, Emerson believed that half of both suicides and admissions to mental hospitals "could be prevented, chiefly through guidance of behavior and emotions in childhood and adolescence."[23]

Ferrari, founder of the Italian League for Mental Hygiene, proclaimed:

The mental prophylaxis of the new generation is certainly the greatest claim to honor, and will be the real glory, of the American movement for mental hygiene. For, if for a long time now we have been preoccu-pied with the young people who fell ill or who had become perverts, the idea of taking care of youth in its entirety, even of those who are not ill and who perhaps never will be, could be born only in North America, because of the "freshness" and the courage with which she faces facts and problems, and also because of her great riches.[24]

Few speakers went as far as Dr. André Repond, president of the Swiss National Committee for Mental Hygiene. He attributed physicians' opposi-tion to mental hygiene to its "psychological nature," which physicians had lost sight of "owing to the influence of the purely materialistic medical and scientific advances of the last decades." The tasks of mental hygiene "em-brace practically every form of human activity" and aimed to change "so-called normal" people's memory, thoughts, emotions, and instincts. Mental hygiene allows psychiatrists to come out of their isolation, to use their knowledge and to submit it "to the test of facts." It was "also the opportu-nity of a belated, but necessary and noble revenge on the other branches of medicine, which always considered psychiatry as belonging to an inferior or-der. Indeed it may well be, that through mental hygiene, the crowds who were ensnared by religious and charlatan medications will return to the path of scientific medicine, now misunderstood on account of its materialism and lack of soul."[25]

Several speakers introduced notes of doubt. Even Ferrari admitted that it was not "at all easy to see how mental hygiene can intervene and successfully influence" the conflict commonly occurring between parents and children. Sir Hubert Bond, commissioner of the Board of Control in England, in com-menting on Haven Emerson's paper, questioned whether the "vista held out is not too rosy." It would be better to define mental hygiene as a public health measure—the preservation of mental health, not the prevention of mental illness.[26]

Adolf Meyer, in his paper, "Organization of Community Facilities for Prevention, Care and Treatment of Nervous and Mental Diseases," tried to give a balanced view and called for a rational, practical approach, although he criticized the mental hygiene movement for straying too far from psychia-try and medicine in its need to go beyond them in promulgating reforms and educating the public. Meyer attempted to explain why Americans tended to become so enthusiastic about the prevention of mental disorders: it repre-sented a turn from a static focus on institutional treatment of mental pa-tients to a concern for "health, happiness, and efficiency of the rank and file of people." This spirit drew its impetus from several sources: a new achieve-ment or discovery, a change in general philosophy or goals, or a "personality that impresses a new stamp on the attitude and policies and mobilization of persons disposed to muster the available opportunities—either a movement largely of optimists and opportunists, toward what we might expect of an exuberant temperament; or a movement more of steady and systematic growth and construction." In the United States especially, "a buoyant pioneer spirit to this day gives opportunities to individuals of the most varied preparation to cultivate their courage of naïve vision, and to harvest the realization of their personal plans." The result was "tendencies of an almost kaleidoscopic variety," shaped by "a mixture of humanitarian, fiscal, and medical factors" and leading to, among other things, "almost Utopian promises of prevention," along with "archaic traditions" (such as trial by jury for commitments to mental hospitals).

No special prominence was given in Meyer's short history of the mental hygiene movement to Beers' role; his book and his activities in founding the National Committee are seen as influential events in a continuum of effort by numerous people. It is clear, however, that Meyer would categorize Beers among those of "exuberant temperament" and strong personality who create movements out of their "personal plans" and "naïve vision." And although he says little about the National Committee, here and there can be discerned criticism of its turn away from efforts "to secure adequate facilities for more rigid scientific control and creative work in psychiatry" toward independence from psychiatry and an unbalanced concentration on child guidance. Meyer conceded that the mental health movement should concern itself with organizing the "entire mental-health service and at the same time . . . reach into all the educational and industrial and court and home spheres, the work-distribution and license offices, the marriage license and advice centers, etc."—work that required "many more special work centers, as well as a favorable state and civic community spirit; and an active promotion of research and teaching as well as of service centers." He cautioned against using disease to define health, "as is done by certain psychotherapeutic cults and especially by psychoanalysis," and he did not conceive of psychiatry and mental hygiene replacing sociology, education, and the "religious-moral work of the community." There was enough to do within the sphere of sound psychiatric research and teaching, combined with service.[27]

‡

Clifford Beers had no doubts about the value of the mental hygiene movement and, besides, had long before abdicated, as Meyer would have wished, to the medical staff of the National Committee the direction of its work. He knew what the staff was doing and kept up with current trends, but his main concerns were with promotion, organization, and fund-raising. He had become, in a sense, an entrepreneur for whom the object was to keep his business going and ever expanding, for whom there were no limits to growth in this field that he considered so crucial. The congress, which he considered an unqualified success, spurred him to new projects: not only a second congress in Paris, but serious efforts to establish an international institute of mental hygiene at Yale University. As was his practice in launching new enterprises, he started to draw up an "Outline" of such an institute and gathered approving letters from well-known physicians, scientists, and educators. The institute would be an "international center for the collection and dissemination of information on all subjects relating to the mental health, efficiency and the well-being of mankind."[28]

Where the estimated five-million-dollar endowment for the institute would come from, in the midst of a worldwide depression and when the National Committee had yearly to be financed, was another question, and one of which Beers, though as usual optimistic, was well aware. His fund-raising work, burdensome before, would become even more so, especially as the International Committee had been firmly established at the congress. He was secretary of the National Committee (for which he wanted to start a general membership campaign), the American Foundation for Mental Hygiene, and the International Committee for Mental Hygiene.

‡ 16 ‡

Traveling and Family Troubles

Beers wanted to be freed from routine duties of his secretarial positions to devote his time to raising big money and developing his projects, and he knew just the man to become his executive secretary — the efficient (though, according to others, hucksterish and amoral) Colonel Bullis, who, financially pressed, had changed his mind about working for Beers. After some haggling and a "scene," Beers got half a year's salary for Bullis from a contribution and the American Foundation gave the other half, so that Bullis really worked for Beers rather than the National Committee. When Bullis worried about how Williams, who did not have a high opinion of him, would take his presence, Beers wrote Williams off as being so involved in his private practice and so uninvolved with the National Committee that no one cared much what he said. Besides, Williams was leaving at the end of the year. Bullis then accepted the job.[1]

This cavalier attitude toward Williams reflected a growing dissatisfaction, in Beers as well as others, with Williams' performance as medical director.[2] Williams may have stayed away from the National Committee offices as much to avoid Beers as because of outside preoccupations. He found Beers difficult to take, although it is said that he had no ill feeling toward him, regarding him as a sick man who went through more or less yearly cycles of ups and downs that included slight feelings of paranoia; by 1930 Beers was becoming more difficult, more crotchety.[3] Basically, though, Williams left the National Committee because, Beers said, his interest had waned. Beers, though he did initiate an unsuccessful move to oust Williams six months before he was due to go, had none of the strong feelings against him that he had had toward Meyer and Salmon. As for the next medical director, Beers wanted to have a strong say in his choice, but it was Ruggles who first suggested Clarence Hincks, the director of the Canadian National Committee. Beers at first demurred: Hincks did "not consider himself much of a psychiatrist and is not thought of as one by many 100% psychiatrists." Later he changed his mind.[4]

Hincks and Beers had much in common. They were both successful salesmen of mental hygiene and good money raisers, and they both suffered from mental disorders. Hincks several times a year went into a depression that kept him inactive and during which his loyal colleagues tried to carry out the programs he initiated during his up periods.[5] During the negotiations between Hincks and the National Committee, Beers told Hincks not to mention his "dull" periods; if his wife didn't notice them they could not be too bad, and there was no point telling the executive committee about it. Beers himself had such episodes but he still managed to accomplish as much as most of his associates.[6]

By this time, the summer of 1930, after the exhilaration of the congress, there seems to have been increased notice of Clifford's mental state. He had, as he said, for a long time undergone periodic swings — great activity in the fall and winter, tapering off by late spring, and then almost total inactivity by summer, when he usually went off for a quiet stay in Maine, a hiatus also forced upon him by the virtual impossibility then of reaching potential donors. When he had to, he did plunge into activity in the spring and summer, but increasingly he tended to rest during the summer — sit, do a little fishing, some driving, and a little painting, which he had begun to take up.[7] In August 1933 he wrote to Paul McQuaid about an award proposed for him: "In my present mood I should feel embarrassed to receive an honor publicly. Only when I am in my proper role is that easy to do. I always feel this way in summer and wonder if I'll ever again be interested in my work. But I always am." His state was such that it was "difficult for me to realize that I have done anything worthwhile."[8]

After the International Congress in 1930 he was so exhausted and wound up — notwithstanding his telling Hincks that the prospect of his coming to the National Committee had put him "in the happiest state of mind I have ever known at this time of year in all my years of work" — that Clara Beers begged Hincks to postpone a planned meeting in Montreal. "Only once before in my life have I interfered in National Committee affairs and this isn't really an interference but a suggestion," she wrote. Clifford was so tired and "intense over everything and I know he would have it on his mind thinking up points and arguments. . . . This two months in Maine of absolute relaxation have always set him up for the winter and he needs these more than ever this year." Would Hincks please destroy the letter, as "Clifford would be furious if he knew I was writing you."[9]

As it worked out, a September meeting proved better for all concerned, and Beers could rest easily, especially as in July he received some very good news. In January it had been announced that the estate of Conrad Hubert, manufacturer of searchlight batteries, would be distributed by a committee composed of Calvin Coolidge, Alfred E. Smith, and Julius Rosenwald. Sixteen hundred organizations and institutions applied for a part of the money. Beers, learning of this opportunity late, had to submit the National Committee's application within forty-eight hours, but through Dr. Bernard Sachs it was placed by Rosenwald among the first eight to ten requests. Finally in July the news came that the National Committee would get two hundred and fifty thousand dollars.[10]

This was a wonderful accomplishment, but since nearly half the money was already committed, attention still had to be given to fund-raising, which the National Committee was turning over again to professionals, the John Price Jones Company, which had had a good deal of success for philanthropic organizations. Beers, wary of professionals after the Boston fiasco and, despite his weariness of fund-raising, never keen to surrender his monopoly of it, objected: the campaign they visualized was too big and too expensive; their literature was no good; the National Committee should have more to say; they were interfering in National Committee business; and, most of all, they had attacked his mental stability in order to keep him from interfering. In the end, the contract with the Jones Company was terminated.[11]

Beers did as much as he could to see that Hincks, whom he had come to see as "the only man in the world suited to the job" of director of the National Committee, got it.[12] Hincks, though, seems to have anticipated trouble with Beers and tried to set down at the outset a basis for their working together. They must cooperate, talk problems out freely, and present a united front. Hincks would always consider Beers the "Founder and . . . fountainhead of the whole Mental Hygiene movement. From the standpoint of distinction that has been worthily won, you will always have first place." Hincks only wanted a reasonably free hand in program-planning, in consultation with the whole group. During the past thirteen years he had had no boss, and his mind worked best when the sky was his limit. "Indeed, I am of the same temperament as yourself." Soon Hincks made it clear that he wanted to control both administration and funding, though he would collaborate with Beers in the latter. "I find the two things so fit into one another . . . [that] my task would be enormously complicated if it were split up into two."[13]

Beers claimed to be delighted. Hincks' ideas and methods were as close to his own as he could reasonably expect. "I shall get myself out of the National Committee work as rapidly as possible, so you [and Bullis] may both have free swing. I say this because I have confidence in both of you."[14]

This cheerful letter was written two weeks after a Beers family tragedy. After suffering from manic-depression for years, William Beers, Clifford's older brother, committed suicide at the end of August 1930. Clifford had probably been involved in placing William in hospitals through the years, but his interest seems to have been minimal in comparison with his concern for Carl, who was incurably ill and needed financial help. By the 1920s William was able to function fairly well and had resumed his career as a successful businessman until the stock market crash, when he became depressed over his losses. On Clifford's advice he entered Bloomingdale Hospital; a few months later he was found hanging from a tree on the hospital grounds.

William was the brother most like himself—a gregarious Yale man who never missed a reunion, a successful salesman, witty, talkative—but the two were not very congenial. Still, Clifford was interested in William's child (however much he deplored any of the Beers brothers daring to have children) and not unconcerned about William himself. But his death did not seem to move Clifford deeply; perhaps he found it too painful. The most that he said, in reply to a letter of condolence, was, "We have had so many mental afflictions in our family that they no longer jolt me—though they are of course, saddening." He doubted that William "would ever have recovered because he was making no effort to do so, and if he had recovered it is doubtful if he, with his make-up, would have stayed well. Will had many fine traits and abilities, but he lacked persistency and ability to interest himself in any one thing for very long at a time. By habit he evaded issues much as *Dr. Salmon* did!" Here we see the personality traits that Beers considered essential to his own mental health.[15]

He pushed forward with plans for the new era of the National Committee under Hincks and Bullis, when new members would be needed for the staff and also on the executive committee, with whose composition Beers was much concerned. Since under Hincks the emphasis of the National Committee would be on research, it was suggested that Meyer be elected president. Beers had long felt that a psychiatrist rather than a general physician should be president, but Meyer would decidedly not be his choice. In a tactful way Beers suggested that the idea be dropped in the interest of progress and harmony.[16] It was good to have Meyer participate in meetings and lend his name to great undertakings like the International Congress, but Beers would not consider working with him again.

Beers did look forward to Dr. Ralph Noble coming from Australia to be general director of the International Committee and director of the National Committee's new division on psychiatric education and research, with a professorship at Yale. The Beerses were thinking of returning to New Haven to live, near old friends and relations. Clifford would commute to New York as necessary, and, with Noble in New Haven, would open an office there of the International Committee, which would lead to the creation of the International Institute there and eventually the transfer of certain functions of the International Committee, the National Committee, and the American Foundation for Mental Hygiene. With the National Committee in the hands of his friends Hincks and Bullis, he felt free to "cut loose, as it were" from it and turn his attention to other things. He had had enough of National Committee chores.[17]

The most exciting new project was a trip to Hawaii, via California, and then, at Noble's invitation, to New Zealand and Australia. The Hawaii tour, under the aegis of the governor and financed by the American Foundation, originated in a request to the National Committee from the secretary of the Territorial Conference of Social Work for an outstanding leader from the mainland to come and sow a "seed in this outpost for the better understanding and treatment of those mentally and emotionally afflicted."[18]

Before leaving on such a long trip Beers wanted to arrange matters so that the affairs of all his organizations would be taken care of. He had the International Committee for Mental Hygiene and an International Foundation for Mental Hygiene incorporated. (The latter organization was established to function on an international basis just as the American Foundation for Mental Hygiene did in the United States.)[19] At the National Committee, Beers had great confidence in Hincks, and Bullis was working out well, his efforts directed mainly at reorganizing the office and making it more efficient.[20] At the same time as Bullis was trying to cut costs, Beers proposed to raise them by hiring another associate secretary to handle his personal correspondence and work for the foundation. The man he wanted was his old friend and benefactor, Victor Tyler, by then a successful businessman more or less retired and receptive to such an offer. After a struggle the new arrangements were approved, the American Foundation voting $6,000 for its new associate secretary, Victor Tyler, and $7,500 toward Bullis' salary. Bullis would be the executive officer of both the National Committee and the American Foundation.[21] By these moves Beers was not only ensuring the smooth working of his and the National Committee's affairs in his absence, he was laying the groundwork for shaping his own work to exclude routine and administrative responsibilities and to free him to do what he wanted.

Just when everything seemed right to leave for Hawaii, Clara had trepidations. She hadn't been feeling well for months, but the main thing bothering her (perhaps brought on by William's suicide) was her ability to take care of herself should anything happen to Clifford. Somewhat embarrassed, though not too much, Beers sought assurances from Mary Bok about his fate after 1936, when the ten years of guaranteed salary would be over. "Tell your wife I'll stand between her and disaster at any time," she told him.[22] How delicate Clara Beers was is questionable. Her life could not have been too hard, as a good part of the year was spent at the Hotel Holly, where she had few household duties, and at Belgrade Lakes, where they lived in a modest cabin and ate in a communal dining hall. Her diary records, for example, that a few days before leaving for California she came into New York for three days running for dinner, the theater, a concert, and movies, and on the fourth went to see a movie in Jersey City. Then for a few days she packed and closed up the Englewood house and went out to lunch and shopping. In Hawaii and California, her constant complaints notwithstanding, she enjoyed an almost continual round of luncheons, teas, dinners, and sightseeing.[23]

Beers himself may have been feeling somewhat uneasy about going "half way round the world and back."[24] It was not uncommon for him to try to get at the National Committee's "enemies" when he was suffering from anxiety, and this time, just before leaving in the middle of January 1931, he sent to Frankwood Williams, the outgoing medical director of the National Committee, an unusually vindictive and nasty letter in which he settled old scores and let Williams know who was now in control.[25] But the trip west, which turned out to be very pleasant and gratifying, apparently dissipated Beers' rancor, for none of his threats against Williams were carried out.

The Beerses traveled to California by train and then by boat to Honolulu, where they were entertained by the governor and other notables and friends. They toured the islands and enjoyed the exotic food and exquisite flowers, in spite of Clara's complaints and Clifford's foot trouble. Clifford also attended various meetings and spoke before an audience of over two thousand people.[26] The trip to Australia was canceled because economic conditions made it unlikely that any of Beers' activity there could be followed by "constructive efforts requiring financial support," but the visit to Hawaii did strengthen the organization of a mental hygiene committee there, and the governor became interested in improving conditions at the Territorial Hospital near Honolulu.[27] At the end of March, Clifford and Clara sailed for Los Angeles, and aboard ship Clifford's fifty-fifth birthday was celebrated with friends. In California, Clifford met people interested in mental hygiene and spoke to three hundred people at a hastily organized Los Angeles meeting. He stayed longer than planned in California because of a difficult situation there. Political interference was threatening the state's mental institutions, and the fragmented mental hygiene groups were too weak to do anything about it. There was a need, Beers thought, for one statewide mental hygiene organization, and he sought to help create one.[28]

Upon his return to New York, the hope he had had that Bullis and Tyler's presence at the National Committee would free him from secretarial burdens was not realized. Because of the heavy correspondence regarding the proposed Second International Congress and other international work, Beers fell even further behind than usual in answering his mail, and of course he had still to keep watch over the National Committee affairs, to the point where he demanded the right to attend all meetings of all standing committees. To the charge that he dominated the work of the National Committee, he pleaded guilty, but his only motive was to protect its interests. All he wanted was the right to present his ideas; if they were good ones and, as a consequence, he dominated the situation, so be it. "If Dr. Hincks or any of the other psychiatrists want to end my so-called domination, let them come along with a sufficient number of original and sound ideas to put me out of business." He would welcome the chance if he could feel sure that the National Committee's work was going along safe lines. These feelings were expressed in a long confidential communication to Vic Tyler, who was to pass on its contents to Hincks.[29]

Beers seemed to have no quarrel with the direction in which Hincks was taking the National Committee or with Hincks' assuming active responsibility for fund-raising. The operating expenses of the National Committee had been through the years financed by individual gifts, a source that, as the economic depression deepened and Beers slackened his efforts, was drying up; prospects for financing special projects were also declining. Hincks, with Bullis' help and Beers' knowledge, was actively soliciting support from foundations, especially from the Rockefeller Foundation and the General Education Board. To their officials, Hincks explained that the National Committee would focus on three major areas: developing educational programs and literature for teachers and parents, training leaders in the field, and fostering research. Later he proposed that it undertake mental hygiene work among the unemployed. A great deal of work was still needed in behalf of hospitalized psychotics, but the "more important social task for the National Committee is the furtherance of positive mental hygiene programs" beyond early diagnosis and treatment of disorders to the "possibilities of directly influencing the lives of individuals through the home, the school, the recreational and leisure time agencies, and adult education."[30]

Foundation officials waited to see what "the energetic new president of the National Committee" would do. They were convinced that psychiatry was an important field but were wary of the National Committee's "overselling mental hygiene" to the public and were unwilling to grant it a monopoly on public education in mental health. Their main concerns were training psychiatric personnel for research and teaching, promoting fundamental research, especially in psychobiology, and developing academic departments of psychiatry.[31] Nevertheless, despite skepticism about the broad social aims sketched by Hincks, the General Education Board was impressed enough by him and by the urgency of the National Committee's financial plight to give it money for 1932 and 1933.[32]

Beers seems not to have been involved in any of this negotiation and program development. International work claimed most of his attention. In the spring of 1932 he responded to a call for help from French friends trying to plan the next international congress of mental hygiene. Beers' presence in Paris to create "real cooperation" among quarreling French psychiatrists was "indispensable." He almost at once took ship with Clara for Paris, from where he wrote to his friend Orlando Willcox, chairman of the finance committee of the International Committee for Mental Hygiene, a long account of the affair which he hoped would someday "form a part of my unexpurgated autobiography."[33] It seems that influential psychiatrists, high French health officials, and lay people active in mental hygiene opposed the domination of the French movement by Dr. Toulouse and his only close associate, Dr. Genil-Perrin—both members of the International Committee and friends of Beers—who were considered ineffectual and whose leadership of the second congress would doom it to failure. If Beers could bring in leading psychiatrists, he would unify the French movement and ensure government subvention of the second congress.

Beers quickly saw the picture and got to work, helped by his friend William Hoggson, who left Italy to join him in Paris, "for I have always had Beers' interests, aims and welfare close to my heart." Through delicate maneuvering Beers succeeded in neutralizing Toulouse and Genil-Perrin by involving a more representative group of psychiatrists in the planning for the congress. "Beers launched his first offensive at his meeting on May 29th," Hoggson wrote Russell, "and when it was apparent he was getting the support of the right men and organizations, the opposition seemed to melt away, and everything is harmonious."[34] Toulouse succumbed gracefully; Genil-Perrin flew into a rage. But Beers managed things well enough that both men appeared to be more cordial to him than ever, which he attributed to their awareness that he had actually lifted a burden from them.[35] The French health ministry was satisfied enough to ask Hoggson for a list of Beers' achievements, presumably as documentation for awarding him the Legion of Honor, and Clifford and Clara were asked by delegates from many countries (Holland, Belgium, Italy, Spain, Switzerland, and others) to come "to help them—promising a very fine time, if they would."[36] But saving mental hygiene in France was exhausting enough; Beers had a heavy correspondence to attend to and various documents to prepare for meetings of the International Committee's governing board and of the organizing group for the second congress. Clara was worn out by social obligations, and Clifford was too busy to take more than three sightseeing trips during their five weeks in Paris. Their stay also enabled him to attend to the publication of the French translation of *A Mind That Found Itself,* which was to be a distinguished edition, with a preface by André Maurois, whom he met.

The climax of the trip was Beers' speech before a meeting in the Great Amphitheater of the Sorbonne under the auspices of the French League for Mental Hygiene and the recently founded Society for Social Hygiene. The minister of health presided, and the president of the Republic attended.[37]

Beers found the Paris trip a "great experience" but enervating: "This setting is almost too complex and active for steady diet." He was ready, though, to attend another international meeting in Rome the next year; Ferrari assured him an audience with Mussolini, and perhaps even the pope would want to meet the founder of mental hygiene.[38]

The success of his work in Paris and the acclaim he received at the Sorbonne strengthened Beers' intention to give most of his time to international activities and to develop both the American Foundation and the International Foundation. Upon his return he told Russell that the National Committee no longer held his interest as before: "Never again will I assume that load even if it shuts up shop—which it won't."[39]

Beers' achievements in Europe impressed Russell greatly. He advised Bullis to reproduce for distribution Beers' letter to Willcox and Hoggson's letter to himself. "Organized mental hygiene is taking on very large proportions and it seems to me that the next International Congress is of vital significance to European problems. I would be glad to think that I might perhaps attend it," Russell wrote. Always generous, he expressed his satisfaction directly to Beers: "You sized up the situation and met it in a masterful way, and I only hope that the foreign direction of the work has gotten into strong and wise hands. I feel sure nothing could have been accomplished without your personal touch."[40]

Still Beers did not trust his success. "I have seldom produced a big result in my work," he told Willcox, "without Fate taking some kind of a swat at me, which, incidentally, has seemed only to stimulate me to further action of a constructive sort."[41]

‡

Fate did take a swat, a powerful one. The day before Clifford and Clara left for home, news came that George Beers' body had been found in the Housatonic River near Stockbridge, Massachusetts.[42] George had been depressed and anxious in recent years and had been in communication with various psychiatrists and heads of mental hospitals; his wife also suffered from "nervous exhaustion." Yale University granted George a leave in 1931 so that he and Louise could travel, the ancient remedy for melancholia. In George's case it was ineffectual; he remained depressed and talked of suicide. Finally he called Dr. William B. Terhune, of Austen Riggs' clinic in Stockbridge, and agreed, despite his lack of faith in psychiatry or hospitals, to enter the clinic for a few weeks to recover from what was called a "minor neurotic upset." He came up that evening and was admitted; the next morning he did not appear for breakfast and was finally discovered in the river. A suicide note explained that he had chosen Stockbridge because the people there would handle the matter tactfully.[43]

As he had after William's suicide, Clifford seemed unaffected. But his associates had not seen him immediately after he received the news, since he was in Europe and then had a week on the Atlantic Ocean to compose himself. At home, he threw himself into his work. Mental hygiene, he remarked, taught that the "best way to handle a sorrow is to do something constructive about it." With respect to suicide the great need was to "educate persons of wealth," especially those who had experienced the pain of the suicide of loved ones, to support a program of suicide prevention.[44] Upon the advice of psychiatric friends, Clifford abandoned his plans for such a program, though a couple of years later Hincks mentioned that the National Committee was becoming interested in suicide prevention and had been reviewing literature in the field.[45]

Beers knew that his stoicism was a protective device. "So many distressing illnesses and deaths have occurred in my family that I am no longer able to react to them as emotionally as one would expect. That is a protection," he told Mary Bok. The mental health movement had helped him to be not "unduly disturbed" by the loss. "I have deliverately [sic] and successfully, blocked it out of my consciousness, by choosing to think of George as still alive," especially as it was so hard to believe him dead. "If I permitted myself to visualize the situations in which George was during the last, fatal week of his life, I could harrow my feelings. I'm not doing that. It would be too disturbing." The best way to honor George's memory was to carry on work in mental hygiene.[46]

Beers was actually deeply affected by George's death, and he appreciated the irony of the suicide of a second brother, this time the best-loved one, and the one most in sympathy with his work and most knowledgeable about it. He also wanted to absolve himself from guilt for it. All this is clear from the long account of the tragedy he composed for friends who sent him condolences. He wrote it "in justice to [George's] memory, to show that he did not end his life without first seeking 'psychiatric' protection against himself and his suicidal impulse."[47]

George might have been saved, Clifford wrote, if he had taken Clifford's advice a year before to put himself under Terhune's care at Stockbridge "for a daily talk at least which, in my opinion, would have bucked up his morale and kept his morbid ideas under control until improved health blotted them out." Clifford had even arranged secretly with Terhune to treat George without frightening him, but George could not bring himself to go to Stockbridge or anywhere else for treatment. This resistance, Clifford believed, derived from George's unhappy experiences with the mental institutions where his brothers had been placed. Clifford claimed that George's travels had been taken against his advice and proved deleterious to his condition, but when Clifford set off for France, George seemed to be improving; his usual brief letters did not indicate to Clifford that he was feeling worse. Upon arriving home, Clifford discovered that a week before his death George, feeling he had "lost control of himself," had gone to see Dr. Ernest Russell, son of Dr. William Russell, to ask to be admitted to New Haven Hospital at once; under his clothes he wore pajamas and had brought his toothbrush. Despite knowledge of the family history and a previous talk with George, Russell told him that he did not require hospital treatment, nor was there a bed available; instead George should take a sedative and go to see Austen Riggs at Stockbridge. Such advice was a mistake, Clifford noted: the patient's estimate of his condition, not the psychiatrist's, should be the basis for judgment, particularly if the patient was suicidal. Clifford did not intend to publicize the matter, but he hoped that some psychiatrist would write a "timely" article on the subject. It was the "irony of Fate" that "members of my own family have been unable to receive benefit from the work I started."

Still, if Clifford had not stayed longer than planned in Paris he might have saved George's life.[48]

To his Belgian friend, Dr. Auguste Ley, Clifford described in detail how he had tried to help George. Years of dealing with psychiatrists and mental illness had made George so distrustful of both that he would not get help, despite Clifford's urging. If Clifford had been home he would have seen to it that he was sent to a "closed" rather than an "open" hospital like Austen Riggs, where he could not be protected against himself. Clifford felt like the "proverbial minister who fails to 'sell' religion inside his own family circle."[49]

Both Dr. Terhune and Dr. Ernest Russell wrote letters of explanation to Beers, the latter concerned that Beers' version of the suicide had been written without first consulting him. He stated that George had seen him several times without revealing his suicidal impulses.[50] Beers remained unconvinced, although a trip to New Haven to see Louise Beers and the family and a statement from Chittenden persuaded him that George would not have submitted to lengthy hospitalization and that his suicide was probably "inevitable considering his strong feelings on these matters."[51]

To believe this was comforting. George had shown utmost devotion to Clifford, who expressed his appreciation not only in his book but in numerous speeches that he made through the years. Yet when George began to break down, Clifford did not take the kind of vigorous action that George had taken thirty-one years before when Clifford himself attempted suicide. Clifford Beers' stock of support for others was limited: he needed too much himself. He would do what he could for his brothers and aunts in the way of recommending doctors and hospitals and sending money, but basically he needed the family to support him. The same was true of his good friends — Vic Tyler, Paul McQuaid, William James, William Hoggson, Russell Chittenden — all of whom were enormously helpful and intensely loyal to him and made few demands upon him in return. In their marriage, Clara subordinated herself to his needs; he probably could not have lived with a more assertive woman. He could never become deeply enough committed to someone else to forget himself or his own interests. The men he worked with — Meyer, Salmon, Williams, and, in time, Hincks, and Bullis — were critics as well as helpers and so lost the possibility of becoming close personal friends. Only those who could consistently support him remained close to him. It could be said that his limited ability to become involved with people — except to a degree with Clara — on a personal and sympathetic level was his greatest protection against the misfortunes that plagued his family. He did not control his emotions concerning family affairs and tragedies so much as mute them: he anaesthetized himself emotionally. He could certainly express emotion — witness his warm letters to Clara and the heated and hurt-filled displays during the infighting at the National Committee. But his feelings tended to be in connection with what he perceived as his own interests and welfare or those of the National Committee and his other organizations, which served as extensions of himself or as his children, as he called them.

George's death raised the question of Clifford's own future. Three brothers dead, two by suicide, and a fourth demented. What would be his own fate? His mental health, he insisted, was good, and "with a virtually new career ahead of me in the international field, [it] can remain good, for I am never so happy as when engaged in new activities of a creative type."[52] He needed the stimulation of the international work, not only because of its intrinsic interest for him, but because the National Committee's prospects were growing bleaker with the economic situation. If it was forced to cut back, Beers should, as William James once said, be in a position to "sail the seas with God." This he could do under the banner of the International Committee and the American Foundation, which was "still flying high." The first congress had been costly, but future ones would be less so if the host countries would pay the bills.[53] His desk was piled with foreign correspondence; he kept close control over the International Committee's affairs and chose, upon consultation, any new members to be appointed. That summer he tried to learn French so that he could "speak it even a little bit" and also read the nearly completed French translation of *A Mind That Found Itself.*[54]

The French edition was to be called *Un Esprit qui se trouve,* a title suggested by Paul Valéry. The problem was to get a good publisher, which might be more likely if the American Foundation would pay the cost of printing, for which it did appropriate eight hundred dollars.[55] Almost simultaneously a Polish translation was in progress, and if Beers could raise the money the book would also be translated into Swedish.[56] By that time the copyright had been bought from him by the American Foundation for Mental Hygiene (in January 1931); royalties would go to the foundation instead of to him. He toyed with the idea of reducing the size of the book and perhaps issuing a second volume covering the history of the mental hygiene movement, though when he would write it he did not know.[57]

His correspondence remained voluminous, but Beers' activity in behalf of the movement, national and international, slowed down. Because of the economic situation, the establishment of an International Institute at Yale had to be postponed. He did not have "sufficient mental hygiene to ask for five million dollars when people were convinced that to-morrow they will not have five thousand dollars."[58] It was almost impossible to raise large sums from individuals. As for the National Committee, recourse had to be to foundations like the General Education Board and the Carnegie Corporation, from which Hincks pried grants. Beers did not begrudge Hincks' success: "Great news . . . and great work on your part in all of the negotiations," he wrote. "You have worked miracles this year. . . . These gifts have saved the ship. Best wishes and thanks for standing on the burning decks — where I used to have to stand virtually alone!"[59]

In spite of his wish to have things go smoothly at the National Committee without his intervention, Beers found he had to "still be militant on occasion" to protect its interests. In this case it was the new division of psychiatric education, financed by the American Foundation and headed by his friend Ralph Noble, that was threatened, and, to Beers' knowledge, by Noble himself. Without consulting Hincks or Beers, Noble was, according to Beers, working to establish an independent "Commission on Psychiatry and Medicine" to take over the work of the division of psychiatric education, which some psychiatrists apparently believed had not a high enough professional standing to be effective. On the contrary, Beers insisted, the National Committee enjoyed "the reputation of being the finest combination of scientific and humanitarian work ever carried on in this country." The time was ripe to convert it into an "almost new type of scientific-humanitarian-welfare organization" unique in this country's history. The division of psychiatric education remained, but Noble did not.[60]

The National Committee was in no position to do large-scale pioneering. By the end of 1933 its professional staff (exclusive of people on special projects) had been reduced to three, the general operating budget pared down to thirty thousand dollars, and the *Mental Hygiene Bulletin,* a pet interest of Beers', had suspended publication for the year. Other than the foundations there were no substantial sources of support. It was, nevertheless, still an active organization. By then it was engaged primarily in promoting psychiatric education, running demonstration child guidance clinics (financed by the Commonwealth Fund), conducting a special project on teacher placement and a research project on dementia praecox, providing consultation services for national, state, and community organizations, publishing *Mental Hygiene,* and acting as an information clearinghouse on all aspects of mental illness and mental health.[61] Hincks did get funding for 1934 from the General Education Board,[62] but the crisis was only postponed another year, when the Rockefeller people would be scrutinizing ever more closely the value and the viability of the National Committee.

Beers' own guaranteed income was affected by the depression. First, the money came in more installments of fewer dollars each; then, to save income tax, a trust fund was set up with Beers as beneficiary.[63] In February 1933 Beers was informed that the trust must suspend payments to him altogether as long as prevailing business conditions continued, news he withheld from Clara until receiving assurances from Mrs. Bok and the American Foundation that his salary would be paid.[64]

Not helping the National Committee's situation was an article published by Frankwood Williams in *Psychoanalytic Quarterly* which he wanted to place in revised form in *Mental Hygiene.* Entitled "Is There a Mental Hygiene?" the piece claimed that the mental hygiene movement was "artificial," not having developed spontaneously out of a growing consciousness of social need felt by either a large body of psychiatrists or the general public. Rather, it originated with one person who pressed his strong feelings of urgency upon others, who in turn impressed it upon others, "until a movement of some magnitude was inaugurated," but one that had little real significance for the work of the educators, psychologists, lawyers, and social welfare workers associated with it. Further, the National Committee engaged not so much in mental hygiene work as in social psychiatry, "the application of psychiatric knowledge, principles and methods to the better understanding and conduct of social problems." Where mental hygiene appeared spontaneously, it did so outside the organized movement and in the form of the question, "What are the motivations of human conduct?" to which the movement had few answers; conventional psychiatry or neurology did not have them, either. The only possible road lay through analysis of infantile sexuality by psychoanalytic methods.[65]

At another time such an article, written by a man who had been medical director of the National Committee for eight years and assistant director for five years before that, might not have mattered as much as it did in 1932, with the National Committee barely holding on. Beers considered its publication dastardly and agreed with Hincks that it should not appear in *Mental Hygiene,* not only because it might affect fund-raising but also because it challenged the National Committee just when it was trying to strengthen its programs to promote positive mental health. It was, Beers felt, very bad taste for Williams to support mental hygiene as long as he drew a good salary from the National Committee but to damn it after leaving it. The best response would be to consign his article to a "deserved oblivion." On that account, Beers, speaking for other National Committee activists as well, turned down a request to publish a response to Williams in the *Mental Hygiene Bulletin.*[66]

Williams' paper expressed the zeal of the newly converted: psychoanalysis, itself subject to doubts and questions, nullified all his previous commitments. There was also naiveté in his distinction between "artificial" and "spontaneous" social movements, especially in a problematic, taboo-ridden area like mental illness. Whether any such movement could be "spontaneous" and could go anywhere without the single-minded leadership Beers provided is questionable; whether it could do so without a base of interested and knowledgeable people as well is also debatable. Such a group of psychiatrists and other professionals did exist in 1908; without them Beers would not have been able to exploit his book and galvanize support as he had. He knew this and also knew how difficult it was to get broad support from the public for mental hygiene. He did have a penchant for going after a few influential patrons, but he also felt this was more realistic. At the same time he was proud of being called, as in a tribute to him by Clarence Farrar in the *American Journal of Psychiatry,* the "apostle of a new era in mental medicine and human welfare" who emerged from his illness in 1903 with a "mind energized and touched with a new light." Nor would he protest Farrar's statement that "rarely has a great movement been so truly the shadow of a single creative spirit as in this instance."[67] Williams had touched a sensitive nerve by questioning Beers' achievements — his pioneering work in founding the movement as well as its expansion to encompass prevention and education. Although Meyer felt that Williams and others led the National Committee too far from psychiatry, he did acknowledge its value in raising public awareness and improving conditions. Williams evidently thought that it had not gone far enough away from conventional psychiatry, indeed that it had gone nowhere — an evaluation difficult for Beers to swallow, particularly at a time not only of crisis for the National Committee but of ever greater popular recognition of his accomplishments.

‡ 17 ‡

Twenty-Five Years After:
Fame and Honors

Williams' article was a slap at Beers, and one he would not forget, but it was not so stinging as it might have been. Soon afterward he received the gratifying news that he was to be awarded the Cross of the Knight of the Legion of Honor of France in November 1932. Wanting to make the most of it, for his own sake and that of the cause, Beers asked White to try to reach the French ambassador in Washington with a request to award the ribbon at the embassy. White complied, and the award was made at the French Embassy by the ambassador, with White, Hincks, and Bullis in attendance.[1]

By this time Beers had become the elder statesman of mental hygiene and something of a celebrity, a role he enjoyed and now had the leisure to cultivate. From the time his book first came out and the National Committee was founded, he had had a good press. The *New York Times, World,* and many other newspapers regularly reported his achievements and reviewed editions of his book, so that by the 1930s his press scrapbook contained an impressive file of newspaper articles and magazine stories, including a lead article in the May 1930 *Survey Graphic,* "The Genius of Clifford W. Beers," with a full-page photograph of him.[2] Writers and public men would write to him for advice or send him manuscripts on mental hygiene. Several books by well-known writers included material on him (some of it edited by him upon request). For example, J. K. Winkler's *Mind Explorers* contains a chapter about Beers entitled "The Prophet of the Mental Hygiene Movement," and Harry Elmer Barnes, the historian and sociologist, in *Can Man Be Civilized?* gave an account of the origin and development of the mental hygiene movement. In *Love in the Machine Age,* Floyd Dell was laudatory of Beers, as was Dr. James A. Tobey, the director of the health service of the Borden Company and former secretary of the National Health Council, in *Riders of the Plague.* (Tobey, at Beers' insistence, deleted much of the material on him in favor of more discussion of Pinel, Tuke, Dix, and Salmon.) Sociologist Ernest R. Groves, in *Understanding Yourself,* recommended *A Mind That Found Itself* to his readers and dedicated his *Readings in Mental Hygiene* (edited with Phyllis Blanchard) to Clifford Beers and Frankwood Williams.[3]

269

In 1929 Beers made *Who's Who in America,* and in 1934 the *National Cyclopedia of American Biography* decided to include a biographical sketch of him, which cost him two hundred dollars.[4] His features were displayed on a plaque included in the mental hygiene exhibit, "Century of Progress," at the Chicago World's Fair of 1933, a replica of which he was able to obtain for himself.[5] One of a series of placards on health and hygiene prepared by the Metropolitan Life Insurance Company for permanent display at the Smithsonian Institution carried three portraits — Pinel, Dix, and Beers — next to a reproduction of the famous painting of Pinel striking the chains off patients at the Salpêtrière.[6] Metropolitan Life also devoted several pages to Clifford Beers in its pamphlet, *Health Through the Ages,* placing him in the company of Hippocrates, Moses, Lister, and Pasteur.[7]

A Mind That Found Itself was preserved for posterity in the cornerstone of the new Fairfield State Hospital, Newtown, Connecticut, on the occasion of which Beers delivered an address.[8] Various organizations asked him to speak, and Newton Baker invited him to serve as a sponsor of the National Conference of Protestants, Catholics, and Jews to be held in Washington in 1932. Although honored, Beers declined on grounds of unfamiliarity with the subject, eradication of religious and cultural prejudice. (He also may not have been able to afford the required contribution.) Generally he turned down requests to serve on the boards or as an officer of organizations, although when he considered it worthwhile he would willingly give advice and moral support. It was his policy not to "take an active part in any organization other than those in mental hygiene."[9]

‡

Much of his time in 1933 and 1934 was given to organizing his biggest public relations campaign, the twenty-fifth anniversary of the movement. The celebration was triple: the silver jubilees of his book and of the Connecticut Society in 1933 and of the National Committee in 1934. The events were commemorated by anniversary dinners (one in New Haven and the next in New York), a special edition of his book, and a mass of tributes to him that were eventually published in book form. He originated, organized, and orchestrated all these activities.

Through Mrs. Cyrus L. Sulzberger he arranged for the *New York Times* to publish an article on him in its magazine for April 30, 1933, in connection with the Connecticut Society dinner on May 6. Beers considered the piece "one of the best" ever published on his work. He also succeeded in getting editorials in the *Times,* the *New York Evening Post,* and *Time Magazine.*[10]

A few days after the New Haven anniversary meeting Beers received, at Welch's suggestion, the Gold Medal of the National Institute of Social Sciences in recognition of his "services for the benefit of mankind in establish-

ing and promoting work of the National Committee for Mental Hygiene."
Beers asked that Haven Emerson in his presentation address—Welch was
too ill to do the honors—mention Salmon's part in "laying the sound scientific basis for the work . . . so many assume I did it *all!*" His usual witty self,
Beers accepted the honor "as a symbol for this cause. I don't wish to have
any false modesty. I assume this is a full-weight gold medal. I cannot decide
what percentage belongs to me personally and what to my wife who stood by
me these thirty years."[11]

‡

By this time Beers was flying high, so much so as to hamper Hincks in
properly organizing and financing the National Committee. This Hincks intimated to Dr. Alan Gregg, director of the division of medical sciences of the
Rockefeller Foundation, in their discussions of continued support for the
National Committee.[12] At this time, when the foundation was seriously
looking into the National Committee's condition—its accomplishments, effectiveness, organization, financial support, and future prospects—and with
doubts being expressed by various people as to its current effectiveness,[13]
Beers was planning for the committee a gala twenty-fifth anniversary dinner
in the Grand Ballroom of the Waldorf-Astoria.

By working very hard, Beers managed to get a large attendance, 625
people, and the affair received extensive press coverage locally and nationally. A good many notables came besides Beers' friends, colleagues, benefactors, and old stand-bys in the mental health movement.[14]

Among the speakers was Adolf Meyer, whose wife and daughter also attended. Gradually drawn again into the movement through his participation
in the International Congress, and genuinely admiring what Beers had accomplished through the years, Meyer had resumed contact with him on a
cordial if not really friendly basis. In planning the dinner speeches, Beers
had had in mind a light, reminiscent talk by Meyers on the origin of the mental hygiene movement. He should have known better. Meyer took the occasion to deliver a thoughtful, serious, humanistic address, "The Birth and Development of the Mental Hygiene Movement." He discussed the coalescence
of forces that had produced the movement—the revitalization of psychiatry,
the advent of psychiatric social work, and the "strong and vital impetus" and
"untiring and unswerving determination" of a "sensitized layman," Clifford
Beers. He then went on to analyze the problems the movement faced and the
direction it took. The key obstacle was resistance to the "core of the new
movement—respect for and practical interest in the whole, undivided human being." Medicine and science, on the one hand, were orthodox and dogmatic in their "mechanistic materialism and elementalism." On the other
hand, lay people were dogmatic and orthodox in their monopoly of things

mental, emotional, and moral. With the orthodoxy went aversion, on the part of the medical profession and the great foundations supporting medical research, to give "serious attention to insanity as a disease." It seemed impossible to get support for other than humanitarian, practical mental hygiene work, so that the sought-for balance between lay organization and activity and sound scientific investigation could not be maintained, although much good work was done. The picture was beginning to change, but only slowly.

Meyer's talk was a call, in the days of the New Deal, for what he called a "fair deal" for mental health, for an integrated concept of human life, for recognition by science and medicine and by those who supported and guided their development that the "whole of man, as individual and group" was their "central concern" and "greatest task and opportunity," "for after all man is the most important issue that civilization of today should consider its concern, if we are to make the grade from a lapse into chaos to a livable society." Scientific research, professional training, clinical work, social work, and public education must be coordinated; the issue was not money but the willingness of existing organizations to collaborate. Finally, tribute must be paid to Clifford Beers and other pioneers and workers in mental health, a "great movement."[15]

Beers, the final speaker, gave a completely different sort of talk — informal, amusing, personal, egocentric, digressive — though not without seriousness. He discussed the financial needs of the National Committee and defended its neutrality on controversial subjects like birth control, sterilization, and psychoanalysis; he also called upon mental hygiene societies to do work in relation to world peace and described his proposed International Institute of Mental Hygiene. He also talked about himself, his interests, his ideas, his state of mind, and his motivations. "I have a tremendous reaction to unfairness and injustice, whether I am the victim or someone else, and I immediately go into action, and I *stay* in action." Whenever a crisis threatened the National Committee he welcomed it: "I have sat in the office of our National Committee when we didn't know how we could pay the bills and other people were getting panicky, when I have said, 'The crisis isn't bad enough yet. . . . We have to wait until we haven't got *any* money. . . . ' Then I get eloquent and I get very active and dynamic, and thus far all these crises have been met." Indeed he was no longer so involved as before in the National Committee because the challenge of disbelief in his success was gone, he said.

This analysis was somewhat disingenuous. Beers was selective in the injustices to which he responded, and it had been a long time since he was deeply concerned with any beyond those he considered perpetrated against himself in the National Committee. In his younger days he had met conflict and crisis with relish, but for a number of years the opposite had been true: he found such situations debilitating; he thrived on success and praise. He was aware of his mood swings, and, perhaps because he was in a high at the time and also because he was always sensitive on the issue of his mental health, he discussed them openly at the dinner: "I have been very busy lately and when I am busy I get speeded up. I want to get speeded up. . . . Lately, and it has happened lots of times during the twenty-five years, elevators seem very slow and telephone connections seem unusually slow." Because of his age, though, he was planning to slow down, to return to live in New Haven and spend a few days a week in New York, which he was mentioning to forestall any "disturbing rumors" about his mental health that would arise when he actually did "slack up a bit."[16]

He had been busy, not only with organizing and publicizing the two anniversary dinners, but with putting through the press a new book that constituted, in effect, a festschrift for himself: *Twenty-Five Years After: Sidelights on the Mental Hygiene Movement and Its Founder,* published in 1934 by Doubleday, Doran (but paid for by two donors). This was a compilation of some six hundred tributes to Clifford Beers, plus a preface by the editor, Wilbur Cross, governor of Connecticut and formerly Sterling Professor of English Literature and dean of the graduate school at Yale; an introduction by William Welch, who had solicited the tributes; reprints of Cross' and Winslow's speeches at the 1933 anniversary meeting in New Haven; statements of the aims, activities, and officers of the National Committee, International Committee, American Foundation, and International Congress; and a directory of mental hygiene societies. At Beers' suggestion the book was dedicated to the memory of Welch, who had just died, and who had been a steadfast friend through the years; just a few months earlier he had told Beers, "Like William James, I esteem it an honor to have been associated with you in your great adventure—and for you—I wish continued success."[17]

When the idea of publishing these tributes originated and with whom is not certain, albeit Beers is far and away the best candidate. He knew all about the project, planned it, edited and revised the letters, and secured the money to publish it. Welch was to be the editor but in name only; when he died Cross took over, but Beers continued to do all the work: "I, as the hero of the book must *seem* not to know what is going on in regard to the publication of the tributes." His anonymity notwithstanding, Beers sometimes took a direct hand in prodding recalcitrant contributors, suggesting what they might write, and even drafting letters for them to send.[18]

The book was issued in a limited edition of a thousand copies and for presentation only; Beers considered it bad taste to sell a book devoted to praising himself, and he realized that a limited edition of letters honoring a living man would not be reviewed. He would give a copy to each contributor of a letter, offer it to those donating five dollars or more to the National Committee, and in general use it in promoting gifts to the movement. "We cannot afford to spend about $3,000 just for glorification of the Founder!"[19]

The combined magic of Welch's name and Beers' achievements had resulted in a body of tributes from an impressive group of men and women who constituted the academic, medical, psychiatric, philanthropic, and social work elite of the United States and Western Europe. The psychologist Gardner Murphy expressed the consensus of the contributors in one sentence: "Clifford Beers's autobiography is a great book, and the conception of mental hygiene is one of the great conceptions of the century."[20]

In preparing the volume Beers became surfeited with praise and requested that contributors "stress the importance of mental hygiene work and soft pedal any reference to my part in the movement because, for one reason, I have already more personal tributes than I can properly digest."[21] His modesty did not go so far as to lead him to include in the book a letter from an unnamed sociologist who criticized the "elements of hero worship in the situation which suggests that Mr. Beers merely symbolizes and leads a movement which events have proved indispensable in the present state of social organization and change and in the present state of medical and psychiatric knowledge." In a postcard agreeing to have his letter published he further wrote, "I confess it beyond me how any person or organization can spend so much, even in prosperity, on self-glorification." Beers did not agree; the letter was omitted from the volume.[22] *Twenty-Five Years After* remained a book of nearly undiluted praise.

‡

At approximately the same time as *Twenty-Five Years After* came out, and with funds from the same donors for its publication, the twenty-fifth anniversary edition of *A Mind That Found Itself* appeared, also published by Doubleday, Doran, to favorable press notices.[23] Beers had written to book review editors all over the country soliciting reviews for the new edition, so that a new generation could become aware of it. The writer Herschel Brickell, a friend of Clifford's who had first become acquainted with him in connection with mental hygiene work in Mississippi years before and had written a letter for *Twenty-Five Years After,* devoted his book-reviewing column in the *New York Evening Post* to *A Mind That Found Itself.* Upon receiving this new edition, Brickell wrote, he meant simply to glance at it, but "I read it once more and I was again deeply impressed by the sheer fascination of Mr. Beers' narrative, and with its impressive merit as literature. . . . In fact, I find it somewhat hard to understand how John Dewey, Charles A. Beard and Edward Weeks overlooked 'A Mind That Found Itself' when they were compiling their lists of the twenty-five most influential books of our generation. Obviously Mr. Beers and the book have worked together, but the influence of the book alone has been very great." Brickell later listed the book among his choices for the ten best American autobiographies.[24]

Beers asked Cyrus L. Sulzberger, through Mrs. Sulzberger, to use his influence to have the *New York Times* feature *A Mind That Found Itself* in some way. Beers realized that he could not ask "Mr. John Chamberlain to feature this *old* book in his column, when so many new books are appearing, but may it not be possible for the Times to treat the 25th Anniversary Edition (22nd printing) . . . editorially, perhaps on the basis of the influence it has exerted and its standing as a unique document?" Chamberlain did review *A Mind That Found Itself*. "Twenty-two printings," he wrote, "failed to exhaust curiosity in the book. Justifiably so." As William James had said, it read like fiction. "For sheer horror, parts of it challenge comparison with Céline's far more literary 'Journey to the End of Night.'"[25]

Through the successive new editions, and especially the twenty-fifth anniversary one, which Beers not only managed to have noticed in influential reviewers' columns but which he also distributed widely to friends and potential friends of the mental hygiene movement, people were still discovering *A Mind That Found Itself*. A condensed version in *Reader's Digest* (with corrections by Beers)[26] made the book even more widely known, as did an account of the movement that appeared in *True Story* in March 1935. And through the various translations, people abroad would soon be able to read it. The French edition and the Polish, Czech, and German translations were in progress; in 1938 came finally a firm request for Italian rights.[27] There was even a Braille version, which Beers discovered when he met Helen Keller in 1934. He was thrilled to know this, he told her, as he considered his book a good story for the blind, depicting as it did a triumph over obstacles and handicaps.[28]

With all his public relations tactics, Beers was very careful about the kind of publicity he might get. He wanted none that veered from the image he wished to project of himself or that might misrepresent his views or those of the National Committee, which he always strove to keep neutral on controversial issues.[29] To a reporter from the *Boston Evening Transcript* who wanted to interview him, Beers said that he disliked interviews and would rather give several pages of information that could be used instead, plus other material to be worked into a magazine story that the *Transcript* could publish some time later.[30] He did, however, grant an interview and send information about his family to a writer planning to do a profile of him for the *New Yorker* (which was apparently never published).[31]

In 1936 the Philip Morris radio program wanted to dramatize *A Mind That Found Itself,* with Beers commenting on his own work. "This, as you can see," the producer wrote, "would give your book and your institution a tremendous coast to coast publicity boost." Beers refused. "My story in written form has done good, but its high spots lifted out and radioed would do harm."[32] After further negotiations, Beers got the National Committee's executive committee to back him by voting unanimously to deny permission to dramatize his story then or in the future; its nature precluded its "ever being dramatized."[33]

Subsequently he refused a request to make his autobiography into a motion picture. "Any dramatization would, of necessity, give emphasis to the most disturbing parts of my narrative and would, in consequence, give a wrong impression in regard to hospital conditions as they now are in many of the more enlightened states in this country. Quite aside from these reasons, I, as the central figure in the story, naturally would not care to see it put on the screen, or stage, or given wing over the radio."[34] Beers had even opposed the dramatization of the founding meeting of the Connecticut Society for Mental Hygiene that was planned for its thirtieth annual meeting.[35] His antipathy to any representation of himself extended to an insistence that his book never be illustrated by anyone but himself, and he was also very particular about photographs of him that were to be published.[36] Clara Beers respected and shared her husband's sensitivity to exposing himself to the public except in his own words or images. After his death a dramatization of his life, "My Name Is Legion," did appear with her approval, but only after it was written so that the central figure never appeared on the stage.

Apart from his inhibitions about dramatic depictions of himself, Beers' methods of promoting himself and his book may seem unusually aggressive, and they may have been for someone in his position at that time. They became quite common a generation or so later, when such behind-the-scenes public relations became a prerequisite for popular success, to the point of becoming professionalized. Beers seems almost egomaniacal in his pursuit of attention because evidence exists of his machinations (as it may not for other public figures) and because he served as his own best press agent. He used the public relations techniques of politicians and entertainers to reach a scholarly, professional, highly educated public, in the interest of a humanitarian cause, and with a good deal of success.

‡ 18 ‡

Personal Interests

The mid-1930s were somewhat less hectic years for Beers than the previous twenty-five, but they were neither inactive nor fruitless. Beers' intimate involvement with the National Committee diminished, but he still knew what was going on and took a hand in its affairs when he thought he had to. He also did international work, helped to further the mental hygiene movement in various states, and became involved in several special projects.

‡

Occupying a good deal of his time was the Second International Congress, which was postponed from 1935 to 1936 and finally 1937, because of both the international situation and lack of enthusiasm. In contrast to the first congress, the program of the second, planned in France, was strictly psychiatric, with little attention to social psychiatry and mental hygiene; the British, excluded from the planning, had a small role in the proceedings, as did the Americans, whose participation would also be limited by a scarcity of funds. Then, no one could be sure where Hitler might move, and there was a problem about the congress's policy toward Nazi eugenics theories, which disturbed Bernard Sachs. The "man from Munich," he wrote Beers, "whom you have put down as the first speaker on the Condition and Role of Eugenics in the Prevention of Mental Diseases, is Ernst Rudin . . . the most outspoken and rabid Nazi protagonist . . . who heads a whole group of men who are now openly making eugenic doctrines conform with the race purity doctrines of the present German regime." Beers regretted the choice of a man with a "narrow, Nazi point of view"; however, the decision was not his but that of the executive committee of the congress in Paris, and just then (1935) nothing short of war between France and Germany could get Rudin off the program.[1]

Beers would not forget Sachs' message. He kept up with world events but was not deeply involved in them; in politics he was a Theodore Rooseveltian progressive (harking back to his youth), against governmental "competition

277

with private business" but for "adequate Government regulation,"[2] rather than a Franklin D. Roosevelt liberal. Generally he identified with the interests of the businessmen and corporation lawyers with whom he associated and from whom he needed to pry money; his views on most things tended to be conventionally conservative upper-middle-class. But although he had been something of an admirer of Mussolini in the 1920s, by 1935 he was not, and he deplored Hitler and Nazism.

Fighting was fierce in Spain's civil war, but general war did not break out. The congress was set for July 1937, and a month earlier Clifford and Clara Beers sailed for England, but without the old enthusiasm. In London, Beers fulfilled an old yearning—to be introduced to royalty, in this case the Duke of Kent. But this event, like other entertainments, meetings, and newspaper interviews, fell flat. Even Paris, previously so exciting, was a disappointment. Not all his good friends were there, he had to watch his expenditures closely, the congress was small (only two to three hundred people), and he was an honored guest rather than an organizer.[3]

The congress proceedings did prove interesting, and Beers was able to help prevent the Nazi ideologue Rudin from being elected to a vice-presidency of the International Committee. Rudin had, in his opinion, "hurt his reputation as a scientist by his Nazi propaganda in reference to eugenics and sterilization." Adolf Meyer also helped to put Rudin in his place by giving a "good speech on sterilization, following a radical talk on that subject by Dr. Rudin."[4] Because of the international situation, it was suggested that the third congress be held in Rio de Janeiro, which Beers did not favor but which seemed the best place. In any case he did not intend to go and had his physician advise him against it for reasons of health. He also doubted that the third congress could be held under the threat of war that hung over Europe in 1938.[5] War did prevent its convening, then or ever; by the end of the war, in 1945, Beers was dead and the National Committee was shortly to merge with other organizations to form a new movement.

Much as Beers tried to stay politically neutral, the events in Europe, as the Rudin affair indicated, could not be ignored. The German translation of *A Mind That Found Itself,* sponsored by Beers' friend André Repond of Switzerland and completed in 1938, could not find a publisher in Germany because the translator was Jewish. (It was finally published in Switzerland in 1941 as the second volume in the series "Psychohygiene.")[6] Some members of the National Committee were concerned not only about Nazi racial theories but about their victims, who included Jewish psychologists and psychiatrists.[7] Perhaps because in 1938 the danger that European Jews, especially German Jews, faced from the Nazis was not fully appreciated in the United States, Beers, by no means an anti-Semite, shared the traditional insensitivity of non-Jews toward the Jewish fate, and he did not exert himself to help. Indeed, he discouraged foreign physicians from coming to the United States unless they had independent incomes; jobs were unavailable, he explained to an Italian psychiatrist, probably Jewish, partly because many mental hospitals were run by governments, which usually required U.S. citizenship of staff members.[8] One National Committee member, the Columbia University psychologist R. S. Woodworth, wrote Beers of the problems the Jewish refugees would create by competing with Americans for jobs: "Not only is the Jewish minority afraid of the majority, but the majority is afraid of the Jews because of their ability along certain lines, their tendency to crowd certain professions, and their solidarity."[9] Beers expressed similar doubts, albeit ascribed to others, in replying to a request for support of a law in behalf of Jewish children. One of the questions people asked him, he said, was, "Even if Jewish children won't at first take jobs that present residents of this country need, will they not be taking such jobs within a very few years?" He responded, "How can I combat these objections?" This was in 1939, the eleventh hour for getting Jews out of Germany and occupied countries.[10] It did not seem to occur to Beers that the argument could be used to prohibit all immigration, or that if these children were excluded they might be killed.

The National Committee did help a few very prominent German Jews to come to the United States,[11] and at the end of 1938 (after the Munich agreement and the imminent fall of Czechoslovakia to the Germans, with accompanying persecution of the Jews there), on the prompting of Haven Emerson, it took an official stand against Nazism. Addressed to President Roosevelt and signed by Ruggles, president of the National Committee, the statement expressed "horror at the persecution of the Jews and Catholics of Germany" and protested such actions as destructive of a nation's mental health.[12] As expected, controversy arose within the National Committee over the propriety of sending such a declaration, over its form and style, and over the scientific validity of its statements. National Committee members intimately involved in its work voted overwhelmingly in favor of sending a revised form of the declaration. Beers supported the original and then the revised document.[13]

‡

Another project in which Beers was involved during the mid-1930s was a book, sponsored by the American Foundation for Mental Hygiene and by himself—Albert Deutsch's classic *The Mentally Ill in America: A History of Their Care and Treatment from Colonial Times.*[14] In 1934 Deutsch, a writer and researcher who as a result of his work on a history of public welfare was struck by the lack of a popular history of the care, treatment, and prevention of mental illness in the United States, came to see Beers. He wanted the National Committee to collaborate with him on such a work; for a thousand dollars he would waive royalty rights but wanted an honorarium if the book sold well. Beers liked the idea and suggested that Deutsch send him a letter outlining the project, which Deutsch did.[15]

Beers hoped to get the American Foundation for Mental Hygiene to pay

Deutsch; if not, he would try to find a donor or pay him out of his own pocket. Pending a decision, he employed Deutsch, then badly in need of money, for four weeks at thirty-five dollars a week to help prepare *Twenty-Five Years After* for the publisher and to edit his Connecticut Society anniversary speech. Beers' publisher was impressed by Deutsch's outline of his proposed book and expressed interest. The American Foundation then hired Deutsch to collaborate with Beers in preparing a popular history of the treatment of the insane from colonial days to the present.[16]

Actually Deutsch wrote it, Beers entering the picture only when the manuscript was nearly finished. At that time, in the spring of 1935, Beers sent a large part of the manuscript to psychiatric authorities for comment. After the readers had all agreed on the manuscript's high quality, Beers was able to persuade the American Foundation trustees to give Deutsch five hundred dollars at once; if Beers could raise the money to publish the book and it sold well, he intended to recommend further payment.[17]

Until the last chapter came in all went smoothly. That chapter, dealing with contemporary developments, stirred controversy. First, objections were made to what were considered unsubstantiated (and too favorable) remarks on the treatment of the criminally insane in Mexico and the Soviet Union, especially the latter. Deutsch deleted the offending passages.[18] More in dispute was his positive assessment of psychoanalysis, which affronted that still passionate opponent of Freud, Bernard Sachs. Beers, always sensitive to the reaction of physicians on professional matters, became worried. The chapter must be made "bomb-proof"; Deutsch must get expert opinions and revise it to suit. Otherwise the American Foundation, which had the legal right to edit the book, might reconsider publishing it.[19]

After a struggle, Deutsch finally made the changes, and Beers went to work to ensure the book's success. With his wide contacts he could get knowledgeable people to read the manuscript and give opinions about portions that dealt with their special fields of interest.[20] He also searched out and obtained illustrations and had friends read proof and do the index.[21] Doubleday, Doran published the book in 1937, with the copyright held by the American Foundation for Mental Hygiene and with an introduction by William A. White; only Deutsch's name appeared on the title page as author. In his foreword he acknowledged the grant awarded by the foundation and particularly thanked Clifford Beers "for his innumerable services" and "splendid cooperation."[22]

After its publication Beers worked to promote the book, including plugs for himself and his autobiography, in both the mass media and in the mental health and psychiatric community, where he made use of his many acquaintances.[23] Although Deutsch did not earn royalties, he did gain a reputation through the book and went on to make a career of writing about mental illness, with his later stories in the popular media initiating a reawakening of concern over the condition of the hospitalized mentally ill. *The Mentally Ill in America* went through three printings in the first edition and in 1949 was issued in a second edition, revised and enlarged, by Columbia University Press. It became the standard comprehensive work on the subject.

Apart from Deutsch's book, which was a special case, Beers made it a rule, with very few exceptions, not to read manuscripts sent to him and would turn down requests to write introductions to books. He felt he had insufficient psychiatric knowledge. When occasionally a publisher asked his opinion of a manuscript, he would refer the publisher to a psychiatrist, and he told one former mental patient turned author that it would be preferable for his book to be introduced by a reputable psychiatrist than by another former mental patient, even if the latter was Clifford Beers. His policy was never to express himself on stories of mental breakdowns except his own.[24]

‡

Beers became more preoccupied with himself as he approached late middle age. When it came to his work and his book he had always been vigorous in promoting himself, especially during the twenty-fifth anniversary years, when he was at the height of his fame. What was different now was his concern with himself in a personal way. Encroaching old age, which he dreaded, together with declining health, seems to have been crucial in this change. After the National Committee's jubilee dinner in November 1934 he did not feel well. His physician diagnosed arteriosclerosis and resultant myocardial degeneration, for which he was given digitalis and advised to avoid excessive stress and to relax more. Another problem was glaucoma in his right eye.[25] Although he accompanied Hincks to Canada to appear at the Canadian National Committee's annual meeting, he turned down, on doctor's orders, other speaking engagements. Then he went to Atlantic City for three days to "cool off," after which his pace slowed "so much that some of my associates at the office noticed it."[26] He felt that, aside from health problems, even men as dynamic as he must slacken their tempo as they reached their sixties, or face being removed entirely from the scene. He was also tired of the old quest for money. He could still rouse himself to go after contributions when there seemed to be a good opportunity, but the days of intense fund-raising efforts were, he hoped, over. Even before his health began to deteriorate and he had turned to other things, he had publicly expressed himself on the matter. In the *Survey Graphic* article of 1930 he was quoted as calling himself the National Committee's "ambulatory endowment." "For years I have had a tin cup as a watch-charm . . . and I am sick of the noise it makes. I might as well be a goat with a bell on it."[27]

His own financial security was a problem. In 1932 the National Committee had agreed to purchase an annuity for him, a matter that would become crucial as 1936, the last year of Mary Bok's guarantee of his salary, approached. Even before then it was a worry, as the Boks did not pay his salary for 1933 and 1934 (which was taken care of by the American Foundation). An annuity would not only give the Beerses some security, it would enable Clifford to retire early. From 1933 to 1935 he campaigned for it. *Twenty-Five Years After* was planned in part as a device to raise money for himself, and he approached various foundations for contributions.[28] A selling point was his declining health. When his glaucoma was diagnosed he asked the ophthalmologist, Dr. William H. Wilmer of Johns Hopkins, to send him a letter advising that he must relax and work in a less tense way. Such a letter could be used to secure a guaranteed salary for him for the next ten years from one or more foundations and thus enable him to slow down enough to "*help* keep my present limited degree of glaucoma under control" and make him independent of the organization he founded. Wilmer obliged, with the reservation that physical causes should be sought for the glaucoma. Still, Beers should relax more. "The nerve tension at which [you have] been living, I think, has a very important bearing upon the glaucoma."[29] After seeing this letter Russell recommended to Albert Milbank that the Milbank Fund help Beers; Chittenden also wrote a supporting letter, and a similar appeal was apparently made to philanthropist Edward S. Harkness.[30]

Shortly thereafter Beers had Dr. Harlow Brooks, his physician and an old friend, write Wilmer of his alarm over Beers' arteriosclerosis, "which is more advanced than his years justify" and which might well account for the glaucoma and was caused in his opinion by economic insecurity. The condition could be stabilized if Beers could be relieved of his excessive worries and the details of his work and have time to devote himself to the "really important executive and creative work which his position demands."[31] Beers also planned to request outstanding National Committee members, plus the "Tribute Committee" for *Twenty-Five Years After,* to sponsor his requests for money from Harkness and John D. Rockefeller, Jr., and he had asked Mary Bok to put the remaining $38,500 of her ten-year pledge into the American Foundation's Beers annuity fund.[32]

The situation by 1935 had become critical. There was no money for Beers' salary (which had already been reduced to $8,000), and hardly any money yet in the annuity fund. Beers had to borrow money to live on. Because of the decline in the Milbank Fund's resources, he reduced his request to them from $75,000 to $25,000; finally in May 1935 the fund voted $21,467.71 toward a life annuity that would give him $1,666.67 a year. The Boks then contributed altogether the $38,500 owed from Mary Bok's pledge. Under a rather complicated arrangement, the prospect by the end of the year was that there would be available to Beers from various sources (including a legacy from his cousin Caroline Dudley, who died in 1934) enough investment in annuities to yield him $6,000 a year for life (with the hope that this could eventually be raised to meet but not exceed the full amount of his salary, $8,000, and with provision for Clara Beers if he should die.[33] Everyone was very pleased, and Beers wrote triumphantly of his accomplishment to a friend, "I am telling you these things because when I talked with you I had the feeling that you thought I was handing you another of my so-called 'delusions of grandeur' and I am sure you will not find fault with me for giving you this added proof of how terribly normal I am all of the time."[34] In raising money, especially for himself, Hincks marveled, Beers was "a master without equal."[35]

The Beerses were by then in fairly good shape financially. The promise of $6,000 a year was an excellent one at the time (it was well above the national average income), and there was other income coming in as well. At the end of 1935 the final settlement of his cousin's estate gave Clifford some "surplus" money beyond that invested in the annuity; a few months later he bought fifteen hundred dollars in stocks to add to his small holdings, and the next year he bought more and also received some stocks in a legacy. He had also by 1935 been able to pay off the mortgage on his Englewood home, and he managed Clara's money so that it yielded good returns. In the depths of the depression Clifford was able to send two hundred dollars a year to the Yale Alumni Fund, and Clara was buying a necklace at Tiffany's, ordering a hat from McCreery's (a Fifth Avenue store), and choosing shirts and underwear for Clifford at Wanamaker's.[36]

The entire annuity Beers had aimed for had not been obtained, but he had accomplished a good measure of security for himself and Clara at the same time as he reduced his workload, so much so that his physician found his condition much improved. He was "getting on far better than we expected and as well as we have any right to hope for."[37] By then Clifford was the only Beers brother left. Carl, who had been supported in the Connecticut State Hospital at Middletown after George's death by their cousin Caroline Dudley and after her death by a trust fund she left, finally died in November 1935, an event that Clifford seemed to take in stride. He had interested himself in Carl's welfare to the end, and then he wrote to the superintendent of the hospital to thank him for the "kind and good care" Carl had received there for twenty-three years.[38]

‡

The reduced intensity of his work enabled Beers to get on better with the National Committee staff, particularly his secretaries. Theresa Frega, after nine battling years with him, finally resigned in May 1934 because of temperamental differences between them and because he demanded that she work irregular hours and under great pressure for weeks at a time. Her successor, Elizabeth S. Royce, did better, but left after a year for another job.

"Surely," she wrote Beers, "I do not need to tell you that the relation with you during the past year has been a happy one for me." He replied that she had taught him what a real secretary and assistant could be. Most of his difficulties with previous secretaries, he said, were due not so much to his own behavior as to their failure to render service willingly and cheerfully.[39] His next and last secretary, Bianca Artoni, brought peace to the National Committee during her work there from 1934 to 1939. This was much appreciated by the older members of the staff, who told her they tried not to antagonize Beers, as he was prone to making scenes. Beers appreciated her enough to pay her doctor's bills out of his own pocket and to obtain extra pay for her so that she could take a vacation. He also would help other staff members in personal ways.[40]

But if he did not explode so frequently, he was still not easy to work for. He would appear at the office in mid-afternoon, "his inside coat pockets on both sides bulging with papers,"[41] and if the mood hit him, work until eight or nine o'clock in the evening, puffing away at his pipe. Miss Artoni was expected to work along with him, taking dictation for his many letters. Saturday or even Sunday might be working days for him, whereas during the week he might stay away from the office or go home early. It was hard on his secretary, but then he allowed her to alter her hours to suit. One day when his overtime demands interfered with her hairdressing appointment, he gave her the money to go to a Fifth Avenue beauty salon during her lunch hour.[42] And his sense of humor, which never left him, mitigated hard feelings, as did his generosity.

Beers had never been a systematic worker, as a long-time employee at the National Committee, Paul Komora, recalled. Instead he "plunges vigorously into whatever project he happens to be interested in, hacking away at his objectives until he attains them." He worked at things in order of importance, so that his desk became a mess.[43] Only before leaving for Maine each summer would he work consistently in order to catch up with his mail, but he would never quite finish and would have to leave the job to Miss Artoni. He procrastinated so much that when he left for Paris in 1937 she had to go down to the ship to take dictation until it sailed. "I'll answer it, tomorrow," was his usual response to a letter. When he did answer he would rewrite his own letter ten or twelve times until it seemed perfect enough to sign; even then he might redo it a few more times, so that a pile of rejected and revised versions would accumulate on his desk, all in the interest of wanting to leave perfect documents for posterity and for his eventual biographer.[44] For similar reasons he felt self-conscious about his speeches, which were not only repetitious but "very discursive and all over the lot." He did what he could to prevent their being recorded verbatim so that "posterity" would not "wonder how a person who could talk so loosely was able to write a book which literary critics have pronounced good."[45]

He had become less concerned about his writing in favor of a new form of self expression, painting. Aside from driving his car (a used car he bought in 1928) and fishing during the summer he had had no real hobbies. The movement and his life with Clara had totally absorbed him. When he was forced to slacken his pace, he rediscovered the pastime that had so intrigued him thirty years before at the Hartford Retreat.

During the summer of 1933, many of his old friends at Belgrade Lakes being absent, he decided, on Winston Churchill's recommendation to middle-aged people in *Amid These Storms,* to try oil painting. His friends, as friends do, praised his first ventures; in any case, he reported to Mary Bok, it was good fun and gave "one the feeling that something is being created whether it is or not." Mrs. Bok was kind, as always, referring to Leopold Stokowski's first painting: he had proudly shown her a sunset, "but it looked more like a poached egg to me."[46]

Beers could not take anything he did casually, so that although he had no thought of becoming a professional artist (as he had many years before), he did think he had talent. As usual, he sought confirmation from experts, whose encouragement was sufficient for him to stage an exhibit of his paintings in his home for his friends. The move of the National Committee office to Rockefeller Center along with all the other national health organizations appealed to him because he could then visit art galleries during lunch hours.[47]

After the twenty-fifth anniversary dinner of the National Committee, he had a photograph of one of his snowscapes printed, with a quotation from his after-dinner speech, on the verso, complete with insertions of audience reaction, like "laughter, More laughter," and sent it out to friends and acquaintances.[48] His main motive was to promote the National Committee in a "flank attack" on pocketbooks, but he thought it would do him "no harm in certain quarters to be thought of as an 'artist' rather than as one who is always playing an aggressive role in the movement."[49] He was probably not aware of any unfavorable impression that he was making. At the Rockefeller Foundation one official commented, "Instead of giving money to this man he should be first candidate for investigation," and another noted, "Tell LMD to read 'The mind that found itself' by Beers. Maybe it's lost again."[50]

Beers kept painting, mainly during the summer and sometimes on weekends, and by December 1935 he had produced enough to enter eighteen oils in the Yale Club's First Annual Amateur Art Show. To his delight, he took second prize for oils, the jury judging them notable for their "atmosphere, freedom, and sense of space." Now that he considered himself a real artist, he and Clara went to the Beaux Arts Ball, he as a Chinese mandarin, she in oriental costume.[51]

Beers worked up a description of the Yale Club award, including the quotation from Churchill that had first spurred him to try painting, and edited by Paul McQuaid (who persuaded him to exclude excerpts from his twenty-fifth anniversary dinner speech). He sent copies of this out, together with a photograph of the prize paintings, as New Year's greetings to hundreds of "interested" people. Encouraged by the responses of friends and acquaintances, he planned to distribute a thousand copies as part of his "'art as a hobby' campaign!" He sent his "message" to, among others, Harvey Cushing, A. A. Brill, John Dewey, Simon Flexner, Harry Emerson Fosdick, Governor Herbert Lehman, Mrs. John D. Rockefeller, Jr. (a patron of the arts), and Presidents Angell of Yale and Conant of Harvard. He even mailed one to Churchill, together with copies of congratulatory notes (some of them solicited) and an account of the art exhibit.[52] Churchill did not reply.

To Eugene O'Neill, whom he had met briefly in New Haven years before and who had spent a summer on Belgrade Lakes, the subject of several of the paintings, Beers wrote about the pleasures of painting as a hobby. He planned to develop a method to instruct anyone to paint quickly and without ever having to mention perspective, composition, or "any of the rules of the game." Then he would write an article on the subject. O'Neill replied, saying that some of Beers' paintings had vividly renewed his memories of Belgrade Lakes. As to taking up painting, O'Neill was not so sure: "I'll keep pictures and quote as a reminder — for by the time this cycle of plays I'm working on is finished, I have a strong hunch I'll need to take on one hobby at least to take my mind off the damned drama — though it's hard to imagine myself ever being capable of painting even a barn door."[53]

Beers even suggested that the twenty-seventh annual luncheon of the National Committee invite Austen Riggs to speak on play and hobbies in relation to mental hygiene, after which Beers would show some of his own paintings — a project that did not work out. He also proposed using painting as a hobby to cure "'nervous indigestions,'" and in 1937 turned up unannounced at Clarence Farrar's hospital in Toronto, his object being to introduce painting as occupational therapy. He could teach anyone to paint in a very short time; to illustrate he completed a seascape on the spot. He gave paintings as gifts to staff members and friends, including Mary Bok, and proposed bestowing them on anyone who gave one hundred thousand dollars to the mental hygiene movement.[54]

This preoccupation with art worried Russell, who tactfully suggested, in a letter marked "Personal," that Beers not "over-feature" his "undoubted talent as an artist" to the point where he would be identified as an artist rather than a mental hygiene worker. "We wish . . . to retain you as the center of the mental hygiene movement." Have no fear, Beers answered. During the year he did not spend very much time painting, and as an amateur painter he could reach potential donors to the cause more easily than as a money raiser pure and simple.[55]

Beers hoped to turn his painting to account for the movement, especially during the summer, for it was not good form to ask the rich for money while they were on vacation. So when he and Clara were invited to Seal Harbor to show his paintings to James Angell and to demonstrate his method of teaching others to "paint a picture at the first attempt," he used the occasion to meet Mr. and Mrs. Edsel Ford, who were interested in art. He eventually sold them, for a friend, a Christian Schussele watercolor,[56] but as for a contribution, the Fords were no more inclined to give to the National Committee than their parents had been years earlier.

Painting also broadened the Beerses' social life and brought them a new friendship, that of the New York portrait artist Henry Rittenberg. Rittenberg, wanting to meet "this interesting man, Mr. Beers," had himself introduced to Beers and then read his autobiography and other literature that Beers sent him. He was so affected by *A Mind That Found Itself* that he painted Beers' portrait as a contribution to the cause.[57] For several years Rittenberg retained ownership of the portrait, which Beers thought was wonderful. It was used in subsequent editions of *A Mind That Found Itself,* while Beers paid the insurance;[58] its present whereabouts are unknown. There were apparently two more versions painted, one of which hangs in the Payne Whitney Psychiatric Clinic at New York Hospital. A good likeness, it captures something of Clifford Beers' intensity but is somewhat formal and stiff.

Beers appointed himself agent for Rittenberg, trying, with some success, to get commissions for him. He persuaded the widow of William A. White, who died in 1937, to have him memorialized in a Rittenberg portrait, paid for by subscriptions from White's friends, for which Mrs. White felt "deeply grateful."[59] Beers also convinced the board of governors of New York Hospital to have Russell sit for his portrait, and got Rittenberg a commission to paint Dr. Arthur W. Rogers, head of the Rogers Memorial Sanitarium, Oconomowoc, Wisconsin; at Beers' urging the *New York Times* placed Rittenberg's portrait of Dr. Bernard Sachs in its picture section.[60]

Beers realized that his own painting was amateurish, and it afforded him mainly personal satisfaction, plus the opportunity to meet interesting or important people. His aim was as simple as his approach to technique: to produce photographic likenesses or mood pieces. Modern trends in art—abstractionism, cubism, expressionism—left him bewildered. His taste in plays and films did not go beyond the popular hits of the day, and on radio he very much liked the Rudy Vallee show. His and Clara's small home in Englewood was finely furnished in conventional upper-middle-class style, the paintings and watercolors as traditional as the furniture. Nor did his taste in literature develop greatly with the years. Asked by Lewis Gannett his opinion of books deserving best-seller status, he had to confess, "I read comparatively few books and am therefore not in a position to give any list worth mentioning." Each morning he went through the *Times* or the *Herald Trib-*

une, and he regularly read the *Saturday Evening Post, Fortune, Forbes Magazine,* the *New Yorker,* and *Time.* Occasionally he would read novels, including *Gone with the Wind,* which held his attention "because of my southern ancestry."[61]

Painting filled a certain void in his life. He was in his sixties, he and Clara had no children, George was dead, the mental hygiene movement, albeit established as a legitimate cause, was limping along financially and there was not much he could do about it; international work was stymied by the rise of Hitler and the threat of war in Europe. Painting was the new enthusiasm that he always needed. If he could link it in with the movement, all the better. To Dr. Frederick Peterson, the physician and poet and early sponsor of the National Committee, who sent him an inscribed copy of his *Creative Re-education,* he wrote that he did not take up painting for therapeutic purposes, "except, possibly, as it may serve a useful and healthful purpose when, years hence," he retired. "I suppose that almost everything I have done since leaving a mental hospital in 1903 has been, for me, a sort of creative re-education."[62]

✠ 19 ✠

The Mentally Ill Intrude

Besides the many letters Beers received praising his book, his increased fame brought numerous requests for help from people with mentally ill friends and relatives and from the mentally ill and formerly mentally ill themselves. Some applicants came to his office or telephoned him; many more wrote. There was also a noticeable rise in complaints addressed to him or to the National Committee about conditions at mental hospitals. This increase reflected both the successes and the failures of the mental hygiene movement; Beers' response indicates the directions his thinking and activities had taken through the years. That more people were asking for help with psychiatric problems testified to the effect mental hygiene education was having and also to the legitimacy and authority the National Committee had been able to achieve among the informed lay public. That more complaints about hospital abuses came in says something less positive about the ability of the movement to effect enduring changes in the care of hospitalized patients, especially in the face of financial stringency. As to the efficacy of the National Committee's preventive work, it was too soon to tell.

The work of the National Committee from the mid-1920s into the 1930s had made mental hygiene respectable, indeed had raised it into almost an ideology among some people looking for answers to human problems. And Clifford Beers had grown in prestige along with the National Committee and his other organizations, which, despite all their financial problems, had remained the center of mental hygiene activity in the United States and abroad. As Adolf Meyer pointed out, however, the shift to prevention, education, and social work meant some degree of disregard for hospital psychiatry and for the hospitalized patient, a trend apparent in the 1920s under Williams and accelerated under Hincks. Initially Beers' celebrity had derived from his revelations about his own experiences with hospital abuses. As time went on, he continued to draw upon his own life in soliciting money, but his commitment became less to reform than to his organizations per se, less to other people's troubles than to his own career and welfare.

Circumstances early forced Beers to abandon investigating and reforming; that was one reason why Meyer, who abhorred exposés and scandals, would work with him. Only early in his career did Beers serve ex-patients directly — in Connecticut, where he did aftercare work to appease Meyer and mark time until he could go into action on a national scale. With all his struggles with Meyer over the bilateral (lay and medical) composition of the National Committee, participation of lay people (including himself) in planning and executing its programs was small. Salmon, Williams, and Hincks — physicians all — guided the National Committee, together with the influence, implicit and explicit, of the foundations on which it depended. The decision to legitimize the movement and the need to find financial support by encompassing within it leading physicians and psychiatrists, including hospital superintendents, as well as leaders in business and social welfare, tied Beers and the National Committee to the medical and social establishment — albeit an enlightened section of it — and thus inhibited militant action toward improving hospital care. Reliance on rich donors, who could be quickly educated as to mental hygiene, and the great foundations, conservative in their outlook, meant that circumspection was in order. Without support from the medical community and money from the rich, Beers could never have activated his organization; mental illness had limited mass appeal. It would be the job of his movement, once established, to build popular awareness and support. At the same time, he relished his contacts with important people and sought praise from them. Instead of the business entrepreneur he had aimed to be in his youth, he had become the entrepreneur of mental hygiene, the captain of a philanthropic enterprise.

Soon after leaving the Connecticut State Hospital, he wrote in 1910, he had decided to "pay more attention to general conditions than to continue to worry over the smaller things," that is, individual cases of abuse of mental patients. His movement would see to that: "As soon as the public is informed regarding the improved methods of treatment, all institutions both public and private, will of necessity have to adopt them."[1] The years passed, but the bad conditions did not. There was no great popular outcry after *A Mind That Found Itself* came out, and the public proved difficult to reach. Beers did try to generate broad support for mental hygiene in organizing and running the Connecticut Society for Mental Hygiene; once he moved to the national level he devoted himself almost exclusively to organizing, public relations, and fund-raising for the National Committee among a small group of people. Apart from contributing money to the National Committee, on occasion exerting pressure on legislatures for funds for mental health, and joining local mental hygiene societies (with the minimal obligation to pay dues and attend an annual dinner), there was, in his view, little role for lay people in the movement. He adopted the outlook of the psychiatrists he worked with that improvements would come through investigations and reports by experts, through raising standards by upgrading the training of psychiatrists, and through the influence of the highly placed and powerful. He neither encouraged lay people to go into mental hospitals as volunteers and to help in aftercare work, as Meyer had suggested, nor, beyond his first efforts in Connecticut, urged the interested public to band together to press for the reforms he advocated. And although he talked about broadening the base of the National Committee, the time never seemed ripe. He operated only on the higher levels, associating mainly with superintendents of leading hospitals and officials of the American Psychiatric Association, as well as officials in foundations, government agencies, and welfare organizations — all institutions that would be susceptible to critical scrutiny by a militant reform group.

Under Salmon's administration, the National Committee devoted much attention to conditions in hospitals. The hospital surveys, drafting of model legislation, and standardization of nosology, nomenclature, and statistics in mental hospitals helped improve conditions which in some states Salmon found to be "the most appalling survivals of neglect of mental disease" in the United States.[2] Beers approved of this work and even pushed for the National Committee to do more than conduct surveys. But eventually he became less deeply involved in the content of the National Committee's work except as it might affect its reputation or its existence. By the mid- and late 1920s, when it veered more sharply toward preventive programs, he was preoccupied with international organizing.

Hospital psychiatry remained the "Cinderella of Medicine."[3] More hospital beds were filled by mental patients than by those suffering from all other diseases combined, yet hospital psychiatry, as Meyer lamented, was not where medical research money went. Although strides had been made in raising both the quality and number of trained psychiatrists, the most talented considered private psychiatric practice, which had expanded as psychoanalytic and other psychotherapeutic systems found popular and professional acceptance, more attractive and more lucrative than hospital work. Treating psychotic patients was discouraging because there were few therapeutic techniques, and public indifference kept budgets too low to effect many environmental changes. The new psychological theories and renewed interest in social questions that pointed to possible success in overcoming mental illness by prevention through education and social change made working with the community at large more appealing to mental hygiene workers than hospital work. Beers knew how little was understood about mental disorders and their cure, he shared the general pessimism, and he was ready to shift his focus to prevention and education — areas he had always considered crucial, in his own case as well as others.

‡

He did spend time listening sympathetically to the stories of the hundreds of troubled people who came to see him and would reply to letters from them and try to help them through referrals to hospitals and physicians. Always disclaiming psychiatric expertise, he would give substantive advice only if he felt competent to do so, and sometimes after he had consulted with his psychiatrist friends. The many letters in his files testify to his prudence and good judgment in handling requests for aid or advice. If he in some way knew the correspondents or was acquainted with their friends or relatives, he would exert himself doubly, but he did try to respond to everyone. A high school teacher wrote to Ruggles in 1934 about Beers' willingness to give generously of his time to work out, if he could, solutions to personal problems: "His counsel was given on a social parity that gave you a feeling of strength and confidence in your ability to control the problem and see it through."[4] In one case, Beers tried to help a paranoid woman and was for several years bombarded with letters and calls from her alternately expressing love and threats; finally he extricated himself and learned to be more wary. When someone asked for help for a former patient, he refused after assessing the situation: "The fact that this man is looking for someone to hear all his troubles until they are cleared up is reason enough for anyone except a psychiatrist to steer clear of him. Please don't think me hardhearted. I simply know when to stay outside of situations I cannot improve — though I'm not always successful in doing this as it is shown by Mrs. H--'s pursuit of me over a period of years."[5]

In referring those in need of professional help, he would try to match his advice to the financial state of the applicant; for those without much money he would suggest state hospitals or send the person to a private psychiatrist who would not charge high fees or would accept indigent patients without fee. Those who could afford it, he would steer to Butler Hospital in Providence, which was headed by Arthur Ruggles, and sometimes to the Westchester Division of New York Hospital (the old Bloomingdale Hospital), run by another old friend, William Russell. That he did not in the 1930s suggest another prestigious institution, the Hartford Retreat, illustrates his growing conservatism and entrenchment in the "old boy" network.

The Hartford Retreat had a dynamic, young new chief, Dr. C. Charles Burlingame. Eclectic in his psychiatric approach, Burlingame subscribed to Meyer's dictum that "it is the patient whom we must treat, not merely the disease; but it is the patient as seen in his total environment."[6] Pending the day when science would discover the biochemistry of mental disorders, Burlingame effected sweeping changes. He employed every therapeutic and diagnostic technique as soon as it was medically established and set up full clinical and laboratory facilities, a psychotherapy section, workshops for patients, a swimming pool, and a small golf course. In six years he built more new facilities than had been constructed in the previous sixty. His new department of educational therapy served as a model for other institutions: under its auspices well-known writers, artists, and intellectuals gave lectures and readings; leading clergymen delivered Sunday sermons; experts like Ely Culbertson, the bridge master, gave lessons. There were fashion shows, horse races, and all sorts of activities designed to contribute toward creating the "meticulously normal" environment that Burlingame sought. He also replaced the custodial attendants with psychiatric aides, college-educated young people who looked upon themselves as guiding rather than guarding the patient.

These and other spectacular accomplishments in the midst of a general economic depression reflected not only Burlingame's salesmanship, organizing ability, and originality in tackling old problems, but the appearance of new hope in psychiatry. The new optimism was sparked by increasing acceptance of Freud's ideas (notwithstanding opposition from neurologists) and also by the new, tangible "narcosis therapies," first sleep treatment and then insulin and Metrazol (electric) shock therapy. To communicate news of modern developments to the general medical profession, still for the most part uninterested in psychiatry, Burlingame initiated *The Digest of Psychiatry and Neurology,* and through his encouragement of scientific investigation the Retreat became widely known as a research center.[7]

This was the man of whom Clifford Beers disapproved. To an acquaintance who complained of the high cost (a thousand dollars a month) of his sister-in-law's care at the Retreat, Beers, trying to maneuver her transfer to Butler Hospital, wrote that he found little good to say about the Retreat or its medical superintendent. "Dr. Burlingame and I are by temperament verbally antagonistic toward each other on occasion." In another instance Beers, asking Ruggles whether he had facilities for a transfer patient, said, "I do not suppose that Dr. Burlingame would kiss me on both cheeks if he could read this letter but I feel quite at ease in entering upon the negotiations mentioned above, because the human element at the Hartford Retreat has evidently been somewhat lost sight of in the re-organization of that institution."[8] What he meant by this criticism he did not say. Ruggles' response was in kind:

> I am very much interested in what you have done toward interesting the
> . . . family in Butler Hospital. I think we could provide adequate accommodations but, of course, you must remember that I must not get in wrong with Hartford Retreat by appearing to solicit patients now there. Frankly and confidentially, I do feel they have left out some of the human element there. If the . . . [family] decide to make a change—which, of course, any patient or family is entitled to do—I would

suggest their coming here and letting us show them what we have. I appreciate very much your efforts in our behalf.[9]

The extent to which Beers had become removed from vital concern with mental hospitals and the problems of their patients as a class may be seen in his responses to complaints and suggestions sent to him in the 1930s, when he might have done something spectacular to help improve hospital care and community attitudes. The complaints and proposals he received resembled his own a quarter of a century earlier, but he had lost his youthful capacity for indignation. He was not insensible to the problems and did not ignore them, but they were not high on his list of priorities. When he did address himself to them, it was through the familiar mode of working through the top people.

In 1931, fresh from the acclaim he had received in Hawaii and California, he did not reply to a letter from the Chicago Humane-Education Society asking for an investigation into alleged mistreatment of mental patients. Instead he forwarded the letter to the executive secretary of the Illinois Society for Mental Hygiene, a friend, who reported that the Humane-Education Society's charges against a private asylum were proved unfounded and that it was not a member of the Council of Social Agencies. So unrespectable was the Humane-Education Society that at one of its recent meetings an osteopath spoke; other speakers were equally of "low standing professionally." She would, however, make contact with them if Beers so advised.[10] This seems to have been the end of the matter as far as he was concerned.

To a former teacher, evidently also a former mental patient, who wrote to him about abusive physicians and attendants in mental hospitals, Beers, ignoring the complaints about the physicians, acknowledged that the National Committee should "take action in this important matter" of attendants and that the letter had "re-aroused" his own interest in the problem. He promised to bring it before the appropriate committee of the National Committee, and possibly as a consequence of his action a special subcommittee was created to look into mental hospitals, especially the state hospitals, where most patients were. Beers advised his correspondent to drop the subject: As an individual he could not do much more than what he had done; the material he had provided was too emotionally charged to be published; and it was not healthy to brood over problems that one could not cope with alone. Only a person with organizational connections could hope to accomplish much, and even the National Committee could do little more than investigate conditions in the face of opposition to change from a hospital's medical staff. Nor could Beers help the man find a job: "My feeling is that each recovered patient must go out and get his own job — just as I had to do when I left the hospital way back in 1903."[11]

His correspondent understandably called Beers' letter "one of the most cold-hearted, futile, caddish, empty little screeds." The man who long ago battled the "swinish brutality of hyenas who were fattening on human misery" was no more. "I was told some time ago that no psychiatrist would be in the least worried about any reports sent in to you," which turned out to be true. "The wheel has gone full circle and while you no doubt wish to and possibly do actually raise the standards of thinking along psychiatric lines, I am certain that you are of no use whatever to those victims of a system of which you are now a part and concerning whose brutality, cowardice, and incompetence you have become so complacent." Beers had not said a "single manly, honest word" about the brutality reported to him. He "neither knew nor cared." Nor had the National Committee developed ways to help former patients get jobs. "Your priggish and sniffish assertion that you went out and got a job . . . hardly tallies with your own statement . . . that it was due to the extraordinary . . . kindness of Hoggson that you found work." And what of the help that Phipps gave? Beers should thank God that he dealt with men like James, Phipps, Lounsbury, and Welch instead of one like himself. "I feel that the way that you have managed this business from start to finish is rather despicable." And Beers' suggestion to teach again without pay was "masterly in view of the fact that I told you that as a result of injuries in the state hospital I have lost the use of my voice."[12] Beers apparently did not reply.

To reports of abuse in a Pennsylvania hospital he admitted that the practices of thirty years earlier still prevailed in numerous mental hospitals; he again ignored the complaints about psychiatrists. If the National Committee still had the money to carry out surveys as it had in its early years, he said, standards of care could be raised at least in some hospitals, but unfortunately the foundations no longer supported such work, despite the willingness of the organization to reenter this field.[13] The only advice he could offer was for his correspondents to keep in touch with state mental health officials and the state mental hygiene committee.

Several years later, when the National Committee had gone back into mental hospital survey work, Beers did step in more directly to try to remedy a situation reported in a letter that greatly impressed him. It was from Richard H. Hughes, a student at Antioch College who was fulfilling his work-study requirement by working as an attendant at the New Jersey State Hospital at Trenton. In Hughes' concern for the brutality shown by the regular attendants toward the tubercular patients for whom he cared, and in the intelligence and ability his analysis of the situation demonstrated, Beers recognized real talent. "I am sure," wrote Hughes, "that, along with education and better working conditions for attendants there is needed either a higher type of attendant or some system that would make impossible, even with the present low-grade, sadistically inclined type of hospital employee, the heartbreaking cruelty and inhumanity which prevails at the present time."[14] The result was a conference between Hughes and the director of the National Committee's work with mental hospitals. Hughes' statements were convincing enough for Beers to get Dr. William J. Ellis, director of the New Jersey Department of Institutions and Agencies, who had a reputation for improving the state's institutions, to promise to look into the matter. Beers told Ellis that if his department's information-gathering proved successful, the same method might be used elsewhere by institutions willing to engage in self-surveys, as letters telling of poor treatment of mental patients came to the National Committee all the time. Arrangements were also made for Hughes to see a member of the board of the Trenton State Hospital. Beers expected improvements to follow, and he congratulated Hughes on performing a real service. "I, strangely enough, was in a position to get prompt action from the powers that be in New Jersey."[15]

In 1933 the *New York Times* article about Beers brought a letter from a Connecticut physician, an old friend of the Beers family, that discussed conditions in mental hospitals. "I have for years realized . . . that at least 90% of unfortunates in our State Institutions are deplorably treated by unsympathetic incompetence, and are virtually prisoners that should have their liberty under an environment of sympathetic kindness and consideration." These included many old and feeble but not insane people. Beers acknowledged that many state hospital patients could live in the community if they had financial support and family care. "Such cases make great demands on one's sympathy but with things as they are the best things cannot always be done for a given case." He invited the old physician for a talk at the National Committee office.[16]

Another correspondent faulted the National Committee for failing to work with mental hospitals or to follow up complaints made in behalf of individual patients. The value of preventive work was dubious. "Can prevention succeed before it is thoroughly understood what is to be prevented?" It was more important to be concerned about the declining recovery and discharge rates and rising admission and readmission rates. Without improvement in treatment of patients, "no real progress in ANY phase is possible." Beers, in reply, defended the National Committee, though admitting that it had not been very active in this connection in recent years. But some work had been done, and staff members had been working with officials in various states and had done a study of mental hospitals during the depression.[17]

In the early 1930s Beers and the National Committee did try to help the people struggling to raise standards in mental hospitals and eliminate political interference in various states—California, Hawaii, Indiana, Missouri, and Florida—and later in Maryland, Georgia, and Alabama. This was not the direction, however, that Hincks wanted to take; it was forced upon the National Committee by circumstances. In 1933 Hincks had told Rockefeller Foundation officials that the American Psychiatric Association seemed willing to assume greater responsibility for the original objective of the National Committee, improving care of the institutionalized insane, and that it was more important for the National Committee to further positive mental hygiene through education and social work.[18] Why Hincks thought an organization of psychiatrists could muster the enormous energy needed to improve conditions in mental hospitals he did not say. His appraisal of the American Psychiatric Association was overoptimistic, his program for the National Committee proved to be somewhat vague, and reports of intolerable conditions and political chicanery in state hospitals eventually could not be brushed aside. By 1936, the National Committee, searching for programs that would please the Rockefeller Foundation, and having become involved, together with foundation officials, in investigating a particularly bad hospital situation in Maryland, established, with foundation support, a division of mental hospital services.[19]

Before then, Beers thought that progress was being made and that in time humane and scientific care would prevail: "the organized movement for higher standards of care in State Hospitals, inaugurated a quarter of a century ago . . . has begun to produce results."[20] So he rejected a critical article on hospitals submitted to *Mental Hygiene,* "Ten Centuries in an Insane Asylum." Such an exposition of the author's experiences, admittedly well written and accurate, "would do harm . . . since thousands of relatives of patients in mental hospitals . . . would or might assume that conditions in *all* mental hospitals" were bad. Instead the author should place the article in the hands of responsible state officials or, better, visit the director of his state's bureau of mental health. "If progress is to be made in any state, it must come largely through officials who have authority to deal in an official way with 'abuses.'"[21] To another correspondent who wanted to do something full-time for the mentally ill, he wrote, "It is difficult, if not impossible, for anyone to do very much who has not had special training in the field of mental hygiene or psychiatry, but everyone can help who takes the trouble to bring to the attention of others the existence of the National Committee for Mental Hygiene and persuades people to read my autobiography."[22] "I don't know what to suggest," he told another inquirer, "unless it be to familiarize yourself with the teachings of mental hygiene and to influence others" to do the same. One could also help by contributing money to the movement.[23] At the National Committee itself, he doubted that lay people could do much, as "only persons who have had a formal training in psychiatry or mental hygiene work are employed."[24]

Although their stated goal had been to provide proper treatment and extend mental hygiene to all, regardless of color, Beers' and the National Committee's interest in mental hospitals and mental patients never extended to a long-neglected group, blacks. Beers, with his conventional middle-class outlook and his southern sympathies, was not sensitive to the special plight of blacks, who usually received the worst treatment and experienced the worst neglect. When in 1937 a "well-meaning, young coloured woman," a former patient in mental hospitals, approached him to help establish a hospital for "Professional Negroes," he told her she would have to find wealthy backers interested in the "welfare of your race." A year later she saw Beers and an official of the National Committee to discuss starting a mental hospital for "Negroes" in the South; they could help her with advice but would not, as a matter of National Committee policy, sign their names to a list of those interested in this project. Beers also discouraged her from starting a mental hygiene committee in White Plains, New York, advising the executive secretary of the New York State Committee on Mental Hygiene to treat her "kindly" but to dissuade her.[25] In this particular case Beers' attitude was probably influenced by a judgment of the young woman's condition; in any case, the real needs of blacks for better care, which he could not but acknowledge once he was made aware of them, he evidently felt should be taken care of by their own people. Neither he nor the National Committee ever did anything special for them.

‡

Beers' conservatism extended to proposals to organize former mental patients in their own behalf, an interesting development of the 1930s. In August 1931 he received a letter from Dr. L. Cody Marsh, late of Kings Park State Hospital (Kings Park, New York) and of Worcester State Hospital, eventually recognized as a pioneer in group psychotherapy in mental hospitals. In an article published in 1931 in *Mental Hygiene,* Marsh had discussed his "Group Treatment of the Psychoses,"[26] which he had developed to give patients a feeling of group solidarity and of shared problems. He wrote to Beers to ask the National Committee to organize "an ex-patient league" or make a small grant for him to do so, with the National Committee's help. He had successfully organized the patients in Kings Park Hospital, and the superintendent of Worcester State Hospital, where Marsh used to hold meetings of patients, was trying to establish contact between the community and the hospital in order to break down fear and suspicion of the patients and find homes for those who could be discharged. Marsh, interested in the "sociological approach to mental disease," was convinced that "if so-called insanity is to be baptized with respectability, which is now the case with formerly untouchable things such as tuberculosis, cancer, and leprosy, the patient himself must be willing to come out into the open and admit that he has suffered from mental disease without any sense of shame or apology."[27] Beers took four months to reply to this letter.

He promised to bring the proposals before the scientific administration committee of the National Committee but could not himself support it.

Prejudice against mental illness and suspicion of recovered patients, though lessened, was still too widespread for anyone to benefit from joining an ex-patient organization. "Without taking undue credit to myself, I believe I am one of the few who have ever successfully capitalized a mental breakdown and I, as you know, did not try to capitalize it in my own interests, though as things have turned out, I have received unexpected personal benefits from and through my work." A history of mental illness was "without question" a detriment to its former sufferers. "Even I, whose attitude toward recovered patients is a generous, and, I believe, intelligent one, would look askance at applicants for work if I were the head of a business concern and were asked to take them into my employ. There would, of course, be exceptional cases but, as a group, recovered patients are sadly handicapped in the way indicated. To organize a league and have its members label themselves, as it were, would, I fear, do them more harm than good." Organizing the patients within the hospital is a "most helpful and inspiring thing. My feeling of doubt, however, is in regard to the desirability of keeping patients linked up too closely with a mental hospital after they have returned to society, though they should, of course, be encouraged to return to a hospital for advice and also for treatment should that later be needed."[28]

Only Clifford Beers could confess his past and still succeed in the world. The prospect that others could do as he had done no doubt threatened his unique claim to fame. Besides, the existence of ex-patients' organizations, with the criticism of hospital conditions and calls for reforms they would inevitably bring, might compete with the National Committee and call into question the success he boasted for the mental hygiene movement. Such doubts are not palatable when one is nearing sixty and has received the Légion d'Honneur. And, however much Beers was wrapped up in his movement, however much he exploited his own personal history and talked about eliminating the stigma of mental illness, he must still have felt the need to deny it by dissociating himself from others in the same plight. Otherwise he could not have written the way he did to Marsh.

Interestingly, at the time he wrote this reply, Beers had started once again to write a "continuing sequel" to *A Mind That Found Itself,* with the object of describing "dramatic incidents that have occurred in connection with the launching and development of what is now known as 'The Mental Hygiene Movement'" and to "give a continuing picture of the mental processes and mental spectrum, as it were, of an acute observer and singularly articulate person who lost his mind, found it again, and, as events have proved, made effective use of it in the interests of a great cause." This person "in his work and in his methods of work has shown signs of real genius, or certainly a genius for doing the work in which he has engaged with such success."[29]

After many more pages devoted to establishing his genius, Beers wrote, on the day after his letter to Marsh, a dreamlike sequence (originally described in 1905 at the Hartford Retreat) that seems designed to confirm that no one could expect to complete successfully with him: In heaven, "when careers are being offered for me to choose from and they offer the one that I have lived, I ask the Master of Ceremonies if they did not have some career of a somewhat milder and less painful nature." There were two such careers but Pinel and Dix chose them after deciding that the one set aside for Clifford Beers "was too painful" for them. So he had to accept the only career left, that of crusading ex-patient.[30]

Marsh was not deterred by Beers' response. He had gone ahead with his plan, he informed Beers, and already had some thirty ex-patients ready to come out into the open. "You know, the psychology bound up in the 'Foreign Legion' of the French I think obtains here. One can capitalize one's unfortunate past and put up even greater efforts and heroism than he who has no 'past.'" Marsh had also continued his "classes" or "institutes" for people with personal, vocational, or social difficulties, with psychoneuroses, or with a history of psychoses who wanted to know about mental hygiene or just about the "art of living." His "social-educational" approach was cheaper than individual psychotherapy and also escaped the "odium which attaches to the Mental Hospital, the Psychiatric Clinic, and even the private psychiatric consultation."[31]

It might be argued that, in discouraging Marsh and others, Beers missed the opportunity to build a movement that could have strengthened efforts to improve the conditions of mental patients in and out of hospitals and on a sustained, consistent basis. Beers' original push for reform, as well as campaigns before and after his, met with indifferent success partly because they failed to involve a deeply interested constituency, those who had suffered from mental illness—patients, former patients, and their friends and relatives. Leaders of reform movements traditionally appealed for support not to the victims of appalling conditions but to elite groups in positions of power or with access to those in authority—the rich, other liberal reformers and social workers, and politicians and government officials. Because of their single-minded, even fanatical devotion to their cause, such leaders could accomplish a good deal—hospital care for the neglected insane in Dorothea Dix's time and the promotion of psychiatry and mental hygiene in Clifford Beers'. But when their energies waned so did their movements, leaving the mentally ill friendless and forgotten, if not quite so badly treated, to be rediscovered by another generation in a new era of social change.

There were, to be sure, other forces operating to cause this cycle, and of course there is no assurance that, had the victims themselves and their relations—those with the keenest, most direct, and most abiding interest in the matter—been actively involved, conditions would have improved more substantially and less ephemerally. Whether such a group could have been organized in the first place, given the stigma and shame attached to mental illness and the poverty of most of its sufferers, is another question, especially for the nineteenth century. But it might have been possible in the first half of the twentieth, in a new era of mass movements and when the development of psychology and psychiatry and of public awareness about mental hygiene had prepared the ground. Precedents existed in the community health center idea that grew in part out of the settlement house movement. For some of its originators, the central idea of the health centers was to involve community residents in their own health programs, with the extent of local participation seen as an indication of the level of health in the community. Politics and health were held to be interdependent, and the health centers, each serving from thirty to forty thousand people, were to act as coordinating agencies for all other groups likely to help meet the health needs of residents. By the 1920s the red scare in the United States that followed the Bolshevik Revolution had made community participation too dangerous an idea, and it disappeared from the health center movement.[32]

Not all the health centers that sprang up in cities at the turn of the century involved the participatory concept; many were sponsored and run by the same kinds of people who supported the mental health movement. Beers himself had in 1919 proposed a comprehensive community mental health demonstration project, encompassing diagnosis, treatment, and care of disturbed people. It involved local organizations and agencies in planning and execution, but not the community residents in general — and certainly not the inmates, patients, handicapped, orphans, and others to be helped, that is, those "unfortunates" looked upon conventionally as passive objects rather than active participants. As much as Beers himself had, as a patient, insisted on not being treated as a thing to be manipulated, he did not extend that feeling to others once he had come out of his dependent situation. His plan nevertheless did exhibit an attempt to integrate modern concepts of mental health and psychiatry with community needs on many levels; when it failed to get support from the Rockefeller Foundation he dropped it and did not pick it up again.[33]

Although the community mental health center idea was not revived until the 1960s, when ex-patients' organizations also sprang up, along with lawsuits in behalf of hospitalized patients, a notable organization of former patients and their friends was started in Chicago in 1937, several years after Marsh wrote to Beers. It was led by Dr. A. A. Low of the Illinois Psychiatric Institute. When released patients, whose recovery Low attributed to the new insulin and Metrazol shock treatments, complained of the hostility they encountered in the outside world, he proposed that they form an organization to remove the stigma of mental illness by educating the public. With himself as president and with the support of their relatives and of prominent Illinois physicians and public welfare officials, thirty former patients organized Recovery, Inc. Working quietly, it was quickly able to change state civil service application forms to eliminate requirements for applicants to reveal a history of mental illness, and it began an effort, with the endorsement of the state Department of Public Welfare, to improve commitment proceedings in Illinois. In July 1938 Recovery began publishing *Lost and Found,* a newsletter edited by Low, and soon its meetings were attracting two hundred patients and their friends.[34]

In January 1939, Low, who had worked independently of Beers and the National Committee, discussed in *Lost and Found* Beers and the mental hygiene movement.[35] Beers' public career, Low said, had originally had two aims: the prevention of mental illness and the humane treatment of the insane. Aftercare "played little if any part in Beers' program," a deficiency arising from the paucity of recovered patients, who were just now becoming numerous because of the introduction of shock treatment. Recovery was a continuation of Beers' work. "We physicians were in a quandary because we were trained in the tenets of Beers' strategy. There was a general staff: the psychiatrist and mental hygienist. But there was no army for the general staff to lead in battle. Now the army had appeared on the plain and we, acquainted with the tactics of headquarters only, did not know what to do with it. And the army grew, and its demands became more insistent. Something had to be done." Hence, Recovery. "An Army needs leaders, and does well to win for itself a friendly hinterland of sympathizers, well wishers and sponsors. But the actual fighting and campaigning cannot be done by outsiders, no matter how sympathetic and well disposed. The very principle of an army is self-help." Beers had piled victory upon victory, vanquishing the system of restraint and humanizing the "system of hospital treatment; he forced the introduction of voluntary commitment and in some states the system of temporary detention." The founding of psychopathic hospitals and development of psychiatric social services and child guidance and mental hygiene clinics also owed much to him directly or indirectly. Nevertheless the war was not won; the stigma of mental illness remained, and as long as the courts stamped the families of the insane as officially tainted, the stigma would remain. Clifford Beers was not superannuated; a general staff was still needed and the "conservative ideas for which he stands are still our guide," but the movement must go forward.

So it did, with similar associations founded elsewhere in Illinois, with *Lost and Found* eventually distributing fifteen hundred copies, and with Recovery members speaking on radio programs sponsored by the Illinois Society for Mental Hygiene. The American Association for the Advancement of Science discussed Recovery at its 1938 meeting, and University of Chicago sociologist E. W. Burgess called it "the most intelligent and thoroughgoing attempt to deal with the problems of the community to which the cured patient must return." Recovery was more than just a continuation of Clifford

Beers' work; its meaning for the mental hygiene movement could "hardly be overestimated," Burgess said.[36]

Similar organizations were founded in other states, although few survived very long, and the movement began to receive recognition, including favorable comments in the National Committee's *Mental Hygiene* and in the *American Journal of Psychiatry*. Recovery found, however, that its attempts to educate the public through radio broadcasts and public lectures proved unsuccessful. A new set of goals was adopted, embodying the concept of self-help.[37] At the same time, *Lost and Found* was discontinued with the November-December 1940 issue after two and a half years of publication; in 1946 Low's influence waned after he left the Illinois Psychiatric Institute.[38] Recovery lived on, grew, and still exists, though its lost ties to the state hospitals were not reestablished until the activist 1960s.

It is likely that Clifford Beers was not aware of the existence of Recovery; there is no mention of it in his papers. When Low's analysis of his role, something to which he would ordinarily have responded if he knew about it, appeared, Beers was not only deeply involved in a new National Committee crisis, but he was beginning to feel very ill. By the time Recovery had become at all prominent he was out of the picture. Whether he would have been more sympathetic to its activities than he had been to Marsh's proposal is problematic. He was always impressed by success and by the approval of "important" people, so perhaps Recovery might have won, if not his whole-hearted endorsement, a measure of sanction from him.

It is perhaps unfair to criticize Beers for his conservatism, for not seeing that other ex-patients like himself and their friends might be a powerful impulse for change. It was only in the 1960s that it began to be realized that manipulation of powerless people, even for their own good, was not only expensive but usually ineffective, that people must be and could be actively involved in improving their own lives. Radical thinkers and activists had had this idea for a long time, but their aim was structural change—total revolution —something that middle-class reformers, even those of more liberal stripe than Clifford Beers, were not interested in and indeed shied away from. At the beginning, Beers' activities, motivated by a wish to reach the general public and to effect far-reaching reforms in mental hospitals, were circumscribed by the difficulty of doing so, by the need for money and sponsorship, and by the advice he took from knowledgeable and well-connected people who helped him then and could help him in the future. Once his National Committee was established, it took on a life of its own as a small organization run by medical men trying to effect change indirectly through studies, publications, training, and demonstration projects and becoming increasingly dependent on foundation support. Beers was the only lay person prominently and actively involved with its work. Through the years he chafed under the yoke of the psychiatrists and physicians he had to work with, but he did not or could not do much to change the situation. He could not help but know that, to use Low's metaphor, he had organized a general staff but few troops. Circumstances aside, however, would he have wanted to lead soldiers who were, in his view, handicapped—former inmates of mental hospitals? Such an army would not in his eyes reflect glory upon its commander. A man seeking to prove his mental soundness for over twenty-five years would not relish the idea of commanding a collection of people who needed to do the same.

✤ 20 ✤

Final Years:
Crisis and Collapse

There was increasing doubt whether even the general staff would survive the lingering economic depression which had dried up funds for so many organizations like the National Committee and forced them to curtail their activities. It was discouraging to Beers that, after all the work and the success, the National Committee should still be insecure. If it should go under he believed that some similar organization would have to be created to take its place, so great was the need for mental hygiene work. He predicted at one time that the American Foundation would probably outlive the National Committee, which "might at some future time find its field . . . usurped by federal or state action . . . no one can safely predict what will happen in the future if certain political trends [the New Deal] should continue to grow in force."[1]

Whatever his glum feelings, Beers was not about to allow the National Committee to die, and throughout the thirties he always kept its financial needs in mind and tried to find funds when he could. From its beginnings to 1938, the National Committee's total income came to more than $4 million, of which more than half was granted by foundations, mainly the Commonwealth Fund, the Rockefeller Foundation, the Milbank Memorial Fund, and the Supreme Council of Scottish Rite Masons (which supported research in schizophrenia), with others giving lesser sums. Over $1 million had come in as individual contributions, for which Beers was mainly responsible, and the American Foundation for Mental Hygiene received $232,500 up to 1938, largely through his efforts. From 1920 to 1930 he had brought into the National Committee an average of $78,245 annually, compared with $139,329 that came from foundations. There was also income from *Mental Hygiene* subscriptions and the sale of mental hygiene literature and National Committee memberships.[2]

With the depression, total income was reduced drastically and dependence on foundations became nearly complete. From 1931 to 1935 private individuals' contributions declined by approximately 90 percent, to $7,185.67 a year, and foundation support fell to $57,599.31 a year, mainly from the

305

General Education Board and the Rockefeller Foundation, with much smaller sums donated by the Carnegie Corporation, the Rosenwald Fund, the Friedsam and New York Foundations, and the Masons.[3] Without the Rockefeller Foundation the National Committee could not function. The foundation's officials were interested in developing psychiatry, and in three stages: discovering and training first-rate people who would then teach physicians and lay people and carry out research; developing research and training centers; and sponsoring clinical applications of psychiatry. The subsidies to the National Committee were only a small portion of the foundation's total grants in psychiatry, which went mainly to support academic and hospital research and training programs in medical schools. Despite reservations about the National Committee's viability (doubts shared by officials of the Carnegie Corporation), the Rockefeller Foundation continued to support it because it was still providing services that no other agency could or would provide. It was still the center of mental hygiene activity, training, and information-gathering and dissemination, and of public education in psychiatry and mental hygiene in the United States, although some of these functions, the foundation's leaders came to think, should be the responsibility of the federal government.[4] In 1936, partly because of problems in Maryland's mental institutions and partly because some foundation officials thought the National Committee's central interest should again be the improvement of care in mental hospitals, which had suffered from cutbacks during the depression, the Rockefeller Foundation financed the establishment of the National Committee's division of mental hospital services for a three-year period.[5]

At the same time, officials at the Rockefeller Foundation kept criticizing Hincks' leadership, of whose deficiencies Beers was aware. In 1935, analyzing the situation for Ruggles, he said that the National Committee under Hincks had no strong leadership, no clear direction, and no consistent planning. Besides his tendency to go off in various directions and not see programs through to completion, Hincks often was away in Canada, leaving Bullis, an office and business manager, to make decisions for which he was not qualified. A competent medical officer, Beers believed, was needed to complement Hincks' strengths in promotion and public education. That the National Committee's base of support could be broadened significantly, something the Rockefeller Foundation had been urging for years, he doubted, but he felt it was worth trying to get more individual contributions in order to impress the foundation. He was aware of the criticism that he interfered in the National Committee's work, to which he pleaded guilty. But he was always supported by the ablest members of the board, and without him the National Committee "would have gone to smash." He was the only one continuously on the job and alert to danger, ready to bring important matters to the attention of the executive committee. Once the National Committee could become "a proper organization with a fulltime psychiatrist, with Bullis as Executive Officer and a Planning Committee to lay down safe lines of action," he would retire to New Haven.[6]

Beers' evaluation coincided more or less with that of Rockefeller Foundation officials,[7] but the problems persisted, and he did not move decisively to change the situation at the National Committee until the Rockefeller Foundation four years later acted on its threats to cut off funds.

As Alan Gregg, the influential chief of the foundation's division of medical sciences, noted in an analysis of the connection between foundations and organizations like the National Committee, once a relationship of dependency was set, it became difficult for the recipient organization to realize that the relationship might end, no matter how much the foundation warned that the goal was financial independence. Such an organization could expend a great deal of energy trying to do things to please the foundations (whatever the assurances that the organization was free of foundation control), especially if the organization was doing work that the foundations wanted done but could not or did not care to undertake themselves. The result was a certain fiscal irresponsibility on the part of the organization's administrators, a situation that was not good either for them or for the foundations. At one point Gregg had to scold Bullis for publicity that blurred the identity of the National Committee, to the extent that a newspaper referred to it as the "Rockefeller Foundation of Mental Hygiene."[8]

In line with its approach to giving — to encourage recipients to find other sources of support — the Rockefeller Foundation, as it had done in the 1920s, gradually reduced its subsidies to the National Committee, so that things became desperate by 1937 and 1938, with deficits of ten thousand dollars or more looming in the general budget. Beers thought the crisis would be weathered and roused himself to do what he could, although the decline in the stock market at the end of 1937 did not help. He sent out appeals for both large and small contributions and tried to establish, again without result, contacts with wealthy people — Edsel Ford, John Hay Whitney, and Pierre DuPont, for example. As he had many times before, he wanted board members to become more actively involved in fund-raising (something Gregg also urged) and to help him secure interviews with prospective donors.[9] He also worked out a plan to speak to women's clubs. He thought he had done as well as could be expected through his mail subscriptions, at least enough to impress foundation officials, but the latter considered this effort to build up a roster of small subscribers and in general to get wider support "desultory"; the money received was used ill-advisedly, in their view, to solicit more money instead of developing local mental hygiene organizations, which could be an eventual source of support.[10]

Bullis and Hincks came up with unrealistic or inappropriate schemes for new activities, some of which Beers vetoed when he heard about them. To

Bullis' idea of setting up a clearinghouse or institute dealing with shock therapy information, Beers said that shock therapy was not yet established and such a connection with it might damage the National Committee's reputation; it was "not a *medical* society and it should not get mixed up in *strictly* medical *matters*." The executive committee agreed.[11]

A serious controversy arose over a proposal to accept money from the Distilled Spirits Institute to study alcoholism. Hincks and Bullis, especially the latter, were pushing the project, with support from various National Committee board members. It was not unethical, they claimed, for the National Committee to have such sponsorship; other medical groups had done research with money from business groups. Beers, along with Russell and Willcox, strongly opposed the idea. He went into action, urgently soliciting opinions from his friends on the board. Chittenden worried that such backing would endanger the National Committee's "good name and standing"; Sachs was "emphatically . . . [and] utterly opposed," as was William A. White. Haven Emerson wrote a sharp letter to Bullis, stating that studies done under the auspices of commercial organizations were practically all discredited, and he doubted whether the National Committee could survive the opprobrium that such a connection would bring. The scientific administration committee voted unanimously in favor of a survey of facilities for care and treatment of alcoholics but split on the issue of accepting money for it; the final decision was against asking the Distilled Spirits Institute. Bullis hoped to change this decision; Beers worked to kill the idea for good, enlisting the aid of the Boks as well as others. "Thumbs down on liquor money," Curtis Bok wrote. Beers asked Mary Bok to write a letter countering the argument that the National Committee could take such funds if other donors would not be offended. The idea that money from anywhere could be accepted if the National Committee could get away with it should be fought. Mrs. Bok complied. There the issue ended. The National Committee would have to struggle along without the distillers.[12]

From 1936 to 1938 Beers, sometimes with Hincks and Bullis, took to the field in response to requests for help from mental hygiene advocates and also, no doubt, to comply with Rockefeller Foundation suggestions that the National Committee work more with local groups and become more involved in improving hospital conditions, which were, in Beers' view, "nearly as bad" as when the organization was founded in 1909 and were again the target of surveys by its new division of mental hospital services.[13]

In the spring of 1936 he and Clara combined a trip south to see old friends, and to inspect a sanitarium that Aunt Mame might be placed in, with "organizing work" in Georgia, North Carolina, and Virginia. In North Carolina, Beers spoke before six hundred people at Chapel Hill, and at Salem College the students, about one-third of them having read his book, were a responsive audience. His appearances helped to reinvigorate the movement in that state; he also extracted a promise from Dr. D. Clay Lilley of Winston-Salem to introduce him to the "big fortunes" there and to officials of the Winston-Salem Foundation.[14]

Soon afterwards he went to Milwaukee to address the Wisconsin Society for Mental Hygiene, and in 1938 he promised to help a New Jersey activist establish a mental health movement there.[15] He also became, confidentially and unofficially, involved in an investigation into conditions in the Milledgeville, Georgia, State Hospital and became active in organizing a mental hygiene society in that state, work that was helped by the impression his autobiography made on the chairman of the Georgia State Board of Welfare.[16] In Alabama, where his "splendid book" and the "inspiring influence of [his] life and work" allegedly influenced the governor and leading lawmakers to get the legislature to vote unanimously five hundred thousand dollars for the state hospitals and the state school for mentally deficient children, he aided a group of citizens trying to improve hospital conditions and start a mental hygiene movement; he also hoped to interest wealthy people there to contribute to the National Committee. A visit to Alabama included the usual social functions, with a birthday lunch for Beers in the governor's mansion and dinner with the wealthy sister-in-law of the leader of the mental hygiene activists in the state, an event "which in course of time may pay a dividend."[17] Hincks and Bullis were to join the Beerses in Alabama, and to ease the pressure of the trip Beers allowed them to drive his car down to Birmingham to meet him and Clara. Because his car was very precious to him, he gave them, much to their amusement, a "To Whom It May Concern" letter as evidence of his permission to use it, plus four pages of instructions on how to drive and care for it.[18]

Beers also resumed searching for an endowment for the American Foundation. In 1938 he learned from a friend how close he had come to getting several million dollars from Elizabeth Milbank Anderson, one of the National Committee's first benefactors and founder of the Milbank Memorial Fund. Mrs. Anderson had intended that she and Mrs. Henry O. Havemeyer (wife of the sugar magnate and art collector) would each give two million dollars to the National Committee and then raise a fifth million from among their friends, but she was persuaded by her cousin and executor, Albert Milbank, to give him a free hand in establishing the Milbank Fund as planned. After recounting what might have been, which Beers took as encouragement that someone else with vision and public spirit would eventually come along to endow the movement, his friend criticized Beers' fund-raising approach as being anachronistic. Mental hygiene could not appeal to the small giver, and the big giver was too vulnerable to stock market vicissitudes; foundations were the only answer. If Beers must appeal to individuals he should be more specific about where the money would go and the practical results to be expected. Businessmen understood facts and needed a motive for giving.[19]

Beers could not change, and he stuck to his formula: "As I look back, my occasional success in getting large gifts has been due almost entirely to the impression made during my talks, plus the effect made by my book, read either before or afterwards."[20]

Through mailings, some personal solicitation, and trips to the field, he helped the National Committee survive through 1938, for which year he secured ten thousand dollars to erase the deficit, with the help of a last-minute contribution extracted from Marshall Field.[21] When the National Committee needed him he would always help, and he expected to continue to do so in 1939, when a deficit was again expected.

‡

That new year did not begin well. Early in January, Alan Gregg informed Hincks that the Rockefeller Foundation would terminate its grants to the National Committee both for general expenses and for the support of the division of mental hospital services at the end of the year. Gregg explained the foundation's position: Its policy was to keep its freedom to undertake new projects in early stages of development, which meant that support of such projects must eventually be discontinued to release funds for new ones. A project's continued need for support after an appropriate period of assistance demonstrated either failure to fulfill the promise of independence or the discharge of its primary purpose. Both conditions seemed to operate in the National Committee. The foundation's term grants for the past twenty years were justified by the National Committee's success in its "original and central task" of awakening interest in mental health, which task might well be considered accomplished. In the matter of achieving independence the picture was less positive; the National Committee had not been able to reach financial self-sufficiency or stability. The foundation did not feel that it ever would or, by implication, should. Aside from mental hygiene propaganda, many of the National Committee's activities could perhaps be as effectively administered by the American Psychiatric Association, the U.S. Public Health Service, the National Research Council, or foundations interested in psychiatry and neurology.[22] In other words, the National Committee, having achieved what it initially set out to do and unable to do all the other things it tried to do, should go out of business.

The foundation had originally supported the National Committee's division of mental hospital services because, at the time, the Public Health Service could not act so freely and effectively as the National Committee and surveys were needed to counter "the lowering of hospital standards during the depression." The hospital survey work "represented, in effect, a return to the . . . earliest activities of the [National] Committee," and the division was a "good, useful and conscientious part of a very unstable organization."

By 1939, however, its worth having been proven, the division's work should be taken over by the government, which the Public Health Service agreed to do with the help of the National Committee.[23]

A confidential Rockefeller Foundation report discussed the relationship between the foundation and the National Committee:

> Despite repeated warnings the Committee remained dependent upon the Foundation and continued to suffer from this status of a dependent intermediate set-up. Behind this unsatisfactory record lay such factors as the depression, the doubtful judgments and temperamental inconsistency of some of its executive personnel, the inherent difficulties of the mental hygiene field as such, and a gradually evident lack of sober and solid policy within the organization.

The National Committee was credited with standardizing hospital care of the insane and mentally deficient, acting as a clearinghouse of information, and stimulating better teaching of psychiatry and wider awareness of the needs of the insane for therapy and prevention. "Its failures were in personnel and in policy as an organization, not in outliving its potential usefulness, or neglecting its ideals. It should have done fewer things better, spread less, sought and saved for endowment, and built up through service to state societies the status of an indispensable national service institution." The sum total of Rockefeller Foundation support was more than it should have been by perhaps one-fourth or one-fifth. "By how much the rest of the aid helped a growing movement it is hard to say—but probably by a great deal."[24] Gregg also implied to Hincks privately that the National Committee, afraid of being called conservative, had been too flighty; in many of its plans it was "already 15 or 20 years ahead of the times." If it was to go on, the best thing would be "to get some program of procedure and stick to it until it was finished."[25]

One might argue that if the foundations, the federal government, and the American Psychiatric Association had been ready to expand their own mental health programs, then the National Committee, notwithstanding its weaknesses, would have been able to carve out a place for itself more in keeping with its resources. As it was, in the face of the slowness of others to act and the immensity of the work to be done, the National Committee did go in various directions, the emphasis changing with the successive medical directors. Whatever justification the Rockefeller Foundation's criticism had, and however much some of it seemed to describe Clifford Beers, the fault could not be laid to him. He had had little direct influence on the substantive work of the National Committee, and he had for years been striving to place it on a stable basis through an endowment. As he said, commenting on the foundation's action, had someone put a "golden spoon" in the National Committee's mouth, "the movement would have gone ahead much faster—and we on the inside would have been set free to do work instead of having to fight crisis after crisis." Instead they had been forced to rely on the "possessor of the biggest spoon of all, the Rockefeller Foundation."[26]

Still, Beers felt that the National Committee would survive. As always, he tried to turn the disaster to account. He had Gregg add to his letter to Hincks a sentence expressing confidence in the National Committee and sent a copy to Marshall Field in hope of getting a contribution from him. Field sent twenty-five hundred dollars.[27]

Beers also became more involved in the National Committee's affairs, which meant, mostly, looking into what Hincks and Bullis were doing, as he assumed, probably rightly, that the Rockefeller Foundation's criticism was aimed primarily at Hincks and indirectly at Bullis. He still liked Hincks as a friend but realized, as he told Gregg, that his judgment was not always dependable[28] and that he had scattered his energies at the National Committee; he also was spending more time in Canada than in New York. As for Bullis, he was very discouraged by the Rockefeller Foundation's decision, a feeling he expressed in letters sent out of the National Committee office. Beers took the liberty of reading them and following them up by his own, saying that Bullis had given too "gloomy a picture" of the National Committee's financial condition, and that it was "not quite accurate" to say that the foundation withdrew its support, "at least not permanently." The National Committee was still viable and could operate without the foundation subsidy.[29] (However unethical his spying on Bullis may have been, Beers was not wrong in what he said; the appointment later of a new medical director who impressed Gregg with his good sense predisposed Gregg to consider again making grants for specific projects if the National Committee could meet its administrative expenses.)[30] Beers also reprimanded Bullis for handling professional matters in Hincks' absence and in his name.[31]

Bullis' worst offenses, in Beers' view, were dubious business ventures that either took time away from the National Committee or exploited his position there, or both. He established, counter to a directive from the executive committee of the National Committee, an International Speech Defect Institute that people erroneously connected with the National Committee, was president of Reconciliation Tours, Inc. (an agency designed to encourage travel between the Soviet Union and the United States), and was treasurer of Allied Optical Service, a discount eyeglass service for employees of business firms and other organizations.[32] Beers in principle opposed any exploitation of the National Committee, "intentionally or otherwise," for the financial advantage of its staff or the use of its name for any purpose but its own. He himself avoided "expressing opinions on the books of others because I cannot speak as an individual because of my close connection and identification with our National Committee."[33] Both the International Speech Defect Institute and the Allied Optical Service threatened to sue the National Committee for damages, the president of the latter demanding a seventy-five-dollar settlement from Beers and a temporary place on the staff of the National Committee at twenty-five dollars a week to enable him to restore his reputation and liquidate Allied Optical Service with honor. Nothing came of all these threats, responsibility for which Beers attributed to Bullis, who "does not yet feel that he had done anything out of the ordinary. I need not say more."[34]

Years later Bullis claimed that the fuss over his business ventures was a smokescreen to hide Beers' unhappiness over the National Committee's financial situation and to provide reasons to force him and Hincks out, as Beers had not forgiven them for the Distilled Spirits Institute scheme and for approving the transfer of the hospital surveys, a project dear to his heart, to the Public Health Service.[35] True, Beers had been upset by the alchoholism proposal and was at first categorically opposed to the delegation of the hospital survey work to the Public Health Service. He realized that a federal role in mental hygiene was coming, but with his conservative politics and jealous love for the National Committee he did not look upon the prospect with joy, however much he had in his younger days visualized the government as an important element in his grand plan of reform.[36] Nevertheless, when the blow to the division of hospital services came, he did not seem devastated by it; at least the matter did not loom large in his correspondence at the time. Bullis underestimated Beers' distress over the ethical questions raised by Bullis' business dealings and condoned by Hincks and over the effect on foundation executives of the two men's manner of running the National Committee. Their questionable activities were even worse, Beers said, than people already knew about. And neither of them had "had the sense to talk over all matters with me before going ahead" with their projects.[37]

The management of the National Committee must be recast, Beers concluded, because the foundations had "lost confidence in the somewhat erratic and, at times, mercurial leadership of Dr. Hincks on a part time basis."[38] Beers got to work to clean house, which meant building support on the executive committee, several members of which were appalled by Hincks' and Bullis' activities and the damage done to the National Committee's reputation.[39] Through Beers and possibly others, the Rockefeller Foundation people were kept informed of events.[40] Beers heeded advice from Ruggles and others that an "entire change" in the National Committee's management be avoided; after all, said Ruggles, the great accomplishments of Hincks and Bullis should not be dwarfed by the mistakes they made under the "terrific financial strain of recent years." Hincks would be kept on part-time till the end of the year and listed as editor of *Mental Hygiene* until a new medical director was chosen, and Bullis could handle the New York World's Fair mental hygiene exhibit, on an honorarium basis. Beers tried to soften the blow to Hincks by having him take a leave of absence to work in Canada, with the title of "Field Consultant" for the National Committee, and he always considered Hincks the honored founder of the Canadian National Committee.[41]

At an executive committee meeting on the matter, Beers presented his case: Hincks had not been attending to National Committee business and had allowed Bullis to make too many decisions. Hincks then made a statement that was "manly, straight-forward and honorable" and that, in Bullis' recollection, conceded Beers' supremacy at the National Committee. Bullis, however, became emotional, describing how Beers had urged him to come to the National Committee and how hard he and Hincks had worked to get Beers' annuity, an outburst that brought a rejoinder from Beers.[42] Privately Beers told Ruggles that some people who did not know the whole story (that is, the questionable business dealings) thought Bullis was being treated unfairly. If necessary they must be told the truth, for the "good name of the National Committee is of more importance than the good name of anyone who has done things that have hurt its reputation." He, Beers, was acting on the advice of sober people and was therefore not going off half-cocked. Perhaps feeling somewhat guilty about his treatment of Bullis, Beers figured out a way to keep him on temporarily in a minor capacity, as a part-time "Business Manager," even calling him up at four o'clock in the morning on the night after the stormy executive committee meeting to tell him so.[43]

Hincks probably felt relieved to give up the burden of the National Committee.[44] The Canadian National Committee needed him, and he had always felt a special commitment to the Canadian mental hygiene movement. He still wrote friendly, deferential notes to his friend "Beersie," with the hope that "we have luck in both the United States and Canada in rebuilding financial support."[45]

Hincks had not fulfilled his promise at the National Committee. He had taken office in the midst of a depression, and, in a field where informal contacts mattered a good deal, he had the difficulty, as a Canadian, of having to operate in foreign territory. He had tried, with some success, to revitalize the organization and had secured renewed support from foundations. But he lacked force as an administrator and could not establish appropriate working relations with associates; he needed to lean on others and have their friendship but at the same time did not rely enough on expert advice.[46] More important, he could not think through carefully enough and execute his many ideas, a failing that led to a lack of clear direction at the National Committee and made a negative impression on the foundation officials and other leaders in psychiatry whose support the National Committee needed. It also led to an erroneous downgrading in their minds of the entire National Committee staff. It was only when Hincks left that Gregg and others at the Rockefeller Foundation realized that the National Committee had greater possibilities than they had thought. Gregg commented that a symposium organized by the National Committee at an American Association for the Advancement of Science meeting was

> in its organization and the subjects discussed, . . . so much more sensible and comprehensive than anything that the National Committee for Mental Hygiene had submitted to the Foundation in the past eight years that it was perfectly evident that the difficulty with the National Committee lay quite as much in the incompetence of its personnel as in any difficulty of the field as such. This was all the more obvious since . . . some of the secondary personnel in the National Committee for Mental Hygiene did most of the spade work for the Symposium.[47]

Hincks' psychological troubles, of which few people were aware, played some role in his downfall. His swings, from optimistic moods when he was full of plans that were not always feasible to depressed moods when he could not work much and became pessimistic, must have contributed to the instability Gregg and others saw in the National Committee. Beers did know about Hincks' personal problems but minimized them in his pleasure at having a good friend lead the National Committee and take the burden of fundraising from him, and he must also have thought that Hincks could, like himself, snap out of his moods to do what had to be done. Until about 1936 Beers was busy with other things—international work and then the twenty-fifth anniversary projects—so that he was not deeply immersed in National Committee affairs; nor was he in the confidence of foundation officials. When it finally became clear to him that Hincks' leadership, or lack of it, was harming the National Committee, he acted.

With Hincks gone, Beers set out to find a new, full-time medical director to be chief executive officer of the National Committee. From requests for suggestions to National Committee members came a consensus in favor of George Stevenson, director of the National Committee's division on community clinics.[48] Stevenson was an able man but, like Hincks, Williams, and Salmon before him, he had little hospital experience and had spent most of his professional life at the National Committee working in a special field. Although he soon changed his mind, Gregg noted in his diary that Stevenson was not, unfortunately, the "first-rate psychiatrist" needed "for this position which could be one of real significance." There was none such available.[49] Stevenson was, however, well known and respected in the field of child guidance and community mental health. Beers, aware of the reservations people would have about the appointment, tried to strengthen it by collecting letters praising Stevenson and sending them to National Committee members and other interested people, including foundation officials; the letter he highlighted was from Adolf Meyer, under whom Stevenson had studied at Johns Hopkins and the Phipps Clinic. In sending Gregg this collection of testimonials Beers wrote, "It is little short of miraculous that we should have discovered a highly trained and ideal Medical Director, right in our staff, when the need for appointing one arose so suddenly and was so urgent." He also defended the choice to doubters in the National Committee's inner circle.[50]

Beers instructed Stevenson on how to proceed. He should ask for a guarantee of his salary for five years, plus a sufficient sum for general expenses, in order to give himself and the staff the sense of security that they had not had for a long time and freedom from the need to raise funds.[51] One of Beers' motives was his old one of trying to get National Committee members to become active in raising money and also to remove responsibility for such activity from the medical director. No matter how many times Ruggles and others urged that the medical director have full authority over all aspects of the National Committee's operation, Beers always wanted to keep "his" side of the work in his own hands, which had become, however, somewhat shaky. Stevenson concurred, suggesting to the executive committee that Beers have "responsibility for raising funds for the general budget." The promotion brought no salary raise for Stevenson, who continued also to head the division on community clinics. Beers tried to make him feel better about it: it was all right, he said to bring a sandwich for lunch or go to the Automat to eat, as he himself sometimes did.[52]

As part of his campaign to "save" the National Committee, Beers wanted to strengthen the board of trustees by "adding some new members of heavier calibre than appeared . . . during earlier years." Among them would be Meyer, whom Beers asked to join "as a great favor personally" as well as in the name of the board.[53] Beginning with his participation in the First International Congress, Meyer had gradually been drawn back into the orbit of the National Committee. He gave an important address at the twenty-fifth anniversary dinner, and in 1937, his seventieth birthday year, he was named its honorary president. By 1939 he seems to have participated somewhat in National Committee affairs, and Beers kept him informed of events. His acceptance of appointment to the board was gracious: "I know your good will and thoughtfulness in the organization and am glad to accede to your invitation with my thanks," he told Beers. This was probably a true expression of Meyer's feelings and not simply reassurance at a difficult time; Meyer had told others what a good job Beers had done through the years.[54] Beers had evidently buried his old resentments of Meyer and fears of his domineering tendencies, a change that Meyer's cordiality in recent years must have effected; the National Committee, moreover, desperately needed a man like Meyer. Welch was dead, White was dead. There was no one else on its board with such stature.

Beers' reply to Meyer's note contained a personal call for help. "Under the new set-up and with Dr. Hincks no longer responsible for raising funds . . . I am carrying such a burden at present in regard to raising money . . . that I must share this responsibility. Will you help?"[55] At the end of the month Beers had to give up entirely. His glaucoma, his physician said, could not be kept under control unless he relaxed more.[56] He asked to resign from his duties at the National Committee: "I can no longer stand the strain of trying to 'save' the National Committee in crisis as I was able to do when younger and when it was easier to get large gifts." He felt sure his resignation would be accepted, "but the worst of it" was that the unsolved financial problems would still haunt him. He was not "enough of a mental hygienist to forget" what he could not remedy.[57]

‡

Beers was going through a serious emotional breakdown, a condition that had been brewing for a while. He had not been enjoying his travels with his usual relish and had lost some of his optimism. Growing old was not easy: "If, as they say, advancing age has its own compensations, I don't know what they are."[58] To keep his image of youthful vigor he dyed his hair and refused to have diseased teeth extracted. And he exhibited, according to Vic Tyler, "an overbearing egotism which taxed even my long and great affection for him."[59] Always erratic and never easy to get along with, by the end of 1938 he had become even more dictatorial, quarrelsome, and critical, a state which had influenced his relations with Bullis to the point where Clara Beers, who never interfered, asked Mrs. Bullis' forgiveness for Clifford's rudeness:

I have heard very indirectly that you are angry with Clifford — for speaking to your husband like an office boy. I know the incident and don't blame you. But I do hope you will forgive him. He has been greatly overwrought and he speaks quickly, without any thought at all — but he doesn't mean what his words imply. I know by experience believe me! As a child, he was never taught self-control. I regret it and I think he does.[60]

A month earlier she had made him apologize for rudeness to a friend.[61]

During the struggle to oust Hincks and Bullis and reorganize the National Committee, Beers seemed to have snapped back into his active, optimistic self and to have been glad to be in the middle of things again. Although his associates on the executive committee might have had some idea of his problems, their letters do not show an undue concern to humor him, albeit he did manage to get what he wanted from them. His secretary recalled his being obsessed with justifying his position with regard to Hincks and Bullis. He badgered everyone for assurance that he was right and dictated endless memoranda and letters on the subject that he would revise again and again.

He was in such a state that "it was not surprising to anyone" that he finally broke down.[62] He was not only reading other people's mail but going through wastepaper baskets looking for anything that might reflect unfavorably on himself or the National Committee. He was also having trouble sleeping and in general was experiencing anxiety. He kept his feelings to himself, thinking perhaps that they would disappear as he resolved the Hincks-Bullis crisis. Toward the end of March he wrote Gregory Zilboorg, the psychiatrist and writer, that he had just successfully come through "two hectic and disturbing months." He looked forward to Zilboorg's "stimulating company" at dinner, but not until after April 9 could he "dare book up for a given evening," a sign that he was holding himself ready for fund-raising interviews.[63]

He also started to talk about finding an executive secretary to act as his understudy and free him from having to come to the office every day. If "I can keep away . . . for days at a time, I can focus on big game."[64] To this end he made an appointment with the John Price Jones Corporation to discuss the kind of person he was looking for.

By the next month he no longer could work, and he called a psychiatrist friend for an appointment. This was Dr. Ralph Banay, a native of Hungary whom Beers first met in 1929 and who supplied him with information on European psychiatry. From time to time he would treat patients referred to him by Beers, usually people who could not afford to pay.[65] He was surprised that Beers should come to him for help instead of one of the prominent psychiatrists he knew so well. Beers replied, "I trust you," which Banay interpreted as indicating his basic distrust of people and feelings of insecurity about them which made him want to consult someone who was not part of his life and for whom he felt less hostility and suspicion. He was a guarded man who did not reveal himself and tended to ignore unpleasant realities; even Clara Beers probably did not know what was really bothering him. In Banay's view he did best in situations that he controlled and at meetings where the applause and approval reassured him and he could bask in the reflected glory of the prominent people who supported his work. His decline began in the mid-1930s, when he realized that his role in the movement had diminished, that the professionals were taking over even the fund-raising. The very bothersome Bullis-Hincks affair reflected his own inability to give the warmth and loyalty that he accused others of denying to him. Reticent, contentious, dictatorial, censorious, he had, Banay recalled, paranoid tendencies, a consequence of a childhood lacking maternal warmth and affection. He also had sexual problems he was reluctant to discuss. He was friendlier toward men than women and also much more emotionally involved with male associates and friends than with women friends or relatives, whom he saw in rigid moralistic terms and as objects to be protected; sexual interest in women other than his wife was limited to visiting burlesque shows surreptitiously. Troubled always, he used his work with the National Committee to float himself through life, much as some alcoholics use Alcoholics Anonymous.[66]

However much Banay developed insight into Beers' problems, he could not help him very much. He became depressed and developed delusions, with a "sort of suicidal drive," and begged Banay to come to his home and stay with him; he had new locks installed on the doors of all the second-floor bedrooms of the Englewood house.[67] Finally it seemed clear that Beers needed institutional care. A few days after his resignation from the National Committee, he was taken to Butler Hospital to be put under the care of his old friend Ruggles. During the trip Beers was depressed, agitated, and worried that he was a failure and had let everyone down.[68] At the hospital he appeared somewhat exhausted, doubted the wisdom of coming there, and worried that his absence would cause Clara to break down. Nevertheless he signed a voluntary application for admission, dated June 8, 1939, and went passively to the ward and lay down on the bed. The noise of conversation and radio music seemed to disturb him, but he did not feel he deserved the consideration of having them lowered.[69] He was slipping back into the state he had been in thirty-six years before.

Physical examination revealed a "roughened murmur over the body of the heart" which was fully compensated, and pyorrhetic and neglected teeth.[70] He remained depressed, with paranoid tendencies, with some periods of improvement and even light talk. Clara was beside herself, especially at the thought of Clifford's being released and going up to Maine, as Ruggles and then Clifford himself suggested on and off. Belgrade Lakes was too isolated and there would not be enough for him to do. If he had a relapse she would be helpless. "I'm not strong enough to go through another siege. . . . It is thanks to my brother's care and cheering personality that I have come through so far without breaking." She could not cope with Clifford unless he were *"completely recovered."* "I am feeling a reaction myself just now and don't know that I shall be able to see him this week." After an initial lift, Clara's visits evidently disturbed Clifford enough for him to tell her not to come. She thought "it made him feel terribly to have us go away and leave him."[71] He found it hard to write letters. Thoughts passed through his mind, he wrote his secretary, but he could not "transfer them to paper. Indecision is the word for it." He instructed her to work on the documents of last year's annual meetings of the American Foundation and the governing board of the International Committee. "This is not much of a letter, but it carries best wishes to all at the office."[72]

He was preoccupied with the condition of his hair, which he wanted to stop dyeing because it struck him now as a deception; yet he did not want to return to his friends as a white-haired old man. The hospital physicians tried to accommodate him, and Clara sent a package of dyeing materials and wrote that Banay suggested that anything should be done to help restore "'his Ego,' which he seemed to have lost." But he insisted on absolute privacy and made objections to any place offered for the purpose.[73] "He seems," his physician wrote, "to be taking out all his anxiety on this particular problem and it seems to symbolize for him the deeper problems of his present mental illness." Beers himself commented, "This seems a rather picayune sort of thing when I have really so much else on my mind."[74]

He felt hopeless about his condition, arguing that the cards were stacked against his recovering as he had in his youth. He could not get better in the hospital, yet he had no alternative to suggest. He rarely participated in hospital activities and was seclusive, passive, indecisive, and often close to tears. He spoke of having delusional thoughts but would not discuss them. Most of the time he sat in his room or out on the lawn reading. He would not associate with other patients or speak except when directly addressed, and then reluctantly though pleasantly. "From time to time a great deal of material mostly of a paranoidal nature is produced, usually in relation to the work set-up in the past." By October he had become practically mute and totally removed from all ward activities and gave indications of suspecting the identity of those around him and of Clara, whom on one occasion he refused to see because he doubted she was really his wife. He also refused medication and ate poorly, although he denied believing that the food was poisoned. In conversation his face was "always one of cynical distrust." One of his physicians, son of his friend Earl Bond, noted that his symptoms resembled those described in *A Mind That Found Itself*. The similarity became more marked as he lost a great deal of weight, doubted that his suit, now too big, belonged to him, continued to question the identity of everyone, and spent his time sitting in a chair, "with a very anxious and woe-begone expression." He eventually would not even cooperate in a physical examination, his usual comment upon being approached being, "Oh, go away and leave me alone." Shock treatment was considered but rejected as too risky because of his arteriosclerotic condition; he did receive six grains of sodium amytal daily and later insulin to stimulate his appetite.[75]

Clara Beers meanwhile was lonely and heartsick — "Oh, I am homesick for my Dearest!" — and bearing the strain of giving friends like Mary Bok the impression that Clifford had just had a nervous breakdown and would surely recover. Six months after Clifford entered the hospital all that Alan Gregg seemed to know was that he had resigned and had been depressed and tired since.[76] From others, especially outside the United States, his illness was kept altogether secret, which also accounted for the small amount of mail and few visitors he received.[77]

In March 1940 Clara received a cautiously hopeful letter from Dr. C. MacFie Campbell, an old friend who had gone to see Clifford and review his case with Ruggles. Beers was, he said, "somewhat thin and in a rather uncommunicative and depressed condition," but there was an "alertness about him" that was "very reassuring." He even occasionally smiled. Campbell believed that his depression derived partly from his accepting it instead of trying to fight it. It would be best to "emphasize strongly to Clifford the view that although his depression came upon him slowly and in a way that he did not recognize it was occurring, he must now do everything not to prolong it." He had a responsibility to help himself recover. Campbell could not give a prognosis but did suggest that Beers was on the upgrade. Meyer then wrote to Beers of his wish that he, too, could visit him to bring his "reassurance . . . that you will rise to full working capacity and satisfaction of life, as a reward for all the good that you have done for those who are well and those who are sick."[78]

Beers continued nevertheless to be passive and removed, although occasionally, "when his sodium amytal and insulin hit him just right," he would talk "fairly freely" for a short while. His physical condition fluctuated but over the long run deteriorated; his pallor was grayish, and his gums got worse, but Clara refused to allow his teeth to be extracted. On August 3, 1941, he spoke out spontaneously to one of the physicians. He wanted to be sure that a letter would go to his real wife and not the impostor who came to visit him; the hospital was a "colossal fake" and all the so-called doctors impersonators. He talked at length about the food served him, which he saw as sexual symbols (both heterosexual and homosexual), and spoke of his delusion that he, Clara, and all his associates at the National Committee were being prosecuted for questionable activities. The physician recorded the interview "in some detail due to the fact it was one of the few occasions when patient has talked during his stay at this institution." All the physicians could think of to do was to administer shock treatment, again rejected because of the risk to Beers' heart.[79]

He continued as before, "very depressed, retarded, with nihilistic and self-depreciatory ideals" and speaking only in response to a direct question, and then with his face turned away and muttering under his breath. He recovered from his physical disorders enough to eat better, take walks, and attend the hospital's social functions—movies, plays, church services. Even though his teeth were worse and his gums bleeding, a possible source of focal infection, Clara still would not have them removed.[80] Partly because he did not believe in the authenticity of his visitors he did not have many; when Henry Rittenberg sent him a case of ginger ale he told Ruggles, "I can't believe it—no one would want to send me a gift."[81] Toward the end of 1942 he would sit in a catatonic position for hours. Then he spoke again, discussing his illness and admitting that some of his ideas about his body—that his excrement had destructive power, for example—might be delusions, but he was by no means convinced that they were. He became very alert and talked freely to the nurses but only in monosyllables to everyone else, whom he told to "get out." He still believed that letters from Clara were fakes.[82] She visited him about once a month and found the experience trying. "I suppose it is time to be arranging for another visit," she wrote Ruggles, "if you still think once a month is necessary." Clifford was much more responsive during their last visit and when Clara mentioned the car said, "'I shall never drive again' in a rather questioning way." She tried to convince him otherwise; he still insisted that she was an impostor but "frankly admitted" her identity after she called him by his pet name.[83] Ruggles, who had never given up hope, although his staff had little treatment to offer for Beers' mental condition, was happy to hear this news: "You can see now why I have not lost the belief that Clifford can recover."[84]

But soon afterwards Beers suffered fainting spells; then he fainted, fell, struck his head, and was observed to suffer a convulsion in his right arm; he developed pneumonia and died a few days later, on July 9, 1943, at the age of sixty-seven. Cause of death was given as "Terminal bronchopneumonia, Cerebral thrombosis," with the contributing cause "Arteriosclerotic cardiovascular-renal disease." There is no report of an autopsy.[85] Clara Beers survived him by many years, living in Englewood until her death in a nursing home on September 8, 1966, at the age of ninety-two.

In an inscription in a copy of his book Clifford Beers had written his epitaph:

Clifford W. Beers
Author of "A Mind That Found Itself,"
    and founder of the Mental Hygiene Movement.[86]

Epilogue

Clifford Beers died disappointed. He had finally, and again, succumbed to the disorder he had dedicated his life to ameliorating and which had destroyed his brothers. It was as if he could not escape the Beers' family destiny, no matter how he challenged it and, some might say, tempted it by making the world of mental illness nearly his whole existence.

But despite his final disconsolation, Beers' life had been the grand success he had hoped for. Mental illness had not been vanquished, thoroughgoing reforms had yet to come, mass support had still to be mobilized. But a great beginning had been made: he had written a classic autobiography read by thousands of people; he had had the imagination and insight to recognize the many-faceted needs of the field of mental illness and the vision and talent to organize in behalf of its sufferers a movement that captured the interest and support of powerful men and women and reverberated all over the world. He had become famous, and his achievements testified to the message of the mental health movement. That not all he envisaged was accomplished in his lifetime and not all goals reached are other matters. The point is that when he started there was almost nothing; by the time he finished, there was an organized mental health movement that, with all its vicissitudes, was respected and had accomplished a good deal.

Whether Clifford Beers would have made a name for himself had he not become mentally ill in 1900, or, given that, had he afterwards buried his psychiatric history and pursued his youthful goal of business success, is hard to say. It raises the inevitable, perhaps unanswerable but still interesting question: what was the connection between Clifford Beers' life work and his mental disorder?

Before, during, and after his first mental breakdown he was unmistakably the same man. His "normal" personality traits became exaggerated while he was hospitalized — paranoid tendencies during depression and activist, controlling propensities during mania — but these qualities were well marked previously. After being discharged from the hospital he tended to fluctuate between what psychiatrists called normal and excited states, interspersed with periods of depressed activity and moods. But at all times his attitudes and ways of relating to people remained in the configuration that characterized Clifford Beers. He was always one, unitary man, now "excessively" active, now calm, now suspicious, now exhilarated, now despondent. For a few years, at the beginning and then at the end of his adult life, his propensities shaded off into "abnormality" or inability to cope with the demands of daily living, which is termed psychosis.

His early psychosis had an undeniably profound effect on him. It was a crisis that he was able to transform creatively into a meaningful life work that made an impress on the world.[1] However doubtful Beers' sober psychiatric critics were, the title of his book, *A Mind That Found Itself,* was apt. In the course of his struggles with mental illness he did find himself. He emerged from the hospital not only a deeper and more thoughtful man, but one with the need to give his experiences meaning. This he would do by reliving them in the service of exorcising them, not through religious rites but through their secular replacements, the social and medical reforms and research that seemed possible in the United States at the turn of the century. In that sense his recovery had been, as he himself saw it, a rebirth.

The mental health movement was for Beers an extension of himself, a creative response to his own experiences and needs. Upon his discharge from the Connecticut State Hospital the intermittent periods of excitement he experienced made him dissatisfied with the path he had been advised to take — the slow, safe, but tedious building of a business career — and drove him to write his autobiography. Apart from any psychologically cathartic value it may have had, writing his story would be a passport to fame and the prelude to using his organizational and executive talents as the leader of a great new reform movement. When he won approval and encouragement from men like William James, William Welch, and Adolf Meyer, business permanently lost its appeal. In a mental health movement, moreover, his hospital experience could be an asset: he could, by exposing his past and campaigning for an end to the stigma of mental illness, help to remove the shame from himself and, by proving that someone like himself could fully recover, counteract what he always regarded as the unfavorable and unflattering self-portrait in his autobiography. Further, his short relapse in 1905 had been a warning that other periods of excitement or even mania might come upon him. A mental health movement founded by him could not very well reject him if that happened or even if he became mildly erratic or depressed. He could find protection as a star reformer, a courageous crusader vouched for by psychiatrists, supported by the American and then the international scientific elite, and funded by the wealthiest people in the United States. He always needed approval from authority figures: indeed, his whole career in the National and International Committees can be seen in part as a succession of campaigns to amass endorsements from important people.

Like so many people intensely devoted to a cause or a life goal, Beers exhibited the singlemindedness that sets them off from their less driven contemporaries. At the same time, he can be seen as a typical high achiever in the Western, particularly American, tradition, where aggressive, obsessive, competitive striving for success, combined with organizational talent, creative vision, and supersalesmanship, has been admired and rewarded in business and politics, the worlds of power he wanted so much to penetrate. The great leaders of industry and finance whom he esteemed and emulated, however condemned by social critics, have not been regarded as neurotic in their all-absorbing pursuit of power and money. They moved in the mainstream of their society and expressed and reinforced its key values. But Beers' field, mental illness, was considered somewhat odd, even if it did concern itself with a serious and widespread problem. In focusing on such a problem (and being himself an example of it), and with intensity, flamboyance, and self-confidence, he disconcerted some people. His need to succeed, quickly and in a big way, did partly reflect his tendency toward excitement, which when on the rise exploded into activity that could irritate colleagues who seemed to him to be moving with glacial slowness. But where strong commitment, foresight, ability, and keen instinct for the possible leave off and unrealistic exaggeration and untoward energy spurts begin is difficult to tell. It can even be said that Beers' "manic" qualities—his optimism and enthusiasm, his dedication, his energy, his imaginativeness—combined with intelligence and humor, were what made him so attractive, even irresistible, to many people and uniquely fitted him for the work he set out to do.

He could be hard to deal with on a day-to-day basis. His erratic mode of work, mood changes, expansiveness, contentiousness, suspiciousness, underhandedness, egocentricity, and need to dominate could be exasperating, however much he could be charming and lovable and could disarm with a warm smile or self-deprecating wisecrack. Like so many founders and leaders of movements, organizations, and governments, Beers equated the interests of the cause with his own interests, so that he could not easily distinguish loyalty to him personally from loyalty to the National Committee, or differentiate sincere disagreement from disloyalty. He could also sacrifice good colleagues for the cause; the only pangs of conscience he ever seemed to suffer were over the possibly preventable death of George Beers and the "dismissals" of Hincks and Bullis. Yet he was no more (and probably much less) difficult and selfish than many famous reformers. His egoism was perhaps more exposed than theirs. Crusaders need to be hard-driving, even fanatical, to keep pushing unpopular causes, to make things happen, to pull other more mild-mannered, less activist, more "balanced" people along with them. In this respect Beers was probably unusual in being so likable and in being capable of long, devoted friendships, amenable to advice, and willing to work behind the scenes and let famous men have the presidencies and chairmanships.

If he was prone to exaggeration, reformers and radicals have always tended to exaggerate, to claim complete and unconditional solutions, to predict the millennium if society would only adopt their particular program, which is generally presented simplistically in the interests of public relations. Beers followed this tradition, partly out of personal inclination, partly because it would gain attention. When he entered the field, other organizations were also being founded to solve various health and social problems, each giving credence to the others and together helping to create an atmosphere of hope. They were also all competing for funds and attention, a struggle in which Beers would not be outdone. He must offer goods as valuable as any on the market, and he must see to it, just as his models in business and industry had done, that he had no competitors, so that the National Committee and its offshoots must be all-encompassing, must cover most aspects of mental hygiene.

Beers had the audacity of a salesman, the boldness of a man with a cause, and the dynamism and self-confidence of the manic personality. This was evident not only in his choosing to make a career out of a personal tragedy that anyone else would keep a deep secret but in his style throughout his life. It was "big," even when he himself was "small." He conceived grand schemes and then went to the people who could help him realize them. His aim was always to go directly to the best, the most important, the most knowledgeable, the most powerful. So while at Connecticut State Hospital, he wrote to the governor of the state; he later penetrated the presence of Joseph Choate; he secured a momentous interview with William James; he achieved a collaboration with Adolf Meyer; he intrepidly approached business tycoons, university presidents, foundation heads — all in the conviction that he would be taken seriously, that his cause was just and indeed God-given, that his plans were feasible. To sober heads, such temerity in a poor, obscure, formerly psychotic (and perhaps still excited) mental patient, albeit with some family connections and a Yale degree, would be presumption, indiscretion, foolishness. But for Beers it led to success. This was so not only because he came along with his ideas at the right moment, when interested people were ready to act. His immense charm and sense of timing, along with the poignancy of his personal history, were potent factors, as were his earnestness and intelligence. But also very important was his identification with the values of the people he was soliciting: he approached them with utter respect and faith in their judgment and in their potential sympathy for his cause.

Beers was not really a social reformer. Clever rather than intellectually thoughtful, knowledgeable of events rather than socially conscious, he did not delve into social problems and had neither a broad perspective nor a deep awareness of past or contemporary social movements and forces. Although he solicited the support of people like Jane Addams and Julia Lathrop, he was not by nature a critic of society or its ills, a defender of the downtrodden, or a sympathizer with the weak and helpless. His normal response was to support the rich and powerful in any contest with other sectors of society. His activism, much as it was exerted in behalf of a mistreated group, was elitist, and his choice of a field of work came from his personal experiences and needs rather than any ideological or theoretical position. As time went on and psychology became stylish, he accepted the growing idea that all human problems had a mental or emotional component and that therefore the mental hygiene movement could be a vehicle to improve society, which for him did not mean changing the existing social order. War might be eradicated, poverty eliminated, unhappiness mitigated by the enlargement of psychiatric-psychological knowledge and its dissemination among the public through the work of the National Committee and the International Committee for Mental Hygiene. But these groups must not themselves become involved with any controversial or radical issues or look too deeply for the social roots of mental illness: that might spoil the good image of the organizations and alienate their highly placed supporters.[2]

His middle-class attitudes enabled Beers to reach the upper classes and to build his movement, but at the same time they limited its effectiveness. Although highly political in his behavior within his organizations, he did not develop a broadly political approach to the problems of the mentally ill; he did not fully appreciate the importance to their situation of their lack of political power. As a young man in the state hospital he had a glimmering of this, and then in his work for the Connecticut Society for Mental Hygiene he had tried his hand at a legislative campaign. But for the rest of his life he operated mainly within a comparatively small circle of influential people. He believed that the issue was essentially if not exclusively a moral one: it was only necessary to convince the American people, especially the rich, that mental patients were unjustly treated and that prevention of mental illness was feasible, and support for reforms would be forthcoming. Similarly, state and federal governments would do their duty if their officials were educated to the need to do so. That in fact the basis for allocation of resources was not primarily moral, that his movement must also have political power to exert pressure beyond the personal on governments, politicians, and even foundations and wealthy individuals, Beers never really recognized. His concentration on moral suasion presupposed shared goals, values, and interests in society; that different groups or classes might have antagonistic interests and viewpoints that were not always reconcilable was a concept alien to his outlook.

He originally had conceived that a reform organization controlled by lay people and with a large public membership would be the best means of forcing psychiatrists to improve their hospitals and of influencing legislators and governors to support such reform and to give mental hospitals adequate financial resources. But there was no ideological basis for this position, so it did not take much to dissuade him from this plan once he was convinced, by Meyer and others, that no reform of mental hospitals could win the support of the economic, intellectual, and scientific establishments without the approval and active assistance of leading psychiatrists, including hospital superintendents. Since it soon became obvious that the general public could not be counted on to rise up in wrath against the ill treatment of mental patients, the help of those in positions of influence was indispensable, and this required a small organization sponsored by such people and run by psychiatrists, with Clifford Beers as the representative of the lay public. He could readily adapt to such a model: it seemed to make sense, given financial realities and the disabilities of mental hygiene as a popular cause, and it fitted his own social views and style of work. He believed in a harmonious social order in which the upper classes directed the course of events in the best interests of society at large. He saw himself as playing the same role in the mental health movement: eventually the masses would give him financial and moral support, but only under his guidance and once he had educated them to the rightness of the cause. Until then he must depend upon the rich and take the advice of the professionals. He may have chafed under the psychiatrists' regime (and, as he saw it, their constant scrutiny of him) and may have tried to outmaneuver them, but he gave the substantive direction of the National Committee into their hands because he felt this was necessary for its success and respectability.

He did not object to the passive support of lay people but never, after his early efforts, sincerely wanted a membership with any real say in the National Committee's affairs. Wider genuine public participation might alienate the psychiatrists and wealthy donors who gave the movement legitimacy and money. It might also bring in objectionable people. Beers especially wanted nothing to do with former patients in any organizational way. He had worked too hard to prove to the world that a mind could find itself and not get lost again. He was willing to have his autobiography issued again and again and would himself retell his story endlessly. But despite the possible benefit to the movement, no one else could dramatize, illustrate, or otherwise interpret his manic-depressive behavior. It was as if his recounting (as an obviously "sane" man and with his proven success in the world as testimony) was in itself the negation of his past and an affirmation of his present "normal" state, but someone else's would be just the reverse. (The inclusion in successive editions of *A Mind That Found Itself* of documentation of the progress of the mental hygiene movement, together with letters praising his work, came in part out of the same impulse.)

This lifelong need to prove himself "sane" was threatened by the troubles encountered by the National Committee during the 1930s, when Beers was at the summit of his fame. The existence of the National Committee and the respected place it had won was evidence of his mental stability, for it demonstrated that the initial goals he set for himself in 1902–1903 and pursued through the years were realistic. In his mind, if the organization should go under, he might lose his standing as a recovered mental patient and be exposed as a fraud. He understood that economic conditions beyond his control were very much at fault and that mental illness was too complex and mysterious a problem to yield solutions in only one generation. He even came to realize that the scope of the problem was too broad for private philanthropy to handle. This point is important, for whatever criticisms one may lay at the door of Clifford Beers, certainly the failure of the National Committee to fulfill all its original goals should not be one of them. One need only note the inability of the mental health movement today to provide humane and therapeutic care for the bulk of institutionalized patients, as well as those not institutionalized, to realize that despite the large sums of money, new programs, and involvement of the federal government, Beers' objectives are still far from being attained. He had entered a field that still has not resolved many of the basic problems of providing therapeutic and humane care to those needing it, or of preventing the onset of mental disorders in the general public. Beers did not have the solution to these problems; he could not have.

Still, twenty-five years after the mental hygiene movement began, the acceleration of complaints about conditions in mental hospitals and the requests for help from former patients and from others wanting to improve the situation of the mentally ill disturbed him. Not fully attuned to the sufferings of the poor and afflicted and, like so many aging reformers and radicals (before and after him), grown more conservative, more concerned with the survival of the organization he had founded and with which he was identified than with the objects of its efforts, Beers had little to offer in a time of crisis. He was frozen, besides, into a mode of operation — personal fundraising — that could not work well any more, and he was too tired to think of charting new directions for the movement.

What he and most others seemed not to understand was that every reform effort in the field of mental illness had foundered upon the inability to sustain the therapeutic or humane care of the mentally ill for which its leaders originally fought. This was true of reform movements in the eighteenth century, the nineteenth century, and the twentieth. There is an initial strong push for reform, some improvements are made, then backsliding begins, and finally retrogression sets in. Mental illness involves a complex collection of disorders about whose causes, prevention, and treatment little still is definitively known, and, although all disorders are bound up with the social as well as the natural environment and dependent upon material and human resources for their treatment, mental illness seems to be more so perhaps than any other. It has been a relatively long-term, chronic condition involving millions of people, the afflicted and their families, the latter deeply troubled and frequently impoverished by the calamity. Because it has been dealt with during modern times in institutional settings, for the most part state-supported, it has been inextricably intertwined with politics and economics. It seems to be uniquely affected by the sociopsychological environment, so that the social organization of hospitals and attitudes of staffs become themselves key factors in the course of the disorder and the feelings of many patients. Mental illness, besides, is threatening to "sane" people; even in the modern era the heritage of association with sin or the devil has still had potency, and the stigma and the shame remain. Madness has a certain horrible glamour in literature; in real life it is a nuisance, a threat, a burden, an expense. The mad are themselves largely helpless to help themselves, and their friends and relatives are embarrassed and powerless. Only recently have famous people with the power to move others revealed their disabilities and thus educated the public and helped workers trying to launch massive research and health care programs — in poliomyelitis, heart disease, and cancer. Mental illness has been something else; witness the outcry, as late as 1972, when it was revealed that vice-presidential candidate Thomas Eagleton had suffered from depression.

In the pushing and shoving for attention and support among the many causes in a competitive society, the mental health movement has suffered severe disadvantages. Not least among these has been the lack of pressure groups passionately and personally concerned — the relatives and friends of patients and the ex-patients themselves — and willing, in alliance with political activists, to challenge the legal, governmental, and professional establishments in order to effect change. There must also be a realization that when money values predominate over human ones, when society is individualistic and competitive, when power over resources is concentrated rather than dispersed, people who are strange, who are unable to function well, who are antisocial and unlovable, will suffer. Clifford Beers, imaginative and far-seeing as he was, never went this far in his thinking. Very few others have either. No implication is intended that other, differently organized societies have solved the problem of mental disorders or even discovered how to provide humane and therapeutic care for the mentally ill. Each form of social organization places certain strains on people; in the United States the stress on economic success puts a premium upon money-making and achievement of status and engenders lack of sympathy for those who do not so succeed, despite the strength of Judaeo-Christian traditions of charity and a humanitarian political ethos. What seems necessary, besides biomedical discoveries leading to more effective treatment, is that those who are disadvantaged develop mechanisms to fight for their own interests.

With all the limitations of Clifford Beers and his movement, they both added important new elements to the effort to deal with mental disorders. Before his time, no permanent central agency existed to institutionalize reform. It was he who showed the way and demonstrated the need for an integrated national and even international movement in this field, even though he organized only a "general staff." He also significantly contributed toward making public discussion of mental disorders legitimate, informed, and matter-of-fact. The movement helped to introduce mental health considerations into many aspects of American life, such as the schools and the courts, not for sensational exploitation but to develop systematic means of dealing with children's emotional problems. On a personal plane, Clifford Beers was a living refutation of the view that mental disorder forever incapacitated a person for useful public activity. His life experience educated people to the complexities and surprising possibilities that lie within so many men and women whom society tends to discard.

Notes ‡ Index

ABBREVIATIONS

AM: Adolf Meyer

AM Papers: Adolf Meyer Papers, Welch Medical Library, Johns Hopkins University Medical School, Baltimore, Md.

AMTFI: A Mind That Found Itself, by Clifford W. Beers, various drafts and editions as noted

AMTFI, 1st ed.: *A Mind That Found Itself,* by Clifford W. Beers (New York: Longmans, Green, and Co., 1908)

Beers Clinic Papers: Papers in Clifford W. Beers Guidance Clinic, Inc., New Haven, Conn.

CEB: Carl E. Beers

CJ: Clara Jepson

CJB: Clara Jepson Beers

CMHA Archives: Canadian Mental Health Association Archives, Toronto

Conn. Valley Hosp.: Connecticut Valley Hospital, Middletown, Conn. (formerly Connecticut Hospital for the Insane, then Connecticut State Hospital)

CSMH: Connecticut Society for Mental Hygiene

CWB: Clifford W. Beers

CWB Coll.: Clifford W. Beers Collection, Archives of Psychiatry, New York Hospital–Cornell University Medical Center, New York, N.Y.

EM Coll.: Emily Martin Collection, Archives of Psychiatry, New York Hospital–Cornell University Medical Center, New York, N.Y.

1st Int. Cong. MH: First International Congress on Mental Hygiene, Washington, D.C., May 1930

GEB Archives: General Education Board Archives, in RFA

GMB: George M. Beers

HWF: Herbert W. Fisher

IOL: Institute of Living (formerly Hartford Retreat), Hartford, Conn.

MFA: Menninger Foundation Archives, Topeka, Kan., Beers Collection

NAMH Coll.: National Association for Mental Health Collection, Archives of Psychiatry, New York Hospital–Cornell University Medical Center, New York, N.Y.

NCMH: National Committee for Mental Hygiene

RFA: Rockefeller Foundation Archives, Hillcrest, Pocantico Hills, North Tarrytown, N.Y.

TWM: "Troubles with Meyer," by Clifford W. Beers, submitted in confidence to Dr. William L. Russell, Jan. 23, 1910 (carbon copy of typescript), in CWB Coll.

TWS: Thomas W. Salmon

TWS Papers: Thomas W. Salmon Papers, in CWB Coll.

Welch Papers: William H. Welch Papers, Welch Medical Library, Johns Hopkins University Medical School, Baltimore, Md.

White Papers: William Alanson White Papers, National Archives, Washington, D.C.

WJ: William James

Yale: Yale University Library, Beers Collection

Notes

Sources

The main sources for this book have been unpublished manuscript materials, supplemented by published primary sources such as speeches and journal and newspaper articles, and by interviews with people who knew Clifford Beers. Furnishing by far the most information was the voluminous Clifford W. Beers Collection in the Archives of Psychiatry of the New York Hospital–Cornell University Medical Center, New York City. This collection contains Beers' extensive correspondence files, drafts of speeches and other writings, the manuscript of his "Autobiography" (1905), materials dating back to his early years and to his hospital stays from 1900 to 1903, various notebooks he kept, newspaper and magazine clippings, reprints of articles, scrapbooks, and numerous documents relating to the affairs of the National Committee for Mental Hygiene, the National Foundation for Mental Hygiene, and the International Committee for Mental Hygiene. Within this collection are also the Thomas W. Salmon Papers. Also in the Archives of Psychiatry is a valuable group of personal and family papers pertaining to Clifford and Clara Beers collected by Emily Martin, a long-time employee at the National Committee for Mental Hygiene and friend of Clara Beers'. The papers of the successor to the National Committee, the National Association for Mental Health, have also been deposited in the Archives of Psychiatry.

Much personal Beers correspondence exists in the Beers Collection in the Menninger Foundation Archives, Topeka, Kansas, and the Beinecke Library at Yale University contains several manuscript drafts of *A Mind That Found Itself*. These drafts, together with the various published editions of the book, constitute a key source. For Beers' work in the Connecticut Society for Mental Hygiene the papers in the Clifford Beers Guidance Clinic, Inc., New Haven, Connecticut, have useful material, and the archives of the Connecticut Association for Mental Health contain the minutes of the early years of the Connecticut Society for Mental Hygiene. The archives of the Canadian Mental Health Association in Toronto yielded information relating to Beers' work in Canada and his relationship with Clarence Hincks. *Twenty-Five Years After,* a compilation of tributes to Beers (Garden City, N.Y.: Doubleday, Doran & Company, 1934), has various descriptions of his personality and his work.

The Beers Collection in the Archives of Psychiatry is fairly complete for Beers' correspondence, as he customarily requested and received from his correspondents his own letters for his files (or kept carbon copies) as well as conscientiously retaining letters sent to him. The papers of several of his associates (such as Adolf Meyer, William Welch, Julia Lathrop, and William A. White) are, however, fruitful sources of correspondence between these and other people that discuss Beers and his activities. For Meyer's viewpoint, his *Collected Papers* (ed. Eunice E. Winters, vols. 2–4 [Baltimore: Johns Hopkins Press, 1951–1952]) are invaluable. Beers' relationship with William James, which James' biographers have ignored, is illuminated in the material in the Beers Collection, some of which is duplicated in the James Papers at Harvard University. The opening of the Rockefeller Foundation Archives while this book was being written added an important dimension to the research, as did access to hospital records of Clifford Beers, his brother Carl, and his aunt, Henrietta Cooke Robinson.

All unattributed sources in the notes are from the Beers Collection in the Archives of Psychiatry of the New York Hospital–Cornell University Medical Center.

Chapter 1. Early Years

1. CWB to Louise Beers, Sept. 18, 1902.

2. CWB to Mrs. Clara G. Stillman, June 12, 1935; to Gov. Abriam S. Chamberlain, Mar. 12, 1903, p. 2. Information about the Beers family is also contained in the CEB Case Records, State Records Center, Rocky Hill, Conn. (microfilm), and H. C. Robinson Case Records, Conn. Valley Hosp.

3. CWB, "My Autobiography," in "Note Book #1, Hartford, Jan. 1905," p. 9 (hereafter cited as CWB, "Autobiography"); CWB to Arthur Lucas, Jan. 31, 1938.

4. CWB to Mrs. Clara G. Stillman, June 12, 1935; H. C. Robinson Case Records, Conn. Valley Hosp.

5. Ibid.; CWB to Arthur Lucas, Jan. 31, 1938.

6. H. C. Robinson Case Records, Conn. Valley Hosp.; CWB to GMB, Sept. 16, 1902.

7. H. C. Robinson Case Records, Conn. Valley Hosp.

8. CWB to H. W. Fisher, July 11, 1906; to Dr. Thomas, Apr. 10, 1903, p. 4.

9. CWB to GMB, fragment on gray paper, n.d. (later than 1902, perhaps early 1903), p. 11, CWB Coll.; CWB, *AMTFI,* 1st draft (excerpts), Aug. 26, 1905, p. 37, Yale; also childhood letters, Jan. 31, 1883(?) and 1888, from CWB to Aunt Mame, in CWB Coll.

10. Stewart Means to William H. Welch, in *Twenty-Five Years After: Sidelights on the Mental Hygiene Movement and Its Founder,* ed. Wilbur L. Cross (New York: Doubleday, Doran & Company, 1934), p. 249.

11. H. C. Robinson Case Records, Conn. Valley Hosp.; Means to Welch, in *Twenty-Five Years After,* p. 249; CWB Case Records, Conn. Valley Hosp.

12. See, for example, CWB to Mother, June 8, 30, July 6, 1903.

13. CWB, *An Intimate Account of the Origin and Growth of the Mental-Hygiene Movement* (New York: National Committee for Mental Hygiene, 1931), pp. 2–3; CWB, "Address Delivered at the Opening Evening Session of the First International Congress on Mental Hygiene, Washington, D.C., May 6, 1930," p. 12, rpt. from *Mental Hygiene,* 15 (Oct. 1931): 673–84.

14. CWB to Mrs. Robert A. Beers, Mar. 5, 1903.

15. Ruth Almond, "Beers Outline," CWB Coll.; Means to Welch, in *Twenty-Five Years After,* p. 249.

16. CWB to Father and Mother, June 10, 1903.

17. "Some Intimate Aspects of the Origin and Growth of the Mental Hygiene Movement," unpub. version [no. 1] of a talk, n.d. [1933?], typescript, p. 14; CWB to Mother, Mar. 18, 1903; CWB, Remarks at 1st Int. Cong. MH, May 6, 1930, in typescript draft of proceedings (carbon copy), p. 16.

18. See, for example, CWB to Aunt Mame, Sept. 8, 1902, p. 7.

19. "Robert Bostwick Ruggles 1762–1823," appended to a letter from CWB to Mrs. Clara G. Stillman, June 12, 1935; some of the information came from a genealogy compiled in 1897 by his Aunt Eliza White Beers Dudley.

20. *Address of Mr. Clifford Whittingham Beers, Founder of the Connecticut Society for Mental Hygiene and of the Mental Hygiene Movement, at the Laying of the Corner Stone of the Fairfield State Hospital, Newtown, Connecticut, June 10, 1931,* p. 2; H. Edmund Bullis, interview, 1966.

21. CWB, "Autobiography," p. 15.

22. Ibid., pp. 9–11; CWB to Arthur Lucas, Jan. 31, 1938. Clifford Beers' oldest brother, George M. Beers, confirmed that Clifford suffered a near fatal attack of diphtheria and described the rheumatism as of the muscular type but did not mention cholera (CWB Case, Summary, Aug. 14, 1903, Conn. Valley Hosp.).

23. CWB, "Autobiography," pp. 15–17; CWB to Paul McQuaid, Apr. 30, 1906; *AMTFI,* 2nd ed., p. 32.

24. CWB, "Autobiography," pp. 17–19.

25. CWB to Uncle Sam, Aug. 22, 1903.

26. CWB to GMB, Sept. 17, 1902.

27. CWB, *AMTFI,* 1st draft, Yale, p. 11; CWB to F. C. Earle, Oct. 12, 1902; to Mrs. Bok, Dec. 22, 1937.

28. CJB to Mrs. Bullis, Dec. 22 [1938?].

29. CWB, "Autobiography," p. 20; CWB to GMB, Mar. 18, 1903, Sept. 16, 1902, pp. 22–23, 17.

30. CWB, "Autobiography," p. 20; also *AMTFI,* 1st ed., p. 6.

31. CWB, "Autobiography," pp. 20–21; *AMTFI,* 2nd ed., p. 9.

32. Newspaper clippings enclosed in GMB to CWB, Sept. 6, 1905.

33. CWB, "Autobiography," pp. 21–22; *AMTFI,* 1st ed., p. 7; *AMTFI,* 1st draft, Yale, p. 13. In his unpublished "Autobiography" he says that a cramp in his hand forced an interruption of the match and that he then won when play was resumed (pp. 22–23).

34. CWB to Dr. Richard [Henry P.] Stearns, Sept. 18, 1902, pp. 37–38; CWB "Autobiography," p. 12.

35. TWM, p. 440.

36. CWB Case, Summary, Aug. 14, 1903, Conn. Valley Hosp.; CWB, "Autobiography," p. 20; CWB to GMB, Sept. 16, 1902.

37. CWB Case, Summary, Aug. 14, 1903; also his Case Records, Conn. Valley Hosp.; CWB, "Autobiography," p. 69.

38. CWB, "A Continuation Sequel to *AMTFI,*" Dec. 7, 1931, pp. 19–21; CWB to GMB, May 27, 1903.

39. CWB, "Autobiography," p. 24; *AMTFI,* 1st ed., p. 8.

40. CWB, "Autobiography," pp. 24–25; *AMTFI,* 1st draft, Yale, p. 16.

41. CWB, "Autobiography," pp. 25–28. Beers noted in his "Autobiography" (p. 29) that he cared for Sam for two years; Conn. Valley Hosp. records say a year and a half.

42. CWB, "Autobiography," pp. 28–29.

43. CWB to GMB, May 27, 1903. In this letter, written as he was recovering from his manic state at Conn. Valley Hosp., he comments on George's silent suffering when his business affairs "were on the verge of collapse": "When you were 25 or 26 you had your troubles all right. Sam at 26 had his. Will at about the same age was far from well. At 24 I started in on a siege."

44. CWB, "Autobiography," pp. 36, 25–26, 29; *AMTFI,* 1st ed., p. 9. Neurasthenia was a concept developed by Dr. George M. Beard and popularized by Dr. S. Weir Mitchell. It was defined by Beard as "nervous exhaustion," a "chronic, functional disease of the nervous system, the basis of which is impoverishment of nervous force; deficiency of reserve, with liability to quick exhaustion, and a necessity for frequent supplies of force; hence the lack of inhibitory or controlling powers, physical and mental — the feebleness and instability of nerve action and the excessive sensitiveness and irritability, local and general, and the vast variety of symptoms, direct and reflex." See George M. Beard, *American Nervousness: Its Causes and Consequences; a Supplement to Nervous Exhaustion (Neurasthenia)* (New York: G. P. Putnam's Sons, 1881; rpt. ed., New York: Arno Press and the *New York Times,* 1972), pp. 55–59; George M. Beard, *Sexual Neurasthenia (Nervous Exhaustion): Its Hygiene, Causes, Symptoms and Treatment,* 5th ed., with formulas (New York: E. B. Treat & Company, 1898; rpt. ed., New York: Arno Press and the *New York Times,* 1972), p. 36.

45. CWB, "Autobiography," pp. 30, 35–36.

46. CWB, summary from excited letters (mimeographed) [1906–07?], p. 15; *AMTFI,* 1st ed., pp. 9–10.

47. CWB, "Autobiography," pp. 30–32. Any disorder that could produce such results in such a variety of colors is unknown to any authority questioned on the subject.

48. CWB, "Some Intimate Aspects of the Origin and Growth of Mental Hygiene Movement" (1934) (typescript, final draft?), pp. 2–3; CWB Case Records, Conn. Valley Hosp., note that he was excused from recitation from Nov. 1895 to Jan. 1896; CWB, "Autobiography," p. 32.

49. CWB Case, Summary, Aug. 14, 1903, Conn. Valley Hosp.; Dr. Arthur Sanford Cheney to Dr. Henry S. Noble, Nov. 18, 1902; CWB to GMB, Sept. 16, 1902.

50. CWB, "Autobiography," p. 33; CWB Case, Summary, Aug. 14, 1903, Conn. Valley Hosp.

51. CWB to Conn. Valley Hosp., Apr. 25, 1903.

52. CWB to Mr. [?] Coggershall, Sept. 22, 1902; Paul A. McQuaid to Welch, Mar. 10, 1933, in *Twenty-Five Years After,* p. 247; CWB to GMB, Nov. 14, 1902; to Conn. Valley Hosp., Apr. 25, 1903.

53. CWB, "Autobiography," p. 32; CWB Case, Summary, Aug. 14, 1903, Conn. Valley Hosp.

54. CWB to Stearns, Sept. 18, 1902; Ham to Cliff, Apr. 24, 1903.

55. Yale University, Sheffield Scientific School, *Bulletin of the Class of 1897,* 1 (Apr. 3, 1913): 219, 248; Yale University, Sheffield Scientific School, *The '97 Class Book,* comp. E. A. Bredt et al. (New Haven: Lee Adkins Co., 1897), p. 219.

56. CWB Case, Summary, Aug. 14, 1903, Conn. Valley Hosp.

57. McQuaid to Welch, in *Twenty-Five Years After,* p. 247; to CWB, Mar. 30, 1903.

58. McQuaid to Welch, in *Twenty-Five Years After,* p. 247.

59. CWB Case, Summary, Aug. 14, 1903, Conn. Valley Hosp.; CWB to Vic [Tyler], Aug. 13, 1903; *AMTFI,* 1st draft, Yale, p. 23; CWB to GMB, Sept. 3, 1902.

60. Billy to CWB, Aug. 25, 1898; CWB to Conn. Valley Hosp., Apr. 25, 1903.

61. CWB to Mother, Sept. 15, 1898.

62. Ibid.; CWB to Mother, May 25, 1900.

63. CWB to Frank Coombes, Sept. 21, 1902; CWB, "Autobiography," p. 39.

64. CWB to GMB, Sept. 17, 1902.

65. CWB to Frank Coombes, Sept. 21, 1902, p. 3; to Conn. Valley Hosp., Apr. 25, 1903; *AMTFI,* 1st draft, Yale, pp. 27–28; CWB to Mother, May 25, 1900; to GMB, May 27, 1903.

66. CWB to GMB, Sept. 17, 1902; see also CWB to GMB, May 27, 1903.

67. CWB Case Records, IOL.

68. *AMTFI,* 1st ed., pp. 12–13; CWB Case, Summary, Aug. 14, 1903, Conn. Valley Hosp.; CWB to GMB, Sept. 17, 1902; to Stearns, Sept. 18, 1902, p. 45.

69. CWB to Mrs. Richard Morgan, Sept. 29, 1902; to Dr. Denton [?] F. Morgan, Sept. 21, 1902; CWB, "Autobiography," p. 35.

70. CWB, "Autobiography," pp. 40–41; CWB to Richard Morgan, Oct. 1, 1902; *AMTFI,* 1st ed., p. 13.

71. *AMTFI,* 1st draft, Yale, p. 28; CWB, "Autobiography," p. 42.

72. CWB, "Autobiography," pp. 42–44, 38, 45; *AMTFI,* 1st ed., pp. 14–15.

73. CWB, "Autobiography," pp. 45–48.

74. *AMTFI,* 1st ed., pp. 17–18; CWB, "Autobiography," pp. 49–50.

75. CWB, "Autobiography," pp. 51–56, 65–67, 60–64.

76. CWB to Mrs. Arthur Hofheimer, May 12, 1937.

77. CWB, "Autobiography," p. 76. Dr. Walter Alvarez in *Minds That Came Back* (Philadelphia: J. B. Lippincott Company, 1961, pp. 34–35) thought that George Beers had made a

mistake in employing the nurse who had tended Clifford at Grace Hospital. This breach of promise snapped the only remaining tie that held Clifford in contact with the real world: "He could not believe that his brother could have done such a thing, and hence the man who did it could not be his brother; he had to be an impostor. This is typical of the logic of the insane." Alvarez's views are also typical of early nineteenth-century American psychiatric thinking on the subject of truthfulness in dealing with mental patients.

Chapter 2. Stamford Hall

1. Norman Dain, "American Psychiatry in the 18th Century," in *American Psychiatry, Past, Present, and Future,* ed. George Kriegman, Robert D. Gardner, and D. Wilfred Abse (Charlottesville: University Press of Virginia, 1975), pp. 15–21; Norman Dain, "Three Centuries of Vicissitudes in Community Mental Health," paper presented at "The Community Imperative," a national conference on the public response to community care for the mentally disabled, Washington, D.C., June 1, 1978, pp. 1–5 (in press).

2. CWB to Uncle Sam, Aug. 22, 1903 (draft).

3. *AMTFI,* 1st ed., p. 45.

4. Givens to Noble, May 13, 1903.

5. *AMTFI,* 1st ed., pp. 39, 45, 41; CWB, "Autobiography," p. 88.

6. CWB, "Autobiography," pp. 88, 92; *AMTFI,* 1st ed., p. 45; CWB to GMB, Sept. 16, 1902.

7. CWB, "Autobiography," p. 93; *AMTFI,* 1st ed., p. 48. Hodgson also deeply disturbed Beers by forcibly placing muffs on his hands to restrict their movement. Before doing so Hodgson said, Beers recalled, "Mr. Beers we are sorry but we think it best to put these 'muffs' on you at night. You won't again try to do what you did in New Haven, will you?" ("Autobiography," p. 94). In the published version of this story, Beers complained bitterly about this humiliation, which made him weep for the first time since his suicide attempt. Out of "mistaken delicacy of feeling" the physician had not given him sufficient reason for the restraint; if only he had been told in "plain English" that he was insane and had tried to kill himself it would not have been so bad (*AMTFI,* 1st ed., p. 43). An early manuscript draft, however, contains the admission that Beers' embarrassment arose from his thinking that the muffs were applied because he was erroneously thought to be in the habit of masturbating, then still considered damaging to mental health ("Autobiography," pp. 94, 95).

8. Frank B. Wordin, "Autobiography," Sept. 17, 1907, p. 22 (MS sent to CWB, who acknowledged it in letter to Wordin, Sept. 17, 1907).

9. Ibid., pp. 19–20, 28–30.

10. CWB to F. B. Wordin, June 24, 1906; Wordin to CWB, June 30 [1906?], July 1906; CWB to Wordin, July 14, 1906; Wordin to CWB [n.d.], Aug. 18, 1907; Wordin, "Autobiography," pp. 11, 16–18.

11. *AMTFI,* 1st ed., pp. 52, 55; Wordin, "Autobiography," pp. 36–37; Wordin to CWB, July 1906.

12. A. J. Givens to GMB, Dec. 20, 1900; *AMTFI,* 1st ed., p. 53.

13. Wordin, "Autobiography," pp. 33–34.

14. Emil Kraepelin, *Manic Depressive Insanity and Paranoia,* trans. R. Mary Barclay, from 8th German ed. of the "Text-book of Psychiatry," vols. 3 and 4, ed. George M. Robertson (Edinburgh: E. & S. Livingstone, 1921), p. 205.

Chapter 3. The Hartford Retreat

1. CWB, "Autobiography," pp. 98–99; *AMTFI,* 1st ed., p. 56.

2. CWB, "Autobiography," pp. 101–02; *AMTFI,* 1st ed., p. 61.

3. Victor Morris Tyler to William Welch, Mar. 7, 1933, in *Twenty-Five Years After: Sidelights on the Mental Hygiene Movement and Its Founder,* ed. Wilbur L. Cross (New York: Doubleday, Doran & Company, 1934), p. 377; H. C. Robinson Case Records, Conn. Valley Hosp. George Beers had also had his difficult times in his mid-twenties but had apparently weathered the crisis in his business career so bravely that no one realized, Clifford told him, "what a stiff proposition you were up against" (CWB to GMB, May 27, 1903).

4. Francis J. Braceland, *The Institute of Living, The Hartford Retreat, 1822–1972* (Hartford: Institute of Living, 1972).

5. CWB to Wordin, May 3, 1903; CWB Case Records, IOL; CWB, "Autobiography," p. 102; *AMTFI,* 1st ed., pp. 62–64.

6. *AMTFI,* 1st ed., pp. 66–67, 63, 64; CWB Case Records, July 15, 1903, Conn. Valley Hosp.

7. Braceland, *Institute of Living,* p. 133.

8. *AMTFI,* pp. 65–66; CWB, "Autobiography," pp. 103–04.

9. CWB Case Summary, Case Records, IOL.

10. CWB, "Autobiography," pp. 106–07; CWB to Richard Morgan, Sept. 28, 1902.

11. *AMTFI,* 1st ed., pp. 71–72.

12. CWB Case Records, IOL; also CWB to Aunt Mame, Sept. 8, 1902.

13. CWB, "Autobiography," pp. 107–14; CWB to Richard Morgan, Sept. 28, 1902; *AMTFI,* 1st ed., pp. 76–79 (quotation from p. 79). *AMTFI,* (1st ed., pp. 76–77) says that George did not write but only telephoned.

14. CWB Case Records, Aug. 30, 1902, IOL.

15. See discussion of this point and of the description in *AMTFI* below in chapters 6 and 7.

16. CWB to GMB, Sept. 3, 1902; CWB Case Records, Sept. 4, 11, 12, 1902, IOL; *AMTFI,* 1st draft, Yale, p. 136; *AMTFI,* 1st ed., pp. 84–85; CWB to Aunt Mame, Sept. 8, 1902, p. 7; to Marshall J. Embler, Sept. 14, 1902; to Arthur Brewer 2nd, about Sept. 14, 1902; to Stearns, Sept. 18, 1902.

17. Fragment of letter to former fellow employee, n.d. [Jan. 1903?]; CWB, "Autobiography," pp. 118–19.

18. CWB, "Autobiography," pp. 118–19.

19. CWB Case Records, Sept. 8, 1902, IOL.

20. Ibid., Sept. 13, 1902; GMB to CWB, Sept. 12, 1902; CWB to GMB, Oct. 12, 13, 1902.

21. CWB, fragment in ink, pp. 3–8, probably 1903; CWB to Aunt Mame, Sept. 17, 1902; to Stearns, Sept. 18, 1902, pp. 7–11, 19, 12, 36, 40, 49; also CWB, "Autobiography," p. 121; CWB to GMB, May 10, 1903; to Conn. Valley Hosp., Apr. 25, 1903.

22. *AMTFI,* 9th draft, Yale, p. 119; *AMTFI,* 1st ed., p. 92.

23. CWB to GMB, to M. J. Embler, to A. Brewer, all Sept. 14, 1902 (these letters may not have been mailed); to Judge Livingston W. Cleveland, Sept. 17, 1902. See also CWB to Annie E. Cooke, to H. K. Lines, to Frederic G. Gilbert, all Sept. 14, 1902.

24. CWB to GMB, Sept. 17, 1902.

25. CWB to Stearns, Sept. 18, 1902, p. 22; also pp. 26–28.

26. Ibid., pp. 50–61, 78–89.

27. *AMTFI,* 1st ed., p. 98; CWB, "Autobiography," pp. 125–27.

28. CWB to Frederic E. Earle, Oct. 4, 1902; to Richard Morgan, Oct. 1, 1902, pp. 12e–12h; to Mrs. R. Morgan, Sept. 29, 1902, pp. 8h, 8e, 8g.

29. CWB, "Autobiography," pp. 131–32; CWB Case Records, Sept. 25, Oct. 7, 1902, IOL; CWB, Diary, 3″ x 5″ card, Oct. 4, 1902; CWB to GMB, Oct. 6, 1902, 3 P.M.; *AMTFI,* 1st ed., pp. 102–03.

30. See Stearns' discussion of *folie circulaire* (later called manic-depressive psychosis) in his *Lectures on Mental Diseases* (Philadelphia: P. Blakiston Son & Co., 1893), pp. 253–56; see also Braceland, *Institute of Living,* chap. 7.

31. CWB, fragment, after mid-Feb. 1903, p. 7.

32. CWB Case Records, IOL; CWB to GMB, Oct. 10, 1902; *AMTFI,* 1st ed., pp. 111–14; CWB, "Autobiography," pp. 133–37, 139; CWB to GMB, May 10, 1903. According to the hospital case records, the day of the alleged choking was October 19; CWB in *AMTFI,* 1st ed., p. 133, says it was the 18th, and also in letter to GMB, May 10, 1903.

33. CWB, "Autobiography," pp. 140–46, 148; CWB to GMB, May 10, 1903; CWB Case Records, IOL; *AMTFI,* 1st ed., p. 133; CWB to Pres. Theodore Roosevelt, Feb. 12, 1903; to Conn. Valley Hosp., Apr. 25, 1903, p. 6; *AMTFI,* 1st ed., pp. 133 ff. In the ninth draft of his book Beers mentions that the jacket was finally adjusted to make him more comfortable (*AMTFI,* 9th draft, Yale, p. 159).

34. CWB Case Records, Oct. 25, 1902 ff., IOL; CWB, "Autobiography," p. 150; CWB to Conn. Valley Hosp., Apr. 25, 1903; to Pres. Roosevelt, Feb. 12, 1903; to GMB, May 10, 1903, p. 10.

35. CWB to Conn. Valley Hosp., Apr. 25, 1903, pp. 1–7.

36. CWB, "Autobiography," pp. 148–50, 152; CWB to Gov. Chamberlain, Mar. 12, 1903, p. [9]; to John Coe, Apr. 8, 1903; Braceland, *Institute of Living,* chap. 7.

37. Stewart Paton, *Psychiatry: A Text-Book for Students and Physicians* (Philadelphia: J. B. Lippincott, 1905), pp. 367, 383, 370, 364–65; Nathan G. Hale, Jr., *Freud and the Americans: The Beginnings of Psychoanalysis in the United States, 1876–1917* (New York: Oxford University Press, 1971), p. 67. See also J. Rogues de Fursac, *Manual of Psychiatry,* trans. A. J. Rosanoff, 3rd U.S. ed. from the 3rd French ed., rev. and enl. (New York: John Wiley & Sons, 1911), p. 346.

38. A Ross Defendorf, *Clinical Psychiatry: A Text-Book for Students and Physicians,* abstracted and adapted from the 6th German ed. of Kraepelin's "Lehrbuch der Psychiatrie" (New York: Macmillan Company, 1904), pp. 312–15. A variant spelling for this author's name is Diefendorf, which is the form I have used in the text.

39. CEB to F. E. Earle, Oct. 4, 1902, pp. 10–11; CWB, fragment in ink, late 1902 or early 1903, pp. 3–8 (quotation from p. 5).

40. CWB, "Autobiography," pp. 119–21; CWB to GMB, May 10, 1903, Jan. 29, 1903. In the latter letter, written several months after Beers left the Retreat for the Connecticut State Hospital, he dates the refusal of writing materials as September 1, 1902, but on September 17 and 18 he was still writing voluminous letters. And, though at some point between October 1 and November 8, 1902, Dr. A did refuse him paper and pencil, the overactive Beers scribbled on any scrap he could find, including the Book of Psalms, which Dr. A did let him have (*AMTFI,* 1st ed., pp. 95–96).

41. CWB to GMB, May 10, 1903.

42. *AMTFI,* 1st ed., pp. 110–11.

43. CWB to GMB, Jan. 29, 1903.

44. Later CWB told Adolf Meyer that Samuel Merwin had contributed $1,883.52 to his hospital expenses (CWB to AM, July 21, 1908).

Chapter 4. Connecticut Hospital for the Insane

1. CWB Case Records, Conn. Valley Hosp.

2. CWB Case, Summary. Aug. 14, 1903, Conn. Valley Hosp.

3. *AMTFI,* 1st ed., pp. 143–44.

4. CWB to GMB, Nov. 14, 1902; also Nov. 12, 1902.

5. CWB to GMB, Nov. 14, 1902.

6. CWB Case Records, Nov. 8, 1902, Conn. Valley Hosp.; fragment of a letter to former fellow employee, n.d. [Jan. 1903?], p. 12. In *AMTFI* he acknowledged that he was elated and occupied with writing letters, drawing, and continually talking.

7. *AMTFI,* 1st ed., p. 145; CWB Case, Summary, Aug. 14, 1903, Conn. Valley Hosp.

8. CWB Case Records, Nov. 20, 1902.

9. Ibid., Nov. 21, 22, 1902.

10. *AMTFI,* 1st ed., pp. 143, 146–51; CWB to Conn. Valley Hosp., Apr. 25, 1903, p. 9.

11. CWB Case, Summary, Aug. 14, 1903; Case Records, Nov. 24, 27, 1902, Conn. Valley Hosp.; also CWB to Mrs. S. E. Merwin, Mar. 6, 1903 (incomplete).

12. CWB to Chamberlain, Mar. 12, 1903; to Conn. Valley Hosp., Apr. 25, 1903, p. 9; to GMB, May 10, 1903; *AMTFI,* 1st ed., p. 156.

13. *AMTFI,* 1st ed., p. 160; also CWB to Mother, Aug. 3, 1903.

14. *AMTFI,* 1st ed., pp. 183–86; see also CWB to Dr. Noble, Dec. 30, 1902.

15. Marion Kenworthy, interview, 1966.

16. *AMTFI,* 1st ed., pp. 169, 153; CWB to Dr. Thomas, May 2, 1903.

17. CWB to Chamberlain, Mar. 12, 1903; *AMTFI,* 1st ed., pp. 162–64.

18. *AMTFI,* 1st ed., pp. 169 ff.; CWB to GMB, Feb. 24, 1903; to Chamberlain, Mar. 12, 1903; also to Conn. Valley Hosp., Apr. 25, 1903, pp. 11–12.

19. *AMTFI,* 1st ed., pp. 187–89; CWB to Conn. Valley Hosp., Apr. 25, 1903; CWB Case Records, Dec. 18, 1902, Conn. Valley Hosp.

20. CWB Case, Summary, Aug. 14, 1903, Conn. Valley Hosp.; also Case Records, Feb. 16, 1903.

21. CWB to GMB, Jan. 29, Feb. 26 [?], fragment, 1903.

22. CWB to Aunt Em (Mrs. Merwin), Mar. 6, 1903, pp. 14–15; *AMTFI,* 1st ed., pp. 190–91. There are examples of his poetry in the CWB Coll.

23. CWB to Editor, *Life,* July 14, 1903.

24. Fragment of CWB letter after mid-Feb. 1903, pp. 4–6.

25. CWB's letter of Mar. 5 to his mother was written from Ward 5S (violent ward); the next day, Mar. 6, he was writing to Mrs. Samuel E. Merwin from Ward 2S.

26. CWB to GMB, late Feb. or early Mar. 1903, fragment; see also CWB to Mrs. S. E. Merwin, Apr. 2, Mar. 6, 1903 (incomplete).

27. CWB to Mrs. Robert A. Beers, Mar. 5, 1903.

28. N. Cooke to Mame, Mar. 21, 1903.

29. GMB to CWB, Mar. 7, 1903; CWB to GMB, late Feb. [?] 1903, fragment; to Mrs. Robert Anthony Beers, Mar. 1, 1903; CWB Case Records, Feb. 16, 1903, Conn. Valley Hosp.; M. Kenworthy, interview.

30. In group of pictures and notes, Jan.–Feb. 1903.

31. CWB to Roosevelt, Feb. 12, 1903.

32. CWB to Mrs. Samuel E. Merwin, Mar. 6, 1903 (incomplete); to Wm. J. Hoggson, Mar. 16, 1903.

33. CWB to Mother, Sept. 8, 1903; to Dr. Jerome Gill Atkinson, Mar. 23, 1903, p. 7; see also note at end of CWB to Chamberlain, Mar. 12, 1903, and note on CWB to GMB, Mar. 18, 1903.

34. See, for example, folders for Mar. 1903; McQuaid to CWB, Mar. 18, 1903.

35. CWB to GMB, Mar. 14, 1903.

36. CWB to GMB, Mar. 18, 1903. Clifford also wanted to write to women friends and once sneaked out a letter to one, for which George rebuked him: women did not like to correspond with an inmate of a mental hospital (CWB to G. Wallard Kellam, Mar. 24, 1903; to GMB, Mar. 28, 1903).

37. McQuaid to Welch, in *Twenty-Five Years After: Sidelights on the Mental Hygiene Movement and Its Founder,* ed. Wilbur L. Cross (New York: Doubleday, Doran & Company, 1934), pp. 247–48; letters from CWB's friends are in folders for Mar. 1903, CWB Coll.

38. CWB to John W. Coe, Mar. 23, 1903; to Chamberlain, Mar. 12, 1903.

39. Ibid.

40. CWB to Coe, Mar. 23, 1903; to Governor, Mar. 24, 1903.

41. CWB to Dr. H. S. Noble, Mar. 15, 1903; "Declaration of Independence," Mar. 21, 1903; CWB to GMB, Mar. 18, 1903; to Augustus G. Nung, Mar. [19?], 1903; group of letters and fragments on lined paper, Mar. [21?], 1903; see also McQuaid to CWB, Mar. 18, 1903.

42. CWB to Paul A. McQuaid, Mar. 20, 1903, 12:30 P.M.

43. CWB to Dr. A. C. Thomas, Mar. 16, 1903; CWB Case Record, Apr. 10, 1903, Conn. Valley Hosp.

44. CWB to GMB, Mar. 18, 1903; to Augustus G. Nung, Mar. 19, 1903.

45. CWB to A. R. Diefendorf, Dec. 28, 1936; to Diefendorfer [sic], May 12, 1903.

46. CWB to Dr. Thomas, Mar. 22, 1903, 8:15 A.M.

47. Ibid., 7 P.M.

48. McQuaid to Whit, Mar. 24, 1903.

49. CWB to McQuaid, Mar. 26, 1903.

50. GMB to CWB, Mar. 28, 1903.

51. CWB to Thomas, Mar. 28, 1903; to GMB, Mar. 30, 1903.

52. John [Veitch] to GMB, Wednesday [April 1?, 1903]; Sunday [Apr. 5?, 1903]; CWB to Mother, Mar. 31, 1903.

53. CWB to Thomas, Mar. 29, 1903, two letters; to Dr. Noble, Mar. 29, 1903; to Thomas, Apr. 8, 1903; to GMB, Apr. 1, 1903; to Conn. Valley Hosp., Apr. 25, 1903.

54. CWB to GMB, Apr. 1, 1903; John [Veitch] to GMB, Sunday [Apr. 5?, 1903].

55. Ibid.

56. CWB to Thomas, Apr. 10, 1903.

57. CWB to Father, Apr. 20, 1903.

58. CWB to Thomas, Apr. 26, 1903; Coe to CWB, Apr. 7, 1903; GMB to CWB, Apr. 24, 1903; CWB to Thomas, Apr. 22, 1903; *AMTFI,* 1st ed., pp. 204–05.

59. CWB to Coe, Apr. 8, 1903.

60. CWB to Thomas, Apr. 24, 1903.

61. CWB, Memorandum, Apr. 25, 1903.

62. CWB to Coe, June 16, 1903 (draft); to Richard Morgan, May 3, 1903; to Coe, May 8, 1903.

63. *AMTFI,* 1st ed., pp. 204–08; quotation from p. 208.

64. Henry S. Noble to CWB, Dec. 26, 1904.

65. CWB to Morgan, May 3, 1903.

66. CWB to Thomas, Noble, Apr. 26, 1903; to Coe, May 8, 1903.

67. CWB to Morgan, May 3, 1903.

68. CWB to Mr. Elms, May 1903; to Levi Abernethy, May 1, 1903.

69. J. S. . . . to GMB, May 5, 1903.

70. CWB to Thomas, May 2, 1903.

71. CWB to Thomas, May [30?], 1903; CWB, Case Records, [May ?] 5, 1903; see also CWB to Thomas, May 9, 12, 1903.

72. CWB to GMB, May 10, 1903; see also CWB to Noble, May 24, 1903.

73. CWB to Thomas, May 21, 1903.

74. CWB to Thomas, June 8, 1903.

75. CWB to Wordin, May 3, 1903; to Elizabeth Chamberlain, May 13, 1903; to GMB, May 27, 23, 1903.

76. CWB to Morgan, May 3, 1903.

77. Coe to CWB, June 12, 1903; CWB to Coe, June 16, 1903 (draft).

78. CWB to Vic Tyler, Aug. 13, 1903 (unfinished).

79. CWB to Father, June 23, 1903; also to Mother, June 8, 1903.

80. CWB to Parents, June 10, 1903.

81. Various letters, June–Sept. 1903; *AMTFI,* 1st ed., p. 210.

82. CWB to Mother, Aug. 3, 1903; to Father, Aug. 8, 1903; CWB Case, Summary, Aug. 14, 1903, Conn. Valley Hosp.; CWB to Mother, Aug. 6, 1903; *AMTFI,* 1st ed., pp. 211, 209; see also letters, July–Aug. 1903.

83. GMB to Father, June 23, 1903; to Mother, June 30, 1903; to CWB, June 23, July 10, 1903; CWB to GMB, July 16, 1903.

84. GMB to CWB, July 27, 1903.

85. CWB to Miss Purdon, Aug. 15, 1903.

86. CWB to GMB, Sept. 8, 1903.

Chapter 5. Back in Circulation

1. CWB Case Records, Sept. 9, 1903, Conn. Valley Hosp.; Case Summary, Aug. 14, 1903.

2. *AMTFI,* 1st ed., pp. 256–57; CWB to Mrs. Jepson, Aug. 29, 1908; to Clara, fragment, n.d., #128; fragment [9]; to CJ, Sept. 22, 1908; note, Dec. 25, 1908, on copy of Gibbons to CWB, Nov. 28, 1908, all in MFA.

3. *AMTFI,* 1st ed., pp. 257–58; CWB, "General Outline to be followed in concluding my story," July 19, 1906; *AMTFI,* 1st draft, Yale, p. 259; CWB to Bert Fisher, July 21, 1906.

4. *AMTFI,* 1st draft, Yale, pp. 259–60, 262–65; *AMTFI,* 1st ed., p. 285; CWB to Mother, Feb. 14, 1904; to GMB, Jan. 1904, in Notebook #1, Hartford.

5. *AMTFI,* 1st ed., p. 260; CWB to GMB, Jan. 19, 1904; to Mother, Feb. 14, 1904.

6. GMB to CWB, Feb. 18, 1904.

7. *AMTFI,* 1st draft, Yale, p. 256; CWB, "General Outline to be followed in concluding my story," July 19, 1906; CWB, Notebook, 3″ x 5″ [no. 1, 1905].

8. Just six months earlier Beers had written W. J. Hoggson's brother, Noble Foster Hoggson, from the hospital at Middletown that he intended to study art and had asked for comments on some artistic work he would send (CWB to N. F. Hoggson, June 4, 1903).

9. W. J. Hoggson, "The Dreams of a Business Man," Apr. 1932, typescript (carbon copy), pp. 37–38; W. J. H[oggson], typescript of talk, 3/5/23, 2 pp.

10. *AMTFI,* 1st ed., pp. 257–59.

11. CWB to Victor Morris Tyler, Jan. 2, 1905, p. 4.

12. "To CWB," Jan. 6–10, 1905, p. 6, in CWB, "Note Book #1, Hartford, Jan. 1905"; CWB, fragment, after Jan. 1905, 5 typed pages; *AMTFI,* 1st draft, Yale, pp. 266–68; *AMTFI,* 1st ed., p. 263.

13. Hoggson quoted in *AMTFI,* 1st draft, Yale, pp. 266–68, also pp. 263–64.

14. *AMTFI,* 1st ed., p. 264; CWB to GMB, Jan. 3, 1905, copy; CWB report of telephone conversation with GMB, Jan. 3, 1905, 12:45 P.M.

15. *AMTFI,* 1st ed., pp. 264–65, 268; CWB to Fisher, July 21, 1906, p. 9; to Tyler, Jan. 2, 1905.

16. CWB, "To whom it may concern . . . ," Yale Club, Jan. 1–Jan. 3, 1905, pp. 40–41; CWB to Fisher, July 21, 1906, pp. 10–11.

17. CWB to Tyler, Jan. 2, 1905; *AMTFI,* 1st draft, Yale, p. 268; CWB to Fisher, July 21, 1906, p. 13.

18. *AMTFI,* 1st ed., p. 266; CWB to Fisher, July 21, 1906, p. 13; *AMTFI,* 1st draft, Yale, p. 270; also Noble Foster Hoggson to CWB, Nov. 15, 1907.

19. CWB to Father, Jan. 5, 1905; also *AMTFI,* 1st draft, Yale, p. 272–73; *AMTFI,* 1st ed., p. 269.

20. CWB to Aunt Mame, Jan. 5, 7, 9, 1905; to Father, Jan. 5, 1905; to Mother, Jan. 6, 1905; Francis J. Braceland, *The Institute of Living, The Hartford Retreat, 1822–1972* (Hartford: Institute of Living, 1972), p. 139.

21. CWB, *AMTFI,* 6th draft, Yale, p. 351.

22. GMB to CWB, Jan. 5, 1905; *AMTFI,* 1st draft, Yale, pp. 273–74; "To CWB," Jan. 6–10, 1905, p. 13, in CWB, "Note Book #1, Hartford, Jan. 1905"; *AMTFI,* 6th draft, Yale, p. 357.

23. CWB, "Autobiography," p. 1.

24. "To CWB," Jan. 6–10, 1905, pp. 4–5, in CWB, "Note Book #1, Hartford, Jan. 1905."

25. Fragment, in CWB's hand, pp. 140–42, inserted in CWB, "Note Book #1, Hartford, Jan. 1905"; "To CWB," Jan. 6–10, 1905, ibid., pp. 6, 18.

26. Fragment in CWB's hand, pp. 140–41, inserted ibid.; "Quotations from 'Insanity—Its Causes and Prevention,' by Dr. H. P. Stearns," Jan. 21, 1905, pp. 4–7, ibid.

27. CWB to McQuaid, Apr. 30, 1906, p. 19.

28. "Quotations from 'Insanity—Its Causes and Prevention,'" p. 11, in CWB, "Note Book #1, Hartford, Jan. 1905."

29. "To CWB," Jan. 6–10, 1905, pp. 7, 15, ibid.

30. CWB to Father, Jan. 19, 1905; to Mother, Jan. 12, 1905.

31. "To CWB," Jan. 6–10, 1905, pp. 8–12, 19–20, in "Note Book #1, Hartford, Jan. 1905"; CWB, "Autobiography," pp. 2–8.

32. CWB to Mother, Jan. 17, 1905; to Father, Jan. 19, 1905.

33. CWB Case Records, IOL.

34. *AMTFI,* 6th draft, Yale, p. 345.

Chapter 6. Writing the Autobiography

1. *AMTFI,* 6th draft, Yale, pp. 354–55; CWB, Notebook, 3″ x 5″ [no. 4, 1905].

2. CWB to HWF, July 21, 1906, p. 17; GMB to CWB, Mar. 9, Aug. 9, 1905; CWB to Judge R. W. Taylor, Mar. 8, 1906; also Taylor to GMB, Mar. 27, 1905.

3. Stewart Paton, *Psychiatry: A Text-book for Students and Physicians* (Philadelphia: J. B. Lippincott, 1905), p. 365; for CWB's reading list see CWB to McQuaid, Apr. 30, 1906, pp. 21–22.

4. CWB to W. J. Hoggson, Sept. 22, 1905, p. 2; to Vic Tyler, Mar. 25, 1905; *AMTFI,* 1st ed., pp. 282–83; CWB, Notebook, 3″ x 5″ [no. 3], Aug. 5, 1905, [no. 4], Mar. 29, Feb. 22, 1905, [no. 1], 1905. Beers' description of the pressure to write, lack of fatigue, newfound fluency, and plans to produce numerous books in a new career as author is not atypical of manic persons. For a recent similar description by a former mental patient see Robert Dahl, *Breakdown* (New York: Ace Books, 1959), pp. 118–23.

5. CWB to Lounsbury, July 31, 1905.

6. In August he spoke modestly of three poems that he wrote as being technically imperfect and yet having poetic quality (CWB to Mother, Aug. 25, 1905).

7. *AMTFI,* 1st ed., p. 283; CWB, Notebook, 3″ x 5″ [no. 4], July? 1905, [no. 5], Aug. 1905; CWB to Aunt Em, July 30, 1905; CWB, Notebook, 3″ x 5″ [no. 3], 1905. "F. L." remains unidentified.

8. CWB to Father, Mar. 29, 1905; to A. L. Comstock, July 31, 1906; CWB, "Open Letter #1, to the President of These United States," June 16, 1906, p. 18 [not sent].

9. Walpole quoted in CWB to Robert C. Jeffcott, Oct. 21, 1937 (copy). See Barbara Sicherman, "The Quest for Mental Health in America, 1880–1917" (Ph.D. dissertation, Columbia University, 1967), which takes a similar position on CWB's feelings (pp. 294–95).

10. Paton, *Psychiatry,* pp. 370, 367; *AMTFI,* 1st draft, Yale, p. 1; CWB, Notebook, 3″ x 5″ [no. 4], 1905.

11. CWB to Mother, July 1, 1905; to Rev. Richard Whittingham, Sept. 10, 1905, p. 4; CWB, Notebook, 3″ x 5″ [no. 4], Mar. 29, 1905.

12. CWB to W. J. Hoggson, July 26–27, 1905.

13. CWB, Notebook, 3″ x 5″ [no. 2], 1905, [no. 3], July 21, 1905; CWB to Lounsbury, Aug. 1, July 31, 1905.

14. CWB, Notebook, 3″ x 5″ [no. 2], Aug. 15, 1905; *AMTFI,* 1st ed., pp. 283–84; CWB, "Note Book #1, Hartford, Jan. 1905," p. 68.

15. CWB to Choate, Aug. 18, 1905; *AMTFI,* 1st ed., pp. 283–85.

16. CWB, Notebook, 3″ x 5″ [no. 2], Aug. 20, 7, 1905; CWB to Mother, Aug. 21, 1905; to Rev. Whittingham, Sept. 10, 1905.

17. "Hours of Dictation," in *AMTFI,* 1st draft, Yale; CWB to Judge Taylor, Mar. 28, 1906, p. 4; Caroline [?] H. Bartlett to CWB, Mar. 5, 1936; *AMTFI,* 1st draft, Yale, p. "(ss)"; CWB to W. J. Hoggson, Sept. 22, 1905, pp. 2, 8–10.

18. *AMTFI,* 1st ed., pp. 286–87.

19. GMB to CWB, Aug. 29, 1905; CWB to W. J. Hoggson, Sept. 22, 1905, p. 4.

20. CWB to Rev. Whittingham, Sept. 29, 1905.

21. To a fellow patient Beers wrote asking for an account of their "first meeting and everything else that happened" at the hospital (CWB to . . . , Sept. 10, 1905). In reply to a similar request, his former caretaker at Stamford Hall, Frank Wordin, offered the use of the detailed records his aunt had kept during Beers' stay at her home (Frank B. Wordin to CWB [1906]). From the Beers family physician came a recounting of Beers' medical history before he attempted suicide (A. S. Cheney to CWB, Mar. 22, 1907).

22. Diefendorf to CWB, Sept. 13, 1905; Albert A. Thomas to CWB, Nov. 24, 1905.

23. CWB to Rev. Whittingham, Sept. 10, 1905, pp. 7–8; W. J. Hoggson to CWB, Sept. 25, 1905; CWB to Hoggson, Sept. 26, 1905; to Judge Taylor, Mar. 8, 1906.

24. *AMTFI,* 1st ed., pp. 287–88; CWB to Judge Taylor, Mar. 8, 1906, p. 2.

25. CWB to Judge Taylor, Mar. 8, 1906, pp. 8–9; CWB, "To whom it may concern . . . ," Yale Club, Jan. 1–3, 1905, p. 46; CWB to Miss O'Shaughnessy, Nov. 29, 1905, in *AMTFI,* 6th draft, Yale, pp. 6–8.

26. GMB to CWB, Feb. 18, 1906.

27. See, for example, A. Guyot Cameron to CWB, Feb. 1, 1908; Vic Tyler to CWB, Sept. 21, 1905; HWF to CWB, Jan. 4, 1906; Alfred D. Smith to CWB, Mar. 13, 1906.

28. Page to CWB, Mar. 8, 1906.

29. CWB to Page, Sept. 18, 1906; to McQuaid, Apr. 30, 1906.

30. Page to CWB, Feb. 14, Mar. 18, 1906.

31. *AMTFI,* draft entitled "Reason Triumphant," 1907, p. 1 following p. 370; HWF to Professor Irving Fisher, May 28, 1906.

32. HWF to CWB, Mar. 11, 1906; CWB to HWF, Mar. 21, 1906; HWF to CWB, Mar. 31, 1906, pp. 11–12; CWB to HWF, June 6, 1906; HWF to CWB, June 6, 1906.

33. See, for example, in MFA: CWB to Mrs. William James, June 29, 1912 (typed copy of a copy); to Mr. and Mrs. Acker and Mrs. Marks, July 19, 1912 (copy); to [CJ], Mar. 9, 1911; CWB, "Some Intimate Aspects of the Origin and Growth of the Mental Hygiene Movement," unpub. version [no. 1], p. 5.

34. Note, Dec. 25, 1908, on copy of Gibbons to CWB, Nov. 28, 1908, MFA; Walter E. Coe to CWB, Feb. 1, 1907; CWB to Alfred D. Smith, Mar. 30, 1906; CWB to CJ, calling card, Dec. 14, 1906, on list of holdings in EM Coll.

35. Fragment of letter, Nov. 11, 1906, in CWB's handwriting; CWB, typed fragment, n.d. [1905?], 3 pp.; HWF to CWB, Mar. 31, 1906; also Diefendorf to CWB, Sept. 13, 1905.

36. HWF to CWB, Aug. 5, 1906. Later, revising the first edition, Beers intended, at the suggestion of a psychiatrist, to tell more about his boyhood, "so that physicians, especially, may get a better insight into the conditions which preceded my mental collapse," but he did not (penciled note on p. 6 of *AMTFI,* 1st ed., copy in CWB Coll. with CWB's notes).

37. HWF to CWB, Dec. 5, 1906; CWB to HWF, Dec. 7, 1906, pp. 1–2.

38. CWB to HWF, July 11, p. 4, Nov. 22, 1906; CWB, typed summary from excited letters (mimeographed) [1906–07?]; CWB, "General Outline to be followed in concluding my story," July 19, 1906; AM to CWB, Apr. 23, 1908.

39. CWB to WJ, June 9, 1906; to Mother, Aug. 30, 1906.

40. CWB to HWF, May 16, 1906, pp. 5–6; CWB, "Open Letter #1, To the President of These United States, June 16, 1906 + Supplement, To Whom It May Concern."

41. CWB to HWF, Aug. 25, 1906, pp. 1-4; to Judge Taylor, Mar. 8, 1906, p. 10; to HWF, June 12, 1906.

42. CWB to HWF, Aug. 6, 1906, pp. 9-10; HWF to CWB, June 14, 1906.

43. CWB to HWF, June 28, 1906; Annie Trumbull Slosson to CWB, June 23, 1906; HWF to CWB, July 1, 1906.

44. CWB to HWF, July 11, 12, 1906; to Comstock, July 18, 5, 1906; HWF to CWB, July 8, 1906.

45. CWB to HWF, May 31, 1906; to Dr. Page, July 16, 1906; to WJ, June 9, Aug. 12, 1906.

46. *The Diary of Alice James,* ed. Leon Edel (New York: Dodd, Mead, 1964); Gay Wilson Allen, *William James, a Biography* (New York: Viking Press, 1967), pp. xii, 122, 124, 330-31, 227, 166-67, 302-03, 305, 312.

47. CWB to WJ, June 9, 1906.

48. WJ to CWB, July 1, 1906 (typed copy). The letter quoted in *AMTFI,* 1st ed., pp. vii-viiii, was revised for publication and is slightly different.

49. CWB to WJ, July 1, Aug. 12, 1906 (copy). His father, worried about the effect of all this mental activity on Clifford's health, now admitted that he would feel proud to see his projects succeed (CWB to Father, July 20, 1906); Carl E. D. [Caroline E. Dudley] to CWB, July 12, 1906.

50. CWB to WJ, Aug. 12 (copy), July 1, 1906; to Mancel Clark, July 8, 1906.

51. CWB to Page, Sept. 18, 1906; Diefendorf to CWB, Oct. 8, 1906.

52. CWB to WJ, June 6, July 10, 1906; to Comstock, July 18, 1906, p. 12; to WJ, July 10, 1906 (copy in longhand); Carl E. D. to CWB, July 12, 1906.

53. CWB to Comstock, July 18, 31, 1906; to HWF, June 15, July 15, 21 (p. 42), Sept. 16, Oct. 11 (p. 5), Aug. 6, 26, Nov. 26, Dec. 7, 1906; HWF to CWB, Aug. 5, Nov. 25, 1906.

54. CWB to HWF, Oct. 11, 1906; to Wm. H. Baldwin, Jan. 7, 1907; to Messrs. Hoggson Bros., Jan. 27, 1907; to [?], Nov. 11, 1906 (incomplete); to WJ, Jan. 27, 1907.

55. CWB to HWF, Feb. 5, Mar. 3, 1907; to Diefendorf, Mar. 6, 1907; to Chittenden, Mar. 1, 1907; to Taylor, Nov. 25, 1907 (copy); CWB, Summary of interview with Wm. James, Mar. 1, 1907 (16 pp. in pencil); copy of WJ letter of introduction in CWB to HWF, Mar. 1907.

56. CWB to Ada [Comstock], Mar. 21, 1908; WJ to CWB, Oct. 30, 1907 (copy).

57. CWB to WJ, Jan. 27, Mar. 11 (copy), Mar. 21, 1907; to HWF, Mar. 1907; to McQuaid, Apr. 9, 1907; WJ to CWB, Mar. 17, 1907 (copy).

58. CWB to WJ, Feb. 21, 1907; to Aunt Mame, Mar. 1, 1907; to WJ, Mar. 4 (draft), 21, 24, 1907.

59. CWB to Longmans, Green & Co., Mar. 15, 1907 (copy?); to Aunt Mame, Mar. 13, 1907. Actually Diefendorf, without telling Beers, had contacted Macmillan, whose manager was interested (Diefendorf to CWB, June 3, 5, 1907).

60. CWB to Longmans, Green, Mar. 24, 1907 (draft); to WJ, Mar. 24, 1907 (copy).

61. Lounsbury to CWB, Mar. 24, 1907; W. L. Cross to CWB, Feb. 25, 1907 (copy); TWM, p. 11; Cross to [?], June 10, 1942 (carbon copy), Cross Papers, Yale University; Hadley to CWB, Feb. 25, 1907 (copy); also CWB to Page, Mar. 7, 1907 (copy).

62. CWB to Longmans, Green, Mar. 12, 1907 (draft); to HWF, Feb. 28, Mar. 3, 1907.

63. CWB to McQuaid, Apr. 8, 1907 (copy); to CJ, Apr. 21, 1907, MFA; on skepticism of family see Carl to CWB, Mar. 21, 1907.

64. CWB to Uncle Sam, Aug. 22, 1903; to HWF, Mar. 11, 1907; to Aunt Mame, Mar. 13, 22, 1907; to Ada, Mar. 21, 1907; Carl D. to CWB, Mar. 21, 1907; *AMTFI,* 1st ed.

65. CWB to HWF, Apr. 12, 1907, Dec. 23, 1906, Jan. 4, 1907.

66. Carl D. to CWB, Mar. 21, 1907.

67. CWB to HWF, Mar. 29, 1907; HWF to CWB, Mar. 26, 1907; also HWF to CWB, fragment, 10 pp., about May 1907.

68. His comments are mainly in a long letter to CWB, June 7, 1907.

69. CWB to Charles T. Holman, Aug. 3, 1937. On the other hand, a modern writer commenting on Beers' book writes that psychiatrists "could have saved him a world of anxiety" by telling him that because of his temporary insanity when he attempted suicide there could be no legal charges against him. "This, in a moment, could have relieved him of most of his mental suffering. It would have helped him greatly if someone had kept telling him why it was advisable and for his own good that he be kept shut up for a while." (Walter Alvarez, *Minds That Came Back* [Philadelphia: J. B. Lippincott, 1961], p. 36.)

70. Noble to CWB, Aug. 8, 1906.

71. CWB to HWF, June 9, 17, 1907; to McDonald, June 10, 1907 (copy).

72. McDonald to CWB, Sept. 6, 1907.

73. *AMTFI,* 1st draft, Yale, p. cc; *AMTFI,* 1st ed., p. 91.

74. McDonald to CWB, Sept. 6, 1907; CWB to McDonald, Sept. 13, 1907, 2 versions, unsigned (copies?).

75. CWB to HWF, June 10, 1907; HWF to CWB, June 17, 1907; CWB to Noble, Aug. 1, 1906 (copy); Noble to CWB, Aug. 8, 1907 (copy); CWB to HWF, June 17, 1907. An eminent former chief of the Retreat, writing its history in 1972, judges that the Retreat episodes in Beers' book, true or not, "did neither him nor the hospital any good." By implication the impression is given that Clifford, "high" when he wrote the book and certainly so during the experiences he related, could not have been trusted to write a wholly valid account. (Francis J. Braceland, *The Institute of Living, The Hartford Retreat, 1822–1972* (Hartford: Institute of Living, 1972), pp. 134–35.

76. CWB, Address, 24th Anniversary, H.P.P.C., Apr. 17, '37 (typescript); Otto M. Marx, "American Psychiatry Without William James," *Bulletin of the History of Medicine,* 42 (Jan.–Feb. 1968): 52–61.

77. Paton, *Psychiatry,* pp. 1, 10; CWB to Paton, May 20, 1907; Paton to CWB, May 20, 1907; CWB, "Address Delivered at the 70th Birthday Dinner for Dr. Adolf Meyer" [1937?] (typescript), p. 2; CWB to HWF, Sept. 24, 1907.

78. Nathan G. Hale, Jr., ed., *James Jackson Putnam and Psychoanalysis: Letters Between Putnam and Sigmund Freud, Ernest Jones, William James, Sandor Ferenczi, and Morton Prince, 1877–1917* (Cambridge: Harvard University Press, 1971), pp. 11, 12, 347; Adolf Meyer, *Collected Papers,* ed. Eunice E. Winters, vol. II, *Psychiatry* (Baltimore: Johns Hopkins Press, 1951), pp. 174, 215, 228.

79. CWB to AM, Sept. 24, 1907, AM Papers; to CJ, Oct. 3, 1907, MFA.

80. CWB to Judge Taylor, Nov. 25, 1907; to HWF, Oct. 23, 1907; CWB, Address, 24th Anniversary, H.P.P.C., Apr. 17, '37 (typescript).

81. CWB to AM, Oct. 16, 1907, AM Papers; to J. M. Mosher, Sept. 29, 1907; to George Blumer, Nov. 28, 1910, in TWM, I, 31; to CJ, Oct. 3, 1907, MFA; to AM, Oct. 7, 1907, AM Papers.

82. Handwritten postscript in AM to CWB, Oct. 10, 1910.

83. AM to Dr. Bancroft, Oct, 28, 1910, AM Papers.

84. Meyer review of *AMTFI* in *North American Review,* Apr. 1908, in "Index to Excerpts — Reviews of *AMTFI,*" CWB Coll. On the Bull Pen Meyer wrote: "Wherever the more complex difficulty of dealing with groups of patients is handled in a summary fashion 'by wards,' where the individual is submerged in a compact of compromises, nothing but the utmost care will prevent real hardships. The pattern of a ward is apt to be shaped according to the demands of the patients who cause the most trouble, that is, the more or less chronic cases. If a ward is in such a condition as the 'Bull-Pen' described in the book, the official visits are short and the chances of an inquiry into individual needs by the physician small and almost hopeless. These wards have existed so long that, like restraint, they are considered inevitable by those who have grown up with them."

85. Meyer to C. B. Farrar, July 20, 1943 (typed, unsigned), Private Papers of C. B. Farrar; HWF to CWB, Apr. 14, 1907; CWB to HWF, Apr. 16, 1907, Aug. 6, 1906.

86. *AMTFI,* 1st ed., pp. 79, 81–82.

87. The CWB Coll. copy of the first edition of *AMTFI* has a note on the flyleaf in CWB's hand saying that the volume contains changes to be incorporated into the third edition. On p. 79 is a penciled note concerning the addition of the explanatory footnote. On p. 81 CWB penciled the insertion "largely ???" before the word "regaining," and underlined "reason" and placed an "x?" in the margin. The sentence as published in the third edition, however, reads the same as in the first.

88. *AMTFI,* 1st ed., pp. 79–81.

89. CWB to HWF, Oct. 23, 1907; to Comstock, Oct. 27, 1907.

90. Andrew Carnegie, *The Gospel of Wealth and Other Timely Essays,* ed. Edward C. Kirkland (Cambridge, Mass.: Belknap Press of Harvard University Press, 1962), p. 40; Carnegie is quoted in Joseph Frazier Wall, *Andrew Carnegie* (New York: Oxford University Press, 1970), p. 832. In Jan. 1907 CWB reproduced in multiple copies the relevant passage from Carnegie's essay (CWB Coll.)

91. TWM, I, 26; CWB to WJ, July 31, 1907 (copy); Simon Flexner and J. T. Flexner, *William Henry Welch and the Heroic Age of American Medicine* (New York: Viking Press, 1941), pp. 269–71.

92. CWB to WJ, July 31, 1907 (copy); to Paton, July 22, 1907 (copy); to Anson Phelps Stokes, Jr., July 25, 1905 [1907].

93. CWB to Aunt Mame, Sept. 23, 1907; to Paton, July 25, 1907; CWB, penciled notes, Sept. 22–Oct. 10, 1907, 3 pp. on 4″ x 7″ graph paper; Welch quotation in CWB to AM, Oct. 14, 1907. On Barker's interests see AM, "Barker, Lewellys Franklin, M.D., 1867–1943," *Journal of Nervous and Mental Disease,* 98 (1943): 336–39, in AM, *Collected Papers,* III, 554–57; Lewellys F. Barker, "The Psychic Treatment of the Functional Neurosis," *International Clinics,* 17th ser., 1 (1907): 15–16, cited in Nathan G. Hale, Jr., *Freud and the Americans: The Beginnings of Psychoanalysis in the United States, 1876–1917* (New York: Oxford University Press, 1971), p. 139; Sicherman, "Quest for Mental Health in America," p. 265.

94. CWB to Paton, July 25, 1907; to Stokes, Aug. 14, 1907; to Ada, Aug. 16, 1907; to Stokes, Aug. 9, 1907; to Mosher, Sept. 29, 1902.

95. CWB to AM, Oct. 16, 1907; to HWF, Oct. 23, 1907; to Prof. L. S. Barker, Nov. 5, 1907; F. T. Gates to CWB, Oct. 30, 1907.

96. CWB to HWF, Oct. 23, 1907; to WJ, Sept. 29, 1907; fragment in CWB's hand, Mar. 9, 1908; CWB to AM, Oct. 16, 1907; to WJ, Nov. 8, 1907 (copy).

97. CWB to WJ, Nov. 15, 1907 (copy); WJ to CWB Oct. 30, 1907 (typed copy). Carbon copies in typescript of both letters used in *AMTFI,* with James' signatures and corrections, are in CWB Coll., Nov. 1907 folder.

98. CWB to AM, Oct. 26, 1907, AM Papers; AM, "To Whom It May Concern," Oct. 27, 1907 (copy).

99. Stokes to CWB, Nov. 16, 1907; CWB to WJ, Nov. 22, 1907; to James A. MacDonald, Dec. 17, 1907; to Wm. V. Thorne, Dec. 15, 1907; to J. H. Glenn, Nov. 4, 1907; TWM, pp. 93–95, contains copy of CWB to Glenn, Feb. 25, 1908.

Chapter 7. Publication of *A Mind That Found Itself*

1. *AMTFI,* pp. vii, [xi]. The CWB Coll. contains draft of new version of Lounsbury's letter, Jan. 26, 1908, with note by CWB to the effect that the Mar. 24, 1907, letter had been revised in Lounsbury's presence.

2. *AMTFI,* pp. 289, 290, 318.

3. Anson Phelps Stokes, "The Beginnings of Mental Hygiene," Address Delivered at

350 ‡ Notes to Pages 88–94

the Founders Dinner of the Connecticut Society for Mental Hygiene, May 5 [1938?], pp. 4–5.

4. See Bert Kaplan, ed., *The Inner World of Mental Illness* (New York: Harper and Row, 1964) for a sampling of first-person ex-patient literature; other such excerpts and an extensive bibliography of this literature are in Walter Alvarez, *Minds That Came Back* (Philadelphia: J. B. Lippincott, 1961).

5. Albert Deutsch, *The Mentally Ill in America: A History of Their Care and Treatment from Colonial Times,* 2d ed., rev. and enl. (New York: Columbia University Press, 1949), pp. 306–07.

6. Trans. and ed. with introduction and discussion by Ida Macalpine and Richard A. Hunter (London: Dawson, 1955).

7. *Perceval's Narrative: A Patient's Account of His Psychosis, 1930–32,* ed. Gregory Bateson (Palo Alto: Stanford University Press, 1961), pp. v–vii.

8. *A Narrative of the Treatment Experienced by a Gentleman, during a State of Mental Derangement; Designed to Explain the Causes and the Nature of Insanity . . .* (London: Effingham Wilson, 1838), pp. 1–2.

9. William L. Parry-Jones, *The Trade in Lunacy: A Study of Private Madhouses in England in the Eighteenth and Nineteenth Centuries* (London: Routledge & Kegan Paul, 1972), pp. 230–31; *Perceval's Narrative,* p. viii.

10. Stokes, "Beginnings of Mental Hygiene," p. 6; CWB to GMB, Feb. 14, 1908.

11. See Scrapbook of clippings about *AMTFI* and also Excerpts from reviews of *AMTFI,* carbon copy of typescript, part I (78 pp.), both in CWB Coll.

12. *Boston Herald,* Mar. 14, 1908, in newspaper clippings, EM Coll.

13. CWB to GMB, Feb. 14, 1908; CWB, *Some Intimate Remarks, Delivered at the 25th Anniversary Dinner of the National Committee for Mental Hygiene, November 14th, 1934* (New York: National Committee for Mental Hygiene, 1935; rpt. from *Mental Hygiene,* 19, no. 9 [Jan. 1935]): 3–4; see also CWB to AM, Mar. [?], 1908, Mar. 14, 1908 (typed copy), letter dated Sunday [Mar. 1908], AM Papers.

14. CWB to Noble, Mar. 16, 1908.

15. WJ to CWB, Mar. 25, 1908 (copy).

16. *New York Times,* Mar. 22, 1908, p. 7.

17. Ibid.

18. Letter dated New York, Mar. 22, 1908, in *New York Times,* Mar. 24, 1908, p. 6.

19. WJ to CWB, Mar. 25, 1908 (copy); CWB to AM, Mar. 28, 1908 (typed copy), AM Papers.

20. CWB to AM, Mar. 23, 28, 1908 (typed copies), AM Papers.

21. *New York Times,* Mar. 30, 1908, p. 6.

22. CWB to GMB, Feb. 14, 1908; AM to CWB, Apr. 1, 1908.

23. *Baltimore Sun,* Apr. 26, 1908; *Cleveland Plain Dealer,* May 10, 1908, in Scrapbook of clippings about *AMTFI.*

24. Nathan G. Hale, Jr., *Freud and the Americans: The Beginnings of Psychoanalysis in the United States, 1876–1917* (New York: Oxford University Press, 1971), pp. 234–35. For periodical reviews see *Nation,* 27 (Mar. 19, 1908): 265–66; *Dial,* 44 (May 1, 1908): 278; *Independent,* 65 (Sept. 17, 1908): 663; *Outlook,* 88 (Mar. 21, 1908): 654–55; *American Review of Reviews,* 37 (Mar. 21, 1908): 383–84; *Literary Digest,* 36 (Apr. 4, 1909): 489. Final quotations from *Outlook* review.

25. CWB to GMB, Feb. 15, 1908.

26. *North American Review,* 188 (Apr. 1908): 611–14.

27. See, for example, *Lancet* review in Excerpts from reviews of *AMTFI,* carbon copy of typescript, pt. 1, pp. 14 ff.

28. Earl D. Bond, interview, 1966.

29. Wordin affidavit, Mar. 16, 1908; J. Franklin Wallace affidavits, Jan. 26, Mar. 6, Nov. 8, 1907; also CWB to Wallace, Nov. 1, 6, 1906. In Mar. 1908, near the time of his book's publication, Beers "had a very satisfactory interview with Dr. Givens," who had not heard about the book. "I guess he'll hear enough in future to make him wish my project had remained a delusion of grandeur," Beers reported to Meyer (CWB to AM [Mar. 1908], AM Papers).

30. CWB to AM, Feb. 20, 1908 (typed copy), AM Papers; AM to Noble, Feb. 13, 1908; to CWB, Feb. 18, 1908.

31. *Psychological Bulletin,* 5 (1908): 283–84, in AM, *Collected Papers,* ed. Eunice E. Winters, vol. IV (Baltimore: Johns Hopkins Press, 1951), pp. 254–55.

32. *American Journal of Insanity,* 65 (July 1908): 224, 216.

33. Ibid., pp. 222–23.

34. Ibid., pp. 223–25.

35. The authors of the preface to the German translation of *AMTFI,* Drs. Heinrich Meng and André Repond, who had met Clifford Beers several times, describe his ego as having undergone a total change during his illness; he was liberated from his hypochondria and developed self-discipline, self-education, self-reliance, and helpfulness (CWB, *Eine Seele die sich Wiederfand: Autobiographie des Begründers der "Geistigen Hygiene"* [Basel: Benno Schwabe & Co., 1941], p. 12). Years later Anton T. Boisen, in *The Exploration of the Inner World,* described his own illness and others' as successful struggles to resolve problems, resulting in "a socially valuable new self" (New York: Harper & Brothers, 1936; rpt. ed., 1962). Ernest Becker, in *The Revolution in Psychiatry: The New Understanding of Man* (Glencoe, Ill.: Free Press, 1964) sees Clifford Beers as creating meaning through his mental illness. "Beers staged a series of small dramas and one grandiose drama, including a counterspy game in which he enlisted a fellow patient. In these, each of his significant daily acts was connected to a broad pattern, and given abiding significance. . . . Hence even taking a pill becomes an act loaded with meaning, and *under the control of one's powers.* One was not a mere pawn of the doctor passively swallowing pills, but a locus of worldly control" (p. 93). Here we do not have a new personality emerging but an attempt to express oneself by creating a world in which the self is the center of all things. In a recent account of mental disorder that reflects the ideas and practices of the radical British psychiatrist R. D. Laing (Mary Barnes and Joseph Berke, *Mary Barnes: Two Accounts of a Journey through Madness* [New York: Ballantine Books, 1971]), Barnes characterizes her schizophrenic breakdowns as "going down" and "coming up," as rebirth, as liberation, leading to fulfillment as a painter. Laing himself came to regard schizophrenia as a form of liberation and transcendence. See his *Politics of Experience* (New York: Ballantine Books, 1967).

36. See, for example, CWB to AM, Oct. 29, 1907, AM Papers.

37. *American Journal of Insanity,* 65 (July 1908): 225, 226, 216, 227.

38. *Journal of Abnormal Psychology,* 5 (Apr.–May 1910): 39, 41.

39. Morton Prince to CWB, May 21, 29, 1908.

40. CWB to Prince, May 31, 1908 (copy).

41. M.E.T. to CWB, May 16, 1908; Mrs. W.D. to CWB, July 31, 1908; CWB to H.C.C., Apr. 22, 1908, Beers Clinic Papers; to Mrs. R.C.M., Mar. 26, 1908, Beers Clinic Papers.

42. Dr. Frank W. Page to CWB, May 5, 1908 (copy).

43. N.S.F. [Newell S. Ferry] to CWB, July 22, 1909 (copy); CWB to Edmund A. Christian, June 9, 1933; Christian to CWB, July 14, 1933 (2 letters). The widow of a St. Louis asylum superintendent wrote about her late husband's unappreciated humane policies (Emily Foote Runge to CWB, May 24, 1908).

44. Knox Maddox to CWB, May 27, 1908 (copy); John T. Mitler to CWB, May 23, 1908 (copy?).

45. Dr. William Russell to CWB, May 10, 1908; Welch to CWB, May 24, 1908.

46. Letters to CWB, all in 1908, from Weir Mitchell, Apr. 2 (copy); James B. Angell, Mar. 2; J. G. Schurman, Mar. 27; L. Farrand, Apr. 25; Jacob Riis, Apr. 3, 10 (copy); R. Yerkes,

Apr. 11 (copy); CWB to President T. Roosevelt, Mar. 4, 1908 (copy); Wm. Loeb, Secretary to the President, to CWB, Mar. 9, 1908; Ethel Roosevelt to Welch, Feb. 14, 1933, in *Twenty-Five Years After: Sidelights on the Mental Hygiene Movement and Its Founder,* ed. Wilbur L. Cross (New York: Doubleday, Doran & Company, 1934), p. 113.

47. CWB to AM [Mar. 1908], AM Papers; to WJ, Apr. 8, 1908; Excerpts from reviews of *AMTFI,* carbon copy of typescript, pt. II, pp. 137–39; copy of WJ letter in CWB to Aunt Mame, Apr. 21, 1908.

Chapter 8. A Reform Movement Launched

1. It should be noted that the description in this and following chapters of the Beers-Meyer collaboration differs from that presented in Eunice E. Winters, "Adolf Meyer and Clifford Beers, 1907–1910," *Bulletin of the History of Medicine,* 43 (Sept.–Oct. 1969): 414–43. Winters did not examine the Beers Collection and did not fully exploit the Meyer-Beers correspondence in the Meyer Papers; nor did she cite the two-volume typed version of Beers' "Troubles with Meyer" (TWM), to which she was given access.

2. AM, "To Whom It May Concern," Oct. 27, 1907, draft in AM's hand in AM Papers; typed copy in CWB Coll.

3. CWB to Irving Fisher, Feb. 18, 1936.

4. AM, "British Influences in Psychiatry and Mental Hygiene," the Fourteenth Maudsley Lecture, delivered before the Royal Medico-Psychological Association on May 17, 1933, in his *Collected Papers,* ed. Eunice E. Winters, vol. III (Baltimore: Johns Hopkins Press, 1951), p. 422 (rpt. from *Journal of Mental Science,* 79 [1933]).

5. At the time *AMTFI* came out, CWB received a letter from someone of radical persuasion who wanted him to collaborate on another book, "The Call of the Insane." Taking "decided exception" to his correspondent's opinion that abuses in mental hospitals were "inherent in this damnable capitalistic system" and that therefore "radical reforms" could not be expected, CWB advised him to adopt his own moderate and understated methods to win approval of his work. (George S. Gelvin to CWB, Mar. 18, 1908; CWB to Gelvin, Aug. 21, 1908.)

6. CWB to L. S. Barker, Nov. 5, 1907 (carbon copy).

7. CWB to HWF, June 24, 1906, Apr. 3, 1907; HWF to CWB, Mar. 26, 1907.

8. Barbara Sicherman, "The Quest for Mental Health in America, 1880–1917" (Ph.D. dissertation, Columbia University, 1967), pp. 52–53, 12–13, 60–65 (quotation from pp. 60–61).

9. CWB, Notebook, 3″ x 5″ [no. 5], Aug.–Sept. 1905, contains a citation to the *Proceedings* of the National Conference of Charities and Corrections for 1880 (vol. 7, pp. 141–51), in which was published information about the founding of the National Association for the Protection of the Insane. His remarks on his discovery of the National Association are contained in the text of a speech before the National Conference on Charities and Corrections, May 6, 1912.

10. AM to CWB, Apr. 23, 1908; Russell to CWB, Jan. 16, 1908.

11. CWB to WJ, Apr. 16, 1907 (draft 2); CWB, "Autobiography," p. 8.

12. HWF to CWB, Oct. 29, 1907.

13. CWB to AM, Oct. 26, 1907 (copy); to WJ, Apr. 16, Nov. 22, 1907 (draft 2); to Taylor, Nov. 25, 1907; to Stokes, Dec. 1, 1907.

14. CWB to AM, Nov. 14, 1907; to WJ, Nov. 22, 1907; to Taylor, Nov. 25, 1907; AM to CWB, Dec. 27, 6, 1907.

15. CWB to WJ, Nov. 22, 1907; WJ to CWB, Nov. 25, 1907.

16. Higginson to WJ, Dec. 4, 1907 (copy); Peabody to WJ, Dec. 12, 1907; WJ to CWB, Dec. 16, 1907; Peabody to CWB, Dec. 28, 1907.

17. CWB to WJ, Nov. 22, 1907; to Taylor, Nov. 25, 1907.

18. CWB to Taylor, Nov. 25, 1907; to Stokes, Dec. 1, 1907; AM to CWB, Dec. 6, 1907.

19. Abbott to CWB, Dec. 12, 1907; CWB to Abbott, Dec. 18, 1907 (copy); Abbott to CWB, Dec. 19, 1907.

20. Mitchell to CWB, Dec. 19, 1907.

21. Lathrop to CWB, Jan. 2, 1908; Hoch to CWB, Jan. 4, 1908.

22. See list of acceptances, Jan. 25, 1907 (carbon copy).

23. Welch quoted in CWB, red memo book, 2¼″ x 4¾″, Jan. 21, 1908; Welch to Rob. de Forest, to Mr. Devine, to Dr. [J. S.] Billings, all Feb. 17, 1909; WJ to CWB, Jan. 9, 1908.

24. Clipping from *New York Sun,* Mar. [23?], 1908 (dateline Mar. 21).

25. CWB to George McAneny, Jan. 10, 1908.

26. See list appended to CWB to Stokes, Mar. 14, 1908 (mimeographed).

27. CWB to Gates, Mar. 9, 1908 (copy); Gates to CWB, Mar. 13, 1908; CWB, Report of interview with Starr Murphy in Excerpts from reviews of *AMTFI,* carbon copy of typescript, pt. II, pp. 54–55.

28. Page to CWB, May 14, 1907; WJ to CWB, Dec. [4?], 1908 (copy).

29. Clipping from *New York Sun,* Mar. [23?], 1908 (dateline Mar. 21); also CWB to McAneny, Jan. 10, 1908.

30. See CWB to Stokes, Apr. 7, 1908.

31. See CWB to Arthur Hadley, Mar. 28, 1908 (copy); to Gifford Pinchot, Feb. 28, 1908; Paton to CWB, May 30, 1907; Welch to CWB, May 24, 1908; AM to Noble, Feb. 13, 1908.

32. CWB to WJ, Apr. 8, 1908; see also CWB to AM, Sunday, Mar. 23, [1908], E. Winters version, p. 2, AM Papers; CWB to Stokes, Apr. 7, 1908.

33. Walcott to WJ, Apr. 12, [1908] (copy); WJ to CWB, Apr. 16, 1908 (copy).

34. See Sicherman, "Quest for Mental Health in America," pp. 281 ff.; John Chynoweth Burnham, "Psychiatry, Psychology, and the Progressive Movement," *American Quarterly,* 3 (Winter 1960): 457–65.

35. See Sicherman, "Quest for Mental Health in America," pp. 285–86; Richard H. Shryock, *National Tuberculosis Association, 1904, 1954* (New York: National Tuberculosis Association, 1957); S. Adolphus Knopf, *A History of the National Tuberculosis Assocation: The Anti-Tuberculosis Movement in the United States* (New York: National Tuberculosis Association, 1922); Frank J. Bruno, *Trends in Social Work* (New York: Columbia University Press, 1948); Robert H. Bremner, *From the Depths: The Discovery of Poverty in the United States* (New York: New York University Press, 1956); Allen F. Davis, *Spearheads for Reform: The Social Settlements and the Progressive Movement, 1890–1914* (New York: Oxford University Press, 1967); Roy Lubove, *The Professional Altruist: The Emergence of Social Work as a Career, 1880–1930* (New York: Atheneum, 1971).

36. Lubove, in *The Professional Altruist,* has a perceptive discussion of the evolution of social work.

37. AM, "The Birth and Development of the Mental Hygiene Movement," *Mental Hygiene,* 19 (Jan. 1935): 30; AM, "British Influences in Psychiatry and Mental Hygiene," in his *Collected Papers,* III, 419.

38. Quoted in Sicherman, "Quest for Mental Health in America," pp. 290, 289, from AM, "After-Care and Prophylaxis and the Historical Physician," *Journal of Nervous and Mental Disease,* 24 (Feb. 1907): 113–16.

39. AM, "Thirty-Five Years of Psychiatry in the United States and Our Present Outlook," president's address read at the eighty-fourth annual meeting of the American Psychiatric Association, in his *Collected Papers,* II, 8–9 (rpt. from *American Journal of Psychiatry,* vol. 85 [1928–1929]).

40. AM, "Birth and Development of the Mental Hygiene Movement," p. 29.

41. *American Journal of Insanity,* 64 (July 1907): 6.

42. AM, "The Role of the Mental Factors in Psychiatry," in his *Collected Papers,* II, 581–90 (rpt. from *American Journal of Insanity,* 65 [1908]: 39–52).

43. Nathan G. Hale, Jr., *Freud and the Americans: The Beginnings of Psychoanalysis in the United States, 1876–1917* (New York: Oxford University Press, 1971), p. 99.

44. George M. Beard, *American Nervousness: Its Causes and Consequences; a Supplement to Nervous Exhaustion (Neurasthenia)* (New York: G. P. Putnam's Sons, 1881; rpt. ed., New York: Arno Press and the *New York Times,* 1972); S. Weir Mitchell, *Doctor and Patient* (Philadelphia: J. B. Lippincott Company, 1888; rpt. ed., New York: Arno Press, 1972); see also Richard D. Walter, *S. Weir Mitchell, M.D. — Neurologist: A Medical Biography* (Springfield, Ill.: Charles C Thomas, 1970), chap. 9.

45. Dorothy Ross, *G. Stanley Hall, the Psychologist as Prophet* (Chicago: University of Chicago Press, 1972), pp. 160–61, 179.

Chapter 9. The Connecticut Society and Founding the National Committee

1. CSMH, Minutes, May 6, 1908; CWB to WJ, June 16, Nov. 13, 1908; CWB, "Some Intimate Aspects of the Origin and Growth of the Mental Hygiene Movement," unpub. version [no. 1] of a talk [1933?], typescript, pp. 9–10.

2. *New Haven Journal Courier,* May 7, 1908; *New Haven Evening Register,* May 7, 1908; CSMH, Minutes, June 4, 1908; copy of *Evening Register* editorial, May 6, 1908 in CWB Coll.

3. AM to CWB, May 5, 1908, in TWM, p. 68.

4. 1st Preliminary Prospectus, in pencil, May 1908.

5. CSMH, Minutes, June 4, Nov. 12, 1908; CWB to WJ, June 16, 1908; to Dr. Newell S. Ferry, Aug. 15, 1908.

6. CWB to WJ, June 16–18, 1908.

7. CWB to CJ, June 30, 1908, MFA.

8. AM to CWB, June 1, 1908, in TWM, pp. 140–41.

9. July 19, 1908, scrapbook of clippings, CWB Coll.

10. Welch to CWB, July 10, 1908; Barker to CWB, July 2, 1908; CWB to WJ, June 16, 1908; to John S. Phipps, June 24, 1908; George E. Goden, Secretary, to CWB, Aug. 4, 1908, in CWB, "Account of the Organization of the NCMH," in Excerpts from reviews of *AMTFI,* carbon copy of typescript, pt. II, p. 185; CWB to AM, Oct. 19, 1908, in TWM, pp. 198–99.

11. CWB to Welch, July 13, 1908 (copy).

12. AM to CWB, June 25, 1908, in TWM, p. 142.

13. AM, "Opening of the Henry Phipps Psychiatric Clinic," Introduction to the Special Number of the *American Journal of Insanity,* 69 (1913): 835–36, in his *Collected Papers,* ed. Eunice E. Winters, vol. II (Baltimore: Johns Hopkins Press, 1951), p. 176; AM, "Thirty-Five Years of Psychiatry in the United States and Our Present Outlook," ibid., II, 9, 220; AM, "Stewart Paton," ibid., III, 551–52 (rpt. from *Journal of Nervous and Mental Disease,* 95 [1942]: 518–23). C. B. Farrar, in a memoir of Paton, confirmed that Paton had taught Welch about psychiatry ("Historical Notes: I Remember Stewart Paton," *American Journal of Psychiatry,* 118 [Aug. 1960]: 160–62).

14. CWB to AM, July 8, 1908; AM to CWB, July 9, 1908.

15. CWB to WJ, July 31, 1908.

16. CWB to AM, July 21, 1908 (copy with penciled comment sent to WJ, July 22, 1908); see also CWB to Rev. Whittingham, Sept. 25, 1908 (copy).

17. AM to CWB, July 29, 1908, in TWM, p. 163; AM to CWB, Apr. 23, 1908.

18. TWM, pp. 164–65.

19. CWB to WJ, Aug. 12, 1908.

20. WJ to CWB, Aug. 16, 1908.

21. CWB to WJ, Aug. 31, 1908.

22. Favill to CWB, Oct. 5, 1908 (copy); see CWB to AM, Oct. 12, 1908 (copy) re letter from Lathrop on founding an Illinois society.

23. It is unlikely that Beers was aware of the similar work of Herman M. Biggs in New York or of Dr. Lawrence F. Flick of Philadelphia, who with others started local and state anti-tuberculosis societies in the late 1890s (Richard H. Shryock, *National Tuberculosis Association, 1904, 1954* [New York: National Tuberculosis Association, 1957], p. 57).

24. CWB to AM, Oct. 12, 1908 (copy); also CWB to Julia Lathrop, Oct. 12, 1908, Rockford College Archives.

25. AM to CWB, Oct. 18, 1908 (copy).

26. AM to Lathrop, Oct. 22, 1908, Rockford College Archives.

27. Henry Phipps to CWB, Oct. 21, 1908; CWB to WJ, Dec. 17, 1908; AM to CWB, Dec. 19, 22, 1908.

28. CWB to CJ, Oct. 1, 1908, EM Coll.; see also CWB to CJ, Oct. 3, 1907, and poem in CWB's hand, July–Sept. 1907, EM Coll.

29. CWB to [CJ], Oct. 20, 27, 1908, EM Coll.; to CJ, May 19, 1912, MFA; CJ to CWB, Oct. 1, 1908, 8 P.M., letter no. 5; CJ to K [CWB], Oct. 11, 1908, both in EM Coll.

30. For biographical information on Clara Jepson and her family see Emily L. Martin, "Clara Louise Jepson Beers (December 20, 1874–September 8, 1966), a Biographical Sketch," prepared at the request of the American Foundation for Mental Hygiene, Inc. (New York: 1966, mimeographed copy).

31. CWB, Notebook, 3" x 5", brown, 1905.

32. CWB to Dearest [CJ], May 8, 1910; to CJ, May 18, 1910, both in EM Coll.; CWB to CJ, Sept. 3, 1909, MFA.

33. Welch to CWB, Nov. 30, 190[8].

34. CWB to AM, Oct. 27, 1908 (copy); see also AM to CWB, Oct. 27, 1908 (copy).

35. AM to CWB, Nov. 9, 1908; AM to CWB, n.d. (probably Nov. 1908); CWB to WJ, Nov. 25, 1908. Dr. Noble also thought that prevention would prove more difficult than Beers implied (Noble to CWB [probably Nov. 1908]).

36. Bryce to WJ, Nov. 9, 1908; George P. McLean to Gov. George L. Lilley, Nov. 25, 1908; McLean to Pinchot, Nov. 25, 1908; Welch to Cardinal Gibbons, Nov. 27, 1908 (copy); Gibbons to CWB, Nov. 28, 1908 (copy); CWB to Gibbons, Dec. 15, 1908; CWB to Welch, Dec. 19, 1908, all in CWB Coll.; note on copy of Gibbons to CWB, Nov. 28, 1908, in CWB to CJ, Dec. 25, 1908, MFA. Using Pinchot's name, Beers composed a letter to the newly elected president of the United States, William H. Taft, to whom he wished to send his book; appropriate to Pinchot's interests he spoke of the need to conserve the mental as well as physical resources of the nation. This letter was never sent. (CWB to President of the U.S.A., Nov. 29, 30, 1908.) By this time, Pinchot informed Beers, Theodore Roosevelt had read *AMTFI*, but nothing came of it (Pinchot to CWB, Nov. 30, 190[8?] [copy]).

37. See, for example, Mary E. M. Morrell to CWB, Sept. 19, 1909; H. H. Osborne to National Society for Mental Hygiene, Oct. 6 [1908?]; Jessie G. Farrell to CWB, Dec. 6, 1908; Charles P. Hone to CWB, Oct. 24, 1908 (copy).

38. CSMH, Minutes, Nov. 13, 1908.

39. Ibid.; Mary Meyer to CWB, Mar. 16, 1908, in TWM, p. 116.

40. "An Example of the Kind of Work That Is Done by the After Care Committee of the Connecticut Society for Mental Hygiene," unsigned typed single page; CWB to AM, Jan. 18 (copy), 27, 1909.

41. AM to CWB, Jan. 19, 1909, in TWM, pp. 236, 241.

42. CSMH, Minutes, Nov. 13, 1908.

43. CWB to WJ, Nov. 25, Dec. 17, 1908.

44. AM to CWB, Mar. 23, 1909, CWB Coll.; AM to CWB, Jan. 16, 1909, in TWM, p. 232; AM to CWB, Mar. 27, 1909, Winters summary, AM Papers; CWB, re bill, Mar. 11, 1909, CWB Coll.; Russell to CWB, Mar. 14, 1909, in TWM, pp. 318-19.

45. AM to CWB, Dec. 22, 1908.

46. CWB to AM, Dec. 22, 1908 (copy).

47. CWB to AM, Dec. 23, 31, 1908; AM to CWB, Jan. 16, 1909, in TWM, p. 233.

48. CWB to AM, Jan. 27, 1909, in TWM, p. 238; Noble to CWB, Feb. [?], 1909, in TWM, pp. 242-43.

49. CWB to WJ, Feb. 8, 1909. Before *AMTFI* was published, Beers, then appealing to Rockefeller through Gates, had asked James to send page proofs of the book to Strong. Beers could not do it for fear Gates would think he was going over his head to Rockefeller. All Beers wanted was to interest Strong, as a psychologist, in the movement. "Then having secured his support, there will be two roads open to me when the time comes to secure part of the Rockefeller fortune in behalf of the cause." (CWB to WJ [before Feb. 1908], [typed copy, first page missing], filed with Rockefeller appeal in TWM.)

50. WJ to CWB, Feb. 9, 1909 (copy).

51. WJ to CWB, Feb. 14, 1909; Strong to CWB, Feb. 11, 1909; CWB to WJ, Feb. 12, 1909.

52. AM to CWB, Feb. 15, 1909; CWB to WJ, Feb. 18, 1909; to AM, Mar. 1, 1909 (copy).

53. CWB to Walter Wyman, Feb. 15, 1909; *AMTFI*, 9th ed., pp. 266-71; "Meeting for the Founding of a National Committee of Mental Hygiene" [minutes], Feb. 19, 1909, CWB Coll.; CWB to CJ, Feb. 19, 1909, EM Coll.

54. CWB to WJ, Feb. 18, 1909; Welch to CWB, Feb. 9, 1909.

55. "Meeting for the Founding of a National Committee of Mental Hygiene" [minutes], Feb. 19, 1909.

56. CWB to CJ, Feb. 19, 1909, EM Coll.

57. CWB to WJ, Feb. 22, 1909.

58. AM to CWB, Feb. 27, 1909; WJ to AM, Feb. 24, 1909; AM to WJ, Feb. 26, 1909 (copies), AM Papers; CWB to Veitch, Mar. 2, 1909.

59. CWB to AM, Mar. 1, 1909 (copy sent to WJ).

60. AM to CWB, Mar. 2, 1909 (copy).

61. CWB to AM, Mar. 4, 1909.

62. WJ to CWB, Feb. 21, 1909 (copy).

63. CWB to WJ, Feb. 22, 1909.

64. CWB to Mrs. Stephen T. Cooper, July 2, 1909, Beers Clinic Papers.

65. WJ to AM, Feb. 24, 1909 (copy), AM Papers.

66. AM to WJ, Feb. 26, 1909 (copy), AM Papers.

67. WJ to AM, Feb. 27, 1909, 2 letters (copies), AM Papers.

68. AM to WJ, Mar. 2, 1909 (copy), AM Papers.

69. CWB, penciled note to WJ, on copy of CWB to Meyer, Mar. 1, 1909.

70. WJ to AM, Mar. 3, 1909; AM to CWB, Apr. 3, 1909; CWB to AM, Apr. 5, 1909 (copies), AM Papers.

71. CWB to Aunt Mame, Mar. 30, 1909.

72. CWB to AM, Dec. 24, 1908 (copy); M. Meyer to CWB, Dec. 27, 1908.

Chapter 10. "The Ox and the 'Wild Ass'"

1. CWB to AM, [mid-Mar.] 1909; AM to CWB, Mar. 15, 1909, in TWM, pp. 314-15; CWB to WJ, Apr. 1 or 2, 1909, in TWM, p. 322.

2. WJ to CWB, Apr. 4, 1909, in TWM, pp. 322-23; CWB to WJ, Apr. 6, 1909; AM to CWB, Apr. 12, 13, 1909, in TWM, pp. 336-39; Chittenden to CWB, Apr. [?], 1909, in TWM, p. 323; CWB to Russell, Apr. 19, 1909, in TWM, pp. 346-48.

3. AM, Drafts of Rockefeller appeal, no. 4a [Oct.-Nov. 1909?]; AM, "Reasons for a Start as a Private Organization," [1909]. Meyer was just not convinced that the National Committee was on the right track; logically his position would lead to beginning work on a small scale, with requests for larger sums as progress was made.

4. CWB, Address, 24th Anniversary, H.P.P.C., Apr. 17, '37 (typescript), p. 312.

5. CWB to Aunt Mame, May 9, 1909; to WJ, May 9, 1909; AM to CWB, May 17, 1909, in TWM, pp. 357–59; AM, "Forecast of the Work and a Statement of the Needs of the National Committee for Mental Hygiene," in TWM, pp. 380–86.

6. WJ to Rockefeller, June 1, 1909, in TWM, pp. 247–49.

7. WJ to Rockefeller, June 1, 1909 (copy in CWB's hand); AM, "Forecast of the Work," in TWM, pp. 380–86; CWB to Stokes, May 24, 1909, in TWM, p. 367; AM to CWB, May 25, 1909, in TWM, p. 368.

8. CWB to Meyer, report of conversation with Stokes, June 19, 1909 (copy).

9. AM to CWB, June 29, 1909; WJ to CWB, June 27, 1909, in TWM, p. 401; CWB to Ellenbogen, Oct. 30, 1909, in TWM, pp. 482–83; CWB to Dr. G. C. Ferrari, July 9, 1909.

10. CWB to AM, Sept. 14, 19, 1909; CWB, "The Number of the Insane," Apr. 9, 1909 (part of Rockefeller appeal); CWB to AM, Sept. 19, 1909 (part of Rockefeller appeal); AM to CWB, Sept. 27 (copy), 28, 1909.

11. CEB Case Records, State Records Center, Rocky Hill, Conn. (microfilm).

12. CWB to AM, Aug. 1, 1909 (copy); CWB to Mrs. Jepson, Aug. 25, 1909, MFA.

13. CWB to Mrs. Jepson, Aug. 25, 1909, MFA.

14. The list of possible topics was wide-ranging, encompassing a history of mental illness and its treatment from ancient times, an analysis of contemporary knowledge and trends, a discussion of past reform movements and the present one, and proposed chapters on hospital administration, model legislation, and almost everything else connected with the subject of mental illness (CWB to Paton, Sept. 14, 1909, in TWM, pp. 316–435; to AM, Sept. 30, 1909, AM Papers).

15. CWB to AM, Oct. 7, 1909; report of interview with Stokes, Oct. 7, 1909, both in TWM, pp. 447–49.

16. CWB to Stokes, Oct. 8, 1909, in TWM, pp. 449–54.

17. TWM, pp. 458–59.

18. AM to CWB, n.d. [1909?]; CWB to WJ, Oct. 19, 1909; to Meyer, Oct. 14, 1909, both in TWM, pp. 461–64.

19. Stokes to CWB, Oct. 20, 1909, in TWM, p. 465; CWB to AM, Oct. 21, 1909, in TWM, p. 467.

20. CWB to AM, Oct. 27, 1909; AM to CWB, Apr. 1909; CWB to AM, Oct. 21, 1909, in TWM, pp. 465, 468; AM to CWB, Oct. 25, 1909; CWB to Paton, Oct. 23, 1909.

21. Paton to CWB, Oct. 25, 1909, in TWM, pp. 469–71.

22. CWB to AM, Oct. 27, 1909, in TWM, pp. 473–75; Russell to CWB, Nov. 27, 1909; CWB to AM, Nov. 14, 1909, Winters Summary, AM Papers; CWB to AM, Nov. 4, 1909, in TWM, p. 475; AM to CWB, Oct. 25, 1909 (copy); AM to WJ, n.d., in TWM, p. 608.

23. CWB to AM, Oct. 21, 1909, in TWM, p. 465.

24. CWB to AM, Nov. 8, 1909, AM Papers; CWB to AM, Nov. 3, 1909.

25. CWB to Lathrop, Nov. 26, 1909; Paton to CWB, Nov. 28, 1909; CWB to AM, Nov. 27, 1909, AM Papers; to Louise Nearing, Sept. 29, 1909, Beers Clinic Papers.

26. TWM, pp. 515–16; CWB to AM, Nov. 26, 1909, in TWM, p. 521; AM to CWB, Nov. 29, 1909, in TWM, p. 324; AM to CWB, Nov. 29, 1909; to Paton, Dec. 3, 1909.

27. AM to CWB, Nov. 29, 1909 (copy).

28. CWB to Gibbons, Nov. 29, 1909 (copy); T. R. Whitney to CWB, Nov. 30, 1909.

29. TWM, p. 530; Phipps to CWB, Nov. 30, 1909.

30. CWB to Paton, Dec. 1, 1909 (copy), AM Papers; AM to Paton, Dec. 3, 1909, AM Papers; TWM, pp. 543–45; CWB to Paton, Dec. 10, 1909, in TWM, p. 551.

31. CWB to AM, Dec. 14, 1909, Feb. 3, 8, 1, 1910, all in AM Papers.

32. CWB to AM, Jan. 13, 1910, AM Papers; CWB to CJ, Jan. 22, 1910.

33. CWB to AM, Jan. 22, 31, Feb. 1, 1910; Pollock to CWB, Feb. 4, 1910, all in AM Papers; CWB to Mrs. Ketchum, Mar. 8, 1910, Beers Clinic Papers.

34. CWB to Mr. and Mrs. P. A. McQuaid, Dec. 31, 1909; also report of conversation with AM, Dec. 26, 1909, in TWM, p. 569.

35. CWB to Dearest!, Dec. 20, 1909.

36. CWB to WJ, Jan. 11, 1910; AM to Paton, Dec. 11, 1909, AM Papers; CWB to WJ, Feb. 28, 1910.

37. CWB to WJ, Feb. 28, 1910.

38. CWB to AM, Feb. 18, 1910, in TWM, p. 584; to WJ, Apr. 28, 1910; Stokes to AM, Feb. 21, 1910, in TWM, p. 584.

39. AM to Blumer, Feb. 19, 1910 (copy).

40. CWB to WJ, Feb. 28, 1910.

41. Chittenden to AM, Feb. 25, 1910, AM Papers; Blumer to AM, Feb. 25, 1910 (copy).

42. CWB to WJ, Feb. 13, 1910. Apparently Beers told others about his new scheme; one correspondent turned down a suggestion from him that a Massachusetts Society be organized with outside help: "Would it not be better that Mass. should finance her own Association?" (Henriette Cushing to CWB, Feb. 27, 1910 [copy]).

43. AM to Blumer, Feb. 26, 1910, in TWM, pp. 594–95; AM to Stokes, Feb. 25, 1910 (copy); AM to Dr. H. B. Favill, May 8, 1910 (copy).

44. In 1902, describing the initiation of a new program at the Pathological Institute for the New York state hospitals, Meyer said, "After long hesitation . . . and only after I received full assurance that the intention was serious, and that no preemptory creation but a judicial growth out of actual felt needs and existing opportunities was looked for did I undertake the task." ("Aims and Plans for the Pathological Institute for the New York State Hospitals," paper read on Ward's Island, Dec. 1, 1902, in AM, *Collected Papers,* ed. Eunice Winters, vol. II [Baltimore: Johns Hopkins Press, 1951], p. 91.)

45. AM to WJ, Feb. [26?], 28, 1910, in TWM, p. 610; AM to WJ, early Mar. 1910, in TWM, pp. 607–10; CWB to AM, Mar. 6, 1910.

46. AM to Chittenden, Mar. 3, 1910.

47. CWB to WJ, Mar. 4, 1910; also Mar. 6, 1910, in TWM, p. 614.

48. WJ to CWB, Mar. 3, 1910 (copy), [early 1910].

49. WJ to CWB, Mar. 4, 11, 1910.

50. Ralph Barton Perry, *The Thought and Character of William James,* briefer version (New York: George Braziller, 1954), p. 362.

51. CWB to WJ, Jan. 16, 1910.

52. WJ to CWB, Jan. 17, 1910 (copy). In later years CWB collected messages and letters from James, of which he accumulated some "thirty or forty" (CWB to W. S. Carter, June 20, 1933).

53. Henry P. Walcott to WJ, Mar. 6, 1910 (copy); WJ to CWB [1910]; CWB to WJ, Mar. 10, 1910; WJ to CWB, Mar. 5, 1910.

54. AM to CWB, Mar. 12, 1910, AM Papers.

55. TWM, pp. 625–27; AM to Stokes, Mar. 12, 1910, AM Papers.

56. AM to Bancroft, Apr. 4, 1910, Winters Summary, AM Papers.

57. Mary C. Acker to CWB, Mar. 9, 1910 (copy with note at bottom in CWB's hand).

58. Blumer to Emerson, Apr. [1910].

59. CWB to WJ, Mar. 18, 1910.

60. AM to Chittenden, Apr. 10, 1910, AM Papers.

61. CWB to GMB, Apr. 18, 1910.

62. AM to Favill, May 8, 1910. Mary Meyer wrote Beers that she believed her husband could do most for the cause by devoting himself to his clinic (Mrs. Meyer to CWB, May 28, 1910, in TWM, p. 700).

63. Gay Wilson Allen, *William James, a Biography* (New York: Viking Press, 1967), pp. 480–81; WJ to CWB, May 24, 1910 (copy of postcard).

64. CWB to Dearest, May 19, 1910, MFA; CWB to CJ, May 8, 1910; see also CWB to CJ, Aug. 7, 1910, EM Coll.

65. CWB to AM, June 10, 1910, in TWM, p. 707.

66. AM to Bancroft, Apr. 4, 1910, AM Papers.

67. Russell to AM, July 13, 1910 (copy), AM Papers; AM to Russell, July 13, 1910.

68. AM to Russell, July 13, 1910; TWM, p. 710; AM to CWB, Aug. 14, 1910.

69. CWB to Louise, Aug. 15, 1910.

70. CWB to AM, Sept. 6, 1910, in TWM, p. 713.

71. Ibid.

72. CWB to Louise Nearing, July 12, 1910 (copy), Beers Clinic Papers; see also CWB to Mrs. H. M. Arnold, May 31, 1910 (copy?), Beers Clinic Papers, in which he advised that at present the decision was against establishing state mental hygiene societies.

73. Manhattan Hotel Meeting, Sept. 12, 1910, in TWM, pp. 720–22, 732–33.

74. AM to CWB, Dec. 10, 1910; AM to Favill, Dec. 10, 1910.

75. Favill to Chittenden, May 26, 1910, confidential; CWB to Dearest, May 19, July 31, 1910, MFA.

76. CWB to AM, Dec. 19, 1910; AM to Favill, Dec. 28, 1910.

77. For example, talk by Phyllis Greenacre at Payne Whitney Psychiatric Clinic, New York City, Feb. 1969; talk by Oskar Diethelm at Payne Whitney Psychiatric Clinic, 1968. So terrified of Meyer were new staff members that dead silence reigned during the first staff meeting of every year, and when Meyer took his vacation during the summer no patients were admitted.

78. AM, "Mental Abnormalities in Children During Primary Education," in his *Collected Papers,* IV, 329, 333 (rpt. from *Transactions of the Illinois Society for Child Study,* 1895); AM, "Mental and Moral Health in a Constructive School Program," ibid., p. 366 (rpt. from *Suggestions of Modern Science Concerning Education,* 1925); Barbara Sicherman, "The Quest for Mental Health in America, 1880–1917" (Ph.D. dissertation, Columbia University, 1967), p. 385.

79. For an examination of the health center movement see Lucy Michelle Candib, "A Social Study of the Health Center Movement: A New Approach to Public Health History" (B.A. thesis, Harvard University, 1968).

80. Oskar Diethelm, "History of Swiss Psychiatry," talk at Payne Whitney Psychiatric Clinic, 1972, and personal conversation. Meyer, recollecting his problems during the early years at the Phipps Clinic, said, "I found myself engaged in the development of a partly supported private university hospital for study and treatment and teaching and research, with an organization that had to be maintained at a level of expense putting upon us a serious responsibility of earning 60 per cent to 70 per cent of our support from our exclusively voluntary patients — an economic situation quite different from what I had been accustomed to (when working in state hospitals). As a matter of fact, I should have liked best a model of community hospital as a basis for service, teaching, and research. But American communities were not prepared to finance a project for which they as yet saw no need." (AM, "Thirty-Five Years of Psychiatry," in his *Collected Papers,* II, 13.) This was a need that Clifford Beers wanted a national organization to dramatize.

81. "Visit with Dr. Meyer in Baltimore," carbon copy of typescript, probably by Paul O. Komora or Earl Bond, TWS Coll.

82. CWB, "Some Intimate Aspects of the Origin and Growth of the Mental Hygiene Movement," unpub. version [no. 1] of talk, n.d. [1933?], p. 10; CWB, "Some Intimate Aspects of the Origin and Growth of the Mental Hygiene Movement," typescript version of talk [no. 2], with notes by CWB, n.d. [1933?], p. 6.

83. CWB, Address, 24th anniversary, H.P.P.C., Apr. 17, 1937 (typescript), pp. 2–5.

Chapter 11. Phipps "To the Rescue"

1. CWB to C. E. B[each]; to [Jessie I. Belyea], Mar. 25, 1911, Beers Clinic Papers; to Belyea, July 23, June 8, 1912; C. E. B[each] to Belyea, Dec. 30, 1930; CWB to Charles B. Kellogg, Jan. 16, 1911 (copy).

2. Dr. A. A. Atkinson to CWB, Sept. 10, 1910, Beers Clinic Papers; CWB to Atkinson, Sept. 26, 1910, Beers Clinic Papers; to Atkinson, May 5, 1911; Atkinson to CWB, May 3, 1911; CWB to Atkinson, Oct. 5, 1910 (copy), Beers Clinic Papers; Atkinson to CWB, Sept. 28, 1910, Beers Clinic Papers.

3. For example: CWB to C. E. B[each], May 25, 1911; in Beers Clinic Papers: CWB to Favill, Dec. 16, 1908 (copy); to John Petnot, Apr. 20, 1911 (copy); to Miss A., June 20, 1910; to Mrs. S., Aug. 11, 1910; field worker to Miss C., May 10, 1910.

4. CWB to Russell, Jan. 23, 1911; to CJ, Jan. 17, 1911, card, EM Coll. The typed version has been cited as TWM. Clara did want Clifford to write about his work in a sequel to *AMTFI,* but it is unlikely that "Troubles with Dr. Meyer" was what she had in mind.

5. CWB, Summary of minutes of third annual meeting of the NCMH, Jan. 28, 1911; also CWB to Hoch, Feb. 1, 1911; to Jane Addams, Jan. 17, 1911.

6. CWB to Stokes, Jan. 25, 1911.

7. CWB to Hoch, Feb. 1, 1911 (copy).

8. Barker to Chittenden, Mar. 31, 1911.

9. CWB to Addams, Feb. 27, 1911; Addams to CWB, Mar. 1, 1911; also CWB to Hoch, Feb. 3, 1911; Hoch to CWB, May 26, 1911 (copy).

10. CWB to Lathrop, Aug. 14, 1911; Stokes to [?], Nov. 1, 1911.

11. CWB to Lathrop, Aug. 14, 1911; Favill to CWB, Nov. 27, 1911.

12. Hoch to Welch, Nov. 10, 1911; CWB to Hoch, Jan. 16, 1911 (copy); Hoch to CWB, Jan. 18, 1911 (copy); CWB to Addams, Feb. 27, 1911; to Hoch, Apr. 24, 1911; see also Barbara Sicherman, "The Quest for Mental Health in America, 1880–1917" (Ph.D. dissertation, Columbia University, 1967), pp. 319–20.

13. CWB to Hoch, May 26, 1911: "please have this rewritten on your letter head and returned to me"; draft from Hoch to CWB, May 26, 1911, follows.

14. Stokes to CWB, June 8, 1911.

15. Russell to Morris Loeb, June 26, 1911 (copy); CWB to Paton, July 10, 1911 (copy); Loeb to CWB, July 10, 1911 (copy); Phipps to Chittenden, July 14, 1911 (copy); GMB to CWB, July 28, 1911; Phipps to CWB, Oct. 19, 1911.

16. CWB to Gates, Nov. 1, 1911 (copy); Stokes to Gates, Nov. 1, 1911; Chittenden to Gates, Nov. 1, 1911; Gates to CWB, Nov. 3, 1911.

17. CWB, Address, 24th anniversary, H.P.P.C., Apr. 17, 1937 (typescript), p. 4.

18. Welch to CWB, Nov. 4, 1911; letter to Phipps, prepared Nov. 8, 1911; CWB to Welch, Nov. 6, 1911; Welch to Russell, Nov. 22, 1911. This last letter, a request for such assurance, may have been *pro forma,* as Russell sent his assurance on Nov. 21 (Russell to Welch, Nov. 21, 1911 [copy]), or possibly one of the two letters is misdated.

19. CWB to Welch, Nov. 13, 1911; AM to Barker, Dec. 21, 1911; Welch to CWB, Nov. 17, 1911.

20. John Koren to CWB, Nov. 27, 1911; CWB to Koren, Nov. 29, 1911; to Hoch, July 11, 1912; to Noble, Sept. 30, 1912; to Russell, Sept. 30, 1912; *Summaries of the Laws Relating to the Commitment and Care of the Insane in the United States* (New York: National Committee for Mental Hygiene, 1912).

21. CWB, Summary of these events, attached to Welch to CWB, Nov. 4, 1911.

22. Phipps to CWB, Dec. 5, 1911.

23. CWB, "Verbatim Account of My Interview with Mr. Phipps," Dec. 11, 1911; CWB to Dearest, Dec. 11, 1911, 5:20 P.M. The next day the check arrived, with Phipps' note that it was "to be exclusively for your own use" (Phipps to CWB, Dec. 12, 1911).

24. CWB to GMB, Dec. 25, 1911; to Mrs. James, Dec. 30, 1911 (copy); to Welch, Apr. 5, 1912; Welch to Gates, May 17, 1912.

25. CWB to Lathrop, Aug. 14, 1911 (copy).

26. CWB to George Blumer, president, CSMH, Jan. 16, 1913, carbon copy of longer of two letters of same date.

27. "Suggestions" appended to CWB to Blumer, Jan. 16, 1913, carbon copy of shorter of two letters of same date.

28. "The Meaning of the Mental Hygiene Movement as Shown by Work of Societies for Mental Hygiene," to be delivered at the Southern Sociological Congress, New Orleans, Apr. 1916 (typescript), p. 9.

29. Blumer to CWB, May 9, 16, 1913; CWB to W. E. Blackman, Dec. 30, 1913, Mar. 6, 1914, Beers Clinic Papers.

30. Belyea to Blackman, Mar. 10, 1913, Beers Clinic Papers; CWB to Mary Bok, Feb. 7, 1927.

31. CWB to CJ, Feb. 24, 1915.

32. CWB, Transcript of remarks at First International Congress on Mental Hygiene, May 6, 1930 (carbon copy of typescript), p. 15.

33. CWB, draft of speech, May 6 [1912], Chicago, pp. 1–4.

34. CWB to Dearest [probably in Feb. 1912], MFA.

35. CWB to Dearest, June 1, 1911, MFA; Apr. 15, 1912, EM Coll.; June 5, 1912.

36. CWB to Dearest, June 1, 1911, MFA; also July 31, 1910, CWB Coll.

37. Emily L. Martin, "Clara Louise Jepson Beers (December 20, 1874–September 8, 1966), a Biographical Sketch," prepared at the request of the American Foundation for Mental Hygiene, Inc. (New York: 1966, mimeographed copy), p. 4; correspondence between CJ and her parents, 1902–1903 (29 letters), EM Coll., especially CJ to Father and Mother, June 21, 1903; Papa to My own dear Clara, Jan. 18, 1903; also CWB to CJ, Mar. 19, 1909, EM Coll. When Clara was a woman of thirty-seven, her father addressed her as "dear little 'Baby'" and "my little Clara" and at the time of her marriage six months later, "My baby Daughter" (B. Jepson to CJ, Dec. 19, 1911, June 28 or 29, 1912, EM Coll.).

38. Photograph included in box of correspondence between CJ and her parents, 1902–1903 (29 letters), EM Coll.

39. CJ to [Philip], [1901?], not sent, EM Coll.

40. Martin, "Clara Louise Jepson Beers," p. 5.

41. For example: CWB to CJ, Oct. 1, 1908; CJ to CWB, Oct. 1, 1908, letter no. 5, EM Coll.; CJ to K, Oct. 11, 1908; CWB to CJ, Dec. 24, 1908, EM Coll.

42. For example, CWB to CJ, Mar. 19, 1909, Dec. 24, 1908.

43. CWB to Dearest, Jan. 1, 1910, EM Coll.

44. CWB to CJ [July 1911?] (incomplete); CJ to My darling, July 14, 1911, both in EM Coll.

45. CWB to CJ, fragment [probably Mar. 1910]; Your loving Father to My dear little "Baby," Dec. 19, 1911, EM Coll.

46. B. Jepson to CWB, July 12, 1912; to CJ [between June 1912 and 1914], both in EM Coll.

47. CWB to Phipps, June 26, 1912; to Mrs. William James, June 29, 1912 (copy of a copy); to Mr. and Mrs. Acker and Mr. and Mrs. Marks, July 19, 1912, all in MFA.

48. Bullis, interview.

49. According to a psychiatrist whom Clifford saw toward the end of his life, he stayed faithful to Clara, his only sexual adventures being visits to burlesque shows (Dr. Ralph Banay, interview, 1966).

Chapter 12. The National Committee in Action

1. Bond, interview.

2. CWB to Welch, Nov. 6, 1911.

3. Information about Salmon is derived mainly from Earl D. Bond, with the collaboration of Paul O. Komora, *Thomas W. Salmon, Psychiatrist* (New York: W. W. Norton, 1950). Beers also supplied biographical information about Salmon in his draft of a letter (incomplete) to Dr. Samuel S. Marquis, Dec. 22, 1913.

4. Barbara Sicherman, "The Quest for Mental Health in America, 1880–1917" (Ph.D. dissertation, Columbia University, 1967), p. 388; Norman Dain, *Concepts of Insanity in the United States, 1789–1865* (New Brunswick, N.J.: Rutgers University Press, 1964), pp. 99–104.

5. Haven Emerson, "Thomas William Salmon, 1876–1927, A Tribute," delivered at 18th annual meeting of the National Committee for Mental Hygiene, Nov. 10, 1927, in 1st Int. Cong. MH, *Proceedings,* ed. Frankwood E. Williams (New York: International Committee for Mental Hygiene, 1932), I, 513–15; Bond, *Thomas W. Salmon,* p. 43; see also William L. Russell, "A Brief Account of the Life and Work of Dr. Salmon," *Mental Hygiene,* 10 (Oct. 1927): 673–80.

6. Sicherman, "Quest for Mental Health in America," p. 358.

7. CWB to Marquis, Dec. 22, 1913, incomplete draft, p. 8.

8. Sicherman, "Quest for Mental Health in America," pp. 348–55, 364.

9. CWB to Marquis, Dec. 22, 1913, incomplete draft.

10. CWB, "An Intimate Account of the Origin and Growth of the Mental-Hygiene Movement," in 1st Int. Cong. MH, *Proceedings,* I, 507.

11. This and the following more detailed summary of the National Committee's activities are derived from George K. Pratt, *Twenty Years of the National Committee for Mental Hygiene* (New York: National Committee for Mental Hygiene, 1930); Thomas W. Salmon, "Summary of the Work, Plans and Needs of the National Committee for Mental Hygiene, Inc." [1921] (carbon copy of typescript); Sicherman, "Quest for Mental Health in America," pp. 318 ff.; and material in the CWB Coll. and the RFA.

12. Salmon, "Summary" [1921], pp. 2–3.

13. Minutes of the 4th annual meeting of the NCMH, New York City, Feb. 21, 1912, p. 21.

14. McLean and Welch remarks in "First Convention of Societies for Mental Hygiene . . . ," May 25, 1914 (stenographic transcript).

15. William A. White, *The Principles of Mental Hygiene* (New York: Macmillan Co., 1917; rpt. ed.: New York, Arno Press and the *New York Times,* 1972), pp. v–vi.

16. CWB, Notebook, 3″ x 5″, 1913.

17. Clipping from *Every Week,* Nov. 8, 1915, pp. 10–11, in CWB Coll.

18. H. C. Robinson case records, Conn. Valley Hosp.; Emily Martin, conversation.

19. CWB to Editor, *New Haven Evening Register,* Jan. 17, 1913 (carbon copy); CWB to Russell, Jan. 17, 1913; Sidney Minor to CWB, Jan. 16, 1913.

20. See, for example, CWB to Ansley Wilcox, May 16, 1914 (carbon copy).

21. CWB, Notebook, 2½″ x 5½″, Jan. 9, 1914.

22. CWB, Notebook, 2½″ x 4½″, 1915. Beers recalled that after his first important interview with Elizabeth Milbank Anderson, the first big donor after Phipps, he "was fagged for a week" (CWB to CJB, Dec. 7, 1934, MFA).

23. William Graves to William A. White, Apr. 8, 1914; White to Graves, Apr. 10, 1914 (copy), White Papers, Personal Correspondence.

24. Allan Nevins and Frank Ernest Hill, *Ford: Expansion and Challenge, 1915–1933* (New York: Charles Scribner's Sons, 1957), pp. 494–95, 332n; CWB, Notebook, 3″ x 5″, 1913; CWB to Marquis, Dec. 22, 1913, incomplete draft; CWB to CJ, Dec. 30, 1913.

25. CWB to Marquis, Dec. 22, 1913, incomplete draft; Russell H. Chittenden to Elizabeth Milbank Anderson, June 13, 1916 (carbon copy); also oblique reference to Rockefeller Foundation's role contained in confidential postscript to CWB to E. M. Anderson, Feb. 11, 1915 (carbon copy).

26. CWB to CJ, Dec. 30, 1913.

27. CWB to TWS, Jan. 24, 1916.

28. CWB to Marquis, Dec. 22, 1913, incomplete draft; to CJ, Dec. 30, 1913; and the following material in RFA, all dated 1913: Jerome D. Greene to CWB, June 21; CWB to Greene, June 25; Welch to Mr. Rockefeller, June 29; Chittenden to Greene, June 30; Homer Folks to Starr J. Murphy, July 22; Greene to Stokes, Aug. 18; Stokes to Greene, Aug. 19; Bannard to John D. Rockefeller, Jr., Oct. 15; CWB to John D. Rockefeller, Jr., Oct. 16; CWB to Greene, Oct. 17, 21; Chittenden to Greene, Oct. 17; Greene to Chittenden, Dec. 6, 9; John Koren to Greene, Dec. 20; Memorandum by Mr. Greene on National Committee for Mental Hygiene, Dec. 11; J. D. G. [Greene], Memo. on National Committee for Mental Hygiene, Dec. 16; Excerpts from Rockefeller Foundation board meeting minutes, 10/22/13, 12/20/13.

29. CWB, Account of the development of the mental hygiene movement, written in 1930 or shortly thereafter (typescript fragment), p. 95.

30. Ibid., pp. 95–96, 106; CWB to Mrs. Anderson, Feb. 11, 1915 (carbon copy).

31. Ibid.

32. Excerpts from Rockefeller Foundation board minutes, 1/14/15; Memorandum, Dec. 29, 30, 1914; S. Flexner to Greene, Mar. 2, Oct. 19, Nov. 17, 1914; Greene to Flexner, July 28, Aug. 17, Oct. 30, 1914; Greene to AM, Sept. 14, 1914; Welch to Greene, Dec. 22, 1914; Stokes to Greene, Nov. 23, 1914, all in RFA.

33. AM to Greene, Sept. 11, 17, 1914, RFA.

34. Memorandum, Dec. 29, 1914, RFA.

35. CWB to Anderson, Feb. 11, 1915 (carbon copy).

36. See, for example, Greene to Salmon, July 26, 1916, RFA.

37. Greene, Memorandum, Feb. 17, 1915; to Hoch, Nov. 5, 1916; also Greene to Flexner, Feb. 17, 1915, and Greene's remarks, Feb. 17, 1915, enclosed in CWB to Greene, Feb. 23, 1915, all in RFA.

38. Flexner to Greene, Mar. 2, Oct. 19, Nov. 17, 1914; Greene to Flexner, July 28, Aug. 17, Oct. 30, 1914; Greene to AM, Sept. 14, 1914; Paton to Flexner, Oct. 13, 1914, enclosed in Flexner to Greene, Oct. 19, 1914; Greene to TWS, May 11, 25, 8, 1916; to Charles B. Davenport, Mar. 9, 1916; to Katharine Tweed, May 8, 11, 1916; to Helen Hartley Jenkins, Aug. 3, 1916; TWS to Greene, May 8, 1916, all in RFA.

39. CWB to Welch, Nov. 17, 1914, CWB Coll.; same letter enclosed in Stokes to Greene, Nov. 23, 1914, CWB Coll.; Welch to Greene, Dec. 22, 1914, RFA.

40. CWB, Account of the development of the mental hygiene movement (typescript fragment), pp. 104–05; Bond, *Thomas W. Salmon,* p. 152.

41. Greene, Memorandum, Feb. 17, 1915; CWB to Greene, Feb. 23, 1915; Excerpts from Rockefeller Foundation board minutes, 9/14/15; CWB to Greene, Sept. 17, 1915, all in RFA.

42. Anderson to Otto T. Bannard, Nov. 23, 1916 (copy); see also copies of correspondence between CWB and Mrs. Anderson and account of interview with her, sent to GMB, June 13–Nov. 23, 1916.

43. Bannard to Anderson, Dec. 5, 1916 (copy); Dr. William B. Coley to CWB, Nov. 27, 1916; also CWB to Barker, Dec. 1, 1916; copies of letters from the following to Anderson, all in 1916: Chittenden, Dec. 2; Barker, Dec. 5; W. B. Coley, Dec. 2; William J. Hoggson, Dec. 2.

44. CWB to GMB, Dec. 7, 1916; also notes on copy of CWB to Arthur G. Milbank, Dec. 7, 1916, and on copies of Anderson correspondence.

45. CWB to Anderson, Dec. 3, 1916 (typed copy of handwritten letter).

46. The following all in CWB Coll., all dated 1916: Chittenden to TWS, June 11 (copy); to CWB, June 11; TWS to Chittenden, June 17; to CWB, June 11; Chittenden to CWB, July 11; CWB to Dr. Kirby, Mar. 26 (copy); Kirby to CWB, Apr. 12 (copy), Apr. 18 (telegram); also the following in RFA, all dated 1916: TWS to Greene, June 5; Greene to Hoch, June 26; Hoch to Greene, June 26; Greene to TWS, June 26, 17, July 26; TWS to Greene, July 21 (enclosing Kirby to Greene, July 15).

47. Sicherman, "Quest for Mental Health in America," pp. 321-22; CWB, *Purposes, Plans and Work of State Societies for Mental Hygiene* ("Publication No. 6") (New York: National Committee for Mental Hygiene, 1915).

48. "Program of the First Convention of Societies for Mental Hygiene . . . May 25, 1914"; "First Convention of Societies for Mental Hygiene . . . May 25, 1914," both in CWB Coll.

49. CWB to Dearest, Feb. 24, 1915.

50. CWB, Account of the development of the mental hygiene movement (typescript fragment), pp. 107-09; CWB, "The Number of the Insane," Apr. 9, 1909, p. 18 (later known as Appeal to J. D. Rockefeller, 30 pp.).

51. Blumer to CWB, Mar. 2, 1915.

52. Verso of Blumer to CWB, Mar. 2, 1915; CWB, Account of the development of the mental hygiene movement (typescript fragment), pp. 110-12.

53. CWB to Chittenden, Sept. 4, 1915.

54. CWB to Chittenden, Sept. 5, 1915.

55. Oskar Diethelm, conversation, 1972.

56. CWB to Chittenden, Sept. 5, 1915.

57. CWB to Russell, Dec. 19, 1915.

58. Bond, interview; William B. Terhune, interview, 1971; Kenworthy, interview.

59. CWB, Account of the development of the mental hygiene movement (typescript fragment), pp. 114-15; TWS to Greene, June 5, 1916, RFA; TWS to wife, Aug. 15, 1918, TWS Papers.

60. CWB, Account of the development of the mental hygiene movement (typescript fragment), pp. 113-15; also Chittenden to CWB, June 11; to TWS, June 11 (copy); TWS to Chittenden, June 17 (copy); Chittenden to CWB, July 4; CWB to Kirby, Mar. 26, all dated 1916.

61. CWB to GMB, Feb. 15, 1917.

62. "Proceedings of the 9th Annual Meeting of the NCMH, Inc.," Feb. 7, 1917, pp. 19-22.

63. *Mental Hygiene,* 1 (Jan. 1917): 1.

64. Lewellys S. Barker, "The Wider Field of Work of the National Committee for Mental Hygiene," ibid., pp. 4-5.

65. CWB, "Organized work in Mental Hygiene," ibid., p. 81.

66. Ibid., pp. 88-95.

67. "Report of Committee on Mental Hygiene," *American Journal of Insanity,* 74 (Oct. 1917): 294; Sicherman, "Quest for Mental Health in America," chap. 5; TWS, "Mental Hygiene," *American Year Book,* 1916, pp. 395-98; ibid., 1919, pp. 424-30; TWS, "Mental Hygiene," in *Preventive Medicine,* ed. Milton J. Rosenau, 3rd ed. (New York: D. Appleton & Co., 1917), pp. 331-61; AM, "Organization of Community Facilities for Prevention, Care, and Treatment of Nervous and Mental Diseases," in his *Collected Papers,* ed. Eunice E. Winters, vol. IV (Baltimore: Johns Hopkins Press, 1951), p. 273.

68. Paton to CWB, Oct. 8, 1923.

69. Pratt, *Twenty Years,* pp. 15-16; Edward A. Strecker, "II. Military Psychiatry: World War I, 1917-1918," in *One Hundred Years of American Psychiatry* (New York: Published for the American Psychiatric Assocation by Columbia University Press, 1944), pp. 385-416.

70. CWB, Account of the development of the mental hygiene movement (typescript fragment), pp. 115-17.

71. *Mental Hygiene,* 1 (July 1917): 333.

72. CWB to GMB, May 1, 1917; Rupert Blue, Surgeon General, to NCMH, May 22, 1917; Edwin R. Embree to CWB, Dec. 6, 1917, 2 letters (copies); also *War Work and Other Special Activities of the National Committee for Mental Hygiene, Inc.* (New York: Printed for Private Distribution, 1918).

73. CWB, "Summary of the Financing of the Work of the National Committee for Mental Hygiene since 1907 . . ." (note in pencil at top: July 20, 1920), pp. 6-7.

74. CWB to GMB, Feb. 15, May 1, 1917.

75. Quoted in Bond, *Thomas W. Salmon,* p. 105.

76. CWB to GMB, Nov. 4, 1914, Feb. 15, May 7, 1917, May 25, 1918; also June 26, 1917.

77. CWB to GMB, May 1, 7, 1917.

78. CWB to GMB, Apr. 28, July [19?], 1920, May 22, 1918, May 26, 1920.

79. H. O. Payne (Mrs. Owen S. Payne), "Clifford Beers," May 7, 1951, pp. 1–2 (typescript), in personal collection of C. B. Farrar, M.D., Toronto.

80. CWB to CJB, Feb. 26, 1918, Feb. 24, 1915; to GMB, May 7, 1917; to CJB, Feb. 26, 1918.

81. CWB to AM, Feb. 5, 1909.

82. CWB to Coley, Nov. 28, 1916; to GMB, Jan. 15, 1917, both in CWB Coll.; CWB to Greene, Jan. 6, 1917, RFA; to GMB, Mar. 17, 1917; to Bannard, Apr. 21, 1917 (copy), both in CWB Coll. Greene did write a strong letter to Mrs. Straight praising the National Committee's work under Salmon as "one of the most fruitful and beneficent activities in the whole range of public health and social welfare work" (Greene to Mrs. Willard Straight, Jan. 16, 1917 [carbon copy], RFA).

83. CWB to CJB, Feb. 26, 1918; *Toronto Globe,* Feb. 27, 1918.

84. CWB to Clarence Hincks, Mar. 6, 1918; Emily Martin, interview, 1966.

85. CWB to TWS, Jan. 4, 1920; "Minutes of the Rockefeller Foundation," 1/23/18, RFA; "Quotations from Letters and Cables from Dr. Salmon," Apr. 30, 1918 (note at top in CWB's hand: To E. R. Embree from C. W. Beers), in Embree to Williams, Apr. 5, 1918, RFA.

86. CWB, "Summary of the Financing of the Work of the National Committee for Mental Hygiene Since 1907," pp. 2–3.

87. CWB to Bannard, Boley, and Hoggson, Mar. 15, 1918; Coley to CWB, Mar. 15, 1918; Bannard to CWB, Mar. 15, 1918; CWB to Bannard, Mar. 19, 1918.

88. Minutes of the Joint Meeting of the Executive and Finance Committees, Feb. 26, 1919; CWB to Bannard, Feb. 27, 1919 (sent to GMB); CWB to GMB, Feb. 27, 1919.

89. CWB to Hincks, Mar. 28, 1918, CMHA Archives; CWB to GMB, Apr. 13, 1918.

90. Hincks to Dr. C. K. Clarke, Apr. 21, 1918, CWB Coll.; "Quotations from Letters and Cables from Dr. Salmon," Apr. 30, 1918, RFA.

91. CWB to GMB, May 10, 1918, CWB Coll.; to Embree, May 15, 1918, RFA.

92. Embree to CWB, May 15, 1918 (carbon copy), RFA.

93. CWB to Hincks, June 18, Nov. 23, 1918, CMHA Archives; CWB to GMB, Nov. 4, 1918.

Chapter 13. "Canning Salmon and Bottling Beers"

1. Robert H. Felix, *Mental Illness, Progress and Prospects* (New York: Columbia University Press, 1967), pp. 37–39.

2. "Some Reasons Why an Appropriation for Reconstruction Work . . . Is Absolutely Necessary," in CWB to Embree, Dec. 2, 1918; CWB to Embree, Dec. 4, 1918, including telegram from Pearce Bailey and Frankwood E. Williams to CWB, Dec. 3, 1918, all in RFA; CWB to GMB, Jan. 22, 1919.

3. Earl D. Bond, with the collaboration of Paul O. Komora, *Thomas W. Salmon, Psychiatrist* (New York: W. W. Norton, 1950), p. 145; TWS to Mrs. Salmon, Dec. 18, 1918, Jan. 5, 1919, TWS Papers.

4. Waldemar E. Nielsen, *The Big Foundations* (New York: Columbia University Press, 1972), pp. 53–55.

5. Bond, interview.

6. TWS to Mrs. Salmon, Jan. 5, 1919 (copy), Jan. 26, 1919, Aug. 25, 1918, Feb. 9, 1919, TWS Papers; TWS to Vincent, Apr. 9, 1919, enclosing copy of TWS to Dr. Walter B. James,

Apr. 9, 1919, RFA; Bond, *Thomas W. Salmon,* pp. 107, 110, 151–52, 156–57. An old friend of Salmon's, Dr. Joseph G. Wilson, described him as "very emotional; he could fly off the handle easily" ("Visit with Dr. Joseph G. Wilson" [typescript], TWS Papers).

7. TWS to Mrs. Salmon, Jan. 5, 1919, TWS Papers.

8. Bond, *Thomas W. Salmon,* pp. 86–87; TWS to Mrs. Salmon, Jan. 31, 1919 (copy), TWS Papers. A copy of the resolution, Feb. 8, 1918, is in RFA, with editorial corrections in CWB's hand.

9. TWS to Vincent, Apr. 24, 1919, RFA; Bond, *Thomas W. Salmon,* pp. 156–57; "Minutes of the Rockefeller Foundation," 5/5/19, RFA.

10. Hincks to CWB, Mar. 24, 1919; CWB to Hincks, Apr. 5, 1919; Hincks to CWB, Apr. 12, 1919, all in CWB Coll.; CWB to Hincks, Nov. 21, 1919, "Confidential," CMHA Archives.

11. "Minutes of the Rockefeller Foundation," May 21, 1919; W. B. James to Vincent, May 17, 1919, both in RFA.

12. TWS to Embree, Sept. 5, 1919, RFA.

13. CWB to Hincks, Apr. 17, Aug. 24, 1919, CMHA Archives; Haviland to CWB, Dec. 2, 1919, Oct. 28, 1920.

14. E. F. Gildea, "Notes on Thomas Salmon," p. 14, TWS Papers.

15. Vincent to TWS, Oct. 27, Nov. 12, 1919; TWS to Vincent, Nov. 14, 1919 (telegram), all in RFA; CWB to TWS [Nov. 13, 1919]; TWS to CWB, Nov. 14, 1919, both in TWS Papers.

16. [TWS], "Rockefeller Foundation: Organization and Work for 1920 of Division of Mental Hygiene," Nov. 15, 1919; W. B. James to Vincent, Nov. 17, 1919, enclosing *"Statement"* (with penciled note: by Dr. Walter B. James, 11/19/19), all in RFA.

17. CWB, "A Community Demonstration in Mental Hygiene" [1919], enclosed in CWB to Embree, Nov. 19, 1919, RFA.

18. Embree to W. B. James, Dec. 3, 1919, RFA.

19. Embree to TWS, Dec. 4, 1919, Jan. 20, 1920 (copy); TWS to Embree, Dec. 6, 1919, all in RFA. Russell said later that obtaining adequate treatment for mentally ill war veterans was Salmon's primary object at this time ("A Brief Account of the Life and Work of Dr. Salmon," *Mental Hygiene,* 10 [Oct. 1927]: 520–21). See also postscript (p. 4) of CWB to Welch, Aug. 4, 1921, and postscripts to copy of Vincent to TWS, July 25, 1921, sent to Welch by CWB, all in Welch Papers.

20. CWB to TWS, Jan. 3, 1920, CWB Coll.; TWS to Embree, June 7, 1920; Embree to TWS, June 21, 1920, both in RFA.

21. CWB to GMB, May 26, July 19, 1920.

22. CWB, "Summary of the Financing of the Work of the National Committee since 1907"; CWB to Haviland, Oct. 28, 1920 (copy).

23. CWB to GMB, Nov. 29, Aug. 2, Dec. 6, 1920; Sept. 7, 1921.

24. Vincent to TWS, Mar. 4, 1921; TWS to Embree, Jan. 5, 1921; Embree to TWS, Jan. 18, 1921, all in RFA.

25. Embree to TWS, Apr. 29, 1921, RFA; CWB to Welch, Aug. 4, 1921, plus enclosures: copies of V. V. Anderson to TWS, Mar. 23; TWS to Embree, Apr. 16; Embree to TWS, Apr. 29, all 1921, Welch Papers.

26. TWS to Vincent, May 4, 1921 (copy), RFA. The foundation accepted his resignation with appreciation for his services and praise for him as "a pioneer and leader" in mental hygiene ("Minutes of the Rockefeller Foundation," May 21, 1921 [copy], RFA).

27. TWS to Raymond B. Fosdick, June 18, 1921; also July 19, 1921 ("not sent"); Bond, *Thomas W. Salmon,* pp. 174, 186; CWB to Welch, Aug. 4, 1921, p. 4, Welch Papers; also note in copy of Vincent to TWS, July 25, 1921, sent by CWB to Welch, Welch Papers; Embree to TWS, Dec. 17 (copy), Apr. 29, 1921, RFA.

28. Nielsen, *Big Foundations,* pp. 53–56, 406–25; CWB to Welch, July 11, 1921, "Confidential," Welch Papers.

29. Russell to Dr. Walter E. Fernald, Apr. 19, 1921 (a letter sent by Russell to every executive committee member); CWB to Russell, Apr. 21, 1921; CWB to GMB, May 25, 1921.

30. CWB, "Memorandum in reference to the $100,000 bequest of the late Elizabeth Milbank Anderson," Mar. 22, 1922; CWB to Albert G. Milbank, May 12, 1921 (carbon copy). In the Mar. 22, 1922, memorandum Beers revealed that in 1917 he had confidentially suggested to Mrs. Anderson that she provide for the National Committee in her will as security in case it did not obtain the endowment toward which she had conditionally pledged $100,000.

31. Vincent to TWS, July 20, 1920 (carbon copy); Minutes of the Rockefeller Foundation, 1/21/21, both in RFA; CWB to GMB, Apr. 21, 1921.

32. CWB to GMB, May 25, Aug. 21, Sept. 7, 1921; to Welch, July 12, 1921 (copy); to Van Dyke, Nov. 17, 1921; to Eliot, Dec. 2, 1921 (carbon copy); Eliot to CWB, Dec. 3, 1921; CWB to Cross, Dec. 17 (carbon copy), July 9, 1921 (copy); to GMB, Aug. 21, 1921; Cross to CWB, Sept. 12, 1921.

33. Scott M. Cutlipp, *Fund Raising in the United States: Its Role in American Philanthropy* (New Brunswick, N.J.: Rutgers University Press, 1965), pp. 39–41, 104; "Minutes of the Meeting of the Executive Committee," July 1, 1921.

34. "Report of the discussion of the plan for a campaign for funds considered at the joint-meeting of the Executive and Finance Committees of the National Committee for Mental Hygiene, held on June 9, 1921."

35. CWB to TWS, Aug. 15, 1921.

36. TWS to CWB, Sept. 6, 1921; to Dr. Luis Casamajor, Sept. 29, 1921.

37. CWB to Keen, Jan. 3, 1922; to Dr. James, Dec. 17, 1921 (carbon copy); TWS to CWB, Dec. 19, 1921 (telegram), Jan. 7, 1922; also Keen to CWB, Dec. 19, 27, 31, 1921.

38. CWB, "Journal Notes on Boston Engagements during Financial Campaign" [early Feb. 1922].

39. CWB to TWS, Jan. 16, 1921; Keen to TWS, Jan. 17, 1922; to CWB, Jan. 24, 1922.

40. Paul E. Fitzpatrick to CWB, Feb. 1, 1922; CWB to Dr. Owen Copp and Dr. S. P. Duggan, Jan. 29, 1922.

41. CWB to CJB, Jan. 25, 1922, MFA.

42. CWB to Copp and Duggan, Jan. 29, 1922 (not sent); to Campbell, Feb. 5, 1922; Russell to CWB, Feb. 3, 1922; TWS to CWB, Feb. 4, 1922; Copp and Duggan, "Report to the Executive Committee" [after Feb. 18, 1922]. According to Beers, Salmon criticized his using photographs made in connection with a National Committee survey in interviews with the McCormick family; Salmon also rebuked Beers for his methods of dealing with Mrs. Harriman and the foundations (CWB, Confidential statement, Dec. 11, 1923 [copy], pp. 5–6).

43. CWB, Memorandum submitted to Dr. Duggan . . . on Feb. 28, 1922 (carbon copy of typescript); CWB, Memorandum submitted to Dr. Duggan, Feb. 28, 1922 (penciled draft), pp. 7–8.

44. CWB, "A Crisis, the Cause of it and a Remedy for it," Feb. 1922 (penciled draft, "not used"); CWB, "In refutation of statements and contentions of Mr. Keen in his letter of Feb. 28/22," Mar. 2, 1922.

45. CWB, "Submitted by Clifford W. Beers," Mar. 10, 1922; CWB, "Submitted by Clifford W. Beers" [after Mar. 10, 1922] (penciled draft).

46. CWB to Chittenden, Mar. 11, 1922.

47. Ibid.

48. Dr. G. Harold Ward to CWB, Mar. 17, 1922; Ward to CWB, Apr. 13, 1922; W. B. James to Ward, Hill, Pierce & Wells, Apr. 25, 1922 (copy); unsigned letter to Russell, Apr. 25, 1922 (copy, by James?); CWB to GMB, Sept. 17, 1922; to Paton, Jan. 27, 1923; Williams to CWB, Mar. 8, 1923 (copy); Transcript of meeting ("Mr. Duggan presiding as chairman"), [Feb. 5, 1923], pp. 36, 39–40.

49. Fernald to CWB, Apr. 10, 1922.

50. Thomas W. Farnam, Secretary of Yale University, to CWB, Apr. 12, 1922; CWB to Farnam, Apr. 15, 1922 (copy?).

51. Carbon copy of Phelps' and Angell's remarks, inserted in copy of Yale commencement exercises, 1897; Duggan to CWB, July 19; Judson S. Bradley to CWB, June 23 (copy); Russell to CWB, June 19, all 1922.

52. CWB to Carl, June 8, 1922 (copy).

53. "Program of the First Convention of Societies for Mental Hygiene . . . May 25, 1914"; CWB to Embree, Mar. 6, 1918, RFA; see also TWS telegram to CWB in "Quotations from Letters and Cables from Dr. Salmon," Apr. 30, 1918, RFA.

54. CWB to GMB, Jan. 19, 28, 1919.

55. W. B. James to Embree, Jan. 31, 1919, including a list of persons invited, with notes in CWB's hand, in RFA; clipping, *New York Sunday World,* Feb. 19, 1919.

56. CWB to Dr. C. K. Clarke, Mar. 5 (copy), Mar. 13, 1919.

57. Clarke to CWB, Mar. 17, 1919; Hincks to CWB, Mar. 17, 21, 22, 1919.

58. Dr. Genil-Perrin to CWB, June 11, 1921.

59. Hincks to Duggan, June 17, 1922; to CWB, Apr. 7, 1922; "The National Council for Mental Hygiene," rpt. from *Journal of Mental Science,* July 1923, attached to letter from W. B. James to Beardsley Ruml, Oct. 29, 1923, RFA.

60. Rachel Grant-Smith, *The Experiences of an Asylum Patient* (London: George Allen & Unwin, 1922), p. 29.

61. Helen Boyle to CWB, Mar. 30, 1922; CWB to Stokes, May 12, 1922 (draft).

62. CWB to Stokes, May 12, 1922 (draft); to Noble, May 19, 1922; CWB, "Summary and Forecast," May 7, 1922.

63. Noble to CWB, June 8, 1922 (copy).

64. CWB to Duggan, June 27, 1922 (copy).

65. CWB to Mrs. Jenkins [before Oct. 1, 1922] (draft); to Noble, May 19, 1922.

66. Hincks to CWB, Sept. 1, 1922; Clarke to CWB, Dec. 4, 1922.

67. CWB to Chittenden, Nov. 1, 6, 16, 1922; to GMB, Nov. 16, 1922.

68. Fernald to CWB, Nov. 8, 1922.

69. CWB to Chittenden, Dec. 10, 1922; to Russell, Dec. 25, 1922.

70. CWB, "A Plan; Addressed to those who attend the informal conference at the home of Dr. Walter B. James on . . . January 8th . . . " [late 1922 or early 1923] (carbon copy), CWB Coll.; Williams to Russell, Nov. 23, 1922; to TWS, Nov. 23, 1922; Dr. Owen Copp to Russell, Jan. 16, 1923, all in EM Coll.

71. Russell to CWB, Jan. 10, 1923.

72. Copp to Russell, Jan. 16, 1923, EM Coll.

73. CWB to TWS, Jan. 14, 1923 (carbon copy); enclosure, 3 typed pp. (carbon copy), in CWB to Kirby, Jan. 17, 1923; TWS to CWB, Jan. 15, 1923; CWB to Russell, Jan. 17, 1923.

74. Russell to CWB, Jan. 16, 1923; CWB to Russell, Jan. 17, 1923.

75. CWB to TWS, Jan. 18, 1923.

76. CWB to Owen Dawson, Jan. 21, 1923; Williams to Fernald, Apr. 14, 1923.

77. TWS to Dr. Walter James, Jan. 22, 1923, TWS Papers.

78. CWB to Fernald, Jan. 31, 1923.

79. Hincks to CWB, Dec. 16, 1923.

80. CWB to Hincks, Apr. 17, 1919, CMHA Archives.

81. CWB to Williams, Jan. 11, 1931, postscript.

82. Record of a talk by Salmon in 1921 or 1922 (p. 12) in White Papers, Personal Papers.

83. TWS to Paton, June 26, 1922, TWS Papers; Bond, interview; Paton to TWS, Aug. 12, 1922; Clarence B. Farrar, "I Remember Stewart Paton," *American Journal of Psychiatry,* 117 (Aug. 1960): 160–62.

84. Meyer also thought that Salmon had veered off the correct course by going into social

psychiatry at the expense of supporting research in mental hospitals, the front line of psychiatry, but at the National Conference of Social Work in 1925 he praised Salmon's surveys and on the whole approved the National Committee's "dynamic conception of man" (AM, *Collected Papers,* ed. Eunice E. Winters, vol. IV [Baltimore: Johns Hopkins Press, 1951], pp. 257–72).

85. CWB to R. Noble, May 19, 1922.

Chapter 14. Branching Out

1. "International Mental Hygiene," revised verbatim report of the informal talks at the luncheon-meeting of the Organizing Committee of the International Committee for Mental Hygiene (in process of formation), New York City, Dec. 11, 1922 (mimeographed), pp. 6, 3, 7–8.

2. CWB to Mrs. John Wood Blodgett, Feb. 6, 1928.

3. Payne, "Clifford Beers," Farrar Collection.

4. Williams to Fernald, Apr. 14, 1923; Fernald to CWB, Apr. 23, 1923.

5. CJB, Diary, 1923.

6. Clippings from *Chicago Tribune,* Paris ed., June 22, 1923; CJB, Diary, 1923; CWB to GMB, June 9, 1923.

7. Clarke to Russell, June 3, 1923; CWB to GMB, June 7, 1923.

8. CWB, "Explanatory," appended to Clarke to Russell, June 3, 1923 (copy).

9. Clarke to Russell, June 3, 1923; "The National Council for Mental Hygiene," rpt. from *Journal of Mental Science,* July 1923, attached to James to Ruml, Oct. 29, 1923, RFA; Alice M. Windram to CWB, Oct. 19, 1923; CWB to Chittenden, Nov. 5, 1923; Chittenden to CWB, Nov. 6, 1923; CWB to Windram, Nov. 9, 1923; Welch to CWB, Nov. 14, 1923.

10. CWB to GMB, June 7, 13, 1923; Charles C. Clarke to CWB, Sept. 19, 1923.

11. CWB to Blodgett, Dec. 29, 1923; Ferrari to CWB, Nov. 9, 1923 (translation); CWB to GMB, June 10, 1932; Payne, "Clifford Beers," p. 2, Farrar Collection.

12. CWB to GMB, July 15, 28, 1923.

13. "The National Council for Mental Hygiene," rpt. from *Journal of Mental Science,* July 1923, attached to James to Ruml, Oct. 29, 1923, RFA.

14. CWB to Duggan, Aug. 22, 1923.

15. Duggan to CWB, Sept. 10, 1923; Fernald to CWB, Nov. 20, 30, 1923.

16. Russell to CWB, Nov. 12, 1923; CWB to Russell, n.d. (copy).

17. CWB to Russell, Dec. 11, 1923 (copy).

18. CWB, "Confidential" statement, Dec. 11, 1923 (carbon copy).

19. CWB to Russell, Dec. 11, 1923; to Fernald, Dec. 22, 1923 (copy).

20. CWB to Elizabeth N. Chase, Jan. 1, 1924.

21. CWB to TWS, Nov. 1, 1923; Welch to CWB, Nov. 14, 1923 (and copy); letterhead, Williams to Embree, Jan. 24, 1925, RFA; CWB to Blumer, Jan. 2, 1924.

22. CWB to Chase, Jan. 1, 1924; "Excerpts" from Minutes of the joint meeting . . . , Dec. 21, 1923.

23. CWB to Embree, Dec. 29, 1923, RFA; to Hincks, Dec. 31, 1923, CWB Coll.

24. Russell Doubleday to Hoggson, Feb. 28, 1923 (copy).

25. CWB to Chase, Jan. 1, 1924 (copy): Blumer to CWB, Jan. 4, 1924.

26. CWB to GMB, Jan. 29, Feb. 12, 1924; letters to CWB from H. O. Payne and Emily F. Robbins, Jan.–Feb. 1924; "Quoted from Minutes of Joint Meeting of Executive & Finance Committees, Held June 24, 1924" (carbon copy); draft of letter from Frederic W. Allen in CWB's hand [June? 1924].

27. CWB to Emily Robbins, Feb. 7, 1924 (copy).

28. CWB to Embree, Mar. 13, 19, 21, May 23, June 1, 1924; Welch to Vincent, May 12, 1924; Embree to CWB, May 26, 1924 (carbon copy), all in RFA.

29. CWB to Embree, June 1, 1924, RFA.

30. "Summary of our talk," penciled draft in CWB's hand [1924?].

31. CWB to GMB, May 26, 1924; to Rev. Karl Reiland, May 26, 1924; Marshall Field to Frederic W. Allen, Sept. 18, 1924.

32. Payne, "Clifford Beers," Farrar Collection.

33. CWB to TWS, Apr. 8; to Williams, May 17; to Russell, May 22; to Chittenden, May 22, all 1924.

34. CWB, "At the Office," June 7, 1924 (penciled draft); CWB to Chittenden, Oct. 29, 1924; Chittenden to CWB, Oct. 22, 1924 (copy).

35. Hincks to CWB, Sept. 18, 1924 (personal); Embree to Williams, Nov. 12, 1924 (carbon copy), RFA; Hincks to CWB, Dec. 1, 1924; to Williams, Dec. 1, 1924 (copy); to CWB, Dec. 8, 1924.

36. Hincks to CWB, Dec. 8, 1924, Mar. 9, 1925 (copy); to Williams, Dec. 1, 1924.

37. Hincks to CWB, Mar. 9, 1925; CWB to Hincks, June 23, 1925; to Pres. James R. Angell, Yale University, June 18, 1925 (carbon copy); to GMB, Oct. 2, 1925; to Dr. N. C. Winternitz, Dean, Medical School, Yale University, July 1, 1925 (carbon copy).

38. Hincks to CWB, June 22, 1925 (confidential); CWB to Hincks, June 23, 1925 (confidential).

39. Hincks to CWB, Feb. 11, 1925.

40. CWB to GMB, May 26, Mar. 5, 26, 1925.

41. CWB to GMB, Aug. 27, 1926; to Phelps, Apr. 21, 1926; Phelps to Mary [Bok], Apr. 11, 1926.

42. CWB to GMB, May 23, 1925; to Dr. Charles P. Emerson, May 23, 1926 (copy of telegram); Emerson to GMB, May 25, 1926 (telegram).

43. CWB to GMB, Aug. 27, 19, 1926; Phelps to Mary Bok, June 24, 1926; CWB, "The Perfect Gift," Sept. 15, 1926 (carbon copy of typescript, confidential), pp. [4–5].

44. CWB, "The Perfect Gift," Sept. 15, 1926, p. [12]; CWB to W. C. Bok, July 2, 26, 29, 1926; to GMB, Aug. 19, 1926.

45. This account is based on the story related by Clifford to George Beers in two long letters written just after his visits with Mrs. Bok (Aug. 19, 27, 1926); in a later version prepared for distribution among his colleagues in the movement ("The Perfect Gift," Sept. 15, 1926), Clifford claimed that Curtis Bok made no direct suggestion to his mother, nor had he, Clifford Beers, hinted at the possibility of a personal gift.

46. CWB to GMB, Aug. 30, Sept. 5, 1926.

47. CWB to CJB, Oct. 24, 1917; CWB to Welch, winter 1925–1926 (never sent); comment on this letter by CWB, Feb. 9, 1927.

48. Quoted in Roy Lubove, *The Professional Altruist: The Emergence of Social Work as a Career, 1880–1930* (New York: Atheneum, 1971), p. 190; see also p. 85.

49. CWB to GMB, Aug. 27, 19, 1926; to Mrs. Bok, Sept. 3 (draft), Aug. 16, 1926; GMB to CWB, Sept. 5, 1926; CWB to GMB, Sept. 7, 1926.

50. CWB to Vincent, Nov. 16, 1926, RFA; in a later mimeographed version of the Bok gift, "The Story of the Perfect Gift" [late Nov. or Dec. 1926], Beers further played down his own role in the affair.

51. Charles L. Dana to Williams, Nov. 22, 1926 (copy).

52. CWB to Ruggles, Nov. 28, 1926.

53. John Chynoweth Burnham, *Psychoanalysis and American Medicine, 1894–1918: Medicine, Science, and Culture (Psychological Issues,* V, no. 4, Monograph 20) (New York: International Universities Press, 1967), p. 7; Barbara Sicherman, "The Quest for Mental Health in America, 1880–1917" (Ph.D. dissertation, Columbia University, 1967), p. 224.

54. Nathan G. Hale, Jr., *Freud and the Americans: The Beginnings of Psychoanalysis in the United States, 1876–1917* (New York: Oxford University Press, 1971), pp. 347, 350–52, 441.

55. Emerson to CWB, Dec. 6, 1926.

56. CWB to Ruggles, Apr. 19, 1927; Austen Fox Riggs to CWB, Apr. 12, 1927 (copy), White Papers, Miscellaneous Correspondence and Papers.

57. CWB to White, Apr. 18; to Ruggles, Apr. 19; to GMB, Apr. 21, all 1927; White to CWB, Apr. 20, 1927, White Papers, Miscellaneous Correspondence and Papers.

58. CWB, *Some Intimate Remarks . . .* , Nov. 14th, 1934 [1935], pp. 7-8.

59. Walters to Ruggles, Feb. 3, 1927, in "The American Foundation for Mental Hygiene, Incorporated," n.d., "Confidential," presentation copy from CWB to GMB, Aug. 4, 1928, p. 39; CWB to Mrs. Bok, Jan. 7, Feb. 7, 1927.

60. CWB to Ruggles, Feb. 18, 1927.

61. CWB to Mrs. Bok, Jan. 7, Mar. 24, May 14, 1927.

62. CWB to Mrs. Bok, May 14, 1927; CWB, "A Brief Account of My Trip . . . ," June 10, 1927; CWB to GMB, May 21, 1927.

63. CWB, "A Brief Account of My Trip," June 10, 1927.

64. CWB to GMB, June 16, 21, 1927.

65. G. C. Ferrari to CWB, June 28, 1927 (copy).

66. CWB to Mrs. Salmon, Aug. 22, 1927; to Sol M. Stroock, May 1, 1935; Virgil V. Johnson to CWB, May 4, 1935; CWB to Mrs. Salmon, May 10, 1935; Helen A. Salmon to Dr. Burlingame, Jan. 11, 1938; CWB to Helen A. Salmon, Jan. 14, 1938; see also Mrs. Salmon to CWB, Mar. 13, 1936; CWB to Mrs. Salmon, Mar. 20, 1936.

67. CWB to Hincks, Oct. 3, 1927.

68. Bond to CWB, Mar. 6, 1928; CWB to Bond, Mar. 8, 1928; to Hincks, Mar. 26, 1928.

69. CWB to Ruggles, Mar. 20, 1928; National Committee for Mental Hygiene, "Submitted in Confidence" (prospectus for a foundation for mental hygiene) [1927?]; extract from letter of Mr. Applegate to Ruggles, Mar. 7, 1928.

70. CWB to Mrs. Bok, July 15, May 24, 1928; to W. C. Bok, Mar. 5, 1928; to Ruggles, Mar. 20, 1928. The trustees of the foundation were mainly men with a special knowledge of mental hygiene (including Beers); its officers were all officers of the National Committee: Welch was honorary president of the foundation; Ruggles was chairman; James Angell, the Rt. Rev. William Lawrence (former Episcopal bishop of Massachusetts), and Russell were vice-presidents; Frederic W. Allen was treasurer and Beers, secretary.

71. "The American Foundation for Mental Hygiene, Incorporated," n.d., "Confidential," presentation copy from CWB to GMB, Aug. 4, 1928.

72. *The American Foundation for Mental Hygiene, Inc.,* rpt. from the "Mental Hygiene Bulletin" [1938], pp. 6-7.

73. CWB to GMB, July 23, Dec. 12, 22, 1928; *The American Foundation for Mental Hygiene, Inc.,* rpt. from the "Mental Hygiene Bulletin" [1928]; CWB to GMB, Nov. 9, 1928.

74. CWB to Dr. William H. Wilmer, Feb. 6, 1929; see also CWB to Dr. Forrest C. Tyson, Feb. 27, 1929; to GMB, Dec. 22, 1928.

75. CWB to M. Bok, June 5, July 11, 1929.

76. Gretta Palmer to CWB, May 18, 1931; CWB to G. Palmer, June 21, 1931.

77. CWB to Mrs. Bok, 1929 (not sent).

78. CWB, "A Summary of Crises in the Financial History of the National Committee," June 10, 1929; CWB to Cyrus H. McCormick, July 8, 1929.

79. CWB to GMB, Dec. 12, 1928; "Minutes of Meeting, Committee on Organization," Apr. 26, 1929.

80. Welch to CWB, May 13, 1929; CWB to Welch, May 14, 1929 (copy of longhand letter); to GMB, May 12, 1929; to Mrs. Bok, June 5, 1929; to GMB, Nov. 9, 1928; to President Hoover, July 11, 1929. Hoover's secretary acknowledged the book's receipt and said that the president hoped soon to read it (Lawrence Rickey to CWB, July 13, 1929).

81. CWB to GMB, Aug. 4, 1929; Maurice Craig to CWB, July 29, 1929 (copy of radiogram); CWB to Osborne A. Day, Aug. 26, 1935.

82. Mary Bok to CWB, Aug. 20, Sept. 7, 1929; CWB to GMB, Sept. 5, 1929.

83. CWB to Robbins, Oct. 11, 1929; to Mrs. Bok, Nov. 9, 1929; Hincks to CWB, Nov. 16, 1929; CWB to John M. Hart, Nov. 27, 1929; Herbert Sedgwick to CWB, Nov. 15, 1929; clipping from *New York Times,* Nov. 17, 1929; CWB to Clarence Gardner, Nov. 30, 1931 (carbon copy); invitation and program for Mr. and Mrs. George M. Beers; William Welch, Introductory remarks at the National Committee's 20th Anniversary Dinner, Nov. 14, 1929 (carbon copy of typescript).

84. Welch and Angell quoted in an undated, untitled memorandum [1932?] initialed in pencil, "CWB," and on upper right corner, "E.G."

85. Thomas W. Lamont to CWB, Oct. 7, 1929.

86. CWB to Mrs. Bok, Dec. 23, 1929, CWB Coll.; Howard Moran to Welch, Feb. 14, 1930; C. W. Howe to Welch, Feb. 15; CWB to Moran, Feb. 20; to Welch, Feb. 24; J. M. Glenn to Howe, Apr. 4; Edward T. Devine to Howe, Apr. 5 (copy); H. Edmund Bullis to Welch, July 15, all in 1930 and all in Welch Papers; 1st Int. Cong. MH, *Proceedings,* I, 48–49; Walters to CWB, Dec. 16, 1929 (carbon copy); CWB to Walters, Dec. 17, 1929 (carbon copy).

Chapter 15. The First International Congress on Mental Hygiene

1. Bond, interview.
2. 1st Int. Cong. MH, *Proceedings,* I, 22–23, vii–xii, xv–xviii.
3. Ibid., pp. 31, 32.
4. Bullis, interview.
5. Bond, interview.
6. Bullis, interview.
7. CWB, Int. Cong., May 9, 1930 (typescript).
8. Hincks to Myron Weiss, Apr. 28, 1933.
9. Bullis, interview. The photograph had to compensate for Hoover's declining to address the congress; through Welch and probably others Beers had tried to have the president speak and also to grant him a private audience. When Hoover refused the invitation Beers confessed to Welch that the president had probably been pressed too hard. (CWB to Welch, Apr. 6, 20, 1930; also Feb. 26, 1930, Welch Papers.)
10. 1st Int. Cong. MH, *Proceedings,* I, 30.
11. Ibid., pp. 524–25, 499–501.
12. Ibid., pp. 501–13.
13. Ibid., pp. 28–29.
14. Clipping from *Time,* May 19, 1930; see also clippings for Nov. 15, 1933; clipping from *Washington Post,* May 7, 1930.
15. Thomas B. Applegate to A. W. Packard, Feb. 17, 1930, RFA.
16. "From TBA's Diary," Mar. 21, 1930, RFA.
17. "Dinner to the Delegates of the International Congress on Mental Hygiene," May 13, 1930, Hotel Brevoort, New York City (copy of typescript), pp. 21–22.
18. Simon Flexner and J. T. Flexner, *William Henry Welch and the Heroic Age of American Medicine* (New York: Viking Press, 1941), p. 349; Welch quoted in n. 7, p. 507.
19. Quoted by Hincks in "Special Meeting, Board of Directors of the National Committee for Mental Hygiene," New York City, July 1, 1930, p. 19.
20. 1st Int. Cong. MH, *Proceedings,* I, 24.
21. Ibid., p. 10.
22. One psychiatrist who had acted as an interpreter at the Congress later scolded Beers because the mental hygiene movement did not sufficiently concentrate on prevention and did not dare to touch on the "economic, social, moral causes of mental disorders." He intended to go to the Soviet Union to see for himself what had been accomplished there (B. Liber to CWB, Sept. 1, 1931.)

23. 1st Int. Cong. MH, *Proceedings,* II, 217–18, 223; I, 790–92; II, 284–85; I, 227.

24. Ibid., II, 96.

25. Ibid., I, 281–85.

26. Ibid., II, 104–05; I, 234.

27. Ibid., I, 237–57.

28. CWB, "Outline of the International Institute of Mental Hygiene" (prepared . . . in consultation with a number of advisors), 1931; see also CWB to Welch, June 20, 1931, on the location of the institute at Yale (Welch Papers).

Chapter 16. Traveling and Family Troubles

1. Kenworthy and Bullis, interviews; CWB to members of Board of Directors and Executive and Finance Committees of the NCMH, June 4, 1930; to GMB, July 18, 1930; to Wild, July 24, 1930; to Ruggles, Dec. 26, 1932.

2. CWB, 1st Int. Cong., May 6, 1930 (typed version, carbon copy), p. 22; CWB, "In re deficit of the International Congress" [1930] (Confidential).

3. Ibid.; Bullis, Martin, Bond, and Kenworthy, interviews.

4. CWB, "In re deficit of the International Congress"; "Special Meeting, Board of Directors of the National Committee for Mental Hygiene," New York, July 1, 1930; CWB to Wild, July 27, 1930; to Ruggles, June 23, 1930; Ruggles to CWB, June 24, 1930.

5. Dr. Jack Griffin, interview, 1933; also Bullis, interview. (Griffin was for years Hincks' assistant in the Canadian National Committee and then his successor.)

6. CWB to Hincks, Sept. 14, 1930.

7. CWB to GMB, July 18, 1930; Bullis, interview; also Mabel W. Swan to CWB, Jan. 15, 1935.

8. CWB to Mac, Aug. 25, 1933, MFA; to Dr. Watson, Aug. 11, 1933.

9. CWB to Hincks, July 3, 1930; CJB to Hincks, July 4, 1930.

10. Bullis, interview; "To Those Members of the Board of Directors for Mental Hygiene Who Are to Be Present at the Special Meeting of the Board . . . October 8th" [1930], p. 1; CWB, 1st Int. Cong., May 6, 1930, p. 2; CWB to Wild, July 10, 1930; to Ruggles, July 12, 1930.

11. Scott M. Cutlipp, *Fund Raising in the United States: Its Role in American Philanthropy* (New Brunswick, N.J.: Rutgers University Press, 1965), pp. 43, 169–70; CWB to Hincks, Oct. 1, 2, 1930; to W. J. [Hoggson], Nov. 27, 1930.

12. CWB to Ruggles, Aug. 10, 1930, NAMH Coll.; to Hincks, Aug. 10, 1930; to Wild, Sept. 7, 1930; to Hoggson, Nov. 27, 1930.

13. Hincks to CWB, Aug. 22, 1930; Hincks' remarks, untitled MS, n.d. (probably early 1931), at a meeting of NCMH executive committee, p. 5.

14. CWB to Hincks, mid-Aug. 1930.

15. CWB to Wild, Sept. 7, 1930; Bullis, interview; Margaret H. Wagenhals, interview by telephone, 1966.

16. CWB to Dr. Charles P. Emerson, Oct. 20, 1929 (copy); to Ruggles, Nov. 5, 1930.

17. Ruggles to Noble, Oct. 2, 1931; CWB to Mrs. Bok, Nov. 8, 1930; to Angell, Nov. 8, 1930 (draft).

18. Merle Scott to Williams, Feb. 14, 1929; CWB to Ruggles, Nov. 29, 1930; Ruggles to CWB, Dec. 1, 1930; CWB, "A Little Story" [ca. Jan. 1931], p. 2.

19. CWB to Ruggles, Jan. 3, 1931; to GMB, Jan. 9, 1931.

20. CWB to Ruggles, Nov. 29, 1929; Bullis, interview.

21. CWB to W. J. Hoggson, Nov. 27, 1930; CWB, "A Little Story" [ca. Jan. 1931], p. 2; CWB to Ruggles, Nov. 29, 1930 (copy).

22. CWB, penciled note on envelope, Dec. 19, 1930; CWB to M. Bok, Dec. 18, 1930 (draft).

23. CWB to W. J. Hoggson, Nov. 1, 1932; CWJ, Diary, 1931.

24. CWB to John I. Downey, Jan. 8, 1931.

25. CWB to Williams, Jan. 11, 1931.

26. CJB, Diary, 1931.

27. CWB, New Year's Greeting to members NC and others, 1931, 15 pp.; CWB to Hincks, Nov. 25, 1931 (carbon copy).

28. CJB, Diary, 1931; CWB to Hincks, Apr. 11, 1931.

29. CWB to Vic [Dec. 1931?], "Confidential."

30. Memorandum of interview of Doctor Hincks with Mr. Frank, Oct. 2, 1933, GEB Archives, RFA.

31. See, for example, the following, all in RFA: "From MM's Diary," Jan. 30, 1932, with note by A.G.; "Medical Sciences—Program and Policy—Psychiatry," Excerpt from Agenda for RF meeting, Apr. 11, 1933 (DR 469); Alan Gregg, "Mental Health," Memorandum Regarding Program in the Field of Human Personality, Mar. 17, 1932.

32. For Hincks' relations with the Rockefeller Foundation and the General Education Board, see, for example, in RFA: "From MM's Diary," Jan. 30, 1931; Memorandum from R. A. Lambert to A. Gregg, Oct. 13, 1931; Trevor Arnett, Memorandum of interviews, Feb. 17, 26, 1932; Hincks to Lawrence K. Frank, Mar. 17, 1932; LKF, Memorandum of interviews with Hincks and Bullis, Mar. 17, 1932, with attachments (GEB Archives); Hincks to Arnett, Mar. 30, 1932; W. W. Brierley to Hincks, Apr. 18, 1932 (carbon copy).

33. René Sand to CWB, May 30, 1932; CWB to O. Willcox, May 31, 1932.

34. W. J. Hoggson to Russell, June 2, 1932.

35. CWB to Willcox, May 31, 1932.

36. Hoggson to Russell, June 2, 1932.

37. CWB to Hoggson, June 13, 1932; to Bullis, June 24, 1932; Harold L. Williams to CWB, June 29, 1932.

38. CWB to Bullis, June 24, 1932; to GMB, June 10, 1932.

39. International Committee for Mental Hygiene, Inc., "To the European members of International Committee for Mental Hygiene and others interested in its work," June 24, 1932, p. 3; CWB to Russell, July 11, 1932.

40. Russell to Bullis, June 11, 1932; to CWB, July 7, 1932.

41. CWB to Willcox, May 31, 1932.

42. *Hartford Courant,* June 24, 1932.

43. GMB to Dean Charles E. Warren and Treasurer Thomas W. Farnum, Feb. 16, 1931; Warren to GMB, Feb. 16, 1931; Dr. William B. Terhune to CWB, July 1, 1932, all in CWB Coll.; GMB to Dr. R. L. Leek, Feb. 10, June 20, June 27, 1931, in CEB Case Records, State Records Center, Rocky Hill, Conn.; Dr. William B. Terhune, interview.

44. Bullis, Wagenhols, Bond, interviews; CWB to Russell, July 11, 1932; CWB, "Postscript—Confidential," July 9, 1932, p. 6.

45. White to CWB, June 25, 1932; Hincks to Dr. John A. Ferrell, June 5, 1934.

46. CWB to Mrs. Bok, July 2, 1932; CWB, "Postscript—Confidential," July 9, 1932, p. 3.

47. Ibid.

48. Ibid.

49. CWB to Dr. Auguste Ley, Aug. 10, 1932.

50. E. F. Russell to CWB, July 12, 1932.

51. Bullis to White, July 14, 1932; CWB, "Copy of paragraph in letter to Louise," July 22, 1932.

52. CWB, "Postscript—Confidential," July 9 & 11, 1932, p. 3.

53. CWB to Russell, July 11, 1932; CWB, Proceedings of Meeting of European Members of the Int. Comm., held 5 P.M., Sunday, May 29, 1932, p. 17.

54. CWB to René Charpentier, Aug. 17, 1932, Jan. 13, 1933; to Dr. Carrado Tumeati, Jan. 13, 1933; to Aunt Mame, July 23, 1932; to Sanda Alexandria, July 26, 1932.

55. CWB, note, June 1932, MFA; CWB to René Sand, Aug. 25, 1932; to W. J. Hoggson, Nov. 1, 1932.

56. Dr. W. Winiarz to CWB, Aug. 22, 1932; see also R. Sand to CWB, Aug. 25, 1932; CWB to Bontelleau, Director, Librairie Stack, Aug. 27, 1932; Mme. Neumann-Rahn to CWB, Aug. 11, 1932.

57. CWB to Hoggson, Nov. 1, 1932.

58. CWB, Talk at meeting of European members of International Comm., Sunday, May 29, 1932, after-dinner speech, p. 16.

59. CWB to Hincks, Dec. 24, 1932.

60. CWB to Russell, Mar. 16, 15, 1933.

61. CWB to Dr. Mary O'Malley, Feb. 7, 1933; the following from RFA: Memorandum of interview of Doctor C. M. Hincks with E. E. Day and L. K. Frank, Nov. 22, 1933; Hincks to Dr. Edmund E. Day, Nov. 11, 1933; to Alan Gregg, Nov. 11, 1933; Memorandum of interview with Dr. C. M. Hincks, Oct. 15, 1934.

62. CWB to Hincks, Dec. 15, 1933, GEB Archives.

63. M. Bok to CWB, June 30, 1932; CWB to M. Bok, July 2, 1932; C. W. Hooven to CWB, July 13, 1932; CWB to Bullis, July 17, 1932; Mary A. Reed to CWB, Oct. 7, 1932; to M. Bok, Oct. 18, 20, 1932; to Willcox, Nov. 25, 1932.

64. Trustees William Curtis Bok, Cary Williams Bok, Clement Warren Hooven to CWB, Feb. 2, 1933; CWB to Mrs. Bok, Feb. 17, Mar. 4, 1933; M. Bok to CWB, Feb. 27, 1933.

65. Williams, "Is There a Mental Hygiene?" *Psychoanalytic Quarterly,* 1 (Apr. 1932): 113–20; Williams to Hincks, June 11, 1932; Hincks to Williams, June 15, 1932.

66. CWB to Dr. Milton A. Harrington, Mar. 29, 1933.

67. Clarence B. Farrar, "Twenty-five Years of Mental Hygiene," *American Journal of Psychiatry,* 13 (Nov. 1933): 695.

Chapter 17. Twenty-Five Years After

1. Laurence V. Benet to CWB, Nov. 28, 1932; Joseph Delaitre to CWB, Dec. 26, 1932; CWB to White, Dec. 5, 1932; Bullis, interview; photographs of presentation of Legion of Honor in EM Coll.

2. *Survey Graphic,* 17 (May 1930): 117–19, 167, 170.

3. Winkler and Barnes chapters in CWB Coll.; Floyd Dell, *Love in the Machine Age: A Psychological Study of the Transition from Patriarchal Society* (New York: Farrar & Rinehart, [c. 1930]); James A. Tobey, *Riders of the Plague* (New York: Charles Scribner's Sons, 1930), pp. 294 ff.; *Twenty-Five Years After: Sidelights on the Mental Hygiene Movement and Its Founder,* ed. Wilbur L. Cross (New York: Doubleday, Doran & Company, 1934), pp. 365–66; CWB to Groves, July 15, 1935; Ernest R. Groves and Phyllis Blanchard, *Readings in Mental Hygiene* (New York: Henry Holt and Company, 1937).

4. Winfield S. Davis to CWB, Dec. 17, 1928; CWB to Mayflower Pub. Co. for Who's Who, Jan. 28, 1929; to NCAB, Dec. 11, 1934; R. B. Carter to CWB, Dec. 21, 1934.

5. Josephine Merkel to CWB, Sept. 14, 1933; CWB to Helen L. Myrick, Sept. 18, 1933; Myrick to CWB, Nov. 20, 1933.

6. CWB to Dr. Augustus Knight, Sept. 19, 1933; Albert G. Brenton to CWB, Sept. 22, 1933.

7. *Health Through the Ages* (New York: Metropolitan Life Insurance Company, Home Office, 1933), pp. 56–59, enclosed in CWB to Wilhelmina Broemer, Sept. 18, 1933, Welch Papers.

8. *Address of Mr. Clifford Whittingham Beers, Founder of the Connecticut Society for Mental Hygiene and of the Mental Hygiene Movement, at the Laying of the Corner Stone of the Fairfield State Hospital, Newtown, Conn.,* June 10, 1931.

9. Everett R. Clinchy to CWB, Sept. 10, 1932; CWB to Clinchy, Sept. 25, 1931; to Carey Schory, Oct. 23, 29, 1931.

10. Rachel H. Sulzberger to CWB, Mar. 31, 1933; CWB to Mrs. Cyrus L. Sulzberger, Apr. 3, 1933; to Robert L. Duffus, May 2, 1933; Duffus to CWB, Dec. 28, 1931; CWB to Rt. Rev. William Theodotus Capers, June 9, 1933; to White, Apr. 8, 1933; to Henry R. Luce, Apr. 8, 1933; MacLean Hoggson to Henry R. Luce [Apr. 1933] (copy); Hincks to Myron Weiss, Apr. 28, 1933.

11. C. Stuart Gager, Pres., National Institute of Social Sciences, to Welch, Apr. 7, 1933; Secretary to Dr. Welch to Gager, Apr. 17, 1933 (copy); Bullis to Wilhelmina Broemer, May 12, 1933, all in Welch Papers; CWB to Emerson, May 3, 1933, CWB Coll.; Presentation Address by Dr. Haven Emerson . . . to CWB, National Institute of Social Sciences, May 11, 1933, CWB Coll.; clipping from *New York Times,* May 12, 1933, EM Coll.; CWB, Speech Given at the Annual (Gold Medal) Dinner of the National Institute of Social Sciences, May 11, 1933, CWB Coll.

12. The Rockefeller Foundation, "From AG's Diary," Oct. 31, 1934, RFA.

13. Bullis to Gregg, Nov. 2, 3, 1934; "From AG's Diary," Dec. 6, 7, 20, 1934, all in RFA.

14. *List of Guests, Twenty-fifth Anniversary Dinner of the National Committee for Mental Hygiene . . .* [1934].

15. AM, *Collected Papers,* ed. Eunice E. Winters, vol. IV (Baltimore: Johns Hopkins Press, 1951), pp. 281–87.

16. CWB, *Some Intimate Remarks . . .* , Nov. 14, 1934 [1935].

17. CWB to Cross, May 28, 1939; *Twenty-Five Years After,* p. [v]; Welch to CWB, Oct. 26, 1933.

18. CWB to V. Tyler, Feb. 25, 1934; to William B. Terhune, Oct. 21, 1933; to Gregg, Nov. 1, 1934, RFA; to K. Herman Bouman, Nov. 14, 1933; to Hugh Young, Mar. 19, 1934; to Lloyd Thompson, Feb. 28, 1934; to Katherine Tucker, Mar. 23, 1934.

19. CWB to Emily Sanford, Nov. 8, 1934; to John Wood Blodgett, June 26, 1934; to Harry P. Robbins [Aug. 12, 1934]; to Mac, Aug. 19, 1934, MFA.

20. *Twenty-Five Years After,* p. 265. Absent from the contributors was Frankwood Williams, whom Beers finally did invite to send a letter after hearing that he wanted to. But Williams did not answer his first letter or a second (CWB to Williams, Mar. 5, Apr. 5, 1935).

21. CWB to Dr. Lloyd Thompson, Feb. 28, 1934.

22. "The Story of an Imperfect Tribute," letter to Welch, Feb. 15, 1933, and postcard, both with CWB to Cross, Apr. 21, 1934; CWB to Cross, June 11, 1934.

23. CWB to members of executive committee, Aug. 22, 1934; Henry T. Downey to CWB, Apr. 24, 1935.

24. *Twenty-Five Years After,* pp. 50–51; clipping from *New York Evening Post,* Apr. 12, 1935; CWB to Brickell, Apr. 15, 1935.

25. CWB to Mrs. Cyrus L. Sulzberger, Apr. 16, 1935; also CWB to Brickell, Apr. 15, 1935; *New York Times,* May 14, 1935, p. 19.

26. Kenneth W. Payne to CWB, May 29, 1935.

27. H. E. Maule to CWB, Jan. 10, 1938.

28. CWB to Helen Keller, Dec. 4, 1934.

29. See, for example, Dr. Frederick L. Patry to CWB, Nov. 17, 1934; CWB to Patry, Nov. 19, 30, 1934; to H. E. Barnes, Mar. 10, 1932; Barnes to CWB, Mar. 11, 1932; Katharine Moss Fisher to CWB, Sept. 28, 1933; CWB to K. M. Fisher, Oct. 24, 1933.

30. John A. Green to CWB, Apr. 1, 1935; E. Bigelow Thompson to CWB, Mar. 29 [1935]; CWB to Thompson, Apr. 2, 1935.

31. Correspondence between CWB and Clara G. Stillman, June 5, 7, 12, 1935.

32. Charles Martin to CWB, July 14, 1936.

33. CWB to Charles Martin, Nov. 13, July 18, Oct. 16, 1936; to Miss Artoni, July 18, 1936;

C. Martin to CWB, Oct. 21, 1936; also C. Martin to CWB, Dec. 7, 1936; CWB to Bullis, Aug. 14, 1936.

34. CWB to Leo Feinberg, Dec. 17, 1937.

35. CWB to Dr. Pratt, Apr. 13, 1938.

36. See, for example, CWB to Edwin Oviatt, Apr. 6, 1933; to Farrar, Nov. 11, 23, 1933; Farrar to CWB, Nov. 14, 1933; CWB to W. H. Marshall, Nov. 17, Dec. 21, 1933.

Chapter 18. Personal Interests

1. Bullis to Russell, Nov. 20, 1936; CWB to Mrs. and Miss Simes, Aug. 16, 1937; Bullis to F. Williams, June 18, 1935; Minutes of a Special Meeting of the Executive Committee of the National Committee, Oct. 4, 1935; CWB to Dr. René Charpentier, Oct. 19, 1935; to Dr. Lauren H. Smith, Nov. 6, 1936; Sachs to CWB, June 29, 1935; CWB to Sachs, July 9, 1935.

2. CWB to Senator W. Warren Barbour, Mar. 1, 1935.

3. CWB to Bullis, July 20, 1937.

4. CWB to Bullis, July 6, 20, 1937.

5. Leon V. Arnold to CWB, May 11, 1938; Dr. E. Krapf to CWB, Sept. 16, 1938; CWB to Dr. Mario A. Sborbi, Nov. 15, 1938; to Dr. Harlow Brooks, Apr. 19, 1938; H. Brooks to CWB, n.d.

6. Repond to CWB, Jan. 15, 1938; the German edition was *Eine Seele die sich Wieder-fand; Autobiographie des Begründers der "Geistigen Hygiene,"* published in Basel by Benno Schwab & Co., with a foreword by Heinrich Meng and André Repond.

7. For example, Dr. Ernst Birnbaum to CWB, Nov. 11, 1938.

8. CWB to Dr. Maria Rossi, Dec. 20, 1938, Feb. 11, 1939; to André Repond, Feb. 11, 1939.

9. R. S. Woodworth to CWB, Dec. 21, 1938.

10. CWB to Dr. Marion E. Kenworthy, Mar. 22, 1939.

11. See, for example, Bullis to Dr. Vance Murray, May 2, 1939; to G. Howland Shaw, May 2, 1939; Ernst Birnbaum to Bullis, June 1, 1939.

12. Bullis to Ruggles, Nov. 18, 1939; Haven Emerson to CWB, Dec. 21, 1938; Ruggles to F. D. Roosevelt [Nov. 1939], suggested draft.

13. See, for example, Willcox to CWB, Nov. 29, 1938; Ira S. Wile, M.D., to CWB, Nov. 19, 1938; Abraham Meyerson, M.D., to CWB, Nov. 1938; Harry Pelham Robbins to CWB, Dec. 20, 27, 28, 1938.

14. (New York: Doubleday, Doran, 1937).

15. Deutsch to CWB, Apr. 11, 1934.

16. CWB to Deutsch, Apr. 16, 30, 1934; Russell Doubleday to CWB, Apr. 27, 1934; CWB to Dr. Mortimer Raynor, Oct. 15, 1934.

17. CWB to White, May 14, 1935; Deutsch to CWB, July 23, Aug. 12, 1935; CWB to Ruggles, Aug. 31, 1935; to Deutsch, Oct. 4, 1935. Beers tried unsuccessfully to obtain a foundation grant for Deutsch and, through Mary Bok, to have a condensed version of the chapter on Dorothea Dix published in the *Ladies' Home Journal* (CWB to M. Bok, Mar. 23, 1936; to Editors, *Ladies' Home Journal,* Apr. 3, 1936; Stuart Rose to CWB, Apr. 10, 1936).

18. Russell to CWB, Oct. 14, 1935; Artoni to CWB, July 27, 1936; Bond to CWB, Jan. 18, 1937; Sachs to CWB, Jan. 19, 1937; Sheldon Glueck to CWB, Jan. 19, 1937; Ruggles to CWB, Jan. 19, 23, 1937; H. P. Robbins to CWB, Jan. 21, 1937.

19. Sachs to CWB, Jan. 30, 1937; CWB to Ruggles, Jan. 22, 1937; to Deutsch, Jan. 22, 1937; Deutsch to CWB, Jan. 23, 1937; CWB to Ruggles, Jan. 23, 1937; Ruggles to CWB, Jan. 25, 1937; CWB to Willcox, Jan. 25, 1937; to Deutsch, Jan. 27, 1937.

20. For example, CWB to Bond, Mar. 4, 1937; Bond to CWB, Mar. 4, 1937; C. C. Burlingame to CWB, Mar. 21, 1937.

21. CWB to Dr. Clements C. Fry, Apr. 6, 1937; to Bond, Mar. 19, 1937; Bond to CWB,

Mar. 26, 1937; CWB to Dr. G. W. Brown, Mar. 4, 1937; Brown to CWB, Mar. 4, 1937; CWB to McQuaid, Mar. 3, 1937; George L. Banay to CWB, Mar. 22, 26, 1937.

22. Albert Deutsch, *The Mentally Ill in America: A History of Their Care and Treatment from Colonial Times* (1937), pp. xvi–xvii.

23. CWB to Deutsch, June 14, 1937; Deutsch to CWB, June 29, 1937; CWB to Bullis, July 6, 1937.

24. See, for example, CWB to Richard H. Thornton (of Holt and Co.), Oct. 7, 1935; to P. C. Smith, Apr. 14, 1936; to Cheryl Crawford, Jan. 2, 14, 1938. One exception was a manuscript by a physician who worked in mental hospitals; Beers tried to help the author edit the book and have it published (CWB to Esther H. Stone, Jan. 15, 1937; Esther K. Nichols to CWB, Jan. 26, 1937; CWB to Carrington North, Feb. 4, 8, 1938; North to CWB, Feb. 14, 25, 1938; Stone to CWB, Oct. 21, 29, 1936).

25. Dr. Harlow Brooks to Dr. William H. Wilmer, Dec. 29, 1934; CWB to Wilmer, Oct. 23, 1934; Wilmer to CWB, Jan. 11, 1935.

26. CWB to Ruggles, Dec. 6, 1934; Hincks to CWB, Dec. 8, 1934; CWB to Dr. Ralph P. Truitte, Jan. 7, 1935; Elizabeth S. Royce to E. Bubek, Jan. 15, 1935; CWB to Anne M. Wickman, Jan. 16, 1935; to Mrs. John Arthur Green, Jan. 25, 1935; to Dr. Harlow Brooks, Feb. 1, 1935.

27. CWB to Dr. Milton C. Winternitz, Jan. 23, 1935; Ross, "The Genius of Clifford W. Beers," *Survey Graphic,* 17 (May 1930): 119, 167.

28. E. Edmund Bullis, "Memorandum to the Trustees of the American Foundation for Mental Hygiene," Feb. 2, 1932 (carbon copy); Bullis to Willcox, Feb. 23, 1932 (carbon copy); CWB to M. Bok, Feb. 17, 1933; to Mr. Burke [1933]; to J. S. Burke, Apr. 15, 1935.

29. CWB to Wilmer, Oct. 29, 1934 (confidential); Wilmer to CWB, Oct. 31, 1934; CWB to Wilmer, Nov. 1, 1934.

30. Russell to Albert G. Milbank, Nov. 8, 1934; Chittenden to CWB, Jan. 13, 1935; [CWB?] to Harkness, Oct. 30, 1934.

31. Dr. Harlow Brooks to Wilmer, Dec. 29, 1934.

32. CWB to Ruggles, Apr. 5, 1935; also to Dr. Livingston Farrand, Mar. 22, 1935; to Mrs. Bok, Nov. 9, 1934.

33. A. G. Milbank to Ruggles, May 23, 1935; CWB to Milbank, May 27, July 26, 1935; to M. Bok, July 2, 29, 1935; to H. P. Robbins, July 19, 1935; to E. S. Royce, Aug. 7, 1935; to Cary W. Bok, May 29, Aug. 12, Oct. 3, 1935.

34. CWB to John A. Kingsbury, July 9, 1935.

35. Hincks to CWB, July 26, 1935.

36. CWB to Arthur B. Brooks, Dec. 10, 1935; to Bullis, Aug. 14, 1936; to Marcus Goodbody, Feb. 16, Nov. 2, 1937; to Franklyn B. Kirkbride, Jan. 20, 1937; to Mr. and Mrs. Arthur H. Ham, May 3, 1938; to James S. North, June 1, 1936; Robert S. Tipping to CWB, Jan. 22, 1935; CJB, Diary, Mar. 9, 1936.

37. Dr. H. Brooks to Wilmer, Dec. 15, 1935.

38. CWB to Osborne A. Day, Aug. 26, Sept. 23, 1935 (copies); to Dr. R. L. Leak, Dec. 14, 1935 (copy); to Frederic C. Walcott, Sept. 18, 1935 (copy); Leak to CWB, Nov. 2, 1935; Walcott to CWB, Sept. 20, 1935; Day to CWB, Sept. 7, 1935; to Walcott, Aug. 16, 1935.

39. CWB to Miss Frega, May 6, 1934; Royce to CWB, Aug. 29, 1935; CWB to Royce, Aug. 31, 1935.

40. Bianca Artoni Avela, interview, 1966; CWB to Bianca Artoni, June 22, 1937; to Ogden Miller, Apr. 2, 1935.

41. Paul Komora to Dr. Donald A. Laird, Mar. 25, 1940.

42. Avela, interview.

43. Komora to Laird, Mar. 25, 1940.

44. Avela, interview.

45. CWB to Stanley D. Noble, June 16, 1936.

46. CWB to Hincks, Oct. 10, 1933; to Mrs. Bok, Aug. 11, 1933; M. Bok to CWB, Aug. 14, 1933.

47. CWB to F. E. Williams, Dec. 11, 1933; Everett V. Meeks to CWB, Dec. 4, 1933; CWB to J. Scott Williams, Sept. 22, 25, 1933; J. S. Williams to CWB, Sept. 22, 1933; CWB to Arthur W. Wolfe, Mar. 26, 1934; to Aunt Mame, Apr. 1, 1934.

48. CWB to McQuaid, Jan. 2, 6, 1935 [1936?]; to C. Farrar, Jan. 25, 1935; to Fred C. Abbott, Feb. 4, 1935, for example.

49. CWB to McQuaid, Feb. 1, 1935; to Alice C. Greene, Feb. 5, 1935.

50. Handwritten notes on CWB to Lefferts M. Dashiell, Jan. 21, 1935, RFA.

51. CWB to Arthur B. Brooks, Dec. 10, 1935; CWB to Edwin S. Oviatt (editor, *Yale Alumni Weekly*), Jan. 21, 1936; CWB, "My Kind of Art," on verso of photograph of Yale Club art exhibit, 1935.

52. CWB to McQuaid, Jan. 2, 6, 1935 [1936?]; CWB to Jonas Lie, Feb. 21, 1936; to Evelyn H. Schiorring, Jan. 14, 1936; J. B. Conant to CWB, Oct. 26, 1937; CWB to Rev. Harry Emerson Fosdick, Feb. 20, 1936; to Winston S. Churchill, Feb. 29, 1936.

53. CWB to Eugene O'Neill, Mar. 2, 1936; O'Neill to CWB, Mar. 5, 1936.

54. CWB to Austen Fox Riggs, Oct. 2, 1936; [Bullis?] to Hincks, Oct. 19, 1936; CWB to Elizabeth Trotter, Jan. 27, 1936; Clarence B. Farrar, interview, 1966; CWB to White, Mar. 3, 1936; to Milbank, July 26, 1935.

55. Russell to CWB, Feb. 18, 1936; CWB to Russell, Feb. 19, 1936.

56. CWB to Bullis, Sept. 3, 9, 10, 1936; Edsel Ford to CWB, Oct. 8, 1936; to H. R. Rittenberg, Dec. 11, 1936, EM Coll.; CWB to Bullis and Hincks, Sept. 12, 1936; to Mrs. Edsel Ford, Sept. 10, 1936; to Bullis, Sept. 10, 1936.

57. Meeting, Scientific Administration Committee of the National Committee, May 27, 1936; CWB to Rittenberg, Dec. 10, 12, 1936; to Austen Riggs, May 9, 1936; to Vic Tyler, Mar. 21, 1936.

58. CWB to Dr. Alexis Carrel, Oct. 20, 1936; to Bowers & Co., Jan. 13, 1937.

59. CWB to Mrs. W. A. White, Mar. 29, 1937; Arnold Barbour to CWB, Apr. 1, 1937; CWB to Barbour, Apr. 1, 1937; to Rittenberg, Jan. 7, 1938; Lola P. White to CWB, May 15, 1938, NAMH Coll.

60. CWB to Barklie Henry, May 10, 1937; Mackey Wells to CWB, June 16, 1936; Jas. C. Hasell to CWB, June 17, 1936; CWB to John H. Finley, Nov. 8, 15, 1937; Clipping, *New York Times,* Nov. 14, 1936.

61. CWB to Lewis Gannett, June 13, 1935; to Mrs. George Beers, Dec. 10, 1937; to Bullis, Aug. 12, 1937.

62. CWB to Dr. Frederick Peterson, Mar. 23, 1936; to Dr. Charles T. Burnett, June 24, 1936.

Chapter 19. The Mentally Ill Intrude

1. CWB to Helen W. Arnold, June 30, 1910, Beers Clinic Papers.

2. TWS to Vincent, Mar. 15, 1920, p. 4, RFA.

3. Quoted in Francis J. Braceland, *The Institute of Living, The Hartford Retreat, 1822–1972* (Hartford: Institute of Living, 1972), p. 192.

4. James E. Cattell to Ruggles, Nov. 14, 1934.

5. CWB to Bullis, Aug. 21, 1937.

6. Quoted in Braceland, *Institute of Living,* p. 186.

7. For a description and evaluation of Burlingame's administration see Braceland, *Institute of Living,* chap. 9, and Winkler and Norton, "History of the I.O.L." [ca. 1935] (typescript at Institute of Living), chap. 2.

8. CWB to W.H.C., May 12, 1938; to Ruggles, Oct. 16, 1935.

9. Ruggles to CWB, Oct. 17, 1935.

10. E. C. Does to CWB, Aug. 29, 1931; CWB to Helen L. Myrick, Sept. 25, 1931; Myrick to CWB, Oct. 9, 1931.

11. CWB to S.C., Dec. 13, 1932, Feb. 18, 1933; S.C. to CWB, Jan. 3, 1933.

12. S.C. to CWB, Feb. 25, 1933.

13. Dr. Roland N. Klemmer to CWB, June 1, 1933; Marie Lautz to CWB, June 20, 1933; CWB to Klemmer, June 21, 1933; to Lautz, June 24, 1933.

14. Richard H. Hughes to CWB, June 26, 1938 (copy).

15. CWB to Hughes, June 29, July 7, 1938; Samuel Hamilton to CWB, July 9, 1938; William J. Ellis to CWB, July 11, 1938; CWB to Hughes, July 12, 1938; to Ellis, July 18, 1938; Hughes to CWB, July 26, 1938; Ellis to B. Artoni, July 20, 1938; CWB to Hughes, July 29, 1938 (copy). For a discussion of Ellis' work in New Jersey, see James Leiby, *Charity and Correction in New Jersey: A History of State Welfare Institutions* (New Brunswick, N.J.: Rutgers University Press, 1967), chap. 12.

16. Dr. De Mork to CWB, June 27, 1933; CWB to De Mork, June 27, 1933.

17. Charlotte Osann to CWB, June 24, 1935; CWB to Osann, June 25, 1935.

18. Memorandum of Hincks interview with L. Frank, Oct. 2, 1933, GEB Archives, RFA.

19. See note 5, chap. 20, below.

20. CWB to Helanie Potratz, Dec. 9, 1933.

21. CWB to L. A. Marsh, Mar. 19, 1934.

22. CWB to Anthony M. Olinger, Nov. 7, 1935.

23. CWB to John W. Tucker, Oct. 20, 1937.

24. CWB to Dr. Henry C. Casper, Jr., Apr. 27, 1939.

25. R.A.K. to CWB, Oct. 6, 1937; Sept. 12, 21, 1938, Feb. 16, 1939; CWB to R.A.K., Oct. 6, 1937, Sept. 13, 15, 1938; CWB to Katharine G. Ecob, Mar. 6, 1939.

26. *Mental Hygiene,* 15 (April 1931): 328–29.

27. L. Cody Marsh to CWB, Aug. 8, 1931; CWB to Marsh, Dec. 16, 1931.

28. CWB to Marsh, Dec. 16, 1931; William A. Bryan to William Frazier, Dec. 10, 1931. Dr. Bardwell H. Flower recalled Marsh's meetings with patients at Worcester Hospital but not his attempts to organize them (interview, 1973); nor did psychologist David Shakow, who also knew Marsh there (interview, 1973). Franz G. Alexander and Sheldon T. Selesnick, in *The History of Psychiatry: An Evaluation of Psychiatric Thought and Practice from Prehistoric Times to the Present* (New York: Harper & Row, 1966), evaluate Marsh's role (p. 335). It may be that Beers' cold response to Marsh was caused in part by negative information he had heard about him. Although I have no evidence of this for 1931, when the two men corresponded, there is a letter in the Beers Collection of four years later from a woman who visited Kings Park Hospital, where Marsh was still working. She reported, with disapproval, that he was more an evangelist than a physician, that his patients' meetings were like revival meetings and not taken too seriously by staff or patients. Yet she did speak of the importance of his principles of "hope and optimism," and she obviously had her own theory of treatment that she was pressing. (Emily K. Hottenstein to CWB, Feb. 15, 1935). Dr. Flower confirmed to me the revivalist quality of Marsh's work with patients at Worcester State Hospital.

29. CWB, "A Continuing Sequel to *AMTFI,*" Dec. 7, 1931, pp. 4–5.

30. CWB, "In Reference to New Book," Dec. 17, 1931, Confidential.

31. Accouncement attached to Bryan to Frazier, Dec. 10, 1931; Marsh to CWB, Aug. 3, 1932.

32. L. Z. Boyajian, "History Strikes Again," paper delivered before the Section on the History of Psychiatry and the Behavioral Sciences of the Dept. of Psychiatry, New York Hospital-Cornell University Medical Center, Apr. 18, 1974, pp. 9–10; see also Lucy Michelle Candib, "A Social Study of the Health Center Movement: A New Approach to Public Health History"

(B.A. thesis, Harvard University, 1968), which, while limited in its appreciation of the full scope of the problems faced by the health center movement, is interesting and ground-breaking in its research.

33. See above, pp. 197–98, for a more detailed description of this project.

34. *Lost and Found,* 1 (July 1938): 2, 17–18, 31; (Sept. 1938): 45–47; 2 (Nov. 1938): 81, 82. Low's work is described in his biography by Neil and Margaret Rau, *"My Dear Ones"* (Englewood Cliffs, N.J.: Prentice-Hall, Inc., 1971).

35. *Lost and Found,* 2 (Jan. 1939): 7–9.

36. Ibid., pp. 11, 25; E. W. Burgess, "The Sociological Aspects of Mental Health Administration," in American Association for the Advancement of Science, *Mental Health,* ed. Forest Ray Moulton and Paul O. Komora, Publication of the American Association for the Advancement of Science, no. 9 ([Lancaster, Pa.]: Published for the American Association for the Advancement of Science by the Science Press, 1939), pp. 357–58.

37. *Lost and Found,* 3 (July–Aug. 1940): 118–19; (Nov.–Dec. 1940): 151–52, 156–59.

38. Shakow, interview.

Chapter 20. Final Years

1. CWB, "The Mental Hygiene Movement," 1938, p. 6; CWB to Joseph H. Peck, Dec. 21, 1937.

2. "Memorandum Regarding Finances of the National Committee for Mental Hygiene During Its Twenty-Seven Years History," appended to Emmet Dougherty to Bullis, Dec. 17, 1936, CWB Coll.; "The National Committee for Mental Hygiene, Inc., Grants and Contributions from the Beginning of Its Active Work in 1912 to July 1, 1938," with note in CWB's hand, "To Dr. Gregg—from C. W. Beers," RFA.

3. "Appendix A, Present Financial Status of the National Committee for Mental Hygiene," in Hincks to Albert G. Milbank, Feb. 6, 1936.

4. "The Strategy of Our Program on Psychiatry," typescript with penciled note at end: A.G.? [Alan Gregg], 1938?, and note on p. [1]: From Nov. 1, 1937, Confidential Monthly Report to the Trustees, RFA; Alan Gregg, "What Is Psychiatry?" Dec. 3, 1941, RFA; "From A.G.'s Diary," Oct. 27, 1938, Jan. 10, 1939; "Staff Conference," Dec. 15, 1935, all in RFA.

5. All the following from RFA: "From A.G.'s Diary," June 11, Oct. 15, 21, 1935; Memorandum of Interview, Dec. 9, 1935, of Gregg with Dr. C. M. Hincks and Dr. Ross McClure Chapman; Gregg, "National Committee for Mental Hygiene," Oct. 25, 1935; "Medical Sciences — Program and Policy—Psychiatry; Excerpt from Director's Report on Program, Part of Agenda for Trustees' Meeting," Dec. 11, 1935, p. 10; Gregg to Ivan, Jan. 9, 1936, with enclosures; Hincks to Gregg, Jan. 9, 1936 (telegram); RAL to Gregg, Jan. 11, 1936; Gregg to Hincks, Mar. 10, 1936; Hincks to Gregg, Mar. 20, 1936; F. P. Keppel (president, Carnegie Corporation), "Memorandum for Dr. Gregg's Information," Apr. 3, 1936; Gregg, Memorandum of interview, Baltimore, Apr. 9, 1936; Gregg to Hincks, Apr. 20, 1936; "From A.G.'s Diary," Apr. 23, 1936.

6. CWB to Ruggles [Nov. 16, 1935?]; see also Haven Emerson to CWB, Dec. 19, 1934.

7. See, for example AG [Alan Gregg], Memorandum of interview with Dr. Ruggles re National Committee for Mental Hygiene—New York—July 10, 1935, RFA.

8. AG [Gregg], "National Committee for Mental Hygiene, $906,100; 1915–1939," pp. 1–2, RFA; Gregg to Bullis, Nov. 30, 1936, RFA.

9. CWB to Russell, Dec. 22, 1937; Ruggles to CWB, Dec. 24, 1937.

10. CWB to Hincks, May 28, 1937; Bullis to Edwin G. Barey, Jan. 8, 1937; CWB to Ruggles, Feb. 3, 1937, all in CWB Coll.; excerpt from letter from Dr. Alan Gregg to Mr. Max Mason, Mar. 23, 1939, RFA; Gregg, "National Committee for Mental Hygiene, $906,100; 1915–1939," p. 7, RFA.

11. CWB to Ruggles, June 11, 1937; Hincks to Dr. B. Glueck, June 23, 1937.

12. CWB to Chittenden, Dec. 25, 1935; Franklin G. Ebaugh to CWB, Jan. 13, 1936; H. P. Robbins to CWB, Dec. 28, 1936; Bullis to [?], Dec. 23, 1936; Edward A. Strecker to Bullis, Dec. 29, 1936; Chittenden to CWB, Dec. 28, 1936; Sachs to CWB, Dec. 28, 1936; White to CWB, Dec. 28, 1936; Emerson to Bullis, Dec. 31, 1937; Bullis to Emerson, Dec. 30, 1936; C. Bok to CWB, Jan. 12, 1937; CWB to Mrs. Bok, Jan. 16, 1937; M. Bok to CWB, Jan. 20, 1937.

13. CWB to Dr. Karl Reiland, Feb. 15, 1938.

14. CWB to Hincks, Apr. 23, 1936, EM Coll.

15. CWB to Stanley D. Noble, May 28, June 16, 1936; to Dr. M. Ernest Townsend, June 28, 1938.

16. CWB to Reiland, Feb. 15, 1937; Arthur Lucas to CWB, Feb. 8, 1938; Reiland to CWB, Feb. 9, 1938; group of letters between Dr. Ralph E. Wager and CWB, Mar. 1938.

17. CWB to Dr. Floyd J. Thompson, Nov. 29, 1937; Hopson Owen Murfee to Pierre S. DuPont, Nov. 24, 1937; CWB to Artoni, Mar. 31, 1938.

18. CWB, "To Whom It May Concern," Mar. 19, 1938; Bullis, interview.

19. Charles F. Taylor to CWB, Apr. 13, 26, 1938; CWB to Taylor, Apr. 15, 1938.

20. CWB to Dr. Frank O'Brien, Aug. 6, 1938.

21. O'Brien to CWB, Dec. 20, 1938; CWB to Mrs. Fanny S. Hoggson, Dec. 21, 1938.

22. [A. Gregg] to Hincks, Jan. 6, 1939; Ruggles to Bullis, Jan. 13, 1939.

23. "National Committee for Mental Hygiene, Division of Mental Hospital Service, July 1, 1936–June 30, 1939 . . . Appraisal: November 1939," RFA.

24. Gregg, "National Committee for Mental Hygiene, $906,100; 1915–1939," pp. 2–3, RFA.

25. "From A.G.'s Diary," Jan. 10, 1939, RFA.

26. CWB to Frederic C. Wolcott [1939?], draft.

27. CWB to Gregg, Jan. 11, Apr. 22, 1939; "From A.G.'s Diary," Jan. 13, 1939, all in RFA.

28. "From A.G.'s Diary," Jan. 13, 1939, RFA.

29. For example, Bullis to Gladys Rideout, Feb. 1, 1931; to Mrs. J. R. Sala, Feb. 1, 1939; CWB to Rideout, Feb. 6, 1939; to Helen H. Sala, Feb. 8, 1939.

30. "From A.G.'s Diary," Nov. 30, 1939, RFA.

31. Bullis, interview.

32. Ibid.; CWB to Miss Bevier, Nov. 2, 1936; to G. Howland Shaw, Mar. 7, 1939; Shaw to CWB, Feb. 26, 1939; CWB to Ruggles, Feb. 26, 1939; authorized testimonials regarding Allied Optical Service, attached to T. C. Edwards to J. T. Sinky, June 27, 1938.

33. CWB to Ruggles, Feb. 26, 1939; to August C. Fisher, Nov. 17, 1927.

34. CWB to G. H. Shaw, Mar. 7, 1939; to Willcox, Mar. 8, 1939.

35. Bullis, interview.

36. "From A.G.'s Diary," Jan. 13, 1939, RFA; CWB to Peck, Dec. 21, 1937.

37. CWB to H. Robbins, Feb. 8, 1939.

38. CWB to H. Robbins, Feb. 1, 1939.

39. Strecker to CWB, Feb. 26, 1939; Augustus Knight to CWB, Feb. 20, 1939; Shaw to CWB, Feb. 26, 1939.

40. See, for example, from RFA: "From A.G.'s Diary," Jan. 13,, Feb. 23, Apr. 4, 1939; CWB to Gregg, Feb. 22, Mar. 31, 1939; excerpt from letter from Max Mason to Dr. Alan Gregg, Mar. 16, 1939; excerpt from letter from Dr. Alan Gregg to Mr. Max Mason, Mar. 23, 1939.

41. Ruggles to CWB, Feb. 15, 1939; Strecker to CWB, Feb. 28, 1939; CWB to Ruggles, Feb. 17, 1939; to Hincksie, Feb. 2, Mar. 7, 1939. Beers wrote of his regard for Hincks' work in Canada to C. K. Clarke's son, who felt that his father's role as founder had been obscured by Hincks' claim to that status. True, both he and Hincks, Beers said, needed and sought the help of "older men and leaders in launching their projects," but they would have succeeded without them. (CWB to Dr. Eric Kent Clarke, Mar. 28, 1939.)

42. Bullis, interview; Shaw to CWB, Mar. 11, 1939; AM to CWB, Mar. 11, 1939.

43. CWB to Ruggles, Mar. 6, 1939; Bullis, interview; CWB to Dr. Winfred Overholser, Mar. 1, 1939.

44. Banay, interview.

45. Hincksie to Beersie, Feb. 4, 1939.

46. Griffin, interview.

47. Gregg, "Symposium on Mental Hygiene—Appraisal of," June 20, 1939, RFA.

48. CWB to Ruggles, Jan. 31, Mar. 7, 26, 1939; Knight to CWB, Feb. 17, 1939.

49. "From A.G.'s Diary," Apr. 4, 1939, RFA.

50. AM to CWB, Apr. 4, 1939; CWB to Gregg, Mar. 31, 1931, RFA; to Knight, Feb. 7, 1939; to Russell, Apr. 4, 1939.

51. CWB to Stevenson, Mar. 22, 1939.

52. CWB to Ruggles, Mar. 27, 1939; Stevenson, interview; Stevenson to Willcox, Apr. 4, 1939.

53. CWB to AM, Apr. 27, 1939.

54. AM to CWB, Mar. 11, May 1, 1939; Diethelm, interview.

55. CWB to AM, May 3, 1939.

56. Dr. R. Townley Paton to CWB, May 23, 1939.

57. CWB to the Members of the Board of Directors, May 25, 1939; to Shaw, May 26, 1939.

58. CWB to Mrs. Amos F. Barnes, May 24, 1938.

59. Tyler to Dr. C. B. Farrar, Mar. 30 [1951?].

60. CJB to Mrs. Col. Bullis, Dec. 22, 1938.

61. CWB to Lewis B. Winton, Nov. 21, 1938.

62. Avela, interview.

63. CWB to Zilboorg, Mar. 23, Feb. 20, 1939.

64. CWB to Shaw, Mar. 21, 1939.

65. CWB to Dr. Ralph Banay, Feb. 1, 1935, for example.

66. Banay, interview.

67. Banay, interview; observation of Beers home, 1966.

68. Versions of the trip to Providence differ. A letter from Clara Beers to Bullis, written probably in mid-June 1939, says that Banay suggested a trip to Bermuda for Beers, which he opposed, feeling that he "needed quiet instead of change and stimulation." He "had more insight into his condition than anyone." Ruggles suggested a rest home near Providence, and Clara Beers says she "got Dr. Banay to drive him up. *Fortunately,* they stopped at Butler." (CJB to Bullis [mid–June 1939?].) Banay, in an interview, recalled arranging for Beers to go to Butler Hospital; Bullis and Terhune both each recalled that they had driven him up to Providence.

69. CWB file, June 8, 1939, Butler Hosp., Providence, R.I.

70. Ibid.

71. CJB to Bullis [mid–June 1939?]; to Dr. Fitzgerald [late June or early July 1939], CWB file, Butler Hosp.; to Dr. Nichols [late June or early July 1939], CWB file, Butler Hosp.; CJB to [Bullis?], June 27, 1939.

72. CWB to Artoni, Aug. 8, 1939.

73. CJB to Dr. Nichols [early July? 1939]; Ira C. Nichols to CJB, July 11, 1939, both in CWB file, Butler Hosp.

74. CWB file, July 7, 1939, Butler Hosp.

75. Ibid., Aug. 4, 17, Oct. 2, Nov. 2, 1939; Jan. 31, Mar. 2, May 2, 1940; "Visit with Dr. Gregory," TWS Papers.

76. CJB, Diary, Feb. 1940; M. Bok to CJB, Feb. 7, 1940; "From A.G.'s Diary," Nov. 30, 1939, RFA.

77. For example, Dr. C. Helen Boyle to CWB, Apr. 15, 1941; Repond to CWB, Aug. 25,

1941; Heinrich Meng to CWB, Nov. 27, 1941; Miss R. Repond to CJB, Sept. 16, 1949, all in EM Coll.

78. C. McFie Campbell to CJB, Mar. 18, 1940, CWB file, Butler Hosp.; AM to CWB, Mar. 21, 1940.

79. CWB file, Mar. 5, 10, 25, Aug. 3, Sept. 30, 1941, Butler Hosp.

80. Ibid., Mar. 7, 16, Sept. 25, 1942.

81. Ruggles to Rittenberg, Apr. 1, 1942.

82. CWB file, Sept. 7, 25, Dec. 7, 1942, Mar. 8, 1943, Butler Hosp.

83. CJB to Ruggles, Mar. 2, 1943.

84. Ruggles to CJB, Mar. 3, 1943.

85. The death certificate for Clifford Beers in his file at Butler Hospital leaves blank the answer to the question, "Was there an autopsy?" (CWB file, Apr. 10, July 4, 9, 1943, Butler Hosp.).

86. CWB to Marian Pascal, May 14, 1936.

Epilogue

1. Beers' psychosis and its outcome can be seen as an example of what Erik Erikson, in his study of Martin Luther, described as the youthful life crisis (albeit in highly disturbed form), one that Beers turned into a creative, meaningful, acclaimed calling. As Erikson says, comparison between Luther and young mental patients "is oriented toward those moments when young patients, like young beings anywhere, prove resourceful and insightful beyond all professional and personal expectation." (Erik Erikson, *Young Man Luther: A Study in Psychoanalysis and History* [New York: W. W. Norton & Company, 1962], p. 8.)

2. A recent study of the birth control movement makes a somewhat similar point about Margaret Sanger, albeit she had more social consciousness than Clifford Beers (James Reed, *From Private Vice to Public Virtue: The Birth Control Movement and American Society since 1830* [New York: Basic Books, 1978], pp. 138–39).

Index

385

386 ‡ Index

Beers, Clifford W. (*cont.*)
217–18, 220, 223, 225–28, 230–31, 236, 238, 240–41, 243, 256, 260, 265, 272–73, 280, 282, 286, 289, 305, 306, 310, 312, 316, 326–29; as General Secretary of Organizing Committee for the International Congress, 219; in high school, 7, 9, 10–11, 13; honorary degrees of, 207, 240; mania as turning point in life of, 95, 324; as manic-depressive, 33, 36, 77; and marriage to Clara Jepson, 69, 124–25, 160–61, 164, 188; and mental health movement, xxiii, xxix, 197–98; and mental hygiene movement, 181; and Adolf Meyer, 118–24, 127–28, 131, 134–53; as musician, 7, 9, 28, 31; and National Committee, 104, 129, 130–31, 137–38, 141–42, 168, 205, 211–14, 232–33, 277, 281, 312, 317, 319; as philanthropist, 83, 104, 123, 135; physical characteristics of, 9, 10, 14, 51, 222; physical problems of, 317–18, 320–21; as poet, 62, 74; and psychiatry, 234; as public speaker, 126–27, 148, 160, 192, 204, 206, 246, 259, 261, 272, 308, 310; publications and records of, xxiii, 69, 87–99, 154–55, 205; publicity about, 269, 275, 296; as reformer, xxiii, xxvii, xxix, 31, 51, 90, 94, 95, 97, 99, 100–15, 127, 300, 325, 327; religious convictions of, 59, 63, 230; conflict with Rockefeller Foundation, 175, 177–79; silver jubilees of, 285; and state mental societies, 180–81; suicide attempts of, 16–18, 21, 27, 32–33; suits of, 171–72; venereal diseases of, 15, 59; as violent patient, 25, 29, 31–32, 38; and relationships with women, 58, 69, 125, 136–37, 141, 162, 189, 319; and World War I, 187–88, 192
Beers, Clifford W., hospitalizations of: at Butler Hospital, 318–22; in Connecticut Hospital for the Insane, 33–52, 63, 66, 79; at Connecticut State Hospital, 290; at Grace Hospital, 17–18; at Hartford Retreat, 26–39, 43, 48, 50, 55, 56–57, 59–60, 69, 72, 77, 79, 97, 104, 151–52, 300; at Stamford Hall, 21–24, 36, 76; at Wallingford, 24–26. *See also Mind That Found Itself, A*
Beers family: mental health of, 58, 63, 136, 150, 161, 164, 171, 188, 200, 242, 256, 264–65
Beers, George, 12, 17, 26, 28–32, 35, 37, 40,

Beers, George (*cont.*)
41, 46–48, 49–52, 54–55, 61, 82, 108, 121, 155, 158, 181, 187, 189, 191, 212, 232, 233, 241, 325; breakdown of, 70; as legal guardian of CWB, 18, 25, 44; illness of, 120, 161; suicide of, 262–63, 264
Beers, Ida Cooke, 3–6, 16–17, 58, 63
Beers, Robert, 3, 5–6, 18, 25, 130
Beers, Samuel, 6, 11, 16, 69; illness of, 11–12, 16, 19, 69; death of, 164
Beers, William, 7, 12–13, 51, 188, 257; illness of, 200; suicide of, 256, 258
Belgian National League for Mental Hygiene, 219
Blacks as mental patients, 297–98
Bloomingdale Hospital, 171–72, 188, 256–57, 292
Blumer, George A., 77, 140, 142–44, 147, 153, 155, 157, 181, 184, 225
Bok, Edward William, 231–33, 237, 240
Bok, Mary Louise Curtis, 231, 258, 263, 285, 286, 308; contributes to National Committee, 232, 242, 282
Bok, W. Curtis, 231, 238
Bond, Dr. Earl D., 94, 166–67, 238
"Boston School," 80
Boyle, Dr. Helen, 211, 219, 222
Brickell, Herschel, 274–75
Brill, Abraham A., 235, 245, 286
British National Council for Mental Hygiene, 219, 222
Bullis, H. Edmund, 245, 246, 307, 312, 314, 317, 325; as business manager for National Committee, 306
Butler Hospital, 77, 292, 293, 318–22

Campbell, Dr. C. McFie, 182, 184, 203, 320
Canadian National Committee for Mental Hygiene, 190, 196, 209, 219, 221, 229, 254, 281, 314
Carnegie, Andrew, 83–84, 104, 118, 129, 174
Carnegie Corporation, 265, 306
Carnegie Scientific Research Centers, 102
Cheney, Dr. B. H., 10–13, 16, 18
Chittenden, Russell H., 74, 106, 108, 130, 142–43, 145–48, 155, 157, 206, 228, 264, 282, 308; as treasurer of National Committee, 175
Choate, Joseph, 64–65, 106, 326
Clarke, Dr. C. K., 192, 210, 219, 221
Coe, John W., 47–48, 51

CONTEMPORARY COMMUNITY HEALTH SERIES